IDENTITY MATTERS
Rhetorics of Difference

IDENTITY MATTERS
Rhetorics of Difference

Lillian Bridwell-Bowles
in collaboration with
Kathleen Sheerin DeVore and Holly Littlefield
The University of Minnesota–Twin Cities

 Prof. Easton is a socialist!

Prentice Hall, Upper Saddle River, New Jersey 07458

Library of Congress Cataloging-in-Publication Data

Bridwell-Bowles, Lillian.
 Identity matters : rhetorics of difference / Lillian Bridwell-
Bowles ; in collaboration with Kathleen Sheerin DeVore and Holly
Littlefield.
  p. cm.
 Includes bibliographical references (p.).
 ISBN 0–13–243288–9
 1. Readers—Social sciences. 2. Pluralism (Social sciences)—
Problems, exercises, etc. 3. English language—Rhetoric—Problems,
exercises, etc. 4. Difference (Psychology)—Problems, exercises,
etc. 5. Identity (Psychology)—Problems, exercises, etc. 6. Group
identity—Problems, exercises, etc. 7. Readers—Psychology.
8. College readers. I. DeVore, Kathleen Sheerin. II. Littlefield,
Holly, 1963- . III. Title.
PE1127.S6I35 1998
808′.0427—dc21   97–30620
                                                                                      CIP

Executive editor: Charlyce Jones-Owen
Executive editor: Leah Jewell
Production liaison: Fran Russello
Editorial/production supervision and interior design: Joan Saidel/
 P. M. Gordon Associates, Inc.
Prepress and manufacturing buyer: Mary Ann Gloriande
Cover director: Jayne Conte
Marketing manager: Rob Mejia
Copy editor: Sherry Babbitt
Cover and interior art credit: Arlene Burke-Morgan, "Works of Love." Photographed by
 Rik Sferra. Reprinted with permission of the artist.

This book was set in 10/12 Baskerville by Carlisle Communications, Ltd.
and was printed and bound by Courier Companies, Inc.
The cover was printed by Phoenix Color Corp.

 © 1998 by Prentice-Hall, Inc.
 Simon & Schuster/A Viacom Company
 Upper Saddle River, New Jersey 07458

Printed in the United States of America

10 9 8 7 6 5 4 3 2 1

ISBN 0-13-243288-9

Prentice-Hall International (UK) Limited, *London*
Prentice-Hall of Australia Pty. Limited, *Sydney*
Prentice-Hall Canada Inc., *Toronto*
Prentice-Hall Hispanoamericana, S. A., *Mexico*
Prentice-Hall of India Private Limited, *New Delhi*
Prentice-Hall of Japan, Inc., *Tokyo*
Simon & Schuster Asia Pte. Ltd., *Singapore*
Editora Prentice-Hall do Brasil, Ltda., *Rio de Janeiro*

Dedicated to all of our students,
who have taught us so much
about writing, identity, and difference

Contents

Overlapping Identities: An Alternative Table of Contents

In the table of contents, we have grouped selections as they appear in the text, in the chapter dealing with their primary focus; however, many of the essays examine more than one identity issue. Thus the table of contents below, organized by the topics of each chapter, lists additional, related selections found elsewhere in the book. For example, if you are writing a long paper on a racial topic, you would want to read the essays in Chapter 2 plus the others listed below as having connections to race. Such a table of contents is necessary because so many of the variables that help us construct our identities are influenced by or interact with others. The number of the chapter where you can find the selection is in parentheses.

RACE AND ETHNICITY

CLASS

GENDER AND SEXUALITY

Acknowledgments

Kathleen Sheerin DeVore and Holly Littlefield are two of the most gifted writing instructors I have had the privilege to work with, and their flair for imagining questions and activities to accompany these essays will be obvious to the students who use this material. They are writers themselves, as well as avid readers, so they live the kinds of lives that we are inviting students to share. During our collaboration we each discovered new avenues for reading and writing, thanks to our very different identities and life choices. Their contributions from inception through incubation to completion of this project were an invaluable source of support to me.

Christy Glendenning and Kim Donehower are two other writing instructors who also contributed readings and questions to this volume, and who enlivened our discussions of identity, diversity, and our own differences. We valued the time they spent on this project.

Craig Wagner came in off the streets as a temporary worker to help us prepare the manuscript and showed us one of the reasons why corporate America needs to create more full-time jobs with benefits for liberal arts majors. But we are glad he came along to us when he did, and we wish him the very best with his enormous writing and technological talents.

Our families, including Kathleen's newborn and Holly's youngsters, survived weekend mornings and midweek evenings without us as we poured tea and argued over various selections each of us had contributed. We thank them all, especially Rick Bowles, who often made the tea and vanished.

My son, Joel Bridwell, gave me the original idea for this book when he told me about an essay he had to write in first-year composition at St. Olaf College. He said he struggled to "write like a woman" and to see the world from a different perspective in this course. It opened his eyes to new ways of knowing and confirmed, yet again, my commitment to writing as a way of learning about ourselves, forever.

We also thank all of our supporters at Prentice Hall—Charlyce Jones-Owen, Allison Reeves, Mary Jo Southern, Patricia Castiglione, Fred ("PermDude") Courtright, Leah Jewell, Joan Saidel, and most especially Harriett Prentiss, the world's most helpful development editor.

Lillian Bridwell-Bowles
The University of Minnesota
April 1997

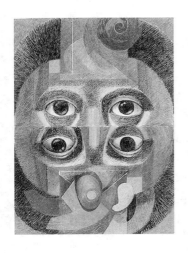

CHAPTER I

Identity and Writing in College

the purpose of the text↓

This book is about reading and writing your way to a better understanding of yourself, your culture, and your education. It is also about understanding the cultures and lives of those whose identities may be constructed differently. During your college years, perhaps more than any other time in your life, you have the freedom to interrogate your own beliefs and attitudes and to examine the multiple factors that determine your identity. In addition, you will be exploring career choices, making decisions about lifestyles, or maybe even changing directions. In all of these endeavors, and for the rest of your life, you will be well served if you have a set of critical strategies for reading and writing. You already use many critical approaches intuitively, and you probably already have some conscious strategies. This book will give you an opportunity to name these strategies, to practice them, and to add new ones.

WRITING TO LEARN

We believe there is no better way to come to know yourself than through the process of writing. As you write for yourself in journals and early drafts of essays, you will come to understand your own positions better. In particular, you will be exploring some of the factors that contribute to your identity, to your way of perceiving the world. Reading your thoughts on paper gives you a chance to reflect on them critically, before you share them. When you share your public writing in more polished drafts, you will learn how your ideas and

Goal: to be able to see the world through others' eyes

opinions affect other people, and you will get feedback about the accuracy of your information.

Key terms

Considering identity in a multicultural society at the turn of the century gives you an unlimited number of things to write about, but these topics also contain potential pitfalls. Terms such as "multicultural," "cultural pluralism," "diversity," and "political correctness" are "loaded" and subject to attack from both the Left and the Right. "Cultural diversity" can simply imply something descriptive, for example, that people in a given culture come from various backgrounds; however, it can also imply something political, for example, that minority groups are seeking to replace "traditional American values" with different values or that the "dominant culture" is imposing "hegemony" on those who are different. To write effectively about ourselves and complex social issues, we need to analyze our own positions and anticipate the ways they will be received by readers who differ from us in radical ways.

WRITING TO COMMUNICATE

When we go public with our ideas, we need a repertoire of rhetorical approaches. Writing within the academy is changing as society changes (although which comes first, we can't answer), and the kind of writing that you do in college demands more from you as a "rhetorician," a person who understands how messages can be communicated effectively in a wide variety of situations. Not only will you be called upon to produce various kinds of writing (e.g., essays, personal explorations, objective research reports, lab reports, essay exams), but you will also be asked to define a number of personas that may be new for you (e.g., "expert," "feminist," "practitioner" in a field). You may also have to write for people whose intellectual and political positions differ dramatically from your own. Some theorists have even declared the "death of the author" because it is so difficult to imagine a singular writing "self" with any agency in such a complicated world. We aren't worried about the death of the author—a trip to any local library or bookstore (or the Internet) will reassure even the most anxious among us that writers are still finding ways to express themselves honestly and powerfully. But we do acknowledge that the rhetorical challenges are more complex. The selections in this book illustrate some of the ways writers have constructed themselves as writers and their audiences as readers. As you try them on for size, some will fit and others won't.

We like the metaphor of becoming a *"rhetorical shape-shifter,"* moving cautiously from one form and medium to another, changing perspectives as necessary to understand multiple points of view, while at the same time staying in touch with your "self," maintaining your position even when it may not be popular or easy—or interrogating it when you think there may be a reason to change. You may have difficulties because the "self" who is writing is changing. You will need to decide when to stand firm and when to experiment with a new position. As instructors, we like to encourage students to take some risks with

[handwritten margin notes: what does it mean to "take risks"? / What is good writing? / Expectations? → you have? / I have? / — for yourself, for myself]

their writing. In Chapter 10 we describe some fairly traditional ways of design-
ing essays, which we hope will serve you well in many settings, and some experimental ones, which might be more appropriate when you are exploring
new territory or a new approach. If you want to take a major risk in a piece of
writing, we encourage you to talk it over with your instructor so that you can
determine what the consequences—or rewards—might be.

FACTORS THAT INFLUENCE IDENTITY

[handwritten: try new things (lenses)]

As you write, we invite you to take on a number of different personas. The
writers included in this collection represent many different subject positions.
They will move you from one set of assumptions to another. Much critical theory within the academy demands that we analyze the concept of "difference"
in various social contexts through the lenses of race, class, and gender. No matter what the issue, some academics believe that we must analyze issues in these
terms, yet most of us have not spent much time asking what the terms mean.

How, for example, do we define "race" in this country? Most of us might
find it hard to believe that some people still literally apply the "one drop rule"
("If you have one drop of African blood, you are a Negro and therefore a
slave"—or subject to whatever laws apply to African Americans at the time).
And yet, according to Michael Omi and Howard Winant (1986), as late as 1982
a woman in Louisiana appealed to have herself legally reclassified from black
to white, but was denied because she was 1/32 black. Despite the occasional
anachronistic judgment such as this, we have no accepted biological definitions of the term "race." And yet many people think their identities as "African
American" or "white" or "Latina/Latino" or "Asian American" or "Native
American" are the most important thing about themselves. Their social construction of their identities—their cultural ways of thinking of themselves—focus on their racial or ethnic heritage. *[handwritten: Race cant be defined]*

The way we construct the categories has changed fairly often in the United
States. "White," as David Roediger (1994) has pointed out, is a fairly recent social construction, like the other categories. Before the term "white" came into
common usage, people were thought of as "Irish immigrants," "Polish immigrants," and so on. Others see themselves as hybrids, neither one nor another,
but a combination of races or ethnicities that they want to continue to name very
carefully. In other cases, some people want to create a category called "hybrid"
or "mixed blood." Still others resist all labels, thinking of themselves as "citizens
of the world," so varied in their histories as to defy classification.

What are we to make of other terms such as "ethnic group" or "community"? Nearly everyone seems to belong to multiple communities these days. In
this book, individual writers refer to all of the racial and ethnic communities
above as well as to others such as the "disabled community," "the deaf community," "the Gay/Lesbian/Bisexual/Transgender community," "the little
people community," and just lately, "the blue-collar community."

[handwritten: there are many aspects that make us]

depending on context

Prejudices and discrimination are based on racial, ethnic, and social distinctions, whether they can be "scientifically" or "legally" defined or not. Classification is an important business—money and opportunity can hinge on one's ability to define oneself as a member of a particular racial group. In most settings in the United States today, you might have more opportunities if you are perceived as "white." In others, especially when affirmative action laws are applied, it might be to your advantage to claim membership in a particular ethnic group. For example, as Native Americans have found ways to market gambling casinos because of the special federal status of reservations, some people have worked very hard to establish their Native American roots so that they can share in the profits. Careful attention to naming, classifying, and defining is crucial as you read and respond to the essays in these chapters.

We also include essays and fictional pieces that expand the number of lenses through which you can view difference, including religion and spirituality, age, ability or disability, regionalism, and nationalism. Clearly, there are additional factors that have influenced the development of your personal identity, and you will want to add them to your analyses. For example, all of us have been significantly molded by family experiences or by our birth order among siblings. Increasingly, studies of twins reared apart are revealing the significance of genetics in determining personality and behavior. You may want to design a research project about some of these factors, in addition to the ones in the book.

We invite you to consider all the factors that have affected you and the factors in your future that will continue to cause you to change and grow. The most powerful intellectual growth occurs when you identify a passion, something you must know, and nearly always this passion is about something personal. We invite you to connect the personal to your intellectual pursuits as you practice the craft of writing.

CONTROVERSY

The selections in this anthology present controversial social issues that we have to deal with if we are to create a more peaceful and productive world for the new millennium. In classes ranging from first-year composition to advanced "writing-intensive" courses, these essay topics can lead to stimulating argument, discussion, and problem-solving on personal and/or private levels and in social and/or professional settings. They can just as easily lead to confrontation and shut down communication. My colleagues and I invite you to consider how people with different perspectives might appropriately communicate with each other. We think that much is left to discover about how we can improve communication within the academy and in society.

INTERCONNECTEDNESS

We also want to show the interconnectedness of identity issues. We don't think you can fully analyze race, for example, without considering class, gen-

Each Identifying factor has more "branches" that stem

der, regionalism, religion, age, ability, and nationalism. Neither can we think about gender without considering how our constructions of it vary depending upon our socioeconomic status, our age, our sexual orientations, our race or ethnic background, our experience of regionalism, and so on. One path through this book is to explore one issue fully, describing how the other issues are related to it. The questions and topics after each reading often refer you to other selections throughout the book, so that you can make these connections. For example, class issues are the focus in Chapter 3, but there are also essays that deal with class in every other chapter. See the alternative table of contents for a listing of the essays that deal with each topic.

CROSS-DISCIPLINARITY

Such as Gender → sexual orientation

The selections in this book will give you a cross-disciplinary look at eight major social issues. They explore the kinds of disciplinary and professional "rhetorics" and "discourses" that are possible within and outside the academy. If you are just beginning your college education, this process may help you as you begin identifying possible majors; if you are further along, you will be able to compare the ways your field approaches a problem to the methods used in other fields.

By "rhetorics" and "discourses," we mean the ways people analyze, package, and present ideas and information when they attempt to communicate. Throughout this volume, you will be challenged to analyze the ways different essayists, journalists, fiction writers, and specialists address the same topics. You will be asked to compare and contrast their ways of working and their choices of genres. As a person seeking an advanced education, you will want to be able to see connections across fields, not just the particular points of view in your own major, discipline, or profession. Later in this chapter, there is a list of rhetorical questions that can help you analyze the rhetoric of a particular discourse. You can use them as you read the essays in this book or as you define the "rhetorical situation" for your own writing. Every attempt to communicate is governed by factors such as the authority of the writer, the audience, the reasons for writing, and so on. See page 579 for a listing of the different genres we have included in the book.

CRITICAL READING

You will need to use critical methods typical of the various courses you will take (or are taking) as you respond to the writers gathered here. They themselves come from a wide range of fields—law, medicine, literature, journalism, creative writing, and many more. As you reflect on these particular writers' points of view, also consider how their views of situations are shaped by their disciplinary or professional perspectives. For example, what does it mean to think about "class" from the point of view of a sociologist? a feminist? a psychologist?

an artist? a scientist? How are their perspectives also shaped by their personal history? Do they include personal experience in their writing?

Critical reading calls for an active approach. In other settings, you probably breeze through a good novel or an interesting magazine article with pure recreation or escape as your only goal. The kind of reading you will be doing here will sometimes please and entertain you (we hope), but it should also stretch your mind. We challenge you to go beyond predictable or "typical" responses as you think and write about this type of reading.

Reading researchers often find that successful college students don't simply move through passages one time and then put down their books. Somewhere along the line, they have acquired "active learning" strategies that help them read and think more critically. Here are some suggestions:

- Preview the article, predicting answers to questions such as the ones we have proposed: Who is the writer? Why did the writer write this? How will the writer prove his or her point? Where was the work initially published? What does this suggest about what I'll find here?
- Take notes in the margins and underline or highlight key passages. Writing a short paraphrase or key phrase in the margins to describe a difficult passage is often more helpful than simply highlighting it.
- Reread the whole essay if you have time, or at least reread key passages.

You can also use the rhetorical questions listed in this chapter for more extended critiques. In the introduction to each chapter, we have suggested a particular focus on one or two of the kinds of rhetorical questions.

PROMPTS TO GET YOU STARTED

Throughout the book we offer opportunities for you to write informally for yourself, to explore your own voice and stance before you go public. After each selection, we offer you some topics "For Journaling and Discussion." You will write informally about these questions in a journal or response log (see suggestions in Chapter 10). You will probably not be evaluated for your writing style or form when you respond to these questions. They are instead intended to help you "think on paper" or to record your observations for class discussion. Under the heading "For Research and Exploration" you should find questions and projects that will lead to public or formal writing.

RHETORICAL QUESTIONS

Finally, we provide a set of rhetorical questions that you can use to guide your thinking about all of the topics contained in this anthology. You can always use them to interrogate a piece of writing, no matter what the topic. These techniques are habits of mind that well-educated people possess and polish throughout their lives. Some writers report that they think about these ques-

Be engaged

tions consciously; others have learned through experience to take them into account intuitively. You can apply these questions both to the essays you read and to those you write. As your instructor assigns sections of the book, or as you work your way through it on your own, we suggest that you review the questions, at least briefly, before you begin writing about any of the topics.

Just to be practical, however, we propose that you focus on one or two kinds of questions in each chapter. Even though it may be ideal to take them all into account every time you write, you may find it helpful to focus on a few as you practice your craft. *Writing strategies*

↓

Context

In what setting does this conversation take place?
Where has this essay been published?
How are conversations about this topic different in other settings? How are they similar?
Where might you publish or distribute something you would write about this topic?

Authority *Who are they?*

Whose voice is being heard on this issue?
Which voices are not represented, underrepresented, and overrepresented? Would everyone agree? Who would not? Why?
What gives you authority to speak or write on this topic?
Because you are different from this writer, how is your authority different?
What could you do to get your readers to give you more authority?

Stance

What are the writer's attitudes? beliefs? philosophies? political positions?
How would you describe the writer's stance toward the readers?
Are the readers insiders or outsiders?
Does the writer seek common ground or confrontation with the readers?
What position(s) might you take?
How would you most effectively communicate your position(s) to different audiences?
Are you limited to just one position, or do you want to keep several options open?

Audience

Who are the intended readers of this essay?
Are they all alike? Are they like you?
Who else might read about this topic, and how would a different audience change the essay?

Pick / choose your tools

Whom do you wish to address as you write about these issues? Are multiple audiences involved?

What attitudes, beliefs, and knowledge do your audiences have about the topic?

How do their positions mesh with yours?

Purpose

Why has the author written this essay?

Does this essay call for action?

What is the writer's purpose?

Do you think the goal is achieved?

What kind of action might follow from this reading?

Why would you want to write something about this topic?

What kind of action might you call for in your response?

Methodology

What has the writer done to gather material?

What way of studying the problem is identified in the essay?

What kinds of insight are possible using the methodology in this essay?

Are there other methods that are more relevant? more interesting? more reliable? more credible?

Is a combination of methods better than a single approach?

What kind of information is not likely to be revealed by this methodology?

What sources or data are most appropriate? How do you find them?

How might a writer from an entirely different field or discipline approach this topic?

Form, Communicative Strategy, and Style

What form has the writer of the essays chosen? magazine feature? short story? autobiographical essay? research report?

What are the characteristics of this form?

What are its patterns of organization? types of arguments? types of evidence?

What function does each paragraph serve?

Which terms need careful definition?

Is there anything unusual about this writer's sentences? word choices? style?

Is the essay written in "standard" English? Why or why not?

How are outside sources documented?

Are the tone and style formal or informal? intimate or distant? humorous or serious? biased or objective?

How might certain readers be affected if the word choices, usage, style, and tone changed?

How might you be affected if you were asked to alter something you
had written?
What form will your writing take?

The last chapter in this book contains suggestions about effective writing
processes and descriptions of the various forms your writing can take. You will
find descriptions of formats and styles, as well as recommendations for documenting outside sources. The chapter also contains suggestions about ways to
use technology to conduct research on the topics we have suggested at the end
of each reading.

A FINAL COMMENT ON OUR PURPOSES ↓ true

We don't know where America is headed as its demographics change. We
don't know whether we want to retain the "melting pot" metaphor or to adopt
new metaphors like the "salad bowl" to describe how we will deal with our differences as citizens of one nation. Are we *"e pluribus unum"* (out of many, one)?
Or are we destined to become just *"pluribus"* with no way of coming together
as *"unum"*? In this book, we draw together multiple American and international voices to raise questions about the social categories that in part define
us all. Sometimes these voices are in conflict with each other, but no single
voice is more authentic or more representative than any other. Limited space
means we cannot even attempt to achieve equal representation on an issue.
Most books that attempt to do that end up offering what we think of as a "token sampler." America is a melting pot (Blend)

We have tried to capture the complexity of a variety of contemporary debates. Sometimes, when one debate dominates over others, we focus on that
debate. In Chapter 2, for example, on race, half of the selections look at
African American/European American tensions because in the United States
today, most discussions about race relations begin with black/white tensions.
The representation in the chapter reflects the nature of most race debates in
the contemporary United States, but we have tried to extend it to other settings
as well. In Chapter 4, on gender and sexuality, however, we open up the lens
to consider questions beyond the usual "battle of the sexes." We think the typical analyses of males versus females are often based on faulty assumptions
about "essential" qualities of either sex, most of which vanish when we take a
closer look at other factors such as race, class, ability, and nation. While "He
said/She said" and "Venus versus Mars" conversations take up a lot of space in
the popular media, we give attention to more complex issues. In a sense, every
chapter in this book is a work in progress. If we produce a subsequent edition
of this anthology, we can imagine that these balances will shift in interesting
ways, some of which are not even predictable now.

When an individual or a group has been marked as "different" or "other"
by the dominant group, it is often out of their "otherness" that they first tell

(margin, left) "Salad bowl" Mix but still individual

(margin, right) melting into the "norm"

their stories. Blacks, blue-collar workers, women, old people, the disabled, southerners, and immigrants are marked as "others" in the United States, and they often take center stage in our chapters. If you belong to one or more of these groups, you will see a variety of options for presenting yourself. If you belong to groups that occupy positions closer to the center or dominant position in society, then analyzing those who are labeled as different will help you to understand how your position is defined in contrast to theirs.

Each writer (and each reader) is never defined just by race or gender or class, ability or disability, or region, nation, or religious/spiritual group. We all have multiple identities. We are African American-male-upper class; we are Jewish-blue-collar-lesbian; we are Presbyterian-middle-aged-white; we are every possible combination. In certain settings, one of these identities may come to the foreground. When a lesbian enters a room full of heterosexual couples, she may immediately put her lesbian identity in the foreground. It is the thing that most marks her as "other" in that situation. Or she may choose to keep this part of her identity confidential and instead foreground her professional credentials to establish her authority in a work setting. A Latina may focus on her ethnic heritage in a white setting, but choose to emphasize her age at a multi-aged family gathering. Every distinction informs every other. We are complicated beings. The more we can learn to interact with each other in complex terms, not just on inflammatory single issues, the better we will function as individuals in complex communities.

It is our great hope that you will be changed in some way by the work that you do with this book. This was our reason for compiling it. We believe in social change and we have hope for the future, but not without improved critical thinking and communication. We do not expect that you will agree with everything you read here. We do not want you to. As collaborators, we often disagreed. But our collaboration continued because we maintained our respect for each other and found ways to argue through lively discussion, debate, and writing. We wish for you the energizing experience that we had, and we hope you are changed forever in some way that will help us all in the twenty-first century. *Life changing book?*

REPRESENTATIVE IDENTITY REFERENCES

In this collection of essays, you will find many ideas for further reading and research into the specific topic of each chapter. To help you with the overall question of how these ways of thinking influence your sense of identity, we have provided a list of helpful books and articles that make this connection. You may find this list useful as you pursue some of our suggestions under "For Research and Exploration" at the end of each essay.

Achieving Independence: The Challenge for the 21st Century—A Decade of Progress in Disability Policy. Washington, DC: National Council on Disability, 1996.

Identity shape shifters
Different parts show

Sources (work cited)

Ackelsberg, Martha A. "Identity Politics, Political Identities: Thoughts Toward a Multicultural Politics." *Frontiers* 16.1 (1996): 87–100.

Albrecht, Lisa, and Rose M. Brewer. *Bridges of Power: Women's Multicultural Alliances.* Philadelphia: National Women's Studies Association by New Society Publishers, 1990.

The Americans with Disabilities Act: Title II Technical Assistance Manual. Washington, DC: U.S. Department of Justice, Civil Rights Division, 1996.

Arber, Sara, and Maria Evandrou, eds. *Ageing, Independence, and the Life Course.* London: British Society of Gerontology, 1993.

Aronowitz, Stanley. *The Politics of Identity: Class, Culture, Social Movements.* New York: Routledge, 1992.

Barkun, Michael. *Religion and the Racist Right: The Origins of the Christian Identity Movement.* Rev. ed. Chapel Hill: University of North Carolina Press, 1997.

Barton, Len, ed. *Disability and Society: Emerging Issues and Insights.* New York: Longman, 1996.

Boyarin, Jonathan. *Thinking in Jewish.* Chicago: University of Chicago Press, 1996.

Brewer, Marilyn B., and Wendi Gardner. "Who Is This 'We'? Levels of Collective Identity and Self Representations." *Journal of Personality and Social Psychology* 71.1 (1996): 83–93.

Campbell, Jane. *Disability Politics: Understanding Our Past, Changing Our Future.* New York: Routledge, 1996.

Chandler, Daniel. "The Construction of Identity in Personal Home Pages on the World Wide Web." 5 paragraphs plus many links. World Wide Web. n.d. Available at http://www.aber.ac.uk/%Edgc/munich.html.

Cornell, Stephen. "The Variable Ties That Bind: Content and Circumstance in Ethnic Processes." *Ethnic and Racial Studies* 19.2 (April 1996): 265–289.

Ehrenreich, Barbara. *Fear of Falling: The Inner Life of the Middle Class.* New York: Pantheon, 1989.

Epstein, A. L. *Ethos and Identity.* London: Tavistock, 1987.

Espiritu, Yen Le. *Asian American Panethnicity: Bridging Institutions and Identities.* Philadelphia: Temple University Press, 1992.

Esposito, John L. *Islam and Democracy: Religion, Identity, and Conflict Resolutions in the Muslim World.* New York: Oxford University Press, 1996.

Friedan, Betty. "Beyond Gender." *Newsweek* 126.10 (1995): 30–32.

Fugita, Stephen, and David O'Brien. *Japanese American Ethnicity: The Persistence of Community.* Seattle: University of Washington Press, 1991.

Gergen, Kenneth J. *Realities and Relationships.* Cambridge: Harvard University Press, 1994.

———. "Social Construction and the Transformation of Identity Politics." 37 paragraphs. World Wide Web. 7 April 1995. Available at http://www.swarthmore.edu/SocSci/kgergen1/text8.html.

Gillis, John R., ed. *Commemorations: The Politics of National Identity.* Princeton: Princeton University Press, 1994.

Hooks, Bell. *Black Looks: Race and Representation.* Boston: South End Press, 1992.

———. *Teaching to Transgress: Education as the Practice of Freedom.* New York: Routledge, 1994.

Journal of Aging and Identity. New York: Human Sciences Press, 1996.

Lerda, Valeria Gennaro, and Tjebbe Westendorp. *The United States South: Regionalism and Identity.* Rome: Bulzoni, 1991.

Levine, Lawrence. *Highbrow/Lowbrow: The Emergence of Cultural Hierarchy in America.* Cambridge: Harvard University Press, 1988.

McCarthy, Cameron, and Warren Crichlow, eds. *Race, Identity, and Representation in Education.* New York: Routledge, 1993.

McNaron, Toni. *I Dwell in Possibility: A Memoir.* New York: Feminist Press, City University Press of New York, 1991.

———. *Poisoned Ivy: Lesbian and Gay Academics Confronting Homophobia, 1964–1994.* Philadelphia: Temple University Press, 1997.

Moraga, Cherrie, and Gloria Anzaldua. *This Bridge Called My Back: Writings by Radical Women of Color.* Watertown, MA: Persephone Press, 1981.

Myrsiades, Kostas, and Jerry McGuire. *Order and Partialities: Theory, Pedagogy, and the "Postcolonial."* New York: State University of New York Press, 1995.

National Organization for Women [NOW]. "NOW World Wide Web Home Page." World Wide Web. n.d. Available at http://www.now.org.

Omi, Michael, and Howard Winant. *Racial Formation in the United States: From the 1960s to the 1980s.* New York: Routledge, 1986.

O'Sullivan, Patrick. *Religion and Identity.* London: Leicester University Press, 1996.

Pinsker, Sanford. "Cooling the Polemics of the Culture Warriors." *The Chronicle of Higher Education* 42.32 (May 3, 1996): A56.

Racial and Ethnic Diversity in America's Elderly Population. Washington, DC: U.S. Department of Commerce, Economic and Statistics Administration, Bureau of the Census, National Institute on Aging, 1993.

Rajchman, John. *The Identity in Question.* New York: Routledge, 1995.

Roediger, David. *Toward the Abolition of Whiteness.* New York: Verso, 1994.

Roth, John K. *American Diversity, American Identity: The Lives and Works of 145 Writers Who Define the American Experience.* New York: Holt, 1995.

Sleeter, Christine. *Multicultural Education as Social Activism.* New York: State University of New York Press, 1996.

Sollors, Werner, ed. *The Invention of Ethnicity.* New York: Oxford University Press, 1989.

Stout, Daniel A., and Judith M. Buddenbaum, eds. *Religion and Mass Media: Audiences and Adaptations.* Thousand Oaks, CA: Sage Publications, 1996.

Thompson, Becky W., and Sangeeta Tyagi. *Beyond a Dream Deferred: Multicultural Education and the Politics of Excellence.* Minneapolis: University of Minnesota Press, 1993.

Tilly, Charles, ed. *Citizenship, Identity, and Social History.* New York: Cambridge University Press, 1996.

Warhol, Robyn R., and Diane Price Herndl. *Feminisms.* New Brunswick, NJ: Rutgers University Press, 1991.

Waters, Mary C. *Ethnic Options: Choosing Identities in America.* Berkeley, CA: University of California Press, 1990.

West, Cornel. *Race Matters.* New York: Vintage Books, 1994.

"Who Are We?" Special issue of *Diogenes*, 44/1.173 (September 1996).

Young, Robert B. *No Neutral Ground: Standing by the Values We Prize in Higher Education.* San Francisco: Jossey-Bass, 1997.

CHAPTER 2

Race and Ethnicity

Race is undefined

(handwritten margin note, left side, vertical): can't do it - Inability

Theorists who have written about race differ dramatically in the ways they approach the subject. Biologists and sociologists, for example, often point out the folly of even trying to define the term "race" scientifically. Many people prefer the term "ethnicity" because it avoids genetic heritage and focuses on one's sociocultural history, which can be described more accurately. Increasingly, some members of our society want to define themselves as "hybrids," not fitting into simple racial or ethnic groups. Despite these trends that might suggest a blurring of color categories, Cornel West, a philosopher and professor of African American studies, argues that race is the single most important defining factor in American society. In every chapter of this book, the question of definition is important. This should be the starting place for your analyses. In what ways do these writers define "race"?

Whether one is "a person of color," "a hybrid," "an ethnic," "a hyphenated American," or "white," race relations in this country affect our daily lives—our sense of who we are, our opportunities, our entitlements, our belief systems, and our futures—individually and collectively. Reacting to the lack of leadership during the riots in Los Angeles in 1992, West argues, "Whoever *our* leaders will be as we approach the twenty-first century, their challenge will be to help Americans determine whether a genuine multiracial democracy can be created and sustained in an era of global economy and a moment of xenophobic frenzy. . . . Either we learn a new language of empathy and compassion, or the fire this time will consume us all" (West 13). He invokes Ralph Ellison

(handwritten margin note, right side, vertical): We have to get along

(handwritten note at bottom): Race Relations: Differences, Relationships, & Effectors

on the conflict that whites feel about their own identity—"a deep uncertainty as to who they really are"—and the result—using "the presence of black Americans . . . as a marker, a symbol of limits, a metaphor for the 'outsider' " (in West 3).

SUMMARIES OF SELECTIONS ON RACE AND ETHNICITY

As we selected essays for this chapter, we were trying to present complicated images of racial experience; we want to challenge you to avoid stereotypes and simplistic solutions as you write about the subject. For example, in "Parents and Family," **Lise Funderburg** collects a range of biracial oral histories that help to break down the notion of "purity" of whiteness and blackness. In her book, she also collects references to historical law on miscegenation as she illustrates the motivations, triumphs, and problems of biracial couples and their biracial children.

David Mura's experience of raising his Japanese American daughter further illustrates the complexities of hybridity. In "Secrets and Anger?" he describes himself as Japanese, "a person of color," and his wife as "white," and gives examples of the ways he and his daughter have a different experience as Americans than white Americans do, despite many "liberal" friends' attempts to claim that they, too, "know what prejudice is."

Sherman Alexie's character John, in the essay "Integration" from his novel *Indian Killer,* is another kind of hybrid—all Native American by birth, but raised by white adoptive parents. His experience of difference surfaces when he tries to date white girls in his parochial school. By his senior year, this "successfully integrated Indian boy" is escaping to the restroom on a daily basis to bite his tongue and lips until they bleed.

Richard Rodriguez is often viewed as a "representative" spokesperson for Mexican Americans, but he is often also attacked by members of this community for being "unrepresentative." In his essay "India," he reflects on his own hybridity and range of perspectives. He writes, "Mexico initiated the task of the twenty-first century—the renewal of the old, the known world, through miscegenation. Mexico carries the idea of a round world to its biological conclusion."

In "Confessions of a Wannabe Negro," **Reginald McKnight** recalls his emerging awareness of himself as "black" when he developed a crush on a girl with hair as "white as sunlight on a web." He describes his inability to be "white" enough in some settings and "black" enough in others, and finally uses Trey Ellis's term to describe himself, and everyone, as a "cultural mulatto." All he has learned about black people, he says, "told me very little about who I am, let alone who we are. We're too big for that, and as individuals too complex."

Gary Indiana complicates the images of "white" as he compares his father's pretentious WASP grandparents to his mother's freewheeling, working-class Catholic family in "Memories of a Xenophobic Boyhood." He believes that people in his community rarely thought of themselves as white until some-body else wasn't: "I suppose that's the white thing: never having to define what you are, while other people scramble to define themselves in relationship to you." And yet the whites in his community always found other ways to establish hierarchy and prejudice—religion, class, sexual preference—ingenious ways to determine who was "whiter" than someone else.

Patricia Williams pokes fun at the Cinderella story when she describes the ways her "best white friend" tries to turn her into a "trophy-wife-in-waiting" on her way to a posh party. The shoe just doesn't fit, as she describes in "My Best White Friend: Cinderella Revisited," even though "M.B.W.F." tells her cheerfully, "Now, now, we're all sisters under the makeup." Williams deals with the differences in their constructions of race, gender, and class, but implies that these very differences may be what makes their friendship work.

Although "Our Next Race Question" explores the economic, historical, and social influences that complicate race relations in the United States, most of the comments by **Jorge Klor De Alva, Earl Shorris,** and **Cornel West** examine the highly personal assault on the individual's sense of self that results from living in a racist society. They also offer several perspectives on the process of naming various racial and ethnic groups.

RHETORICAL QUESTIONS Critical thinking

As you read these selections, focus on the ways the writers establish their *authority* to speak on these issues and how they position themselves within the essay—their *stance* toward their readers. See Chapter 1 for a discussion of the rhetorical questions that guide the explorations in this book.

How is each writer, character, or speaker presented? as a member of one racial or ethnic group? as a hybrid? Are the individuals in the selections aware of their own positions? What gives them the authority to speak on each of these topics? Examine the biographical statements on each author (or do further exploration) to determine why they would be granted authority to speak. What would happen if white people wrote some of the essays about being black or Latino/Latina or Japanese American? Because he is white, does Gary Indiana have the same status as an authority on racial questions as the others? Why or why not?

And finally, what is your position vis-à-vis race? As you respond to the selections in the chapter, focus on your own *stance* and your *authority* to speak on questions of race and ethnicity. Who will care about your experiences? Keeping a running record of your responses to the exploratory questions at the end of each selection should lead you to answers to some of these questions.

If you write a formal paper on a topic that grows out of your readings in this chapter, consider how many other identity issues are related to race or ethnicity. How important are class, gender, age, religion, ability, region, or nationality to the points you want to make? What will you omit so that you can focus your paper?

You will find comments about race and ethnicity in the other chapters as well. See the alternative table of contents for a listing of some of the related essays in other chapters.

[REFERENCE MLA: WORKS Cited

West, Cornel. *Race Matters*. New York: Vintage Books, 1994.]

Parents and Family

Lise Funderburg

Funderburg, herself biracial, writes about issues of community and identity. In the book from which this excerpt is taken, Black, White, Other: Biracial Americans Talk about Race and Identity, *she observes that "as flawed as every definition of race probably is, the emotions and consequences of those definitions are very real," noting that sweeping generalizations about racial confusion in children of mixed-race relationships "reflect the laziness of a society that, if given the choice, will often oversimplify rather than appreciate complexities and coexisting realities." Funderburg lives in Brooklyn, New York.*

One time I got the flour out, and when my dad came home, I had covered myself in flour, from head to toe. My dad asked me what I was doing, and I told him, "I'm gonna be one color."

And he said, "Why are you going to be white?"

I said, "Because we don't have any black powder." And he looked at me, and he just kind of shook his head, and I asked him, I said, "Dad, what am I?" And he told me that I was a beautiful little girl.

"No, Dad, that doesn't work. What am I really?"

"What do you want to hear? What do you want to be?"

"I don't know what I want to be. I just don't understand why I have to be anything; I don't understand what's going on."

Finally he told me, "Well, you're black and you've got really nice hair. Does that sound good?"

"Well, I guess so."

And he said, "Okay, that one will work for a couple of years. Go with it."

—Sandra Shupe . . . .

It takes two people to create a biracial child: a mother and a father. Like all parents, they may be largely responsible for shaping how their children see themselves and the world. What parents teach about race comes, in part, from their own experience of race.

Few interracial couples escape all the land mines that are historically placed in their paths: from being disowned by both sides of the family to the occasional stare or muttered comment on the street. While some couples would respond to such treatment with bitterness or might even retreat from each other, others remain steadfast in their commitment to one another and to the family they have created together.

It wasn't until 1967, in the U.S. Supreme Court's *Loving* v. *Virginia* decision, that remaining antimiscegenation laws (still on the books in sixteen states at the time) were overruled. Richard and Mildred Loving were the appellants in the case. In 1958 the newlywed Lovings were arrested in their Virginia hometown for being married to each other. She was black, he was white. Rather than face incarceration, they moved back in with their respective parents, then moved together to Washington, D.C., where they lived for several years. The Virginia judge's ruling also ordered that they never visit Virginia together. Miserable in their exile, they asked for help from Robert Kennedy, then attorney general of the United States. Kennedy directed them to the American Civil Liberties Union, where two lawyers took on their case. Nine years later, the Lovings and their lawyers changed the law of the land.

Laws against miscegenation existed in America as early as 1661. By and large, they targeted only groups that were not allowed to marry Whites, sometimes reflecting regional concerns. (Laws in Arizona prohibited Whites from marriages with Negroes, Mongolians, Indians, Malay, or Hindu people; Oregon prohibited Whites from marrying anyone more than one-half Indian or one-quarter Negro, one-quarter Chinese, or one-quarter Kanaka [Hawaiian].) In some states, including Maryland and Louisiana, legislators also wrote in provisions against Indians and Blacks marrying, probably to prevent the formation of a coalition between the two oppressed groups.

Laws and the threat of social censure never successfully precluded interracial relationships and the conception of biracial children. Still, since the *Loving* decision, black-white marriages have increased dramatically: According to the census, they jumped 378 percent from 1970 to 1992 (from 65,000 to 246,000).

If such families almost certainly invite some level of criticism and rejection, why have people continued to cross racial lines? Are interracial couples visionaries, living out a utopian ideal? Are they retaliating against or perpetuating an earlier American miscegenation: the slave master's rape of the slave? While the preponderance of racial mixing in early U.S. history was between white men and black women, today, according to the census, 85 percent of black-white interracial marriages reverse that configuration. Does this gender shift speak to alliances of power and powerlessness or something else altogether? Somewhere in the answers to why these couples come together lie clues to what information they will give their children about race.

This chapter presents [a number of] oral histories . . . . For many people, their first (and longest-lasting) impressions of race come from parents and family;

for biracial children, the very existence and nature of their parents' relationship often provides a paradigm for understanding or valuing race. The parents' relationship might communicate that love transcends racial barriers, and serve as evidence that people can bridge what have been considered immutable gaps in color, culture, and experience. On the other hand, parents may behave in ways that cement divisions and distinctions, and not always intentionally. "I used to wonder if my mother really liked black people that much," one woman said about her white parent.

Many black-white couples think they and their children are all part of the same experience: that they are equal participants in their multiracial family. They expect that their children will experience the world as they do, and that the views they hold, their children can hold, too. Mindy Thompson Fullilove is a psychiatrist who has studied racial-identity formation in biracial people (and is herself biracial). She explains what she found to be the more accurate dynamic between parents and children:

> The parents' perspective on this problem is really different from the kids' perspective. That's what's most striking. The parents, at best, think they've done something wonderful in putting together a family that defies racial convention. For them it's an issue of love conquering all or an affirmation of what they wish for themselves over and above the conventions of society. For the parents it's this consciously chosen thing to live in this way; but the kids didn't choose, they just have to grow up in the midst of it. That's a really important distinction, because the parents tend to think it's the same for the kids as it is for them. And it's truly not . . . .

Some of the following stories suggest that whatever parents' intentions may have been, what their children have learned may not be what their parents intended to teach.

ROSA EMILIA WARDER
Age: 34
Residence: Oakland, California
Occupation: Foundation writer and development coordinator;
Children's book author

Rosa Emilia Warder grew up in San Francisco's upper western addition neighborhood, which was, at the time, racially and ethnically mixed. Her parents were three times removed from the mainstream: an interracial couple, artists, and political radicals. Rosa was a red-diaper baby, the only child of two Communists who met through their political activities.

Even Warder's name was a political statement. *Rosa* honored Rosa Parks, who launched the Montgomery, Alabama, bus boycott of 1955. *Emilia* was a feminized tribute to Emiliano Zapata, a Socialist Mexican revolutionary. Repercussions of her parents' political affiliations came early on. In the early 1960s, when Warder saw that a little girl her age resembled a poster of Africans she had seen on the Communist party nursery walls, she told the girl that she was African. "I thought she was beautiful," Warder says. "That was not something she wanted to hear in 1962, so she decked me."

Because Warder had fair skin and long braids, some black children taunted her, once calling her a "honkey nigger" as they tied her hair to a railing. For the

most part, white children simply ignored her. Warder's parents taught her to recognize both sides from a positive vantage point. "I identify as African-American and
European-American," she says. "I've never thought of myself specifically as white or
black. As a kid I remember wanting to be one or the other during different periods. Now I assume that people see me as black or African-American or whatever—
people of color—whatever their phrase of the moment is. That doesn't really affect
what I know, and it's not something I really spend any time thinking about."

My mother is the European-American member of the family. She grew up in
Bend, Oregon, which is still a very homogeneous white community. She grew
up in a fairly wealthy cattle-ranching family and left home when she was twenty
to go to study art at Reed College. Then she worked her way to California,
where she met my father.

My father grew up in Abilene, Kansas, where he was in one of two black
families. His parents died by the time he was thirteen. He grew up with aunts
and uncles after that point, and then joined the navy. He was a jazz musician
during World War II, and he worked his way to California; my parents met in
the early fifties, at a jazz club where he was playing. My mother was an artist.
She was doing sketches of musicians and he was playing. In terms of how their
families reacted, my father's family—being just his sister and the aunts and the
uncles that were still alive—were really pretty accepting of Nancy, my mother,
and their marriage.

My mother's family, on the other hand, was totally not accepting and disowned her when she did get married. That was an interesting contradiction,
because there are a lot of illegitimate children in my mother's very upper-crust
family who were kind of ignored, and so it was just part of that whole history of
denial and strange goings-on. So I actually have never met anyone from my
mother's half of the family. My mother has a younger sister who's still alive who
I've never met, she has a younger brother who I've never met, who are all somewhere in Oregon. Every time I'm up there, I think I might walk right past them
on the street and I would never know.

My mother's still alive. Growing up she was red-haired, blue eyes, looks
very Irish, although she's not, she's actually Scottish and English. Now she's totally snow-haired, but she's seventy-two years old. She looked basically very red-
haired, pale-skinned, kind of an English-looking woman. My father was fairly
chocolate-skinned, darker-skinned.

My parents stayed married until my father died in 1980. It was not a ter-
rific marriage, necessarily. My father was ill pretty much the last twenty-five
years of his life. He had diabetes and every complication that went with it, from
cataracts and glaucoma to circulatory problems, eventually prostate problems
and then strokes. So it was not an easy marriage at all, just from the health
standpoint, and then with the dynamics of him not being able to work a lot of
the time as well. He taught music, which was good; it kept his mind alive, but
was not particularly financially rewarding, and he wasn't able to travel anymore
on the road with bands because of his dietary needs and insulin needs. So it
was more of a care-giver relationship the last twenty years or so.

A lot of the biracial families I know are divorced. I mean, a huge percentage. It's hard for me to say exactly what percentage, but I know as a kid, of my contemporaries who were biracial, my family was the only family that was intact, and I really think the main reason was that my mother wouldn't leave my father because he was so ill.

When I was a kid, my parents would take turns getting arrested for sit-ins in San Francisco. Downtown San Francisco is tremendously different from the way it was then, and my mother used to do things like follow black people downtown to see where they were working so that she would be able to say to others, "There's a possibility you can get a job there." Race was something that was discussed. A lot of what my parents would say to me was around struggle. It was a reaffirmation for me that the way things are doesn't mean you're anything less than anyone else; that you can be whatever you want to be; that we're fighting so things will be better for you than they are for other black people. I don't know if it's turned out that way, but that was the idea.

I heard speeches by Malcolm X, and I remember a time when my parents felt that Martin Luther King was not as important as Malcolm X because he was the one who was really doing the most militant work.

My mother was angry at times about being told that she was sort of an honorary black person. That really used to piss her off, because she did not want to have her whiteness discounted. She just wanted to be a white person who wasn't being an idiot. I remember those kinds of conversations coming up, but between the two of them I don't really remember any conflict around that. I was always told that I was African-American and European-American, and those were the actual terms they used—which I guess was unusual at the time—because they were so entrenched in the political rhetoric.

I was always a mixed child. I never heard the word *biracial* until I was much older. Pretty much, "mixed" was used, or the whole range of everything I was, and I didn't only know I was white and black. I knew I was Jamaican, French, Scottish, English, Modoc Indian—I knew all the pieces, the whole picture. And being in San Francisco, I went to very international places. Part of nursery school was in Chinatown; I still know certain Christmas carols in Chinese. I went to Jewish community center camps and the after-school programs. I danced in a very white European ballet company, played music more with the black and Latin kids when I was a teenager, so I had a chance to be everywhere, and that seemed real, the way it should be.

I think the biggest contributors to my racial identity would be my parents. Because they were both artists, they were so interested in culture, and both came from such different cultures, I had an almost visceral experience of what that was. I remember sitting on my mom's lap at symphony concerts for kids in San Francisco, and hearing her talk about how she learned to play this when she was a child, the dance, going to art galleries. She still is a working artist. I knew where that part of my culture came from; I knew what parts of Europe it came from. She was a fanatic reader, so she would pass things—still passes things—on to me, and the same thing with my father. The music was a part of our lives: There were always music classes going on in the house, there was K-JAZ playing all the time in the car, and then the civil rights stuff they did often had me in child-care clusters with books and materials and posters on the walls that were very revolutionary-minded.

I was seven or eight when I started to realize that people were different cultures and colors, and there were injustices based on what you look like. I remember watching the sixties riots on television and talking about them with my parents. My mother kept a file on old magazines: *Jet,* newspapers, magazines—stuff that was printed in the late sixties that has all the original articles about the civil rights movement from pretty early on. Ten years ago she gave me the file, and I instantly knew what it was.

If nothing else, having this background probably makes me a less bigoted, racist person in a society where it's damn hard not to be racist. I just did not have that option of saying, "Well, I'm not going to associate with you," because I'd cut off half of my life. That's probably the number one benefit.

EMMA BAKER
Age: 62
Residence: South Carolina
Occupation: Retired teacher

Emma Baker (a pseudonym) is the oldest person who appears in this [selection]. Because of her family's lifelong silence about the circumstances of her birth, she asked at first that her name and picture not be used. But after much deliberating (and some coaxing), she decided to provide a picture of herself. "What happened, happened," she told me. Until our interview, she says the only person she'd ever spoken to extensively about her racial identity was a curious niece to whom she is particularly close. The niece once asked—when the two of them were alone—why her aunt's siblings all had such darker skin than her aunt did.

Baker has never identified as anything other than black, although she is old enough to have lived through the terms *Negro* and *Colored.* "I do not like the word *black,*" she says, "because there are so many different colors of black, if you will, starting from the color of the true black Africans, all the way up to just about white.

"I prefer 'Afro-American.' Some of our leaders are going to 'people of color,' and that's a lot to say. To say 'black' is shorter, but Afro-American or just American, is fine."

A family friend said that my mother worked for this white family in a nearby town. My mother stayed in their house; it was maybe ten miles from where her mother lived. She had no transportation during those times to get back and forth and the pay was very little, so they probably had some shanty stuck back somewhere for her to sleep.

This family friend said that the man for whom she worked is or was my father. I guess, my mother being black, she couldn't say no, because she worked for the family. I don't think it was a matter of how she felt towards him.

If it's true, I think it was a matter of—from what I've read of this happening, and I've read many books about this same kind of thing—where the master would go to the cabin where the black woman was. It was not a matter in some instances of how she felt about him, emotionally, it was just that she was trained to do that. She was black and he was white and she was supposed to do what he said.

At home, when I brought up the subject as to who my father was and where he was, it was a no-no. It was just like a dirty word, so from an early age I knew not to say anything more about my father. My other sisters, who were half-sisters of course, were darker than I. There was one who was lighter but not as light as I am.

This [family] friend, who was about twelve years older than I, told me when I was a teenager that this man was my father, or at least this is what she heard the older people say. During that time, the houses were little that Blacks lived in, and some parents would talk, not in front of their children, but the children would be maybe in the next room, listening, and they kind of knew what was going on.

When I became an adult, I used to shop at a supermarket, and this same family friend who told me who my father was—yet I didn't know if that was true—said it was rumored that he had a brother that worked in this store. This man was always polite to me. He cut meat, and when I went in there, being a Black, I was not treated like the other Blacks. He didn't give me anything because it was not his store, but he was more courteous, he cut better pieces of meat for me and that sort of thing.

From the way he behaved towards me, a young black lady, it just made me think that perhaps he was my uncle. Nothing was ever said, but he was always courteous, and it was not that he was trying to make out with me, not that kind of thing. Even the other people who worked in the store, they all acted the same way this man did, so maybe he told them who I was. But they treated me differently, and I always wondered why—I thought that maybe what this young lady had told me was the truth.

The word *father* I could never use. Kids would come to school and have on a dress—this still kind of grabs me, and I'm sixty-two years old—they would have on a little dress and I would say, "Oh, that's pretty." And they would say, "My daddy bought it." Like I said, those two words, *father* and *daddy*, were words that I didn't have in my vocabulary.

I was poked fun or picked at in school by some, and others who were my friends did not talk. There were some, though—you always, always had this—those who were darker would pick, would jeer. I was called names: "half-white bitch," "half-white monkey." And there were other names, let's see . . . "your mother crossed the fence" and that sort of thing. I never fought, I was not a fighter, and I wouldn't go back home and tell. I didn't say anything. I didn't want to hurt my mother. In my world, you're not quite white and you're not quite black.

SONIA TROWERS
Age: 23
Residence: Philadelphia, Pennsylvania
Occupation: Law student

Sonia Trowers's mother, a nurse, is from British Columbia, and her father, a microbiologist, is from Jamaica. They recently celebrated their twenty-fifth wedding anniversary. Trowers and her younger sister grew up in New Rochelle, New York, where their parents still reside.

Of all the people I interviewed, Trowers's complexion would fall at the browner end of the spectrum. "As opposed to other biracial children," she says, "you can't necessarily look at me and tell. I'm not one of those people constantly being asked, 'What are you?' "

Trowers's father telephoned me the day after his daughter responded to my advertisement in her university newspaper. He wanted to check me out, to see if I was legitimate. What else had I written? Who was my publisher? Why had I decided to write this book? His parental concern satisfied, he launched into stories about his two daughters, about their achievements and their earlier experiences with color. When Sonia was eight, he said, the two of them went to do some errands. A stranger approached and asked her what she was. "I'm a CanJam," her father remembered her saying proudly.

When we met for the interview, I asked her why she had responded to my ad. She said that whenever she sees television programs on biracial people, the portrayal of them is always negative. In fact, she said, she thought the particular people who were featured "would be screwed-up regardless of what color their parents were." Those people, in her opinion, make it easier for others to argue against interracial marriage and dating. She saw my book as a forum where she could show that there are normal biracial people in the world, who don't think "this is a big deal."

When my mom finished nursing school, she traveled all throughout Europe and then came to New York and happened to find a job for six months. My dad had just finished getting his second degree, and they both were working at the same hospital. They met, fell in love. But she already had a job she was supposed to start in Canada, and so they decided she would come back afterward and they would get married. So that's how they got together.

I think they got married around twenty-nine—that's kind of old for those days—and had me about four years later.

In terms of their families, the funny thing about that is my Jamaican grandmother has the typical West Indian prejudice as far as it comes to African-Americans. So for my grandmother, thank God, my dad was saved. God forbid he should have married some black American woman. For her, this was seventh heaven.

My mother's family is very, very religious. They were Baptists. Or was it Methodist? We're Presbyterian. They were very, very religious in the true sense. Not just, "Oh, we go to church every Sunday." And so they never had any problems with the marriage. I mean, my mom is the most naive thing in the whole entire world. She grew up on a farm in Canada. She really has no clue what's going on in the real world, and that's how her family is, too. They just really truly view everyone as God's creations. My mom said they never voiced any negative feelings; their only concerns were whether she was going to be able to deal with how *other* people were going to react to her.

The majority of that may stem from the fact that they're not specifically from this country, but also that religious thing is a one-in-a-million find. In New Rochelle, the church we went to was Presbyterian, and some neighbors of ours also go there, people that live a few houses down from us. They would always sit in the same row and were always very nice to us. Then we come to find out their daughter started dating this biracial guy. Her parents were *totally* against it. She wanted to go to college; they told her if she didn't break up with this guy, they weren't going to pay for her to go to school. He was biracial, very light-skinned, but they automatically classified him as black. That's when I stopped going to that church. I thought that was the most hypocritical thing in the world, that I could be sitting next to these people, worshiping with them, but obviously, when it really came down to it, they really thought they were a whole lot better than me. At that point, I just told my mother, "I'm not going there anymore." That whole thing really turned me off big-time. I can't even speak to those people anymore. I'd much rather have people in my face, telling me "I think I'm better than you."

My sister and I went to Catholic grammar school, and we were the only people of color in the whole entire first through eighth grade. I guess that's when things started to get a little bit weird. I started to realize I was different from everyone else, and I remember at that time my dad would always explain and I always knew that I was mixed. I never really had any problem with that. I knew who I was. But at that young age, I do remember going to school, and everyone had straight hair and I didn't have straight hair. Things like that seemed really important at the time. To me, at that young age, having a white mother was something that made me a little bit better. I was a little bit closer to what everybody else was.

The weirdest thing is I was always very popular. I never really had racial problems with other people. I might have had racial problems within myself, seeing as I was the only black person, and maybe once in a while people called me Oreo, but no one ever really made offensive comments . . . .

My high school years were the best, most unconfusing years of my life. I made so many great friends that I'm still friends with now; I hung out with this group of fifteen kids, and half of them were black and half of them were white and we were all friends and we all liked the same music and liked to do the same things. It was weird because when I left the Catholic school, I was under the assumption that you had to go this way or that way. So I didn't really expect to go to public school and have a lot of white friends, but that's exactly how it worked out. Most of the white people I hung out with were Jewish. There's some determining factor in that; I don't know exactly what it is. I don't know if it's that Jewish people sometimes also might see themselves as a persecuted race or whatever, but all the good friends I've had who've been white have been Jewish.

* * *

It's weird. I don't know if this makes sense: I always consider myself mixed, but I also consider myself black because the way I was brought up was that that's how people were going to view me. And I think it worked perfectly for me, probably because of the way that I look. Just because I was always going to be accepted by the black community, you know? There were iffy situations where I could or could not be accepted by the white community, and so I always had the comfort of knowing that I fit into the black community. But I always did identify myself as mixed. If someone asked me, I would always say, "I'm mixed. My father's black, my mother's white." But I definitely felt comfort that I knew there was somewhere I definitely fit in.

I guess I had always had this naive attitude about race, how it didn't really matter. And going down south for college was a whole new experience I had never expected, like going into a store and all of a sudden all the clerks are following you around, and people finding out that I was mixed and just thinking it was the oddest thing in the world. They couldn't believe that wasn't still illegal. I really do believe that up until that point, in my head, everything was fine with how I'd grown up, but I guess that was naive because I was living in a very small world. I expected that everyplace else was the same as where I grew up and there weren't all these problems.

Also, it was the first time I was around black people who talked really negatively about Whites. I didn't believe that there were really prejudiced people out there or people that would look at me weird because I was mixed or hold it against my parents because they had made this crazy decision. I had my first really negative feeling towards Whites in general when I went down south.

When I first got to college and would talk about race issues, people would look at me like I was crazy. They would be like, "You have been living in this little glass box; where the hell have you been?" So I really started to have problems, because I can really honestly say that for a while there, I really started to become very antiwhite because of the experiences I had. Had I had all these experiences when I was younger, then I would have expected and been prepared to deal with it. But for a while I was very antiwhite and had problems with that because I always felt very guilty. But then I would think my mother is the exception to the rule. She's different than the majority of the people there. I really had problems with that; I really felt guilty about it . . . .

I have these friends who were part of the Five Percenter Movement. It's a black movement similar to Islam, but they consider it not to be religious. And they consider they're the five percent that are on the right track and the other ninety-five percent of us are people who are totally lost. We don't realize that the white man's the devil, and the only way we're going to help ourselves is to kill off all the people who aren't of color—then everything will be okay. And these people were almost brainwashed. And I have this one friend who I had gone to high school with, and then I came back home and he had this new name and all these crazy ideals. I sat down with him and I said, "You really believe all these people are the devil? You really believe they hate us and are totally hostile?"

"Yes, yes, I believe that."

But he was someone who had been over to my house a few times, and I put it to him: "You met my mother. You really believe that my mother is really sitting there hating you and hating me and wanting us to drop dead and doing everything she can to keep us down?" He never really said, "Oh you're right, I agree with you," but I could see that maybe made the wheels start turning in his head that you can't just put things in such a generalized manner.

Same thing with mixed people. So many people say to me when they find out I'm mixed, "My God, you're so normal to be mixed! Everyone that I know who's mixed is so confused and you're the most normal person!"

I'm like, "How can you generalize?" You just can't do that; it's impossible.

I'm very outspoken and very independent, and I think my parents didn't have to be as concerned as maybe other people were because they always knew from day one who the hell I was.

But when things would happen, I would tell them both. My mother couldn't believe it, she'd be shocked; my dad would laugh and think it was funny. They were always receptive to hearing it. I don't think they would ever specifically ask me, but I think that's because whenever funny things or different things came up, I was always open with them, so they knew that if I was having a problem, I would address it to them.

DANIELLE WILLIAMS
Age: 22
Residence: San Francisco, California
Occupation: Junior paralegal

Danielle Williams says that not a day goes by without her being reminded of her biracial identity. As a result, it is a topic of paramount importance to her.

Regrettably, she says, her father's general irresponsibility toward her and her older sister has helped form her view of all black men, something she has struggled to break free from in the last few years. Her mother's supportiveness and sensitivity throughout Williams's childhood has just recently started to fall short of her needs. As Williams expands her racial identity, exploring how much black and biracial fit in her life, she feels alone, except for the comfort she gains from confiding in her sister Simone.

My parents met when they were still in high school. They had mutual friends, and they'd hang out at the same diner in New Haven. I don't really know much more about their courtship, so to speak, but they were married in August '66, and my mother's family—she's white Irish-Catholic, and my father's black—completely disowned her. She was married at eighteen. My father was nineteen, I believe. She moved out of her house, lived with her in-laws. My father was in the army at the time, and then he was sent to Germany. She lived with his parents and worked a couple of jobs to save up money. Finally she moved to Germany to be with him. They lived there for a year on the army base, and that's where my older sister was born. . . .

So here's my mother, eighteen years old, living in Germany, barely speaking German, just picking it up as she's there, and having this child with this black person. I don't think my father's family was too hip on the idea either, but they're much more accepting. They let my mother live with them, and they really took her in and taught her a lot. My maternal grandparents had done everything for my mother and her sister: They didn't have to make a bed, they didn't have to lift a finger, so my mother was not only thrust into leaving her home, leaving her family, but she didn't know how to do anything. My father's family really nurtured her and taught her how to cook and take care of things.

After Germany, my parents came back and lived in West Haven, Connecticut. Things quickly declined between them. They were separated, they went back and forth and in an attempt to get back together they had me, which was planned, I'm happy to know. By the time I was three, my parents were divorced, and the relationship between my mother and father was nonexistent. They couldn't speak to each other or be in the same company.

As a small child, I was conscious of race when I walked down the street and people didn't think my mother was my real biological mother. When I was around five or six at a baby-sitter's house, this black child was making fun of me and calling me a "high-yellow baby." I wasn't going to tolerate that, and I whipped around and pulled up my sleeve and I was like, "What are you talking about? Don't you know that I'm white?" My mother was the center of my universe when I was little, as for most children, and my father was not around, and my mother's white. Not only personally but visually I wanted to emulate her in every way possible. So it was at a very young age that I knew that I was different.

Having friends in grammar school was not easy, especially black friends, because they accepted me but there was always that difference. And then with white friends there was always that difference. I thought, "Well, who's going to understand me?" I thought, "Maybe black students will, because I don't look white," and my hair was a little Afro, I had little patchy skin, and I looked either mixed or a lot of people thought I was Puerto Rican. But there was always that distance between my black friends in grade school and myself, just sort of like, "Yeah, we like you, but you're not really like us; your mom's white."

Because I was raised by a white person and because most of the people I was surrounded by were white, that became my culture. I had proper English; I didn't talk the way a lot of inner-city young black children I went to school with did, and my clothes were probably different, too. All these differences were there, no matter how much I tried to find this connection, to say, "Look, maybe I'm half-white, but people look at me and don't think that. There's gotta be some sort of connection here. We're discriminated against—whether people think I'm Spanish or mixed or black—we're both discriminated against because of what we look like. So there's got to be a connection." . . .

*   *   *

All through my college years at Smith there were racial problems. My senior year was very disturbing. A black freshman was harassed by women in her house, who took this black baby doll, cut off her head, and hung it over this woman's bed. They followed her in the bathrooms—horrifying things one would not expect from the polite, Miss Proper Smith Woman. The administration and the community refused to believe it was anyone within the Smith community. Well, it was. Through these incidents and through our Thursday night black dinner and black TV night, I started becoming more into my blackness and more into my black friends, more into learning about black culture, black leaders, black literature, and I started feeling really good about who I was, but at the same time it brought distance between my white friends and between my mother and I.

When we had racial problems at school, I'd talk to her about it. Of course she was supportive, in the way that she could be, but she just couldn't understand because she's white. Part of me understands that. I *do* understand that, and I'm not angry because she can't understand, but it's difficult. I guess part of it makes me angry because I can't talk to her about it. She doesn't walk down the street and experience what I experience, and that's just a fact. It was very difficult in my senior year, because I was becoming close with these black women, and identifying that within myself.

I sort of have this new term: I would say that I am a "black-slash-biracial" woman. And a lot of times you might hear me say, "Well, look, I'm a black woman, this-this-this-this," but then if someone says, "What are you?" I'll say, "Oh, I'm biracial." And that might sound confusing to some people. It's confusing to me.

I am *two* things, you know? And then people say, "Well, you're not. You're biracial." But people don't make it into one thing. It's not a legally noticed race. That's why I like the word *mulatto*. Because mulatto means only black and white. When you say biracial, it's a mixture of any two, and for me, being mulatto is so special that I want an official word, just as white people have white and black people have black, and Japanese and whatever. When I say "mulatto" or whatever, I want people to say, "I know what that is." Growing up, people didn't know what mulatto meant. I had to explain it.

But now I really feel more like a black woman, some days, and other days I feel like a biracial woman, and that difference comes when I come in contact with black people who won't accept me for being a black/biracial person. To them, I'm not black enough. Take the Rodney King trials. When I talk to some of the black people I work with about it, if they want to say, "All white folk this, white folk that," I see them kind of look at me first. They don't want to step on my toes, and then they feel a little distance from me.

But I feel okay when they say that sort of thing because I say it myself. And in some ways, I don't trust white people. I'm not going to assume that someone's guilty before proven innocent, so to speak, but I have to keep my distance. Then at the same time, I have to keep my distance from black people, not as much as I feel right now a distance from white people, but a distance because I can't associate with black people who hate white people or who are separatists. I would definitely say that at this point in my life I am the marginalized tragic mulatto.

That might sound really dramatic and poetic, but I don't have a community that I can call my own and that understands both sides. For that, I'm grateful that I have my sister. I wish I knew more biracial people who felt like I do. I have a very close friend who's biracial—but he identifies as black—and it's wonderful because he's the first black male that I've *ever* in my life been close to. There was a time when I was afraid to go out with black guys because my father had set this image. When I was a kid riding around in cars with him, he'd do that catcalling to women and just reinforce the stereotypical image of black men—that they're always sexually aggressive and offensive, treating women like objects, which I'm sure white men did, too, at the time.

Sometimes I wish I was one or the other, but being biracial has made me a stronger person and has kind of given me my own special gold card because I can understand black culture and white culture. I can talk to white people and talk so they'll understand me, and I can talk with my brothers and sisters, and they'll understand me, too, to a certain extent on both sides. And so it's a very special thing and a place to be, but it's a very lonely place, too . . . .

SIMONE J. WILLIAMS
Age: 25
Residence: Boston, Massachusetts
Occupation: Day-care teacher

Simone Williams is Danielle's [page 26] older sister. She says they used to have very different outlooks on life, but that has begun to change. "The older we get, the more we come to a middle base where we can basically relate. She was like: white guys, rock and roll, ripped jeans, T-shirts. I was more of the outdoors person; she's more of the pocketbook-jewelry person. I was mostly into black guys, and I knew my father the most. She really didn't know her father."

Most people who know their fathers try to date people who are similar to their fathers, which is my syndrome. My sister does not have it because she was not affected by it, and I think her mind is much broader and open compared to mine. But then you go through life, you go through experiences, and you become influenced and things change you, and if a man is as black as coal I will not touch him because of these experiences I have had. If he is light-skinned, maybe a couple of shades darker than me, fine. It sounds narrow-minded and I know it is, but it comes from trying to have a relationship or friendship with my father and having it always end up in lies and being disgusted by it.

I was such a daddy's little girl. I can remember when my parents were still together, when Danielle was a little baby, and they were at a party and they had an argument and I had a choice. My mother came to me upset and she said, "Simone, I'm leaving. I'm going home with your sister. Are you coming with me, or are you staying with your father?" And I said, "I'm staying with Daddy," and I thought it was the greatest thing. I had a great time at this party; he took me to his sister's house, so I got to see my cousin, got to play Barbies, and I just thought Daddy was the best person in the world because he took me out.

I was really young, gosh, younger than four or five, but I do remember it like yesterday. It's crazy, but there are those little moments that I really savored, and so when he did go away, I blamed my mother. I told her I hated her; I was very, very disturbed by this. I think out of the two of us children I suffered the most emotionally because I *knew* him and Danielle didn't really have much attachment to him, and all she really knew was her mother, so nothing was really being taken away from her, and the person she loved, her mother, was being hurt.

So I used to feel like it was Mommy and Danielle over here, and Simone over here, because my buddy was gone. Where's Dad, you know? Then when I got to fourteen, I realized he was a jerk and I took away his visitation rights. I told my mother, "Please go to court, call your lawyer. I'm sick of this. I don't want to see him anymore. If I have to go to court with you, I will." It didn't come to that, but she was astonished that a fourteen-year-old had come to her and said these things.

The day before my seventeenth birthday and the day before my eighteenth birthday, both days I ran into my father. I saw him when I was almost seventeen, and I was surprised, shocked, happy, scared—all these feelings—and I just stood there and he said, "Hello, Simone." And I said, "Hi, Dad." And he goes, "How are you?" I said, "Fine." And then I don't remember what it was—I think because it was a negative—but he said something that hurt me and I ended up walking away from him. And he disappointed me. It's been how many years from fourteen to seventeen, and you're going to say something negative to me? What kind of a person are you? Day before my eighteenth birthday, I see him again, and I thought, "A year later, I do not forget, okay?" I'm walking on the sidewalk, he's driving in a car, and he's screaming out the window, "Hey, Simone! Hey, Simone!" And I see that it's him. Well, I don't want to be bothered with him, so I ignore him, so he gets louder and people are starting to watch. So I say to a guy who's standing there, "Excuse me sir, this man is bothering me. Can you please call the cops or something?"

SETH PRICE
Age: 28
Residence: New York, New York
Occupation: Restaurateur

During the time Seth Price lived with his father, from ages six to eighteen, he believes he was influenced more by his father's identity as a painter—more concerned with art than material comfort—than his identity as a black man. Price, although almost exclusively exposed to his black relatives, arrived at a distinctly nonracial identity. "I feel different than just about most of the people I meet," he says. "I don't feel like I'm black; I don't feel like I'm white. I just sort of feel an affinity to lots of people, like, 'Ah, I sort of know that.' "

I was born in Manhattan; my mom was white. She's English and Irish and French mixed. She lived on Ninety-sixth Street on the West Side, and she's the daughter of an alcoholic and a not physically blind, but mentally blind mother. And my dad was black from Jamaica, Queens. I don't really remember where we lived for the first three or four years.

They met in the High School for Art and Design. They were seventeen, and they never got married. Their parents didn't want them to be together at all, on either side. My mother's parents kicked her out of the house when she decided to keep me, and her sisters basically decided not to talk to her. She ended up living with friends and stayed with an aunt while she had me.

My mother's parents have passed away, and I never met them, but from what my [paternal] stepgrandmother tells me, they were both having a really hard time with it and giving my mother no support. They didn't like Blacks. And her father was a semiviolent alcoholic. He never beat my mother, but he would rant and rave and would break things. He used to go on about every other race than his own, even to the point of being prejudiced against his wife because she wasn't Irish.

And my father's father—he's a very stubborn and a sort of violent man—wasn't giving anyone any support either.

The story gets sort of muddy for me at this point, but when I was two or three, my stepgrandmother on my father's side ended up adopting me. She decided she would take care of me and it would be best for my mother to sort of disappear. And that's what happened.

On my father's side of the family, there was an openness but also a non-trusting of Whites. They would have friends, but what was unsaid was that when the chips came down, white friends wouldn't be standing there, so they were never equals. My grandmother, my grandfather's first wife, would say things like, "They're the ones you always work for and you just have to keep that in mind." She made comments about my mother, but in the sense of mothers talking about their sons' girlfriends or wives. Sometimes you'd hear the words, "He always picks white people," but then it wouldn't go any further than that. Like if he would have picked a black woman, it would have turned out just dandy. And my stepgrandmother had white friends she played bingo with. If she drank, which she did when I was younger, she would come home and say things like, "They're so two-faced." I didn't understand the context of it, but there was some bitterness. I always got this sense of disappointment.

So my stepgrandmother had me while my dad was in school—he'd turned down a basketball scholarship to go to art school, which his dad wasn't very happy with. He went to Pratt, in New York, and then Mills College, in California. When he graduated, they decided it was time for me to go live with him. I was six. They took me on a vacation to visit my father in California and then told me I was staying. And he was a hippie kid, I guess, doing lots of drugs, experimenting with religions, and trying to decide what he was going to do with his life. I'm sure he wasn't more than twenty-three. We were Buddhists for a while, and we were some Korean religion and also the Church of Scientology.

Hinduism was interesting, and there was the Muslim religion for a while. We went through a lot of stages. But throughout all of this, he was always responsible. I never saw him out of control. Always, in my experience, if he said he was going to show up somewhere, he showed up.

I don't know exactly why I mostly date Latin and white women. I think maybe they look like my mother; I always wanted to be with my mother. When I was younger, I had always wanted to find her, and I would ask my father basically once a year or once every six months, where was she? And he would always say he didn't know; he thought she was in New York. And I would go, "Well, do you have the phone number?"

On my seventeenth birthday he bought me a drink in a nice restaurant and told me that he had found my mother. He had put an ad in *The Village Voice* with her maiden name and his phone number, and she had called. So she flew out to the West Coast and we met.

Six months after that I decided I was moving to New York to see her. I stayed with her for about six months and then got a place on my own. For me it was a completion. Definitely. Because I had felt incomplete not having a mother.

FOR JOURNALING AND DISCUSSION

1. Funderburg says, "Many black-white couples think they and their children are all part of the same experience . . . . " Choose any two of the autobiographies she presents and discuss the problems with this perception.
2. What is the author's purpose? Does she seem to encourage or discourage mixed-race marriages, or to assert any one position on the issue?
3. What has been your own experience with mixed-race stereotypes—as a target, perpetrator, or observer? Describe an incident and explore what you learned from it.

FOR RESEARCH AND EXPLORATION

1. Funderburg introduces these histories by noting that the *Loving* v. *Virginia* decision of 1967 marked the end of antimiscegenation laws. Individually or in a small research team, explore your school's law library for data on the end of such laws in your state.
2. The "Emma Baker" section is markedly different from the other histories in the essay. Look at David D. Cooper's "The Changing Seasons of Liberal Learning" in Chapter 6, and explain how the complexities of age and generational difference change Emma's story from the others in the essay.
3. This selection includes one male voice among many female voices, and Funderburg notes that "while the preponderance of racial mixing in early U.S. history was between white men and black women, today, according to the census, 85 percent of black-white interracial marriages reverse that configuration." Research the intersection of gender and feminism in the civil rights movement to offer possible explanations for this trend.

Secrets and Anger?

David Mura

Mura is a poet and the author of Turning Japanese: Memoirs of a Sansei. *He is himself a third-generation Japanese American, whose parents were interned during World War II, when people of Japanese descent on the west coast were forcibly removed from their homes and imprisoned in camps. He has received many awards for his writing, including two Literature Fellowships from the National Endowment for the Arts, two Bush Foundation Fellowships, and a Discovery/The Nation Poetry Prize. His poems and essays have been published widely in national journals and magazines including* The Nation, The Utne Reader, The New York Times, Mother Jones, *and* The American Poetry Review. *Mura lives in St. Paul, Minnesota, with his wife and daughter.*

On the day our daughter was born, as my wife, Susie, and I waited for the doctor to do a cesarean section, we talked about names. Standing at the window, I looked out and said, "Samantha, the day you were born was a gray and blustery day." We decided on Samantha Lyn, after my sisters, Susan Lynn and Lynda. I felt to give the baby a Japanese name might mark her as too different, especially since we live in St. Paul, where Asian Americans are a small minority. I had insisted that her last name be hyphenated, Sencer-Mura. My wife had argued that such a name was unwieldy. "What happens when Samantha Sencer-Mura marries Bob Rodriguez-Stein?" she asked. "That's her generation's problem," I said, laughing. *Just a name can make a difference?*

I sometimes wish now we'd given her a Japanese middle name, as Susie had wanted. Perhaps it's because I sense that the world Samantha's inheriting won't be dominated by the melting-pot model, that multiculturalism is not a project but a reality, that in the next century there will no longer be a white majority in this country. Or perhaps I simply feel guilty about having given in to the dominant culture once again.

He made a decision in order to "fit in"

I am working on a poem about my daughter, about trying to take in her presence, her life, about trying to link her with my sense of the past—my father and mother, the internment camps, my grandparents. I picture myself serving her sukiyaki, a dish I shunned as a child, and her shouting for more rice, brandishing her *hashi* (a word for chopsticks, which I never used as a child and only began to use after my trip to Japan). As I describe Samantha running through the garden, scattering petals, squashing tomatoes, I suddenly think of how someone someday will call her a "gook," that I know this with more certainty than I know she'll find happiness in love.

I speak to my wife about moving out to the West Coast or to Hawaii, where there would be more Asian Americans. In Hawaii, more than a third of the children are *happa* (mixed race); Samantha would be the norm, not the minority. I need to spend more time living in an Asian-American community: I can't tell its stories if I'm not a part of it. As I talk about moving one evening, Susie starts to feel uneasy. "I'm afraid you'll cross this bridge and take Sam with you, and leave me here," she says.

"But I've lived all my life on your side of the bridge. At most social gatherings, I'm the only person of color in the room. What's wrong with living awhile on my side of the bridge? What keeps you from crossing?"

Susie, a pediatric oncologist, works with families of all colors. Still, having a hybrid daughter is changing her experience. Often when she's in the grocery with Sam, someone will come up to her and say: "Oh, she's such a beautiful little girl. Where did you get her?" This has happened so often Susie swears she's going to teach Sam to say: "Fuck you. My genes came all the way over on the *Mayflower*, thank you."

These incidents mark ways Susie has experienced something negative over race that I have not. No one asks me where Sam came from: they assume I'm her father. For Susie, the encounters are a challenge to her position as Samantha's biological mother, the negation of an arduous pregnancy and the physical work of birth and motherhood. For me, they stir an old wound. The people who mistake Sam for an adopted child can't picture a white woman married to an Asian man. *Her mixed baby they think is adopted*

Six ways of viewing identity: Identity is a social and historical construction. Identity is formed by political and economic and cultural exigencies. Identity is a fiction. Identity is a choice. Identity may appear unitary but is always fragmentary. Identity is deciding to acknowledge or not acknowledge political and economic and cultural exigencies.

When I address the question of raising my daughter, I address the question of her identity, which means I address the question of my identity, her mother's, our parents', and so on. But this multiplication of the self takes place along many lines. Who knows where it stops? At my grandparents? At the woman in the grocery store? At you, the imagined reader of this piece?

In the matrix of race and color in our society, there is the binary opposition of black and white. And then there are the various Others, determined by race or culture or gender or sexual preference—Native Americans, Hispanic Americans, Asian Americans, Japanese Americans, women, men, heterosexuals, homosexuals. None of these definitions stands alone; together they form an intricate, mazelike weave that's impossible to disentangle.

Are we a knot, a puzzle, or a melting pot?

I wrote my memoir, *Turning Japanese,* to explore the cultural amnesia of Japanese Americans, particularly those of the third generation, like myself, who speak little or no Japanese. When I give readings, people often ask if I'm going to raise Samantha with a greater awareness of Japanese culture than I received as a child. The obvious answer is yes. I also acknowledge that the prospects of teaching her about Japanese culture feel to me rather daunting, and I now have more sympathy for my nisei parents, whom I used to criticize for forgetting the past.

And yet, near the end of my stay in Japan, I decided that I was not Japanese, that I was never going to be Japanese, and that I was not even going to be an expert on Japanese culture. My identity was as a Japanese American. That meant claiming the particularities of Japanese-American history; it meant coming to terms with how the dominant culture had formed me; it meant realizing my identity would always be partially occluded. Finally, it meant that the issues of race were central to me, that I would see myself as a person of color.

Can I teach these things to my daughter? My Japanese-American identity comes from my own experience. But I am still trying to understand that experience and still struggling to find language to talk about the issues of race. My failures are caused by more than a lack of knowledge; there's the powerful wish not to know. How, for instance, can I talk to my daughter about sexuality and race? My own life is so filled with shame and regret, so filled with experiences I would rather not discuss, that it seems much easier to opt for silence. It's simpler to pretend multiculturalism means teaching her *kanji* [a Japanese writing system] and how to conjugate Japanese verbs.

I know that every day Samantha will be exposed to images telling her that Asian bodies are marginalized, that the women are exotic or sensual or submissive, that the men are houseboys or Chinatown punks, kung fu warriors or Japanese businessmen—robotlike and powerful or robotlike and comic. I know that she will face constant pressure to forget that she is part Japanese American, to assume a basically white middle-class identity. When she reaches adolescence, there will be strong messages for her to dissociate herself from other people of color, perhaps from the children of recent Asian immigrants. She may find herself wanting to assume a privilege and status that come from not calling attention to her identity or from playing into the stereotype that makes Asian women seem so desirable to certain white men. And I know I will have no power over these forces.

Should I tell her of how, when I look at her mother, I know my desire for her cannot be separated from the way the culture has inculcated me with standards of white beauty? Should I tell her of my own desire for a "hallucinatory whiteness," of how in my twenties such a desire fueled a rampant promiscuity and addiction to pornography, to the "beautiful" bodies of white women? It's all too much to expect Samantha to take in. It should not even be written down. It should be kept hidden, unspoken. These forces should not exist.

* * *

He wants differRent expeRiences foR his child

Samantha's presence has made me more willing to speak out on issues of race, to challenge the status quo. I suppose I want her to inherit a different world than the one I grew up in.

One day last year, I was talking with two white friends about the landmark controversy over the Broadway production of *Miss Saigon*. Like many Asian Americans, I agreed with the protest by Actor's Equity against the producer's casting. I felt disturbed that again a white actor, the British Jonathan Pryce, was playing a Eurasian and that no Asian-American actor had been given a chance to audition for that role. Beyond that, I was upset by the Madame Butterfly plot of *Miss Saigon,* where an Asian woman pines for her white male lover.

Both my friends—Paula, a painter, and Mark, a writer—consider themselves liberals; Mark was active in the antiwar movement during the sixties. He was part of my wedding and, at the time, perhaps my closest male friend. But neither agreed with me about *Miss Saigon.* They argued that art represented freedom of the imagination, that it meant trying to get inside other people's skin. Isn't color-blind casting what we're striving for? they said.

"Why is it everyone gets so upset when a white actor may be denied a role?" I asked. "What about every time an Asian-American actor tries out for a part that says 'lawyer' or 'doctor' and is turned down?"

But reverse discrimination isn't the answer, they replied.

I don't recall exactly what happened after this. I think the argument trailed off into some safer topic, as such arguments often do. But afterward, I felt angrier and angrier and, at the same time, more despairing. I realized that for me the fact that Warner Oland, a Swede, played Charlie Chan was humiliating. It did not show me that art was a democracy of the imagination. But for Paula and Mark, my sense of shame was secondary to their belief in "freedom" in the arts.

When I talked to my wife about my anger and despair, she felt uncomfortable. These were her friends, too. She said I'd argued before with them about the role of politics in art. Mark had always looked ruefully at his political involvement in the sixties, when he felt he had gone overboard with his zealous self-righteousness. "He's threatened by your increasing political involvement," Susie said. She felt I should take our disagreement as just another incident in a long friendly dialogue.

But when I talked with a black friend, Garth, who's a writer, he replied: "Yeah, I was surprised too at the reaction of some of my white artist friends to *Miss Saigon*. It really told me where they were. It marked a dividing line."

For a while, I avoided talking about my feelings when Paula and Mark came by. Susie urged me to talk to them, to work it out. "You're trying to get me to have sympathy with how difficult this is for them or for you, how this creates tensions between you and them," I said. "But I have to have this conversation about *Miss Saigon* with every white friend I have. Each of you only has to have it with me." My wife said that I was taking my anger out on her—which, in part, I was.

Tone: Challenging Ranting

NOT THE SAME SITUATION

Finally, in a series of telephone calls, I told Paula and Mark I not only felt that their views about *Miss Saigon* were wrong but that they were racially based. In the emotionally charged conversations, I don't think I used the word "racist," but I know my friends objected to my lumping them together with other whites. Paula said I was stereotyping them, that she wasn't like other whites. She told me of her friendships with a few blacks when she lived back East, of the history of her mother's involvement in supporting civil rights. "It's not like I don't know what discrimination is," she said. "Women get discriminated against, so do artists." Her tone moved back and forth between self-righteousness and resentment to distress and tears about losing our friendship.

Mark talked of his shame about being a WASP. "Do you know that I don't have a single male friend who is a WASP?" he said. I decided not to point out that, within the context of color, the difference between a WASP male and, say, an Irish Catholic, isn't much of a difference. And I also didn't remark that he had no friends of color, other than myself. I suppose I felt such remarks would hurt him too much. I also didn't feel it was safe to say them.

A few months later, I had calmer talks with Mark, but they always ended with this distance between us. I needed some acknowledgment from him that, when we began talking about race, I knew more about it than he did, that our arguing about race was not the same as our arguing about free verse versus formal verse. That my experience gave me insights he didn't have.

"Of course, that's true," he said. "I know you've had different experiences." But for him, we had to meet on an equal basis, where his views on race were considered at the start as just as valid as mine. Otherwise, he felt he was compromising himself, giving away his soul. He likened it to the way he gave away his self in his alcoholic family, where he denied his own feelings. He would be making himself a "victim" again.

At one point, I suggested we do some sessions with a therapist who was counseling him and whom I had also gone to. "No," said Mark. "I can't do that now. I need him on my side."

I can still see us sitting there on my front steps, on a warm early-spring day. I looked at this man with whom I'd shared my writing and my most intimate secrets, with whom I'd shared the process of undergoing therapy and recovery, and I realized we were now no longer intimates. I felt that I had embarked on a journey to discover myself as a person of color, to discover the rage and pain that had formed my Japanese-American identity, and that he would deny me this journey. He saw me as someone who would make him a victim, whose feelings on race were charged with arrogance and self-righteousness. And yet, on some level, I know he saw that my journey was good for me. I felt I was asking him to come on that journey with me.

Inevitably I wonder if my daughter will understand my perspective as a person of color. Will she identify with white friends, and be fearful and suspicious of my anger and frustration? Or will she be working from some viewpoint I can't quite conceive, some line that marks her as a person of color and white and neither, all at the same time, as some new being whose experiences I will have to listen to and learn from? How can I prepare her for that new identity?

Will it be fair or accurate or helpful for me to tell her, "Unless the world is radically different, on some level, you will still have to choose: Are you a person of color or not?"

It took me many months to figure out what had gone down with Paula and Mark. Part of me wanted to let things go, but part of me knew that someday I'd have to talk to Samantha about race. If I avoided what was difficult in my own life, what would I be able to say to her? My black friend Alexs and I talked about how whites desperately want to do "the victim limbo," as he called it. Offered by many as a token of solidarity—"I'm just the same as you"—it's really a way of depoliticizing the racial question; it ignores the differences in power in this country that result from race. **Different struggles**

When white people engage in conversation about racism, the first thing they often do, as Paula did with me, is the victim limbo: "I'm a woman, I know what prejudice is, I've experienced it." "I'm Jewish/working class/Italian in a WASP neighborhood, I know what prejudice is." The purpose of this is to show the person of color that he or she doesn't really experience anything the white person hasn't experienced, that the white person is a victim too. But Alexs and I both knew that the positions of a person of color and a white person in American society are not the same. "Whites don't want to give up their privilege and psychic comforts," said Alexs. "That's really why they're so angry. They have to choose whether they're going to give up power or fight for it."

Thinking this through, though, does not assuage the pain and bitterness I feel about losing white friendships over race, or the distance I have seen open up between me and my white friends. Nor does it help me explain to my daughter why we no longer see Paula or Mark. The compensation has been the numerous friendships that I've begun to have with people of color. My daughter will grow up in a household where the people who visit will be from a wider spectrum than were those Japanese Americans and whites who visited my parents' house in the suburbs of Chicago.

Not that teaching her about her Asian-American self has become any easier. My wife has been more conscious than I've been about telling Sam that she's Japanese. After playing with blond Shannon, the girl from next door, Sam said: "She's not Japanese, Mom. We're Japanese." "No," said Susie. "Daddy's Japanese, and you're part Japanese, but I'm not Japanese." Sam refused to believe this: "No, you're Japanese." After a few minutes, Susie finally sorted out the confusion. Sam thought being Japanese meant you had black hair.

For many liberal whites, what seems most important in any discussion of race is the need for hope, the need to find some link with people of color. They do not see how much that need serves as a tool of denial, how their claims of solidarity not only ignore real differences but also blot out the reality of people

[margin note: Even though our identities all are different, we are all humans (imperfect)]

of color. How can we move forward, they ask, with all this rage you seem to feel? How can you stereotype me or group me in this category of whiteness?

I tell them they are still unwilling to examine what being white has meant to their existence. They think their rage at being classified as a white person is the same rage that people of color feel when they are being stereotyped. It is not. When whites feel anger about race, almost always they are feeling a threat to their comfort or power.

In the end, whites must exchange a hope based on naiveté and ignorance for one based on knowledge. For this naive hope denies connections, complexities. It is the drug of amnesia. It says there is no thread from one moment to the next, no cause and effect. It denies consequence and responsibility.

For my wife, this journey has been a difficult one. The arguments we have over race mirror our other arguments; at the same time, they exist in another realm, where I am a person of color and Susie is white. "I realize that in a way I've been passing too," she said a few months ago. "There's this comfort I've got to give up, this ease." At her clinic, she challenges the mainly white children's books in the waiting room, or a colleague's unconscious assumptions about Hmong families. More and more, she finds herself at gatherings where she as a white person is in the minority.

Breaking through denial, seeing how much needs to be changed, does not have to blunt the capacity for hope. For both of us, our daughter is proof of that capacity. And if I know that someday someone will call Samantha a gook, I know today she's a happy child. The love her mother and I share, the love we bear for her, cannot spare her from pain over race, and yet it can make her stronger. Sam will go further than we will, she will know more. She will be like nothing I can imagine, as I am like nothing my parents imagined.

Today my daughter told me she will grow up and work with her mother at the hospital. I'll be a grandpa and stay home and write poems and be with her children. Neither race nor ethnicity enters into her vision of the future. And yet they are already there, with our hopes, gathering shape.

FOR JOURNALING AND DISCUSSION

1. When Mura writes, "I suddenly think of how someone, someday will call her a gook, that I know this with more certainty than I know she'll find happiness in love," why do you think he is so certain of this?
2. The experience of having a mixed-race child causes Mura to confront his own understandings of race, a project that leads to the loss of two white friends. Describe any loss of friends you have suffered over discussions of race or race-related issues.
3. Mura explains "the victim limbo" that occurs when whites try to claim the same knowledge of prejudice that people of color have. He notes, "It's really a way of depoliticizing the racial question; it ignores the differences in power in this country that result from race." What are some of these differences in power? Do you agree or disagree with this claim?

FOR RESEARCH AND EXPLORATION

1. Mura briefly mentions that members of his family were incarcerated at Japanese internment camps during World War II. Research this period of American history and interview relatives who were alive at this time for their memories—or lack thereof—of Japanese American internment.
2. Mura alludes to his own earlier interest in pornography and a socially constructed attraction to white women. Read Patricia Williams's essay in this chapter as well as Jessica Hagedorn's piece in Chapter 4, and discuss the influences of race and gender on definitions of beauty.
3. After reading Lise Funderburg's essay, which begins this chapter, attempt a narrative response to Mura's fears about the persona of his daughter. Consider especially Funderburg's focus on how different mixed-race children's experiences are from those of their parents.

Integration   *the process of merging*
Sherman Alexie   *or combining*

Alexie was born into a Spokane/Coeur d'Alene Indian family in Spokane, Washington. His father held a variety of jobs, including truck driver and logger, for the Spokane tribe; his mother is a social worker. Alexie graduated with a degree in American studies from Washington State University. Since 1992 he has published seven collections of stories and poetry, including The Lone Ranger and Tonto Fistfight in Heaven, *which won the Lila Wallace–Reader's Digest Writer's Award. His first novel,* Reservation Blues, *appeared in 1995. He is married and lives in Seattle. This story, which was first published in* Granta, *will appear in his second novel,* Indian Killer, *which he is now completing and will be published by Atlantic Monthly Press.*

the setting

The sheets are dirty. An Indian Health Service hospital in the early sixties. On this reservation or that reservation. Any reservation, a particular reservation. Antiseptic, cinnamon and danker odors. Anonymous cries up and down the hallways. Linoleum floors swabbed with gray water. Mop smelling like old sex. Walls painted white a decade earlier. Now yellowed and peeling. Old Indian woman in a wheelchair singing traditional songs to herself, tapping a rhythm on her armrest, right index finger tapping, tapping. Pause. Tap, tap. A phone ringing loudly from behind a thin door marked PRIVATE. Twenty beds avail-

Reservations in the same condition

able, twenty beds occupied. Waiting room where a young Indian man sits on a couch and holds his head in his hands. Nurses' lounge, two doctors' offices and a scorched coffee pot. Old Indian man, his hair bright white and unbraided, pushing his IV bottle down the hallway. He is barefoot and confused, searching for a pair of moccasins he lost when he was twelve years old. Donated newspapers and magazines stacked in bundles, months and years out of date, missing pages. In one of the exam rooms, an Indian family of four, mother, father, son, daughter, all coughing blood quietly into handkerchiefs. The phone still ringing behind the PRIVATE door. A cinder-block building, thick windows that distort the view, pine trees, flagpole. A 1957 Chevy parked haphazardly, back door flung open, engine still running, back seat damp. Empty now.

The Indian woman on the table in the delivery room is very young, just a child herself. She is beautiful, even in the pain of labor, the contractions, the sudden tearing. When John imagines his birth, his mother is sometimes Navajo. Other times she is Lakota. Often she is of the same tribe as the last Indian woman he has seen on television. Her legs tied in stirrups. Loose knots threatening to unravel. The white doctor has his hands inside her. Blood everywhere. The nurses work at mysterious machines. John's mother is tearing her vocal cords with the force of her screams. Years later she still speaks in painful whispers. But during his birth she is so young, barely into her teens, and the sheets are dirty.

The white doctor is twenty-nine years old. He has grown up in Iowa or Illinois, never seeing an Indian in person until he arrives at the reservation. His parents are poor. Having taken a government scholarship to make his way through medical school, he now has to practice medicine on the reservation in exchange for the money. This is the third baby he has delivered here. One white, two Indians. All of the children are beautiful.

John's mother is Navajo or Lakota. She is Apache or Seminole. She is Yakama or Spokane. Her dark skin contrasts sharply with the white sheets, although they are dirty. She pushes when she should be pushing. She stops pushing when they tell her to stop. With clever hands, the doctor turns John's head to the correct position. He is a good doctor.

The doctor has fallen in love with Indians. He thinks them impossibly funny and irreverent. During the hospital staff meetings all of the Indians sit together and whisper behind their hands. There are two white doctors on staff, though only one is on duty at any particular time. There are no Indian doctors, but a few of the nurses and most of the administrative staff are Indian. The doctor often wishes he could sit with the Indians and whisper behind his hand. But he is a good doctor and maintains a personable and professional distance. He misses his parents, who still live in Iowa or Illinois, and often calls them and sends postcards of beautiful, generic landscapes.

The doctor's hands are deep inside John's mother, who is only fourteen and bleeding profusely where they have cut her to make room for John's skull. The sheets were dirty before the blood, but her vagina will heal. She is

[handwritten margin note: Doesn't know about his parents]

[handwritten note at bottom: Unaware of his identity, the "who I am?"]

screaming, of course, because the doctor could not give her painkiller. She had arrived at the hospital too far into labor. The Chevy is still running outside, rear door flung open, back seat damp. The driver is in the waiting room. He holds his head in his hands.

"Are you the father?" a nurse asks the driver.

"No. I'm the driver. She was walking here when I picked her up. She was hitchhiking. I'm just her cousin. I'm just the driver."

The phone behind the PRIVATE door is still ringing. John's mother pushes one last time, and he slides into the good doctor's hands. Afterbirth. The doctor clears John's mouth. John inhales deeply, exhales, cries. The old Indian woman in the wheelchair stops singing. She hears a baby crying. She stops her tapping to listen. She forgets why she is listening, then returns to her own song and the tapping, tapping. Pause. Tap, tap. The doctor cuts the umbilical cord quickly. A nurse cleans John, washes away the blood, the remains of the placenta, the evidence. His mother is crying.

"I want my baby. Give me my baby. I want to see my baby. Let me hold my baby."

The doctor moves to comfort John's mother. The nurse swaddles John in blankets, takes him from the delivery room and carries him past the old Indian man who is dragging his IV down the hallway and looking for his long-lost moccasins. John is carried outside. The flag hangs uselessly on its pole. No wind. The smell of pine. Inside the hospital John's mother has fainted. The doctor holds her hand, convinces himself that he loves her. He remembers the family of four coughing blood into handkerchiefs in the exam room. The doctor is afraid of them.

With John in her arms, the nurse stands in the parking lot. She is white or Indian. She watches the horizon. Blue sky, white clouds, bright sun. The slight whine of a helicopter in the distance. Then the violent what-what of the blades as it passes overhead, hovers briefly and lands a hundred feet away. In the waiting room the driver lifts his head from his hands when he hears the helicopter. He wonders if there is a war beginning.

A man in a blue jumpsuit steps from the helicopter. Head ducked and body bent, the man runs toward the nurse. His features are hidden behind the face shield of his helmet. The nurse meets him halfway and hands John over. The jumpsuit man covers John's face completely, protecting him from the dust that the helicopter has kicked up. The sky is very blue. Specific birds land away from the flying machine. These birds are indigenous to that reservation, wherever it is. They do not live anywhere else. They have purple-tipped wings and tremendous eyes, or red bellies and small eyes. The nurse waves goodbye as the jumpsuit man runs back to the helicopter. She shuts the rear door of the Chevy, reaches through the driver's open window and turns the ignition key. The engine shudders to a stop. She pauses briefly at the door before she walks back inside the hospital.

Race = Trauma

The jumpsuit man holds John close to his chest as the helicopter rises. Suddenly, as John imagines it, this is a war. The gunman locks and loads, strafes the reservation with explosive shells. Indians hit the ground, drive their cars off roads, dive under flimsy kitchen tables. A few Indians, two women and one man, continue their slow walk down the reservation road, unperturbed by the gunfire. They have been through much worse. The what-what of the helicopter blades. John is hungry and cries uselessly. He cannot be heard over the roar of the gun, the chopper. He cries anyway. This is all he knows to do. Back at the clinic his mother has been sedated. She sleeps in the delivery room while the doctor holds her hand. The doctor finds he cannot move. He looks down at his hand wrapped around her hand. White fingers, brown fingers. He wonders at their difference. The phone behind the PRIVATE door stops ringing. Gunfire in the distance. *Race Relationship*

The helicopter flies for hours, it could be days, crosses desert, mountain, freeway. Flies over the city. Seattle. The skyscrapers, the Space Needle, water everywhere. Thin bridges running between islands. John is still crying. The gunner does not fire, but his finger is lightly touching the trigger. He is ready for the worst. John can feel the distance between the helicopter and the ground below. He stops crying. He loves the distance between the helicopter and the ground. He feels he may fall but he somehow loves that fear of falling. He wants to fall. He wants the jumpsuit man to release him and let him fall from the helicopter, down through the clouds, past the skyscrapers and the Space Needle. But the jumpsuit man holds him tightly, and John does not fall. He wonders if he will ever fall.

The helicopter circles downtown Seattle, moves east past Lake Washington and Mercer Island and hovers over Bellevue. The pilot searches for the landing area. Five acres of green, green grass. A large house. Swimming pool. A man and woman waving. Home. The pilot lowers the chopper and sets down gracefully. Blades making a storm of grass particles and hard-shelled insects. The gunner's eyes are wide open, scanning the tree line. He is ready for anything. The jumpsuit man slides the door open with one arm and holds John in the other. Noise, heat. John cries again, louder than before, wanting to be heard. Home. The jumpsuit man steps down and runs across the lawn. The man and woman are still waving. They are white and handsome. He wears a gray suit and colorful tie. She wears a red dress with large black buttons. *Literal Home—Yes*

John is crying when the jumpsuit man hands him to the white woman, Olivia Smith. The white man in the gray suit, Daniel Smith, grimaces briefly then smiles. Olivia Smith pulls her shirt and bra down. She has large, pale breasts with pink nipples. John's birth mother has small, brown breasts and brown nipples. John knows there is a difference. He takes the white woman's right nipple in his mouth. He pulls at her breast. It is empty. Daniel Smith wraps his left arm around his wife's shoulders. He grimaces and smiles again. Olivia and Daniel Smith look at the jumpsuit man, who is holding a camera.

She can't provide what he needs

Flash, flash. Click of the shutter. Whirr of advancing film. All of them wait for the photograph to form, for light to emerge from shadow. *Still in*

John attended St. Francis Catholic School from the very beginning. His shoes always black topsiders polished clean. His black hair very short, nearly a crew-cut, just like every other boy in school. He was the only Indian in the school but he had friends, handsome white boys who were headed off to college. John would never speak to any of them after graduation, besides the one or two he came across in a supermarket, movie theater, restaurant.

"John, buddy," the white boys always said. "How you doing? God, what has it been? Five, six years? It's good to see you."

John could step outside himself during those encounters. At first he listened to himself say the right things, respond in the right way. "I'm good. Working hard? Nah. Hardly working!" He laughed appropriately. Promised to keep in touch. Shared a nostalgic moment. Commented on the eternal beauty of the Catholic girls from way back when. Occasionally he could not stand to see his friends from high school, and more and more their voices and faces were painful to him. He began to ignore their greetings, act like he had never seen them before and walk past them.

John had danced with a few white girls in high school. Mary, Margaret, Stephanie. He had fumbled with their underwear in the back seats of cars. John knew their smell, a combination of perfume, baby powder, sweat and sex. A clean smell on one level, a darker odor beneath. Their breasts were small and perfect. John was always uncomfortable during his time with the girls and he was never sorry when it was over. He was impatient with them, unsure of their motives and vaguely insulting. The girls expected it. It was high school, and boys were supposed to act that way. Inside, John knew that he was simple, shallow and less than real.

"What are you thinking?" the girls always asked John. But John knew the girls really wanted to tell John what *they* were thinking. John's thoughts were merely starting points for a longer conversation. His thoughts were no longer important when the girls launched into monologues about their daily activities. They talked about mothers and fathers, girlfriends, ex-boyfriends, pets, clothes and a thousand other details. John felt insignificant at those times and retreated into a small place inside of himself until the girls confused his painful silence with rapt interest.

The girls' fathers were always uncomfortable when they first met John and grew more irritated as he continued to date Mary, Margaret or Stephanie. The relationships began and ended quickly. A dance or two, a movie, a hamburger, a few hours in a friend's basement with generic rock music playing softly on the radio, cold fingers on warm skin.

"I just don't think it's working out," she would say to John, who understood. He could almost hear the conversations that had taken place.

"Hon," a father would say to his daughter. "What was that boy's name?"

People don't understand where he comes from. He is viewed as a "problem child"

"Which boy, Daddy?"

"That dark one."

"Oh, you mean John. Isn't he cute?"

"Yes, he seems like a very nice young man. You say he's at St. Francis? Is he a scholarship student?"

"I don't know. I don't think so. Does it matter?"

"Well, no. I'm just curious, hon. By the way, what is he? I mean, where does he come from?"

Making assumptions

"He's Indian, Daddy."

"From India? He's a foreigner?"

"No. Daddy, he's Indian from here. You know, American Indian. Like bows and arrows and stuff. Except he's not like that. His parents are white."

"I don't understand."

"Daddy, he's adopted."

He has a problem with race but uses adoption as a cover-up

"Oh. Are you going to see him again?"

"I hope so. Why?"

"Well, you know. I just think. Well, adopted kids have so many problems adjusting to things, you know. I've read about it. They have self-esteem problems. I just think, I mean, don't you think you should find somebody more appropriate?"

The door would click shut audibly. Mary, Margaret or Stephanie would come to school the next day and give John the news. The daughters would never mention their fathers. There were a few white girls who dated John precisely because they wanted to bring home a dark boy to their uptight parents. Through all of it John had repeatedly promised himself that he would never be angry. He didn't want to be angry. He wanted to be a real person. He wanted to control his emotions so he often had to swallow his anger. Once or twice a day he felt the need to run and hide. In the middle of a math class or a history exam he would get a bathroom pass and quickly leave the classroom. His teachers were always willing to give him a little slack. They knew he was adopted, an Indian orphan, and was leading a difficult life.

His teachers gave him every opportunity, and he responded well. If John happened to be a little frail, well, that was perfectly understandable, considering his people's history. All that alcoholism and poverty, the lack of God in their lives. In the bathroom John would lock himself inside a stall and fight against his anger. He'd bite his tongue, his lips, until sometimes they would bleed. His arms, legs and lower back tensed. His eyes closed tightly. He was grinding his teeth. One minute, two, five, and he would be fine. He could flush the toilet to make his visit seem normal, then slowly wash his hands and return to the classroom. His struggles with his anger increased in intensity and frequency until he was requesting a bathroom pass on a daily basis during his senior year. But nobody noticed. In truth, nobody mentioned any strange behavior they may have witnessed. John was a trailblazer, a nice trophy for St. Francis, a successfully integrated Indian boy.

Easier to ignore issues

He was an "exception"

FOR JOURNALING AND DISCUSSION

1. Alexie introduces his painful and specific narrative with generalities and shifting details: the setting is "this reservation or that reservation," his mother is "sometimes Navajo. Other times she is Lakota," and the doctor is from "Iowa or Illinois." How do these generalities affect your reading of the text?
2. Alexie describes his dating experiences as moments of particular isolation and exclusion. Why is dating often an especially racist moment? How does dating disturb families and cultural norms?
3. This story ends with John biting his tongue in the bathroom of his high school, swallowing his anger, as Alexie describes him as "a successfully integrated Indian boy." Describe what you feel at the end of the story, and explain why the ending "works" or does not work, narratively.

FOR RESEARCH AND EXPLORATION

1. The aggressive adoption of Native American children by white families was extremely common into the 1970s in the United States. Research this practice and report on the reasons why it stopped.
2. Interracial adoption is a much-debated contemporary issue. Research how this topic has been treated in the popular press in your city or state over the past five years.
3. In "Fetal Alcohol Syndrome," Chapter 7, Michael Dorris describes this condition largely through a discussion of his experiences with his adopted son Abel. Compare the very different representations of Native American adoption in the issues Dorris and Alexie discuss. What are the differing purposes of each author?

India

Richard Rodriguez

Rodriguez is the author of Hunger of Memory. *He works as an editor at the Pacific News Service in San Francisco and is a contributing editor for* Harper's *and the Sunday "Opinion" section of the* Los Angeles Times. *He also appears on the "NewsHour with Jim Lehrer" as an essayist. Rodriguez currently lives in San Diego.*

At sunrise the next day, the time the Indians appointed, they came according to their promise, and brought us a large quantity of fish with certain roots . . . . They sent their women and children to look at us . . . .

Álvar Núñez Cabeza de Vaca

I used to stare at the Indian in the mirror. The wide nostrils, the thick lips. Starring Paul Muni as Benito Juárez. Such a long face—such a long nose—sculpted by indifferent, blunt thumbs, and of such common clay. No one in my family had a face as dark or as Indian as mine. My face could not portray the ambition I brought to it. What could the United States of America say to me? I remember reading the ponderous conclusion of the Kerner Report in the sixties: two Americas, one white, one black—the prophecy of an eclipse too simple to account for the complexity of my face.

Mestizo in Mexican Spanish means mixed, confused. Clotted with Indian, thinned by Spanish spume.

What could Mexico say to me?

Mexican philosophers powwow in their tony journals about Indian "fatalism" and "Whither Mexico?" *El fatalismo del indio* is an important Mexican philosophical theme; the phrase is trusted to conjure the quality of Indian passivity as well as to initiate debate about Mexico's reluctant progress toward modernization. Mexicans imagine their Indian part as deadweight: the Indian stunned by modernity; so overwhelmed by the loss of what is genuine to him—his language, his religion—that he sits weeping like a medieval lady at the crossroads; or else he resorts to occult powers and superstitions, choosing to consort with death because the purpose of the world has passed him by.

One night in Mexico City I ventured from my hotel to a distant *colonia* to visit my aunt, my father's only sister. But she was not there. She had moved. For the past several years she has moved, this woman of eighty-odd years, from one of her children to another. She takes with her only her papers and books—she is a poetess—and an upright piano painted blue. My aunt writes love poems to her dead husband, Juan—keeping Juan up to date, while rewatering her loss. Last year she sent me her *obras completas,* an inch-thick block of bound onionskin. And with her poems she sent me a list of names, a genealogy braiding two centuries, two continents, to a common origin: eighteenth-century Salamanca. No explanation is attached to the list. Its implication is nonetheless clear. We are—my father's family is (despite the evidence of my face)—of Europe. We are not Indian.

On the other hand, a Berkeley undergraduate approached me one day, creeping up as if I were a stone totem to say, "God, it must be cool to be related to Aztecs."

I sat down next to the journalist from Pakistan—the guest of honor. He had been making a tour of the United States under the auspices of the U.S. State Department. Nearing the end of his journey now, he was having dinner with several of us, American journalists, at a Chinese restaurant in San Francisco. He said he'd seen pretty much all he wanted to see in America. His wife, however, had asked him to bring back some American Indian handicrafts. Blankets. Beaded stuff. He'd looked everywhere.

The table was momentarily captured by the novelty of his dilemma. You can't touch the stuff nowadays, somebody said. So rare, so expensive. Somebody else knew of a shop up on Sacramento Street that sells authentic Santa Fe. Several others remembered a store in Chinatown where moccasins, belts—"the works"—were to be found. All manufactured in Taiwan.

The Pakistani journalist looked incredulous. His dream of America had been shaped by American export-Westerns. Cowboys and Indians are yin and yang of America. He had seen men dressed like cowboys on this trip. But (turning to me): Where are the Indians?

(Two Indians staring at one another. One asks where are all the Indians, the other shrugs.)

I grew up in Sacramento thinking of Indians as people who had disappeared. I was a Mexican in California; I would no more have thought of myself as an Aztec in California than you might imagine yourself a Viking or a Bantu. Mrs. Ferrucci up the block used to call my family "Spanish." We knew she intended to ennoble us by that designation. We also knew she was ignorant.

I was ignorant.

In America the Indian is relegated to the obligatory first chapter—the "Once Great Nation" chapter—after which the Indian is cleared away as easily as brush, using a very sharp rhetorical tool called an "alas." Thereafter, the Indian reappears only as a stunned remnant—Ishi, or the hundred-year-old hag blowing out her birthday candle at a rest home in Tucson; or the teenager drunk on his ass in Plaza Park.

Here they come down Broadway in the Fourth of July parades of my childhood—middle-aged men wearing glasses, beating their tom-toms; Hey-ya-ya-yah; Hey-ya-ya-yah. They wore Bermuda shorts under their loincloths. High-school kids could never refrain from the answering Woo-woo-woo, stopping their mouths with the palms of their hands.

In the 1960s, Indians began to name themselves Native Americans, re-calling themselves to life. That self-designation underestimated the ruthless idea Puritans had superimposed upon the landscape. America is an idea to which natives are inimical. The Indian represented permanence and continu-ity to Americans who were determined to call this country new. Indians must be ghosts.

I collected conflicting evidence concerning Mexico, it's true, but I never felt myself the remnant of anything. Mexican magazines arrived in our mail-box from Mexico City; showed pedestrians strolling wide ocher boulevards be-neath trees with lime-green leaves. My past was at least this coherent: Mexico was a real place with plenty of people walking around in it. My parents had come from somewhere that went on without them.

When I was a graduate student at Berkeley, teaching remedial English, there were a few American Indians in my classroom. They were unlike any other "minority students" in the classes I taught. The Indians drifted in and out. When I summoned them to my office, they came and sat while I did all the talking.

I remember one tall man particularly, a near-somnambulist, beautiful in an off-putting way, but interesting, too, because I never saw him without the current issue of *The New York Review of Books* under his arm, which I took as an advertisement of ambition. He eschewed my class for weeks at a time. Then one morning I saw him in a café on Telegraph Avenue, across from Cody's. I did not fancy myself Sidney Poitier, but I was interested in this moody brave's lack of interest in me, for one, and then *The New York Review*.

Do you mind if I sit here?

Nothing.

Blah, Blah, Blah . . . *N. Y. R. B.*?—entirely on my part—until, when I got up to leave:

"You're not Indian, you're Mexican," he said. "You wouldn't understand."

He meant I was cut. Diluted.

Understand what?

He meant I was not an Indian in America. He meant he was an enemy of the history that had otherwise created me. And he was right, I didn't understand. I took his diffidence for chauvinism. I read his chauvinism as arrogance. He didn't see the Indian in my face? I saw his face—his refusal to consort with the living—as the face of a dead man.

As the landscape goes, so goes the Indian? In the public-service TV commercial, the Indian sheds a tear at the sight of an America polluted beyond his recognition. Indian memory has become the measure against which America gauges corrupting history when it suits us. Gitchigoomeism—the habit of placing the Indian outside history—is a white sentimentality that relegates the Indian to death.

An obituary from *The New York Times* (September 1989—dateline Alaska): An oil freighter has spilled its load along the Alaskan coast. There is a billion-dollar cleanup, bringing jobs and dollars to Indian villages.

> The modern world has been closing in on English Bay . . . with glacial slowness. The oil spill and the resulting sea of money have accelerated the process, so that English Bay now seems caught on the cusp of history.

The omniscient reporter from *The New York Times* takes it upon himself to regret history on behalf of the Indians.

> Instead of hanging salmon to dry this month, as Aleut natives have done for centuries . . . John Kvasnikoff was putting up a three thousand dollar television satellite dish on the bluff next to his home above the sea.

The reporter from *The New York Times* knows the price modernity will exact from an Indian who wants to plug himself in. Mind you, the reporter is confident of his own role in history, his freedom to lug a word processor to some remote Alaskan village. About the reporter's journey, *The New York Times* is not censorious. But let the Indian drop one bead from custom, or let his son straddle a snowmobile—as he does in the photo accompanying the article—and *The New York Times* cries Boo-hoo-hoo-yah-yah-yah.

Thus does the Indian become the mascot of an international ecology movement. The industrial countries of the world romanticize the Indian who no longer exists, ignoring the Indian who does—the Indian who is poised to chop down his rain forest, for example. Or the Indian who reads *The New York Times*.

Once more in San Francisco: I flattered myself that the woman staring at me all evening "knew my work." I considered myself an active agent, in other words. But, after several passes around the buffet, the woman cornered me to say she recognized me as an "ancient soul."

Do I lure or am I just minding my own business?

Is it the nature of Indians—not verifiable in nature, of course, but in the European description of Indians—that we wait around to be "discovered"?

Europe discovers. India beckons. Isn't that so? India sits atop her lily pad through centuries, lost in contemplation of the horizon. And, from time to time, India is discovered.

In the fifteenth century, sailing Spaniards were acting according to scientific conjecture as to the nature and as to the shape of the world. Most thinking men in Europe at the time of Columbus believed the world to be round. The voyage of Columbus was the test of a theory believed to be true. Brave, yes, but pedantic therefore.

The Indian is forever implicated in the roundness of the world. America was the false India, the mistaken India, and yet veritable India, for all that—India—the clasp, the coupling mystery at the end of quest.

This is as true today as of yore. Where do the Beatles go when the world is too much with them? Where does Jerry Brown seek the fat farm of his soul? India, man, India!

India waits.

India has all the answers beneath her passive face or behind her veil or between her legs. The European has only questions, questions that are assertions turned inside out, questions that can only be answered by sailing toward the abysmal horizon.

The lusty Europeans wanted the shortest answers. They knew what they wanted. They wanted spices, pagodas, gold.

Had the world been flat, had the European sought the unknown, then the European would have been as great a victor over history as he has portrayed himself to be. The European would have outdistanced history—even theology—if he could have arrived at the shore of some prelapsarian state. If the world had been flat, then the European could have traveled outward toward innocence.

But the world was round. The entrance into the Indies was a reunion of peoples. The Indian awaited the long-separated European, the inevitable European, as the approaching horizon.

Though perhaps, too, there was some demiurge felt by the human race of the fifteenth century to heal itself, to make itself whole? Certainly, in retrospect, there was some inevitability to the Catholic venture. If the world was round, continuous, then so, too, were peoples?

According to the European version—the stag version—of the pageant of the New World, the Indian must play a passive role. Europe has been accustomed to play the swaggart in history—Europe striding through the Americas, overturning temples, spilling language, spilling seed, spilling blood.

And wasn't the Indian the female, the passive, the waiting aspect to the theorem—lewd and promiscuous in her embrace as she is indolent betimes?

Charles Macomb Flandrau, a native of St. Paul, Minnesota, wrote a book called *Viva Mexico!* in 1908, wherein he described the Mexican Indian as "incorrigibly plump. One never ceases to marvel at the superhuman strength existing beneath the pretty and effeminate modeling of their arms and legs and backs . . . . The legs of an American 'strong man' look usually like an anatomical chart, but the legs of the most powerful Totonac Indian —and the power of many of them is beyond belief—would serve admirably as one of those idealized extremities on which women's hosiery is displayed in shop windows."

In Western Civilization histories, the little honeymoon joke Europe tells on itself is of mistaking America for the extremities of India. But India was perhaps not so much a misnomer as was "discoverer" or "conquistador."

Earliest snapshots of Indians brought back to Europe were of naked little woodcuts, arms akimbo, resembling Erasmus, or of grandees in capes and feathered tiaras, courtiers of an Egyptified palace of nature. In European museums, she is idle, recumbent at the base of a silver pineapple tree or the pedestal of the Dresden urn or the Sèvres tureen—the muse of European adventure, at once wanderlust and bounty.

Many tribes of Indians were prescient enough, preserved memory enough, or were lonesome enough to predict the coming of a pale stranger from across the sea, a messianic twin of completing memory or skill.

None of this could the watery Europeans have known as they marveled at the sight of approaching land. Filled with the arrogance of discovery, the Europeans were not predisposed to imagine that they were being watched, awaited.

That friend of mine at Oxford loses patience whenever I describe my face as mestizo. Look at my face. What do you see?

An Indian, he says.

Mestizo, I correct.

Mestizo, mestizo, he says.

Listen, he says. I went back to my mother's village in Mexico last summer and there was nothing mestizo about it. Dust, dogs, and Indians. People there don't even speak Spanish.

So I ask my friend at Oxford what it means to him to be an Indian.

He hesitates. My friend has recently been taken up as amusing by a bunch of rich Pakistanis in London. But, facing me, he is vexed and in earnest. He describes a lonely search among his family for evidence of Indian-ness. He thinks he has found it in his mother; watching his mother in her garden.

Does she plant corn by the light of the moon?

She seems to have some relationship with the earth, he says quietly.

So there it is. The mystical tie to nature. How else to think of the Indian except in terms of some druidical green thumb? No one says of an English matron in her rose garden that she is behaving like a Celt. Because the Indian has no history—that is, because history books are the province of the descendants of Europeans—the Indian seems only to belong to the party of the first part, the first chapter. So that is where the son expects to find his mother, Daughter of the Moon.

Let's talk about something else. Let's talk about London. The last time I was in London, I was walking toward an early evening at the Queen's Theatre when I passed that Christopher Wren church near Fortnum & Mason. The church was lit; I decided to stop, to savor the spectacle of what I expected would be a few Pymish men and women rolled into balls of fur at evensong. Imagine my surprise that the congregation was young—dressed in army fatigues and Laura Ashley. Within the chancel, cross-legged on a dais, was a South American shaman.

Now, who is the truer Indian in this picture? Me . . . me on my way to the Queen's Theatre? Or that guy on the altar with a Ph.D. in death?

We have hurled—like starlings, like Goths—through the castle of European memory. Our reflections have glanced upon the golden coach that carried the Emperor Maximilian through the streets of Mexico City, thence onward through the sludge of a hundred varnished paintings.

I have come at last to Mexico, the country of my parents' birth. I do not expect to find anything that pertains to me.

We have strained the rouge cordon at the thresholds of imperial apartments; seen chairs low enough for dwarfs, commodious enough for angels.

We have imagined the Empress Carlota standing in the shadows of an afternoon; we have followed her gaze down the Paseo de la Reforma toward the distant city. The Paseo was a nostalgic allusion to the Champs-Elysées, we learn, which Maximilian recreated for his tempestuous, crowlike bride.

Come this way, please . . . .

European memory is not to be the point of our excursion. Señor Fuentes, our tour director, is already beginning to descend the hill from

Chapultepec Castle. What the American credit-card company calls our "orientation tour" of Mexico City had started late and so Señor Fuentes has been forced, regrettably,

" . . . This way, please . . ."

to rush. Señor Fuentes is consumed with contrition for time wasted this morning. He intends to uphold his schedule, as a way of upholding Mexico, against our expectation.

We had gathered at the appointed time at the limousine entrance to our hotel, beneath the banner welcoming contestants to the Señorita Mexico pageant. We—Japanese, Germans, Americans—were waiting promptly at nine. There was no bus. And as we waited, the Señorita Mexico contestants arrived. Drivers leaned into their cabs to pull out long-legged señoritas. The drivers then balanced the señoritas onto stiletto heels (the driveway was cobbled) before they passed the señoritas, *en pointe,* to the waiting arms of officials.

Mexican men, meanwhile—doormen, bellhops, window washers, hotel guests—stopped dead in their tracks, wounded by the scent and spectacle of so many blond señoritas. The Mexican men assumed fierce expressions, nostrils flared, brows knit. Such expressions are masks—the men intend to convey their adoration of prey—as thoroughly ritualized as the smiles of beauty queens.

By now we can see the point of our excursion beyond the parched trees of Chapultepec Park—the Museo Nacional de Antropología—which is an air-conditioned repository for the artifacts of the Indian civilizations of Meso-America, the finest anthropological museum in the world.

"There will not be time to see everything," Señor Fuentes warns as he ushers us into the grand salon, our first experience of the suffocating debris of The Ancients. Señor Fuentes wants us in and out of here by noon.

Whereas the United States traditionally has rejoiced at the delivery of its landscape from "savagery," Mexico has taken its national identity only from the Indian, the mother. Mexico measures all cultural bastardy against the Indian; equates civilization with India—Indian kingdoms of a golden age; cities as fabulous as Alexandria or Benares or Constantinople; a court as hairless, as subtle as the Pekingese. Mexico equates barbarism with Europe—beardedness—with Spain.

It is curious, therefore, that both modern nations should similarly apostrophize the Indian, relegate the Indian to the past.

Come this way, please. Mrs. . . . Ah . . . this way, please.

Señor Fuentes wears an avocado-green sports coat with gold buttons. He is short. He is rather elegant, with a fine small head, small hands, small feet; with his two rows of fine small teeth like a nutcracker's teeth, with which he curtails consonants as cleanly as bitten thread. Señor Fuentes is brittle, he is watchful, he is ironic, he is metropolitan; his wit is quotational, literary, wasted on Mrs. Ah.

He is not our equal. His demeanor says he is not our equal. We mistake his condescension for humility. He will not eat when we eat. He will not spend when we shop. He will not have done with Mexico when we have done with Mexico.

Señor Fuentes is impatient with us, for we have paused momentarily outside the museum to consider the misfortune of an adolescent mother who holds her crying baby out to us. Several of us confer among ourselves in an attempt to place a peso value on the woman's situation. We do not ask for the advice of Señor Fuentes.

For we, in turn, are impatient with Señor Fuentes. We are in a bad mood. The air conditioning on our "fully air-conditioned coach" is nonexistent. We have a headache. Nor is the city air any relief, but it is brown, fungal, farted.

Señor Fuentes is a mystery to us, for there is no American equivalent to him; for there is no American equivalent to the subtleties he is paid to describe to us.

Mexico will not raise a public monument to Hernán Cortés, for example, the father of Mexico—the rapist. In the Diego Rivera murals in the presidential palace, the Aztec city of Tenochtitlán is rendered—its blood temples and blood canals—as haughty as Troy, as vulnerable as Pompeii. Any suggestion of the complicity of other tribes of Indians in overthrowing the Aztec empire is painted over. Spaniards appear on the horizons of Arcadia as syphilitic brigands and demon-eyed priests.

The Spaniard entered the Indian by entering her city—the floating city—first as a suitor, ceremoniously; later by force. How should Mexico honor the rape?

In New England the European and the Indian drew apart to regard each other with suspicion over centuries. Miscegenation was a sin against Protestant individualism. In Mexico the European and the Indian consorted. The ravishment of fabulous Tenochtitlán ended in a marriage of blood—a "cosmic race," the Mexican philosopher José Vasconcelos has called it.

Mexico's tragedy is that she has no political idea of herself as rich as her blood.

The rhetoric of Señor Fuentes, like the murals of Diego Rivera, resorts often to the dream of India—to Tenochtitlán, the capital of the world before conquest. "Preconquest" in the Mexican political lexicon is tantamount to "prelapsarian" in the Judeo-Christian scheme, and hearkens to a time Mexico feels herself to have been whole, a time before the Indian was separated from India by the serpent Spain.

Three centuries after Cortés, Mexico declared herself independent of Spain. If Mexico would have no yoke, then Mexico would have no crown, then Mexico would have no father. The denial of Spain has persisted into our century.

The priest and the landowner yet serve Señor Fuentes as symbols of the hated Spanish order. Though, in private, Mexico is Catholic; Mexican mothers may wish for light-skinned children. Touch blond hair and good luck will be yours.

In private, in Mexican Spanish, *indio* is a seller of Chiclets, a sidewalk squatter. *Indio* means backward or lazy or lower-class. In the eyes of the world, Mexico raises a magnificent museum of anthropology—the finest in the world—to honor the Indian mother.

In the nave of the National Cathedral, we notice the floor slopes dramatically. "The cathedral is sinking," Señor Fuentes explains as a hooded figure approaches our group from behind a column. She is an Indian woman; she wears a blue stole; her hands are cupped, beseeching; tear marks ream her cheeks. In Spanish, Señor Fuentes forbids this apparition: "Go ask *padrecito* to pry some gold off the altar for you."

"Mexico City is built upon swamp," Señor Fuentes resumes in English. "Therefore, the cathedral is sinking." But it is clear that Señor Fuentes believes the sinkage is due to the oppressive weight of Spanish Catholicism, its masses of gold, its volumes of deluded suspiration.

Mexican political life can only seem Panglossian when you consider an anti-Catholic government of an overwhelmingly Catholic population. Mexico is famous for politicians descended from Masonic fathers and Catholic mothers. Señor Fuentes himself is less a Spaniard, less an Indian, perhaps, than an embittered eighteenth-century man, clinging to the witty knees of Voltaire against the chaos of twentieth-century Mexico.

Mexico blamed the ruin of the nineteenth century on the foreigner, and with reason. Once emptied of Spain, the palace of Mexico became the dollhouse of France. Mexico was overrun by imperial armies. The greed of Europe met the Manifest Destiny of the United States in Mexico. Austria sent an archduke to marry Mexico with full panoply of candles and bishops. The U.S. reached under Mexico's skirt every chance he got.

"Poor Mexico, so far from God, so close to the United States."

Señor Fuentes dutifully attributes the mot to Porfirio Díaz, the Mexican president who sold more of Mexico to foreign interests than any other president. It was against the regime of Porfirio Díaz that Mexicans rebelled in the early decades of this century. Mexico prefers to call its civil war a "revolution."

Mexico for Mexicans!

The Revolution did not accomplish a union of Mexicans. The Revolution did not accomplish a restoration of Mexicans to their landscape. The dust of the Revolution parted to reveal—not India—but Marx *ex machina,* the Institutional Revolutionary Party, the PRI—a political machine appropriate to the age of steam. The Institutional Revolutionary Party, as its name implies, was designed to reconcile institutional pragmatism with revolutionary rhetoric. And the PRI worked for a time, because it gave Mexico what Mexico most needed, the stability of compromise.

The PRI appears everywhere in Mexico—a slogan on the wall, the politician impersonating a journalist on the evening news, the professor at his podium. The PRI is in its way as much a Mexican institution as the Virgin of Guadalupe.

Now Mexicans speak of the government as something imposed upon them, and they are the victims of it. But the political failure of Mexico must be counted a failure of Mexicans. Whom now shall Señor Fuentes blame for a twentieth century that has become synonymous with corruption?

Well, as long as you stay out of the way of the police no one will bother you, is conventional Mexican wisdom, and Mexico continues to live her daily life. In the capital, the air is the color of the buildings of Siena. Telephone connections are an aspect of the will of God. Mexicans drive on the sidewalks. A man on the street corner seizes the opportunity of stalled traffic to earn his living as a fire-eater. His ten children pass among the cars and among the honking horns to collect small coins.

Thank you. Thank you very much. A pleasure, Mrs. . . . . Ah. Thank you very much.

Señor Fuentes bids each farewell. He accepts tips within a handshake. He bows slightly. We have no complaint with Señor Fuentes, after all. The bus was not his fault. Mexico City is not his fault. And Señor Fuentes will return to his unimaginable Mexico and we will return to our rooms to take aspirin and to initiate long-distance telephone calls. Señor Fuentes will remove his avocado-green coat and, having divested, Señor Fuentes will in some fashion partake of what he has successfully kept from us all day, which is the life and the drinking water of Mexico.

The Virgin of Guadalupe symbolizes the entire coherence of Mexico, body and soul. You will not find the story of the Virgin within hidebound secular histories of Mexico—nor indeed within the credulous repertoire of Señor Fuentes—and the omission renders the history of Mexico incomprehensible.

One recent afternoon, within the winy bell jar of a very late lunch, I told the story of the Virgin of Guadalupe to Lynn, a sophisticated twentieth-century woman. The history of Mexico, I promised her, is neither mundane nor masculine, but it is a miracle play with trapdoors and sequins and jokes on the living.

In the sixteenth century, when Indians were demoralized by the routing of their gods, when millions of Indians were dying from the plague of Europe, the Virgin Mary appeared pacing on a hillside to an Indian peasant named Juan Diego—his Christian name, for Juan was a convert. It was December 1531.

On his way to mass, Juan passed the hill called Tepayac . . . .

Just as the East was beginning to kindle
To dawn. He heard there a cloud
Of birdsong bursting overhead
Of whistles and flutes and beating wings
—Now here, now there—
A mantle of chuckles and berries and rain
That rocked through the sky like the great Spanish bell
In Mexico City;
At the top of the hill there shone a light
And the light called out a name to him
With a lady's voice.
Juan, Juan,
The Lady-light called.
Juan crossed himself, he fell to his knees,
He covered his eyes and prepared to be blinded.

* * *

He could see through his hands that covered his face
As the sun rose up from behind her cape,
That the poor light of day
Was no match for this Lady, but broke upon her
Like a waterfall,
A rain of rings.
She wore a gown the color of dawn.
Her hair was braided with ribbons and flowers
And tiny tinkling silver bells. Her mantle was sheer
And bright as rain and embroidered with thousands
of twinkling stars.
A clap before curtains, like waking from sleep;
Then a human face,
A mother's smile;
Her complexion as red as cinnamon bark;
Cheeks as brown as persimmon.

Her eyes were her voice,
As modest and shy as a pair of doves
In the eaves of her brow. Her voice was
Like listening. This lady spoke
In soft Nahuatl, the Aztec tongue
(As different from Spanish
As some other season of weather,
As doves in the boughs of a summer tree
Are different from crows in a wheeling wind,
Who scatter destruction and
Caw caw caw caw)—
Nahuatl like rain, like water flowing, like drips in a cavern,
Or glistening thaw,
Like breath through a flute,
With many stops and plops and sighs . . . .

Peering through the grille of her cigarette smoke, Lynn heard and she seemed to approve the story.

At the Virgin's behest, this Prufrock Indian must go several times to the bishop of Mexico City. He must ask that a chapel be built on Tepayac where his discovered Lady may share in the sorrows of her people. Juan Diego's visits to the Spanish bishop parody the conversion of the Indians by the Spaniards. The bishop is skeptical.

The bishop wants proof.

The Virgin tells Juan Diego to climb the hill and gather a sheaf of roses as proof for the bishop—Castilian roses—impossible in Mexico in December of 1531. Juan carries the roses in the folds of his cloak, a pregnant messenger. Upon entering the bishop's presence, Juan parts his cloak, the roses tumble; the bishop falls to his knees.

In the end—with crumpled napkins, torn carbons, the bitter dregs of coffee—Lynn gave the story over to the Spaniards.

The legend concludes with a concession to humanity—proof more durable than roses—the imprint of the Virgin's image upon the cloak of Juan Diego . . . .

A Spanish trick, Lynn said. A recruitment poster for the new religion, no more, she said (though sadly). An itinerant diva with a costume trunk. Birgit Nilsson as Aïda.

Why do we assume Spain made up the story?

The importance of the story is that Indians believed it. The jokes, the vaudeville, the relegation of the Spanish bishop to the role of comic adversary, the Virgin's chosen cavalier, and especially the brown-faced Mary—all elements spoke directly to Indians.

The result of the apparition and of the miraculous image of the Lady remaining upon the cloak of Juan Diego was a mass conversion of Indians to Catholicism.

The image of Our Lady of Guadalupe (privately, affectionately, Mexicans call her La Morenita—Little Darkling) has become the unofficial, the private flag of Mexicans. Unique possession of her image is a more wonderful election to Mexicans than any political call to nationhood. Perhaps Mexico's tragedy in our century, perhaps Mexico's abiding grace thus far, is that she has no political idea of herself as compelling as her icon.

The Virgin appears everywhere in Mexico. On dashboards and on calendars, on playing cards, on lampshades and cigar boxes; within the loneliness and tattooed upon the very skins of Mexicans.

Nor is the image of Guadalupe a diminishing mirage of the sixteenth century, but she has become more vivid with time, developing in her replication from earthy shades of melon and musk to bubble-gum pink, Windex blue, to achieve the hard, literal focus of holy cards or baseball cards; of Krishna or St. Jude or the Atlanta Braves.

Mexico City stands as the last living medieval capital of the world. Mexico is the creation of a Spanish Catholicism that attempted to draw continents together as one flesh. The success of Spanish Catholicism in Mexico resulted in a kind of proof—a profound concession to humanity: the *mestizaje*.

What joke on the living? Lynn said.

The joke is that Spain arrived with missionary zeal at the shores of contemplation. But Spain had no idea of the absorbent strength of Indian spirituality.

By the waters of baptism, the active European was entirely absorbed within the contemplation of the Indian. The faith that Europe imposed in the sixteenth century was, by virtue of the Guadalupe, embraced by the Indian. Catholicism has become an Indian religion. By the twenty-first century, the locus of the Catholic Church, by virtue of numbers, will be Latin America, by which time Catholicism itself will have assumed the aspect of the Virgin of Guadalupe.

Brown skin.

Time magazine dropped through the chute of my mailbox a few years ago with a cover story on Mexico entitled "The Population Curse." From the vantage point of Sixth Avenue, the editors of Time-Life peer down into the basin of

Mexico City—like peering down into the skull of a pumpkin—to contemplate the nightmare of fecundity, the tangled mass of slime and hair and seed.

America sees death in all that life; sees rot. Life—not illness and poverty; not death—life becomes the curse of Mexico City in the opinion of *Time* magazine.

For a long time I had my own fear of Mexico, an American fear. Mexico's history was death. Her stature was tragedy. A race of people that looked like me had disappeared.

I had a dream about Mexico City, a conquistador's dream. I was lost and late and twisted in my sheet. I dreamed streets narrower than they actually are—narrow as old Jerusalem. I dreamed sheets, entanglements, bunting, hanging larvaelike from open windows, distended from balconies and from lines thrown over the streets. These streets were not empty streets. I was among a crowd. The crowd was not a carnival crowd. This crowd was purposeful and ordinary, welling up from subways, ascending from stairwells. And then the dream followed the course of all my dreams. I must find the airport—the American solution—I must somehow escape, fly over.

Each face looked like mine. But no one looked at me.

I have come at last to Mexico, to the place of my parents' birth. I have come under the protection of an American credit-card company. I have canceled this trip three times.

As the plane descends into the basin of Mexico City, I brace myself for some confrontation with death, with India, with confusion of purpose that I do not know how to master.

Do you speak Spanish? the driver asks in English.

Andrés, the driver employed by my hotel, is in his forties. He lives in the Colonia Roma, near the airport. There is nothing about the city he does not know. This is his city and he is its memory.

Andrés's car is a dark-blue Buick—about 1975. Windows slide up and down at the touch of his finger. There is the smell of disinfectant in Andrés's car, as there is in every bus or limousine or taxi I've ridden in Mexico—the smell of glycerine crystals in urinals. Dangling from Andrés's rearview mirror is the other appliance common to all public conveyance in Mexico—a rosary.

Andrés is a man of the world, a man, like other working-class Mexican men, eager for the world. He speaks two languages. He knows several cities. He has been to the United States. His brother lives there still.

In the annals of the famous European discoverers there is invariably an Indian guide, a translator—willing or not—to facilitate, to preserve Europe's stride. These seem to have become fluent in pallor before Europe learned anything of them. How is that possible?

The most famous guide in Mexican history is also the most reviled by Mexican histories—the villainess Marina—"La Malinche." Marina became the lover of Cortés. So, of course, Mexicans say she betrayed India for Europe. In the end, she was herself betrayed, left behind when Cortés repaired to his Spanish wife.

Nonetheless, Marina's treachery anticipates the epic marriage of Mexico. La Malinche prefigures, as well, the other, the beloved female aspect of Mexico, the Virgin of Guadalupe.

Because Marina was the seducer of Spain, she challenges the boast Europe has always told about India.

I assure you Mexico has an Indian point of view as well, a female point of view:

> *I opened my little eye and the Spaniard disappeared.*
> *Imagine a dark pool; the Spaniard dissolved; the surface triumphantly smooth.*
> *My eye!*
> *The spectacle of the Spaniard on the horizon, vainglorious—the shiny surfaces, clanks of metal; the horses, the muskets, the jingling bits.*
> *Cannot you imagine me curious? Didn't I draw near?*

European vocabularies do not have a silence rich enough to describe the force within Indian contemplation. Only Shakespeare understood that Indians have eyes. Shakespeare saw Caliban eyeing his master's books—well, why not his master as well? The same dumb lust.

WHAT DAT? is a question philosophers ask. And Indians.

Shakespeare's comedy, of course, resolves itself to the European's applause. The play that Shakespeare did not write is Mexico City.

Now the great city swells under the moon; seems, now, to breathe of itself— the largest city in the world—a Globe, kind Will, not of your devising, not under your control.

The superstition persists in European travel literature that Indian Christianity is the thinnest veneer covering an ulterior altar. But there is a possibility still more frightening to the European imagination, so frightening that in five hundred years such a possibility has scarcely found utterance.

What if the Indian were converted?

The Indian eye becomes a portal through which the entire pageant of European civilization has already passed; turned inside out. Then the baroque is an Indian conceit. The colonial arcade is an Indian detail.

Look once more at the city from La Malinche's point of view. Mexico is littered with the shells and skulls of Spain, cathedrals, poems, and the limbs of orange trees. But everywhere you look in this great museum of Spain you see living Indians.

Where are the *conquistadores*?

Postcolonial Europe expresses pity or guilt behind its sleeve, pities the Indian the loss of her gods or her tongue. But let the Indian speak for herself. Spanish is now an Indian language. Mexico City has become the metropolitan see of the Spanish-speaking world. In something like the way New York won English from London after World War I, Mexico City has captured Spanish.

The Indian stands in the same relationship to modernity as she did to Spain—willing to marry, to breed, to disappear in order to ensure her inclusion in time; refusing to absent herself from the future. The Indian has chosen to survive, to consort with the living, to live in the city, to crawl on her hands and knees, if need be, to Mexico City or L.A.

I take it as an Indian achievement that I am alive, that I am Catholic, that I speak English, that I am an American. My life began, it did not end, in the sixteenth century.

The idea occurs to me on a weekday morning, at a crowded intersection in Mexico City: Europe's lie. Here I am in the capital of death. Life surges about me; wells up from subways, wave upon wave; descends from stairwells. Everywhere I look. Babies. Traffic. Food. Beggars. Life. Life coming upon me like sunstroke.

Each face looks like mine. No one looks at me.

Where, then, is the famous conquistador?

We have eaten him, the crowd tells me, *we have eaten him with our eyes.*

I run to the mirror to see if this is true.

It is true.

In the distance, at its depths, Mexico City stands as the prophetic example. Mexico City is modern in ways that "multiracial," ethnically "diverse" New York City is not yet. Mexico City is centuries more modern than racially "pure," provincial Tokyo. Nothing to do with computers or skyscrapers.

Mexico City is the capital of modernity, for in the sixteenth century, under the tutelage of a curious Indian whore, under the patronage of the Queen of Heaven, Mexico initiated the task of the twenty-first century—the renewal of the old, the known world, through miscegenation. Mexico carries the idea of a round world to its biological conclusion.

For a time when he was young, Andrés, my driver, worked in Alpine County in northern California.

And then he worked at a Lake Tahoe resort. He remembers the snow. He remembers the weekends when blond California girls would arrive in their ski suits and sunglasses. Andrés worked at the top of a ski lift. His job was to reach out over a little precipice to help the California girls out of their lift chairs. He would maintain his grasp until they were balanced upon the snow. And then he would release them, watch them descend the winter slope—how they laughed!—oblivious of his admiration, until they disappeared.

FOR JOURNALING AND DISCUSSION

1. Rodriguez's wide-ranging narrative inscribes traces of "disappeared" Indians on sites ranging from Mexico City to the mirror's reflection of his own face. What does he cite as some of the various causes of this erasure?
2. The author describes the images of the Virgin of Guadalupe and La Malinche, Cortés's guide and mistress. Compare and contrast these images of Mexican femaleness with those you can find in a sexualized history of Mexican colonization.

3. While mostly exploring the meaning of his "Indianness" in this piece, Rodriguez also traces Spanish, Mexican, European, and American influences in the form-ing of his identity as well as in the ways in which the categories form each other. Explore the various racial, cultural, and ethnic traces in your own identity for-mation.

4. Rodriguez explores gender as well as ethnic identity when he describes contes-tants in the Señorita Mexico pageant and the men they pass on the street. He writes, "The Mexican men assumed fierce expressions, nostrils flared, brows knit. Such expressions are masks—the men intend to convey their adoration of prey—as thoroughly ritualized as the smiles of beauty queens." What does he mean here? Draw on examples from your own experience for your answer.

5. What is the effect of Rodriguez's final image of blond California girls skiing down the snowy slope, wholly oblivious of the Mexican lift operator?

FOR RESEARCH AND EXPLORATION

1. Rodriguez writes, "Spain had no idea of the absorbent strength of Indian spiri-tuality," when he explains the centrality of the Virgin of Guadalupe to Mexican culture. Research the history of this figure, and offer an explanation for its cen-trality.

2. The essay that concludes this chapter, "Our Next Race Question," begins by claiming that in fifteen years Latino Americans will outnumber African Americans as the largest minority group in America. The category of "Latino" continues to erase the classification of "Indian" that Rodriguez works to recover. To explore this erasure further, interview members of your school's or your city's Latino population about Indian traces in their family histories.

3. Itabari Njeri's essay "Sushi and Grits" in Chapter 9 addresses the issues of ethnic identity and the conflict of multiculturalism in the United States. Read that essay and compare it to Rodriguez's narrative; in your comparison, suggest what both au-thors seem to be saying about race in a multicultural United States.

Confessions of a Wannabe Negro *?*

Reginald McKnight

McKnight won the O. Henry and The Kenyon Review Award for Literary Excellence for his story "The Kind of Light That Shines on Texas," and re-ceived a Thomas J. Watson Foundation Fellowship and a 1991 National Endowment for the Arts Grant for Literature. His first collection of short sto-

Reginald McKnight, "Confessions of a Wannabe Negro" from Gerald Early, ed., *Lure and Loathing: Essays on Race, Identity, and the Ambivalence of Assimilation.* Reprinted with the permission of the au-thor, c/o Christina Ward Literary Agent.

ries, Moustapha's Eclipse, *was awarded the 1988 Drue Heinze Literature Prize. McKnight is also the author of the critically acclaimed novel* I Got on the Bus *and is currently associate professor of English at Carnegie Mellon University, in Pittsburgh, where he lives.*

I can't say when I first noticed my blackness. Such things fall upon one like sleep, appear like gray hairs on the head. One moment we are not aware of some aspect of our being, and the next we are saying that we have never known ourselves any different. I do, however, remember the very day I noticed that my blackness made me different. There was this girl named Marsha on whom I had what you could call a crush, young as I was. Her hair was white as sunlight on a web, her eyes were as blue as plums. This was so long ago, thirty years or better, that I can't remember the context within which all of this took place, but I do remember that it happened in school, and I remember that we were indoors, queued next to a row of windows that cast light only on Marsha. I stood in line dead next to her, inhaling her Ivory soap and whole-milk scent, watching the light set fire to that delicate hair. Some kid behind me had been trying to engage me in a conversation for more than five minutes, but I was having little of it. I only wanted to consume Marsha's presence. But, through sheer persistence, the kid broke through. I heard him say, " . . . born in California, just up the road. Where was you born?" "Germany," I answered, and drifted back to Marsha, her elbows, the backs of her knees, the heels of her saddle shoes. Then she turned around . . . to look at me . . . to speak to me . . . to cast her radiance my way. She said, "Coloreds can't be born in Germany." Of course I felt humiliated, embarrassed, angered. My stomach folded in on itself, my hands trembled, my face burned. I couldn't have explained it to you then, but I had never felt this way before, never felt singled out on account of my color, and at first I thought Marsha had misunderstood me, so I replied, "I didn't say I was German, I said I was *born* in Germany." But she stuck to her guns, empty as their chambers were, saying, "You're just a liar! Colored people do not come from Germany." And I told Marsha, as gently as I could, of course, that I most certainly had been born in Germany. Just ask my mother, etc., etc. But the more I asserted my claim, the more incredulous Marsha, and then a growing number of my schoolmates, became. I remember one boy telling me that he was Catholic, and that, " . . . um, in the Catholic Church? um, if you lie? um, you'll, ah go to H.E.L.L." I had only one supporter that morning, a kid whose name I can no longer recall. She tried to defend me by announcing that though she was Chinese she'd been born in Tennessee. Marsha, for some reason, saw no logic in this, and said, "Well, maybe so, but that doesn't mean a colored can be born in Germany."

I was six, I think.

A few years later I remember walking home from school with my neighbors, my friends, the Weatherford kids, Ginny, Kathelynn, and Junior. The

Notices he's different

Weatherford kids were white, but at the time I didn't think of them as white. If I thought of them in terms of a class, or a type, or a category at all, I thought of them as Southerners, children, friends, and so forth. The afternoon was windless, cool. The bone-dry, yellow, tan, and evergreen of a typical Colorado autumn. We strode down the sidewalk, mindful of little outside the foursquare of ourselves. Junior, as he usually did, boasted about some impressive thing he had done or had thought that day in school. Kathelynn and Ginny bickered about which of them had made the bigger mess that morning in the room they shared. I bounced my Car 54 lunch box off my thigh, pretending to listen to Junior, while giving my full attention to his sisters, and somehow being aware of the magpie-fashion hollering of the flock of boys who walked behind us half a block or so back. Though they themselves drew no nearer to us, their words incrementally became more distinct to me. Dummy in the blue shirt. Dummy in the blue shirt. Dummy in the blue shirt, they were saying, and I knew they were talking about me, even though I was wearing not a blue shirt but a blue sweater. It made no difference that I was the only one of the four of us wearing blue. I would have known even if all four of us had been swathed from collar to ankle in blue. Dummy in the blue shirt. Dummy in the blue shirt. "Hey, Dummy, turn around." "Yeah, look at us, Dummy!" "Hey, look at us!" "Were you too dumb to take a bath this morning, Dummy?" "Yeah, you sure are dirty." "Phew! I can smell you from here."

Of course the Weatherford kids heard this too, and one or two of them told me I ought not turn around. I thought that was a good idea. Junior, my man Junior, turned around, though, and hollered back, "You're the dummies . . . . Shut up!" Then he turned to me and said, "They're the dumb ones, not you." Just then a chunk of feldspar, the size of an eight-year-old's fist, zinged a couple of feet over my head and skittered down the sidewalk several feet ahead of us, and came to rest in the grass. "Hey, Dummy, turn around."

"Just ignore them, Junior," Ginny said.

This nonsense went on for several blocks, ending only when we turned right, heading down our own street. Just before we turned, however, I finally did glance back at the kids. They appeared to be a couple of grades ahead. I didn't recognize any of them. Neither did I expect to.

I said nothing to my family about this, that day, but the following morning I told my mother about the incident while she was knocking a few naps out of my hair with a very small-toothed comb. It wasn't till I was about three quarters of the way through the story that I realized I'd made a mistake. In the first place, my mother has never been a "morning person," and she went about all her morning tasks with great flame and fury even when things were running smoothly. But as my story unfolded I noted she began combing my hair with increasing vehemence. It felt as though some great bird were swooping down on me, clutching my head with its blade-sharp talons, and by degrees, plucking the bone away to get to the meat. Quite honestly, I had expected her to lay the comb aside, set me on her lap, and coo rather than caw. But Mama said,

Bird Metaphors

"What were you doing? Were you acting like a dummy?" And I said, "No, ma'am, I was just walking." "Well," she said, combing with still greater heat, "you must've been doing something, boy." I was pretty sure my scalp had begun bleeding. "Hold still, boy," she said. Then, "I tell you *what*—if I *ever* catch you acting the fool at school or anywhere else, I'll skin you alive—you hear me?" And I said, "Yes, ma'am, I did, but I didn't do a thing except walk home from school." "I said hold still, boy! You better not be lying to me, Reginald." I was in tears by this time and all I could manage to say was what I'd already said before, that I'd just been walking, and so forth. Then, in a last-ditch effort for sympathy, I mentioned the rock they'd chucked, and that it had just barely missed hitting me smack on the head. "Well, why didn't you throw one back?" Mama said, and then she said she'd be damned if she was going to raise anybody's sissy. But I heard something catch in her throat, and she laid the comb on the rim of the basin, then rested her hands on my shoulders. I was too ashamed of my tears to look up into the mirror and at her reflection. She turned me about, drew me into her warm bosom, held me, talked about how ignorant some people were, that I shouldn't let a bunch of stupid boys upset me, that the world could sometimes be a tough, mean, petty place and I was just going to have to toughen up right along with it. She said a few more things, which I can no longer remember, but I do remember that her warmth and the sounds that issued from her throat, dozy, lugubrious, made my belly heat up and glow, made my legs tremble, made me want to sleep. But Mama said, "Come on now, son, you got to be strong." She took me by the shoulders again, turned me back around, and resumed working on my hair.

I think I was about eight then.

And by this time I thought I was getting it, thought I had discovered the difference, and what it meant, but in that same year I made a second discovery, something that made it clear to me that I was different, but not different in the way I thought I was. That year my grandfather took ill and the air force granted my father a special two-month leave so my mother and he could go to Waco and tend to family needs. At first I was delighted, for I thought my father's leave meant a leave from school for me and my siblings. I was wrong, of course. One of the very first things my parents did when we got to Waco was enroll my sisters and me in school, and for the first time in my life I attended a segregated school.

For the first two or three days it was quite nice. The teacher seemed to adore me, unlike previous teachers I had had, the majority of whom treated me with a benign indifference. But with this new teacher, Mrs. Wood, it appeared I could do no wrong. She enjoyed having me read aloud, often stopping me midsentence and asking my classmates to mark the way I'd pronounced a particular word. The schoolwork seemed easy to me, and Mrs. Wood would invariably make positive comments on my work as she handed our assignments back to us. To this day I don't know whether I did well in school because the school, as some of my friends have suggested, was substandard, or because, as others have said, for once I'd felt comfortable amid my peers and didn't feel like the usual dummy in the blue shirt. Perhaps it was both. Perhaps it was coincidence. I can't be sure because in those days I was a very quiet kid, very shy. I felt no comfort in the teacher's special attention. I felt no comfort amid my peers, whether black or white, and I don't recall the work being significantly different from what I'd had at previous schools. It was the first school I ever attended, however, that permitted the practice of corporal punishment. Perhaps that made all the difference.

In any case, one afternoon, as I was leaving the campus at the end of the school day, two boys jumped me from behind and tried to tackle me to the ground. Not only was I surprised by the attack, but I was surprised by the ineptitude of my attackers. Neither of them attempted to slug me even though several onlookers standing nearby were hollering, "Hit 'im. Hit that white paddy. Hit that boy." One of my attackers, as he gripped me in a headlock, kept saying, "You think you something good, huh? You think you the teacher's pet, huh?" The other one said, "Git his legs, git his legs, git his legs." And he finally decided to get my legs himself and they brought me down, though I had boy number one in the headlock, rather than he me. Boys as small as we were could hardly do one another any harm, but all the dust we kicked up, all the pounding we exchanged, all the yelping of our spectators, not to mention the surprise of the attack, had me extremely agitated. Extremely nonplused too, because I wasn't clear as to whether they were simply playing, Texas style, or really trying to do me harm. While I lay prone, still holding the one boy in the headlock, and as the other boy, rather than slugging me, tried to peel my arms from around his friend's head, my Uncle Bill, who was responsible for picking me up from school each day, approached us and very coolly asked me, "You okay?" I felt the grips of both boys slacken a notch, but as I would not let go, they would not let go.

"Awright," said Uncle Bill, "that's enough. I got some errands to run." Then Bill hoisted me up by my belt, swung me over his shoulder, and carried me to my grandfather's old Willie.

As the Jeep vibrated away from the school, I noticed, after a while, that I had been staring at the backs of my hands, and alternately glancing at the hands of my uncle. After a while I said, "Uncle Bill, do you think I look white?" And without looking at me, he said, "Do you think you look white?"

"Don't look white to me," I said.

"Me neither," he said.

And I didn't. I don't. I'm the color of a well-worn penny, as dark as, or darker than, any of my classmates in that Texas school. What on earth could they have meant? As the old woody rolled down the street, rattling the windows of Piggly Wigglys, hardware stores, barbershops and five-and-dimes, streets in this part of Waco where whitefolk were seldom seen, rarely thought of, I recalled a conversation I'd had just a week or so before with a classmate, this bullet-headed boy who sat two seats in front of me in Mrs. Wood's class. We were at lunch, and I remember being fairly amazed at what his lunch consisted of, rice buried in sugar (sugar?) and milk (milk?), two boiled eggs, and an orange. We were just getting acquainted, and he began by asking me the usual sort of questions: Where you from? Where's that? Why you move here? and so on. Then rather suddenly he asked me—and it seemed so incongruous to the previous questions—"Is your mama white?" And I said no. "Your daddy white?" No, I told him. "Hm," the boy said, "then why you talk so funny?" and he waited for my reply. I really didn't know what to say, but ended up with "I don't know. I don't think I talk funny." Then he asked me, "Why you walk so funny? Walk like you afraid to move, like you Frankenstein. Walk like a whiteboy." He chugged his milk, then wiped his mouth with the heel of his hand. "You act funny, too."

I turned toward my uncle and said, "Uncle Bill, what's a white paddy?" Bill shrugged, shook his head. "Aw, it's a whole lot of things, Reggie. Someone who looks white or acts white. Someone who acts sidicty, you know, like he better than everybody else. Something like that. Those boys are just ignorant, Reggie. They don't know nothing about nothing. Somebody don't act the way they do or look or think the way they do, and they wanna call him white paddy. You take my advice: Don't even study people like that."

But I did study them, as I suppose they studied me. I studied people both black and white, both critical and congratulatory. I studied the buck-toothed, tube-headed, freckle-faced whiteboy named Mike who called me nigger when I struck out in a softball game in the fourth grade. That happened in Colorado. It was the first time anyone ever called me nigger. I studied the two little Waco black girls who tossed rocks at me and my cousin Valencia as they chanted, "White paddy, white paddy." I remember the relief I felt, though it was only momentary, when I thought the girls meant that both Valencia and I were white paddies. It turns out I was mistaken, though. They meant just me. What mystified me at the time was that they hadn't even heard me speak, hadn't seen me walk. What were they seeing? I asked myself. How could I hide it? What was I doing? I studied the Colorado brother who, in school one day, replied to my "What's happ'nin', man?" with "Tom." And he coolly rolled away like mercury on glass, leaving me utterly bamboozled. I didn't know the guy, had never seen the guy before. Another high school acquaintance, a guy named Keith, used to joke with me, from time to time, by calling me Uncle Tunk. I studied him, too, discovering that he sincerely liked me but just thought I acted white. I studied the white boys in Louisiana who called me Charlie Brown, Coony, Nigra, Hippy Nigger, Boy, Monkey, Spade, Jig, who sincerely disliked me, and thought of me as typically black. I studied the six kids who spat on me as I walked past their bus parked in front of the school one day. As I approached the bus, each of them poked his head out the window and chanted, "Fuck a duck. Screw a penny. Nigger's dick's as good as any!" And then they showered me with their poetic residue. I must admit that though I studied the poem I never quite understood the intent. The spittle, though, was as legible as big black lettering on a yellow school bus . . . .

"Uncle Tom" – Those who act or want to be white (Negative) the cabin

He wanted to discover himself

I think these people have been trying to suggest to me that though I exhibit blackness I perform it rather poorly. I believe they are trying to tell me that there are a limited number of valid ways to express blackness, and that my own expression of it is, at best, shaky. Trey Ellis talks about this sort of thing in his essay "The New Black Aesthetic." Ellis says, "It wasn't unusual for me to be called 'oreo' and 'nigger' on the same day . . . . I realized I was a cultural mulatto."[1] But when I say that I am a cultural mulatto, I don't mean to suggest that the majority of blacks in this country (or anywhere else) have some unwitting propensity toward resisting cross-cultural influences in the same way that a duck's oily feathers resist water. In a certain sense all Americans are mulattoes of one shade or another. But when whites "do blackface," people don't so much as blink (though a few would call them nigger lovers; a few would accuse them of exploiting black art/culture for lucre and fame or power and diversion). I daresay they are looked upon by many with a kind of admiration. They are lauded as hip white cats, down whitegirls, soulful purveyors of the "suchness," if not the substance, of negritude. As for blacks who are influenced by expression that is not, as some would say, "preponderantly black," the response is rather more ambiguous. Charlie Pride, for example, or Richie Havens, or Jimi Hendrix, or Tracy Chapman may be praised for their talents, their virtuosity in the "pure" sense, but I know of no one who lauds such artists for their mastery of art forms that could be referred to as decidedly "white," except a handful of rock bands who argue, and quite rightly, that rock is a product of black culture as much as it is of white culture, if not more so. There may or may not be such a thing as "blue-eyed soul," but there is certainly the language for the concept. I know of no such term, however, for blacks who perform, in one way or another, to whatever degree, the white "thing" except for the term "crossover" which applies not only to blacks but to everyone else as well. Why the difference? Are we to conclude that this difference lies in the notion that blackness-as-performance is more neatly extricable from blackness-as-being than whiteness-as-performance is from whiteness-as-being? Is blackness-as-performance somehow regarded as a free-floating entity, belonging to no one in particular, while whiteness-as-performance can, and *should,* only belong to whites? After all, it appears to me that black-influenced whites are very often thought to be deepened and ennobled by such processes, while white-influenced blacks are regarded as weakened, diluted, less black.

Of course, it should come as no surprise that some blacks resent certain other blacks who seem willing to accept Eurocentrism, either in part or whole-sale, given our history of having it shoved down our gullets. But I have seen whites reveal the same sort of resentment toward white-influenced blacks, as if blackness-as-performance belongs to anyone who would grasp it, master it, even extend upon and recreate its various forms, while its opposite doesn't or shouldn't belong to anyone but its primary producers. Are we to suspect, as Timothy Maliqalim Simone does, that whites may be engaged in "a new form of parasitism"? Simone asks, "Is the assumption of black ideas and worldviews simply a virulent means of recuperating white identity, so that it may resuscitate a waning confidence in its legitimacy to dominate others?"[2] Both of these questions are exceedingly difficult to answer, largely because I'm not sure we know what we're talking about when we talk about "everybody." And also because, " . . . like it or not," says Henry Louis Gates, Jr., in a recent *New York Times Book Review* essay, "all writers" (and from here I extrapolate musicians, painters, sculptors, etc., as well as a number of individuals who are not artists—black, white, yellow, etc., etc.) "are 'cultural impersonators.' "[3] It almost goes without saying that the nature of being human has a great deal to do with mimesis, adaptability, absorption, shape-shifting, souleating. $\longrightarrow$

Like Ellis I was reared in predominantly white environments for most of my life. Though there were schools I attended where I was the only black person in the class, or my grade, and on one occasion, the entire school, for the most part I went to schools where the ethnic representation reflected national ethnic proportions. The neighborhoods in which I grew up were also integrated, being, most of them, military bases established or demographically reconstituted after 1947, the year that the armed forces were integrated. As a result of my upbringing, I learned quite early that the meaning of being black is always, always, always a matter of context. On the sliding scale of my personal history I have been adjudged to be both an Uncle Tom and a Hippie Nigger Bigot. In a 1988 interview with Bob Edwards of National Public Radio's *Morning Edition,* I described myself as a victim/beneficiary of the Civil Rights movement. Since that time I have heard others use the term (though I'm not here implying that I coined it. Historians have suggested that there are times in certain societies when things reach a critical mass of sorts, and ideas, more or less, invent themselves) and I've no doubt that the term implies a grudging affirmation that the movement succeeded to a certain degree. It also implies its failure. The term "victim/beneficiary," just like the word "mulatto," connotes the tragic, leaves us with the image of the heart and mind shred in two by the exigencies of two parallel but inherently incompatible worlds. Success is the irresistible force, failure, the immovable object. The result is either a new creature, a fresh-born slippery babe, yet half veiled by its own steam, but leaving us breathless with hope and wonder; or it is a mutant bastard, a monster, without a place, without a voice, illegible, indecipherable, not worthy of our trust; or it is nothing, a heartless, brainless wonder worthy of neither hope nor scorn. Has the successful failure, the failed success of the Civil Rights movement, left blackfolk in the same slough, left us with the same "sense of always looking at one's self through the eyes of others, of measuring one's soul by the tape of a world that looks on in amused contempt and pity" that W. E. B. Du Bois speaks of in *The Souls of Black Folks?* Are we still left with that "double-consciousness . . . two souls, two thoughts, two unreconciled strivings; two warring ideals in one dark body"? I think it has, I think we are, but with one significant difference, a difference, however, that was not promulgated so much in the Civil Rights era, but in the era of Du Bois himself. As Julius Lester puts it:

[margin handwriting: Making other cultures our own]

Dissent and disagreement have been the hallmark of black history. Though Booker T. Washington, the most politically powerful black American in history, sought to control the minds of black folk with that power, W. E. B. Dubois [sic], the preeminent intellectual and the founder of the NAACP, fought publicly with him over whether the minds and souls of black folks were better protected by protest and the vote or accommodationism and economic nationalism. Later, Dubois [sic] and Marcus Garvey, the ideological father of today's black separatists, would not even pretend that they liked or respected each other.[4]

The phenomenon Du Bois talks about ought not really be regarded as mere bifurcation, for it is not the nonblack world alone that is engaged in the act of being touchstone and measuring tape of the black world, but we ourselves. The "double-consciousness" of which Du Bois speaks isn't really so much a double-consciousness as it is a poly-consciousness. Someone who's black like me doesn't feel particularly torn between one thing and another, but rather among a multiplicity of things. For the better part of this century, many of our leaders, and a good many of us who have followed them, have insisted on toeing one ideological, aesthetic, political, spiritual, or intellectual line or another. Many of us have assiduously searched for the essence of blackness and again and again returned to the inner self empty-handed. What does one have to be or do or believe to be truly, wholly, monolithically black? Some have suggested to me that the wearing of European clothing is unblack, while others have preached the Black Gospel while dressed like Young Republicans. Others have said that the consumption of pork is unblack, while others have insisted that to eschew pork is to deny one's cultural roots. Some have insisted that marrying a nonblack spouse is unblack, while others have said, When you get down to it, we're all African. Some would judge one's level of blackness as being manifest in one's level of knowledge of the history and culture produced by blacks, while others say that very few products have been invented in a vacuum, that when one straddles the interstices of culture and history one begins to trace all the borrowings, the purchases, the thefts, the loans, the imitations that lead to the artifacts that one group or another claims as theirs, that when we are honest with ourselves, the best we can say is that this thing or that thing is a product of our species.

Many say that the term "black" itself is inadequate, and substitute for it African American, Afro-American, Afrikan, and so on and on . . . . Many say so much, so often, with such fervor and conviction that I can't tell rectitude from attitude: *"Hey, man, them shoes ain't black." "Look, here, brother, that ain't the way a brother's supposed to talk to a sister." "Dag, 'B,' brothers don't supposed to read that kinda shit." "Hey, don't talk to me about that Africa stuff, cause I've never been to Africa. I don't know the first thing about the place. I'm an American. Period." "Look here, baby, I don't know what that is you listening to, but it ain't music." "Understand something, little brother, I'm the last black man. That's right. You kids don't know a thing about dancing or walking or thinking or making love under the moon. Don't know about knocking whitey the fuck up the side of his head when he needs it. You kids don't know a thing. When I'm dead, that's it. No more black men."* For a long, long time I've let

Fake conversation

myself be pulled from joint to joint, pulled by the joint. I've stood up and praised her praise song, cursed his condemnation, then changed places with myself. Weren't they all authorities, all valid, all experts when held up to my pathetic little narrow-behind wavering blackness? My inability to put it all together, find the center, swim away clean, black, and sanctified was my fault, no? I thought so. But all the while in the back of my head I sensed something missing, felt some still and empty point that was always out of reach. I soon discovered, though, that what was missing was my own voice. **Found himself**

The thing that has accounted for at least half of the trouble that the performance of my blackness has brought me is the way I speak. "*Now, listen to the way Reginald enunciates when he reads that paragraph again, class. Go ahead, Reginald. Start from the top of the page.*" I don't know if Mrs. Wood knew that since the "standard" form of any language is established on political rather than purely elocutionary imperatives, no dialect conveys meaning any better or sounds any better—depending on who's doing the listening—than any other dialect. It's just a matter of which dialect the ruling class chooses to make its own. I know for certain that I didn't know this, way back in second grade. I suppose that to some ears I speak the patois of the ruling class, though to my own ears it is more of an ideolect that has resulted from living in a household in which my father's Alabamese and my mother's rather un-Texaslike East Texas accent, and the various accents of all the places we lived have mixed rather curiously upon my tongue. Nevertheless, people have responded to my use of English as though I were an impostor, a usurper, as if I were puttin' on airs, stubbornly willing myself to speak in a way that wasn't natural to "my kind," and by doing so have marked myself as an adopted (at least adoptable) member of the ruling class.

Some have assumed that I come from a privileged background, upper-middle class, college-educated parents, and so on. And beneath this assumption lies the suspicion that I feel little more than contempt for black people and that I would wish nothing more than to assimilate more deeply into the dominant culture. Well, I would be more than a fiction writer if I say I have never felt anger toward certain black people, or have never admired certain whites, but since I have experienced few constants in terms of my innumerable encounters with members of both groups, there have been few times in my life when I felt any particular way about anyone until I became acquainted with her or him. I have never consciously desired to be white. I have never even imagined what it would be like to be white, outside the confines of what I do as a writer. But there were definitely times I was made to feel I wasn't black enough, and wished somehow that I could get a handle on being so, being properly black. I felt this way, even though, when I want to, I can use my father's dialect, as well as a number of others, that are considered to be more or less black. But I kept silent for a long, long while, not because I had nothing to say, but because I thought I had nothing with which to say it. When I spoke in my own ideolect, I lacked authority. When I borrowed my father's I felt like an impostor, and still lacked authority. Having traveled as much as I have I've acquired a fairly decent ear, but my natural speech is my natural speech, and if I don't fit in because of it, I think that's absurd. And I am beginning to suspect that I am as black as I can possibly be. I don't think it would make any difference, in this respect, if I spoke with an Irish brogue. When I lived in Senegal, a friend who had recently introduced me to his family said to me, "You know, they like you, but they just can't get over the fact that you come from a country where all the black people speak English. English!" I asked him if he had considered the notion that I came from a place where blacks might be just as mystified or surprised as his family that there are countries where nearly everyone speaks (at least some) French. "I see what you're getting at," he said. "But to me, it seems natural for a black person to speak French. But English. Man, that is so strange to them. To me, too, to tell you the truth."

From Marsha with the plum-colored eyes to my friend Mike who wanted me to date his sister, people are trying to tell me, as I say above, that there is something essential that I exhibit but poorly perform. At times this poor performance troubles some people, at times it brings others comfort. From southern "rednecks" to northern "rustnecks," from southern "geechees" to northern "Malcolmists," from the privileged to the dispossessed, I had grown up feeling hard-pressed to find a genuine place for myself, a general consciousness upon which to draw. I felt I had no group with whom I was completely at peace or for whom I held unbending antipathy, no permanent correspondences based on culture, color, class, race, sex, gender. Be this as it may, I never believed that I was wholly unique in terms of how I performed my blackness or perceived my position in the black world. But I am not saying that I had or have "risen above" the constraints or the licenses of culture, class, race, and so on. And I don't mean to suggest that the relative isolation I have experienced has given me any special insights into any of the apparent enclaves through which I have traveled and by which I have been shaped. All I know is that it is my responsibility to carve out a "space" for myself in the black world without giving up my individuality. In fact, the whole idea of there being a world in which the individual does not fit seems, to me, to be antithetical to the very idea of a "world." As Julius Lester puts it, "The intellectual and spiritual health of any group is secured only to the extent that its members are permitted to be themselves and still be accepted as part of the group."[5] It's really very simple, and wholly without climax when you get down to it.

For all I know, there may be some essential blackness, but I tend to think it won't be found within the architecture of any particular ideology. In fact, if it is to be found at all, it will likely be found to be a sort of palimpsest, upon which is written all names, ideas, philosophies, arguments, fears, projections, productions, hopes, extrapolations, histories, even silences. But it ought to be the sort of palimpsest upon which there can be no erasures. I have grown weary of my differentness being used against me, or being used as a lever to force me to the banks of our dark and dusky river of being, when, in actuality, my differentness, my relative uniqueness, expands the black world, makes it more complex, contributes to our wherewithal to survive sudden or gradual changes in the political environment. If we insist on a definition of blackness it will have to be predicated on something other than a set of codified and repeatable performances (though this is not to eschew our traditions), for blackness is a process, ever changing, ever growing. I think only lemmings should move in lockstep.

I am not merely asserting that "We are not all alike." Those who aren't aware of that would not likely read this essay or anything like it. What I am saying is that generalizations from within are every bit as fragmenting as scrutiny from without. From my boyhood I have read and heard all manner of statistical facts and figures about black people. Really, they've told me very little about who I am, let alone who we are. We're too big for that, and as individuals too complex. I'm not so sure we should ever find ourselves in the position of saying this general thing or that general thing about black people, expecting our words to discover the essence of our "true self-consciousness," for when we do, we will be doing no more than talking *about* black people, talking *around* them, never quite getting it right, never pinning us down, never quite turning sound into substance, and never—much like the way sharks course around caged divers—ever able to sink our teeth into flesh.

We are, from the bottom to the top, as polymorphous as the dance of Shiva. We are not a race, not a culture, not a society, not a subgroup, not a "breeding group," or a cline, not even simply an agglomeration of individuals. We are, in my mind, a civilization, a collection of cultures, societies, nations, individuals, "races." We are ancient and new, Christian, Muslim, Jew, American, Trinidadian, Zimbabwean, female and male, gay and straight, brilliant and stupid, wealthy and poor, mocha and almond and ripe olive. We are at times a "We" and a "Them," an "Us" and "The Other." Being a civilization does not mean we will always like one another, agree with one another, or even—though this is not wise—listen to one another. But I hope it means that my name will be written on this great palimpsest, my ideas, my contributions, my voice, right next to yours. Let all be included. Let none be cast aside.

NOTES   Welcoming

1. Trey Ellis. "The New Black Aesthetic," *Callaloo,* Spring, 1989.
2. Timothy Maliqalim Simone, *About Face: Race in Postmodern America.* Auronomedia Brooklyn, 1989.
3. Henry Louis Gates, Jr. " 'Authenticity,' or the Lesson of Little Tree," *New York Times Book Review,* November 24, 1991.
4. Julius Lester. "What Price Unity?," *The Village Voice,* September 17, 1991.
5. Ibid.

FOR JOURNALING AND DISCUSSION

1. McKnight describes his first memory of "blackness as difference" occurring in grammar school. Write a detailed account of your own earliest memory of being singled out or marked as different by classmates.

2. McKnight explains the politics of language and notes that "no dialect conveys meaning any better or sounds any better—depending on who's doing the listening—than any other dialect." Explore the politics of language in light of the dialects and other forms of English you speak at home, are learning in this course, and use in your major.

3. McKnight concludes his essay with the notion of African Americans not as a race, culture, or subgroup but as a civilization. After reading "Our Next Race Question," which concludes this chapter, write what you think McKnight's response would be to both Jorge Klor De Alva's and Cornel West's definitions of blackness and race.

FOR RESEARCH AND EXPLORATION

1. One identification of the author would label him an "army brat," moving from base to base with his father's military career. McKnight notes that these neighborhoods were integrated earlier than most, following the integration of the army in 1947. Research the details of this historic integration as well as the contemporary race politics of the military.

2. The author draws heavily from W. E. B. Du Bois's *The Souls of Black Folk*. Read this ground-breaking work, and write a summary and critical response to the text.

3. In "A Real Class Act" in Chapter 3, Julie Charlip writes, "All of us are the products not just of our immediate upbringing but also of the past that our parents and grandparents transmit. She is discussing the complexity of social class and the process of finding where we "fit." Compare Charlip's essay to McKnight's to explore the role of class in his position as a "cultural mulatto."

Memories of a Xenophobic Boyhood

Gary Indiana

Indiana is a well-known film and art critic for The Village Voice, Artforum, *and* Interview, *among other publications. His books include* Horse Crazy, Scar Tissue and Other Stories, White Trash Boulevard, Gone Tomorrow, Rent Boy, *and* Let It Bleed: Essays from 1985–1995. *He lives in New York.*

I recently met a Southern novelist who asked me where I came from. When I told him he said, "Why, that's as close to Tupelo, Mississippi, as you can get, isn't it?" I loved him for saying it, since most people I meet in New York think of New Hampshire as "New England" in the generic Yankee sense of salt-box houses and Mayflower pedigrees, part of a homogenous bloc of nominally liberal states overblessed with vacation lakes and ski colonies. Contrary to this sunny leisure vision, New Hampshire has always been the slum of New England.

You would have to go back to the time of Carnegie and Morgan and J. D. Rockefeller to puzzle out the demographic of the textile belt where I grew up. When my mother's grandparents worked in the Amoskeag and Lawrence mills, the life expectancy of a textile worker was 22 years shorter than that of a textile mill owner, there were thousands of job-related deaths every year and many thousands more job-related injuries, all of them uncompensated; children of 12 were shoved into the factories, where no laws protected them from the myriad biohazards produced by "free enterprise." These children often died within two or three years of starting work. Thirty-six out of 100 adult workers died before the age of 25.

The towns along the New Hampshire–Massachusetts border were thickly settled by the poorest arrivals from Ellis Island, who filtered northward through the industrial plants of New Jersey, New York, and Pennsylvania: Greeks, Italians, Germans, Poles, Irish, Lithuanians, Portuguese. Jay Gould, the Vanderbilts, the Morgans, and the Rockefellers lured them from their European ghettos with newspaper propaganda, advertising the U.S. of A. as a gilded land of limitless opportunity—which for Gould, Vanderbilt, Morgan, and Rockefeller it was. The people who owned the country (including the sprawling corporation known as the U.S. Government) obtained slave labor from abroad with the poor-tired-and-huddled-masses con, and this worked out rather more cheaply for them than actual slavery in the South had for the plantation owners, if we think in terms of investment-to-profit ratios. The suckers even paid their own passage.

My people on my mother's side came down from Canada a decade after the Civil War, first to Augusta, Maine, where they "lived like gypsies," according to one great-aunt, and then to Lowell, Salisbury, Lawrence, and Haverhill in Massachusetts. The newspapers of the day, owned by the Morgan empire, encouraged huge families—with the staggering infant mortality rate and early death in the mills, many births ensured an unflagging work force—and so did the Catholic church; my maternal grandparents knocked out something like a kid a year, and though several of them died, seven made it to adulthood. My mother's first language was French. It wasn't until the early '30s that the children became fluent in English.

The pretensions of my father's parents, who thought they were gentry because they were WASPs and had actually farmed in Vermont before moving to Lowell (where, far from working in the mills, they published an advertising register, something like a hardcover newspaper; they transported this business to Coles Grove, New Hampshire, where they retired on their profits), gave me my first vague notion of class and ethnic distinctions; they might never have said so, but the Edwardses thought my mother's tight-knit, wage-earning siblings vulgarly clannish, poorly educated, and, unforgivably, given to strong drink of a Saturday night—a typically Canuck, RC set of defects my father had avoided with his first wife, Florence.

Though Florence had attempted, on three occasions, to stab my father to death with a pair of upholstery shears, she was pure Anglo-Saxon on both sides, like them, and had given him two perfect male children before being carted off to the asylum.

In actual fact, my father's mother was Welsh, his father Scottish—in a distant sense, at least, products of colonialism, like my mother's family. (That my father's mother was half Jewish is an abiding article of faith in my mother's family; I have never been able to verify or disprove this, but Welsh Jews are rare indeed.) It was a question of the degree of dilution, I suppose, or distance from the "mother country": the Edwardses considered themselves "English," in a way that the Robitailles could never be, simply, French.

The ethnic suet of Coles Grove never produced anything like the racism of Tupelo, Mississippi, though it was similarly stocked with rednecks. There were no lynchings of Italians by Swedes, no luncheon-counter rebuffs to the one Jew and two Lebanese sisters who lived there; no separate water fountains and toilets for French Canadians. There were, less dramatically, in the absence of African or Asian Americans, all manner of ethnic stereotypes, "discrimination" in the sense that a store owner always extended credit to a WASP but seldom to a Portuguese, and, in advance of the current prejudice against gays, phobias about "behavior" ascribed to one or another group. Sometimes these followed religious lines: the Baptists were tightfisted, the Episcopalians jumped-up, the Congregationalists too loose and conciliatory in their affections, the Adventists smarmy and deranged at the same time, and so on. As Catholics—my mother's side; my father and his father were atheists, his mother nominally Baptist—we were, of course, the only people who could enter the Kingdom of Heaven. It was better not to make friends with Protestant children, since they were all going to Hell or Purgatory for eternity, and we wouldn't see them again in the afterlife.

Did we perceive ourselves as "white"?

Yes and no: the early civil rights movement scarcely penetrated our consciousness, though once it did, with TV coverage of Little Rock, it became part and parcel of the subversion perpetrated by the Red Communists. We were not encouraged in any feelings about Negroes, for or against, but their sudden visibility in the shadow play of televised world events meant that the natural order of things was being disrupted by foreigners. The anticommunist hysteria of the McCarthy era colored every waking and sleeping moment of our lives. In the '50s, I think, racial violence in the South reinforced our sense of superiority to the white minions of the Confederacy; the North-South polarity was even invoked in the early '60s to explain the racist Boston politician Louise Day Hicks. She was, my father explained, "shanty Irish from down there," and therefore more ignorant, incredible though it might seem, than the Canucks who lived in Pinardville across the railroad tracks.

A fairly distant branch of my mother's family (Patnaudes or Dammes, I can't remember which) had been involved in labor organizing, was said to be "pinkish" if not downright red, and because they lived over the border "the Massachusetts people," with their educated airs and progressive ideas, merged with Massachusetts itself into a slick, socialist menace. In fact, we gloated over their racial problems, as if they were getting what they deserved from the Negroes, whom we had been clever enough to keep out of New Hampshire. As the bedroom suburbs of Boston spilled over into Windham and Derry and Salem in the late '50s, people who had lived in Coles Grove since the '20s cultivated an intense resentment of virtually anyone from Massachusetts; they were coming to Coles Grove to avoid sales tax, to take advantage of the low property tax, to register their cars for at least 10 dollars less than it cost in Haverhill or Lowell. Never mind that we had moved there from Lowell ourselves a few decades earlier. That was different. True, several of my aunts, uncles, and cousins worked at the GE and Raytheon plants around Lawrence, commuting in the other direction. But the Massachusetts people, who reaped the tax advantage, expected something for nothing. They were taking over the town, voting their own people into Town Hall, burdening the local schools with their snotty brats.

While my WASP grandparents kept their own counsel and seldom expressed a political thought (they lived, my mother opined, in the previous century), the factory workers on my mother's side—and my father, who at that time was part owner of a lumber mill—identified with Joseph McCarthy, an obvious alcoholic with the logical prowess of a seventh grader. Beneath the masochistic niceness with which their social skills began and ended, they shared his insensible xenophobia, a natural extension of their own mistrust of other families. The miserable, flailing, nihilistic rhetoric of McCarthy comfortingly resembled the drunken midnight ravings of my Uncle Norman, whose throat had been ravaged by several cancer operations; he couldn't be fitted for false teeth, and railed incomprehensibly through his gums at things he saw on TV. Joseph McCarthy was like a member of the family, a more lovably trashy anticommunist than Herbert Philbrick, supposed communist cell infiltrator for the FBI (and a big snob, whose "I Led Three Lives" variety store was a 10-minute drive from our house).

Uncle Norman had fought the weasely Japs in the Pacific War, on horrible islands where there was no fresh water or food, and assured us time and again that "death meant nothing to them." This was also true of the Communist Chinese, though not of the Chinese living on Formosa for some reason, nor was it for that matter true of Eddie Lee, who owned the junkyard that had once been the Robert Frost Homestead.

Around 1958, two books began circulating in the town; for a book to circulate, it had to be really something, like *Peyton Place. None Dare Call It Treason* informed us of the worldwide communist menace, virtually untouched by HUAC and the martyred Joe McCarthy, its domestic tendrils planted deep among the heathen, restive Negroes and (who else?) the Jews; *Deliver Us from Evil*, by Dr. Tom Dooley, described the hideous martyrdom endured by Christian missionaries in Red China and (where else?) Vietnam, Laos, and Cambodia.

My family was fascinated by stupidity, half convinced of its own stupidity, and abjectly complicit with stupid things that were plainly over the top. We knew perfectly well there were no missile silos planted around Exeter, but avidly phoned the local Minuteman line to hear a recording that said there were. We relished the crackpot fulminations of Captain Gay, the local head of the Masons, who passed his days regaling the Family Drug lunch counter with vivid tales of Mandingo types ravishing white ladies in shopping mall parking lots. We thrilled to Tom Dooley's descriptions of satanic Chinese communists driving nails through the skulls of Maryknolls. We knew better, but our own provisional, fraught, crawling-into-the-middle-class status rendered our knowing better somehow questionable: did we really have the right to formulate our own opinions, when other people's were so much stronger? We had never traveled, never seen anything except the mills, the factories, the shopping centers, the rocky landscape where you couldn't grow a thing in bulk besides potatoes. What the fuck did we know?

I really believe that people in Coles Grove were barely aware of themselves as "white people" until the demographic shifted in the late '60s, and African Americans in small numbers, Asians in slightly larger ones, moved into the border towns. By the time they arrived, mass media had instilled a better-than-tolerant if not effusively welcoming attitude among us. It's hard to say, really. I never heard the word *nigger* used in my childhood, except by distant white trash relatives when they were drunk; I'm not sure that means anything more than the fact that difficult and alien subjects were considered unspeakable in my family. We were, I think, the most emotionally constipated family that ever existed.

True, "kike" was sometimes applied to George Cohn when he left the room, as in, "The thing I like about George is, he's not a kike." But I don't think the person talking really knew what "kike" meant; it was just something excitingly off-color to say. "Chink" was considered a natural, rather than derisory, description of Eddie Lee, whom we liked because he always bought my brother's secondhand cars after he totaled them.

We were only white when somebody wasn't. European only in the presence of non-Europeans, Northern in contrast to Mediterraneans. But I suppose that's the white thing: never having to define what you are, while other people scramble to define themselves in relationship to you. Yet whites among themselves (and blacks among themselves, Asians ditto, etc.) invariably find something besides race to detest in each other, ethnicity or sexual preference or whatever. I am convinced that my mother's horror over my first sexual passion, for a Portuguese friend of my brother's named Eugene Dutra, had almost as much to do with his class and nationality as with my being queer. The Dutras had an old Ford up on cinder blocks in their front yard, they lived on the bad side of the railroad tracks, and Eugene was . . . well, a dangerously sexual presence, a fact registered by everybody but mentioned by no one (except me, in what I thought was my private diary). He looked different and that made him sexy, and suspect.

We were a timorous and gentle family, as a matter of fact, and we were taught not to hate anybody. At the same time, there were people it was better not to trust, people we and our parents and our grandparents had been fed half-developed, silly notions about, and these notions accounted, basically, for everyone on earth outside our family. A sense of deep inferiority had been bred into us as part of the immigrant experience, and we were hardly pushy about our whiteness: there was no one around to be pushy about it with, for one thing. And for another, the town was owned by people named Adams and Newell and Shepard, had been owned by them since 1721. There wasn't a chance in hell that Quebec gypsies and dirt farmers from Brattleboro would ever be as white as they were.

FOR JOURNALING AND DISCUSSION

1. Indiana begins his essay about his family and their xenophobia by describing the textile mills in which his mother's family worked. Drawing on evidence from the essay, explain the connections Indiana makes between classism and racism.
2. When Indiana writes, "We were only white when somebody wasn't," what is he saying about how "whiteness" was used in land-seizing, slave-holding, and immigrant-recruiting in the United States?
3. Describe a situation from your own experience where, as Indiana writes, "white among themselves (and blacks among themselves, Asians ditto, etc.) invariably find something besides race to detest in each other, ethnicity or sexual preference or whatever." What is a "difference" other than race that you have heard disparaged in your family, and why do you think this occurs?

FOR RESEARCH AND EXPLORATION

1. Much of the essay connects Joseph McCarthy's fear of communism with racism. Research specifics of the McCarthy hearings, and explain how anticommunism and racism are connected.
2. Look at Katherine Newman's "Illegitimate Elites and the Parasitic Underclass" in Chapter 3, and explain how immigration connects to American attitudes about race.
3. Labor and work changes often lead to the changing demographic makeup of an area, as Indiana demonstrates when he traces these shifts in textile-mill New Hampshire. Explore the labor and demographic changes in the city or town in which your campus is located. Try interviewing older residents and exploring

the local historical society to understand better how work is related to racial prejudice.

My Best White Friend: Cinderella Revisited

Patricia Williams

Williams, the great-great-granddaughter of a slave and a white southern lawyer, is a lawyer and professor at Columbia University School of Law. Her book The Alchemy of Race and Rights *is an eloquent autobiographical reflection on the intersection of race, gender, and class.*

My best white friend is giving me advice on how to get myself up like a trophy-wife-in-waiting. We are obliged to attend a gala fund-raiser for an organization on whose board we both sit. I'm not a wife of any sort at all, and she says she knows why: I'm prickly as all getout, I dress down instead of up, and my hair is "a complete disaster." My best white friend, who is already a trophy wife of considerable social and philanthropic standing, is pressing me to borrow one of her Real Designer gowns and a couple of those heavy gold bracelets that are definitely not something you can buy on the street.

I tell her she's missing the point. Cinderella wasn't an over-thirty black professional with an attitude. What sort of Master of the Universe is going to go for that?

"You're not a *racist,* are you?" she asks.

"How could I be?" I reply, with wounded indignation. "What, being the American Dream personified and all."

"Then let's get busy and make you *up,*" she says soothingly, breaking out the little pots of powder, paint, and polish.

From the first exfoliant to the last of the cucumber rinse, we fight about my man troubles. From powder base through lip varnish, we fight about hers.

You see, part of the problem is that white knights just don't play the same part in my mythical landscape of desire. If poor Cinderella had been black, it would have been a whole different story. I tell my best white friend the kind of stories my mother raised me on: about slave girls who worked their fingers to the bone for their evil half sisters, the "legitimate" daughters of their mutual father, the master of the manse, the owner of them all; about scullery maids whose oil-and-ashes complexions would not wash clean even after multiple waves of the wand. These were the ones who harbored impossible dreams of love for lost mates who had been sold down rivers of tears to oblivion. These were the ones who became runaways.

"Just think about it," I say. "The human drama is compact enough so that when my mother was little she knew women who had been slaves, including a couple of runaways. Cinderellas who had burned their masters' beds and then fled for their lives. It doesn't take too much, even across the ages, to read between those lines. Women who invented their own endings, even when they didn't get to live happily or very long thereafter."

My best white friend says, "Get a grip. It's just a party."

I've called my best white friend my best white friend ever since she started calling me her best black friend. I am her only black friend, as far as I know, a circumstance for which she blames "the class thing." At her end of the social ladder, I am *my* only black friend—a circumstance for which I blame "the race thing."

"People should stop putting so much emphasis on color—it doesn't matter whether you're black or white or blue or green," she says from beneath an avocado mask.

Lucky for you, I think, even as my own pores are expanding or contracting—I forget which—beneath a cool neon-green sheath.

In fact, I have been looking forward to the makeover. M.B.W.F. has a masseuse and a manicurist and colors in her palette like Après Sun and Burnt Straw, which she swears will match my skin tones more or less.

"Why don't they just call it Racial Envy?" I ask, holding up a tube of Deep Copper Kiss.

"Now, now, we're all sisters under the makeup," she says cheerfully.

"When ever will we be sisters without?" I grumble.

I've come this far because she's convinced me that my usual slapdash routine is the equivalent of being "unmade"; and being unmade, she underscores, is a most exclamatory form of unsophistication. "Even Strom Thurmond wears a little pancake when he's in public."

M.B.W.F. is somewhat given to hyperbole, but it *is* awfully hard to bear, the thought of making less of a fashion statement than old Strom. I do draw the line, though. She has a long history of nips, tucks, and liposuction. Once, I tried to suggest how appalled I was, but I'm not good at being graceful when I have a really strong opinion rolling up inside. She dismissed me sweetly: "You can afford to disapprove. You are aging *so* very nicely."

There was the slightest pause as I tried to suppress the anxious rise in my voice: "You think I'm aging?"

Very gently, she proceeded to point out the flawed and falling features that give me away to the carefully trained eye, the insistent voyeur. There were the pores. And those puffs beneath my eyes. No, not there—those are the bags under my eyes. The bags aren't so bad, according to her—no deep wrinkling just yet. But keep going—the puffs are just below the bags. Therein lies the facial decay that gives my age away.

I had never noticed them before, but for a while after that those puffs just dominated my face. I couldn't look at myself for their explosive insolence—the body's betrayal, obscuring every other feature.

I got over it the day we were standing in line by a news rack at the Food Emporium. Gazing at a photo of Princess Diana looking radiantly, elegantly melancholic on the cover of some women's magazine, M.B.W.F. snapped, "God! Bulimia must work!"

This is not the first time M.B.W.F. has shepherded me to social doom. The last time, it was a very glitzy cocktail party where husband material supposedly abounded. I had a long, businesslike conversation with a man she introduced me to, who, I realized as we talked, grew more and more fascinated by me. At first, I was only conscious of winning him over; then I remember becoming aware that there was something funny about his fierce infatuation. I was *surprising* him, I slowly realized. Finally, he came clean: he said that he had never before had a conversation like this with a black person. "I think I'm in love," he blurted in a voice bubbling with fear.

"I think not," I consoled him. "It's just the power of your undone expectations, in combination with my being a basically likable person. It's throwing you for a loop. That and the Scotch, which, as you ought to know, is inherently depoliticizing."

I remember telling M.B.W.F. about him afterward. She had always thought of him as "that perfect Southern gentleman." The flip side of the Southern gentleman is the kind master, I pointed out. "Bad luck," she said. "It's true, though—he's the one man I wouldn't want to be owned by, if I were you."

My best white friend doesn't believe that race is a big social problem anymore. "It's all economics," she insists. "It's how you came to be my *friend*"—for once, she does not qualify me as black—"the fact that we were both in college together." I feel compelled to remind her that affirmative action is how both of us ended up in the formerly all-male bastion we attended.

The odd thing is, we took most of the same classes. She ended up musically proficient, gifted in the art of interior design, fluent in the mother tongue, whatever it might be, of the honored visiting diplomat of the moment. She actively aspired, she says, to be "a cunning little meringue of a male prize."

"You," she says to me, "were always more like Gladys Knight."

"Come again?" I say.

"Ethnic woman warrior, always on that midnight train to someplace else, intent on becoming the highest-paid Aunt Jemima in history."

"Ackh," I cough, a sudden strangulation of unmade thoughts fluttering in my windpipe.

The night after the cocktail party, I dreamed that I was in a bedroom with a tall, faceless man. I was his breeding slave. I was trying to be very, very good, so that I might one day earn my freedom. He did not trust me. I was always trying to hide some essential part of myself from him, which I would preserve and take with me on that promised day when I was permitted to leave; he felt it as an innate wickedness in me, a darkness that he could not penetrate, a dangerous secret that must be wrested from me. I tried everything I knew to please him; I walked a tightrope of anxious servitude and survivalist withholding. But it was not good enough. One morning, he just reached for a sword and sliced me in half, to see for himself what was inside. A casual flick, and I lay dead on the floor in two dark, unyielding halves; in exasperated disgust, he stepped over my remains and rushed from the room, already late for other business, leaving the cleanup for another slave.

"You didn't dream that!" M.B.W.F. says in disbelief.

"I did so."

"You're making it up," she says. "People don't really have dreams like that."

"*I* do. Aren't I a people, too?"

"That's amazing! Tell me another."

"O.K., here's a fairy tale for you," I say, and tell her I dreamed I was being held by Sam Malone, the silly, womanizing bartender on "Cheers." He was tall, broad-chested, good-looking, unbelievably strong. My head, my face were pressed against his chest. We were whispering our love for each other. I was moved deeply, my heart was banging, he held me tight and told me that he loved me. I told him that I loved him, too. We kissed so that heaven and earth moved in my heart; I wanted to make love to him fiercely. He put a simple thick gold band on my finger. I turned and, my voice cracking with emotion and barely audible, said, "What's this?" He asked me to marry him. I told him yes, I loved him, yes, yes, I loved him. He told me he loved me, too. I held out my hand and admired the ring in awe. I was the luckiest woman on earth.

Suddenly Diane Chambers, Sam's paramour on "Cheers," burst through the door. She was her perky, petulant self, bouncing blond hair and black-green eyes like tarnished copper beads, like lumps of melted metal—eyes that looked carved yet soft, almost brimming. She turned those soft-hard eyes on me and said, "Oh no, Sam, not tonight—you promised!"

And with that I realized that I was to be consigned to a small room on the other side of the house. Diane followed me as I left, profusely apologetic with explanations: she was sorry, and she didn't mind him being with me once or twice a month, but this was getting ridiculous. I realized that I was Sam's part-time mistress—a member of the household somehow, but having no rights.

Then Diane went back into the master bedroom and Sam came in to apologize, to say that there had been a mixup, that it was just this once, that he'd make it up to me, that he was sorry. And, of course, I forgave him, for there was nothing I wanted more than to relive the moment when he held me tightly and our love was a miracle and I was the only woman he wanted in the world, forever.

"Have you thought of going into therapy?" she jokes.

"As a matter of fact, I have," I say, sighing and rubbing my temples. "On average, we black women have bigger, better problems than any other women alive. We bear the burden of being seen as pretenders to the thrones of both femininity and masculinity, endlessly mocked by the ambiguously gendered crown-of-thorns imagery of "queen"—Madame Queen, snap queen, welfare queen, quota queen, Queenie Queen, *Queen* Queen Queen. We black women are figured more as stand-ins for men, sort of like reverse drag queens: women pretending to be women but more male than men—bare-breasted, sweat-glistened, plow-pulling, sole supporters of their families. Arnold Schwarzenegger and Sylvester Stallone meet Sojourner Truth, the *Real* Real Thing, the Ace-of-Spades Gender Card Herself, Thelma and Louise knocked up by Wesley Snipes, the ultimate hard-drinking, tobacco-growing-and-aspitting, nut-crushing ball-buster of all time . . . . I mean, think about it—how'd you like to go to the ball dressed like a walking cultural pathology? Wouldn't it make you just a wee bit tense?"

"But," she sputters, "but—you always seem so *strong!*"

We have just about completed our toilette. She looks at my hair as though it were a rude construction of mud and twigs, bright glass beads, and flashy bits of tinfoil. I look at hers for what it is—the high-tech product of many hours of steam rollers, shine enhancers, body spritzers, perms, and about eighteen hundred watts of blow-dried effort. We gaze at each other with the deep disapproval of one gazing into a mirror. It is inconceivable to both of us that we have been friends for as long as we have. We shake our heads in sympathetic unison and sigh.

One last thing: it seems we have forgotten about shoes. It turns out that my feet are much too big to fit into any of her sequinned little evening slippers, so I wear my own sensible square-soled pumps. My prosaic feet, like overgrown roots, peek out from beneath the satiny folds of the perfect dress. She looks radiant; I feel dubious. Our chariot and her husband await. As we climb into the limousine, her husband lights up a cigar and holds forth on the reëmerging popularity of same. My friend responds charmingly with a remarkably detailed production history of the Biedermeier humidor.

I do not envy her. I do not resent her.

FOR JOURNALING AND DISCUSSION

1. Williams juxtaposes the Cinderella fairy tale with her mother's stories of slave girls, describing them as "scullery maids whose oil-and-ashes complexions would not wash clean even after multiple waves of the wand." Discuss the new perspectives these other tales cast on the Cinderella story.
2. What does Williams say about white "trophy wives" in the way she describes her "best white friend"? Drawing evidence from the essay, what would you say is her friend's level of awareness about racism?
3. When Williams describes the white man at the cocktail party, she explains his surprise as "the power of your undone expectations." What does she mean?
4. Williams describes the misconceptions and racist myths driving white society's stereotypes of black women defined with the "imagery of 'queen.'" Use examples from your own experience to explain why the "welfare queen" image is so effective and persistent in fueling American racism.
5. The Cinderella fairy tale is a recurring image in this essay, and in that tale good triumphs over evil. What does Williams's focus on the rape of slave women by their masters do to your ideas about white knights and handsome princes?

FOR RESEARCH AND EXPLORATION

1. Williams connects issues of race with patriarchal definitions of beauty. Research feminist discussions of the connections between power (and money) and beauty. The work of Katie Roiphe would be a good starting place.
2. Examine and critique three contemporary women's fashion magazines for their hair, clothes, and makeup ads. Focus especially on issues of race and beauty.
3. In Chapter 4, Sallie Tisdale's "A Weight That Women Carry: The Compulsion to Diet in a Starved Culture" discusses body image and social definitions of beauty. Compare that essay with Williams's to explore the connections between body size and image in relation to race and beauty.

Our Next Race Question: The Uneasiness Between Blacks and Latinos

Jorge Klor De Alva, Earl Shorris, and Cornel West

Klor De Alva is the Class of 1940 Professor of Comparative Ethnic Studies and Anthropology at the University of California at Berkeley. He has written

Jorge Klor De Alva, Earl Shorris, and Cornel West, "Our Next Race Question: The Uneasiness Between Blacks and Latinos" from *Harper's* (April 1996). Copyright © 1996 by Harper's Magazine. Reprinted with the permission of *Harper's*.

or edited fourteen books on anthropology, history, and interethnic relations in the Americas, and is currently working on The Norton Anthology of Mesoamerican Literature.

Shorris is a contributing editor of Harper's Magazine *and the author of ten books, including* Latinos: A Biography of the People; Ofay, *a novel about a black-white love affair; and* Under the Fifth Sun, *a novel about Pancho Villa.*

West is a professor of African American studies and philosophy of religion at Harvard University. He has written eleven books on philosophy, African American studies, and religion, including Race Matters. *His latest book, co-authored with Henry Louis Gates, Jr., is* The Future of the Race.

The angry and confused discourse about American race relations that followed the O. J. Simpson trial may have been passionate, but it blindly assumed (as if the year were 1963 or 1861) that the only major axis of racial division in America was black-white. Strangely ignored in the media backwash was the incipient tension between the country's largest historical minority, blacks, and its largest future one, Latinos.

In fifteen years, Latinos (known to the U.S. Census as Hispanics) will outnumber blacks, as they already do in twenty-one states. Each group constitutes an ever greater percentage of the total population; each is large enough to swing a presidential election. But do they vote with or against each other, and do they hold the same views of a white America that they have different reasons to distrust?

Knowing that questions of power and ethnicity are no longer black-and-white, *Harper's Magazine* invited three observers—a black, a Latino, and a white moderator—to open the debate.

EARL SHORRIS: To begin, would you both answer one question with a yes or no, no more than that? Cornel, are you a black man?

CORNEL WEST: Yes.

SHORRIS: Jorge, do you think Cornel is a black man?

JORGE KLOR DE ALVA: No, for now.

SHORRIS: Apparently we have something to talk about. Jorge, can you tell me why you say, "No, for now?"

KLOR DE ALVA: To identify someone as black, Latino, or anything else, one has to appeal to a tradition of naming and categorizing in which a question like that can make sense—and be answered with a yes or a no. In the United States, where unambiguous, color-coded identities are the rule, Cornel is clearly a black man. Traveling someplace else, perhaps in Africa, Cornel would not necessarily be identified as black. He might be seen as someone of mixed African descent, but that's different from being identified as black. Cornel is only black within a certain reductionist context. And that context, where color is made to represent not so much the hue of one's skin as a set of denigrated experiences—and where these experiences are applied to everyone who ever had an African ancestor—is one I consider to be extremely negative.

WEST: I think when I say I am a black man, I'm saying first that I am a modern person, because black itself is a modern construct, a construct put forward during a particular moment in time to fit a specific set of circumstances. Implicit in that category of "black man" is American white supremacy, African slavery, and then a very rich culture that responds to these conditions at the level of style, mannerism, orientation, experimentation, improvisation, syncopation—all of those elements that have gone into making a new people, namely black people.

A hundred years ago I would have said that I was a "colored man." But I would still have been modern, I'd still have been New World African, I'd still have been dealing with white supremacy, and I would still have been falling back on a very rich culture of resistance, a culture that tried to preserve black sanity and spiritual health in the face of white hatred and job ceilings. I think Jorge and I agree that we're dealing with constructs. And I think we agree in our objections to essentialist conceptions of race, to the idea that differences are innate and outside of history.

KLOR DE ALVA: What advantage has it been, Cornel, for blacks to identify themselves as blacks?

WEST: For one, that identification was imposed. We were perceived as a separate people—enslaved, Jim Crowed, and segregated. To be viewed as a separate people requires coming to terms with that separateness. This category "black" was simply a response to that imposition of being a separate people, and also a building on one's own history, going back to Africa, yes, but especially here in the United States. So when I say, for example, that jazz is a creation of black people, I'm saying that it's a creation of modern people, New World African people. And we've come up with various categories, including black, as a way of affirming ourselves as agents, as subjects in history who create, initiate, and so forth. So in that sense there have actually been some real benefits.

KLOR DE ALVA: When the Europeans arrived in Mexico, they confronted people whose level of social organization was not unlike that of the Romans. Before millions died from newly introduced diseases, the Europeans called them *naturales,* or "natural people." Afterwards the survivors came to be called "Indians," a term the natives did not use until the nineteenth century, preferring to identify themselves by their tribal group. And to the extent that they were able to do that, they managed to maintain a degree of cultural integrity as separate groups. When that ended, they were all seen as despised Indians.

The general label only helped to promote their denigration. Now, I agree that group designations help build a sense of community, but as free and enslaved Africans took on the general labels that oppressed them, they also helped to legitimize their being identified as one irredeemable people. In the United States this unwillingness to challenge what has come to be known as the one-drop rule—wherein anyone who ever had an African ancestor, however remote, is identifiable only as black—has strengthened the hand of those who seek to trap them, and other so-called people of color, in a social basement with no exit ladder.

WEST: When we talk about identity, it's really important to define it. Identity has to do with protection, association, and recognition. People identify themselves in certain ways in order to protect their bodies, their labor, their communities, their way of life; in order to be associated with people who ascribe value to them, who take them seriously, who respect them; and for purposes of recognition, to be acknowledged, to feel as if one actually belongs to a group, a clan, a tribe, a community. So that any time we talk about the identity of a particular group over time and space, we have to be very specific about what the credible options are for them at any given moment.

There have been some black people in America who fundamentally believed that they were wholehearted, full-fledged Americans. They have been mistaken. They tried to pursue that option—Boom! Jim Crow hit them. They tried to press that option—Boom! Vanilla suburbs didn't allow them in. So they had to then revise and recast their conception of themselves in terms of protection, association, and recognition. Because they weren't being protected by the police and the courts. They weren't welcome in association. Oftentimes they were not welcome in white suburbs. And they weren't being recognized. Their talents and capacities were debased, devalued, and degraded. "Black" was the term many chose. Okay, that's fine, we can argue about that. But what are the other options? "Human being?" Yes, we ought to be human beings, but we know that's too abstract and too vague. We need human communities on the ground, not simply at the level of the ideal.

CONSTRUCTING HUMANS

KLOR DE ALVA: Nobody is born black. People are born with different pigmentation, people are born with different physical characteristics, no question about that. But you have to learn to be black. That's what I mean by constructedness.

WEST: But are people born human? Is "human" itself constructed, as a category?

KLOR DE ALVA: Certainly as a category, as a social, as a scientific category, of course it's a construct. The species could have been identified in some other fashion. Since Columbus's landfall you had very extensive debates as to whether indigenous peoples in the Americas were human, like Europeans, or not. The priest Montesinos posed that question to the Spanish colonists in

1511, and Las Casas, a fellow priest, and the theologian Sepúlveda debated the issue at mid-century before Emperor Charles V.

WEST: You see, this historical process of naming is part of the legacy not just of white supremacy but of class supremacy. Tolstoy didn't believe his peasants were actually human until after he underwent conversion. And he realized, "My God, I used to think they were animals, now they're human beings, I have a different life and a new set of lenses with which to view it." So it is with any talk about blackness. It's associated with subhumanness, and therefore when we talk about constructed terms like "black" or "peasant" or "human," it means that the whole thing's up for grabs in terms of constructedness. And if that's so, then all we have left is history.

KLOR DE ALVA: All identities are up for grabs. But black intellectuals in the United States, unlike Latino intellectuals in the United States, have an enormous media space within which to shape the politics of naming and to affect the symbols and meanings associated with certain terms. Thus, practically overnight, they convinced the media that they were an ethnic group and shifted over to the model of African-American, hyphenated American, as opposed to being named by color. Knowing what we know about the negative aspects of naming, it would be better for all of us, regardless of color, if those who consider themselves, and are seen as, black intellectuals were to stop participating in the insidious one-drop-rule game of identifying themselves as black.

WEST: If you're saying that we are, for the most part, biological and cultural hybrids, I think you're certainly right. But at the same time there's a danger in calling for an end to a certain history if we're unable to provide other options. Now, because I speak first and foremost as a human being, a radical Democrat, and a Christian, I would be willing to use damn near any term if it helped to eliminate poverty and provide adequate health care and child care and a job with a living wage, some control at the workplace, and some redistribution of wealth downward. At that point, you can call all black people colored. That's fine with me.

SHORRIS: Are you saying that you're willing to disappear?

WEST: Well, I would never disappear, because whatever name we would come up with, we're still going to have the blues and John Coltrane and Sarah Vaughan and all those who come out of this particular history. And simply because we change the name wouldn't mean that we would disappear.

KLOR DE ALVA: I think that's the wrong emphasis. I think what has happened is that much of the cultural diversity that Cornel mentions has, in fact, disappeared behind this veil that has transformed everybody with one drop of African blood into black. That reductionism has been a much more powerful mechanism for causing diversity to disappear.

WEST: Well, what do you mean by disappearance at this point?

KLOR DE ALVA: Let me answer your question from a slightly different perspective. We have, in the United States, two mechanisms at play in the construction of collective identities. One is to identify folks from a cultural perspective. The other is to identify them from a racial perspective. Now, with the exception of black-white relations, the racial perspective is not the critical one for most folks. The cultural perspective was, at one time, very sharply drawn, including the religious line between Catholics and Protestants, Jews and Protestants, Jews and Catholics, Jews and Christians. But in the course of the twentieth century, we have seen in the United States a phenomenon that we do not see anyplace else in the world—the capacity to blur the differences between these cultural groups, to construct them in such a way that they became insignificant and to fuse them into a new group called whites, which didn't exist before.

WEST: Yes, but whiteness was already in place. I mean, part of the tragedy of American civilization is precisely the degree to which the stability and continuity of American democracy has been predicated on a construct of whiteness that includes the subordination of black people, so that European cultural diversity could disappear into American whiteness while black folk remain subordinated.

KLOR DE ALVA: But everything, even whiteness, must be constructed and is therefore subject to change.

WEST: Categories are constructed. Scars and bruises are felt with human bodies, some of which end up in coffins. Death is not a construct. And so, when we're talking about constructs having concrete consequences that produce scars and bruises, these consequences are not constructed, they're felt. They're very real. Now, in light of that, I would want to accent the strengths of the history of black resistance. One of the reasons why black people are so integral a part of American civilization is because black people have raised a lot of hell. That's very important, especially in a society in which power and pressure decide who receives visibility. By raising hell I mean organization, mobilization, chaos-producing capacity, as in rebellion. That's a very important point. Why is it important? It's important for me because what's at stake is the quality of American civilization, whether it actually survives as a plausible idea.

That's why a discourse on race is never just a discourse on race. Richard Wright used to say that the Negro is America's metaphor. It means you can't talk about one without talking about the nature of the other. And one of the reasons we don't like to talk about race, especially as it relates to black folk, is because we're forced to raise all the fundamental questions about what it means to be an American, what it means to be a part of American democracy. Those are exhausting and challenging questions.

The best of the black intellectual and political tradition has always raised the problem of evil in its concrete forms in America. People like Frederick Douglass, Martin Luther King, and Ella Baker never focused solely on black suffering. They used black suffering as a springboard to raise issues of various other forms of injustice, suffering, and so forth, that relate to other groups—black, brown, white workers, right across the board, you see. During the Eighties, the major opposition to right-wing Reaganism was what? Jesse Jackson's campaigns. Opening up to workers, gay brothers, lesbian sisters, right across the board. Black suffering was a springboard. Why? Because a question of evil sits at the heart of the American moral dilemma. With the stark exception of its great artists—Melville, Faulkner, Elizabeth Bishop, Coltrane, Toni Morrison—American society prefers to deny the existence of its own evil. Black folk historically have reminded people of the prevailing state of denial.

ANGLOS MAY BE OF ANY RACE

SHORRIS:　We've just demonstrated one of the tenets of this conversation. That is, we have discussed almost exclusively the question of blacks in this society. But we started out saying we would have a black-brown dialogue. Why does that happen? And not only in the media. Why did it happen here, among us?

KLOR DE ALVA:　Part of the answer, as Cornel was pointing out, is that blacks are the central metaphor for otherness and oppression in the United States. Secondly, in part I take your question, when focused on Latinos, to mean, Don't Latinos have their own situation that also needs to be described if not in the same terms, then at least in terms that are supplementary?

I'm not sure. The answer goes to the very core of the difference between Latinos and blacks and between Cornel and myself: I am trying to argue against the utility of the concept of race. Why? Because I don't think that's the dominant construct we need to address in order to resolve the many problems at hand. Cornel wants to construct it in the language of the United States, and I say we need a different kind of language. Do you know why, Earl? Because we're in the United States and blacks are Americans. They're Anglos.

WEST:　Excuse me?

KLOR DE ALVA:　They're Anglos of a different color, but they're Anglos. Why? Because the critical distinction here for Latinos is not race, it's culture.

WEST:　Speaking English and being part of American culture?

KLOR DE ALVA:　Blacks are more Anglo than most Anglos because, unlike most Anglos, they can't directly identify themselves with a nation-state outside of the United States. They are trapped in America. However unjust and painful, their experiences are wholly made in America.

WEST:　But that doesn't make me an Anglo. If I'm trapped on the underside of America, that doesn't mean that somehow I'm an Anglo.

KLOR DE ALVA:　Poor whites similarly trapped on the underside of America are also Anglos. Latinos are in a totally different situation, unable to be captured by the government in the "five food groups" of racial classification of Americans.

The Commerce Department didn't know what to do with Latinos: the census takers didn't know what to do with Latinos; the government didn't know what to do with Latinos, and so they said, "Latinos can be of any race." That puts Latinos in a totally different situation. They are, in fact, homologous with the totality of the United States. That is, like Americans, Latinos can be of any race. What distinguishes them from all other Americans is culture, not race. That's where I'm going when I say that Cornel is an Anglo. You can be a Latino and look like Cornel. You can be a Latino and look like you, Earl, or like me. And so, among Latinos, there's no surprise in my saying that Cornel is an Anglo.

WEST: But it seems to me that "Anglo" is the wrong word.

KLOR DE ALVA: Hey, I didn't make it up, Cornel.

WEST: "Anglo" implies a set of privileges. It implies a certain cultural formation.

KLOR DE ALVA: I'm trying to identify here how Chicanos see "Anglos."

WEST: But I want to try and convince those Latino brothers and sisters not to think of black folk as Anglos. That's just wrong. Now, they can say that we're English-speaking moderns in the United States who have yet to be fully treated as Americans. That's fine.

KLOR DE ALVA: My friend, Cornel, I was speaking of one of the more benign Latino names for blacks.

WEST: Let's hear some of the less benign then, brother.

WHAT COLOR IS BROWN?

KLOR DE ALVA: Do you think of Latinos as white?

WEST: I think of them as brothers and sisters, as human beings, but in terms of culture, I think of them as a particular group of voluntary immigrants who entered America and had to encounter this thoroughly absurd system of classification of positively charged whiteness, negatively charged blackness. And they don't fit either one: they're not white, they're not black.

SHORRIS: What are they?

WEST: I see them primarily as people of color, as brown people who have to deal with their blackness-whiteness.

SHORRIS: So you see them in racial terms.

WEST: Well, no, it's more cultural.

SHORRIS: But you said "brown."

WEST: No, it's more cultural. Brown, for me, is more associated with culture than race.

SHORRIS: But you choose a word that describes color.

WEST: Right. To say "Spanish-speaking" would be a bit too vague, because you've got a lot of brothers and sisters from Guatemala who don't speak Spanish. They speak an indigenous language.

KLOR DE ALVA: You have a lot of Latinos who aren't brown.

WEST: But they're not treated as whites, and "brown" is simply a signifier of that differential treatment. Even if a Latino brother or sister has supposedly white skin, he or she is still Latino in the eyes of the white privileged, you see. But they're not treated as black. They're not niggers. They're not the bottom of the heap, you see. So they're not niggers, they're not white, what are they? I say brown, but signifying culture more than color. Mexicans, Cubans, Puerto Ricans, Dominicans, El Salvadorans all have very, very distinctive histories. When you talk about black, that becomes a kind of benchmark, because you've got these continuous generations, and you've got very common experiences.

Now, of course, blackness comprises a concealed heterogeneity. You've got West Indians, you've got Ethiopians. My wife is Ethiopian. Her experience is closer to browns'. She came here because she wanted to. She was trying to get out from under a tyrannical, Communist regime in Ethiopia. She's glad to be in a place where she can breathe freely, not have to hide. I say, "I'm glad you're here, but don't allow that one side of America to blind you to my side."

So I've got to take her, you know, almost like Virgil in Dante's *Divine Comedy,* through all of this other side of America so that she can see the nightmare as well as the dream. But as an Ethiopian, she came for the dream and did a good job of achieving it.

KLOR DE ALVA: So you are participating in the same process as the other Americans, other Anglos—to use that complicated term—that same song and dance of transforming her into a highly racialized American black.

WEST: It wasn't me. It was the first American who called her "nigger." That's when she started the process of Americanization and racialization. She turned around and said, "What is a nigger?"

KLOR DE ALVA: And you're the one who explained it . . .

ONE NIGHT OF LOVE

SHORRIS: Cornel, what do you most worry about in the future?

WEST: I think my fundamental concern is the disintegration of American civilization as black people become more and more insulated, isolated, targeted, and hence subjected to the most brutal authoritarian rule in the name of democracy. And that's exactly where we're headed, so it's not just a fear.

KLOR DE ALVA: I would say that what you've described for America would be true of just about any nation I know, particularly any multicultural nation. It's not something that's unique to the United States. My biggest fear, as this nation moves into an inevitable browning, or hybridization, is that there will be a very powerful minority, overwhelmingly composed of Euro-Americans, who will see themselves in significant danger as a consequence of the way democracy works: winner-take-all. And they will begin to renege on some of the basic principles that created the United States and made it what it is.

SHORRIS: We've been talking about conflicts. Let's stipulate, unless you disagree, that the advantage to the people in power of keeping those at the bottom at each other's throats is enormous. That's the case in all societies. So we have blacks and browns, for the most part, at the bottom. And they are frequently at each other's throats. They're fighting over immigration, fighting over jobs, and so on. A group of young people comes to you and says, "Tell us how to make alliances, give us a set of rules for creating alliances between blacks and browns." What would you answer?

WEST: I'd appeal to various examples. Look at Ernesto Cortés and the Industrial Areas Foundation in Texas or the Harlem Initiatives Together in New York City, which have been able to pull off black-brown alliances of great strength, the "breaking bread" events of the Democratic Socialists of America. Or I'd talk about Mark Ridley-Thomas in South-Central Los Angeles and look at the ways in which he speaks with power about brown suffering as a black city councilman, the way in which he's able to build within his own organization a kind of black-brown dialogue. Because what you really see then is not just a set of principles or rules but some momentum at work.

SHORRIS: But how do you do that? What's the first step?

WEST: Well, it depends on what particular action you want to highlight. You could, say, look at the movement around environmental racism, where you have a whole host of black-brown alliances. With Proposition 187* you had a black-brown alliance among progressives fighting against the conservatives who happened to be white, black, and brown. In the trade-union movement, look at 1199, the health-care workers union, here in New York City. You've got brown Dennis Rivera at the top, you've got black Gerry Hudson third in charge, running things. That's a very significant coordinated leadership of probably the most important trade union in the largest city in the nation. So it depends on the particular issue. I think it's issue by issue in light of a broad vision.

SHORRIS: What is the broad vision?

WEST: Democracy, substantive radical democracy in which you actually are highlighting the empowering of everyday people in the workplace and the voting

---

*Editor's note: Proposition 187, passed by California voters in 1994, was an effort to limit illegal immigration and the demands on state resources made by illegal immigrants. One of the reactions to what some called anti-Latino propaganda during this political campaign was an unprecedented number of applications for naturalization from noncitizen Latinos who have since organized a stronger political presence, which Gregory Rodriguez has described as "the browning of California" (*The New Republic,* September 2, 1996, p. 18).

booth so that they can live lives of decency and dignity. That's a deeply democratic sensibility. And I think that sensibility can be found in both the black and brown communities.

KLOR DE ALVA: Unless there's a dramatic shift in ideology, linkages between people who are identified as belonging to opposing camps will last only for the moment, like the graffiti I saw during the L.A. riots: "Crips. Bloods. Mexicans. Together. Forever. Tonite [*sic*]," and then next to that, "LAPD" crossed out and "187" underneath. That is, the alliances will work only as long as there's a common enemy, in this case the L.A.P.D., whose death the graffiti advocated by the term "187," which refers here to the California Criminal Code for homicide.

As long as we don't have a fundamental transformation in ideology, those are the kinds of alliances we will have, and they will be short-lived and not lead, ultimately, to terribly much. Clearly, the progressive forces within the United States must be able to forge ideological changes that would permit lasting linkages. At the core of that effort lies the capacity to address common suffering, regardless of color or culture. And that cannot be done unless common suffering, as the reason for linkages across all lines, is highlighted in place of the very tenuous alliances between groups that identify themselves by race or culture.

SHORRIS: Let's see if anything happened in this conversation. Cornel, are you a black man?

WEST: Hell yes.

SHORRIS: Jorge, is he a black man?

KLOR DE ALVA: Of course not.

FOR JOURNALING AND DISCUSSION

1. In the original version of this essay, there were many graphs on population, age, income, poverty, and language that have not been reprinted here. How does the omission of the information affect your understanding of the debate between Klor De Alva and West? Did you wish for more evidence as you read the dialogue?
2. When Klor De Alva explains why American race discussions always become discussions about black-white distinctions, he says that blacks are "Anglos." What does he mean by this?
3. In *Talking Back: Race and Representation,* the black feminist critic bell hooks [who does not capitalize her name] writes that while race does not exist, racism does. What do both West and Klor De Alva say about the existence of the category "race"?
4. In the title of the article, "Our Next Race Question," the use of "next" implies we've moved beyond earlier questions of black-white race relations. Do you agree or disagree with this assumption? Draw examples from your own experience to support your claim.

5. In another section of this debate, which does not appear in your excerpt, West argues that many Americans have a "sophomoric, childish" understanding of good triumphing over evil, but says that writers and musicians such as William Faulkner, Toni Morrison, Herman Melville, and John Coltrane have a much more "morally mature view of what it means to be human." From what you can infer about West's philosophy and from what you know about any of the artists he mentions, what do you think he means by this?

FOR RESEARCH AND EXPLORATION

1. In other places, West has written about his concern that we not mask the history of racism. He wants to overcome racial barriers, but he opposes dismantling racist language, for example. Read more about West's views (see his book *Race Matters*). Research Jim Crow legislation and prepare a class presentation on three or four laws that regulated African American lives during this period.
2. In Chapter 7, Edward Dolnick argues in "Deafness as Culture" for distinctions to be made in terms of culture rather than "difference." Compare his argument with Klor De Alva's call to dismantle racial language and West's claim that such dismantling minimizes the history of racism.
3. This article is introduced with the claim that the media portrayed the O. J. Simpson trial merely in terms of black-white tension, thereby ignoring the tension that exists between blacks and Latinas/os. Look at the coverage of the trial in your city's local press and do a rhetorical analysis of the stories you find; do you agree that the issue was reduced to one concerning blacks and whites only?

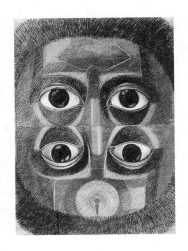

CHAPTER 3

Class

The contemporary United States is often called the "Land of Opportunity," a place where people's choices are not limited by birth into a particular socio-economic class. While this may be part of the American dream (or fantasy), we all know that our nation has a history of class distinctions (free versus slave, craftsman versus apprentice, landowner versus sharecropper). People make class judgments all the time, and yet we do not have clear, universal definitions of class. In his book entitled *Class,* from which we have taken an excerpt and which Julie Charlip discusses in her essay in this chapter, Paul Fussell says that our definitions of the term vary with the status of the person doing the defining. People at the bottom think of money first; those in the middle consider education or job classifications; those at the top focus on tastes, styles, and values.

As you read the selections in this chapter, keep a running list of the ways these writers are using the term "class." When you respond to the essays, you will need to be clear about how you are defining class—or at least about why you are not clear about it. At the end of this introduction, you will find other suggestions about how to focus your writing. Obviously, an important step in your thinking will be to define the ways you think of your own class status.

SUMMARIES OF SELECTIONS ON CLASS

Julie Charlip, in "A Real Class Act: Searching for Identity in the Classless Society," demonstrates how class is complicated by social, cultural, economic, and educational factors as she documents her own struggle to understand herself in terms of differing definitions of "class." She shows how older Marxist theories of class are no longer adequate to account for her own condition—or for the nation's.

classes can be defined in so many different ways

In "To Have and Have Not," **Michael Lind** also argues that we continue to have a very class-based society in the United States despite assertions to the contrary. He examines the factors that are responsible for perpetuating this American class system, including election laws, immigration laws, education, and monetary structures.

Katherine Newman shows the ways in which status systems are based on race and nationality and how they are undermined and complicated by the acquisition of money. In "Illegitimate Elites and the Parasitic Underclass," she explains just how complex the issue of class is and how it reaches beyond economic hierarchies.

In his humorous essay "Speak, That I May See Thee," **Paul Fussell** shows us how dialect, word usage, and other linguistic features mark a person as a member of a particular class.

In **Liliana Heker**'s short story "The Stolen Party," Rosaura is invited to a birthday party for her friend Luciana. Rosaura's mother works as a maid for Luciana's parents. She tries to tell Rosaura that she will be hurt only if she tries to be a part of these rich people's activities—that they really don't want her there, but this is something Rosaura has to find out for herself.

Rivethead by **Ben Hamper** is an angry, funny book. In the excerpt included here, he describes how, despite his own and his family's resolutions that he would never work on the assembly line, he ends up doing exactly that. He discusses how issues of gender involving working-class masculinity are linked to class and how class is a familial and generational issue.

Unlike Hamper, **Dorothy Allison** does not find her class roots funny, even though she often amuses friends with stories about crazy characters from her past. In her fictional "River of Names," she unleashes the violence that was very much a part of her "underclass" childhood. Her relationship to her middle-class lesbian lover and their conversations about class frame her memories in this essay.

G. J. Meyer, in contrast to the other writers, represents a voice from the upper class, even though he is unemployed. In "Dancing with the Headhunters," Meyer describes his experiences as a vice president of a major corporation who is laid off. He's not exactly living in a homeless shelter, but he acknowledges that pain is relative and offers some insights on the current downsizing trend in the corporate United States.

RHETORICAL QUESTIONS

In addition to identifying these writers' *definitions* of class and refining your own, you may find it useful to study other choices these writers have made about their *methods* and *forms*. Four of the essays (Charlip, Hamper, Allison, and Meyer) are personal narratives that use first-hand experience as their primary evidence. When do these writers choose to bring in other sources? theories? data?

Hecker's selection is a short story. What might a writer who cares about class issues accomplish with fiction? Why would she choose fiction over other types of writing? What other fiction have you read that focuses on class issues?

Other fictional pieces appear in other chapters. You might ask the same questions about them.

Lind's article appeared in the magazine *Harper's,* which has a definite "high-brow" audience. As a journalist, he uses current events and statistics as evidence. His tone might be described as "objective" when compared to the personal essays, but a closer analysis will also reveal his own perspective and biases.

Fussell's book combines his experience as both an English professor and a popular writer. Unlike most scholarly writing, this essay addresses the reader as "you" and employs informal constructions such as contractions and terms such as "cornball-elegant." But his use of detail, examples, and illustrations does resemble academic writing. Where do they come from? How does he get his material? Why is his emphasis on language such an important class issue?

Katherine Newman's contribution is a chapter from a book that is typical of a certain kind of anthropology. It is more academic than the other selections included here in that she provides detailed descriptions (often called "thick descriptions" in ethnography), interspersed with her own analyses and interpretations. What other kinds of evidence might an anthropologist use? Why did she make the choices she made? What would it take to change this from a chapter in a book to an article in *Harper's?* in *Newsweek?*

As we mentioned in Chapter One, one of the hardest things about writing well is being able to consider all of the rhetorical choices we describe there, and we are focusing on only one or two in our introductions to each chapter. Obviously, it would help to understand the writer's *purpose* in order to answer the questions about *form* or *method.* As you read these selections, you can work from analyses of forms and methods to a consideration of the author's purpose. As you write informally, you can also explore a variety of approaches and then consider what purposes your material might serve. If you write a formal paper, however, we recommend that you define a purpose first and then choose a form and method to accomplish your goal.

A Real Class Act: Searching for Identity in the Classless Society

Julie Charlip

Charlip grew up in a working-class family in New Jersey. She has a bachelor's degree in journalism and worked for several years as a newspaper

Separating into many groups

reporter before returning to graduate school at the University of California at Los Angeles to get a Ph.D. in Latin American studies.

Marx and Engels wrote, "Society as a whole is more and more splitting up into two great hostile camps, into two great classes directly facing each other—bourgeoisie and proletariat" (10). If only that were true, things might be more simple. But in late twentieth-century America, it seems that society is splitting more and more into a plethora of class factions—the working class, the working poor, lower-middle class, upper-middle class, lower uppers, and upper uppers. I find myself not knowing what class I'm from.

In my days as a newspaper reporter, I once asked a sociology professor what he thought about the reported shrinking of the middle class. Oh, it's not the middle class that's disappearing, he said, but the working class. His definition: if you earn thirty thousand dollars a year working in an assembly plant, come home from work, open a beer and watch the game, you are working class; if you earn twenty thousand dollars a year as a school teacher, come home from work to a glass of white wine and PBS, you are middle class.

How do we define class? Is it a matter of values, lifestyles, taste? Is it the kind of work you do, your relationship to the means of production? Is it a matter of how much money you earn? Are we allowed to choose? In this land of supposed classlessness, where we don't have the tradition of English society to keep us in our places, how do we know where we really belong? The average American will tell you he or she is "middle class." I'm sure that's what my father would tell you. But I always felt that we were in some no man's land, suspended between the classes, sharing similarities with some and recognizing sharp, exclusionary differences from others. What class do I come from? What class am I in now? As an historian, I seek the answers to these questions in the specificity of my past. *whats the def of class?*

A FAMILY HERITAGE *Relationship - class / past*

All of us are the products not just of our immediate upbringing but also of the past that our parents and grandparents transmit. This is why class is never a matter of money alone. (Just ask the people with old money about the nouveau riche.)

My mother was the daughter of Russian Jewish immigrants who came to Lawrence, Massachusetts, in the early 1900s, before the revolution and during the pogroms. Her father died of pneumonia when she was a little girl, leaving her mother to raise five children during the Depression. Her mother ran a corner grocery, and she was too kind-hearted to deny her neighbors credit. The result was little for her own family, and my mother grew up in poverty. She was loath to talk about it, but when pressed she converted what must have been a nightmarish existence into the stuff of a warm-hearted B movie. "Oh, we were poor but happy," she would say. She finally revealed more when a high school history teacher assigned me to interview my parents about the Great Depression. My mother had two strong memories: the sight of families with all their belongings on the street, evicted from repossessed homes, and her sisters chasing the ragman to sell old cloth to get money for food. (It was a lasting legacy. Years later, when she died, I found an entire drawer filled with scraps of fabric cut from clothes she had hemmed.)

Mom's older brother moved to Trenton, New Jersey, and it was there that she met my father. Dad's grandparents had emigrated from Poland and Russia, settling in New York. His father moved to Trenton to seek his fortune, and he found it. They say every family has a story of a fortune made and lost; in mine, it's the story of Grandpa the bootlegger. Grandpa was one of the wealthiest men in Trenton. He had the Trenton police force and high-ranking officials on his payroll. Dad grew up knowing he didn't have to worry about money, yet his father, fearful of the federal authorities, was reluctant to display wealth. He bought old cars, and the family lived in apartments over the stores that were a front for his business. Dad tells colorful stories about working for his father, soaking corks to put in the bottles of "alky," putting liquor labels on bottles. But the only real comforts the wealth provided were the sumptuous meals that Grandpa hosted as patriarch. "He always set a good table," Dad recalled, a legacy Dad continued, along with his love for opera. Eventually, an angry cohort reported Grandpa to the feds, and he lost everything.

While Grandpa's wealth gave Dad a sense of financial security, he knew these ill-gotten gains did not provide him entry into the upper classes. In a touching memoir, Dad recalls that by error he was allowed to attend a junior high school in a rich neighborhood and how he hoped some of the "class" from the other students, the ones from the other side of the tracks, would rub off on him.

THE SMALL BUSINESS BLUES

Grandpa's talent for illegal business didn't carry over into legitimate enterprises, and when he died Harry's Supply Co. was nearly bankrupt, but Grandma begged Dad to take it over. Harry's Supply was a bar, restaurant, and party supply store located in an old downtown building: a long, narrow, high-ceilinged rowhouse that I remember as dusty and grimy, very different from the modern glass-and-chrome stores in the suburbs. The building itself was rented, a fact that puzzled me as a child; just what, I wondered, did my father own?

The staff consisted of Dad, Grandma, the part-time bookkeeper, the truck driver, and the warehouse kid. And, of course, my sister and me—a family business that was quite literally a *family* business.

Father putting himself in bad health for money

Dad worked at the store from nine to five, Monday through Saturday. After dinner and a brief rest, he'd head down to his basement workshop. Dad had hit on the idea of imprinting matches, napkins, and ribbons as novelty items for parties and weddings. The printing process, hot stamping, combined enormous pressure and heat to impress loose type or lines of type through colored foil. I have a chilling childhood memory of Dad crushing his finger in the machine. For him, there was no employer to sue, no workmen's compensation or union benefits; there wasn't even much time to recuperate.

Dad would print until late at night, then get up to face another day at the store. Sunday, his "day off," would be spent mostly printing in that workshop. As a kid, I never really understood the supposed freedom of "being your own boss." It seemed to me that Dad was the prisoner, not the warden, of Harry's Supply. Because Dad couldn't leave the store unattended, there were no vacations. Instead, we went to New York for dinner and a Broadway show twice a year. We really couldn't afford vacations, anyway. As Dad put it, first you paid the employees and the bills; then if there was something left, it was yours. As a result, our resources varied drastically from week to week. Years later, after Dad lost the store to tax problems, he became manager for a former competitor. For the first time, he said, he looked forward to payday.

In Marxian terms, Dad's position as shopkeeper made him petit bourgeois, but what does that mean in actuality? Did that role make him an exploiter profiting from the work of his employees, a conservative force in society? That hardly seems accurate. He worked alongside his employees, for far longer hours and frequently for less money, while championing the liberal causes of change. Simultaneously, in Marxian terms, Dad was an artisan who owned his own tools. But again, what does this mean? That he was a skilled craftsman, an owner of small capital but threatened by the competition of big capital and mass production? In popular stereotypes, the petit bourgeois should have rising prosperity, a comfortable lifestyle imitating the upper classes and disdaining the lower. The artisan should be a worker with greasy hands, more skilled than the assembly-line worker but not in the same league as the middle class. But both Marxian and popular concepts seem simplistic when compared with reality.

Whether in Marxian or popular terms, my own role was clear: I was Dad's employee, owning only my labor power. This was no middle-class set of household chores, make-work designed to teach a sense of responsibility. I didn't receive an allowance; I earned wages. This was my job, a serious and essential part of Dad's business. When I grew up, he had to hire someone else.

I don't remember how old I was when I started work. Before I could count, I sorted matchbooks and paper napkins by color. Later, I packed the printed matches, cut imprinted ribbons, glued ribbons into glasses as novelty items, made car decorations for weddings, and printed on a small machine. I was paid for my work at less than the legal wage. Still, by the time I was twelve I earned enough to buy my own clothes. I also had hand-me-downs from my sister, Lindsey, and my parents would buy the more expensive items, such as winter coats, boots, or a fancy dress for a wedding, but essentially I was on my own. If there were no orders for me to work on, then I couldn't earn money.

Dad paid by the unit for the work I did at home and by the hour during summers when I worked in the store and punched the time clock. At times, Lindsey and I felt exploited. I was probably eight and Lindsey twelve when she convened the first labor negotiations. We sat Dad down and she declared that he either upped our wages or we'd go on strike. He laughed, amused at our youthful savvy. And he gave in. After all, Lindsey was right: if we quit, he'd have to hire "real" employees and pay at least the minimum wage.

Working for a parent, however, is not like working for any other employer; no other boss can forge such bonds of obligation. While the typical employer-employee relationship is impersonal, the family business relationship is patriarchal in the most literal and theoretical sense. Dad and I clashed as I grew up and wanted a social life. I insisted that Dad give me at least forty-eight hours' notice on orders for my work, as he usually did with his own work and that of his nonfamily suppliers. But on more than one Friday night he arrived home with orders due the next day. Already dressed for a party or a dance, waiting for my ride, I would complain bitterly of his unfairness, initially refusing to do the work. With a mixture of Jewish guilt and theater, Dad would blame the late order on my grandmother, whom I could not challenge. He would muse that he would have to do my work after finishing his own at midnight, and finally he would pledge to take me to the dance or party as soon as I finished. I always gave in, and Dad always saw that I made it, however belatedly, to parties and dances. But the responsibility of the work was always there; I could negotiate, but I couldn't quit.

LIFE IN THE 'BURBS

Harry's Supply was in Trenton, but my parents moved to a suburb, Hamilton Township, in 1955. This, however, was no case of white flight or upward mobility to the more affluent suburbs. Unlike the more prosperous communities that ringed Trenton—Ewing Township, Lawrence Township—Hamilton was a largely undeveloped, and therefore inexpensive, area. My father's first choice was to stay in Trenton, but he couldn't afford the housing prices. Instead he bought a small split-level tract home in a brand-new suburb designed for the veterans using their GI loan benefits.

Lindsey and I shared a bedroom and a bed. The small third bedroom was converted into a study for the two of us. A friend of Dad's built unvarnished shelves with a stand for the huge dictionary; two hinged panels pulled down to become our desks. The room was lined with books, mostly Book-of-the-Month

Club selections and *Reader's Digest* condensed books, a few classics but no encyclopedias. The book collection was evidence to me that Dad must have been an avid reader in his youth, but I never saw him read a book. He devoured the local newspapers and an assortment of news magazines, but work left no time for leisure reading.

I read ravenously and uncritically; my parents were happy to see me reading but provided no guidance on my choices. I never knew whether they were allowing me my freedom—Dad wasn't allowed to have comic books as a child—or whether they were unprepared to judge. As a result, I still wince when people mention childhood classics that were not a part of my reading, and I have a deep aversion to the trashy novels that some of my colleagues delight in as respite from the serious, grad-student load.

In my childhood neighborhood, the fathers' occupations—most mothers stayed home—ranged from policeman to pharmacist, from working class to rising middle class. My best friend's father owned a pharmacy. Carol had music lessons, which I envied, and each summer visited her grandmother's beach house in tony Medford Lakes. When I went to the beach with Mom's family, eight aunts, uncles, and cousins piled into a rented apartment or bungalow.

Carol's family moved away to Princeton, following the expected pattern for neighborhoods like ours. These were supposed to be starter homes, where the middle class starts families and careers. Theoretically, there would be promotions and raises, or businesses would succeed and families would move to bigger and better homes. My father would still be in our little split-level had it not been for Interstate 295 cutting a swath directly through our house. After a protracted battle led by my father, we accepted a paltry settlement and moved to a new home in 1969. The new house cost more than the government settlement, and of course interest rates were higher and Dad was older, meaning a twenty-year instead of a thirty-year mortgage. What little savings the family had were wiped out.

③ The new house was bigger (at fifteen I finally had my own room), a three-bedroom ranch in another planned neighborhood with every house one of three models. Outside, it looked like the American Dream. But inside, the front room was virtually empty—there was one chair and my grandmother's cast-off table—and the den in the back was furnished with two rather shabby couches. We finally got a couch for the front room when my uncle gave us his old one.

Ends never met, the furniture was well worn, new clothes were limited, and yet my parents spent enormous amounts of money on food. They bought steak, veal, lamb—the legacy, I'm sure, of Mom's chasing the ragman and Grandpa's admonition always to set a good table. I found these contradictions confusing and viewed them as a middle-class façade pasted over a working-class income, not realizing that working-class incomes often were higher than ours. Nowhere was this contradiction sharper than at the restaurants. Because of Dad's business, we spent many Sundays dining out, patronizing the businesses that patronized Harry's Supply. The meal was a business expense, and Dad usually came away with an order for merchandise. Many of the restaurants were casual, but others were ones we could never have afforded if not for the business connection. My favorite was Princeton's elegant Lahiere's. We dressed in our best clothes and learned to casually order escargots. But Lindsey and I marveled at the other patrons, whose wealth gave them a graceful ease while we carefully, nervously watched our manners.

On the other hand, I once went out to dinner with a group of friends, among them the daughters of a chiropractor. They seemed comfortably middle class to me. They had an above-ground pool, the kids didn't have to work, and their dad didn't work on weekends. But with five children, the family rarely went out to eat. I remember my friends freezing at the array of silverware. I couldn't understand how they could have more money than my family yet not know the social graces. I began to see that there was a complex interconnection between money and lifestyle, between social skills and acceptance. I didn't see then, however, that the obsession with manners is a middle-class phenomenon, as Paul Fussell notes in his book *Class*. The uppers feel entitled to do as they please—just think of the photo by Weegee of the gowned and jeweled dowager with her leg hiked unceremoniously on the table. And for whom did Lahiere's keep loaner ties at the front desk? Certainly not for those who wouldn't dare show up at such a restaurant without one.

I saw more contradictions with a new set of friends across town. We lived in a largely gentile area, and my parents, concerned about my social life, joined the Jewish Community Center and enrolled me in the youth group, B'nai B'rith Girls, which had a brother chapter of "nice Jewish boys," Aleph Zadik Aleph. I had always been amused by the stereotype of rich Jews, so foreign to my life. But at the community center, I thought I was the anomaly among these solidly middle- and upper-middle-class kids. Only three of my friends lived in Hamilton Township; the rest lived in Ewing or Lawrence, the high-income suburbs, or in the one "good" neighborhood left in Trenton. The Trenton girls, of course, did not attend Trenton High School. They were usually enrolled in Villa Victoria Academy, an excellent private Catholic girls' school with so many Jewish students that it closed for the High Holy Days.

Through the community center I became close friends with the daughter of Dad's attorney, a local judge. Her well-appointed home always had a quiet formality about it. In my home the TV was usually on, and we had a tendency to yell across the house. My friend's family was in another league: they had a cleaning woman, they had a boat, and they had enough money for private schools.

Rich friends

THE EDUCATIONAL DIVIDE

Eileen and I started out attending the same high school, but her parents quickly transferred her to the Hun School in Princeton. She read authors that I was not exposed to until college, and the curriculum included a class for girls

Exposed to lower levels of education

called "How to Be a Gracious Member of Society," focusing on such important points as the care and storage of your furs and hosting a dinner party.

I, of course, continued at the local high school, Hamilton High West. The school was declared to be in a "depressed area" because of the adjacent African American neighborhood. There were at least thirty-five students to a class, and sometimes there were not enough books to go around. New college graduates taught there because the federal government reduced their college loans for each year of work in a "depressed area." Certainly no one ever thought of teaching us to be gracious; teachers routinely referred to the students as "animals" and called our parents ignorant. Some of our graduates were college bound, others functionally illiterate.

It was determined from an early age that I would go to college. A teacher at Kisthardt Elementary School, where two grades routinely shared a room and a teacher, told my parents that I was "college material." I was lucky that this was decided in my earliest school years, because students were tracked by perceived ability, and those who were not seen as college material didn't have access to preparatory classes. Many a bright but economically disadvantaged student whose home life was not conducive to studying could be passed over by the tests.

As we entered junior high school, college-bound students were separated from those in business or commercial curricula. I confounded the administration, however, when I insisted on a mix: algebra, junior business training, Spanish, and typing. I had been raised to be practical, and I wanted some tangible skills.

My career goals were vague; all I was sure of was that I loved to write. The only junior high teacher to take an interest in me was an English teacher who encouraged my writing. It was during a typing class in high school that I made my decision. If I spent the rest of my life behind a typewriter, it would be to record *my* words, not someone else's. I decided on journalism largely because I was influenced by my father, who had been founder and editor of his base paper in the Navy and who had longed to be a journalist, but he put those dreams aside to take over the family business. My decision was also a practical one, though. How else could I possibly support myself as a writer?

My family was intent on my attending college, but we understood none of the complexities of preparing for and choosing a school. I relied on my high school guidance counselor, a woman of great enthusiasm but little competence. I dreamed of going away to school and she encouraged me, guiding me to apply to Bates and Colby Colleges in Maine, Wesleyan University in Connecticut, and Ithaca College in New York. I had never heard of them, but I didn't want to go to the local schools, Trenton State College or Rider College. I never even daydreamed about schools like Princeton University, fifteen miles and fifteen light years away. Such schools were for other people, those who came out of the college preparatory academies.

I assumed, however, that I would be accepted and given financial aid at the schools we selected because everyone told me that I was smart enough to do it. I didn't understand that it was a rare student from my high school who could make it beyond Trenton State College because our training was so inadequate. And my grades were erratic. While I excelled in English, history, Spanish, anything that captured my interest and involved writing, I failed miserably at math and science. School administrators informed me that if I could excel in the social sciences and humanities, then I must be struggling in math and the physical sciences out of pure perversity. My parents tried to help, but they had never studied algebra, geometry, chemistry. There were no tutors, and the teachers facing crowded classrooms didn't worry about those of us who fell behind. I was lost and there were no guides. I gave up and huddled in the back of the room with author-philosopher Ayn Rand's *The Fountainhead* hidden inside my algebra book. Further, I tended to neglect my studies in favor of editing an award-winning newspaper for B'nai B'rith Girls and editing the high school newspaper before quitting in a censorship battle.

I also consulted a cousin with a doctorate in psychology, the only person in my family to have an advanced degree and whom I'd met only once. (Although many of my cousins started college, most dropped out.) His advice was to visit every campus for a personal interview to impress them with my enthusiasm and interest. I vividly remember visiting Bates with my mother. It was winter, and it was cold in Maine. She wore her good wool coat, the one to which she had sewn a small mink collar, the one she had had all my life. The dean of students greeted us in his plush office and looked my mother up and down with a sniff of disdain. Clearly he thought we were so far beneath him that he didn't need to mask his scorn. I felt small and inadequate and terribly sorry for Mom.

I was, as expected, rejected by Bates and by Wesleyan, wait-listed by Colby, which meant no financial aid, and accepted to Ithaca with no funding. I was stunned, but I had also learned by then that nothing comes easy. Mom and Dad raised me on a steady diet of such clichés as "Money doesn't grow on trees" and "Nothing comes without hard work." I dreaded what seemed to be my only option, Mercer County Community College, little more than an extension of high school. My sister and her husband lived in Bucks County, Pennsylvania, and he studied at Bucks County Community College, a much better school. High school quality depends on the local tax base, and because Bucks County was affluent, it had a higher caliber of students at the community college and attracted better faculty. I decided to use their address and go to Bucks.

I remember going into the cellar where Dad was working to tell him my plans: go to Bucks, transfer later to another school, and work my way through college. For the first time in my life, I saw my father cry. "It wasn't supposed to be like this," he said. "I've let you down; I was supposed to pay for your education." I was touched but also stunned; I had been raised to make my own way. I didn't feel let down in the least.

Father couldnt provide for his Son (sadly)

THE NEWSPAPER GAME

I landed a newspaper job the same week that I started college and worked twenty-five to thirty hours a week during the semester, full time summers. I earned high grades, and I still dreamed of going away to a big-name, four-year college, but my co-workers dissuaded me. After all, they said, you want to be a journalist and you've already got a job. Go to school in Trenton and keep working here. So I transferred to Rider College, the only local campus offering journalism. It was the easy way out: journalism classes were a snap after two years in the business. I felt that I had my career launched; college meant merely that piece of paper.

Rider was known mostly as a business school, and its journalism department was small. It wasn't until I left for a job in Kansas that I heard about the big journalism programs at midwestern universities. And when I moved on to California, I met reporters who majored in "serious" subjects—political science, economics—and brought that knowledge to journalism. It seemed that I'd learned a trade rather than received an education.

That feeling had been forged at *The Trentonian.* Journalism today may earn some respect, but when I started in 1972, Watergate was just developing and journalism was very suspect. Our old-fashioned tabloid newsroom, where we squashed our cigarette butts on the floor, was more akin to *The Front Page* than *All the President's Men.* Most reporters didn't have college degrees; they joked that journalism graduates had to be retaught everything. Starting there at eighteen, I grew up in a rough-and-tumble newsroom where reporters were skilled workers, perhaps, but certainly not professionals. We had a union, we bargained collectively, we threatened strikes.

As I moved on to other newspapers and journalism became more popular, I saw a trend toward better-educated reporters, self-identified professionals. While the scrappy self-trained reporters could still go far, the ones who ended up covering Washington, working as foreign correspondents, or writing books were often children of the elite. I filled my gaps with avid reading and lots of attitude. (A woman in journalism in the 1970s needed a lot of brass.) I was tough and smart, and since journalism takes you from the gutter to mansions, I learned to function in vastly different situations.

But my attitude, formed in Trenton, was fundamentally working class, and I brought that to Kansas, where I helped organize a union and ended up unofficially blacklisted. When I finally found a job—a union one—in Fresno, California, I jumped at the chance. But in a few years, I was dissatisfied with journalism. It wasn't just Trenton or Wichita or Fresno, I discovered. Partly I was disillusioned, a watchdog for justice fighting with editors who were ambitious climbers and publishers just out to make money. And despite journalism's seemingly endless variety, I began to find that the names changed while the stories remained the same. So I took a leave of absence and went to Central America to find myself.

FROM MANAGUA TO LOS ANGELES

I had first become interested in Central America when I wrote about a Latin America solidarity group in Fresno. They showed films and sponsored lectures, and their information clashed dramatically with the news stories that came across the wires. I decided to see for myself, satisfying my curiosity and my restlessness. I intended to travel throughout Central America, starting in Nicaragua at a school that would help me brush up my Spanish, place me in a private home, and give me guided tours. I fell in love with the country and stayed till my money ran out.

Nicaragua impressed me because the 1979 revolution had brought rapid change, seeming to compress the usual slow movement of history. Coming from a country where most people believe that voting makes no difference and "you can't fight city hall," I found Nicaragua refreshing. Despite dire poverty and US-waged aggression, Nicaraguans believed they held their future in their hands, and they were involved and excited by the prospects.

At thirty years old, twelve years after I began in journalism, I walked into a research institute in Nicaragua and asked how one got a job there. They admired my interest, my writing and editing experience, but wondered what I knew about Latin America and Third World problems. I decided on the spot; I was going back to school.

This time, I had a little more savvy than in my high school days. Deciding to get a master's degree in Latin American studies, I researched the schools and applied to the best, UCLA and the University of Texas at Austin. When I was accepted and UCLA recruited me with a fellowship, I was amazed. Would I really be able to fulfill my dream of attending a major university?

My parents, however, were shocked. Dad couldn't understand why I would leave an award-winning career. The idea of changing careers was alien to him; where I grew up, people kept their jobs for life. In Trenton, the ultimate job was to work for the state, with civil-service security. My mother couldn't understand what I'd do with a master's degree. "Now you're a journalist," she'd say. "When you get this degree, what will you be?"

I thought *they* were naive until I got to UCLA. When I told an adviser that I wanted to use my M.A. to do research, she laughed at me. She said that I would need a Ph.D. and I would have to choose another field because I couldn't get a Ph.D. in Latin American studies. This, I thought, was my big chance. A high-ranking student at UCLA could be accepted at Princeton, Harvard, Yale—a working-class kid from Trenton in the Ivy League! Then my naïveté became clearer. Dr. E. Bradford Burns explained to me that I should consider not just universities but specific departments, indeed, specific fields within departments. The Ivy League schools offered at best one or two historians specializing in Latin America compared to UCLA's four, who included leaders in the field. The important thing, he said, was to find a professor who wanted to work with me; he encouraged me to stay at UCLA, which I didn't even realize has one of the country's top ten history departments. I had never imagined that I would study for a Ph.D., much less that a renowned professor would want to work with me.

I don't think Dr. Burns, who became my chair and mentor, ever realized just how uninformed I was about the machinations of academe. All those years as a journalist had made me adept at soliciting information in a way that sometimes masked my limited knowledge, a skill that prepared me well for graduate school and the often brutal games played by graduate students in seminars.

I needed that ability to pose when I arrived at UCLA because I was terrified. I remember one of my first classes, "The Political Economy of Latin America," taught by the brilliant Dr. Jeffry Frieden. During the first week, a student in the class casually asked a question about the Porfiriato, the period when Porfirio Diaz ruled Mexico. I had never heard the term, and I thought in dismay that I was clearly in over my head. Everyone seemed to know more than I did, to have better educations, to have read works that were never part of my curriculum. By the end of the quarter, however, the other student had dropped out, and I was still there, being encouraged to go on for a Ph.D. That support was crucial. Without mentors to reassure me, answer my questions, help guide me through the system, I would have been lost.

The master's degree confused my parents, but the Ph.D. is something else. They are very proud of their daughter the doctor, the future professor, and so am I. Students who come from privileged backgrounds, and there are many at UCLA, can never understand what it means to me. Graduates of fine colleges, they affect a jaded pose, a grad-school chic, about UCLA. I find UCLA to be a wonderland of knowledge and resources. They have no idea what it is like to go to unknown, inferior schools with limited resources. They are mostly children of the upper class, and they have a sense of entitlement that I will never know and that I will always envy. They have always known they belong at UCLA. I feel grateful that I was allowed in. Despite my accomplishments—awards, fellowships, teaching assistantships—I still have the sneaking suspicion that someone will shout "Fraud!" and send me away. A part of me doesn't believe that I can really know as much as they do or that I will ever fit in. Surely, this is all a mistake, and they will find me out someday. That's why they can take time out to read a bodice ripper while I feel I must read Dostoyevsky. After all, Dostoyevsky has nothing to do with Latin American history but everything to do with a well-read background; the problem isn't knowing the material in class but knowing the references made over cappuccino.

Those graduate students who are to the manor born have been groomed; everything in their backgrounds has prepared them for this life. To me, they are the diners at Lahiere's with their easy grace. They studied Russian in high school, read the classics as undergraduates, traveled extensively. And while I

Poor always work harder

have bested many of them with ease, I will always feel that I have to work harder simply because my background has not entitled me.

Perhaps that is the greatest tragedy of a working-class background, if that is what mine is. The nagging feeling of inferiority intimidates many of us, sometimes to such an extent that fine minds never turn to academe. Some start and don't finish because the environment is so alien and because they can no longer tolerate worrying that they are frauds as they compete with those who are entitled. Graduate school is about more than what you know; it is an elite system designed to maintain the status quo. Social training and attitude matter here. Graduate students are expected to adapt to a system that is arcane and virtually medieval in its form. This is no stretch for the students who dined in eating clubs on the gothic Princeton campus. Ah, but the distance for the student who was just down the road at Rider College!

WHERE DO I BELONG?

What class am I from? How do you reconcile the definition of the bourgeois who owns his own business with the reality of the small businessman and his pile of debts? An employer's outlook with my Dad's labor-leaning, staunchly Democratic views? The opera buff who loves Broadway shows with the supposedly uncultured artisan working with his hands in the cellar? Even Marx and Engels, who defined the dual-class system, recognized the complexities. In part three of *Capital,* Marx notes that even in classically industrialized England, "intermediate and transitional strata obscure the class boundaries" (Bottomore 75). But Marx saw those strata as transitional, disappearing with the march of capitalism and its dualistic structure.

The great Flo Kennedy, the attorney who represented Black Panthers and the prostitutes' organization COYOTE, maintains that there are only those who work and those who don't. If you have to work for a living, Kennedy says, no matter how much money you make you are working class. On some level, she is right. The belief that we are different obscures the socioeconomic truth that a tiny percentage of the elite in this country owns the real wealth and the rest of us are dependent on them. In Kennedy's purely theoretical terms, there is no difference between a blue-collar union worker, my father the small businessman, and a corporate executive making a hundred thousand dollars a year. However, we all know that money does matter. The difference in income buys the wealthier among us opportunities for education, travel, upward mobility, entrance into groups with their own private signs and signals of inclusion and exclusion. It is possible, perhaps, for all of these groups to reach the same political conclusions. But there are differences in our psyches, in our expectations, our sense of entitlement, and the ways we move through the world. Those differences are rarely addressed by political theorists, but they are important.

The reality of class in America is more complex than dualistic models allow. On the surface, my father's small business and our home in the suburbs are the visage of the petit bourgeoisie, the middle class, the American Dream. Beyond that facile categorization is the reality of hard work, little money, limited opportunities, and far more insecurity than that of the blue-collar worker who has a steady paycheck and job benefits.

In *Class*, Paul Fussell notes that even our definition of the term is conditioned by our class standing: "At the bottom, people tend to believe that class is defined by the amount of money you have. In the middle, people grant that money has something to do with it, but think education and the kind of work you do almost equally important. Nearer the top, people perceive that taste, values, ideas, style and behavior are indispensable criteria of class, regardless of money or occupation or education" (3). Fussell comes up with nine classes—top out-of-sight, upper, upper middle, middle, high proletarian, mid-proletarian, low proletarian, destitute, and bottom out-of-sight. It's a tricky business, and I guess my background falls somewhere in the high proletarian to middle range. The middle class, according to Fussell, suffers from psychic insecurity, is concerned about manners and appearances, and includes salesmen and managers; the high proles are the former lower-middle class, skilled workers and craftsmen, who pride themselves on independence.

To what class do I belong now, as I head from grad-school poverty to the rather ill-paid life of the mind? Marx and Engels placed intellectuals somewhat outside the class dialectic, perhaps rising from one of the classes but choosing to ally with one class or the other, the conservatives protecting the interests of the state and the progressives siding with the working class. Similarly, Fussell would call us "category X," not members of a class at all. Formerly called "bohemians," Fussell writes: "You are not born an X person, as you are born and reared a prole or a middle. You become an X person, or, to put it more bluntly, you earn X-personhood by a strenuous effort of discovery in which curiosity and originality are indispensable. And in discovering that you can become an X person, you find the only escape from class" (212–13).

On the latter, of course, Fussell is dead wrong. Scratch an X-person's bohemian, even eccentric, façade, and you'll find attitudes and a sense of self molded by membership in a particular class. I can never escape from my class background, and there's nothing quite like the hallowed, upper-class halls of academe to remind me of it. As a journalist, I was a professional outsider, observing and criticizing. As an academic, however, I must now be an insider, functioning within a system designed by and for the elite. I know all too well the system's effect on me; the question is whether I can affect the system.

WORKS CITED

Bottomore, Tom, ed. *A Dictionary of Marxist Thought.* Oxford: Basil Blackwell, 1985.

Fussell, Paul. *Class.* New York: Ballantine, 1983.

Marx, Karl, and Friedrich Engels. *The Communist Manifesto.* Ed. Samuel H. Beer. New York: Meredith Corp., 1955.

FOR JOURNALING AND DISCUSSION

1. What is "middle class"? How do we define "class"? What are its social (as opposed to monetary) markers?

2. What role does education play in determining class? How does the educational policy of tracking students (placing them into ability groups) perpetuate our class system?

3. Charlip states that for her one of the most difficult parts of graduate school was trying to make up for all the subtle, "cultural" things she didn't know; "the problem isn't knowing the material in class but knowing the references made over cappuccino." This is similar to the experience of anyone moving into a new culture. In what ways do you think that switching classes is more difficult than moving to another country?

4. Reflect on a time when you felt out of place because of class differences. How did you know that you were "out of your class"? How did you feel and react to this situation?

5. Write a personal "class" narrative for yourself. What are the factors—money, education, gender, race, manners, neighborhood, etc.—that have shaped your class identity? Do you usually even think of class as part of your identity?

FOR RESEARCH AND EXPLORATION

1. In Chapter 2, Lise Funderburg talks in "Parents and Family" (from *Black, White, Other*) about the importance of parents helping their biracial children to negotiate the two different worlds they inhabit; parents, she says, can help bridge gaps or "cement divisions." How did Charlip's family help her to negotiate her way into the middle class? How did they hinder her progress? Link her experiences to those of some of the people that Funderburg describes. How have these people all been similarly brought up by their parents?

2. Throughout this piece Charlip makes frequent reference to Karl Marx. Do some research about Marx's views about class. How do they support Charlip's position? Where do you think that they diverge?

3. Interview your parents or grandparents about their own experiences with class. How do they define their social class? What are the markers of class for them? Have they shifted classes in their lifetimes? How did that experience affect them? Do they think that shifting classes is easier or more difficult now than it was when they were young?

To Have and Have Not: Notes on the Progress of the American Class War

Michael Lind

[Handwritten annotations: "?" above "and"; "ESSAY"; "A constant battle"; "Conflict between groups" in left margin; "misleading"]

Lind has worked as an editor for several national magazines, including National Interest, Harper's, *and* The New Republic. *His articles have appeared in* The New Yorker, The Atlantic, The Washington Post, *and other well known periodicals.*

Judging by the headlines that have been leading the news for the last several years, public debate in the United States at the end of the twentieth century has become a war of words among the disaffected minorities that so often appear on the never-ending talk show jointly hosted by Oprah, Larry King, Jenny Jones, and the McLaughlin Group. Conservatives at war with liberals; Christian fundamentalists at odds with liberal Jews; blacks at war with whites; whites at war with Hispanic immigrants; men at war with women; heterosexuals at war with homosexuals; and the young at war with the old. A guide to the multiple conflicts in progress would resemble the Personals pages in *The Village Voice*, with "versus" or "contra" substituted for "seeking" (Pro-Sex Classicists versus Anti-Sex Modernists).

The noise is deceptive. Off-camera, beyond the blazing lights, past the ropy tangle of black cords and down the hall, in the corner offices (on Capitol Hill as well as at General Electric, The Walt Disney Company, and CBS News), people in expensive suits quietly continue to go about the work of shifting the center of gravity of wealth and power in the United States from the discounted many to the privileged few. While public attention has been diverted to controversies as inflammatory as they are trivial—Should the Constitution be amended to ban flag-burning? Should dirty pictures be allowed on the Internet?—the American elites that subsidize and staff both the Republican and Democratic parties have steadfastly waged a generation-long class war against the middle and working classes. . . .

The American oligarchy spares no pains in promoting the belief that it does not exist, but the success of its disappearing act depends on equally strenuous efforts on the part of an American public anxious to believe in egalitarian fictions and unwilling to see what is hidden in plain sight. Anybody choos-

We are all the same?

A connection the over

ing to see the oligarchy in its native habitat need do nothing else but walk down the street of any big city to an office tower housing a major bank, a corporate headquarters or law firm, or a national television station. Enter the building and the multiracial diversity of the street vanishes as abruptly as the sound of the traffic. Step off the elevator at the top of the tower and apart from the clerical and maintenance staff hardly anybody is nonwhite. The contrast between the street and the tower is the contrast between the grass roots and the national headquarters, the field office and the home office. No matter what your starting point, the closer you come to the centers of American politics and society, the more everyone begins to look the same. Though corporate executives, shop stewards, and graduate-student lecturers could not be more different, the people who run big business bear a remarkable resemblance to the people who run big labor, who in turn might be mistaken for the people in charge of the media and the universities. They are the same people. They differ in their opinions—and in almost no other way. Almost exclusively white, disproportionately mainline Protestant or Jewish, most of the members of the American elites went to one of a dozen Ivy League colleges or top state universities. Not only do they have advanced professional or graduate degrees—J.D.'s, M.B.A.'s, Ph.D.'s, M.D.'s—but usually at least one of their parents (and sometimes both) has advanced professional or graduate degrees. They dress the same. They talk the same. They walk the same. They have the same body language, the same gestures. They eat the same food, drink the same drinks, and play the same sports. They read the same publications. They . . . but I should say *we*. As a second-generation professional with an Ivy League diploma, having worked for liberal Democrats and conservative Republicans, business lobbyists and pro-labor intellectuals, among professors and journalists and lawyers and Foreign Service officers, I am a card-carrying member of the overclass. So, in all likelihood, reader, are you.

Amounting, with their dependents, to about 20 percent of the population,[1] this relatively new and still evolving political and social oligarchy is not identified with any particular region of the country. Homogeneous and nomadic, the overclass is the first truly national upper class in American history. In a managerial capitalist society like our own, the essential distinction is not between the "bourgeoisie" (the factory owners) and the "proletariat" (the factory workers) but between the credentialed minority (making a living from fees or wages supplemented by stock options) and the salaried majority. The salaried class—at-will employees, lacking a four-year college education, paid by the hour, who can be fired at any time—constitutes the real "middle class," accounting, as it does, for three-quarters of the population . . . .

. . . The most remarkable thing about our own American oligarchy is the pretense that it doesn't constitute anything as definite as a social class. We prefer to assign good fortune to our individual merit, saying that we owe our perches in the upper percentiles of income and education not to our connections but solely to our own I.Q., virtue, brio, genius, *sprezzatura*, chutzpah,

The middle class — working, No formal education, lower wages

No defined social classes

A defect formed when
Somethings missing

Is it the person or their environment?

gumption. Had we been switched at birth by accident, had we grown up in a ghetto or barrio or trailer park, we would have arrived at our offices at ABC News or the Republican National Committee or the ACLU in more or less the same amount of time. The absence of black and Hispanic Americans in our schools and our offices and our clubs can only be explained, we tell ourselves, not by *our* extrinsic advantages but by *their* intrinsic defects. Compared with us (and perhaps with middle-class East Asian immigrants), most blacks and Hispanics must be disproportionately lazy, even (if Charles Murray and the late Richard Herrnstein are to be believed) disproportionately retarded. What other explanation for their failure to rise can there be? America, after all, is a classless society.

Or rather a two-class society. The belated acknowledgment of an "under-class" as a distinct group represents the only exception to the polite fiction that everyone in the United States, from a garage mechanic to a rich attorney (particularly the rich attorney), belongs to the "middle class." Over the past decade the ghetto poor have been the topic of conversation at more candlelight-and-wine dinner parties than I can recall, but without looking at the program or the wine list it is impossible to tell whether one is among nominal liberals or nominal conservatives. The same kind of people in the same kind of suits go on about "the blacks" as though a minority within a 12 percent minority were taking over the country, as if Washington were Pretoria and New York a suburb of Johannesburg. Not only do the comfortable members of the overclass single out the weakest and least influential of their fellow citizens as the cause of all their sorrows but they routinely, and preposterously, treat the genuine patholo-gies of the ghetto—high levels of violence and illegitimacy—as the major prob-lems facing a country with uncontrollable trade and fiscal deficits, a low savings rate, an obsolete military strategy, an anachronistic and corrupt electoral sys-tem, the worst system of primary education in the First World, and the bulk of its population facing long-term economic decline . . . .

During the past generation, the prerogatives of our new oligarchy have been magnified by a political system in which the power of money to buy TV time has become a good deal more important than the power of labor unions or party bosses to mobilize voters. Supported by the news media, which it largely owns, the oligarchy has waged its war of attrition against the wage-earning ma-jority on several fronts: regressive taxation, the expatriation of industry, and mass immigration. Regressive taxes like the Social Security payroll tax and state sales taxes shift much of the tax burden from the rich to middle-income Americans. After the Reagan-era tax reforms, 75 percent of the American peo-ple owed more taxes than they would have owed had the 1977 tax laws been left untouched; only the wealthiest 5 percent of the public received any signif-icant benefit from the tax cuts . . . .

On the second front of the class war, corporate elites continue to use the imperatives of global free trade as a means of driving down American wages and nullifying the social contract implicit in both the New Deal and the Great Society. U.S. corporations now lead the world in the race to low-wage countries with cheap and politically repressed labor forces. Concentrated in "export-processing zones" in Third World countries, and usually not integrated into the local economy, much of the transnational investment brings together foreign capital and technology with inexpensive and docile labor to manufacture consumer electronics, shoes, luggage, or toys . . . .

Not all nonprofessional jobs can be expatriated to Mexico or Malaysia, and a great many low-skilled services—from truck driving to nursing and sales and restaurant work—still must be performed in America. Accordingly, on a third front of the class war, the American gentry support a generous immigration policy. Enlarging the low-skill labor pool in the United States has the same effect as enlarging the labor pool through the expatriation of American-owned industry. From the point of view of members of the white overclass, of course, this is good news—if mass immigration ended tomorrow, they would probably have to pay higher wages, fees, and tips . . . .

The *Wall Street Journal*, ever mindful of the short-run interests of the overclass, has called for an amendment to the U.S. Constitution consisting of five words: "There shall be open borders." If the United States and Mexican labor markets were merged (together with the capital markets already integrated by NAFTA), then American investment would flow south to take advantage of cheap labor, and tens of millions of Mexican workers would migrate north to better-paying jobs, until wages stabilized somewhere above the contemporary Mexican level (between $4 and $5 a day) but below the current American minimum wage of $4.25 an hour. The numbers of the white overclass would remain fixed, while the pool of cheap labor expanded . . . .

Although the inequalities of income in the United States are now greater than at any time since the 1930s, and although numerous observers have remarked on the fact and cited abundant statistics in support of their observations, the response of the American overclass has been to blame everybody but its nonexistent self—to blame the ghetto, or the schools, or the liberal news media, or the loss of family values. In a characteristic argument that appeared in early April on the Op-Ed page of the *Washington Post* ("Raising the Minimum Wage Isn't the Answer"), James K. Glassman dismissed the idea that public policy can help the majority of workers whose real wages continue to fall: "[T]he ultimate answer lies with workers themselves . . . . Government can help a bit through tax breaks for education, but ultimately the cure for low working wages may be nothing more mysterious than high personal diligence."

In any other democracy, an enraged citizenry probably would have rebelled by now against a national elite that weakens unions, slashes wages and benefits, pits workers against low-wage foreign and immigrant competition—and then informs its victims that the chief source of their economic problems is a lack of "high personal diligence." But for whom could an enraged citizen

[handwritten in right margin: We have jobs that are "lower" in America]

[handwritten: American "upper class" taking advantage]

Recognizes more than 1 ultimate principal (handwritten)

vote? The American overclass manages to protect itself from popular insurgencies, not only through its ownership of the news media but also by its financial control of elections and its use of affirmative-action patronage . . . .

We were taught in civics classes that the United States is a "pluralistic" democracy in which Madisonian "factions" balance one another, ensuring that no single minority or economic interest will prevail. We were lied to. Labor does not balance big business; consumer groups do not balance big business; *nobody* balances big business anymore. Contrary to conservative claims that liberal and left-wing "special interests" dominate Congress, PAC funds come, overwhelmingly, from business. Citizens vote occasionally; dollars vote continually. During the first two months of this year [1995], "soft money" contributions, chiefly from industry, flowed into the coffers of the Republican National Committee at the rate of $123,121 per day, and during the recently ended two-year congressional campaign cycle, then Majority Leader Richard A. Gephardt (D., Mo.) accumulated PAC money in the amount of $1,001,400, while Speaker Newt Gingrich (R., Ga.) received $763,220. As recently as last April, President Clinton appeared at a $50,000-a-couple fund-raiser at Steven Spielberg's home in Hollywood. Because the same economic oligarchy subsidizes almost all of our politicians, our political fights are as inconsequential as TV wrestling.

Armed with the political advantage secured by the purchase of congressmen, senators, and presidents, the overclass shores up its defense against genuinely representative democracy (i.e., a popular coalition uniting middle-class and working-class Americans of all races and regions) by adopting a strategy of divide and rule expressed in the language of multiculturalism. The dynamics of a divided society similar to our own were noted in 1947 by Gunnar Myrdal: "In a society where there are broad social classes and, in addition, more minute distinctions and splits in the lower strata, *the lower class groups will to a great extent take care of keeping each other subdued*, thus relieving to that extent the higher classes of this otherwise painful task necessary to the monopolization of its power and advantages." Centuries before today's multiculturalists adopted the slogan "Celebrate diversity," William Smith, a slave trader, explained his reasons for celebrating diversity among the exploited:

> As for the languages of *Gambia*, they are so many and so different, that the Natives, on either side of the River, cannot understand each other; which, if rightly consider'd, is no small Happiness to the *Europeans* who go thither to trade for slaves . . . . [T]he safest Way is to trade with the different Nations, on either side of the River, and having some of every Sort on board, there will be no more Likelihood of their succeeding in a Plot than of finishing the Tower of Babel.

Unified along the lines of economic interest, the wealthy American minority hold the fragmented majority at bay by pitting blacks against whites in zero-sum struggles for government patronage and by bribing potential black and Hispanic leaders, who might otherwise propose something other than rhetorical rebellion, with the gifts of affirmative action . . . .

*The "5%" dont want*** the minorities to become more powerful* (handwritten)

Feudalism- those who can afford

Meanwhile, behind the Potemkin Village facade of contemporary America, with its five separate-but-equal official races and its racially authentic folk art, the American oligarchy goes busily about the work of constructing its own enclave society, an America-within-America, linked to the international economy and detached from the destiny of the native middle class. What Lewis Lapham has called "the new feudalism" reverses the trend of the past thousand years toward the government's provision of basic public goods like policing, public roads and transport networks, and public schools. In the United States—to a degree unmatched in any other industrial democracy—these public goods are once again becoming private luxuries, accessible only to the affluent few. Federal spending declined in the 1980s for services like law enforcement and government (by 42 percent), for education and training (by 40 percent), and for the transportation infrastructure (by 32 percent); and most of the growth in government spending in recent decades has taken the form of non-means-tested entitlements, like Social Security and Medicare, that benefit middle- and upper-income Americans.

"what if" Situation

If the notion of a neo-feudal United States seems far-fetched, consider the "feudal" elements of modern America. Increasing numbers of affluent white Americans have been withdrawing into gated suburbs, many of them indistinguishable from private cities, whose community associations provide not only security but trash collection, street cleaning, and utilities. The inhabitants have sought permission from local governments to block off public streets with gates and other barriers to traffic (a California appeals court recently ruled that seven metal gates installed by the Los Angeles suburb of Whitley Heights represented an illegal "return to feudal times"—but only *after* their installation had been approved by the Los Angeles City Council). Some of the richer residents within the walls seek not only permission to barricade themselves but exemption from taxes—on the argument that taxes for public municipal services on top of the fees they pay their private community associations constitute "double taxation."

Because the affluent would rather hire mercenary forces than pay for police, the number of private security guards in the United States now exceeds the number of publicly employed policemen. To help those who cannot afford to rent police officers, the right is trying to make it easier to carry concealed weapons at the mall, in the office, and on the subway; holsters and body armor may once again become fashion accessories. A chorus of conservative voices proposes the replacement of public schools with taxpayer-subsidized vouchers to private schools, and the idea of replacing the national highway system with private toll roads is not a fantasy confined to dystopian science fiction. More than ten states now have projects for such roads, which would allow the happy few to drive their expensive cars on state-of-the-art computer-enhanced highways while ordinary Americans fume in traffic on crumbling public streets . . . .

. . . In a more homogeneous society, the growing concentration of power and wealth in the hands of a privileged minority might be expected to produce

"we have got to stop fighting each other"

a strong reaction on the part of the majority. In present-day America, however, no such reaction is likely to take place. Although heavily outnumbered, the unified few rest secure in the knowledge that any insurgency will almost certainly dissipate in quarrels among the fragmented many rather than in open rebellion; during the 1992 Los Angeles riots, black, Hispanic, and white rioters turned on Korean middlemen rather than march on Beverly Hills. The belligerent guests on the never-ending talk show, urged on by the screaming audience, will continue to enact allegorical conflicts, while, off-camera and upstairs, the discreet members of the class that does not exist ponder the choice of marble or mahogany for the walls of the executive suite from which they command. *the "over-class" blames the under for society's problems*

NOTE

1. Defined as individuals with professional or graduate education (which is roughly correlated with high income), and without counting dependents, the members of the overclass account for no more than 5 percent of the U.S. population.

FOR JOURNALING AND DISCUSSION

1. How does the invisibility of the American class structure help to maintain it? Does the fact that few people acknowledge that they are anything other than middle class help to entrench our class divisions even further?

2. Lind claims that as a society we prefer to believe that our successes are a result of our individual merits rather than a product of the educational, class, racial, and other privileges that most middle-class people enjoy. Do you think this holds true for you? To what extent do you think that your success or position in life has been determined by your own inherent merit rather than the fact that you were born into a specific class, race, gender, neighborhood, etc.?

3. Lind claims that the American preoccupation with "trivial" issues such as flag burning and banning dirty pictures on the Internet is being used to divert our attention from more important societal issues. Do you think that this is true? Are the issues he mentions trivial? What are the more important issues that we are not focusing on? Why aren't they getting our attention?

FOR RESEARCH AND EXPLORATION

1. Lind suggests that one of the ways the overclass maintains its position is by diverting attention away from itself toward other conflicts (especially racial ones). Review some of the news stories written about the riots in Los Angeles after the Rodney King trial. Analyze how the media directed our attention away from the issue of poverty and instead painted the riots as a solely racial matter due in large part to conflicts between African and Korean Americans.

2. Lind claims that affirmative action has been little more than a program that operates "by pitting blacks against whites in zero-sum struggles for government patronage and by bribing potential black and Hispanic leaders, who might otherwise propose something other than rhetorical rebellion . . . ." Find evidence either to support

or refute this claim. Has affirmative action helped minority peoples? or just a few chosen minority individuals? Is it one more tool to keep the "masses" in their place?

3. Lind claims that regressive taxation, the expatriation of industry, and mass immigration are the three main tools currently used by our government to maintain the present class structure. Pick one of these three topics and research how it is covered in a leading business magazine such as *Forbes, Fortune,* or *Money.* What views and images are they feeding to their upper-class audience? How are these images being used to perpetuate the status quo?

Illegitimate Elites and the Parasitic Underclass

Katherine Newman

Newman earned a Ph.D. in anthropology at the University of California at Berkeley. She has taught in the School of Law at Berkeley and is currently an assistant professor of anthropology at Columbia University in New York.

I understand some of the factors that have been involved in [the changes we see in Pleasanton[*]]. There's been a lot of foreign investment. People are moving into the community that were never there before. My brother works in the school system, and a quarter of his students are Oriental. Half of them are very, very wealthy Orientals. People who buy homes for $500,000 in cash. Walking into a strange land with bags of money. It's bound to affect the local economy! It inflates the prices of homes all around. I have a friend who's a real estate broker in the area and the stories he tells about the Asian families . . . . He just says, "It's ridiculous!"

—Martin O'Rourke, age 40

The welfare system is absurd. There are guys in New York sitting on curbs smoking joints today. Six-foot-two, 190-pound guys with other 200-pound guys. That's how it works. Second- and third-generation welfare people, that's absurd. Nobody should receive welfare unless they're at least willing to work. It's draining our country; making it third world.

—George McDermott, age 62

Katherine Newman, "Illegitimate Elites and the Parasitic Underclass" (excerpts) from *Declining Fortunes: The Withering of the American Dream.* Copyright © 1993 by Katherine Newman. Reprinted with the permission of HarperCollins Publishers, Inc.

[*]Editor's Note: In the preface to *Declining Fortunes: The Withering of the American Dream,* the book from which this excerpt is taken, Newman describes "Pleasanton" as "one typical suburban community, a town the likes of which could be found in almost any state in the union." The book is based on more than 150 interviews with "ordinary Americans," white-collar professionals and skilled blue-collar workers who come from a variety of ethnic and religious backgrounds.

Neither Martin O'Rourke nor George McDermott considers himself to be a racist; they bridle with indignation when they hear people with opinions like theirs described as bigots. Yet the melting-pot theory to which they subscribe at some level posits only one acceptable path of entry, only one way of making a claim to the good life that lies at the end of the American rainbow. Newcomers must start at the bottom and work their way up.[1] This maxim applies both to new immigrants and to minorities who have long been here but want something better for themselves and their children.

When Martin examines his world critically, however, he does not see an orderly progression of ethnic communities and new immigrants lining up to claim their fair share, with evidence of their hard work in hand. Above himself, Martin sees a group of elites who have exploited the present weakness of the U.S. economy. The price has been paid by hardworking Americans who have forfeited the opportunity to live in their own communities to these interlopers. Casting an eye to the bottom of the social structure, he sees the dangerous classes who inhabit the inner city or segregated suburbs nearby. Chronic welfare dependents, criminals, addicts, women who cannot control themselves, and men who have no attachment to family—these are the denizens of the underclass. They may as well live a million miles from Pleasanton, for all the immediate connection between the two strata.

But the underclass and the politicians who want to do something about poverty in the United States want Martin's tax dollars; they want the people of Pleasanton to support single-parent families; they want to take money from his kids' school and throw it at urban schools in the name of equality. In the best of all possible worlds, Martin might be inclined to help the deserving poor,[2] for he does believe that the disadvantaged deserve some help. But Martin is feeling the pinch; his resources will not stretch to care for his own family the way he thought he would be able to. He wonders whether the middle class, sandwiched in between illegitimate elites and parasitic underclasses, is being played for the fool.

The stresses and strains of raising a family in tight economic times are leading boomers like Martin to push the argument over what has gone wrong with the country beyond the internal conversation over the legitimacy of his generation's expectations. They are looking to place the blame elsewhere, and their gaze reaches above and below. What they find at the end of this exercise is a disturbing departure from traditional virtues and an Alice in Wonderland inversion of the rules that are supposed to lead from the work ethic to the good life.

APPLE PIE VERSUS SUSHI

When Martin was growing up in Pleasanton, the community was almost entirely composed of white ethnics and WASPs. Though they could trace their origins to different nations, the commonalities that bound these suburban-bound refugees from the inner city were more important than the differences.

They were all seeking the same thing and were all doing it the same way: from the sweat of their own brows, or so they see the matter with hindsight. There were people in the community who were rich by Martin's standards, kids whose fathers were doctors or lawyers. Yet even the privileged residents of Pleasanton were people who "made it" by virtue of their own brains. Everyone in Pleasanton—whether the well-heeled doctor or the self-made blue-collar craftsman—looked with satisfaction upon his material accomplishments because these comforts came by virtue of his own efforts,[3] that is, according to the rules of mobility in America.

These moral preconditions for personal accomplishment leave little room in Martin's mind for outsiders to march into his community, or his country, and reorder the traditional route to upward mobility. He believes that natives have to work hard if they are to lay legitimate claim to comfort. Foreigners should be held to the same strictures:

> These are the new Americans. But the difference between the way my parents came to this country and these people is that my grandfather and his kids came with just the clothes on their backs. They had nothing except a few relatives who set them up with work. The Asians that are coming here now come from rich backgrounds. I met one gentleman from Korea whose kids go to school with my kids and his father owned a big textile business. He's opening up a distribution center in the city, and they moved to New Jersey and plunked down a huge amount of money for a beautiful, expensive home in our town.

In essence, Martin believes that the Asians who have leapfrogged their way to the top are as illegitimate in their claims to this comfortable life as his spoiled classmates who expect to be (and sometimes are) set up by Mom and Dad. Neither group has done it the hard way; hence, neither deserves what it has. Success gained that way is not morally justifiable because it fails to express the core values of American culture. Martin's voice betrays his frustration when he reflects on the lack of moral purpose in the Asian ascent of the American class structure. "They have no real reason behind their efforts to push for better," by which he means they are not trying to prove themselves and point to their houses and cars as evidence of their inner worth. By starting at the top, they have no real proving to do. Rewards are going to the undeserving too easily, he figures. The "overprivileged" rich are benefiting at Martin's expense:[4]

> They come into this country with a lot of money and I can't help but think that it's inflating the real estate prices tremendously. This has got to calm down, but I don't know when or how. There are a lot of [native-born] people who are very upset that they can't live in Pleasanton or anywhere nearby. A lot of my friends think that it's absolutely ridiculous that they can't buy houses around here.

Martin knows who is to blame, who has derailed the natural progression from parents to children in the community: the new Asian neighbors . . . .

. . . The boomers who grew up in Pleasanton are generally a well-educated lot; most are white-collar employees. They are supposed to be above crude expressions of nativism. But it is testimony to how deeply they feel the sting of eviction from their community that they focus as much energy as they do on the Asian invader as the source of their problems.

Displacement of this kind is particularly evident among the boomers who were born in the 1960s, graduating from high school in the midst of the recession of the early 1980s. These people, who represent the tail end of the baby-boom phenomenon, have seen the most pronounced ethnic shift in the composition of their town, and they (along with their parents) are most prone to defining this shift, not as a gradual change in the nature of Pleasanton, but as a sharp departure from what Pleasanton should really be. It was supposed to be the kind of place where each generation naturally took the place of the one that came before it. It was supposed to be a place where "real" Americans—descendants of immigrant stock, children of depression survivors—could keep the extended family together by moving in around the corner.[5] If there was room left over after continuity was assured, then they would be happy enough to welcome faces of another color. But as Oran MacDowell sees it, Pleasanton has become a community closed off to its own progeny:

> Every house on my mother's block has been sold to an Oriental. That's a little depressing at times. It's not that they're second-class citizens. But now you're being alienated from your own town. You're not given a chance to move into your town.

Even more galling to Katherine, his wife, is the fact that these families can afford to do exactly what she would like to pull off, but cannot:

> These people are able to move into those houses with one person working. Mom staying home with the kids. For them it's just like back when our parents were growing up. One supporting person. That's all out of the question for us and it's frustrating.

Katherine and Oran cannot imagine having the luxury to buy a house, even one far from Pleasanton. If they are lucky enough to manage that feat someday, it will take both of their earnings to do so. Katherine will not be able to follow her mother's example—or the Japanese example—and stay home with her babies.

Postwar parents did not themselves experience the displacement their children are complaining about. Most stayed put in Pleasanton unless their jobs required a transfer, or they decided to leave for a retirement haven where the taxes are lower. Yet the Pleasanton they have remained in is not the Pleasanton they raised their children in, as they see it. The grandsons of Italy, Ireland, Germany, and France—who came to Pleasanton via the Bronx, Brooklyn, and the less desirable parts of Manhattan—believe the last of their kind have come to this suburban community. All around them houses vacated by these "real" Americans have been bought up by families from India, Korea, and Japan. And though the "natives" of Pleasanton are themselves only one generation removed from the immigrant experience of the early twentieth century, many find they cannot accept these newcomers as today's example of those who follow a familiar pathway from the old country to the new.

The Fieland family is a particularly vocal example of this new nativism.[6] George, the machinist who worked in aerospace, and his wife, Julie (a longtime sales assistant in local department stores), believe that Pleasanton should be a quintessential American town. Its people ought to express the values that made the country great. They should articulate these values in the English language. Only newcomers who visibly aspire to these marks of assimilation should be welcomed with open arms. Until then, the Fielands argue, immigrants should be regarded with suspicion:

JULIE: I can understand why people come here. This is what this country was all about. After all, our own parents were immigrants.

GEORGE: But if you come here you come for a reason, right? You come here for a better life. So why drag all the bad stuff with you? Maybe bad is the wrong word. But if you're so interested in your background and culture, don't leave [the place you come from]. Stay where you are!

The Orientals move in and right away they put up their own signs. I can't read those signs. Business signs, the church down here. Not that I go to that church, but what's the difference . . . . I should be able to read a sign in this country, but they're all kinds of Chinese signs, or Korean, or whatever . . . . You go into any of these stores and it's either Indian or Oriental. If they want to come into this country and make all their money . . . there's no reason why they can't at least have the sign so I understand it. People with money that are leaving their own country and coming here to make [more of it].

The Fielands believe that there can be only one motivation for coming to Pleasanton and that is to become as American as apple pie, to leave the old ways behind and adopt the superior culture of the United States. This is as true, they tell us, for rich immigrants like the East Asians as it is for the poorer ones . . . .

At some level, the Fielands (and their many neighbors who agree with them) realize that these nativist sentiments are not acceptable in polite company, that they run against the grain of the American tradition of tolerance. The unholy attitudes that breed today's anti-Asian fury are the result of racial antagonism, immigrant hysteria, and residual hatred of our enemies from the Second World War. But the rejection of Asian neighbors must also be understood as reflecting the dismay and confusion that postwar parents and their children are experiencing as they bear witness to the breakdown of upward mobility in this country. There would be plenty of room for newcomers—even newcomers of a different culture—if the boomers who expected to follow their parents to Pleasanton (or places like Pleasanton) could still make that journey. Seeing the children sent out into the unknown—or worse, the known and unacceptable—fate of downward mobility, the "natives" react by looking around for the nearest visible agent of this misfortune . . . .

There is a certain irony in all of this. Pleasanton's senior generation, those who were lucky enough to buy when homes were cheap, have been able to sit back and watch the value of their assets skyrocket. Indeed, many of them can look forward to a comfortable retirement because of a near-miraculous increase in their equity, an unexpected windfall. (It is certainly folly to think this came about simply because of foreign investment in towns like Pleasanton.) Hence, as much as they would like to see a drop in property prices so that their children can get into the market, many postwar parents are depending upon this very windfall, sustained in part by foreign investment, to bankroll their twilight years.

How then are we to understand their anger at their neighbors, their sympathy for their own children? Sociological insights into class identity are of little value here.[7] The traditional perspective tells us that class position is a matter of individual occupation, individual income, individual interests. On these grounds, the "Asian invasion" has been nothing but a blessing for Pleasanton's postwar parents. To the extent that it contributed to the inflation of housing prices, it has dropped a great financial benefit in the laps of those "natives" who were already in place when the great escalation began . . . .

Anger and resentment are hot emotions that surface in the "native" parents and boomer children from Pleasanton.[8] Yet their overall attitudes toward the new Americans is more mixed than these vignettes from the housing wars might suggest. Steeped in the work ethic themselves, Pleasanton's postwar parents cannot help but admire the remarkable industry, seriousness of purpose, and high standards that their new neighbors have brought to the community. This is nowhere more evident than in the local schools, where children of Japanese and Korean descent now account for nearly 50 percent of the younger classes. Teachers and parents alike remark upon how well behaved, intelligent, and hardworking these children are. Old-timers in Pleasanton are proud to note that one of the reasons their community is deemed so desirable by foreign families is that its school system has a good reputation. As Mrs. James put the matter:

> Now that the Japanese have moved to town, the [school] system is really terrific. Because they value a good educational system and they're willing to put the time and effort into it . . . . The high school has always been good, but the elementary school system has come a long way and I think the Asian population is responsible for it. Some things about the Asian community drive me up the wall, but as far as their caring about the educational system, you can't beat them. They really care about what happens with their children. And if some of these folks [who complain about Asians] would stop and think about it, a good school system is the equivalent of a good neighborhood.

Nevertheless, underlying this sentiment lurks a fear of intellectual domination by the Asian community. Schools are the proving ground for future success. Those who fail in school or who do not do well enough to make it into a good college pay the price for the rest of their lives. Not that the presence of hardworking Asian students will foreclose further opportunities for longtime Pleasanton residents, but the competition underlines a more general feeling that Americans are falling behind in the international contest for market dominance. If we are surpassed in the schools, say Pleasanton's old-timers, can our downfall in other arenas—jobs, standard of living, industrial clout—be far behind? How do we maintain our advantage in technical fields if our children are unable to compete against foreign brain power? It is bad enough, they say, that this specter haunts us in the international arena: it is worse when that sad fact is the reality in your neighborhood schools.

But what is most galling about the local competition between ethnic groups is that old-timers feel they are being bested at their own game. They want to know the secret of this success. Are Japanese children so much smarter than American children? Are Korean kids constitutionally better at mathematics than their U.S. counterparts? The most frightening and perhaps damning answer Pleasanton parents can come up with is the possibility that Asian families exert the kind of discipline over their children that middle-class Americans long ago yielded. Defensive at the very idea, they turn around and indict their neighbors for preventing children from just being children.

The Krasdales have thought long and hard about this issue. Joan Krasdale's job as a local real estate agent provides a vantage point from which to view the changes in the community. She knows that Asian families have come to this pleasant suburb because they want their children to be well educated. The results are obvious:

> We were talking to a mother who lives in an adjoining town. She mentioned that her son's elementary class is 50 percent Oriental. I was rather shocked or surprised, but I shouldn't have been. If you read the local paper, you read about these kids that are on the high honor roll. They all excel; you'll see all Oriental names . . . . They're very serious. No nonsense.

All to the good, one might imagine. But as Joan and her husband, Norman, continue the conversation, we find that this is not what she thinks of as normal or good for a child:

> JOAN: I think there's no balance in their lives. That tends to make them totally stressed out. They have the drive to be achievers because their parents have put this into their culture. I was reading some statistics about high suicide rates in Japan because they can't face their parents if they don't do well in school . . . . They go crazy if they don't win the prize or don't get into high honors programs.
>
> NORMAN: I'd hate to see my kids run up against them.
>
> JOAN: Our son was a merit scholar in high school, but he was a jock. That was his prime concern, although fortunately for him he scored well [on standardized tests] . . . but if he had had to bear down and compete [in the classroom] like he did in the sports arena, I don't know what would have happened.
>
> NORMAN: I don't think I like what has happened around here. I think that there are too many of them. It doesn't come from prejudice. It just comes because of numbers. We're overloaded now.

As the Krasdales see it, Asian children are not allowed to be kids; their parents push them to be intellectual robots grabbing up honors at every turn. The Krasdales find this approach unnatural, and feel alienated from their Asian neighbors. Japanese and Korean families are defined as "the other," "the foreign," who by some mystical force manage to achieve a discipline that only an alien could want . . . .

Nativism is not a pretty sentiment. It is a selfish and fearful streak in American culture that belies the ideal of welcoming tolerance and diminishes the benefits the United States reaps from including new groups into the fold. Pleasanton's postwar parents do not want to think of themselves in this light and would reject this characterization. Indeed, most consider themselves to be open, unbiased, and sincere in their desire to be inclusive. From their perspective, the Japanese and Koreans would be most welcome if they wanted to join the mainstream. Unfortunately, the signals they see are just the opposite: their Asian neighbors seem to want to keep to themselves. The community institutions that used to guarantee a sense of participation and inclusion have faded away and the old-timers attribute this sad fact to the presence of an alien element that has no interest in block parties, Girl Scout clubs, or the PTA.

Evelyn Maguire is a widow. She moved to Pleasanton forty years ago with her husband and raised her five children there. Evelyn grew up in the Bronx, one of seven Irish Catholic children raised by a widowed mother. She wanted something better for her own kids, so with some regrets she moved out of the city and into a friendly suburban town. Evelyn's husband was a cab driver when they met, but eventually he moved into the security field and ended up as the head of security in a local manufacturing firm. He died in 1974, but while he was alive, Evelyn's husband devoted his weekends to the volunteer fire department and their sons' softball league. These were the kinds of activities that made the Maguires feel a part of the community. As Evelyn sees it, those symbols of community no longer exist because the newcomers refuse to participate:

> We're getting a lot of Orientals in town and it's changed everything. Before the people worked together. We have a volunteer ambulance and a volunteer fire department, and it was terrific. But we can't get anybody to join. The Orientals won't join. They keep to themselves. The woman who lives across the street, I guess in two years I spoke to her once and she looked at me incomprehensible. If their house burned down, the fire department would have to fight it anyway. So they should [do their share] . . . well, anyway, they don't. They're not pulling their weight and they don't get involved. And I think in a small community, people should get involved.

As Lou Campagna, Evelyn's neighbor down the road, sees it, these new people not only fail to involve themselves in these participatory institutions, but are also unfriendly in more casual circumstances:

> They're kinda unsociable. Don't get me wrong, I got nothing against Orientals. But I got nothing but Orientals livin' around me. They seem to stay on their own. You'll be outside doin' something and they'll walk by. You say hello, but it's changed.

Intimacy, neighborliness, friendship, participation—these are the elements of community that the old-timers in Pleasanton value. Their young married years were defined by them, and they are sorely missed. Much has changed in the town since the postwar years, but the ethnic mix is often singled out as the prime mover in the destruction of that sense of belonging.

In truth, most of the clubs and activities that made postwar families feel so much a part of Pleasanton were organized around the children: block parties, Scouts, the PTA. An aging community, where children are no longer around to serve as the social glue, is one in which old-timers are bound to feel a sense of decline or alienation. Without the child-driven voluntary organizations, they have few institutional connections to bring them into sustained contact either with other empty-nested adults or younger families preoccupied with raising children. For all they know, the new Asian families may be active in the very organizations they rarely participate in now that their own children are grown . . . .

Behind the personal experience of generational displacement lies the specter of something much larger: the declining fortunes of the boomers is interpreted as symptomatic of the end of American dominance in international commerce. Pleasanton's boomers and the parents who raised them are convinced that they have been denied an entitlement. They are also certain that their own experience is but a smaller version of a more profound problem: the United States is losing its power, ceding its autonomy, endangering its status as a preeminent nation. "Asian countries," it is asserted with dismay, "are taking over and we are doing nothing to stop it!" We have allowed ourselves to be driven into a corner. Our labor is overpriced, our competition prone to taking unfair advantage of our markets, our government unable or unwilling to stop unhealthy foreign ownership of our productive resources. This can only spell one thing for Americans: the end of affluence . . . .

Johnny Carson, former king of late-night television, captured the fears and furies of Pleasanton's native whites well the night his monologue focused on America's disintegrating economy. "If we'd let the Japanese win the war," said Carson impishly, "maybe we'd still own the Rockefeller Center."[9] The sale of the Rockefeller building was followed in short order by other symbols of the great American sellout. Sony bought the AT&T building. The largest communications companies in Hollywood are acquired by their Japanese counterparts. One after another, the icons of American business deliver themselves into foreign hands. Business may be business, but the transfer of these national symbols is emblematic of our commercial decline, and sends an unwelcome message to the average citizen: we no longer control our destiny.

People who live in communities far from Pleasanton, who may never see a prosperous immigrant population in their midst, follow these events closely. They would agree with suburban soul mates in Pleasanton that the country is on the road to ruin if it sacrifices its most precious resources to other (unscrupulous) nations. Someday, they imagine, we will need to rely upon ourselves again. What will be there for us to depend upon when that day comes? Who else can we really trust? For most Americans, the answer is, No one else is really trustworthy. In Pleasanton, signs of this posture abound: in comments about the superiority of the English language and the denigration of Asian neighbors as unfriendly or as alien types who push their children to succeed where "real Americans" are failing.

Little assistance can be expected from the native-born elites who run the power machine in Washington. This is not because they are somehow uniquely insular, unable to see what has happened to the heartland. Their myopia has more sinister origins, at least in the eyes of some of Pleasanton's more conservative residents. Politicians who are not working on behalf of special interest groups concerned with the poor are on the bandwagon of the homegrown wealthy. Some Pleasanton old-timers are turning to populist candidates who promise to do something about privilege, something to force the rich to do their part. It is to people like Ralph Anderson that the populism of the 1990s is directed, for he is as angry at the rich (and those in Washington who have done their bidding) as he is at the poor:

> Political corruption [is rampant]. Take tax reform . . . it made the rich richer and the poor poorer. The poor get away with almost nothing and the middle guy, like I am, pays the brunt, because the rich people don't pay anything. Leona Helmsley, she says only poor people pay taxes. She was right! She was telling the truth! Now they're talking about reducing the capital gains tax . . . to eliminate any disadvantage to the so-called rich people. It's absurd![10]

Ralph remembers that when he first moved to Pleasanton his property taxes amounted to a modest $400 a year, a manageable burden, particularly for a suburb like Pleasanton, which has no industrial base from which to draw additional revenues.[11] These days the same house costs $4,000 a year in taxes, a sum that falls hard on the shoulders of people like the Andersons who see their retirement prospects compromised by these voracious demands for their dollars.

PARASITES IN THE CITY

As the economy tightened up in the late 1980s, a cry went up across the United States to reform the welfare system. In some states this took the form of cutting off or cutting back on benefits for women who continue having children after being placed on welfare rolls.[12] Some reforms imposed work requirements on welfare recipients. Local initiatives followed on the heels of federal legislation, spearheaded by the chief social scientist on capital hill, Daniel Patrick Moynihan, the Democratic senator from New York and a longtime student of the welfare system. The timing of these amendments was no accident and was, in most respects, unrelated to the financial burden that welfare imposes on state and federal budgets—a cost dwarfed by the cost of the more middle-class entitlement programs, social security and Medicare.[13] Welfare reform got a shot in the arm because it served as a focus for the wrath of people in communities like Pleasanton who have felt increasingly frustrated about their own declining fortunes.

Statistics on teenage pregnancy, high school dropouts, and soaring crime are the daily media diet in households full of people who fled to suburbia to find their own patch of blue sky and green lawn but also to put the problems of the cities behind them. Now, it seems, one cannot escape these problems: the urban underclasses look to be on the verge of exploding, with the Los Angeles riots of 1992 only the beginning.[14] Liberals argue that large-scale disturbances are the inevitable fallout of a decade of deliberate neglect, the erosion of employment opportunities in the nation's cities now bereft of factories that once employed inner-city minorities, and the progressive deterioration of urban school systems.[15] But the liberal argument has had only a limited appeal with the American middle class that supports civil rights but remains too attached to traditional norms of family life and the work ethic to buy the argument that the problems of the urban underclass rest on anyone's shoulders but its own. They were once willing to look the other way and let the War on Poverty go forward because it cost them little; the economy was fat, taxes were relatively low, and the fortunes of the middle class were secure.

In the less favorable climate of the 1980s and 1990s, the conservative posture has won the day: what we need, say the right-wing critics, is to stop coddling people by making it easy to be poor in the United States.[16] We must make welfare more difficult to access and thereby encourage the underclass to get back on its own feet and off the backs of the rest of us. They do not favor draconian measures that leave women and children without food or shelter. But they do believe that the traditional virtues of family integrity and the work ethic have disappeared in the nation's cities, and they insist upon personal responsibility as the cornerstone of individual worth, whatever the origins of contemporary poverty may be. And until these values actively reassert themselves among tax-hungry minorities, Pleasanton will be skeptical, even angry, about the demands of the inner-city underclass.

George McDermott has worked for the past twenty years as a commissioned sales representative for a company that makes home appliances. He has never lived in a big city, having come originally from a suburban community in Pennsylvania. George married his high school sweetheart and together they steadily worked their way up from a small garden apartment in southern New Jersey to a house on Long Island. With a promotion in hand, George and his wife, Jenny, finally had the wherewithal to buy their dream house in Pleasanton, where they subsequently raised three children. By his own admission, George is one of the old-timers in Pleasanton, an Irish Catholic by descent who settled in thirty years ago as one of the postwar upwardly mobiles. George knows he has been fortunate, but he attributes his success to traditional virtues, which he has tried to communicate to his own children:

> I taught my children to be hard workers . . . . My boys started working when they were twelve. They were paperboys. And my next-door neighbor has a cleaning business that my kids worked in when they were fourteen or fifteen . . . . So even through high school they worked. They learned the value of money, they learned to apply themselves. At one point—my sons were runners—they would go out in

the morning and run seven miles, then come home, eat, go to school, come
home, go to work, then come home, eat their dinner, then study and go to bed.

George believes that discipline of this kind is the key to his children's success in
life, and he points with pride to their flourishing careers as pilots and teachers.
However, in his view, these virtues are dying everywhere else in American society.
We are fast becoming a country that, in George's words, is "deteriorating, socio-
logically and graphically." He rails against crime, crowded jails, early parole, and
the short-sighted rejection of the death penalty in a society more inclined to mol-
lycoddle criminals than deal with them in the no-nonsense fashion they deserve.
From his perspective, however, crime is merely the tip of the iceberg. Next on
the list is our misguided generosity toward the able-bodied poor:

> I believe in morality; I believe in ethics; I believe in hard work; I believe in all the
> old values. I don't believe in free handouts . . . . So that whole welfare system falls
> into that [category]. . . . The idea of fourteen-year-old kids getting pregnant and
> then having five children by the time they're twenty is absurd! It's ridiculous! And
> that's what's causing this country to go downhill.

George does not see himself as a racist. Publicly he would subscribe to the
principle everyone in this society deserves a fair shake.[17] But he does not see welfare or its twin policy—affirmative action—as legitimate redress for these historic
wrongs, particularly since they are likely to hit him in the pocketbook or his children in the sweepstakes for job opportunities.[18] What George sees is a loaded
deck: minorities that cannot really compete claim jobs, all sorts of federal programs, and general social sympathy while the rest of the country is left to struggle
on its own. Under these circumstances, the disorganized but virtuous many are
likely to lose out to well-organized, powerful, nameless special-interest groups.

George's neighbors up the street, the Lanackers, do not fully accept his
brand of conservatism. Jane Lanacker's family fled Europe during the war, and
her own experience of refugee life, of the difficulty of making one's way in an
unfamiliar society, has left its mark in the form of a more benevolent spirit.
Jane believes that the government does have a responsibility to assist the less
fortunate to get back on their feet and is discouraged by the resistance of the
White House to take initiatives that would help people help themselves. Her
more Republican, American-grown husband, Walter, accepts her point but believes that while immigrants do dedicate themselves to a life of hard work and
deserved rewards, native-born Americans have forgotten how to do so:

> I had a client who was an immigrant who made good. Hardly spoke English but
> he worked sixteen hours a day, built up a nice pizza shop in Plainview. I had got-
> ten some insurance for him. One day he put a big sign in the window, "Help
> Wanted." He ran ads in the papers. He couldn't get anybody who wanted to learn
> to make pizzas. Five-fifty an hour was pretty decent pay. Nobody wanted to take
> the job . . . . A carpenter who didn't have a job would rather accept welfare ben-
> efits than do some honest work because he felt it was demeaning. I think there's
> something wrong with that. Before I accepted a penny of welfare, I would sweep
> floors just to stand on my own two feet.[19]

The appeal of outsider political candidates like H. Ross Perot lies in the rough seas that seem to envelop "middle guys" like George McDermott: squeezed between the demanding poor and the favored rich, with no one to defend their interests, no one to look out for their well-being.[20] And while life has been pretty good to George and to most of the postwar generation who joined him in Pleasanton, it is dealing a bad hand to their kids. What George sees in protest candidates are people willing to stand up to this system that privileges those at the top and those at the bottom—people willing to challenge the status quo in the name of the hardworking middle class. George longs for the "good old days" when hard work ruled and was properly rewarded, when poor people did what they could to better their lot without asking anything from anyone else, and the rich were at least minimally responsible. Populist politicians who promise to turn the clock back and take no nonsense from anyone are enormously appealing to the George McDermotts of the country. The major parties simply have not been able to convince him that they are challenging the influence that the parasitic underclass and the undeserving rich have brought to bear on public policy.

LIVING WITH CONTRADICTION

It is always tempting to seek coherence in culture. Anthropologists are confused by contradictions and devote many hours and countless pages to the task of reconciling mutually incompatible beliefs, usually by demonstrating that they are not as contradictory as they appear.[21] We like to think that people try to make sense, if not to the scholars they speak to, then at least to themselves. But it is in the nature of our culture, and no doubt of most cultures, to live with incoherence and contradiction. This is not a particularly troublesome feature of social life; it bothers social scientists much more than it bothers people.

When postwar parents and their boomer children knit their brows over what has gone wrong for the younger generation, they focus in on a complex set of problems for which they have few solutions. Kids are spoiled; they expect too much too soon; they aren't willing to work as hard as was the generation hardened by the depression; and they cannot seem to get it through their heads that rewards will come in the fullness of time. At the same time, parents shake their heads, wring their hands, and proclaim that their children are working like maniacs and getting nowhere, that the country is "going to hell in a hand basket," that our politicians cannot rescue us because they are hopelessly corrupt or incompetent.

In the next breath, the same people rail against their neighbors, arguing that they are the frontline troops in an international effort to rob the United States of its economic independence. We can see it happen right in our own backyard, say the elders of Pleasanton. These wealthy foreigners are evicting our children from their own hometown, and there seems to be nothing we can do about it. The international economy becomes visible at the local level, where declining opportunities in the job market (relative to the spectacular upward mobility of postwar parents) and the rising cost of housing have combined to create sharp differences between the generations in their personal experiences of economic well-being. However inconsistent the explanations offered for this unwelcome state of affairs, there is no mistaking the frustration these problems cause. Nor can there be much doubt about the destructive potential of nativist or racially charged explanations themselves. Generations who point fingers at each other, ethnic groups who look with envy upon the accomplishments and possessions of their neighbors, comfortable "middle guys" who flare up at the demands placed upon them to support the less fortunate through their tax dollars—these are the flash points that flare into strained relations, reactionary politics, and violent confrontation.

NOTES

1. Jonathan Rieder shows how this belief shapes the way ethnic whites think about their own social standing relative to African Americans in his book *Canarsie: The Jews and Italians of Brooklyn against Liberalism* (Cambridge, Mass.: Harvard University Press, 1985). On the same point, see Alan Wolfe, *Whose Keeper?* (Berkeley: University of California Press, 1990).

2. See David Matza, "The Disreputable Poor," in *Class, Status and Power: Social Structures in Comparative Perspective,* ed. Richard Bendix and Seymour Martin Lipser (New York: Free Press, 1966), pp. 289–302.

3. In this retrospective tale, the contributions made by the federal government in the form of low-interest mortgages, the GI Bill, and the like are rarely cited, a point discussed at length in chapter 3.

4. This is a variant of a theme that appears in David Halle, *America's Working Man: Work, Home, and Politics among Blue-Collar Property Owners* (Chicago: University of Chicago Press, 1984). Halle talks about blue-collar suspicion of the wealthy; here we see an ethnic twist on the same idea.

5. For a far more complete discussion of anti-Asian legislation and public opinion, see Ellis Cose, *A Nation of Strangers* (New York: William Morrow, 1992).

6. I say new form of nativism only because it is normally found among lower class populations locked in direct economic competition in the labor market. Competition for resources is clearly central to the nativist response of Pleasanton residents to their Asian neighbors, but it is less the result of labor-market conflict and more a matter of intergenerational mobility and international economic decline.

7. In their classic work *The American Occupational Structure* (New York: Free Press, 1977), Peter M. Blau and Otis Dudley Duncan stress that an individual's occupational position is the single best indicator of class.

8. Because this research was based upon the composition of Pleasanton in 1970 and 1980, very few Asian families fell into the interview sample. In those years, there were few nonwhite families in Pleasanton. Were this study to be replicated today, the composition of the sample would be very different.

9. "The Tonight Show," NBC television, December 3, 1990.

10. Ralph's point is amplified in more scholarly studies of tax burdens, some of which show that increasingly taxes are being paid (1) by individuals and less by corporations, particularly those that can take advantage of generous write-off provisions and (2) more by middle- and low-income workers and less by the wealthiest individuals. See

Donald Barlett and James Steele, *America: What Went Wrong?* (Kansas City: Andrews and McMeel, 1992), pp. 47–48.

11. While suburbs began as bedroom communities, newer suburbs have become the focus of manufacturing industries and other economic activities. Suburbs like these, with good commercial sales and high property values, suffer less fiscal strain. Mark Baldassare, *Trouble in Paradise: The Suburban Transformation in America* (New York: Columbia University Press, 1986).

12. For a discussion of these policy initiatives, see Lawrence M. Mead and Laurence E. Lynn, "Should Workfare Be Mandatory? What Research Says," *Journal of Policy Analysis and Management* 9 (Summer 1990): 400–404.

13. Aid to Families with Dependent Children accounted for 0.9 percent of the federal budget in 1991, while food stamps cost the federal purse another 1.5 percent. The states spent 2.2 percent of the revenues on AFDC in the same year. Center on Budget and Policy Priorities quoted in "Politics of Welfare: Focusing on the Problems," *New York Times,* July 5, 1992, pp. 1, 13.

14. See John Kenneth Galbraith, *The Culture of Contentment* (Boston: Houghton Mifflin, 1992); and William Julius Wilson, *The Truly Disadvantaged: The Inner City, the Underclass, and Public Policy* (Chicago: University of Chicago Press, 1987).

15. On this last point, see Jonathan Kozol's indictment of school spending patterns, *Savage Inequalities: Children in America's Schools* (New York: Crown Publishers, 1991).

16. This is essentially the point made by conservatives like Charles Murray, *Losing Ground: American Social Policy, 1950–1980* (New York: Basic Books, 1984); and Laurence Mead, *The New Politics of Poverty: The Nonworking Poor in America* (New York: Basic Books, 1992).

17. Studs Terkel, the well-known oral historian of American culture, provides a longer and more detailed look at the racial divide that separates blacks and whites in the United States in his recent book *Race: How Blacks and Whites Think and Feel about the American Obsession* (New York: New Press, 1992).

18. George would probably react favorably to the kinds of proposals to end welfare issued by authors like Mickey Kaus, even though they involve increasing public sector employment. See Kaus, *The End of Equality* (New York: Basic Books, 1992).

19. In his book on welfare policy, conservative analyst Lawrence Mead argues that America's underclass is growing, not because there are too few jobs to go around, but because the poor are simply unwilling to work in jobs like those described in this quote. Mead gives academic voice to the sentiments of many in the affluent suburbs who are suspicious of the nonworking poor. See Lawrence Mead, *The New Politics of Poverty*.

20. Jonathan Rieder made a similar point in his book *Canarsie: Jews and Italians against Liberalism*. Rieder is speaking of white urban dwellers who moved out of the Lower East Side of New York for less dense communities in Brooklyn, only to discover that minorities were interested in the same area. He explains the resistance of whites to desegregation by saying that they could not flee any farther and were worried that the social problems they left behind in the city would follow them to the community in which they had invested their life savings. The people in Pleasanton are not as lacking in options as Rieder's Canarsians may be. But they share with the working class of Canarsie a sense of being stuck in the political arena with no one to represent their views.

21. Claude Lévi-Strauss, *Structural Anthropology* (1958; New York: Basic Books, 1963). As Lévi-Strauss has shown, however, there are other ways to reduce the dissonance of contradiction. He has raised the examination of oppositional ideas to a high art in his work on mythology.

FOR JOURNALING AND DISCUSSION

1. Consider the use of quotations in this article. Who gets quoted? Who is left out? Why is not a single Asian quoted? What is the effect of this bias?
2. Imagine that you are one of these new immigrants. Write a letter home describing your new country.
3. This article focuses on wealthy immigrants, and most media attention is directed at poor and illegal immigrants. Why do we hear so little about other groups?
4. "Asian children are not allowed to be kids; their parents push them to be intellectual robots grabbing up honors at every turn." Why do many Americans hold this stereotype of Asian children? Why is it important for Americans to believe that Asian children are somehow damaged by their upbringings?
5. Newman describes a middle class that feels "sandwiched in between illegitimate elites and parasitic underclasses . . . ." Link this to Michael Lind's views in "To Have and Have Not" in this chapter about the ways in which our social class structure is maintained. How does this focus on immigrants and the poor keep attention away from those at the very top?

FOR RESEARCH AND EXPLORATION

1. Recently many parts of the country have tried to pass "English only" laws. Do some research into this controversy, and write an essay in which you take a stand and defend one side of the issue.
2. What is the stereotype of the "typical" Asian? Find examples of this stereotype in the media—newspapers, television, film, etc. How do they affect Asian Americans? What is the negative side to being known as the "model minority"?
3. Newman quotes a man who complains that the new immigrants are not learning English. "The Orientals move in and right away they put up their own signs. I can't read those signs . . . . I should be able to read a sign in this country . . . ." Write an essay comparing this perspective with Chang-rae Lee's views in "Mute in an English-Only World" in Chapter 9.

Speak, That I May See Thee

Paul Fussell

For over thirty years Fussell worked as an English professor at Rutgers University and the University of Pennsylvania. He wrote several academic books on poetry, rhetoric, and eighteenth-century England. In 1975, how-

ever, Fussell turned to writing mainstream nonfiction. His account of the aftereffects of World War I, The Great War and Modern Memory, *won a National Book Award and the National Book Critics Circle Award. Since then he has produced several other books dealing with subjects ranging from travel writing to social class and ethics.*

Regardless of the money you've inherited, the danger of your job, the place you live, the way you look, the shape and surface of your driveway, the items on your front porch and in your living room, the sweetness of your drinks, the time you eat dinner, the stuff you buy from mail-order catalogs, the place you went to school and your reverence for it, and the materials you read, your social class is still most clearly visible when you say things. "One's speech is an unceasingly repeated public announcement about background and social standing," says John Brooks, translating into modern American Ben Jonson's observation "Language most shows a man. Speak, that I may see thee." And what held true in his seventeenth century holds even truer in our twentieth, because we now have something virtually unknown to Jonson, a sizable middle class desperate not to offend through language and thus addicted to such conspicuous class giveaways as euphemism, genteelism, and mock profanity ("Golly!").

But at the outset it's well to recognize the difficulty of talking accurately about the class significance of language. It's easy to get it wrong when talking about classes, or traditions, not one's own, the way the Englishman H. B. Brooks-Baker recently got American class usage quite wrong when he offered an "American Section" of upper- and lower-class terms in Richard Buckle's *U and Non-U Revisited* (1978). Mastery of this field takes years, and it's admittedly hard to hear accurately across the Atlantic. Still, Brooks-Baker's list of twenty-six expressions said to be avoided by upper Americans errs dramatically. For example, he tells us that *affair* is a non-upper word for *party.* But any American of any of the classes knows that the two are different things entirely, not different names for the same thing. An *affair* is a laid-on commercial catering event like a bad banquet or reception. Unlike a *party,* you don't go to an *affair* (unless it's a love affair) expecting to have a wildly good time. Again, Brooks-Baker informs the reader that *folding-stuff* is prole for *money.* No, it's simply archaic slang, as much heard today as *mazuma* or *greenbacks.* Brooks-Baker also says that in the U.S.A. proles say *tux,* uppers *tuxedo.* Wrong again. Proles say *tux,* middles *tuxedo,* but both are considered low by uppers, who say *dinner jacket* or (higher) *black tie.* But even getting our hero decently home from his *tuxedo affair* (i.e., *black-tie party*), Brooks-Baker slips up. Proles say *limo,* he asserts, uppers *limousine.* Wrong on both counts. Proles say *big black shiny Cad* (sometimes *Caddy*). Middles say *limousine,* and the thing would be called a *limo* only behind the scenes by those who supply rented ones for funerals, bar mitzvahs, and the like. What, then, is this vehicle called by the upper orders? It's called a *car,* as in "We'll need the car about eleven, please, Parker."

Brooks-Baker's slips are useful reminders of the hazards of interpreting language class signals aright. Alexis de Tocqueville's errors in prophecy also provide a handy warning against overconfidence there. De Tocqueville overestimated the leveling force on language of "democracy," and imagined that this new kind of political organization would largely efface social distinctions in language and verbal style. Looking about him at mid-nineteenth-century America, he thought he heard everyone using the same words, and conceived that the line was ceasing to be drawn "between . . . expressions which seem by their very nature vulgar and others which appear to be refined." He concluded that "there is as much confusion in language as there is in society." But developments on this continent have proved him wrong about both language and democratic society. Actually, just *because* the country's a democracy, class distinctions have developed with greater rigor than elsewhere, and language, far from coalescing into one great central mass without social distinctions, has developed even more egregious class signals than anyone could have expected. There's really no confusion in either language or society, as ordinary people here are quite aware. Interviewed by sociologists, they indicate that speech is the main way they estimate a stranger's social class when they first encounter him. "Really," says one deponent, "the first time a person opens his mouth, you can tell."

Because the class system here is more complicated than in England, less amenable to merely binary categorization, language indicators are more numerous and subtle than merely those accepted as "U" (i.e., upper) or stigmatized as "non-U" by Nancy Mitford in her delightful 1955 essay in *Encounter*, "The English Aristocracy." Still, a way to begin considering the class meaning of language in the U.S.A. is to note some absolute class dividers. Probably the most important, a usage firmly dividing the prole classes from the middles and highers, is the double negative, as in "I can't get no satisfaction." You're as unlikely to hear something like that in a boardroom or premises frequented by "house-guests," or on a sixty-five-foot schooner off Nantucket, as you are likely to hear it in a barracks, an auto-repair shop, or a workmen's bar. Next in importance would rank special ways of managing grammatical number, as in "He don't" and "I wants it." And these are not just "slips" or "errors." They signal virtually a different dialect, identifying speakers socially distinct from users of the other English. The two can respect each other, but they can never be pals. They belong to different classes, and if they attempt to mix, they will inevitably regard each other as quaint and not quite human.

If it's grammar that draws the line between middles and below, it's largely pronunciation and vocabulary that draw it between middles and above. Everyone will have his personal collection of class indicators here, but I have found the following quite trustworthy. Words employed to register (or advertise) "cultural experience" are especially dangerous for the middle class, even *crêpes,* which they pronounce *craypes.* The same with most words deployed to display one's familiarity with the foreign, like *fiancé,* which the middle class prefers to *boyfriend* and delivers with a ridiculous heavy stress on the final syllable: *fee-on-say'*. The same with *show-fur'*, a word it prefers to the upper-class *driver*. Some may think pronouncing the *h* in *Amherst* an excessively finicking indicator of middle-classhood, but others may not. The word *diamond,* pronounced as two syllables by uppers, is likely to be rendered as three by the middle class. Similarly with *beautiful*—three syllables to uppers, but, to middles, *bee-you'-tee-full*. The "grand" words *exquisite, despicable, hospitable, lamentable* invite the middle class to stress the second syllable; those anxious to leave no doubt of their social desirability stress the first, which is also to earn some slight, passing Anglophilic credit. As the middle class gets itself more deeply entangled in artistic experience, hazards multiply, like *patina*, a word it likes a lot but doesn't realize is stressed on the first syllable. High-class names from cultural history pose a similar danger, especially if they are British, like Henry Purcell. President Reagan's adviser Edwin Meese III clearly signaled his class when, interviewed on television, he chose to exhibit his gentility by using the word *salutary* instead of the common *wholesome* or *healthy,* but indicated by his pronunciation that he thought the word *salutory.* That's the pure middle-class act: opt for the showy, and in so doing take a pratfall. Class unfortunates who want to emphasize the largeness of something are frequently betrayed by *enormity,* as in "The whale was of such an enormity that they could hardly get it in the tank." (Prole version: "The whale was so big they couldn't hardly get it in the tank.") Elegance is the fatal temptation for the middle class, dividing it from the blunter usages of uppers and proles alike. Neither of these classes would warn against two people's simultaneously pursuing the same project by speaking of "duplicity of effort." The middle class is where you hear *prestigious* a lot, and to speculate about the reason it's replaced *distinguished* or *noted* or *respected* in the past twenty years is to do a bit of national soul-searching. The implications of *prestige,* C. Wright Mills observes, are really pejorative: "In its origins," he says, "it means dazzling the eye with conjuring tricks." And he goes on: "In France, 'prestige' carries an emotional association of fraudulence, of the art of illusion, or at least of something adventitious." The same in Italy and Germany. Only in the U.S.A. does the word carry any prestige, and looking back, I see that I've depended on *prestige* quite a lot when talking about high-class colleges.

Some of these class dividers are crude. Others are subtle. The upper and upper-middle classes have a special vocabulary for indicating wearisome or unhappy social situations. They say *tiresome* or *tedious* where their social inferiors would say *boring;* they say *upset* or *distressed* or even *cross* where others would say *angry* or *mad* or *sore.* There's a special upper-class diction of approval too. No prole man would call something *super* (Anglophilic) or *outstanding* (prep school), just as it would sound like flagrant affectation for a prole woman to designate something seen in a store as *divine* or *darling* or *adorable. Nice* would be the non-upper way of putting it.

But it's the middle-class quest for grandeur and gentility that produces the most interesting effects. As we've seen, imported words especially are its downfall. It will speak of *a graffiti* and it thinks *chauvinism* has something to do with gender aggression. Pseudo-classical plurals are a constant pitfall: the middles will speak learnedly of *a phenomena* and *a criteria* and *a strata* and (referring perhaps to a newspaper) *a media*. A well-known author is *a literati*. It thinks *context* a grander form of the word *content*, and thus says things like "I didn't like the context of that book; all that blood and gore." Or consider the Coast Guard officer reporting a grievous oil spill in San Francisco Bay; *cross* is too vulgar a term for the occasion, he imagines, and so he says that "several ships transited the area." When after a succession of solecisms of this kind a middle-class person will begin to suspect that he is blowing his cover, he may try to reestablish status by appliquéing a mock-classical plural ending onto a perfectly ordinary word like *process*. Then he will say *process-sees*. The whole middle-class performance nicely illustrates the conclusion of Lord Melbourne. "The higher and lower classes, there's some good in them," he observed, "but the middle classes are all affectation and conceit and pretense and concealment."

All classes except sometimes upper-middle are implicated in the scandal of saying *home* when they mean *house*. But the middle class seems to take a special pleasure in saying things like "They live in a lovely five-hundred-thousand-dollar home," or, after an earthquake, "The man noticed that his home was shaking violently." We can trace, I think, the stages by which *house* disappeared as a word favored by the middle class. First, *home* was offered by the real-estate business as a way of warming the product, that is, making the prospect imagine that in laying out money for a house he was purchasing not a passel of bricks, Formica, and wallboard but snuggly warmth, comfort, and love. The word *home* was then fervently embraced by the customers for several reasons: (1) the middle class loves to use words which have achieved cliché status in advertising; (2) the middle class, like the real-estate con men, also enjoys the comforting fantasy that you can purchase love, comfort, warmth, etc., with cold cash, or at least achieve them by some formula or other; (3) the middle class, by nature both puritanical and terrified of public opinion, welcomed *home* because, to its dirty mind, *house* carried bad associations. One spoke of a *rest home*, but of a *bawdy, whore-fancy,* or *sporting house*. No one ever heard of a *home of ill fame,* or, for that matter, a *cat home*. So out went *house* for the same reason that *madam* has never really caught on in middle-class America. But curiously, users of *home* to describe domestic shelters make one exception. A *beach house* is so called, never a *beach home*. Because of the word's associations with current real-estate scams, a *home,* or something appropriately so designated, does tend to suggest something pretty specific: namely, a small, pretentious, jerry-built developer's rip-off positioned in some unfortunate part of the country without history, depth, or allusiveness. You don't speak of a "two-hundred-year-old white clapboard frame farmhome" in Maine, New Hampshire, or Vermont. *Homes* are what the middle class lives in. As it grows progressively poorer, it sells its *homes* and moves into *mobile homes* (formerly, trailers) or *motor homes*.

Home is by no means the only advertising word embraced by the middle class. "Come into the living forum," you may hear as the corporate wife ushers you into the living room. Or "I think I left your coat in the reception galleria" (front hall). Or "Would you care to go directly up to your sleeping chamber?" And because of its need for the illusion of power and success that attend self-conscious consumerism, the middles instinctively adopt advertisers' *-wear* compounds, speaking with no embarrassment whatever of the family's

footwear
nightwear (or sleepwear)
leisurewear
stormwear
beachwear
swimwear
citywear
countrywear
campuswear
formal wear
eyewear (i.e., spectacles)
neckwear, etc.,

and they feel good uttering the analogous *-ware* compounds:

tableware
dinnerware
stemware
barware
flatware
kitchenware
glassware

or sometimes, when they get into their grand mood, *crystal.* (Uppers, whom the middles think they're imitating, say *glasses.*) Because it's a staple of advertising, the middle class also likes the word *designer,* which it takes to mean *beautiful* or *valuable.* Thus roll paper towels with expensive patterns printed on them cease to be stupid and ugly once they're designated *designer towels.* The Dacron bath towels of the middle class, the ones with the metallic threads, are also usually called *designer towels.*

Advertising diction feeds so smoothly into the middle-class psyche because of that class's bent toward rhetorical fake elegance. Aspiring to ascend, it imagines that verbal grandeur will forward the process. Thus *enormity, salutory, duplicity*—and of course *gourmet.* "The theater still has a certain *nicety* to it," says an actor in a TV interview. He means *delicacy,* but he also means that he's middle-class and slavering to be upper. A fine example of middle-class bogus elegance is the language of a flyer circulated recently to advertise a new magazine aimed at a Northeastern suburb. The town was formerly a fairly classy venue, but it has inexorably been taken over . . . by people who respond enthusiastically to rhetoric like this:

The greater ——— area represents a way of life. It is a lifestyle. It is fine living . . . crystal for a special dinner . . . a gourmet restaurant . . . the joy of a well-written book . . . . It is life at its best . . . quiet elegance . . . creative . . . beauty and grace . . . . ——— *Magazine* will let you share in the dreams, talents, contributions and achievements of a community of people who stand apart from the crowd and set high standards for themselves . . . . ——— *Magazine* is for intelligent, sensitive men, women and children. ——— *Magazine* is you!

One could search widely without locating a more exemplary fusion of insecurity and snobbery, the one propping up the other to produce that delicate equilibrium which sustains the middle class.

Cornball-elegant also is the rhetoric of the airlines and of airports, whose clients are 90 percent middle-class. If one couldn't infer the hopeless middle-classness of airports from their special understanding of the ideas of *comfort, convenience,* and *lug-zhury,* one could from their pretentious language, especially the way they leap to designate themselves "International" or even, like Houston, "Intercontinental." They will do this on the slightest pretext, like having a plane take off now and then for Acapulco or Alberta, while remaining utterly uncontaminated by any sign of internationalism, like dealing in foreign currencies or speaking languages or sympathizing in any way with international styles.

On the aircraft itself, virtually everything said or written accords with the middle-class insistence that words shall be bogus, from such formulations as "motion discomfort" and "flotation device" to "beverages" and "non-dairy creamer." On a recent flight from New York to London, a steward announced, "Smoking is not permitted while you are making usage of the lavatory facilities"—a perfect example, almost a definition, of the middle-class pseudo-elegant style. The little menu cards given out by transatlantic airlines, ostensibly to indicate the components of the meal but actually to tout the duty-free goods (including "designer" neckties and scarves), constitute a veritable exhibition palace of the fake elegant. One I've encountered on a TWA flight does forget itself and slip once, calling beverages *drinks* in a thoroughly upper-class way, but generally it holds the line, especially in describing the meals offered (I have added italics): "FILET TIPS DIJONNAISE. Tidbits of Beef Tenderloin in a *Mild* Creamy Mustard Sauce *Presented with* Pommes Chateau and Petit Pois." Another meal is said to be "*Complemented by* Buttered Broccoli." And then, to cap it all: "Please accept our apologies if *due to previous passenger selections,* your *entree preference* is not available." Or, as a civilized person would put it, "Not all items available," the corollary of "No smoking in the toilets."

But *toilets* does not recommend itself to middle-class speakers, who prefer *lavatories* or *rest rooms,* euphemism as well as elegance being their hallmarks. One of their treasured possessions is a whole vocabulary of euphemized profanity and obscenity, so that when you hear "Holy Cow!" or "Holy Moses!" or hear that someone has done "a whale of a job," you know that a member of the middle class is nearby. It's hard to believe that after the numerous strains and scandals of the mid-twentieth century any relics survive of that class that used to say "O pshaw!" or "Botheration!" when it meant not just "O hell!" but "Shit!"—but we find the American Brigadier General Dozier, back home after weeks of bondage and humiliation at the hands of the most cruel and vicious Italian kidnappers, saying, "It's doggone good to be home." It's the middle class that insists still that *pregnant* be replaced by *expecting* or *starting a family (being in a family way,* on the other hand, is prole), and it has virtually legislated that all the rest of us *make love* instead of what we used to do. But in the face of all this the uppers stand firm. Jilly Cooper reports, "I once heard my son regaling his friends: 'Mummy says *pardon* is a much worse word than *fuck.*' " And of course the middle is where you hear false teeth called *dentures,* the rich called the *wealthy,* and dying called passing away (or *over*). (Proles are likely to be *taken to Jesus.*) Drunks are *people with alcohol problems,* the stupid are *slow learners* or *underachievers,* madness is *mental illness,* drug use is *drug abuse,* the crippled are *the handicapped* (sometimes, by a euphemism of a euphemism, *the challenged*), a slum is *the inner city,* and a graveyard is a *cemetery* or (among those more susceptible to advertising) *memorial park* . . . .

The middles cleave to euphemisms not just because they're an aid in avoiding facts. They like them also because they assist their social yearnings toward pomposity. This is possible because most euphemisms permit the speaker to multiply syllables, and the middle class confuses sheer numerousness with weight and value . . . .

So terrified of being judged socially insignificant is your typical member of the middle class, so ambitious of earning a reputation as a judicious thinker, indeed, almost an "executive," that it's virtually impossible for him to resist the temptation constantly to multiply syllables. He thus euphemizes willy-nilly. Indeed, it's sometimes hard to know whether the impulse to euphemize is causing the syllables to multiply, or whether the urge toward verbal weight and grandeur through multiplication is hustling the speaker into euphemism. The question confronts us when, inquiring what someone does, he answers not that he's a junk man, or even in the junk business, but in the scrap-iron business, or even the recycling business or reclamation industry. Occupational euphemisms always seem to entail multiplication of syllables. In many universities, what used to be the *bursar* is now the *disbursement officer,* just the way what used to be an *undertaker* (already sufficient as a euphemism, one would think) is now a *funeral director,* an advance of two whole syllables. (In raising *funeral director* to *grief therapist,* there's of course a loss of two syllables, but a compensating gain in "professionalism" and pseudo-medical pretentiousness.) *Selling* is raised to *retailing* or *marketing,* or even better, to *merchandising,* an act that exactly doubles its syllables, while *sales manager* in its turn is doubled by being raised to *Vice-President, Merchandising.* The person on the telephone who used to provide *Information* now gives (or more often, does not give) *Directory Assistance,* which is two syllables grander. Some sociologists surveying the status of occupations found that *druggist* ranked sixth out of fifteen.

But when a syllable was added and the designation changed to *pharmacist,* the occupation moved up to fourth place.

Syllable multiplication usually occurs also in the euphemisms by which the middle class softens hard facts or cheerfulizes actuality. It's all in aid of avoiding anything "depressing." But you can aim for the verbally splendid at the same time. Thus *correctional facility* for *prison, work stoppage* or *industrial action* for *strike, discomfort* for *pain, homicide* for *murder, self-deliverance* for *suicide, fatality* for *death. Slum clearance* (three syllables) becomes *urban renewal* (five). *Nuclear device* has it over *atom bomb* both by a lot of euphemism and by two full syllables. Being by nature unmagnanimous (cf. Ronald Reagan), the middle class has always hated to tip, regarding it as a swindle, etc., but when you call a *tip* a *gratuity,* you take a little of the sting out . . . .

The passive voice is a great help to the middle class in multiplying syllables. Thus the TV newsman will say "No injuries were reported" (eight syllables) when he means "No one was hurt" (four). Pseudo-Latinism is another useful technique. *In colleges* has a measly four syllables, but *in academia* has six, just as *in the suburbs* has four but *in suburbia* five, and in addition conveys the suggestion that the speaker is familiar with the classical tongues. (A real Latinist would honor the accusative case and say *in suburbiam,* but let that pass.) Another way of arriving at the goal of adding syllables is simply to mistake one word for another, as the airline steward did with *use* and *usage.* Thus the instructions on a bottle of Calgon Floral Bouquet (formerly *bath salts*) are headed, classily, *Usage Directions.* We can infer the middle-class (rather than prole) origins of most terrorist groups by their habit of leaving behind, after their outrages, *communiqués* rather than *notes,* or even *messages* . . . .

Before turning to a closer examination of the special idiom of the proles, we should note a few more middle-class signals. An excessive fondness for metaphors is one, things like grinding to a halt or running the gamut or boggling the mind, which are never recognized as clichés, and indeed, if they were so recognized, would be treasured all the more. Middle-class speakers are also abnormally fond of acronyms (Mothers United for Fiduciary Security: MUFFS), certainly as an exclusionary mechanism to keep the uninitiated and the impure (i.e., the proles) at a distance, but also as an inclusionary device, to solidify the in-group or corporate or team consciousness (cf. "officers' wives") without which the middle class flies all apart. Although the middles don't quite use such expressions as *milady* and *mine host,* advertisers understand that when such expressions are aimed at them, they will not gag. The middle class likewise thinks quite elegant the expression (corporate?) *over* drinks (or *over* coffee or *over* dinner) rather than *with* or *at:* "Let's discuss it over drinks." (It's the impulse toward metaphor again—fancier than the literal.) The classes not anxious about their own sophistication would more likely say, "Let's have a drink and talk about it." A similar impulse to splendor motivates the middle class to inscribe "Regrets Only" on their social invitations, where the more unpretending classes would say "No's Only," a way of implying less about the implicit desirability of the party. As middles grow worse educated, they tend to employ more pretentious, pseudo-scientific terms to dignify the ordinary or to suggest noble purpose in normal or commonplace behavior: the word *parenting* is an example. Saying *parenting* is virtually the equivalent of telling us on your bumper that you always brake for small animals.

When we hear speakers entirely careless of the former distinction between *less* and *fewer* ("Less white prisoners are in our penal institutions today . . .") or bothering to add the *is concerned* or *goes* to the phrase *as far as* ("as far as the Republican Party . . ."), we know we're approaching the idiomatic world identifiable as prole. Proles signal their identity partly by pronunciation, like the Texan on the Buckley show who said *pro-mis-kitty* and "I am a prole" at the same time. Proles drop the *g* on present participles, saying *it's a fuckin' shame*, as well as the *-ed* on past participles: thus *corned beef* becomes *corn beef* (or better, *corm beef*), and we hear also of *bottle beer, dark-skin people, old-fashion bake beans,* and *Mother's High-Power Beer.* "First come, first serve" is a favorite axiom. Roger Price, the student of Roobs or urban hicks, has located more prole pronunciations. He observes that "in Southern California even newscasters say 'wunnerful' and 'anna-bi-oddicks' and 'in-eress-ting.' The word 'interesting,' pronounced in this manner, with the accent on the third syllable, is the infallible mark of the Roob." Or, as we call it, the prole. To Price other signs of Roobhood are saying

fack	for	fact
fure	"	fewer
present	"	president
oney	"	only
finey	for	finally, and
innaleckshul	"	"nondemocratic"

To say *én-tire*, like the Rev. Rex Humbard, the TV evangelist, is to indicate that you're a high or mid-prole, but to say *merring-gew* when you mean the foamy egg-white stuff on top of pies is low.

Proles of all types have terrible trouble with the apostrophe, and its final disappearance from English, which seems imminent, will be a powerful indication that the proles have won. "Modern Cabinet's," announces a sign in the Middle West, comparable to its Eastern counterpart, "Rutger's Electrical Supply Company." Sometimes the apostrophe simply vanishes, as in *Ladies Toilet.* But then, as if the little mark were, somehow, missed, it, or something like it, is invoked anomalously as if its function were like underlining:

Your Driver: 'Tom Bedricki'
'Today's Specials'
'Tipping Permitted'

Proles like to use words that normally appear only in newspapers. They don't realize that no one *calls* the Pope *the pontiff* except in pretentious journalese, or a senator *a lawmaker,* or the United States *the nation,* or a scholar an *educator.* This last is not objected to by high-school teachers and administrators, who rather embrace it as an elevating professional euphemism. Thus it's purely for social-class reasons that university professors object to being denominated *educators,* because the term fails to distinguish them from high-school superintendents, illiterate young teachers with temporary "credentials," and similar pedagogic riffraff. The next time you meet a distinguished university professor, especially one who fancies himself well known nationally for his ideas and writings, tell him it's an honor to meet such a famous educator, and watch: first he will look down for a while, then up, but not at you, then away. And very soon he will detach himself from your company. He will be smiling all the time, but inside he will be in torment.

Prole fondness for newspaper words tempts them into some extravagant malapropisms. A writer in the London *Sunday Times* not long ago testified to hearing that attempts were being made to *pervert* a strike, and that somewhere a priest had been called in to *circumcise* a ghost:

> Readers notify me of the lady with a painful "Ulster" in her mouth; the shrines you can see in Catholic countries in commemoration of "St. Mary Mandolin"; the police at the scene of a crime, who threw "an accordion" round the street; the touching sight of the deceased George V lying in state on a "catapult" . . . the student who was always to be found "embossed" in a book; the pilot who left his aircraft by means of the "ejaculation seat"; . . . the drowning swimmer who was revived by means of "artifical insemination"; and the rainbow which was said by an onlooker to contain "all the colors of the rectum". . . .

If unexpected silence is one sign of the upper classes (necessary, for example, as Nancy Mitford notes, after someone has said, on departing, "It was so nice seeing you"), noise and vociferation identify the proles, who shout "Wahoo!" at triumphant moments in games (largely hockey and pro football) they attend. Speaking to Studs Terkel, a Chicago policeman (high-prole, probably) indicates his awareness of one important distinction between his class and those below. "If my mother and father argued," he reports, "my mother went around shutting down the windows because they didn't want the neighbors to hear 'em. But they [i.e., the lower sort of proles] deliberately open the doors and open the windows, screaming and hollering . . . ." The prole must register his existence and his presence in public. Thus the conversations designed to be overheard (and admired) in public conveyances, and the prole way of humming tunes audibly, as if hoping to be complimented on pitch, tempo, or attack. The middle class, fearing ridicule or social failure, doesn't do these things: it leaves them to proles, who are not going anywhere. Noise is a form of overstatement, and one reason the upper orders still regard selling anything as rather vulgar is that the art of moving merchandise is so dependent on overstatement. Thus minimal utterance is high-class, while proles say everything two or three times. "Ummmmm" is a frequently heard complete sentence among the uppers.

By what other language signs are proles to be known? By their innocence of the objective case, for one thing. Recalling vaguely that it is polite to mention oneself last, as in "He and I were there," proles apply this principle uniformly and come up with "Between he and I".... Another prole signal is difficulty with the complex sentence, resulting in structures displaying elaborate pseudo-"correct" participles like "Being that it was a cold day, the furnace was on." Because the gerund is beyond their reach, they are forced to multiply words (always a pleasure, really) and say, "The people in front of him at the show got mad due to the fact that he talked so much" instead of "His talking at the show annoyed the people in front." (*People*, however, is not quite right: *individuals* is more likely.) Just as the prole dimly recalls a problem with *like*, he also remembers something about *lying* and *laying*. But what? Because he can't recall, he simplifies his problem and uses *laying* for everything. People thus *lay* on the beach, the bed, the grass, and the sidewalk, without necessarily any suggestion that they're engaged in sexual performances. And there's a final prole stigma. Proles adore being called "*Mr.* [First Name] Prole." Thus proles who have made it to celebrated stations in life are customarily addressed or referred to in public by that title, no matter how inappropriate it may seem to the sophisticated. Thus we hear of "Mr. Frank Sinatra" and "Mr. Howard Cosell." And on the radio: "Ladies and Gentlemen, [portentous pause], Mr. Frank Perdue."

If each class has one word it responds to uniquely, the upper class probably likes *secure* or *liquid* best. The word of the upper-middle class is *right*, as in doing the right thing: "I do want everything right for Muffy's wedding." The middle class likes *right* too, but the word that really excites the middles is *luxury* ("Those beautiful luxury one-room apartments"). *Spotless* (floors, linens, bowels, etc.) is also a middle-class favorite. High proles are suckers for *easy*— easy terms, six easy lessons. And the word of the classes below is *free:* "We never go to anything that's not free," as the low-prole housewife said.

A very little attention to the different idioms of the classes should persuade the most sentimental not only that there is a tight system of social class in this country but that linguistic class lines are crossed only rarely and with great difficulty. A virtually bottomless social gulf opens between those who say "Have a nice day" and those who say, on the other hand, "Goodbye," those who when introduced say "Pleased to meet you" and those who say "How do you do?" There may be some passing intimacy between those who think *momentarily* means *in a moment* (airline captain over loudspeaker: "We'll be taking off momentarily, folks") and those who know it means *for a moment*, but it won't survive much strain. It's like the tenuous relation between people who conceive that *type* is an adjective ("She's a very classy type person") and people who know it's only a noun or verb. The sad thing is that by the time one's an adult, these stigmata are virtually unalterable and ineffaceable. We're pretty well stuck for life in the class we're raised in. Even adopting all the suggestions implied in this chapter, embracing all the high-class locutions and abjuring the low ones, won't help much.

FOR JOURNALING AND DISCUSSION

1. Fussell makes almost no reference to the use of slang in determining class distinctions. Why? What current slang terms are associated with different social classes?
2. Just as upper-class terms are appropriated by the middle class, some lower-class ones are also—especially by teenagers. Why? What does this appropriation suggest about language, class, and rebellion?
3. To what extent does one's accent also mark one's social class?
4. Language is continually changing and shifting. This article was written in 1983. What terms that Fussell mentions are no longer used the way he uses them? Why do you think that these changes have occurred?
5. How does the whole "politically correct" language movement fit into Fussell's theories about language and class?

FOR RESEARCH AND EXPLORATION

1. Much has been written about the importance of the use of "proper, standard" English. Those who do not speak it are generally relegated to the ranks of the lower class. Fussell only briefly discusses the connections between class and "standard" or "proper" grammatical English. Research this issue, and write an essay explaining how grammar is used to regulate social class.
2. Find three automobile advertisements that you feel are clearly aimed at different social classes. Contrast and analyze the language used in each of these ads. How does this fit with Fussell's views about the different classes?
3. In "Confessions of a Wannabe Negro" in Chapter 2, Reginald McKnight describes being told as a child by other blacks that he "sounded white." He frequently was criticized for not being black enough because he didn't "sound black." How does this connect to Fussell's views about language as a social class marker? Why does Fussell spend so little time dealing with the compounding factor of race?

The Stolen Party

Liliana Heker

Heker is an Argentine journalist, editor, and writer. Her first book of short stories, Those Who Beheld the Burning Bush, *was published while she was in her teens. Her novel,* Zona de Clivage, *was published in 1988.*

Rich people = Monkeys?

As soon as she arrived she went straight to the kitchen to see if the monkey was there. It was: what a relief! She wouldn't have liked to admit that her mother had been right. *Monkeys at a birthday?* her mother had sneered. *Get away with you, believing any nonsense you're told!* She was cross, but not because of the monkey, the girl thought; it's just because of the party.

"I don't like you going," she told her. "It's a rich people's party."

"Rich people go to Heaven too," said the girl, who studied religion at school. *Lower class slang*

"Get away with Heaven," said the mother. "The problem with you, young lady, is that you like to fart higher than your ass."

The girl didn't approve of the way her mother spoke. She was barely nine, and one of the best in her class.

"I'm going because I've been invited," she said. "And I've been invited because Luciana is my friend. So there."

"Ah yes, your friend," her mother grumbled. She paused. "Listen, Rosaura," she said at last. "That one's not your friend. You know what you are to them? The maid's daughter, that's what."

Rosaura blinked hard: she wasn't going to cry. Then she yelled: "Shut up! You know nothing about being friends!"

Every afternoon she used to go to Luciana's house and they would both finish their homework while Rosaura's mother did the cleaning. They had their tea in the kitchen and they told each other secrets. Rosaura loved everything in the big house, and she also loved the people who lived there.

"I'm going because it will be the most lovely party in the whole world, Luciana told me it would. There will be a magician, and he will bring a monkey and everything."

The mother swung around to take a good look at her child, and pompously put her hands on her hips.

"Monkeys at a birthday?" she said. "Get away with you, believing any nonsense you're told!"

Rosaura was deeply offended. She thought it unfair of her mother to accuse other people of being liars simply because they were rich. Rosaura too wanted to be rich, of course. If one day she managed to live in a beautiful palace, would her mother stop loving her? She felt very sad. She wanted to go to that party more than anything else in the world.

"I'll die if I don't go," she whispered, almost without moving her lips.

And she wasn't sure whether she had been heard, but on the morning of the party she discovered that her mother had starched her Christmas dress. And in the afternoon, after washing her hair, her mother rinsed it in apple vinegar so that it would be all nice and shiny. Before going out, Rosaura admired herself in the mirror, with her white dress and glossy hair, and thought she looked terribly pretty.

Señora Ines also seemed to notice. As soon as she saw her, she said:

"How lovely you look today, Rosaura."

" Class Relations"

Rosaura gave her starched skirt a slight toss with her hands and walked into the party with a firm step. She said hello to Luciana and asked about the monkey. Luciana put on a secretive look and whispered into Rosaura's ear: "He's in the kitchen. But don't tell anyone, because it's a surprise."

Rosaura wanted to make sure. Carefully she entered the kitchen and there she saw it: deep in thought, inside its cage. It looked so funny that the girl stood there for a while, watching it, and later, every so often, she would slip out of the party unseen and go and admire it. Rosaura was the only one allowed into the kitchen. Señora Ines had said: "You yes, but not the others, they're much too boisterous, they might break something." Rosaura had never broken anything. She even managed the jug of orange juice, carrying it from the kitchen into the dining-room. She held it carefully and didn't spill a single drop. And Señora Ines had said: "Are you sure you can manage a jug as big as that?" Of course she could manage. She wasn't a butterfingers, like the others. Like that blonde girl with the bow in her hair. As soon as she saw Rosaura, the girl with the bow had said:

"And you? Who are you?"

"I'm a friend of Luciana," said Rosaura.

"No," said the girl with the bow, "you are not a friend of Luciana because I'm her cousin and I know all her friends. And I don't know you."

"So what," said Rosaura. "I come here every afternoon with my mother and we do our homework together."

"You and your mother do your homework together?" asked the girl, laughing.

"I and Luciana do our homework together," said Rosaura, very seriously.

The girl with the bow shrugged her shoulders.

"That's not being friends," she said. "Do you go to school together?"

"No."

"So where do you know her from?" said the girl, getting impatient.

Rosaura remembered her mother's words perfectly. She took a deep breath.

"I'm the daughter of the employee," she said.

Her mother had said very clearly: "If someone asks, you say you're the daughter of the employee; that's all." She also told her to add: "And proud of it." But Rosaura thought that never in her life would she dare say something of the sort.

"What employee?" said the girl with the bow. "Employee in a shop?"

"No," said Rosaura angrily. "My mother doesn't sell anything in any shop, so there."

"So how come she's an employee?" said the girl with the bow.

Just then Señora Ines arrived saying *shh shh,* and asked Rosaura if she wouldn't mind helping serve out the hot-dogs, as she knew the house so much better than the others.

"See?" said Rosaura to the girl with the bow, and when no one was looking she kicked her in the shin.

Apart from the girl with the bow, all the others were delightful. The one she liked best was Luciana, with her golden birthday crown; and then the boys. Rosaura won the sack race, and nobody managed to catch her when they played tag. When they split into two teams to play charades, all the boys wanted her for their side. Rosaura felt she had never been so happy in all her life.

But the best was still to come. The best came after Luciana blew out the candles. First the cake. Señora Ines had asked her to help pass the cake around, and Rosaura had enjoyed the task immensely, because everyone called out to her, shouting "Me, me!" Rosaura remembered a story in which there was a queen who had the power of life or death over her subjects. She had always loved that, having the power of life or death. To Luciana and the boys she gave the largest pieces, and to the girl with the bow she gave a slice so thin one could see through it.

After the cake came the magician, tall and bony, with a fine red cape. A true magician: he could untie handkerchiefs by blowing on them and make a chain with links that had no openings. He could guess what cards were pulled out from a pack, and the monkey was his assistant. He called the monkey "partner." "Let's see here, partner," he would say, "Turn over a card." And, "Don't run away, partner: time to work now."

The final trick was wonderful. One of the children had to hold the monkey in his arms and the magician said he would make him disappear.

"What, the boy?" they all shouted.

"No, the monkey!" shouted back the magician.

Rosaura thought that this was truly the most amusing party in the whole world.

The magician asked a small fat boy to come and help, but the small fat boy got frightened almost at once and dropped the monkey on the floor. The magician picked him up carefully, whispered something in his ear, and the monkey nodded almost as if he understood.

"You mustn't be so unmanly, my friend," the magician said to the fat boy.

"What's unmanly?" said the fat boy.

The magician turned around as if to look for spies.

"A sissy," said the magician. "Go sit down."

Then he stared at all the faces, one by one. Rosaura felt her heart tremble.

"You, with the Spanish eyes," said the magician. And everyone saw that he was pointing at her.

She wasn't afraid. Neither holding the monkey, nor when the magician made him vanish; not even when, at the end, the magician flung his red cape over Rosaura's head and uttered a few magic words . . . and the monkey reappeared, chattering happily, in her arms. The children clapped furiously. And before Rosaura returned to her seat, the magician said:

"Thank you very much, my little countess."

She was so pleased with the compliment that a while later, when her mother came to fetch her, that was the first thing she told her.

"I helped the magician and he said to me, 'Thank you very much, my little countess.' "

It was strange because up to then Rosaura had thought that she was angry with her mother. All along Rosaura had imagined that she would say to her: "See that the monkey wasn't a lie?" But instead she was so thrilled that she told her mother all about the wonderful magician.

Her mother tapped her on the head and said: "So now we're a countess!"

But one could see that she was beaming.

And now they both stood in the entrance, because a moment ago Señora Ines, smiling, had said: "Please wait here a second."

Her mother suddenly seemed worried.

"What is it?" she asked Rosaura.

"What is what?" said Rosaura. "It's nothing; she just wants to get the presents for those who are leaving, see?"

She pointed at the fat boy and at a girl with pigtails who were also waiting there, next to their mothers. And she explained about the presents. She knew, because she had been watching those who left before her. When one of the girls was about to leave, Señora Ines would give her a bracelet. When a boy left, Señora Ines gave him a yo-yo. Rosaura preferred the yo-yo because it sparkled, but she didn't mention that to her mother. Her mother might have said: "So why don't you ask for one, you blockhead?" That's what her mother was like. Rosaura didn't feel like explaining that she'd be horribly ashamed to be the odd one out. Instead she said:

"I was the best-behaved at the party."

And she said no more because Señora Ines came out into the hall with two bags, one pink and one blue.

First she went up to the fat boy, gave him a yo-yo out of the blue bag, and the fat boy left with his mother. Then she went up to the girl and gave her a bracelet out of the pink bag, and the girl with the pigtails left as well.

Finally she came up to Rosaura and her mother. She had a big smile on her face and Rosaura liked that. Señora Ines looked down at her, then looked up at her mother, and then said something that made Rosaura proud:

"What a marvellous daughter you have, Herminia."

For an instant, Rosaura thought that she'd give her two presents: the bracelet and the yo-yo. Señora Ines bent down as if about to look for something. Rosaura also leaned forward, stretching out her arm. But she never completed the movement.

Señora Ines didn't look in the pink bag. Nor did she look in the blue bag. Instead she rummaged in her purse. In her hand appeared two bills.

"You really and truly earned this," she said handing them over. "Thank you for all your help, my pet."

Rosaura felt her arms stiffen, stick close to her body, and then she noticed her mother's hand on her shoulder. Instinctively she pressed herself against her mother's body. That was all. Except her eyes. Rosaura's eyes had a cold, clear look that fixed itself on Señora Ines's face.

Señora Ines, motionless, stood there with her hand outstretched. As if

Her childhood is stripped away

Innocence → Experience

she didn't dare draw it back. As if the slightest change might shatter an infinitely delicate balance.

FOR JOURNALING AND DISCUSSION

1. Does Señora Ines intentionally hurt Rosaura as a way of keeping her in her place, or is she completely unaware of how deeply she has injured her?
2. Why does Rosaura's mother instruct her to say that she is the "daughter of the employee" if anyone asks who she is?
3. How do we know that Rosaura is just as class conscious as her mother, even though she claims that class boundaries are not important?
4. Have you ever been in a situation in which you felt "out of your class"? Describe the experience. How did you feel and react?

FOR RESEARCH AND EXPLORATION

1. Using the first person, rewrite this story from another character's point of view—Señora Ines, Luciana, or Rosaura's mother.
2. Write an essay about the subtle ways in which both Señora Ines and Rosaura's mother maintain the "delicate balance" between their social classes.
3. Even though Rosaura has carefully learned how to "pass" as middle class, Señora Ines will not allow her to cross class divisions; in her eyes, Rosaura will remain the maid's daughter no matter what she does. How is this similar to Reginald McKnight's experiences described in "Confessions of a Wannabe Negro" in Chapter 2? Write an essay reflecting on the ways that Rosaura and McKnight both succeed and fail at fitting into a society that does not welcome them.

Connotation depends on the context

Rivethead: Tales from the Assembly Line

Ben Hamper — *"I dont want to quit the shop because Id lose my inspiration to write"*

Hamper worked for six years assembling cars for General Motors in Flint, Michigan. He wrote a column about his experiences at GM for **Mother Jones** magazine, which he developed into the book Rivethead. The documentary film **Roger and Me** detailed the effects of the GM factory closings on Hamper and other workers in Flint.

I was seven years old the first time I ever set foot inside an automobile factory. The occasion was Family Night at the old Fisher Body plant in Flint where my father worked the second shift.

General Motors provided this yearly intrusion as an opportunity for the kin of the work force to funnel in and view their fathers, husbands, uncles and granddads as they toiled away on the assembly line. If nothing else, this annual peepshow lent a whole world of credence to our father's daily grumble. The assembly line did indeed stink. The noise was very close to intolerable. The heat was one complete bastard. Little wonder the old man's socks always smelled like liverwurst bleached for a week in the desert sun.

For my mother, it was at least one night out of the year when she could verify the old man's whereabouts. One night a year when she could be reasonably assured that my father wasn't lurchin' over a pool table at the Patio Lounge or picklin' his gizzard at any one of a thousand beer joints out of Dort Highway. My father loved his drink. He wasn't nearly as fond of labor.

On this night, the old man was present. I remember my mother being relieved. If he hadn't been there, it would have been difficult for her to explain to my little brother and me why we had made this exhaustive trek through Satan's playpen just to ogle a bunch of oily strangers and their grinnin' lineage.

After a hundred wrong turns and dead ends, we found my old man down on the trim line. His job was to install windshields using this goofy apparatus with large suction cups that resembled an octopus being crucified. A car would nuzzle up to the old man's work area and he would be waiting for it, a cigarette dangling from his lip, his arms wrapped around the windshield contraption as if it might suddenly rebel and bolt off for the ocean. Car, windshield. Car, windshield. Car, windshield. No wonder my father preferred playin' hopscotch with barmaids. This kind of repetition didn't look like any fun at all.

And here, all of this time, I had assumed that Dad just built the vehicles all by his lonesome. I always imagined that building adult cars was identical to building cars in model kits. You were given a large box with illustrated directions, a clutter of fenders, wheels and trunk lids, and some hip-high vat of airplane glue. When one was finished, you simply motioned to some boss-type in the aisle: "Hey, bring me another kit and make it a goddamn Corvette this time!"

We stood there for forty minutes or so, a miniature lifetime, and the pattern never changed. Car, windshield. Car, windshield. Drudgery piled atop drudgery. Cigarette to cigarette. Decades rolling through the rafters, bones turning to dust, stubborn clocks gagging down flesh, another windshield, another cigarette, wars blinking on and off, thunderstorms muttering the alphabet, crows on power lines asleep or dead, that mechanical octopus squirming against nothing, nothing, NOTHINGNESS. I wanted to shout at my father "Do something else!" Do something else or come home with us or flee to the nearest watering hole. DO SOMETHING ELSE! Car, windshield. Car, windshield. Christ, no.

Thank God that, even at age seven, I knew what I was going to be when I grew up. There wouldn't be any car/windshield cha-cha awaiting me. I was go-

the constant repition

ing to be an ambulance driver, the most glamorous calling in the world. I would spend my days zooming from one mangled calamity to the next. I would have full license to poke my face into the great American bucket seat blood-fest. The metallic crunch, the spiderweb of cracked glass (no doubt installed by my zombied father), the stupid eyeballs of the ripped and ravaged, the blood and guts of the accordion carnage. Ah, yes. To engage the sweet wail of the sirens. To scoop teeth from out of the dashboard. That would be the life. Everything my mother insisted we avoid when we passed a wreck. "Boys, don't look out the window," she would tremble. I always looked. I had to look.

My mind was set. Someday I'd be an ambulance driver. I would eat at McDonald's every night. I would buy a house right across the street from Tiger Stadium. My old man was nuts. Car, windshield, car, windshield: what kind of idiot occupation was that? *doesnt consider a real job*

As far as I remember, we never returned for another Family Night. It was just as well, for in all likelihood, we'd never have spotted my father. He had this habitual lean for the nearest exit. As soon as my grandmother lined him up for another job, he'd disappear into an eternal crawl for the coldest mug of beer in town. He took turns being a car salesman, a milkman, a construction worker, a railroad hand, a house painter, a mechanic and a landscaper. Each time the suds would devour his sense of duty, he'd get canned or simply quit, and back he'd come to his lumpy retreat on the living room sofa. My grandmother would be less than pleased. *Always on the assembly line*

Frequently mixed in with these dashed occupations were the inevitable sojourns back to the assembly line. It was not the least bit uncommon for a man to be fired at one factory on a Friday and be given the red carpet treatment at another automotive facility across town on Monday. If this is Tuesday, this must be Buick. If this is Thursday, how 'bout AC Spark Plug. During the sixties there were ten or so factories in Flint workin' three shifts per day and in this kind of boomtown climate even the beggars could afford to be choosers. "Sign here, Mr. Beerbreath. So glad to have you collapse on our doorstep."

I can't recall how many times my old man spun through the revolving doors of General Motors. However, around the house, we could always sense when Dad was cleaving through the factory rut. He would enter the house with this bulldog grimace. He'd gobble his meal, arise, put on one of his Arnie Palmer golf sweaters and whisk off for a troll through publand. Often, he wouldn't return for days. Then, suddenly one morning, there he'd be— reekin' of Pabst and pepperoni, passed out in a fetal position on the sofa, wearin' the same cool duds he left home in.

Not surprisingly, this led to a fair amount of friction between my mother and father. I could hear them early in the morning, their ferocious bitching driftin' through the heater vent up and into the bedroom I shared with three of my brothers.

It didn't take a marriage counselor or referee to sift to the bottom of these parental showdowns. Propped up in my bunk, I could easily discern the irrationality of my old man's barbs and the meek desperation of my mother's rebuttals. My father insisted that my mother was yanking the family against him. "You're turnin' the whole bunch of them into goddamn mama's boys!" the old man would rant. "Every one of them acts like I'm some kind of villain."

Meanwhile, my mother would score with a hefty uppercut of fact. "Don't blame me, Bernard. Maybe if you hung around the house more than two nights a month the kids might get to know you." My old man abhorred the truth. It was like some horrible, foreign diction that ripped at his core. The car payment was truth. The telephone bill was truth. The six sleeping children, plus the one sitting bolt upright in his bed, were truth. Worst of all, the cars and windshield were truth. *Stuck @ the job*

Cars, windshields. Cars, fenders. Cars, whatever. The ongoing shuffle of the shoprat. It wasn't as if this profession was a plague that appeared out of nowhere to ensnare my old man. Quite the opposite was true. His daddy was a shoprat. His daddy's daddy was a shoprat. Perhaps his daddy's daddy's daddy would have been a shoprat if only Hank Ford would have dreamed this shit up a little sooner.

My old man's mother had been a shoprat. The same with Uncle Jack and Uncle Gene and Uncle Clarence. Ditto dear old Aunt Laura. My mother's dad had been a shoprat. (If you're wondering what happened to my mother's mother and her sense of duty—well, Christ, somebody had to stay home and pack this clan a lunch.)

Right from the outset, when the call went out for shoprats, my ancestors responded in almost Pavlovian compliance. The family tree practically listed right over on its side with eager men and women grasping for that great automotive dream.

My great-grandfather got the wheel rollin'. In 1910, he began his twenty-year tenure down on Industrial Avenue piecing together mobilized buggies. This was a period right after the invention of the gas-powered engine and long before the introduction of freeway sniping. My great-grandfather would have hung in there longer, but he bumped heads in the thirties with something called the Depression.

My grandfather hired on in 1930. He rode out the turbulence of the Depression and worked as a skilled tradesman for thirty-two years at Buick. He had no plans to retire, but the cancer took him down at age fifty-two. He died one week to the day after he cashed his first pension check.

My other grandfather hitched his way from Springfield, Illinois, to the Vehicle City in 1925. He put in forty years, from Babe Ruth to the Beatles, as an inspector at the Chevrolet Engine plant. He always claimed that the only reason he retired was his disdain for the new breed of autoworkers in the sixties. He referred to them as "candy-asses." I assumed he was remarking about some inedible new brand of chocolate bar.

During the war, my grandmother helped build machine guns at the AC Spark Plug factory. She later switched over to working on aircraft out on

the kids are on the mother's side because their dad is never there

Dort Highway. To this day, my grandmother still helps me change the oil in my Camaro.

My Aunt Laura and her husband Jack put in a combined sixty-five years at the AC plant and the Buick Foundry. Uncle Jack was well known for his lust for overtime, often volunteering to work double shifts and sixteen-hour days. This may provide a valuable clue as to why they never had any children.

For sheer longevity, my Uncle Clarence outdistanced everyone in the family tree. From 1919 till 1964, an amazing span of forty-five years, he answered the whistle over at the Buick Engine plant.

Forty-five years! That's longer than the life expectancy of over two-thirds of the world's population. Forty-five years! Shit, just imagine—from a cradle down in Dixie to his hunched-over demise on the potty—Elvis Presley never even lived that long. Forty-five years! After all of that, what do they give you for a retirement gift? A grandfather clock? An iron lung? A bronzed calendar the size of a Yugo?

With a heritage like that you'd think my old man would have had enough grit and grind floatin' through his gene pool to practically assure his pod development as a full-bloomin' archetype of the species. A purebred shoprat, begotten from sperms that jingle, jangle, jingle to the jungle strains of Greaseball Mecca. The fair-haired boy in the rhinestone coveralls. Spawn of labor. Self-winding fetus with the umbilical lasso looped around the blue-collared neckbone of Mr. Goodwrench.

Apparently, the old man wasn't much for heritage. He tumbled out of the family tree, urinated on it and never looked back. For him, General Motors was nothing more than a recurring nuisance, an occasional pit stop where he could tidy up his bankroll before troopin' out on another aimless binge.

It was unfortunate that my father couldn't combine his love for beer and his dependence on pocket money into one workable formula. After all, he wasn't the only palooka in the family who tipped toward the tapper. The majority of my ancestors were heavy drinkers. Excluding my grandmother, all of them imbibed frequently as hard-laborin' shoprats are wont to do.

My mother's dad was especially skilled at juggling work and play. Monday morning through Friday afternoon he was the consummate provider. Straight home from work, dinner, the evening news and immediately into bed at 7:00 P.M. He arose each weekday at 3:30 A.M., fixed himself some black coffee, turned on the kitchen radio, smoked a handful of Lucky Strikes and waited to leave for work at a quarter to five. This regimen never varied one iota in the forty years he worked for GM.

Come the quittin' whistle on Friday afternoon, a colossal metamorphosis took place. So long, shoprat. Hello, hooligan. As my mother tells it, they never caught more than a staggerin' glimpse of my grandfather on any given weekend. He occasionally dropped in for a quick supper whereupon he would substitute the dinner hour for an excuse to denounce my grandma's cooking, castigate the children and generously mutter "goddamn-it-alls" for the benefit of the rest of the defective universe.

My grandfather surely could be an ornery bastard, but it should be thusly noted that he was always there to answer the bell. He had a wife and three kids to house and feed. He turned the trick daily. He may have had a passionate lust for booze, but it never interfered with his job at General Motors. When he retired, he was a very wealthy man. Devotion, responsibility and duty to the Corporation. The bottle was never far away, but it always rode shotgun.

Seeing as how my old man constructed this formula completely ass-backwards, the entire burden of support fell solely into my mother's lap. While the old man was off baby-sitting barstools, it was left up to my mom to raise and provide for eight kids.

Throughout my youth, my mother worked two jobs a day. Nine to five, she was a medical secretary at a doctor's office. She walked the two miles to work each day because we were too broke to afford a car. By night, she worked as a medical records transcriber, pounding the dictaphone machine for Hurley Hospital in the tiny, makeshift office in the corner of the living room.

It was unfortunate for my old man that my mother was such a strict and loyal Catholic. Consequently, my mother wasn't allowed to practice the pill and the baby faucet was allowed to leak on unabated. The final tally showed five boys and three girls of which I was the eldest. Eight was indeed enough. In fact, eight was plainly too goddamn many. Every time the stork paid a visit, he left a new bundle of joy for my mother and a fresh load in the chamber of the gun pointed at my old man's skull.

It seemed with each new addition to our family, my father slid further and further away from accountability. He liked children, he just didn't have the space for a clan of his own. It was like the cars and the windshield. The equation never balanced out. The undertow of all this repetition was a riddle he could never hope to untangle.

By the age of ten, I realized that my old man was not soon to be confused with Ward Cleaver. I was hip to all his ploys and well aware of his flair for bullshit. His boozin' never particularly bothered me. I figured if my father wanted to go get plowed, it was his decision.

What bothered me was my old man's insistence on fabricating dreadful, transparent lies. We both knew what he was up to so why not just 'fess up and admit the obvious.

I surely would have respected him more if he'd only come up to me on those occasions of rabid thirst and said "Look, son. I feel like some kind of suffocatin' beast. The world is knockin' me around something awful and it's only fuckin' proper that I find a bar at once. I want to get smashed. I want to play footsies with the locals. I want to sing like Dean Martin. I want to drink until they start clickin' the lights off and on and then I wanna weave home and collapse into bed with the weight of the world slidin' off the sheets. You may not understand any of this now, but someday you'll have a world of your own to contend with."

He wishes he got a simple explaination

Gun → mom = Joy dad = more irresponsible

My friends were always amused with my old man's approach to the duties of fatherhood. Most of their fathers were dedicated shoprats, shackled to some factory titty like hornets to honey. Their fathers wouldn't miss a day's work if their spinal cords were severed. Obedience to the Corporation. An honest day's pay for an honest day's toil. Car, bumper. Car, door latch. Car, dipstick.

For them, my father was the mold breaker—the curious renegade who dared to scrunch himself up in fetal bliss, smack dab in the middle of the workday, snoozin' off the effects of another nocturnal creepy-crawl.

After school, we would tiptoe past him, snickering back and forth at the behemoth in full slumber. You had to be very cautious. To awaken the old man from his beer coma would earn you an immediate pass to have your head dislodged. Sometimes, just for laughs, I'd get as close as I possibly dared and jut my middle finger right in his face. The poor bastard was like some dormant circus geek and he never even knew it. No respect for his dad

Of course, my friends preferred to catch my old man in his glorious prime. This usually occurred whenever I'd have a friend over for the night. My old man would weave in while we were watchin' some late-night horror flick and immediately take over the entertainment. After a full night of drinkin', there was nothin' my old man enjoyed more than a captive audience for his sloshed bar chatter. Even if he was playin' to a crowd comprised of two sleep-starved ten-year-olds.

There were the stories about how he broke said pool stick over said chiseler's head and how the babes he hung with had chests the size of pony kegs ("They'd be through with you boys before you ever got it unzipped," he'd chuckle) and how he knew Tiger great Denny McLain on a first-name basis and how Denny better watch his shit cuz these mob pricks were no one to try and slip a change-up by and how he was rapin' the local bookies with his expertise at pickin' the over and under.

It went on and on. Typically, he would conclude these drunken seminars with horrible denunciations of the black race. My old man was a master of deflecting his own guilt onto anyone other than himself. The blacks were his favorite dumping ground. He would blame them for everything. He'd make all these demented assertions about how Hitler was stopped too early because once he ditched all the Jews, he was gonna wipe out the niggers. Fine fodder for festerin' ten-year-old minds. We preferred hearin' about large breasts and the woes of Denny McLain.

Despite the racial garbage, my friends all agreed that my old man's beer blather beat the shit out of listenin' to their fathers whine about what was on television and how the lawn needed trimmin'. Their fathers were as robotic in their home life as they were about their factory jobs. It was as if the shop had hollowed them out and replaced their intestines with circuit breakers. Car, tailpipe. Food, pork chop. Car, brake pad. Rent, Friday. Car, hubcap. Life, toothpaste.

Mike Gellately's father was a good example. Almost every evening after dinner I headed over to Mike's house. He would greet me at the side door and we'd trail through the kitchen on our way up to his bedroom.

Without fail, Mr. Gellately would be propped at the kitchen table—a six-pack of Blue Ribbon at his right elbow, an overloaded ashtray at his left. He would be staring straight ahead at the kitchen sink and his faithful radio would be stationed in front of him, forever tuned in to the Detroit Tigers or Red Wings. Sip, puff, belch. Occasionally, he would startle the homestead by muttering a random "shit" or "fuck." That would be the extent of his nightly vocabulary.

Neither Mike nor I understood the first thing about our fathers. They were like the living dead. Their patterns differed—Mike's old man held a job most of the time, my old man was on some kind of less-paying treadmill—but their ruts were terribly predictable. We grew to hate our fathers.

By the time I approached teenhood, I no longer wanted to be an ambulance driver. I didn't know what the hell I wanted to be. Mike always suggested that we become disc jockeys. I never argued. A disc jockey would certainly lead a glamorous life. Anything had to be better than the cadaver shuffle the factories were peddlin' our fathers.

Even the neighborhood we lived in was a by-product of General Motors. During the boom years of the twenties, houses had to be constructed in order to keep up with the influx of factory workers arriving from the South to find jobs. General Motors built their own little suburb on the north side of Flint. In keeping with their repetitive nature, all the houses were duplicates.

Our neighborhood was strictly blue-collar and predominantly Catholic. The men lumbered back and forth to the factories while their wives raised large families, packed lunch buckets and marched the kids off to the nuns.

My family was no exception. From the very beginning, I was raised a good Catholic boy. Catholic church, Catholic school, Catholic home, Catholic drone. I was baptized, confirmed, anointed and tattooed with ashes all in the hope that one day I might have a spot reserved for me on that glorious flotilla up to the heavens.

No matter how tight the budget was at home, my mother always managed to scrape up the necessary funds to provide for our Catholic education. It was never intended that I grow up to be anything other than a good Catholic man—a steady churchgoer with a steady factory income, a station wagon parked under the elms and a wife with an automatic door on her womb.

St. Luke's Elementary provided a very capable boot camp environment for those who would later deposit themselves in the rigid bustle of factory life. The education-through-intimidation technique favored there was not unlike the jarhead gang mentality of the General Motors floorlords. Our fathers' overseers were brutes with clipboards, sideburns and tangled rhetoric. Our overseers, the sisters of St. Luke's, were brutes with clipboards, sideburns and tangled rosaries.

A pattern was developing. During the seventh and eighth grades at St. Luke's, the nuns divided the students into groups according to intelligence

(margin handwriting:) Made to be a factory worker

constant cycle

and behavior. There were three groups: the obedient eggheads, the bland robots of mediocrity and, my group, the who-gives-a-shit-hey-have-you-heard-the-new-Cream-album-yet-yup-my-daddy's-a-stinkin'-shoprat-too clan.

Being a proud underachiever of the latter grouping, I was relieved of much of the pressure to succeed in life and was left with my drowsy peers to clog up the classroom while we awaited our almost certain fate as future factory nimwits. Not much was expected of us and we went out of our way to ensure that was how it would remain. Consequently, the nuns cut us a great deal of slack figuring that for every Einstein and Aristotle flipped out of the cookie cutter there had to be a couple mental dwarves available to assemble a life's procession of Buicks and Impalas for those on the road to high places. *comfortable "norms"*

Of course this method of reasoning didn't exactly jibe with our parents' outlook on destiny. At report card time, our folks would raise all kinds of hell while cringing over our grades. I suppose it only makes sense that every mom and pop wants more for their tuition dollar than a series of lazy failures guaranteed to pave the lane right into the turd dump of the assembly line. You could achieve that predestination at any public school and save the family till a lootful.

My folks were no exception. My mother would gaze at my report card and the color would leave her face. It was like a slap to the head—a horrible betrayal on my part considering the long hours of work she had put in to assure her son a fine Catholic education.

"An E in Math, a D in History and Science, a D− IN RELIGION?" my mother would howl. "How could any child who attends mass SIX days a week possibly do so poorly in Religion?"

I would make a pathetic attempt to switch to the highlights. "Look, Mom, I did raise my Self-Conduct mark from a D to a C−. And I did receive passing grades in Music and Gym."

"Music and Gym? MUSIC AND GYM! Just what is that supposed to tell me? That you have a secure future singing the national anthem at basketball games? Just wait until your father takes a look at this mess."

I could wait. If there was one thing I detested, it was my old man preachin' to me about my shortcomings as a model Catholic youth. It was such a bad joke. What the hell qualified him to criticize anything I did? I felt that he should reserve his critiques for matters that more closely coincided with his niche in life. Education? Shit. He should have stuck to advising me on the proper methods of wife cheating and check forging and navigating a car with triple vision. And what about the studied art of smoking an entire Winston without ever removing it from your mouth or the precious knack of impersonating a morgue stiff for forty-eight consecutive hours on the living room sofa. This was the kind of heavy data no nun could ever pass along.

I was my father's seed. Technically, I guess that was reason enough for him to meddle with my grade situation.

"You think you're hot shit, don't you, son?" my father would begin. I would shrug nervously. "You think you've got a pretty soft thing going for yourself. Am I right?" I would shake my head slowly.

"Well, the way I see it, you ain't nothin' but a bad actor. You may be snowin' your mother, but I can smell your game a mile away. You wanna play wiseass with me and I'll knock you down a few pegs. Anytime you feel like you can take the old man, I'll be right here. Anytime you wanna wear the pants in the family, you just let me know. I'll be more than willing to put my foot right up your ass. Understand, son?"

"Yes," I would mumble enraged and full of regrets. If only I were eight inches taller and had a reckless set of balls. I could envision myself springing from the interrogation seat and sucker-punching my old man right in the chops. "Here, sweet father of mine, take this busted lip as a loving token of my esteemed adulation and let this punt to the rib cage serve as a loving reminder that your eldest son worships the ground you piss on."

But back to reality or, at least, my father's version of such. "Now, son, you must realize that your mother and I have worked very hard to see that you receive some proper schooling. All this report card tells me is that you don't give a good goddamn one way or the other. You keep this shit up and you'll be just like half the other morons in this city who end up spinnin' their wheels and suckin' some heavy ass down at Chevrolet or over at Buick. You can clown it up now, but you'll be laughin' out of the other side of your mouth once the blisters appear and some bastard starts leanin' over your shoulder with another bumper to fasten down."

I heard this speech often during my formative years. I came to refer to it as my old man's "State of the Hometown" address. Do as I say, not as I did, kid. My friends received similar pronouncements from their fathers. The factories weren't looking for a few good men. They were dragging the lagoon for optionless bumpkins with brats to feed and livers to bathe. An educated man might hang on for a while, but was apt to flee at any given whistle. That wasn't any good for corporate continuity. GM wanted the salt of the earth, dung-heavers, flunkies and leeches—men who would grunt the day away void of self-betterment, numbed-out cyborgs willing to swap cerebellum loaf for patio furniture, a second jalopy and a tragic carpet ride deboarding curbside in front of some pseudo-Tudor dollhouse on the outskirts of town.

Which is to say that being a factory worker in Flint, Michigan, wasn't something purposely passed on from generation to generation. To grow up believing that you were brought into this world to follow in your daddy's footsteps, just another chip-off-the-old-shoprat, was to engage in the lowest possible form of negativism. Working the line for GM was something fathers did so that their offspring wouldn't have to.

In the case of my ancestry, we had been blessed with this ongoing cycle of martyrs. Men who toiled tirelessly in an effort to provide their sons and daughters with a better way of living. Unfortunately, at the same time, our family was also cursed by a steady flow of uninspired descendants who scoffed at alternative opportunity and merely hung around waitin' for the baton to be passed from crab claw to puppy paw.

By deftly flunking my way through St. Luke's Junior High, I was already exhibiting symptoms of one who was pointing squarely to the loading dock of the nearest General Motors outpost. Even my father was accurate with his diagnosis. Another Hamper banging at the gate of idiot industry with a ten-foot scowl and a forehead fresh for stampin'. I could practically hear my great-grandfather yelpin' from his crypt: "Not another one! Hey, don't any of you pricks wanna become lawyers or somethin'? Huh? HUH?" Silent decades drifted by choking on indecision. "Well, piss on ya, I'm going back to sleep. Car, windshield. Car, fuel pump. Car, ignition switch. Car, zzzzzz . . ."

FOR JOURNALING AND DISCUSSION

1. Contrast Hamper's views of Mike Gellately's father with his views of his own dad. Who comes out looking better? Why?
2. How does Hamper's life as a Catholic student mirror the experiences of the assembly line? What point is he making with this juxtaposition? How did his Catholic education perpetuate the social class system?
3. How does gender trap the people in Hamper's community? Both of Hamper's parents in some ways are caught in the trap of the expectations that go with their own gender roles. How are gender expectations yet one more way of maintaining social class structure?
4. What is the function of Hamper's father's racism? Why is racism in poorer communities often much more virulent than in wealthier ones? How does this link to Michael Lind's views about racism as a method of social class control expressed in "To Have and Have Not" earlier in this chapter?

FOR RESEARCH AND EXPLORATION

1. Hamper describes an educational system that clearly tracked him into the lowest performing group. Do some research on the effects of low teacher expectations on student performance. How do your findings fit with Hamper's experiences? How do the schools and their tracking systems serve to further entrench their students' social class positions?
2. Hamper describes a time in Flint, Michigan, when jobs were plentiful; workers needed only show up in order to get employment. Michael Moore's documentary film *Roger and Me* depicts a much different period—one of factory closings, massive layoffs, and downsizing. After viewing Moore's film, write an essay comparing and contrasting Hamper's and Moore's versions of factory life. How do layoffs change the culture? How do both Hamper and Moore paint a picture of an auto industry that clearly does not care about its workers?
3. Hamper is eventually able to escape the trap of his own upbringing and the assembly line, in large part by rejecting many of his parents' values. Compare this with Usry Alleyne's views and experiences in "Atheism and Me: Why I Don't Believe in God" in Chapter 5. He too rejects many of his family's values in order to arrive at a new place.

River of Names   "Flow"?

Dorothy Allison

*Allison has called herself a "cross-eyed working-class lesbian, addicted to vi-
olence, language, and hope." She grew up in South Carolina and has worked
as a writer, editor, and activist. Her books include* Trash, Skin, Bastard
Out of Carolina, *which was nominated for the 1992 National Book Award,
and* Two or Three Things I Know for Sure.

told from a Narrator's POV

Suicide

At a picnic at my aunt's farm, the only time the whole family ever gathered, my
sister Billie and I chased chickens into the barn. Billie ran right through the
open doors and out again, but I stopped, caught by a shadow moving over me.
My cousin, Tommy, eight years old as I was, swung in the sunlight with his face
as black as his shoes—the rope around his neck pulled up into the sunlit
heights of the barn, fascinating, horrible. Wasn't he running ahead of us?
Someone came up behind me. Someone began to scream. My mama took my
head in her hands and turned my eyes away.

Jesse and I have been lovers for a year now. She tells me stories about her childhood, about her father going off each day to the university, her mother who
made all her dresses, her grandmother who always smelled of dill bread and
vanilla. I listen with my mouth open, not believing but wanting, aching for the
fairy tale she thinks is everyone's life.

"What did your grandmother smell like?"

I lie to her the way I always do, a lie stolen from a book. "Like lavender,"
stomach churning over the memory of sour sweat and snuff.

I realize I do not really know what lavender smells like, and I am for a moment afraid she will ask something else, some question that will betray me. But
Jesse slides over to hug me, to press her face against my ear, to whisper, "How
wonderful to be part of such a large family."

I hug her back and close my eyes. I cannot say a word.

I was born between the older cousins and the younger, born in a pause of babies and therefore outside, always watching. Once, way before Tommy died, I
was pushed out on the steps while everyone stood listening to my Cousin
Barbara. Her screams went up and down in the back of the house. Cousin Cora
brought buckets of bloody rags out to be burned. The other cousins all ran off
to catch the sparks or poke the fire with dogwood sticks. I waited on the porch

a miscarriage?

making up words to the shouts around me. I did not understand what was happening. Some of the older cousins obviously did, their strange expressions broken by stranger laughs. I had seen them helping her up the stairs while the
thick blood ran down her legs. After a while the blood on the rags was thin, watery, almost pink. Cora threw them on the fire and stood motionless in the
stinking smoke.

Randall went by and said there'd be a baby, a hatched egg to throw out
with the rags, but there wasn't. I watched to see and there wasn't; nothing but
the blood, thinning out desperately while the house slowed down and grew
quiet, hours of cries growing soft and low, moaning under the smoke. My Aunt
Raylene came out on the porch and almost fell on me, not seeing me, not seeing anything at all. She beat on the post until there were knuckle-sized dents
in the peeling paint, beat on that post like it could feel, cursing it and herself
and every child in the yard, singing up and down,

"Goddamn, goddamn, that girl . . . no sense . . . goddamn!"

Huge family, many deaths

I've these pictures my mama gave me—stained sepia prints of bare dirt yards,
plank porches, and step after step of children—cousins, uncles, aunts; myster-
ies. The mystery is how many no one remembers. I show them to Jesse, not saying who they are, and when she laughs at the broken teeth, torn overalls, the
dirt, I set my teeth at what I do not want to remember and cannot forget.

We were so many we were without number and, like tadpoles, if there was
one less from time to time, who counted? My maternal great-grandmother had
eleven daughters, seven sons; my grandmother, six sons, five daughters. Each
one made at least six. Some made nine. Six times six, eleven times nine. They
went on like multiplication tables. They died and were not missed. I come of
an enormous family and I cannot tell half their stories. Somehow it was always
made to seem they killed themselves: car wrecks, shotguns, dusty ropes,
screaming, falling out of windows, things inside them. I am the point of a pyramid, sliding back under the weight of the ones who came after, and it does not
matter that I am the lesbian, the one who will not have children.

I tell the stories and it comes out funny. I drink bourbon and make myself
drawl, tell all those old funny stories. Someone always seems to ask me, which
one was that? I show the pictures and she says, "Wasn't she the one in the story
about the bridge?" I put the pictures away, drink more, and someone always
finds them, then says, "Goddamn! How many of you were there anyway?"

I don't answer.

Jesse used to say, "You've got such a fascination with violence. You've got so
many terrible stories."

She said it with her smooth mouth, that chin nobody ever slapped, and I
love that chin, but when Jesse spoke then, my hands shook and I wanted nothing so much as to tell her terrible stories.

So I made a list. I told her: that one went insane—got her little brother
with a tire iron; the three of them slit their arms, not the wrists but the bigger

veins up near the elbow; she, now *she* strangled the boy she was sleeping with and got sent away; that one drank lye and died laughing soundlessly. In one year I lost eight cousins. It was the year everybody ran away. Four disappeared and were never found. One fell in the river and was drowned. One was run down hitchhiking north. One was shot running through the woods, while Grace, the last one, tried to walk from Greenville to Greer for some reason nobody knew. She fell off the overpass a mile down from the Sears, Roebuck warehouse and lay there for hunger and heat and dying.

Later, sleeping, but not sleeping, I found that my hands were up under Jesse's chin. I rolled away, but I didn't cry. I almost never let myself cry.

Almost always, we were raped, my cousins and I. That was some kind of joke, too.

> *What's a South Carolina virgin?*
> *'At's a ten-year-old can run fast.*

It wasn't funny for me in my mama's bed with my stepfather, not for my cousin, Billie, in the attic with my uncle, nor for Lucille in the woods with another cousin, for Danny with four strangers in a parking lot, or for Pammie who made the papers. Cora read it out loud: "Repeatedly by persons unknown." They stayed unknown since Pammie never spoke again. Perforations, lacerations, contusions, and bruises. I heard all the words, big words, little words, words too terrible to understand. DEAD BY AN ACT OF MAN. With the prick still in them, the broom handle, the tree branch, the grease gun . . . objects, things not to be believed . . . whiskey bottles, can openers, grass shears, glass, metal, vegetables . . . not to be believed, not to be believed.

Jesse says, "You've got a gift for words."

"Don't talk," I beg her, "don't talk." And this once, she just holds me, blessedly silent.

I dig out the pictures, stare into the faces. Which one was I? Survivors do hate themselves, I know, over the core of fierce self-love, never understanding, always asking, "Why me and not her, not him?" There is such mystery in it, and I have hated myself as much as I have loved others, hated the simple fact of my own survival. Having survived, am I supposed to say something, do something, be something?

I loved my Cousin Butch. He had this big old head, pale thin hair, and enormous, watery eyes. All the cousins did, though Butch's head was the largest, his hair the palest. I was the dark-headed one. All the rest of the family seemed pale carbons of each other in shades of blond, though later on everybody's hair went brown or red and I didn't stand out so. Butch and I stood out then—I because I was so dark and fast, and he because of that big head and the crazy things he did. Butch used to climb on the back of my Uncle Lucius's truck, open the gas tank and hang his head over, breathe deeply, strangle, gag, vomit, and breathe again. It went so deep, it tingled in your toes. I climbed up after him and tried it myself, but I was too young to hang on long, and I fell heavily

getting high on gas

to the ground, dizzy and giggling. Butch could hang on, put his hand down into the tank and pull up a cupped palm of gas, breathe deep and laugh. He would climb down roughly, swinging down from the door handle, laughing, staggering, and stinking of gasoline. Someone caught him at it. Someone threw a match. "I'll teach you."

Just like that, gone before you understand.

I wake up in the night screaming, "No, no, I won't!" <u>Dirty water rises</u> in the back of my throat, the liquid language of my own terror and rage. "Hold me. Hold me." Jesse rolls over on me; her hands grip my hipbones tightly.

"I love you. I love you. I'm here," she repeats.

I stare up into her dark eyes, puzzled, afraid. I draw a breath in deeply, smile my bland smile. "Did I fool you?" I laugh, rolling away from her. Jesse punches me playfully, and I catch her hand in the air.

"My love," she whispers, and cups her body against my hip, closes her eyes. I bring my hand up in front of my face and watch the knuckles, the nails as they tremble, tremble. I watch for a long time while she sleeps, warm and still against me.

<u>James</u> went blind. One of the uncles got him in the face with home-brewed alcohol.

Suicide

Lucille climbed out the front window of <u>Aunt Raylene's</u> house and jumped. They said she jumped. No one said why.

My <u>Uncle Matthew</u> used to beat my Aunt Raylene. The <u>twins, Mark and Luke,</u> swore to stop him, pulled him out in the yard one time, throwing him between them like a loose bag of grain. Uncle Matthew screamed like a pig coming up for slaughter. I got both my sisters in the tool shed for safety, but I hung back to watch. <u>Little Bo</u> came running out of the house, off the porch, feet first into his daddy's arms. Uncle Matthew started swinging him like a scythe, going after the bigger boys, Bo's head thudding their shoulders, their hips. Afterward, Bo crawled around in the dirt, the blood running out of his ears and his tongue hanging out of his mouth, while Mark and Luke finally got their daddy down. It was a long time before I realized that they never told anybody else what had happened to Bo.

Randall tried to teach Lucille and me to wrestle. "Put your hands up." His legs were wide apart, his torso bobbing up and down, his head moving constantly. Then his hand flashed at my face. I threw myself back into the dirt, lay still. He turned to Lucille, not noticing that I didn't get up. He punched at her, laughing. She wrapped her hands around her head, curled over so her knees were up against her throat.

"No, no," he yelled. "Move like her." He turned to me. "Move." He kicked at me. I rocked into a ball, froze.

"No, no!" He kicked me. I grunted, didn't move. He turned to Lucille. "You." Her teeth were chattering but she held herself still, wrapped up tighter than bacon slices.

Full of secrets
No real answers

"You move!" he shouted. Lucille just hugged her head tighter and started to sob.

"Son of a bitch," Randall grumbled, "you two will never be any good."

He walked away. Very slowly we stood up, embarrassed, looked at each other. We knew.

If you fight back, they kill you.

My sister was seven. She was screaming. My stepfather picked her up by her left arm, swung her forward and back. It gave. The arm went around loosely. She just kept screaming. I didn't know you could break it like that.

I was running up the hall. He was right behind me. "Mama! Mama!" His left hand—he was left-handed—closed around my throat, pushed me against the wall, and then he lifted me that way. I kicked, but I couldn't reach him. He was yelling, but there was so much noise in my ears I couldn't hear him.

"Please, Daddy. Please, Daddy. I'll do anything, I promise. Daddy, anything you want. Please, Daddy."

I couldn't have said that. I couldn't talk around that fist at my throat, couldn't breathe. I woke up when I hit the floor. I looked up at him.

"If I live long enough, I'll fucking kill you."

He picked me up by my throat again.

What's wrong with her?
Why's she always following you around?
Nobody really wanted answers.

A full bottle of vodka will kill you when you're nine and the bottle is a quart. It was a third cousin proved that. We learned what that and other things could do. Every year there was something new.

You're growing up.
My big girl.
There was codeine in the cabinet, paregoric for the baby's teeth, whiskey, beer, and wine in the house. Jeanne brought home MDA, PCP, acid; Randall, grass, speed, and mescaline. It all worked to dull things down, to pass the time.

Stealing was a way to pass the time. Things we needed, things we didn't, for the nerve of it, the anger, the need. *You're growing up,* we told each other. But sooner or later, we all got caught. Then it was, *When are you going to learn?*

Caught, nightmares happened. *Razorback desperate,* was the conclusion of the man down at the county farm where Mark and Luke were sent at fifteen. They both got their heads shaved, their earlobes sliced.

What's the matter, kid? Can't you take it?

Caught at sixteen, June was sent to Jessup County Girls' Home where the baby was adopted out and she slashed her wrists on the bedsprings.

Lou got caught at seventeen and held in the station downtown, raped on the floor of the holding tank.

Are you a boy or are you a girl?

On your knees, kid, can you take it?

Caught at eighteen and sent to prison, Jack came back seven years later blank-faced, understanding nothing. He married a quiet girl from out of town, had three babies in four years. Then Jack came home one night from the textile mill, carrying one of those big handles off the high speed spindle machine. He used it to beat them all to death and went back to work in the morning.

Cousin Melvina married at fourteen, had three kids in two and a half years, and welfare took them all away. She ran off with a carnival mechanic, had three more babies before he left her for a motorcycle acrobat. Welfare took those, too. But the next baby was hydrocephalic, a little waterhead they left with her, and the three that followed, even the one she used to hate so—the one she had after she fell off the porch and couldn't remember whose child it was.

"How many children do you have?" I asked her.

"You mean the ones I have, or the ones I had? Four," she told me, "or eleven."

My aunt, the one I was named for, tried to take off for Oklahoma. That was after she'd lost the youngest girl and they told her Bo would never be "right." She packed up biscuits, cold chicken, and Coca-Cola, a lot of loose clothes, Cora and her new baby, Cy, and the four youngest girls. They set off from Greenville in the afternoon, hoping to make Oklahoma by the weekend, but they only got as far as Augusta. The bridge there went out under them.

"An Act of God," my uncle said.

My aunt and Cora crawled out down river, and two of the girls turned up in the weeds, screaming loud enough to be found in the dark. But one of the girls never came up out of that dark water, and Nancy, who had been holding Cy, was found still wrapped around the baby, in the water, under the car.

"An Act of God," my aunt said. "God's got one damn sick sense of humor."

My sister had her baby in a bad year. Before he was born we had talked about it. "Are you afraid?" I asked.

"He'll be fine," she'd replied, not understanding, speaking instead to the other fear. "Don't we have a tradition of bastards?"

He was fine, a classically ugly healthy little boy with that shock of white hair that marked so many of us. But afterward, it was that bad year with my sister down with pleurisy, the cystitis, and no work, no money, having to move back home with my cold-eyed stepfather. I would come home to see her, from the woman I could not admit I'd been with, and take my infinitely fragile nephew and hold him, rocking him, rocking myself.

One night I came home to screaming—the baby, my sister, no one else there. She was standing by the crib, bent over, screaming red-faced. "Shut up! Shut up!" With each word her fist slammed the mattress fanning the baby's ear.

"Don't!" I grabbed her, pulling her back, doing it as gently as I could so I wouldn't break the stitches from her operation. She had her other arm clamped across her abdomen and couldn't fight me at all. She just kept shrieking.

CARRYING THE WEIGHT OF SURVING
-iv-

Many many problems

"That little bastard just screams and screams. That little bastard. I'll kill him."

Then the words seeped in and she looked at me while her son kept crying and kicking his feet. By his head the mattress still showed the impact of her fist.

"Oh no," she moaned, "I wasn't going to be like that. I always promised myself." She started to cry, holding her belly and sobbing. "We an't no different. We an't no different." *psychological Reasons*

Jesse wraps her arm around my stomach, presses her belly into my back. I relax against her. "You sure you can't have children?" she asks. "I sure would like to see what your kids would turn out to be like."

I stiffen, say, "I can't have children. I've never wanted children."

"Still," she says, "you're so good with children, so gentle."

I think of all the times my hands have curled into fists, when I have just barely held on. I open my mouth, close it, can't speak. What could I say now? All the times I have not spoken before, all the things I just could not tell her, the shame, the self-hatred, the fear; all of that hangs between us now—a wall I cannot tear down.

I would like to turn around and talk to her, tell her . . . "I've got a dust river in my head, a river of names endlessly repeating. That dirty water rises in me, all those children screaming out their lives in my memory, and I become someone else, someone I have tried so hard not to be."

But I don't say anything, and I know, as surely as I know I will never have a child, that by not speaking I am condemning us, that I cannot go on loving you and hating you for your fairy-tale life, for not asking about what you have no reason to imagine, for that soft-chinned innocence I love.

Jesse puts her hands behind my neck, smiles and says, "You tell the funniest stories."

I put my hands behind her back, feeling the ridges of my knuckles pulsing. "Yeah," I tell her. "But I lie."

FOR JOURNALING AND DISCUSSION

1. Allison makes some clear links between poverty and violence. Why do you think such links exist?
2. How does the interaction of poverty and violence play itself out on the female members of her family? Who are the victims here? How do they survive?
3. Imagine that Jesse accidentally finds this story. What do you think her response would be? Why has Allison not told her any of the true stories about her background? Will Jesse be able to understand?
4. How might Allison's sexual identity as a lesbian have helped her to escape from her family's cycle of violence and poverty?

FOR RESEARCH AND EXPLORATION

1. Monitor the newspaper or TV news for one week. Examine all the stories dealing with individual acts of violence. How are they class coded? How many seem to be clearly linked to lower-class people? Why do we make these assumptions?
2. Both Allison and Reginald McKnight, in "Confessions of a Wannabe Negro" from Chapter 2, inhabit hybrid positions—neither working nor middle class, neither black nor white. Both struggle with a sense of alienation because of their inability to fit comfortably into either of the worlds they inhabit. How does each one cope? What are their survival mechanisms? Who seems to be the more successful at negotiating the difficult ground between different worlds?
3. There is much research linking poverty to gender, violence, and abuse. Read several articles on this topic. Write an essay showing how the experts' views correlate with Allison's descriptions of the interconnections between poverty, gender, and violence.

Dancing with the Headhunters

G. J. Meyer

Meyer has worked as an editor, newspaper reporter, and public relations specialist. When he was nearly fifty years old he lost his position as vice president of public relations at McDonnell Douglas, a leading aeronautics company. His book Executive Blues: Down and Out in Corporate America *details his experiences as an upper-class, laid-off executive.*

I'm not getting any interviews.

I call and call and call, looking for leads. But when I turn one up and send in my résumé, nothing comes back. When I follow up the résumés with phone calls, secretaries get rid of me so smoothly that before I know what's happened I'm talking into a dead line.

This has been going on for weeks, and it's starting to scare me.

Then one afternoon the phone rings and it's a man I've been trying to reach, a headhunter named Roger Bullard in the Atlanta office of Russell Reynolds. He's looking for a P.R. vice president for Holiday Inns; he's seen my résumé and he has nice things to say about it.

Would I rather meet him in New York or Atlanta? He has offices in both places.

"Your choice," I say. "I'd vote for New York."

I wait while Bullard checks his calendar. "Monday in New York, then. Nine o'clock. Go ahead and make your reservations, and tomorrow call my secretary to confirm."

First thing the next morning I give Bullard's secretary my flight number, tell her I'll be arriving at my hotel on Sunday evening. She gives me the Russell Reynolds address and reminds me to be there at nine.

The offices, when I arrive, are like something out of the London home of a maharaja. All the walls are paneled the expensive way. Sheraton furniture, thick rugs, gleaming parquet floors. I'm gleaming, too: shoes, collar, cuffs. The crease in my trousers could draw blood, and I'm feeling good about the fact that despite my nervousness I managed seven good hours of sleep and an early jog in Central Park.

A mirror near the elevator indicates that I don't look like what I am: a guy out of work, thrown out of two corporations in the past three years, a little bitter, more than a little overeager.

I tell the receptionist that I'm there to see Mr. Bullard. With a slightly quizzical look she answers that he's not in yet, and I say I know I'm early. Moving delicately, not wanting to wrinkle the suit I've carried so carefully a thousand miles, I lower myself onto a leather sofa. Gingerly, keeping my fingertips clear of the ink, I open the *Wall Street Journal* on the coffee table in front of me and settle in to wait.

At nine the receptionist looks over at me, dials her phone, has a brief, inaudible conversation, hangs up, and looks at me again.

"You did say you have an appointment with Mr. Bullard?"

"Yes, I did. Nine o'clock."

"I'm sorry . . . but Mr. Bullard isn't scheduled to be in New York today."

When I call Atlanta, Bullard's secretary sounds almost as shocked as I feel. She can't understand how this could have happened. They were expecting me in New York *next* Monday. She thought that was understood.

In Edvard Munch's painting "The Scream," a solitary, empty-eyed figure stands in a roadway clutching its head, mouth open wide. I hope that's not what I look like as I walk the streets of Manhattan during the next several hours, seeing and hearing nothing, waiting for it to be time to return to La Guardia. But that's how I feel. Without making a sound, I scream all the way back to Wisconsin.

Today is Friday, the thirteenth of September, the ninety-eighth day of my unemployment. Ninety-nine days ago I was vice president for communications of the J. I. Case Company, a multinational manufacturing corporation with sales of more than $5 billion a year. Three years before that I was a vice president at McDonnell Douglas Corporation, a firm that needs no introduction.

And for more than three months now I have been a man with no particular need for an alarm clock, no place where I really need to go in the morning.

This afternoon, to kill a few hours and take my mind off a telephone that will not ring, I play nine holes of golf. For the first time this year it is difficult to find the ball. Pale leaves are beginning to clutter the fairways, making small white objects hard to see. On the day I was let go, the sixth of June, the Wisconsin summer was just beginning. I had expected that finding work would take a few months, during which I would be free to sleep late, to stay away from neckties for a while, to savor the sweetest part of the northern year.

Now it's fall that is just beginning, and I'm no closer to finding work than I was a season ago. I've had shots at jobs, but every shot has missed. I never got a second chance to meet with Roger Bullard. Holiday Inns, he told me, has put its search on hold.

I keep hearing politicians say that the recession is over. A nice thought. But what I see, wherever I look, is more and more good people with good credentials being let go for the first time in their lives and not being able to find work. I know an amazing number of capable, experienced, college-educated, unemployed people. Never in my life have I seen so many people lose their jobs. And I can't name one who has found a new job. Not one.

Ninety-eight days. Three months and a week. Not a long time according to the formula that says a job search is likely to last one month for every $10,000 of annual salary. By this formula, my wait has quite a way to go. The general rule for executive "separation packages" is this: the less you need, the more you get. If your annual compensation has been in six digits for years and the first digit isn't a one anymore, you can expect full pay and benefits for a year and a half, possibly even longer. Six-figure salaries starting with one are good for about a year, six months at a minimum. If your salary is well short of six figures and you have worries about the mortgage and tuition bills, watch out: you're down in dog-eat-dog territory, where they try to get you out the door with as little money as possible.

I have been among the immensely fortunate in this regard. At J. I. Case, after only two and a half years of work, I was promised up to a year with full pay and benefits while I looked for a new job. My wife, Pam, quit her own odious job before we knew mine was in danger and is now trying to get herself established in insurance sales. I hope she succeeds. Though my separation package is a wonderful cushion, it's also temporary, and I'm amazed at how much we've grown used to making and spending every month. Rivers of money flow in and just as quickly flow out: money to keep the kids in school, to keep the house and cars going, to keep all of it insured and the IRS satisfied. I don't like to think about how quickly all this could sink us.

My first job, at age thirteen, was mopping floors in a decrepit drugstore for fifty cents an hour. Twenty years later, I was moving between jobs of a kind my parents could hardly believe, with an income that passed the furthest limits of my imaginings; I've traveled the world, won semi-high honors, had my picture in the papers, floated above the fields of Normandy in a hot-air balloon.

And now, suddenly, I call it a good day if someone will take my phone call or answer my letter.

I know that not one percent of the human beings now alive in the United States of America, not one tenth of one percent of the current inhabitants of Earth, could possibly find me an object worthy of pity. I know too that this is as it should be: imagine feeling sorry for a man whose situation is so tragic that it causes him to play golf on Fridays. Imagine feeling sorry for somebody who is still drawing full pay ninety-eight days after being fired and still has months of full pay ahead of him whether he gets out of bed or not.

And yet I feel sorry for myself constantly. And I want everybody I know to feel sorry for me.

I am ashamed of myself, of all my feelings: murderous rage, envy, fear, and, mostly, shame itself. On a simple level I'm ashamed of myself for being out of work, for getting my family into such a fix, for allowing myself to become an "executive" in the first place and then letting the whole thing go so wrong. I'm ashamed of myself for losing. When I hear the guy next door start his car in the morning and drive away, I'm ashamed to be in bed. I'm ashamed to rake leaves on weekday afternoons, because everybody in the neighborhood will know—as if they didn't already—that I don't have an office to go to anymore. The deeper shame has to do with my weakness in the face of what feels like the most painful crisis of my life but which is, in fact, a mere inconvenience compared with what millions of people face every day.

Yet I'm jealous of anybody who still has the kind of job I used to have, of almost anybody who has a job, period. My envy of the people who put me here and are still drawing their giant salaries and piling up their gigantic pension points is as murderous as my resentment.

I envy people who took fewer chances than I did and are now in the safe if charmless harbors that I set sail from years ago: the post office, the Navy, reporting jobs at daily papers. I also envy people who took more chances than I did and broke free of salaries and corporations and bullshit. I spend a lot of time wondering where I might be today if I had taken more chances.

If envy caused cancer, I'd be dead by Sunday.

Calm down, I tell myself. Stop pacing. Find something sensible to do.

But I find that I can't do any such thing.

What will I be like by Christmas?

I think I can tell you how it will happen, if it's going to happen to you. The first thing they'll do, when they've made their preparations, is to get you out of your office and into a room with some geek from Human Resources.

If you're a vice president, your executioner will be a V.P. also—possibly a senior V.P. Directors are done by directors, managers by managers, et cetera, on down almost to the ranks of the blue-collar folks who even today do actual work for a living even in these United States of America.

From the moment you pass through his door, the H.R. geek will appear to be in visible pain. He wants you to understand that he, too, is a human being, a nice guy, and that his mother didn't raise him for this kind of thing.

(Is it flippant of me to call these people "geeks"? Originally the word referred to individuals who did revolting things for money at carnivals and fairs. I don't think I'm being flippant at all.)

"God," said McDonnell Douglas Corporation's senior vice president for Human Resources ten seconds before he fired me. "God, this is going to be hard." He twisted, literally writhed, in his chair. Then he swung back toward me and quickly got down to his work.

Once the geek has delivered his message and demonstrated the depths of his humanity, he'll get up out of his chair and come around from behind his desk. You'll be drawn up after him by some mysterious force resembling magnetism, and together the two of you will glide out the door and down the hall to some smaller office that you probably never noticed before, where somebody you've never seen is waiting to tell you not to worry, everything is going to be fine.

Sometimes other people are waiting in other little rooms nearby, but if you behave yourself you'll never know about them. There might be a company lawyer, for example. You won't see him unless you say something that indicates a less than perfect willingness to be agreeable. Somebody from security might be hidden in the wings, too.

The stranger awaiting you in the little office, the one telling you that everything is going to be all right, is the outplacement geek. He's been brought in, and will be paid handsomely, to "guide you through your transition."

The assigned outplacement geek will be the nicest of nice guys—one of the main reasons he was called to his profession in the first place. He'll give you a small, slightly rueful smile. He'll say that he understands what a shock this is but that he also knows something important: that it's very likely the start of a better life not just for you but for your whole family. If he was ever fired himself, he'll tell you about it, encouraging you to appreciate how beautifully that worked out in the end. Or he'll tell you about one or two of his past clients—how one of them is now King of Samoa and the other is expected to be nominated for the Nobel Prize next week. He'll ask whether everything will be okay at home, whether you expect to have trouble telling your spouse. When you say no, he'll give you his card and urge you to take things easy for a while, but then to come see him at his office.

"I know it can be hard to believe at a time like this," my first outplacement geek told me, "but it really is true that this could turn out to be the best thing that ever happened to you."

The outplacement geek wants to think of himself as a useful citizen, a kind of midwife, not as an accessory after the fact. Understandable, of course. Not many of our mothers had anything like this in mind for us when they brought us into the world. Not many of us want to do these things we do for pay.

A guy in Connecticut, a friend of a friend, tells me that Gerber Products has a search on. I wait until just after six and try to call the company's vice president for Human Resources, Curtis Mairs. Calling very early or very late in the day is a good tactic: the secretaries are usually off duty then. Today it works: Mairs picks up his own phone, and he doesn't hang up as I hurriedly introduce myself. I say I've heard he's looking for a P.R. exec. Not wanting to repeat what may have been my big mistake with Booz, Allen, I say I'd like the name of the recruiter handling the search.

"You might try Steven Seiden," he says. "In New York," and hangs up. There's a New York listing for Seiden Associates, Inc., in my *Directory of Executive Recruiters*. And it is indeed headed by a Steven Seiden. I spend much of the evening writing and rewriting a letter.

First thing the next morning I call Seiden's office and get his fax number. Then I drive to the EconoPrint shop and have my letter and résumé transmitted. Next I put both into a manila envelope, drive to the post office, and send them off by Priority Mail.

The next night Seiden calls. We talk for a long time. He goes through my résumé line by line, asking for details about everything.

"Well," he says finally, "all of it sounds pretty impressive. On the face of it. As far as it goes."

On the face of it? Does he think I'm pretending to be somebody I'm not?

He asks me to describe my appearance. When I do so, fumblingly, he asks how tall I am. How much I weigh. Whether I have a beard. A mustache. He asks me to send a photo of myself.

What?

We agree that I will also send him samples of my work.

Once again I sit up late composing a letter intended to make me seem brilliant and clever, motivated but not desperate. When I'm satisfied, I put it into an envelope with a fat stack of supporting evidence: corporate annual reports, articles and speeches, official descriptions of my last two jobs, charts of departments I've headed, a survey showing that business editors rated one of those departments among the best in the country after I'd been running it for seven years. Fat yellow envelope in hand, I'm at the post office when it opens in the morning.

Early the following week, Seiden calls to say he's received my envelope, has examined most of the contents, and finds it "very impressive—assuming it all checks out."

Does he think I've forged this stuff?

Days later I arrive home to find a message saying that Seiden wants me to call him.

"Listen," he says when I reach him, "I'm in a meeting and can't talk now. But I want you to know that I really am interested in you for the Gerber thing. I'll be back to you soon. This search is *not*"—the italics are in his voice—"going to go ahead without you. I'll be back to you soon—in hours, not days. You'll hear from me again in hours, not days."

Taking Seiden at his word, I begin to watch the clock. The day ends without another call. The next day ends the same way, and so does the week. Then it's weeks, not days. After a very long time I try to call him, don't get through, leave my name and number.

More than a week after that Pam and I arrive home one Sunday night and find a message on the machine. The voice of Steven Seiden says, in a bored way, that he's returning my call. He has left his home number but cautions me not to disturb him after ten-thirty New York time—precisely the time I hear the message. After a moment of agonizing I decide to wait.

The next morning I call, leave a message, get nothing back. In the evening I call him at home. His wife says in a cheery voice that he's gone out briefly but will call me back soon.

He doesn't. He never calls again. Eventually, many weeks later, an envelope arrives from his office. In it is a copy of the news release announcing that a new vice president of communications has been appointed at the Gerber Products Company.

The winner is from Chicago. I recognize his name. He's the guy who told me about the Gerber search in the first place.

Small world.

This doesn't need to turn out to be the best thing that ever happened to me. I'll be satisfied, I'll be grateful, if it turns out to be something less than a disaster. If it ends with me in a new job that's more than barely tolerable, with my life not totally deranged and Pam and the kids not permanently hurt. If it ends that way I will, so help me, get down on my knees in gratitude.

What I keep thinking about, though, is not exciting new opportunities or the delights that are still to come.

What I think about is Bobby Joyce.

Bobby Joyce lived in my neighborhood when I was a kid and was a year ahead of me in high school. He was a big, good-looking Irishman of the black-haired, white-skinned, Snow White type—cocky, arrogant, unfailingly sarcastic, athletically brilliant. When I picture him I always see him chewing gum, smiling a kiss-my-ass smile. He showed us how it was possible to be cool even in a cassock and surplice. I'm sure he didn't chew gum while serving Mass, but it isn't hard to picture him that way.

Thirty years out of high school, I found myself seated next to another old-timer from the neighborhood, Jimmy Monahan, at some sort of downtown business lunch. Jimmy had been a few years ahead of Bobby Joyce in school, which put him several years ahead of me. He'd always been the friendly sort, though, even to us little guys. When I ran into him he was the advertising manager for an insurance company. He had the creased face and tired, unjudging eyes of a decent man for whom life has not been a picnic. As the luncheon broke up and we were moving toward the door he somehow mentioned Bobby Joyce—how miserable it was, what had happened to him.

I couldn't let it go; I had to ask. Bobby had become an accountant, Jimmy said, and spent decades with the same company before losing his job. After a year of failing to find a new one, Bobby killed himself. He did it by jumping off the Union Avenue viaduct onto some old railroad tracks at the northern edge of the neighborhood where we'd all been schoolboys together.

I don't know what season it happened in. But in my mind's eye I see it as a raw winter's day, a black-and-white turned-up-collar day like some scene from *On the Waterfront*. It's hard to draw a connection between the spent man I see pulling himself up onto the viaduct's concrete railing and the beautiful boy I remember.

Bobby Joyce, uncrowned king of the kids, dead of a year without work.

FOR JOURNALING AND DISCUSSION

1. How does this article play to and feed off of the fears of its upper middle-class audience?
2. Would this story be as effective if it were about an out-of-work plumber? school-teacher? police officer? Why or why not?
3. What understandings does his prolonged unemployment bring Meyer about himself and society in general?
4. How would this piece be different if it were written by a woman?
5. In his book entitled *Executive Blues,* Meyer claims that Americans define themselves by their possessions. We have become "incapable of imagining goals higher or more meaningful than a fine house or a fine car." Is this true of American society as a whole? How does this focus on materialism help to maintain the American class structure?

FOR RESEARCH AND EXPLORATION

1. Carefully look at Meyer's use of rhetoric and language. Write an essay about how he manages to gain our pity and empathy, despite the fact that he is better off than most of his readers can ever hope to be. How does he manipulate the reader to be on his side?
2. Find several articles dealing with layoffs and downsizing. Write an essay describing how differently the topic is approached depending on who is getting laid off—autoworkers versus executives, for example. Also notice the difference depending on the intended audience. For example, consider how *Fortune* covers a downsizing story compared to the ways *Mother Jones* deals with the same issue.
3. Meyer describes feeling as though he has failed as a man—his manhood is linked to his ability to hold down a job and support a family. Connect this to Andrew Kimbrell's views about masculinity in "A Time for Men to Pull Together" in Chapter 4.

CHAPTER 4

Gender and Sexuality

As we take up the topics of gender and sexuality in our society, the complicated problems of definition and representation continue to expose limitations and biases in our perspectives and to raise many questions. At the end of the century, we encounter seemingly endless variations within categories that were once represented as simple, uncomplicated binaries: male versus female, masculine versus feminine. Now we ask, what is gender, and how is it learned? Is it entirely socially constructed, or are there genetic bases for some characteristics? How many genders are there? What do we mean by the sex of a person? How clear are the biological distinctions between male and female? Which sex is a transgender person?

As we have become more aware of the ways gender and sexuality are socially constructed, we have identified more limitations. In the 1970s discussions of gender primarily addressed white, middle-class, heterosexual males and females. In the 1990s these discussions have more overtly acknowledged the tensions bred of omissions. Just as we have recognized the power of the dominant perspective to limit our understandings of race and class, so have we understood how it has obscured knowledge of gay, lesbian, bisexual, and transgender identities. While we again do not attempt equal representation of all voices, in this chapter we do try to present a range of perspectives that are redefining the very categories "gender" and "sexuality."

SUMMARIES OF SELECTIONS ON GENDER AND SEXUALITY

This redefinition is obvious in essays such as **Andrew Kimbrell**'s "A Time for Men to Pull Together." He mirrors some of the rhetoric from the women's movement as he describes a "male mystique" and a plan for male self-discovery. However, Kimbrell's essay highlights the pain of mostly white, middle-class, straight men, and makes little mention of gays and men of color in this new "manifesto." His essay reminds us of the problems of "exclusion" described in feminism more than a decade ago.

In "Are Women Morally Superior to Men?" **Katha Pollitt** debunks " 'difference,' feminism" by asking, "What is female? Nature. Blood. Milk. Communal gatherings. The moon. Quilts." Her criticisms of feminists who argue for inherent differences between women and men, such as Carol Gilligan and Deborah Tannen, will help you to develop a more critical perspective as you consider many of the other essays in this collection.

Several of the other essays are also grounded in social scientific approaches; they suggest contradictory findings and bring the "objectivity" of scientific inquiries about gender into question. **David H. Freedman**'s "The Aggressive Egg" challenges the age-old biological bias that an active sperm "penetrates" a passive egg, a bias that continues to perpetuate perceptions about male sexual activity and female sexual passivity.

Sallie Tisdale complicates the notion that the struggle for self-definition is merely a period of adolescent angst. In "A Weight That Women Carry" she describes a lifetime of dieting, calorie counting, and social stigma, while at the same time suggesting that body image is socially constructed and pointing out that "dieters are the perfect consumers: they never get enough."

The autobiographical and fictional pieces in this chapter explore the conflicts generated when the outside world forces names and categories on people who are attempting to know and name themselves. **Paula Gunn Allen**'s "They Make Their Climb" marks the moment when a fluid and undefined friendship among two adolescent girls is suddenly and violently forbidden by teachers and parents because it veers too close to the adults' fears of lesbianism.

In "A Clack of Tiny Sparks," **Bernard Cooper** struggles with his teenage attraction for a boy in his class, an attraction he fears, given his mother's terror at the thought of someone calling him a "fag."

Norah Vincent reflects on the ways the term "lesbian" has been defined, both inside and outside "the lesbian community," and opts for an individualistic definition of herself. In "A Normal Lesbian" she says her aim is to "be original, and write something that is a profound, intelligent depiction of the human spirit in a lesbian milieu. . . ."

Finally, in "Asian Women in Film" **Jessica Hagedorn** writes, "As I was growing up in the Philippines in the 1950s, my fertile imagination was colonized by thoroughly American fantasies." She traces depictions of Asian women in American films, and finds them, not surprisingly, full of cultural stereotypes that have shaped her own and others' identities.

RHETORICAL QUESTIONS

In this chapter, we propose that you focus on questions of *purpose*. Why should men need a manifesto at this particular time? What was Kimbrell's particular reason for writing one? What is Pollitt's purpose? How effective is Freedman in convincing you of his thesis that cultural stereotypes have been applied to eggs and sperm? Why do you suppose some of the writers have chosen fiction to accomplish their purposes? Can you even guess what their reasons might have been? What kinds of actions might follow from any of these essays? Do you think the writers want to convince you to do something?

If you write about gender, what will your purpose be? Would you want to change someone's mind about something? Would you want to share an unusual perspective and have the reader acknowledge that it is valid, even though the reader's position might be different?

A Time for Men to Pull Together: A Manifesto for the New Politics of Masculinity

Andrew Kimbrell

Kimbrell is an attorney, writer, and activist. He is the author of The Human Body Shop *and* 101 Ways to Save the Earth, *and general editor of* The Green Lifestyle Handbook. *His articles have appeared in* The New York Times, The Washington Post, Harper's Magazine, The Utne Reader, *and numerous other national newspapers and magazines.* The Utne Reader *named Kimbrell "one of America's '100 Visionaries.' " He lectures widely and has appeared on many national news shows. He is the director of the International Center for Technology Assessment in Washington, D.C., and cofounder of the Men's Health Network.*

"Our civilization is a dingy ungentlemanly business; it drops so much out of a man."

—Robert Louis Stevenson

Andrew Kimbrell, "A Time For Men To Pull Together: A Manifesto for the New Politics of Masculinity" from *The Utne Reader* 45 (May/June 1991). Copyright © 1991 by Andrew Kimbrell. Reprinted with the permission of the author.

Men are hurting—badly. Despite rumors to the contrary, men as a gender are being devastated physically and psychically by our socioeconomic system. As American society continues to empower a small percentage of men—and a smaller but increasing percentage of women—it is causing significant confusion and anguish for the majority of men.

In recent years, there have been many impressive analyses documenting the exploitation of women in our culture. Unfortunately, little attention has been given to the massive disruption and destruction that our economic and political institutions have wrought on men. In fact, far too often, men as a gender have been thought of as synonymous with the power elite.

But thinking on this subject is beginning to change. Over the last decade, men have begun to realize that we cannot properly relate to one another, or understand how some of us in turn exploit others, until we have begun to appreciate the extent and nature of our dispossessed predicament. In a variety of ways, men across the country are beginning to mourn their losses and seek solutions.

This new sense of loss among men comes from the deterioration of men's traditional roles as protectors of family and the earth (although not the sole protectors)—what psychologist Robert Mannis calls the *generative* potential of men. And much of this mourning also focuses on how men's energy is often channeled in the direction of destruction—both of the earth and its inhabitants.

The mission of many men today—both those involved in the men's movement and others outside it—is to find new ways that allow men to celebrate their generative potential and reverse the cycle of destruction that characterizes men's collective behavior today. These calls to action are not abstract or hypothetical. The oppression of men, especially in the last several decades, can be easily seen in a disturbing upward spiral of male self-destruction, addiction, hopelessness, and homelessness.

While suicide rates for women have been stable over the last 20 years, among men—especially white male teenagers—they have increased rapidly. Currently, male teenagers are five times more likely to take their own lives than females. Overall, men are committing suicide at four times the rate of women. America's young men are also being ravaged by alcohol and drug abuse. Men between the ages of 18 and 29 suffer alcohol dependency at three times the rate of women of the same age group. More than two-thirds of all alcoholics are men, and 50 percent more men are regular users of illicit drugs than women. Men account for more than 90 percent of arrests for alcohol and drug abuse violations.

A sense of hopelessness among America's young men is not surprising. Real wages for men under 25 have actually declined over the last 20 years, and 60 percent of all high school dropouts are males. These statistics, added to the fact that more than 400,000 farmers have lost their land in the last decade, account in part for the increasing rate of unemployment among men, and for the fact that more than 80 percent of America's homeless are men.

The stress on men is taking its toll. Men's life expectancy is 10 percent shorter than women's, and the incidence of stress-related illnesses such as heart disease and certain cancers remains inordinately high among men.

And the situation for minority men is even worse. One out of four black men between the ages of 20 and 29 is either in jail, on probation, or on parole—ten times the proportion for black women in the same age range. More black men are in jail than in college, and there are 40 percent more black women than black men studying in our nation's colleges and universities. Homicide is the leading cause of death among black males ages 15 to 24. Black males have the lowest life expectancy of any segment of the American population. Statistics for Native American and Hispanic men are also grim.

Men are also a large part of the growing crisis in the American family. Studies report that parents today spend 40 percent less time with their children than did parents in 1965, and men are increasingly isolated from their families by the pressures of work and the circumstances of divorce. In a recent poll, 72 percent of employed male respondents agreed that they are "torn by conflict" between their jobs and the desire to be with their families. Yet the average divorced American man spends less than two days a month with his children. Well over half of black male children are raised without fathers. While the trauma of separation and divorce affects all members of a family, it is especially poignant for sons: Researchers generally agree that boys at all ages are hardest hit by divorce.

THE ENCLOSURE OF MEN

The current crisis for men, which goes far beyond statistics, is nothing new. We have faced a legacy of loss, especially since the start of the mechanical age. From the Enclosure Acts, which forced families off the land in Tudor England, to the ongoing destruction of indigenous communities throughout the Third World, the demands of the industrial era have forced men off the land, out of the family and community, and into the factory and office. The male as steward of family and soil, craftsman, woodsman, native hunter, and fisherman has all but vanished.

As men became the primary cog in industrial production, they lost touch with the earth and the parts of themselves that needed the earth to survive. Men by the millions—who long prided themselves on their husbandry of family, community, and land—were forced into a system whose ultimate goal was to turn one man against another in the competitive "jungle" of industrialized society. As the industrial revolution advanced, men lost not only their independence and dignity, but also the sense of personal creativity and responsibility associated with individual crafts and small-scale farming.

The factory wrenched the father from the home, and he often became a virtual nonentity in the household. By separating a man's work from his family, industrial society caused the permanent alienation of father from son. Even when the modern father returns to the house, he is often too tired and too ir-ritable from the tensions and tedium of work in the factory or corporation to pay close attention to his children. As Robert Bly, in his best-selling book *Iron John* (1990, Addison-Wesley), has pointed out, "When a father, absent during the day, returns home at six, his children receive only his temperament, and not his teaching." The family, and especially sons, lose the presence of the fa-ther, uncle, and other male role models. It is difficult to calculate the full im-pact that this pattern of paternal absence has had on family and society over the last several generations.

While the loss of fathers is now beginning to be discussed, men have yet to fully come to terms with the terrible loss of sons during the mechanized wars of this century. World War I, World War II, Korea, and Vietnam were what the poet Robert Graves called "holocausts of young men." In the battlefields of this century, hundreds of millions of men were killed or injured. In World Wars I and II—in which more than 100 million soldiers were casualties—most of the victims were teenage boys, the average age being 18.5 years.

Given this obvious evidence of our exploitation, it is remarkable that so few men have acknowledged the genocide on their gender over the last century—much less turned against those responsible for this vast victimization. Women have increasingly identified their oppression in society; men have not. Thank-fully, some men are now working to create a movement, or community, that focuses on awareness and understanding of men's loss and pain as well as the po-tential for healing. Because men's oppression is deeply rooted in the political and economic institutions of modern society, it is critical that awareness of these issues must be followed by action: Men today need a comprehensive political program that points the way toward liberation.

LOST IN THE MALE MYSTIQUE

Instead of grieving over and acting on our loss of independence and gen-erativity, modern men have often engaged in denial—a denial that is linked to the existence of a "male mystique." This defective mythology of the modern age has created a "new man." The male mystique recasts what anthropologists have identified as the traditional male role throughout history—a man, whether hunter-gatherer or farmer, who is steeped in a creative and sustaining relationship with his extended family and the earth household. In the place of this long-enduring, rooted masculine role, the male mystique has fostered a new image of men: autonomous, efficient, intensely self-interested, and dis-connected from community and the earth.

The male mystique was spawned in the early days of the modern age. It combines Francis Bacon's idea that "knowledge is power" and Adam Smith's view that the highest good is "the individual exerting himself to his own ad-vantage." This power-oriented, individualistic ideology was further solidified by the concepts of the survival of the fittest and the ethic of efficiency. The ideal man was no longer the wise farmer, but rather the most successful man-eater in the Darwinian corporate jungle.

The most tragic aspect of all this for us is that as the male mystique created the modern power elite, it destroyed male friendship and bonding. The male mystique teaches that the successful man is competitive, uncaring, unloving. It celebrates the ethic of isolation—it turns men permanently against each other in the tooth and claw world of making a living. As the Ivan Boesky–type character in the movie *Wall Street* tells his young apprentice, "If you need a friend, get a dog."

The male mystique also destroys men's ties to the earth. It embodies the view of 17th century British philosopher John Locke that "[land] that is left wholly to nature is called, as indeed it is, waste." A sustainable relationship with the earth is sacrificed to material progress and conspicuous consumption.

Ironically, men's own sense of loss has fed the male mystique. As men become more and more powerless in their own lives, they are given more and more media images of excessive, caricatured masculinity with which to identify. Men look to manufactured macho characters from the Wild West, working-class America, and modern war in the hope of gaining some sense of what it means to be a man. The primary symbols of the male mystique are almost never caring fathers, stewards of the land, or community organizers. Instead, over several decades these aggressively masculine figures have evolved from the Western independent man (John Wayne, Gary Cooper) to the blue-collar macho man (Sly Stallone and Robert DeNiro) and finally to a variety of military and police figures concluding with the violent revelry of *Robocop*.

Modern men are entranced by this simulated masculinity—they experience danger, independence, success, sexuality, idealism, and adventure as voyeurs. Meanwhile, in real life most men lead powerless, subservient lives in the factory or office—frightened of losing their jobs, mortgaged to the gills, and still feeling responsible for supporting their families. Their lauded independence—as well as most of their basic rights—disappear the minute they report for work. The disparity between their real lives and the macho images of masculinity perpetrated by the media confuses and confounds many men. In his book *The Men from the Boys*, Ray Raphael asks, "But is it really that manly to wield a jackhammer, or spend one's life in the mines? Physical labor is often mindless, repetitive, and exhausting. . . . The workers must be subservient while on the job, and subservience is hard to reconcile with the masculine ideal of personal power."

Men can no longer afford to lose themselves in denial. We need to experience grief and anger over our losses and not buy into the pseudo-male stereotypes propagated by the male mystique. We are not, after all, what we are told we are.

At the same time, while recognizing the pervasive victimization of women, we must resist the view of some feminists that maleness itself, and not the current systems of social control and production, is primarily responsible for the exploitation of women. For men who are sensitive to feminist thinking, this view of masculinity creates a confusing and debilitating double bind: We view ourselves as oppressors yet experience victimization on the personal and social level. Instead of blaming maleness, we must challenge the defective mythology of the male mystique. Neither the male mystique nor the denigration of maleness offers hope for the future.

Fortunately, we may be on the verge of a historic shift in male consciousness. Recently, there has been a rediscovery of masculinity as a primal creative and generative force equal to that of the recently recognized creative and nurturing power of the feminine. A number of thinkers and activists are urging men to substitute empathy for efficiency, stewardship for exploitation, generosity for the competitiveness of the marketplace.

At the forefront of this movement have been poet Robert Bly and others working with him: psychologist James Hillman, drummer Michael Meade, Jungian scholar Robert Moore. Bly has called for the recognition and reaffirmation of the "wild" man. As part of Bly's crusade, thousands of men have come together to seek a regeneration of their sexuality and power, as they reject the cerebral, desiccated world of our competitive corporate culture. Another compelling analysis is that of Jungian therapist Robert Mannis, who has called for a renewal of the ethic of "husbandry," a sense of masculine obligation involved with generating and maintaining a stable relationship to one's family and to the earth itself. And a growing number of men are mounting other challenges to the male mystique. But so far, the men's movement has remained primarily therapeutic. Little effort has been made to extend the energy of male self-discovery into a practical social and political agenda.

A MANIFESTO FOR MEN

As many of us come to mourn the lost fathers and sons of the last decades and seek to re-establish our ties to each other and to the earth, we need to find ways to change the political, social, and economic structures that have created this crisis. A "wild man" weekend in the woods, or intense man-to-man discussions, can be key experiences in self-discovery and personal empowerment. But these personal experiences are not enough to reverse the victimization of men. As the men's movement gathers strength, it is critical that this increasing sense of personal liberation be channeled into political action. Without significant changes in our society there will only be continued hopelessness and frustration for men. Moreover, a coordinated movement pressing for the liberation of men could be a key factor in ensuring that the struggle for a sustainable future for humanity and the earth succeeds.

What follows is a brief political platform for men, a short manifesto with which we can begin the process of organizing men as a positive political force working for a better future. This is the next step for the men's movement.

Fathers and Children

Political efforts focusing on the family must reassert men's bonds with the family and reverse the "lost father" syndrome. While any long-term plan for men's liberation requires significant changes in the very structure of our work and economic institutions, a number of intermediate steps are possible: We need to take a leadership role in supporting parental leave legislation, which gives working parents the right to take time from work to care for children or other family members. And we need to target the Bush administration for vetoing this vital legislation. Also needed is pro-child tax relief such as greatly expanding the young child tax credit, which would provide income relief and tax breaks to families at a point when children need the most parental care and when income may be the lowest.

We should also be in the forefront of the movement pushing for changes in the workplace including more flexible hours, part-time work, job sharing, and home-based employment. As economic analyst William R. Mattox Jr. notes, a simple step toward making home-based employment more viable would be to loosen restrictions on claiming home office expenses as a tax deduction for parents. Men must also work strenuously in the legal arena to promote more liberal visitation rights for non-custodial parents and to assert appropriateness of the father as a custodial parent. Non-traditional family structures should also be given more recognition in our society, with acknowledgment of men's important roles as stepfathers, foster fathers, uncles, brothers, and mentors. We must seek legislative ways to recognize many men's commitments that do not fit traditional definitions of family.

Ecology as Male Politics

A sustainable environment is not merely one issue among others. It is the crux of all issues in our age, including men's politics. The ecological struggles of our time offer a unique forum in which men can express their renewed sense of the wild and their traditional roles as creators, defenders of the family, and careful stewards of the earth.

The alienation of men from their rootedness to the land has deprived us all of what John Muir called the "heart of wilderness." As part of our efforts to re-experience the wild in ourselves, we should actively become involved in experiencing the wilderness first hand and organize support for the protection of nature and endangered species. Men should also become what Robert Bly has called "inner warriors" for the earth, involving themselves in non-violent civil disobedience to protect wilderness areas from further destruction.

An important aspect of the masculine ethic is defense of family. Pesticides and other toxic pollutants that poison our food, homes, water, and air represent a real danger, especially to children. Men need to be adamant in their call for limitations on the use of chemicals.

Wendell Berry has pointed out that the ecological crisis is also a crisis of agriculture. If men are to recapture a true sense of stewardship and husbandry and affirm the "seedbearing," creative capacity of the male, they must, to the extent possible, become involved in sustainable agriculture and organic farming and gardening. We should also initiate and support legislation that sustains our farming communities.

Men in the Classrooms and Community

In many communities, especially inner cities, men are absent not only from homes but also from the schools. Men must support the current efforts by black men's groups around the country to implement male-only early-grade classes taught by men. These programs provide role models and a surrogate paternal presence for young black males. We should also commit ourselves to having a far greater male presence in all elementary school education. Recent studies have shown that male grade school students have a higher level of achievement when they are taught by male teachers. Part-time or full-time home schooling options can also be helpful in providing men a great opportunity to be teachers—not just temperaments—to their children.

We need to revive our concern for community. Community-based boys' clubs, scout troops, sports leagues, and big brother programs have achieved significant success in helping fatherless male children find self-esteem. Men's groups must work to strengthen these organizations.

Men's Minds, Men's Bodies, and Work

Men need to join together to fight threats to male health including suicide, drug and alcohol abuse, AIDS, and stress diseases. We should support active prevention and education efforts aimed at these deadly threats. Most importantly, men need to be leaders in initiating and supporting holistic and psychotherapeutic approaches that directly link many of these health threats to the coercive nature of the male mystique and the current economic system. Changes in diet, reduction of drug and alcohol use, less stressful work environments, greater nurturing of and caring for men by other men, and fighting racism, hopelessness, and homelessness are all important, interconnected aspects of any male health initiative.

Men Without Hope or Homes

Men need to support measures that promote small business and entrepreneurship, which will allow more people to engage in crafts and human-scale, community-oriented enterprises. Also important is a commitment to appropriate, human-scale technologies such as renewable energy sources. Industrial and other inappropriate technologies have led to men's dispossession, degradation—and increasingly to unemployment.

A related struggle is eliminating racism. No group of men is more dispossessed than minority men. White men should support and network with African-American and other minority men's groups. Violence and discrimination against men because of their sexual preference should also be challenged.

Men, who represent more than four-fifths of the homeless, can no longer ignore this increasing social tragedy. Men's councils should develop support groups for the homeless in their communities.

The Holocaust of Men

As the primary victims of mechanized war, men must oppose this continued slaughter. Men need to realize that the traditional male concepts of the noble warrior are undermined and caricatured in the technological nightmare of modern warfare. Men must together become prime movers in dismantling the military-industrial establishment and redistributing defense spending toward a sustainable environment and protection of family, school, and community.

Men's Action Network

No area of the men's political agenda will be realized until men can establish a network of activists to create collective action. A first step might be to create a high-profile national coalition of the men's councils that are growing around the country. This coalition, which could be called the Men's Action Network (MAN), could call for a national conference to define a comprehensive platform of men's concerns and to provide the political muscle to implement those ideas.

A Man Could Stand Up

The current generation of men face a unique moment in history. Though often still trapped by economic coercion and psychological co-option, we are beginning to see that there is a profound choice ahead. Will we choose to remain subservient tools of social and environmental destruction or to fight for rediscovery of the male as a full partner and participant in family, community, and the earth? Will we remain mesmerized by the male mystique, or will we reclaim the true meaning of our masculinity?

There is a world to gain. The male mystique, in which many of today's men—especially the most politically powerful—are trapped, is threatening the family and the planet with irreversible destruction. A men's movement based on the recovery of masculinity could renew much of the world we have lost. By changing types of work and work hours, we could break our subordination to corporate managers and return much of our work and lives to the household. We could once again be teaching, nurturing presences to our children. By devoting ourselves to meaningful work with appropriate technology, we could recover independence in our work and our spirit. By caring for each other, we could recover the dignity of our gender and heal the wounds of addiction and self-destruction. By becoming husbands to the earth, we could protect the wild and recover our creative connections with the forces and rhythms of nature.

Ultimately we must help fashion a world without the daily frustration and sorrow of having to view each other as a collection of competitors instead of a community of friends. We must celebrate the essence and rituals of our masculinity. We can no longer passively submit to the destruction of the household, the demise of self-employment, the disintegration of family and community, and the desecration of our earth.

Shortly after the First World War, Ford Madox Ford, one of this century's greatest writers, depicted 20th century men as continually pinned down in their trenches, unable to stand up for fear of annihilation. As the century closes, men remain pinned down by an economic and political system that daily forces millions of us into meaningless work, powerless lives, and self-destruction. The time has come for men to stand up.

FOR JOURNALING AND DISCUSSION

1. Calls for men's movements have often been criticized as "antifeminist backlash"; however, in this piece Kimbrell cites some powerful statistics tracing male suffering under capitalism. Cite some of these statistics, and explain Kimbrell's point about the status of men in a capitalist patriarchy.
2. Kimbrell explains industrialism's role in isolating men from the home and the land. Write an informal family work history going back as many generations as you can. Have your male relatives been estranged from their homes and land?
3. The author claims that men cannot "understand how some of us . . . exploit others, until we have begun to appreciate the . . . nature of our dispossessed predicament," which suggests men must heal themselves first. Write a letter to Kimbrell explaining your agreement or disagreement with this position.
4. Kimbrell notes that "real wages for men under 25 have actually declined over the last 20 years, and 60 percent of all high school dropouts are males," which for many of you means that your parents had a drastically different school and work experience than you have had or will have. What do you think are some of the reasons for this?
5. Describing role models of the "male mystique," Kimbrell cites John Wayne, Sylvester Stallone, and *Robocop*. Can you describe further images of this aggressively masculine and independent man? Can you describe figures who challenge this mystique?

FOR RESEARCH AND EXPLORATION

1. Explore your local press coverage of the Million Man March in October 1995. Compare the march to Kimbrell's notion of the oppression of males. While the march was overtly open to African American males only, Kimbrell's discussion of male subservience in the factory and the office fleetingly mentions race, and seems to imply an oppression of white males. Using your research and Kimbrell's article, explain connections between race and gender.

2. Kimbrell identifies Robert Bly, among others, as leaders of the men's movement. Read and review selections from Bly's influential work *Iron John.*
3. Read Ben Hamper's "Rivethead" in Chapter 3, and write an analysis of Hamper's narrative in light of some of Kimbrell's data on the ways industrialization has affected American males.

Are Women Morally Superior to Men? Debunking "Difference" Feminism

Katha Pollitt

For more than a decade, Pollitt has taken the strongest positions on the thorniest moral issues and the most controversial events, from date rape to surrogate motherhood, to violence against women to the Anita Hill hearings, to fetal rights and mothers' "wrongs." Her pieces delight by their language— the mastery that won a National Book Circle Award for her first book of poems—and by Pollitt's refusal ever to be ponderous. Her publications include the book of poems Antarctic Traveller, *and* Reasonable Creatures: Essays on Women and Feminism. *Pollitt was born in New York City, where she now lives, was educated at Radcliffe College and Columbia University, and has received numerous awards for her poetry. She is currently an associate editor for* The Nation.

Some years ago, I was invited by the wife of a well-known writer to sign a women's peace petition. It made the points such documents usually make: that women, as mothers, caregivers, and nurturers, have a special awareness of the precariousness of human life, see through jingoism and cold war rhetoric, and would prefer nations to work out their difficulties peacefully so that the military budget could be diverted to schools and hospitals and housing. It had the literary tone such documents usually have—at once superior and plaintive, as if the authors didn't know whether they were bragging or begging. We are wiser than you poor deluded menfolk, was the subtext, so will you please-please-please listen to your moms?

To sign or not to sign? Of course, I was all for peace. But was I for peace *as a woman?* I wasn't a mother then—I wasn't even an aunt. Did my lack of nurturing credentials make my grasp of the horrors of war and the folly of the arms race only theoretical, like a white person's understanding of racism? Were mothers the natural leaders of the peace movement, to whose judgment non-mothers, male and female, must defer, because after all we couldn't *know*, couldn't *feel* that tenderness toward fragile human life that a woman who had borne and raised children had experienced? On the other hand, I was indeed a woman. Was motherhood with its special wisdom somehow deep inside me, to be called upon when needed, like my uterus?

Complicating matters was my response to the famous writer's wife herself. Here was a woman in her 50s, her child-raising long behind her. Was motherhood the only banner under which she could gain a foothold on civic life? Perhaps so. Her only other public identity was that of a wife, and wifehood, even to a famous man, isn't much to claim credit for these days. Motherhood was what she had in the work-and-accomplishment department, so it was understandable that she try to maximize its moral status. But I was not in her situation: I was a writer, a single woman, a jobholder. By sending me a petition from which I was excluded even as I was invited to add my name, perhaps she was telling me that, by leading a non-domestic life, I had abandoned the moral high ground, was "acting like a man," but could redeem myself by acknowledging the moral pre-eminence of the class of women I refused to join.

The ascription of particular virtues—compassion, patience, common sense, non-violence—to mothers, and the tendency to conflate "mothers" with "women," has a long history in the peace movement but goes way beyond issues of war and peace. At present it permeates discussions of just about every field, from management training to theology. Indeed, although the media like to caricature feminism as denying the existence of sexual differences, for the women's movement and its opponents alike "difference" is where the action is. Thus, business writers wonder if women's nurturing, intuitive qualities will make them better executives. Educators suggest that female students suffer in classrooms that emphasize competition over cooperation. Women politicians tout their playground-honed negotiating skills, their egoless devotion to public service, their gender-based commitment to fairness and caring. A variety of political causes—environmentalism, animal rights, even vegetarianism—are promoted as logical extensions of women's putative peacefulness, closeness to nature, horror of aggression, and concern for others' health.

In the arts, we hear a lot about what women's "real" subjects, methods, and materials ought to be. Painting is male. Rhyme is male. Plot is male. Perhaps, say some feminists, even logic and language are male. What is female? Nature. Blood. Milk. Communal gatherings. The moon. Quilts.

Haven't we been here before? Woman as sharer and carer, woman as earth mother, woman as guardian of all the small rituals that knit together a family and a community, woman as beneath, above, or beyond such manly concerns as law, reason, abstract ideas—these images are as old as time. Defenders of male supremacy have always used them to declare women inferior to men; covert ones use them to place women on a pedestal as too good for this naughty world. Thus, in the *Eumenides,* Aeschylus celebrated law as the defeat by males of primitive female principles of blood guilt and vengeance, while the Ayatollah Khomeini thought women should be barred from judgeships because they were too tenderhearted. Different rationale, same outcome: Women, because of their indifference to an impersonal moral order, cannot be full participants in civic life.

There exists an equally ancient line of thought, however, that uses femininity to pose a subversive challenge to the social order: Think of Sophocles' Antigone, who resists tyranny out of love and piety, or Aristophanes' Lysistrata, the original women's-strike-for-peace-nik, or Shakespeare's Portia, who champions mercy against the savage letter of the law. For reasons of power, money, and persistent social structures, the vision of the morally superior woman can never overcome the dominant ethos in reality but exists alongside it as a kind of permanent wish or hope: If only powerful and powerless could change places and the meek inherit the earth! Thus, it is perpetually being rediscovered, dressed in fashionable clothes and presented, despite its antiquity, as a radical new idea.

In the 1950s, which we think of as the glory days of traditional sex roles, the anthropologist Ashley Montagu argued in "The Natural Superiority of Women" that females had it all over males in every way that counted, including the possession of two X chromosomes that made them stabler, saner, and healthier than men, with their X and Y. Montagu's essay, published in *The Saturday Review* and later expanded to a book, is witty and high-spirited and, interestingly, anticipates the current feminist challenge to male-defined categories. (He notes, for example, that while men are stronger than women in the furniture-moving sense, women are stronger than men when faced with extreme physical hardship and tests of endurance; so when we say that men are stronger than women, we are equating strength with what men have.) But the fundamental thrust of Montagu's essay was to confirm traditional gender roles while revising the way we value them: Having proved to his own satisfaction that women could scale the artistic and intellectual heights, he argued that most would (that is, should) refrain, because women's true genius was "humanness," and their real mission was to "humanize" men before men blew up the world. And that, he left no doubt, was a full-time job.

Contemporary proponents of "difference feminism" advance a variation on the same argument, without Montagu's puckish humor. Instead of his whimsical chromosomal explanation, we get the psychoanalytic one proposed by Nancy Chodorow in *The Reproduction of Mothering:* Daughters define themselves by relating to their mothers, the primary love object of all children, and are therefore empathic, relationship oriented, non-hierarchical, and interested in forging consensus; sons must separate from their mothers, and are therefore individualistic, competitive, resistant to connection with others, and focused on abstract rules and rights. Chodorow's theory has become a kind of mantra of difference feminism, endlessly cited as if it explained phenomena we all agree are universal. But the central question Chodorow poses—Why are women the primary caregivers of children?—could not even be asked before the advent of modern birth control, and can be answered without resorting to psychology. Historically, women have taken care of children because high fertility and lack of other options left most of them no choice. Those rich enough to avoid personally raising their children often did.

Popularizers of Chodorow water down and sentimentalize her thesis. They embrace her proposition that traditional mothering produces "relational" women and "autonomous" men but forget her less congenial argument that it also results in sexual inequality, misogyny, and hostility between mothers and daughters (because daughters, like sons, desire independence but have a much harder time achieving it). Thus, in an immensely influential book, *In a Different Voice,* Carol Gilligan uses Chodorow to argue that the sexes make moral decisions according to separate criteria: women according to an "ethic of care," men according to an "ethic of rights." Deborah Tannen, in the best-selling *You Just Don't Understand,* claims that men and women grow up with "different cultural backgrounds"—the single-sex world of children's play in which girls cooperate and boys compete—"so talk between men and women is cross-cultural communication." Both Gilligan and Tannen confine their observations to the white middle class—especially Gilligan, much of whose elaborate theory of gendered ethics rests on interviews with a handful of Harvard-Radcliffe undergraduates—and seem unaware that this limits the applicability of their data.

And both massage their findings to fit their theories: Gilligan's male and female responses are actually quite similar to each other, as experimenters have subsequently shown by removing the names and asking subjects to try to sort the test answers by gender; Tannen is quick to attribute blatant rudeness or sexism in male speech to anxiety, helplessness, fear of loss of face—anything, indeed, but rudeness and sexism. Both look only at what people say, not what they do. For Tannen this isn't a decisive objection because verbal behavior is her subject, although it limits the applicability of her findings to other areas of behavior; for Gilligan, it is a major obstacle, unless you believe, as she apparently does, that the way people say they would resolve farfetched hypothetical dilemmas—Should a poor man steal drugs to save his dying wife?—tells us how they reason in real-life situations or, more important, what they do.

But the biggest problem with Chodorovian accounts of gender difference is that they credit the differences they find to essential, universal features of male and female psychosexual development rather than to the economic and social positions men and women hold, or to the actual power differences between individual men and women. In *The Mismeasure of Woman,* her trenchant and witty attack on contemporary theories of gender differences, Carol Tavris points out that much of what can be said about women applies as well to poor people, who also tend to focus more on family and relationships and less on work and self-advancement; who behave deferentially with those more socially powerful; and who appear to others more emotional and "intuitive" than rational and logical in their thinking. Then, too, there is the question of whether the difference theorists are measuring anything beyond their own willingness to think in stereotypes. If Chodorow is right, relational women and autonomous men should be the norm, but are they? Certainly, it is easy to find in one's own acquaintance, as well as in the world at large, men and women who don't fit the models. Difference feminists like to attribute ruthlessness, coldness, and hyperrationality in successful women—Margaret Thatcher is the standard example—to the fact that men control the networks of power and permit only women like themselves to rise. But I've met plenty of loudmouthed, insensitive, aggressive women who are stay-at-home mothers and secretaries and nurses. And I know plenty of sweet, unambitious men whose main satisfactions lie in their social, domestic, and romantic lives, although not all of them would admit this to an inquiring social scientist. We tend to tell strangers what we think will make us sound good.

So why are Gilligan and Tannen the toasts of feminist social science, endlessly cited and discussed? The success of the difference theorists proves yet again that social science is one part science and nine parts social. They say what people want to hear: Women really are different, in just the ways we always thought. Women embrace Gilligan and Tannen because they offer flattering accounts of traits for which they have historically been castigated. Men like them because, while they urge understanding and respect for "female" values and behaviors, they also let men off the hook: Men have power, wealth, and control of social resources because women don't really want those things.

While Chodorow's analysis of psychosexual development is the point of departure for most of the difference feminists, it is possible to construct a theory based on other grounds. The most interesting attempt I've seen is by the pacifist philosopher Sara Ruddick. Although not widely known outside academic circles, her book *Maternal Thinking* makes an argument that can be found in such mainstream sources as the columns of Anna Quindlen in the *New York Times*. For Ruddick it is not psychosexual development that produces the feminine virtues but intimate involvement in child-raising, the hands-on work of mothering. Men too can be mothers if they do the work that women do. (And women can be Fathers—a word Ruddick uses, complete with arrogant capital letter, for distant, uninvolved authority-figure parents.) Mothers are patient, peace-loving, attentive to emotional context, and so on because those are the qualities you need to get the job done, the way accountants are precise, lawyers are argumentative, writers self-centered. Thus mothers constitute a logical constituency for pacifist and anti-war politics, and, by extension, a "caring" political agenda.

But what is the job of mothering? Ruddick defines "maternal practice" as meeting three demands: preservation, growth, and social acceptability.

These rubrics can be used to explain almost anything mothers do, however cruel, dangerous, unfair, or authoritarian—the genital mutilation of African and Arab girls, the foot binding of pre-revolutionary Chinese ones, the sacrifice of some children to increase the resources available for others, as in the killing or malnourishing of female infants in India and China today. In this country, many mothers who commit what is legally child abuse *think* they are merely disciplining their kids in the good old-fashioned way. As long as the practices are culturally acceptable (and sometimes even when they're not), the mothers who perform them think of themselves as good parents. But if all these behaviors count as mothering, how can mothering have a necessary connection with any single belief about anything, let alone how to stop war, or any single set of personality traits, let alone non-violent ones?

We should not be surprised that motherhood does not produce uniform beliefs and behaviors: It is, after all, not a job; it has no standard of admission, and almost nobody gets fired. Motherhood is open to any woman who can have a baby or adopt one. *Not* to be a mother is a decision; becoming one requires merely that a woman accede, perhaps only for as long as it takes to get pregnant, to thousands of years of cumulative social pressure. After that, she's on her own; she can soothe her child's nightmares or let him cry in the dark. Nothing intrinsic to child-raising will tell her what is the better choice for her child. Although Ruddick starts off by looking closely at maternal practice, when that practice contradicts her own ideas about good mothering it is filed away as an exception, a distortion imposed by Fathers or poverty or some other outside force. But if you add up all the exceptions, you are left with a rather small group of people—women like Ruddick herself, enlightened, up-to-date, educated, upper-middle-class liberals.

And not even all of them. Consider the issue of physical punishment. Ruddick argues that experience teaches mothers that violence is useless; it only creates anger, deception, and more violence. Negotiation is the mother's way of resolving disputes and encouraging good behavior. As it happens, I agree that violence is a bad way to teach, and I made a decision never, no matter what, to spank my daughter. But mothers who do not hit their children, or permit their husbands to do so, are as rare as conscientious objectors in wartime. According to one survey, 78 percent approve of an occasional "good, hard spanking"—because they think violence *is* an effective way of teaching, because they think that hitting children isn't really violence, because they just lose it.

Ruddick claims to be describing what mothers do, but all too often she is really prescribing what she thinks they ought to do. "When their children flourish, almost all mothers have a sense of well-being." Hasn't she ever heard of postpartum depression? Of mothers who belittle their children's accomplishments and resent their growing independence? "What mother wouldn't want the power to keep her children healthy . . . to create hospitals, schools, jobs, day care, and work schedules that serve her maternal work?" Notice how neatly the modest and commonsensical wish for a healthy child balloons into the hotly contested and by no means universal wish of mothers for day care and flextime. Notice too how Ruddick moves from a mother's desire for social institutions that serve *her* children to an assumption that this desire translates into wanting comparable care for *all* children. But mothers feature prominently in local struggles against busing, mergers of rich and poor schools, and the placement of group homes for foster kids, boarder babies, and the retarded in their neighborhoods. Why? The true reason may be property values and racism, but what these mothers often say is that they are simply protecting their kids. Ruddick seems to think Maternal Thinking leads naturally to Sweden; in the United States, however, it is just as likely to lead to Fortress Suburbia.

As Gilligan does with all women, Ruddick scrutinizes mothers for what she expects to find, and sure enough, there it is. But why look to mothers for a peaceful constituency in the first place? Why not health professionals, who spend their lives saving lives? Or historians, who know how rarely war yields a benefit remotely commensurate with its cost in human misery? Or, I don't know, gardeners, blamelessly tending their innocent flowers? You can read almost any kind of work as affirming life and conferring wisdom. Ruddick chooses mothering because she's already decided that women possess certain virtues and she wants a non-biological peg to hang them on, so that men can acquire them too. A disinterested observer scouring the world for labor that encourages humane values would never pick child-raising: It's too quirky, too embedded in repellent cultural norms, too hot.

Despite its intellectual flabbiness, difference feminism is deeply appealing to many women. Why? For one thing, it seems to explain some important phenomena: that women—and this is a cross-cultural truth—commit very little criminal violence compared with men; that women fill the ranks of the so-called caring professions; that women are much less likely than men to abandon their children. Difference feminists want to give women credit for these good behaviors by raising them from the level of instinct or passivity—the Camille Paglia vision of femininity—to the level of moral choice and principled decision. Who can blame women for embracing theories that tell them the sacrifices they make on behalf of domesticity and children are legitimate, moral, even noble? By stressing the mentality of nurturance—the *ethic* of caring, maternal *thinking*—Gilligan and Ruddick challenge the ancient division of humanity into rational males and irrational females. They offer women a way to argue that their views have equal status with those of men and to resist the customary marginalization of their voices in public debate. Doubtless many women have felt emboldened by Carol Gilligan's accounts of moral difference: Speaking in a different voice is, after all, a big step up from silence.

The vision of women as sharers and carers is tempting in another way too. Despite much recent media blather about the new popularity of being a victim, most people want to believe they act out of free will and choice. The uncomfortable truth that women have all too little of either is a difficult hurdle for feminists. Acknowledging the systematic oppression of women seems to deprive them of existential freedom, to turn them into puppets, slaves, and Stepford wives. Deny it, and you can't make change. By arguing that the traditional qualities, tasks, and ways of life of women are as important, valuable, and serious as those of men (if not more so), Gilligan and others let women feel that nothing needs to change except the social valuation accorded to what they are already doing. It's a rationale for the status quo, which is why men like it, and it's a burst of grateful applause for womanhood, which is why women like it. Men keep the power, but since power is bad, so much the worse for them.

Another rather curious appeal of difference feminism is that it offers a way for women to define themselves as independent of men. In a culture that sees women almost entirely in relation to men, this is no small achievement. Sex, for example—the enormous amount of female energy, money, and time spent on beauty and fashion and romance, on attracting men and keeping them, on placating male power, strategizing ways around it or making it serve one's own ends—plays a minute role in these theories. You would never guess from Gilligan or Ruddick that men, individually and collectively, are beneficiaries of female nurturance, much less that this goes far to explain why society encourages nurturance in women. No, it is always children whom women are described as fostering and sacrificing for, or the community, or even other women—not husbands or lovers. It's as though wives cook dinner only for their kids, leaving the husband to raid the fridge on his own. And no doubt many women, quietly smoldering at their mate's refusal to share domestic labor, persuade themselves that they are serving only their children, or their own preferences. It's easier than confronting the inequality of their marriage.

The peaceful mother and the "relational" woman are a kinder, gentler, leftish version of the right's crusade for "family values," and both are modern versions of the separate-spheres ideology of the Victorians. Men ruled the world, women ruled the home. In the 19th century, too, some women tried to turn the ideology of sexual difference on its head and expand the moral claims of motherhood to include the public realm. Middle-class women became social reformers, abolitionists, temperance advocates, and settlement workers and even took paying jobs in the "helping professions"—nursing, social work, teaching—which were perceived as extensions of women's domestic role although practiced mostly by single women. These women did not deny that their sex fitted them for the home, but argued that domesticity did not end at the front door of the house, or confine itself to dusting (or telling the housemaid to dust). Even the vote could be cast as an extension of domesticity: Women, being more moral than men, would purify the government of vice and corruption, end war, and make America safe for family life.

Accepting the separate-spheres ideology had obvious advantages in an era when women were formally barred from higher education, political power, and many jobs. But its defects are equally obvious. It defined all women by a single standard, and one developed by a sexist society. It offered women no way to enter professions that could not be defined as extensions of domestic roles—you could be a math teacher but not a mathematician, a secretary but not a sea captain—and no way to challenge any but the grossest abuses of male privilege. Difference feminists are making a similar bid for power on behalf of women today, and are caught in similar contradictions. Once again, women are defined by their family roles. Child-raising is seen as women's glory and joy and opportunity for self-transcendence, while Dad naps on the couch. Women who do not fit the stereotype are castigated as unfeminine—nurses nurture, doctors do not—and domestic labor is romanticized and sold to women as a badge of moral worth.

For all the many current explanations of perceived moral difference between the sexes, one hears remarkably little about the material basis of the family. Yet the motherhood and womanhood being valorized cannot be considered apart from questions of power, privilege, and money. There is a reason a nonearning woman can proudly call herself a "wife and mother" and a non-earning man is just unemployed: The traditional female role implies a male income. Middle-class women go to great lengths to separate themselves from this uncomfortable fact. One often hears them defend their decision to stay at home by heaping scorn on paid employment—caricatured as making widgets or pushing papers or dressing for success—and the difference feminists also like to distinguish between altruistic, poorly paid female jobs and the nasty, profitable ones performed by men. It's all very well for some women to condemn others for "acting like men"—being ambitious, assertive, interested in money and power. But if their husbands did not "act like men," where would they be? Money must come from somewhere; if women leave to men the job of earning the family income (an option fewer and fewer families can afford), they will be economically dependent on their husbands, a situation that, besides carrying obvious risks in an age of frequent divorce, weakens their bargaining position in the family and ensures that men will largely control major decisions affecting family life.

Difference theorists would like to separate out the aspects of traditional womanhood that they approve of and speak only of those. But the parts they like (caring, nurturing, intimacy) are inseparable from the parts they don't like (economic dependence and the subordination of women within the family). The difference theorists try to get around this by positing a world that contains two cultures—a female world of love and ritual and a male world of getting and spending and killing—which mysteriously share a single planet. That vision is expressed neatly in a recent pop psychology title, *Men Are from Mars, Women Are from Venus*. It would be truer to say men are from Illinois and women are from Indiana—different, sure, but not in ways that have much ethical consequence.

The truth is, there is only one culture, and it shapes each sex in distinct but mutually dependent ways in order to reproduce itself. To the extent that the stereotypes are true, women have the "relational" domestic qualities *because* men have the "autonomous" qualities required to survive and prosper in modern capitalism. She needs a wage earner (even if she has a job, thanks to job discrimination), and he needs someone to mind his children, hold his hand, and have his emotions for him. This explains why women who move into male sectors act very much like men: If they didn't, they'd find themselves back home in a jiffy. The same necessities and pressures affect them as affect the men who hold those jobs. Because we are in a transition period, in which many women were raised with modest expectations and much emphasis on the need to please others, social scientists who look for it can find traces of empathy, caring, and so on in some women who have risen in the world of work and power, but when they tell us that women doctors will transform American medicine, or women executives will transform the corporate world, they are looking backward, not forward. If women really do enter the work force on equal terms with men—if they become 50 percent of all lawyers, politicians, car dealers, and prison guards—there may be less sexism (although the example of Russian doctors, a majority of them female, is not inspiring to those who know about the brutal gynecological customs prevailing in the former USSR). And they may bring with them a distinct set of manners, a separate social style. But they won't be, in some general way, more honest, kind, egalitarian, empathic, or indifferent to profit. To argue otherwise is to believe that the reason factory owners bust unions, doctors refuse Medicaid patients, and New York City school custodians don't mop the floors is that they are men.

The ultimate paradox of difference feminism is that it has come to the fore at a moment when the lives of the sexes are becoming less distinct than they ever have been in the West. Look at the decline of single-sex education; the virtual abolition of virginity as a requirement for girls; the equalization of college-attendance rates of males and females; the explosion of employment for married women and mothers even of small children; the crossing of workplace gender lines by both females and males; the cultural pressure on men to be warm and nurturant fathers, to do at least some housework, to choose mates who are their equals in education and income potential.

It's fashionable these days to talk about the backlash against equality feminism—I talk this way myself when I'm feeling blue—but equality feminism has scored amazing successes. It has transformed women's expectations in every area of their lives. However, it has not yet transformed society to meet those expectations. The workplace still discriminates. On the home front few men practice egalitarianism, although many preach it. Single mothers—and given the high divorce rate, every mother is potentially a single mother—lead incredibly difficult lives.

In this social context, difference feminism is essentially a way for women both to take advantage of equality feminism's success and to accommodate themselves to its limits. It appeals to particular kinds of women—those in the "helping professions" or the home, for example, rather than those who want to be bomber pilots or neurosurgeons or electricians. At the popular level, it encourages women who feel disadvantaged or demeaned by equality feminism to direct their anger against women who have benefited from it by thinking of them as gender traitors and of themselves as suffering for their virtue—thus the hostility of nurses toward female doctors, and of stay-at-home mothers toward employed mothers.

Although it is couched in the language of praise, difference feminism is demeaning to women. It asks that women be admitted into public life and public discourse not because they have a right to be there but because they will improve things. Even if this were true, and not the wishful thinking I believe it to be, why should the task of moral and social transformation be laid on women's doorstep and not on everyone's—or, for that matter, on men's, by the you-broke-it-you-fix-it principle? Peace, the environment, a more humane workplace, economic justice, social support for children—these are issues that affect us all and are everyone's responsibility. By promising to assume that responsibility, difference feminists lay the groundwork for excluding women again, as soon as it becomes clear that the promise cannot be kept.

No one asks that other oppressed groups win their freedom by claiming to be extra good. And no other oppressed group thinks it must make such a claim in order to be accommodated fully and across the board by society. For blacks and other racial minorities, it is enough to want to earn a living, exercise one's talents, get a fair hearing in the public forum. Only for women is simple justice an insufficient argument. It is as though women don't really believe they are entitled to full citizenship unless they can make a special claim to virtue. Why isn't being human enough?

In the end, I didn't sign that peace petition, although I was sorry to disappoint a woman I liked, and although I am very much for peace, I decided to wait for a petition that welcomed my signature as a person, an American, a citizen implicated, against my will, in war and the war economy. I still think I did the right thing.

FOR JOURNALING AND DISCUSSION

1. In this piece Pollitt wants to argue against an essential "womanness" because of the limits inherent in any fixed definition. She asks with some sarcasm, "What is female? Nature. Blood. Milk. Communal gatherings. The Moon. Quilts." What does she say is the problem with such definitions?

2. From your own experience, describe your perception of the differences between men and women. Are these biologically inherent differences or learned differences? Use specific examples to support your opinions.

3. Look at David H. Freedman's "The Aggressive Egg" (the next essay in this chapter), especially the section where he explores "biased metaphors" and their effects on scientific inquiry. How does Freedman's discussion apply to metaphors of motherhood and mothering?

4. Pollitt challenges Nancy Chodorow and other "difference feminists" as essentializing *how* women reason rather than *what* they do, thereby supporting feminist Sara Ruddick's claim that when men do what women do, particularly child-rearing, so-called feminine virtues will emerge in men too. From your own experience of being parented, what do you think about this argument?

5. Explaining the popularity of "difference feminism" with many women, Pollitt notes that "most people want to believe they act out of free will and choice. The uncomfortable truth that women have all too little of either is a difficult hurdle for feminists." What do you think about choices available to women today?

FOR RESEARCH AND EXPLORATION

1. Pollitt describes the 1950s as "the glory days of traditional sex roles. . . ." Research reviews of gender roles in this period of American history, immediately following World War II, and offer an explanation of why gender roles were so "fixed" at this time.
2. Pollitt cites both Nancy Chodorow and Deborah Tannen. Find articles on or by each of these writers, and discuss their work on gender difference in relation to Pollitt's argument.
3. Many contemporary talk shows exploit male/female tensions and supposed differences. Watch two or three of these shows, and critique the gender issues underlying the shows' stated subjects.

The Aggressive Egg

David H. Freedman

Freedman is a contributing editor at Discover *magazine, and a regular contributor to* Science, Forbes, Congress of Industrial Organizations, *and* Self. *He has also written for* The Boston Globe, The Washington Post, *and the* Harvard Business Review. *He is the author of* Brainmakers: How Scientists Are Moving Beyond Computers to Create a Rival to the Human Brain. *Freedman lives in Brookline, Massachusetts, with his wife and two children.*

Ah, fertilization—that miraculous process to which we all owe our existence. Let's review: First, a wastefully huge swarm of sperm weakly flops along, its members bumping into walls and flailing aimlessly through thick strands of mucus. Eventually, through sheer odds of pinball-like bouncing more than anything else, a few sperm end up close to an egg. As they mill around, the egg selects one and reels it in, pinning it down in spite of its efforts to escape. It's no contest, really. The gigantic, hardy egg yanks this tiny sperm inside, distills out the chromosomes, and sets out to become an embryo.

Or would you have put it differently? Until very recently, so would most biologists. For decades they've been portraying sperm as intrepid warriors battling their way to an aging, passive egg that can do little but await the sturdy victor's final, bold plunge. But the first description is closer to the truth, insists Emily Martin, a 47-year-old researcher at Johns Hopkins who has spent the past seven years examining the metaphors used to describe fertilization. Martin is not a biologist; she's a cultural anthropologist. But her efforts to spotlight the male-skewed imagery that permeates our views of reproduction have placed her at the center of a growing debate about how cultural myths can turn into scientific myths, and vice versa.

Martin didn't set out to skewer biologists. Actually she was studying biology, among other things, at the University of Michigan in 1965 when a course on Japanese music hooked her on investigating other cultures. After picking up a Ph.D. in cultural anthropology from Cornell in 1971, she spent nine years traveling back and forth between the United States, Taiwan, and China, where she was studying Chinese rituals and social organization. Then, having done the study of a foreign culture that's traditionally expected of anthropologists, and being pregnant with her first child, she started casting about for a new project closer to home. "Studying your own culture is harder," she says, "because everything seems so normal to you."

Not until 1982, while attending a class for expectant parents before the birth of her second child, did Martin stumble on her topic. "It suddenly hit me that the way everyone was talking about their bodies was really weird," she recalls. "It was *the* body, *the* uterus, and *the* contraction—as if these things weren't a part of us. I realized that medical science was in need of some sort of interpretation, and my wedge would be reproductive issues." Martin started off by interviewing dozens of women on their feelings about every aspect of reproduction, from menstruation to menopause. Her book *The Woman in the Body,* published in 1987, explored the relation between images of the body and ideas about oneself. But by 1985 Martin realized that she had been looking at these issues from only one point of view. "I decided to do an ethnographic study in a scientific setting, to see how biologists thought about some of these questions," she says. "Also, I thought I should be including male reproductive processes as well." Fertilization research, she realized, would allow her to cover all the bases.

As she began her background studies, Martin was surprised to find that popular literature, textbooks, and even medical journals were crammed with descriptions of warrior sperm and damsel-in-distress eggs. Martin found that classic biology texts, for example, enthused about the human male's "amazing" productivity—some 200 million sperm every hour—while practically complaining over the "waste" of the 2 million immature eggs present in the human female at birth, only some 400 of which the ovaries ever "shed" for possible fertilization, with the rest destined to "degenerate" over the woman's lifetime.

"The real mystery," says Martin, "is why the male's vast production of sperm is not seen as wasteful."

Less mysterious, in Martin's opinion, was the motivation for such biased language. "Men link potency to strong sperm," she says. "You'd like your sperm to be like you; no wonder everyone believed sperm were torpedoes." In all her searching, Martin came up with only a single depiction of less-than-mighty sperm: Woody Allen's portrayal of a neurotic sperm nervous about his imminent ejaculation in the movie *Everything You Always Wanted to Know About Sex But Were Afraid to Ask.*

Woody Allen aside, the durability of the masterful-sperm imagery astonished Martin. It continued to dominate the contemporary technical and popular literature despite a growing body of evidence that the egg plays anything but a passive role. From the early 1970s on, studies of the sperm and eggs of many species have revealed that molecules released by the egg are critical to guiding and "activating" the sperm—that is, triggering the sperm to release proteins that help it adhere to the egg. In fact, the egg might just as well be called eager as passive. Among many species of lizards, insects, some crustaceans, and even turkeys, the egg doesn't always wait for the sperm's arrival. It can begin dividing without fertilization, and females can reproduce without sperm at all.

Yet none of this had made a dent in biologists' language. "When I asked them about it, they told me I had a point," says Martin. "They claimed the imagery came up only when they needed to explain their research, and not in the lab. But I wanted to know what was really going on."

By 1986 Martin had begun hanging out with a team of researchers at Johns Hopkins who were observing sperm mobility in hopes of coming up with a strategy for a new contraceptive. They had started the year before with a simple experiment—measuring human sperm's ability to escape and swim away from a tiny suction pipet placed against the side of the sperm cell's head. To the team's great surprise, the sperm turned out to be feeble swimmers; their heads thrashed from side to side ten times more vigorously than their bodies pushed forward. "It makes sense," says Martin. "The last thing you'd want a sperm to be is a highly effective burrower, because it would end up burrowing into the first obstacle it encountered. You want a sperm that's good at getting away from things."

The team went on to determine that the sperm tries to pull its getaway act even on the egg itself, but is held down against its struggles by molecules on the surface of the egg that hook together with counterparts on the sperm's surface, fastening the sperm until the egg can absorb it. Yet even after having revealed the sperm to be an escape artist and the egg to be a chemically active sperm catcher, even after discussing the egg's role in "tethering" the sperm, the research team continued for another three years to describe the sperm's role as actively "penetrating" the egg.

Meanwhile, Martin was keeping an eye on two other fertilization groups. They too seemed at times to disregard their own observations when writing about fertilization. Researchers at the University of Wisconsin, for example, described the way sea urchin sperm first make contact with an egg by quickly stringing together protein molecules into a filament that extends out until it reaches the egg. But instead of describing this as an innocuous process of assembly and attachment, the group wrote—in a pioneering paper that otherwise points out the egg's ability to actively "clasp" and "entwine"—that the sperm's filament "shoots out and harpoons" the egg. Likewise, when a researcher at the Roche Institute of Molecular Biology in Nutley, New Jersey, wrote in 1987 of his discovery that mouse eggs carry a molecular structure on their coating that fits inside a complementary structure on the sperm, helping bind the two together, he described the two structures, naturally enough, as a lock and key—but he called the egg's protruding structure the lock and the sperm's engulfing structure the key.

Martin doesn't suggest that these researchers willfully distorted their imagery. In fact, she notes that one of the investigators at Johns Hopkins was her politically correct husband, Richard Cone. What's more, Martin concedes that she herself was slow to recognize the disparity between the discoveries at Johns Hopkins and the way the findings were written up. "It didn't strike me for a few years," she says. But innocent or not, she adds, the cultural conditioning these biologists had absorbed early in their careers influenced more than their writing: it skewed their research. "I believe, and my husband believes, and the lab believes, that they would have seen these results sooner if they hadn't had these male-oriented images of sperm. In fact, biologists could have figured out a hundred years ago that sperm are weak forward-propulsion units, but it's hard for men to accept the idea that sperm are best at escaping. The imagery you employ guides you to ask certain questions and to not ask certain others."

People preparing to dismiss Emily Martin as a humorless feminist have their work cut out for them. At once animated and easygoing in her cramped, cactus-strewn office, Martin chuckles as she goes through an inch-thick file of hapless-egg and macho-sperm imagery clipped from magazines. (In one Gary Larson cartoon, a housewife egg fends off a swarm of sperm trying to get past her by posing as phone repairmen, insurance salesmen, and UPS deliverymen.) "I just think this stuff is a riot," she says. In fact, it's the biologists who seem a little stuffy. Though she usually lectures to students, Martin recalls one lecture she gave to biologists at the Woods Hole Oceanographic Institution in 1990. "It was one of the most painful experiences of my life," she says. "I had gotten to the point where the audience is usually rolling in the aisles, and all I got was stony silence. I could see they were furious. On the other hand, I can understand their feelings; I get defensive when someone criticizes cultural anthropology."

One researcher who doesn't bristle at Martin's jabs is Scott Gilbert, a developmental biologist at Swarthmore College. Though he suggests Martin may go a little overboard in stressing the egg's aggressiveness—for example, he prefers to think of the egg as "engaging in a dialogue" with the sperm rather than gluing it down—he does believe her views are a vast improvement over the conventional explanations. "Most studies clearly show that the sperm is at-tracted by the egg and activated by it," says Gilbert. "But if you don't have an interpretation of fertilization that allows you to look at the egg as active, you won't look for the molecules that can prove it. You simply won't find activities that you don't visualize."

Now that the discrepancy between experiment and interpretation is being brought out into the open, the professional literature seems to be coming around—although a [1991] issue of the biology journal *Cell Differentiation and Development* placed on its cover a Prince Charming sperm delivering a wake-up kiss to a long-eyelashed Sleeping Beauty egg. As for the popular press, Gilbert and Martin cite the same recent example as particularly egregious: an article titled "Sperm Wars" that appeared as a cover story in a national science maga-zine whose name you'd recognize in a minute, which referred to the sperm cell as "a formidable .00024-inch weapon, tipped with a chemical warhead" (see DISCOVER, July 1991). On the other hand, *Developmental Biology,* the most popular college textbook in its subject area, takes great pains to point out the new, equal-opportunity view of fertilization. No wonder: Gilbert wrote it.

One reason the older interpretation is dying hard is that it tends to be self-reinforcing, not only in suggesting ready-made imagery that can skew observa-tions but also in subtly determining who becomes a biologist in the first place. "This business has stopped certain people from entering the field," says Gilbert. "Why would a woman want to continue if people are telling her she's passive?"

Nevertheless, as Martin points out, a growing number of women *are* con-tinuing in biology. But that won't guarantee more evenhanded interpretations. "Scientific training involves a rigorous socialization process that doesn't allow for different perspectives," she says. "It's hard to say that women biologists are any less guilty of these things than men."

Even if biologists do move away from the passive-egg myth, other images are waiting in the wings. These days, says Martin, researchers seem ready to confer a "spider woman" aspect on the egg. "Men have always turned to spider imagery when they are confronted with women who acquire power," she charges. Indeed, her file of magazine clippings contains several images in sup-port of her claim. One striking example: the cartoonish silhouette employed as the emblem of the once-popular *Charlie's Angels* television series, which de-picts the three starring female characters, guns and all, unmistakably merged into the eight-limbed shape of a spider.

Though Martin is the first to insist that much of the fertilization imagery is good for a laugh, she doesn't mean to let scientists dismiss it all as a big joke. "People say, 'Oh, what difference does it make?' as if this stuff doesn't affect any-one," she says. "But our culture *is* affected by these powerful visual images. We all put so much faith in science, and so much of the negative load lands on women."

She notes, as another example, that it's been known since the 1960s that women exposed to toxic chemicals bear children who run a higher risk of serious medical problems. Those findings reinforced the cultural notion that women should be sheltered, and some companies have rules to prevent women of reproductive age from working at jobs that might involve exposure to these chemicals. But only in the past few years have comparable studies shown that men exposed to high levels of lead, vinyl chloride, and about a dozen other chemicals also have children who are at higher risk. "It's the notion of invulnerable sperm," she claims, "that made it take so long for scientists and the public to accept the male role in birth defects and infertility."

Martin has recently shifted her focus to metaphors used in other areas of medical research. For example, she says, "when AIDS was seen as affecting only the 'dregs' of society, scientists described it as a monkey virus. Now that well-to-do white women are getting it, all of a sudden researchers are talking about AIDS being an autoimmune disease." There are, of course, other reasons that researchers' language might change, including a growing knowledge of how the AIDS virus in fact wreaks havoc on the host's immune system. Martin is still studying the literature and observing researchers in immunology labs. For now, she concedes, "all you can do is raise a question. It's often impossible to prove causality."

Although she is no longer studying fertilization imagery, Martin still lectures on the topic because, she contends, "the work shows that science can have social effects. When we anthropomorphize the egg and sperm, when we turn them into a miniature bride and groom complete with personalities, what effect does this have on abortion legislation? These effects aren't intended by scientists, but they happen. They blend moral and scientific issues together in a way that makes me want to stand up and say something."

There's further irony in the traditional metaphors. The notion of fiercely battling, competitive sperm suggests that they're battling each other in a "race" to the egg. In fact, says Cone, they have a hard time making their way through the mucus glop, and like a team of bicyclists they "take turns" up front parting strands of mucus. So in a sense sperm are cooperative. The egg, on the other hand, is the real competitive loner. Only one matures each month, and the one out in front suppresses the maturation of all the others. The macho image of sperm not only obscures this reality; it actually reverses what's been observed.

Can biased metaphors be eliminated from science? Martin doesn't think so. Even if they could be, she doesn't think that antiseptically neutral language would be desirable. Metaphor is, after all, a powerful vehicle for creative thinking. "The goal shouldn't be to clean the imagery out," she says, "but to be aware that it's there." It also helps, she adds, to be able to take a joke. "Humor takes away the sting," she says, "along with the potential for inculcating harmful ideas."

FOR JOURNALING AND DISCUSSION

1. Freedman reports that since the 1970s studies have shown that eggs release molecules that activate the sperm, making them active rather than passive recipients

of sperm "penetration." He continues that "none of this [has] made a dent in biologists' language," and concludes that "the older interpretation is dying hard. . . ." Why does this continue to be largely true?

2. Anthropologist Emily Martin found one biologist writing on reproduction in mice who "called the egg's protruding structure the lock and the sperm's engulfing structure the key." Why is this point significant? How do cultural metaphors like "lock and key" reflect cultural values?

3. Examine your own experience and reading for an example of language that does not reflect scientific or biological reality. Can you come up with any cultural metaphors that reflect cultural bias over reality?

FOR RESEARCH AND EXPLORATION

1. In your school's biomedical library, find a journal article on human reproduction and explore its language for biased metaphors. Write an analysis of what you find.

2. Scientists, Freedman reports, explain the persistence of the biased language that continues to skew scientific research by describing "who becomes a biologist in the first place." Check with your school's biology or premed departments for a gender breakdown of their majors. Try to interview a few students about their experiences with gender bias in their work.

3. Look at Gary Indiana's essay, "Memories of a Xenophobic Boyhood," in Chapter 2. In it he writes, "We were only white when somebody wasn't," which suggests that race does not exist as its own category, but only in relation to someone of differing ethnicity and/or skin color. Compare that position to Emily Martin's work on biased scientific metaphors. Does her discovery of the egg's competitiveness and the sperm's cooperativeness have implication for male and female personality traits?

A Weight That Women Carry: The Compulsion to Diet in a Starved Culture

Sallie Tisdale

Tisdale worked as a registered nurse from 1983 to 1990, after which she began writing about medicine, health, and sexuality. She has been visiting writer at the University of Portland and the University of California at Davis. Tisdale is the author of The Sorcerer's Apprentice: Tales of the Modern Hospital, Harvest Moon: Portrait of a Nursing Home, Lot's Wife: Salt and the Human Condition, *and* Talk Dirty to Me: An Intimate Philosophy of Sex. *She is also a contributor to many national magazines, including* The New Republic, The New York Times, Vogue, The New Yorker, *and* Esquire, *and a contributing editor at* Harper's.

I don't know how much I weigh these days, though I can make a good guess. For years I'd known that number, sometimes within a quarter pound, known how it changed from day to day and hour to hour. I want to weigh myself now; I lean toward the scale in the next room, imagine standing there, lining up the balance. But I don't do it. Going this long, starting to break the scale's spell— it's like waking up suddenly sober.

By the time I was sixteen years old I had reached my adult height of five feet six inches and weighed 164 pounds. I weighed 164 pounds before and after a healthy pregnancy. I assume I weigh about the same now; nothing significant seems to have happened to my body, this same old body I've had all these years. I usually wear a size 14, a common clothing size for American women. On bad days I think my body looks lumpy and misshapen. On my good days, which are more frequent lately, I think I look plush and strong; I think I look like a lot of women whose bodies and lives I admire.

I'm not sure when the word "fat" first sounded pejorative to me, or when I first applied it to myself. My grandmother was a petite woman, the only one in my family. She stole food from other people's plates, and hid the debris of her own meals so that no one would know how much she ate. My mother was a size 14, like me, all her adult life; we shared clothes. She fretted endlessly over food scales, calorie counters, and diet books. She didn't want to quit smoking because she was afraid she would gain weight, and she worried about her weight until she died of cancer five years ago. Dieting was always in my mother's way, always there in the conversations above my head, the dialogue of stocky women. But I was strong and healthy and didn't pay too much attention to my weight until I was grown.

It probably wouldn't have been possible for me to escape forever. It doesn't matter that whole human epochs have celebrated big men and women, because the brief period in which I live does not; since I was born, even the voluptuous calendar girl has gone. Today's models, the women whose pictures I see constantly, unavoidably, grow more minimal by the day. When I berate myself for not looking like—whomever I think I should look like that day, I don't really care that no one looks like that. I don't care that Michelle Pfeiffer doesn't look like the photographs I see of Michelle Pfeiffer. I want to look—think I should look—like the photographs. I want her little miracles: the makeup artists, photographers, and computer imagers who can add a mole, remove a scar, lift the breasts, widen the eyes, narrow the hips, flatten the curves. The final product is what I see, have seen my whole adult life. And I've seen this: even when big people become celebrities, their weight is constantly remarked upon and scrutinized; their successes seem always to be *in spite* of their weight. I thought my successes must be, too.

I feel myself expand and diminish from day to day, sometimes from hour to hour. If I tell someone my weight, I change in their eyes: I become bigger or smaller, better or worse, depending on what that number, my weight, means to them. I know many men and women, young and old, gay and straight, who look fine, whom I love to see and whose faces and forms I cherish, who despise themselves for their weight. For their ordinary, human bodies. They and I are simply bigger than we think we should be. We always talk about weight in terms of gains and losses, and don't wonder at the strangeness of the words. In trying always to lose weight, we've lost hope of simply being seen for ourselves.

My weight has never actually affected anything—it's never seemed to mean anything one way or the other to how I lived. Yet for the last ten years I've felt quite bad about it. After a time, the number on the scale became my totem, more important than my experience—it was layered, metaphorical, *metaphysical,* and it had bewitching power. I thought if I could change that number I could change my life.

In my mid-twenties I started secretly taking diet pills. They made me feel strange, half-crazed, vaguely nauseated. I lost about twenty-five pounds, dropped two sizes, and bought new clothes. I developed rituals and taboos around food, ate very little, and continued to lose weight. For a long time afterward I thought it only coincidental that with every passing week I also grew more depressed and irritable.

I could recite the details, but they're remarkable only for being so common. I lost more weight until I was rather thin, and then I gained it all back. It came back slowly, pound by pound, in spite of erratic and melancholy and sometimes frantic dieting, dieting I clung to even though being thin had changed nothing, had meant nothing to my life except that I was thin. Looking back, I remember blinding moments of shame and lightning-bright moments of clearheadedness, which inevitably gave way to rage at the time I'd wasted—rage that eventually would become, once again, self-disgust and the urge to lose weight. So it went, until I weighed exactly what I'd weighed when I began.

For ages humans believed that the body helped create the personality, from the humors of Galen to W. H. Sheldon's somatotypes. Sheldon distinguished between three templates—endomorph, mesomorph, and ectomorph—and combined them into hundreds of variations with physical, emotional, and psychological characteristics. When I read about weight now, I see the potent shift in the last few decades: the modern culture of dieting is based on the idea that the personality creates the body. Our size must be in some way voluntary, or else it wouldn't be subject to change. A lot of my misery over my weight wasn't about how I looked at all. I was miserable because I believed *I* was bad, not my body. I felt truly reduced then, reduced to being just a body and nothing more.

Fat is perceived as an *act* rather than a thing. It is antisocial, and curable through the application of social controls. Even the feminist revisions of dieting, so powerful in themselves, pick up the theme: the hungry, empty heart; the woman seeking release from sexual assault, or the man from the loss of the mother, through food and fat. Fat is now a symbol not of the personality but of the soul—the cluttered, neurotic, immature soul.

Fat people eat for "mere gratification," I read, as though no one else does. Their weight is *intentioned,* they simply eat "too much," their flesh is lazy flesh. Whenever I went on a diet, eating became cheating. One pretzel was cheating. Two apples instead of one was cheating—a large potato instead of a small, carrots instead of broccoli. It didn't matter which diet I was on; diets have failure built in, failure is in the definition. Every substitution—even carrots for broccoli—was a triumph of desire over will. When I dieted, I didn't feel pious just for sticking to the rules. I felt condemned for the act of eating itself, as though my hunger were never normal. My penance was to not eat at all.

My attitude toward food became quite corrupt. I came, in fact, to subconsciously believe food itself was corrupt. Diet books often distinguish between "real" and "unreal" hunger, so that *correct* eating is hollowed out, unemotional. A friend of mine who thinks of herself as a compulsive eater says she feels bad only when she eats for pleasure. "Why?" I ask, and she says, "Because I'm eating food I don't need." A few years ago I might have admired that. Now I try to imagine a world where we eat only food we need, and it seems inhuman. I imagine a world devoid of holidays and wedding feasts, wakes and reunions, a unique shared joy. "What's wrong with eating a cookie because you like cookies?" I ask her, and she hasn't got an answer. These aren't rational beliefs, any more than the unnecessary pleasure of ice cream is rational. Dieting presumes pleasure to be an insignificant, or at least malleable, human motive.

I felt no joy in being thin—it was just work, something I had to do. But, when I began to gain back the weight, I felt despair. I started reading about the "recidivism" of dieting. I wondered if I had myself to blame not only for needing to diet in the first place but for dieting itself, the weight inevitably regained. I joined organized weight-loss programs, spent a lot of money, listened to lectures I didn't believe on quack nutrition, ate awful, processed diet foods. I sat in groups and applauded people who'd lost a half pound, feeling smug because I'd lost a pound and a half. I felt ill much of the time, found exercise increasingly difficult, cried often. And I thought that if I could only lose a little weight, everything would be all right.

When I say to someone, "I'm fat," I hear, "Oh, no! You're not *fat!* You're just—" What? Plump? Big-boned? Rubenesque? I'm just *not thin*. That's crime enough. I began this story by stating my weight. I said it all at once, trying to forget it and take away its power; I said it to be done being scared. Doing so, saying it out loud like that, felt like confessing a mortal sin. I have to bite my tongue not to seek reassurance, not to defend myself, not to plead. I see an old friend for the first time in years, and she comments on how much my fourteen-year-old son looks like me—"except, of course, he's not chubby." "Look who's talking," I reply, through clenched teeth. This pettiness is never far away; concern with my weight evokes the smallest, meanest parts of me. I look at another woman passing on the street and think, "At least I'm not *that* fat."

Recently I was talking with a friend who is naturally slender about a mutual acquaintance who is quite large. To my surprise my friend reproached this woman because she had seen her eating a cookie at lunchtime. "How is she going to lose weight that way?" my friend wondered. When you are as fat as our acquaintance is, you are primarily, fundamentally, seen as fat. It is your essential characteristic. There are so many presumptions in my friend's casual, cruel remark. She assumes that this woman should diet all the time—and that she *can*. She pronounces whole categories of food to be denied her. She sees her unwillingness to behave in this externally prescribed way, even for a moment, as an act of rebellion. In his story "A Hunger Artist," Kafka writes that the guards of the fasting man were "usually butchers, strangely enough." Not so strange, I think.

I know that the world, even if it views me as overweight (and I'm not sure it really does), clearly makes a distinction between me and this very big woman. I would rather stand with her and not against her, see her for all she is besides fat. But I know our experiences aren't the same. My thin friend assumes my fat friend is unhappy because she is fat: therefore, if she loses weight she will be happy. My fat friend has a happy marriage and family and a good career, but insofar as her weight is a source of misery, I think she would be much happier if she could eat her cookie in peace, if people would shut up and leave her weight alone. But the world never lets up when you are her size; she cannot walk to the bank without risking insult. Her fat is seen as perverse bad manners. I have no doubt she would be rid of the fat if she could be. If my left-handedness invited the criticism her weight does, I would want to cut that hand off.

In these last several years I seem to have had an infinite number of conversations about dieting. They are really all the same conversation—weight is lost, then weight is gained back. This repetition finally began to sink in. Why did everyone sooner or later have the same experience? (My friend who had learned to be hungry all the time gained back all the weight she had lost and more, just like the rest of us.) Was it really our bodies that were flawed? I began reading the biology of weight more carefully, reading the fine print in the endless studies. There is, in fact, a preponderance of evidence disputing our commonly held assumptions about weight.

The predominant biological myth of weight is that thin people live longer than fat people. The truth is far more complicated. (Some deaths of fat people attributed to heart disease seem actually to have been the result of radical dieting.) If health were our real concern, it would be dieting we questioned, not weight. The current ideal of thinness has never been held before, except as a religious ideal; the underfed body is the martyr's body. Even fat people can lose weight, [but] maintaining an artificially low weight for any period of time requires a kind of starvation. Lots of people are naturally thin, but for those who are not, dieting is an unnatural act; biology rebels. The metabolism of the hungry body can change inalterably, making it ever harder and harder to stay thin. I think chronic dieting made me gain weight—not only points, but fat. This equation seemed so strange at first that I couldn't believe it. But the weight I put back on after losing was much more stubborn than the original weight. I had lost by taking diet pills and not eating much of anything at all for quite a long time. I haven't touched the pills again, but not eating much of anything no longer works.

When Oprah Winfrey first revealed her lost weight, I didn't envy her. I thought, she's in trouble now. I knew. I was certain. She would gain it back; I believed she was biologically destined to do so. The tabloid headlines blamed it on a cheeseburger or mashed potatoes; they screamed Oprah PASSES 200 POUNDS, and I cringed at her misery and how the world wouldn't let up, wouldn't leave her alone, wouldn't let her be anything else. How dare the world do this to anyone, I thought, and then realized I did it to myself.

The "Ideal Weight" charts my mother used were at their lowest acceptable-weight ranges in the 1950s, when I was a child. They were based on sketchy and often inaccurate actuarial evidence, using, for the most part, data on northern Europeans and allowing for the most minimal differences in size for a population of less than half a billion people. I never fit those weight charts. I was always just outside the pale. As an adult, when I would join an organized program, I accepted their version of my Weight Goal as gospel, knowing it would be virtually impossible to reach. But reach I tried; that's what one does with gospel. Only in the last few years have the weight tables begun to climb back into the world of the average human. The newest ones distinguish by gender, frame, and age. And suddenly I'm not off the charts anymore. I have a place.

A man who is attracted to fat women says, "I actually have less specific physical criteria than most men. I'm attracted to women who weigh 170 or 270 or 370. Most men are only attracted to women who weigh between 100 and 135. So who's got more of a fetish?" We look at fat as a problem of the fat person. Rarely do the tables get turned, rarely do we imagine that it might be the viewer, not the viewed, who is limited. What the hell is wrong with *them*, anyway? Do they believe everything they see on television?

My friend Phil, who is chronically and almost painfully thin, admitted that in his search for a partner he finds himself prejudiced against fat women. He seemed genuinely bewildered by this. I didn't jump to reassure him that such prejudice is hard to resist. What I did was bite my tongue at my urge to be reassured by him, to be told that I, at least, wasn't fat. That over the centuries humans have been inclined to prefer extra flesh rather than the other way around seems unimportant. All we see now tells us otherwise. Why does my kindhearted friend criticize another woman for eating a cookie when she would never dream of commenting in such a way on another person's race or sexual orientation or disability? Deprivation is the dystopian ideal.

My mother called her endless diets "reducing plans." Reduction, the diminution of women, is the opposite of feminism, as Kim Chernin points out in *The Obsession*. Smallness is what feminism strives against, the smallness that women confront everywhere. All of women's spaces are smaller than those of men, often inadequate, without privacy. Furniture designers distinguish between a man's and a woman's chair, because women don't spread out like men. (A sprawling woman means only one thing.) Even our voices are kept down. By embracing dieting I was rejecting a lot I held dear, and the emotional dissonance that created just seemed like one more necessary evil.

A fashion magazine recently celebrated the return of the "well-fed" body; a particular model was said to be "the archetype of the new womanly woman . . . stately, powerful." She is a size 8. The images of women presented to us, images claiming so maliciously to be the images of women's whole lives, are not merely social fictions. They are *absolute* fictions; they can't exist. How would it feel, I began to wonder, to cultivate my own real womanliness rather than despise it? Because it was my fleshy curves I wanted to be rid of, after all. I dreamed of having a boy's body, smooth, hipless, lean. A body rapt with possibility, a receptive body suspended before the storms of maturity. A dear friend of mine, nursing her second child, weeps at her newly voluptuous body. She loves her children and hates her own motherliness, wanting to be unripened again, to be a bud and not a flower.

Recently I've started shopping occasionally at stores for "large women," where the smallest size is a 14. In department stores the size 12 and 14 and 16 clothes are kept in a ghetto called the Women's Department. (And who would want that, to be the size of a woman? We all dream of being "juniors" instead.) In the specialty stores the clerks are usually big women and the customers are big, too, big like a lot of women in my life—friends, my sister, my mother and aunts. Not long ago I bought a pair of jeans at Lane Bryant and then walked through the mall to the Gap, with its shelves of generic clothing. I flicked through the clearance rack and suddenly remembered the Lane Bryant shopping bag in my hand and its enormous weight, the sheer heaviness of that brand name shouting to the world. The shout is that I've let myself go. I still feel like crying out sometimes: Can't I feel *satisfied?* But I am not supposed to be satisfied, not allowed to be satisfied. My discontent fuels the market; I need to be afraid in order to fully participate.

American culture, which has produced our dieting mania, does more than reward privation and acquisition at the same time: it actually associates them with each other. Read the ads: the virtuous runner's reward is a new pair of $180 running shoes. The fat person is thought to be impulsive, indulgent, but insufficiently or incorrectly greedy, greedy for the wrong thing. The fat person lacks ambition. The young executive is complimented for being "hungry";

he is "starved for success." We are teased with what we will *have* if we are willing to *have not* for a time. A dieting friend, avoiding the food on my table, says, "I'm just dying for a bite of that."

Dieters are the perfect consumers: they never get enough. The dieter wistfully imagines food without substance, food that is not food, that begs the definition of food, because food is the problem. Even the ways we *don't eat* are based in class. The middle class don't eat in support groups. The poor can't afford not to eat at all. The rich hire someone to not eat with them in private. Dieting is an emblem of capitalism. It has a venal heart.

The possibility of living another way, living without dieting, began to take root in my mind a few years ago, and finally my second trip through Weight Watchers ended dieting for me. This last time I just couldn't stand the details, the same kind of details I'd seen and despised in other programs, on other diets: the scent of resignation, the weighing-in by the quarter pound, the before and after photographs of group leaders prominently displayed. Jean Nidetch, the founder of Weight Watchers, says, "Most fat people need to be hurt badly before they do something about themselves." She mocks every aspect of our need for food, of a person's sense of entitlement to food, of daring to *eat what we want*. Weight Watchers refuses to release its own weight charts except to say they make no distinction for frame size; neither has the organization ever released statistics on how many people who lose weight on the program eventually gain it back. I hated the endlessness of it, the turning of food into portions and exchanges, everything measured out, permitted, denied. I hated the very idea of "maintenance." Finally I realized I didn't just hate the diet. I was sick of the way I acted on a diet, the way I whined, my niggardly, penny-pinching behavior. What I liked in myself seemed to shrivel and disappear when I dieted. Slowly, slowly I saw these things, I saw that my pain was cut from whole cloth, imaginary, my own invention. I saw how much time I'd spent on something ephemeral, something that simply wasn't important, didn't matter. I saw that the real point of dieting is dieting—to not be done with it, ever.

I looked in the mirror and saw a woman, with flesh, curves, muscles, a few stretch marks, the beginnings of wrinkles, with strength and softness in equal measure. My body is the one part of me that is always, undeniably, here. To like myself means to be, literally, shameless, to be wanton in the pleasures of being inside a body. I feel *loose* this way, a little abandoned, a little dangerous. That first feeling of liking my body—not being resigned to it or despairing of change, but actually *liking* it—was tentative and guilty and frightening. It was alarming, because it was the way I'd felt as a child, before the world had interfered. Because surely I was wrong; I knew, I'd known for so long, that my body wasn't all right this way. I was afraid even to act as though I were all right: I was afraid that by doing so I'd be acting a fool.

For a time I was thin. I remember—and what I remember is nothing special—strain, a kind of hollowness, the same troubles and fears, and no magic. So I imagine losing weight again. If the world applauded, would this comfort me? Or would it only compromise whatever approval the world gives me now? What else will be required of me besides thinness? What will happen to me if I get sick, or lose the use of a limb, or, God forbid, grow old?

By fussing endlessly over my body, I've ceased to inhabit it. I'm trying to reverse this equation now, to trust my body and enter it again with a whole heart. I know more now than I used to about what constitutes "happy" and "unhappy," what the depths and textures of contentment are like. By letting go of dieting, I free up mental and emotional room. I have more space, I can move. The pursuit of another, elusive body, the body someone else says I should have, is a terrible distraction, a sidetracking that might have lasted my whole life long. By letting myself go, I go places.

Each of us in this culture, this twisted, inchoate culture, has to choose between battles: one battle is against the cultural ideal, and the other is against ourselves. I've chosen to stop fighting myself. Maybe I'm tilting at windmills; the cultural ideal is ever-changing, out of my control. It's not a cerebral journey, except insofar as I have to remind myself to stop counting, to stop thinking in terms of numbers. I know, even now that I've quit dieting and eat what I want, how many calories I take in every day. If I eat as I please, I eat a lot one day and very little the next; I skip meals and snack at odd times. My nourishment is good—as far as nutrition is concerned, I'm in much better shape than when I was dieting. I know that the small losses and gains in my weight over a period of time aren't simply related to the number of calories I eat. Someone asked me not long ago how I could possibly know my calorie intake if I'm not dieting (the implication being, perhaps, that I'm dieting secretly). I know because calorie counts and grams of fat and fiber are embedded in me. I have to work to *not* think of them, and I have to learn to not think of them in order to really live without fear.

When I look, *really* look, at the people I see every day on the street, I see a jungle of bodies, a community of women and men growing every which way like lush plants, growing tall and short and slender and round, hairy and hairless, dark and pale and soft and hard and glorious. Do I look around at the multitudes and think all these people—all these people who are like me and not like me, who are various and different—are not loved or lovable? Lately, everyone's body interests me, every body is desirable in some way. I see how muscles and skin shift with movement; I sense a cornucopia of flesh in the world. In the midst of it I am a little capacious and unruly.

I repeat with Walt Whitman, "I dote on myself . . . there is that lot of me, and all so luscious." I'm eating better, exercising more, feeling fine—and then I catch myself thinking, *Maybe I'll lose some weight.* But my mood changes or my attention is caught by something else, something deeper, more lingering. Then I can catch a glimpse of myself by accident and think only: That's me. My face, my hips, my hands. Myself.

FOR JOURNALING AND DISCUSSION

1. Tisdale, remembering her mother, writes, "She didn't want to quit smoking because she was afraid she would gain weight, and she worried about her weight until she died of cancer five years ago." Why is this line so powerful?
2. This essay looks at the role of the media and endless dieting programs in making people believe that they will be happy if they are thin. Write about your earliest memory of your own body image. Where did you get the most powerful messages about your size?
3. It seems that dieting commercials today are as common as car ads. Watch an evening of TV, and analyze the diet program ads you see. Who's in them? What do they wear, do, and say?

FOR RESEARCH AND EXPLORATION

1. Tisdale writes of the images bombarding her daily: "Today's models, the women . . . I see constantly, unavoidably, grow more minimal by the day." In your school's library find a fashion magazine from the year you were born and another from this year. Write an analysis comparing the images of beauty and body size reflected in the models used in both magazines.
2. Linking American dieting with capitalism, Tisdale writes, "Dieters are the perfect consumers: they never get enough." Research the dieting industry, looking specifically at its profit margins over the past ten years, to understand its emergence as a major business. Do any of the major dieting companies help people?
3. Read both Bernard Cooper's "A Clack of Tiny Sparks" later in this chapter and Richard Rodriguez's "India" in Chapter 2, and compare their examination of bodies to Tisdale's discussion of body size. How do social constructs of sexuality, race, and beauty influence what we are able to "see" of others' identities and our own?

They Make Their Climb

Paula Gunn Allen

Gunn Allen, a Laguna Pueblo/Sioux Indian, is one of the foremost Native American scholars and literary critics. She is the author of Skins and Bones *as well as six other books of poetry, the novel* The Woman Who Owned the Shadows, *the critically acclaimed collection of essays* The Sacred Hoop: Recovering the Feminine in American Indian Tradition, *and* Spider

Paula Gunn Allen, "They Make Their Climb" from the forthcoming novel *Ravens Road*. Originally published in Susan Koppelman, ed., *Women Friendships* (Norman: University of Oklahoma Press, 1991). Copyright © 1991 by Paula Gunn Allen. Reprinted with the permission of the author.

Woman's Granddaughters. *Her most recent book is* Grandmothers of
the Light: A Medicine Woman's Sourcebook. *She is professor of English
at the University of California at Los Angeles.*

It had been the apple tree. The long spring days there. With the girl. They had
watched the village going. They had watched the clouds. When they thirsted
they climbed down from the branches and walked to the nearby spring. Took
a long sweet drink.

Elena had taught Ephanie about the weeds. Which to eat. When they had
gathered prickly pears in the summer, brushing carefully the tiny spines from
the fruit before they ate. They had wandered the mesas and climbed the nearer
peaks. Together they had dreamed. Sharing. They never talked about growing
up. What that would mean.

They had ridden horses. Pretended to be ranchers. Chased the village
cattle around the town. Suffered scoldings for it. Learned to be trick riders.
Roy Rogers and Hopalong Cassidy. Maybe they could be stunt men in
Hollywood if they got good enough at it. If they could learn to jump from the
rooftop onto the horse's back. They had chased the clouds.

Or lying, dreaming, had watched them, tracing faces and glorious beast
shapes in the piling, billowing thunderheads. On July mornings they had gone
out from their separate homes, laughing, feet bare and joyful in the road's
early dust. The early wind cool and fresh, the bright sunlight making promises
it would never keep. They had lain together in the alfalfa field of Elena's father, quiet, at peace.

They were children and there was much they did not know.

In their seasons they grew. Walking the road between their houses, lying
languorous and innocent in the blooming boughs of the apple tree. Amid the
fruiting limbs. And had known themselves and their surroundings in terms of
each other's eyes. Though their lives were very different, their identity was such
that the differences were never strange. They had secret names for each other,
half joking, half descriptive, Snow White and Rose Red, they named themselves, in recognition of the fairness of Elena, the duskiness of Ephanie. In
recognition also of the closeness they shared, those friends.

The events that measured their shared lives were counted in the places
that they roamed, and Ephanie always remembered her childhood that way.
The river, the waterfall, the graveyard, the valley, the mesas, the peaks. Each
crevice they leaped over. Each danger they challenged, each stone, each blade
of grass. A particularity that would shape her life.

They had especially loved the shadows. Where they grew, lavender, violet,
purple, or where those shadows would recede. On the mountain slopes and
closer by, beneath the shading trees. And the blue enfolding distance surrounding that meant the farthest peaks. Shared with them in their eyes, in
their stories, but where, together, they had never been.

In all those years, in spite of distance, in spite of difference, in spite of change, they understood the exact measure of their relationship, the twining, the twinning. There were photographs of them from that time. Because Elena's gold-tinged hair looked dark in the photograph's light, no one could say which was Elena, which Ephanie. With each other they were each one doubled. They were thus complete.

Jump.

Fall.

Remember you are flying. Say you are a bird.

She had said that, Ephanie. Had urged Elena to leap the great crevices between the huge sandstone formations that shaped the mesas they roamed. Some of the leaps were wide and the ground far below. She had always done the leading. Elena, devoted, did what Ephanie decided. Or it seemed that way.

Ephanie didn't want to remember it that way. Wanted the fact to be that Elena had gone on her own windings, ones not of Ephanie's making. And in some cases, that was true. There were some things that, no matter how Ephanie urged them, Elena would not do. Some ways in which she remained safe within her own keeping. Sometimes, when she had adamantly refused, Ephanie would give up and go back to her own home. And it also went, sometimes, the other way.

They did not argue. They did not fight. Elena would do what was of her own wanting. And while it seemed that the dark girl was leading, the fair one did the guiding. And in her quiet, unargumentative, unobtrusive way, she kept them both safe within the limits of their youthful abilities, gave the lessons and boundaries that encompassed their lives.

Kept them safe. Or almost so. Except for that one time that she hadn't. Kept them safe. Had missed some signal. Had turned aside in some way, away or toward, a split second too soon, too late. Had not known in time not to speak. Had not known what her words, in time, in consequence, would create.

Perhaps it had been the shadows that betrayed her. The certain angle of light that somehow disoriented her. Perhaps so accustomed to being safe, she did not know the danger, any danger that might tear the web of their being. Shredding. Shattering. Splintering.

Or maybe it was the sun. The bright, the pitiless, the unwavering sun.

But whatever had disturbed her knowing, her keeping in time with the turns and twists of their sharing, their lives, in that splitting second everyone had abandoned Ephanie. Everything had gone away.

It was on a certain day. They went hiking. Exploring. They went walking. It was an adventure. One they had planned for a long time. Ever since they were small. They planned to walk to Picacho. The peak. That rose, igneous formation, straight up from the surrounding plain. The arid floor of the semi-desert of their homeland.

They wanted to climb the peak. To go to the top. To see. Elena said you could see the next village. The one that was invisible from where they lived. She told Ephanie the story, one she had recounted before. Much of what Ephanie knew about the people and land around them she learned from Elena. She didn't hear much that others told her. Not for many years.

Not that others had not spoken. Had not told her stories, had not given ideas, opinions, methods. They had. Some part of Ephanie recorded what they told her. What they said. But she did not acknowledge it until later. Not for many years. She did not understand how that had happened. But it did.

They had planned in the last days before their journey very well. Deciding what to take. What would not be too heavy to carry. What would not get in their way. What to wear, for comfort and protection, in the heat, against the stone. Which shirts, which length pants, which shoes. They knew they would get thirsty. It was July.

They wore tennis shoes and jeans. Usually they went barefoot from spring well into fall. Every chance they got. But this journey was special. It signified accomplishing. That they were grown. That they knew something, could put it into use.

They took oranges. For the juice. They knew how to use them, slit the rind with a toughened thumbnail, in a circle. Peel the small circle of rind away from the flesh. Press finger into the fruit, firmly, gently. So as not to lose too much juice. The juice was precious. It would sustain them. Then put the opening thus made to their mouths. Sucking. When all the juice was thus taken, they would split open the fruit and eat the pulp. And the white furry lining of the rind. Elena said it was sweet. That it was healthy.

Ephanie never ate an orange that way later. It didn't seem right. She didn't know why she wouldn't. Like her dislike of spiders. Which made no sense either. She remembered how it had gone, that journey, and why they had learned to eat oranges that particular way. She didn't understand her unwillingness to follow that childhood ritual. Not for a long time. And she found the lining bitter. Peeled it carefully away from the fruit all of her adult life. Threw it away.

But she loved the smell of oranges. The orange oil that clung to her hands when she was done. Its fragrance. Its echoing almost remembered pain. She would sniff it, dreaming, empty in thought, empty in mind, on her way to the faucet to wash it off her hands. And in the flood of water and soap she would banish what she did not know. Averting. Avoiding. Voiding. Pain.

They met in the early morning. While the cool wind blew down from the mountain. The way they were going was into the wind. The earth sparkled. The leaves. The sun was just getting started. Like a light from elsewhere it touched their eyes, their hands. They shivered slightly, shaking. They began to walk. Taking the road that curved upward. Upward and out. They were leaving. They knew that. They knew they would never return.

They didn't talk about that intuition, but walked, silent, amiable, close. They listened to the soft padding of their footfall on the dusty road, watched their shadows move, silent, alongside of them. Elena told Ephanie how high the peak was. Much taller than it looked. They speculated about climbing it.

Ephanie was afraid of heights that had no branches to hold on to, but she never let on. She had never let on.

The great isolate rock rose maybe a hundred feet from the ground. Its top was slender, precarious. It stood alone, gray and silent, reaching into the sky. It was a proud rock. A formation. It brooded there on the plain between the villages. It guarded the road to the mountain. Sentinel.

The story it bore was an old one. Familiar. Everywhere. They remembered the old tale as they watched the rock grow larger, approaching it. About the woman who had a lover. Who had died in a war. She was pregnant. Lonely, desperate, she went to Picacho, climbed to the top, jumped to her death. That was one version, the one Elena's Chicano people told.

There was another version, one that Ephanie's Guadalupe people told. The woman was in love with a youth she was forbidden to marry. He was a stranger, and she had fallen in love with him somehow. Maybe he was a Navajo. Maybe he was a Ute. But her love was hopeless from the start. Then the people found out that she was seeing the youth secretly. They were very angry. They scolded her. Said the things that would happen to the people because of her actions. Shamed her. Hurt and angry, she had gone to Picacho. Climbed to the top. Jumped to her death.

Ephanie imagined that climb. The woman finding places to put her hands. Her feet. Tentative, climbing. Tentative but sure. Shaking. She climbed to the place where the rock was narrowest. Where the drop was straight and steep. Dizzy she had stood there, thinking perhaps, of her anguish, of her rage, of her grief. Wondering, maybe, if whether what she contemplated was wise. No one knew what she had been thinking. They must have wondered about it. They must have told themselves stories about what had gone through her mind as she stood, wavering, just on the edge of the narrow rock bridge that connected the two slightly taller peaks of the formation.

From there she could have seen the wide sweep of the land, barren, hungry, powerful as it raised itself slow and serene toward the lower slopes of the mountains to the north beyond Picacho and was there lost to the wilderness of tabletop hills, soaring slopes, green grasses, flowers, shadows, springs, cliffs, and above them the treeless towering peak. Where it became wilderness. Where it came home.

She could have seen that, looking northward. Where the mountain called Ts'pin'a, Woman Veiled in Clouds, waited, brooding, majestic, almost monstrously powerful. Or she could look southward, eastward, toward the lands the people tended, that held and nurtured them. But probably she had not looked outward. Had not seen the sky, the piling, moving thunderheads. The gold in them. The purpling blue. The dazzling, eye-splitting white. The bellies of them pregnant, ripe with rain about to be born. The living promise of their towering strength. For if she had seen them, would she have jumped.

SHE IS SWEPT AWAY

By the time they got to the foot of the peak it was late morning. The sun was high and the earth around them looked flat. Sunbitten. The shadows had retreated to cooler places for the long day. Ephanie, slender, sturdy, brown, and Elena, slender, sturdy, hair tinged with gold, lightly olive skin deepened almost brown by the summer sun, sat down to rest amid the grey boulders that lay in piles at the base of the peak. They ate their oranges. Looked at the climb that faced them, uneasy. The gray rock soared above their heads, almost smooth. Ephanie looked at Elena for reassurance, thinking how beautiful her friend was, sweating, laughing. Wanted to reach out and touch her face. To hold her hand, brown and sturdy like her own. Reached and touched the smooth brown skin, brushed tenderly back the gold-streaked hair.

"When we get home," she said, "let's go to the apple tree and cool off."

"I can't," Elena said. "I have to go with my mother to town. We're going to stay a few days at my sister's." She looked away from Ephanie. Looked at the ground. Ephanie felt uneasiness crawling around in her stomach. She shifted her weight away from Elena. She didn't know why she felt what way. "Let's go on up," she said.

They climbed. Elena went first. Finding places to put hands and feet. They pretended they were mountains, climbing Mount Everest. They didn't have ropes, but they knew about testing rock and brush before trusting weight to them. They climbed over the boulders and up the first stage of the climb. That part was fairly easy. It was steep, but there was a broad abutment that circled most of the peak, as though supporting its slender, massive skyward thrust. The abutment was hard packed dirt, light sandstone and the gray rock, probably volcanic, that formed Picacho.

They came to a resting place, high above the valley floor. It was very hot. They sat and looked around them. The rest of the peak rose above them along a narrow path that rose toward it from where they sat. A sheer drop on either side. Dizzy. Can we cross that. They looked into each other's eyes. Daring. Testing. Their old familiar way. "I don't think I can get across that. It makes me dizzy," Ephanie said. Elena said, since Ephanie had admitted her fear, "just crawl across it. That's what I'm going to do. I'm not going to try and walk across. We can crawl. It's not far." And she began crawling across the smooth sand that lay over the rock bridge that stretched between them and the smooth curving roundness of the farther peak. "Look down," Elena said. "It's really far."

Ephanie, on hands and knees, crept behind Elena. Feeling foolish, scared. Foolish in her fearfulness. Shaking. She did look down. It was a long way to the ground. She imagined falling. Smashing herself on the rocks below. How Elena would manage. Going home to tell them she had fallen. How the woman long ago had fallen. From here.

They got across the narrow bridge and stood up, clinging to the gray rock of the highest point that rose some three feet above their feet. They climbed up on it, scotting their bodies up and then turning to lie stomach-down on the flat peak. They looked down, over the back side of the peak. Saw the mountain a few miles beyond. "Let's stand up," one of them said. They stood, trembling slightly, and looked around. They saw the villages, one north of them, the other, just beyond it to the west.

They rested for awhile, wishing they hadn't left the rest of the oranges down below. They realized they still had to climb back down. The part they were always forgetting. As they examined the descent, Elena said, "Ephanie, there's something I have to tell you." She didn't look at her friend. She looked at her hands. Sweating and lightly streaked where the sweat had washed some of the dust of their climb away. "I can't come over to your place anymore."

The sun was blazing down on them, unconcerned. It was so hot. Ephanie looked at Elena's hands intently. She didn't speak for a long time. She couldn't swallow. She couldn't breathe. For some reason her chest hurt. Aching. She didn't know why. Anything.

She tried to think, to understand. They had been together all their lives. What did Elena mean. She wondered if it was because she had more. Of everything. Dresses, boarding school, a bigger house. A store-owner for a father. A trader.

Elena's father had a small cantina that he owned. But he didn't make a lot of money at it. He drove a school bus, to make ends meet.

Elena's house had three rooms. Besides the kitchen. They were all used for sleeping. One of them they used as a living room too. One of them was very small, hardly large enough for the tiny iron bedstead it held. Five or six people lived there, depending on whether her brothers were both there or not. They didn't have running water, and their toilet was outdoors. Ephanie thought maybe that was what was the matter. That they were growing up. That now that they were nearing adulthood, such things mattered. Were seen in some way that caused anger, caused shame.

When Ephanie didn't say anything for so long, Elena said, "It's because my mother thinks we spend too much time with each other." She looked at Ephanie, eyes shut against her. Not closed, open, but nothing of herself coming through them. Nothing in them taking her in. Ephanie sat, thinking she was dreaming. This didn't make any sense. What could be wrong. What could be happening. How could she not see Elena. Be with her. Who would she be with then, if not Elena.

She put out her hand. Took hold of Elena's arm. Held it, tightly. Swaying. She looked over the side of the peak. Thought about flying. Dropping off. She thought of going to sleep.

She moved so that she could put her hand on Elena's arm. Held her like that, staring. Trying to speak. Not being able to. There were no words. Only too many thoughts, feelings, churning in her like the whirlwind, chindi, dust devils on the valley floor below. "What are you talking about," she finally said. Her voice sounded strange in her ears.

Elena tried to back away, get loose from Ephanie's hand. Pulled away, but not completely. She looked at Ephanie. Her face was wet. Beads of sweat had formed along her upper lip. She wiped them away with the back of her hand. Her eyes looked flat, gave off no light. Her light brown eyes that were flecked with gold. Her brown face had a few freckles scattered over it. They stood out now, sharp.

"You know," she said, her voice low. "The way we've been lately. Hugging and giggling. You know." She looked down at her hands, twisting against themselves in her lap. "I asked the sister about that, after school. She said it was the devil. That I mustn't do anything like that. That it was a sin. And she told my mother. She says I can't come over any more."

Ephanie sat. Stunned. Mind empty. Stomach a cold cold stone. The hot sun blazed on her head. She felt sick. She felt herself shrinking within. Understood, wordlessly, exactly what Elena was saying. How she could understand what Ephanie had not understood. That they were becoming lovers. That they were in love. That their loving had to stop. To end. That she was falling. Had fallen. Would not recover from the fall, smashing, the rocks. That they were in her, not on the ground.

She finally remembered to take her hand off of Elena's arm. To put it in her pocket. She stood up again. Almost lost her balance. How will we ever get down, she wondered. She couldn't see very well. She realized her eyes were blurred with tears. "Why did you do that," she said. "How could you tell anyone? How did you know, what made you ask? Why didn't you ask me." And realized the futility of her words. The enormity of the abyss she was falling into. The endless, endless depth of the void.

"I was scared. I thought it was wrong. It is." Elena looked at Ephanie, eyes defiant, flat and hard, closed.

"Then why did we come today. Why get me all the way up here and then tell me?" Ephanie felt her face begin to crumble, to give way. Like the arroyo bank gave way in the summer rains. She didn't want Elena to see her like that, giving in to anguish, to weakness, to tears.

"I'm sorry." That was all Elena would say.

They got down from the peak the way they had come, using lifelong habits of caution and practice to guide them. In silence they walked the long way back to the village. Elena went inside when they came to her house. Ephanie went the rest of the way, not so far however long it seemed, alone. She went to the apple tree and climbed up into it. Hid her face in the leaves. She sat there, hiding, for a very long time.

FOR JOURNALING AND DISCUSSION

1. Gunn Allen begins this piece by writing, "It had been the apple tree," foreshadowing the story's central experience from the first word. Using specific evidence from the story, explain what the "it" is.
2. Later in the piece she writes, "They had especially loved the shadows." Trace the

recurring description of shadow and light, and explore Gunn Allen's purpose in using these images.

3. There is a story in the middle of this piece of a woman who jumped from the peak of Picacho to her death. Elena's Chicano people told one story about this death, while Ephanie's Guadalupe people told another. Explain the significance of the differences in each.

FOR RESEARCH AND EXPLORATION

1. Compare this story to Bernard Cooper's "A Clack of Tiny Sparks," the next selection in this chapter. Both narratives demonstrate the pain and confusion that youth experience when the dominant culture forces them to adhere to rigid categories of sexuality. Write an essay that incorporates research on adolescent sexuality to explain why many adults are so concerned with the sexuality of teens.

2. When Ephanie tries to make sense of Elena's announcement that she can no longer visit Ephanie's house, she wonders "if it was because she had more. Of everything. Dresses, boarding school, a bigger house. A store-owner for a father. A trader." Look at Liliana Heker's "The Stolen Party" in Chapter 3, and compare the stories to examine how class intersects with sexuality.

3. This piece is very much about the violence of naming and stereotyping. Research the etymology of the word "homosexuality," exploring when and where the term came into use.

A Clack of Tiny Sparks: Remembrances of a Gay Boyhood

Bernard Cooper

Cooper is the author of Maps to Anywhere *and* A Year of Rhymes; *critics compared the latter to* Other Voices, Other Rooms, *Truman Capote's debut work published forty-five years earlier. Cooper received the 1991 PEN/Ernest Hemingway Award and a 1995 O. Henry Award. The following piece is from his memoir,* Truth Serum, *which has been widely excerpted in numerous publications, including* Harper's, The Paris Review, The Los Angeles Times Magazine, *and* The Best American Essays, 1995.

Theresa Sanchez sat behind me in ninth-grade algebra. When Mr. Hubbley faced the blackboard, I'd turn around to see what she was reading; each week a new book was wedged inside her copy of *Today's Equations*. The deception worked; from Mr. Hubbley's point of view, Theresa was engrossed in the value of X, but I knew otherwise. One week she perused *The Wisdom of the Orient,* and I could tell from Theresa's contemplative expression that the book contained exotic thoughts, guidelines handed down from high. Another week it was a paperback novel whose title, *Let Me Live My Life,* appeared in bold print atop every page, and whose cover, a gauzy photograph of a woman biting a strand of pearls, head thrown back in an attitude of ecstasy, confirmed my suspicion that Theresa Sanchez was mature beyond her years. She was the tallest girl in school. Her bouffant hairdo, streaked with blond, was higher than the flaccid bouffants of other girls. Her smooth skin, plucked eyebrows, and painted fingernails suggested hours of pampering, a worldly and sensual vanity that placed her within the domain of adults. Smiling dimly, steeped in daydreams, Theresa moved through the crowded halls with a languid, self-satisfied indifference to those around her. "You are merely children," her posture seemed to say. "I can't be bothered." The week Theresa hid *101 Ways to Cook Hamburger* behind her algebra book, I could stand it no longer and, after the bell rang, ventured a question.

"Because I'm having a dinner party," said Theresa. "Just a couple of intimate friends."

No fourteen-year-old I knew had ever given a dinner party, let alone used the word "intimate" in conversation. "Don't you have a mother?" I asked.

Theresa sighed a weary sigh, suffered my strange inquiry. "Don't be so naive," she said. "Everyone has a mother." She waved her hand to indicate the brick school buildings outside the window. "A higher education should have taught you that." Theresa draped an angora sweater over her shoulders, scooped her books from the graffiti-covered desk, and just as she was about to walk away, she turned and asked me, "Are you a fag?"

There wasn't the slightest hint of rancor or condescension in her voice. The tone was direct, casual. Still I was stunned, giving a sidelong glance to make sure no one had heard. "No," I said. Blurted really, with too much defensiveness, too much transparent fear in my response. Octaves lower than usual, I tried a "Why?"

Theresa shrugged. "Oh, I don't know. I have lots of friends who are fags. You remind me of them." Seeing me bristle, Theresa added, "It was just a guess." I watched her erect, angora back as she sauntered out the classroom door.

She had made an incisive and timely guess. Only days before, I'd invited Grady Rogers to my house after school to go swimming. The instant Grady shot from the pool, shaking water from his orange hair, freckled shoulders shining, my attraction to members of my own sex became a matter I could no longer suppress or rationalize. Sturdy and boisterous and gap-toothed, Grady was an inveterate backslapper, a formidable arm wrestler, a wizard at basketball. Grady was a boy at home in his body.

My body was a marvel I hadn't gotten used to; my arms and legs would sometimes act of their own accord, knocking over a glass at dinner or flinching at an oncoming pitch. I was never singled out as a sissy, but I could have been just as easily as Bobby Keagan, a gentle, intelligent, and introverted boy reviled by my classmates. And although I had always been aware of a tacit rapport with Bobby, a suspicion that I might find with him a rich friendship, I stayed away. Instead, I emulated Grady in the belief that being seen with him, being like him, would somehow vanquish my self-doubt, would make me normal by association.

Apart from his athletic prowess, Grady had been gifted with all the trappings of what I imagined to be a charmed life: a fastidious, aproned mother who radiated calm, maternal concern; a ruddy, stoic father with a knack for home repairs. Even the Rogerses' small suburban house in Hollywood, with its spindly Colonial furniture and chintz curtains, was a testament to normalcy.

Grady and his family bore little resemblance to my clan of Eastern European Jews, a dark and vociferous people who ate with abandon—matzo and halvah and gefilte fish; foods the goyim couldn't pronounce—who cajoled one another during endless games of canasta, making the simplest remark about the weather into a lengthy philosophical discourse on the sun and the seasons and the passage of time. My mother was a chain-smoker, a dervish in a frowsy housedress. She showed her love in the most peculiar and obsessive ways, like spending hours extracting every seed from a watermelon before she served it in perfectly bite-sized, geometric pieces. Preoccupied and perpetually frantic, my mother succumbed to bouts of absentmindedness so profound she'd forget what she was saying midsentence, smile and blush and walk away. A divorce attorney, my father wore roomy, iridescent suits, and the intricacies, the deceits inherent in his profession, had the effect of making him forever tense and vigilant. He was "all wound up," as my mother put it. But when he relaxed, his laughter was explosive, his disposition prankish: "Walk this way," a waitress would say, leading us to our table, and my father would mimic the way she walked, arms akimbo, hips liquid, while my mother and I were wracked with laughter. Buoyant or brooding, my parents' moods were unpredictable, and in a household fraught with extravagant emotion it was odd and awful to keep my longing secret.

One day I made the mistake of asking my mother what a "fag" was. I knew exactly what Theresa had meant but hoped against hope it was not what I thought; maybe "fag" was some French word, a harmless term like "naive." My mother turned from the stove, flew at me, and grabbed me by the shoulders. "Did someone call you that?" she cried.

"Not me," I said. "Bobby Keagan."

"Oh," she said, loosening her grip. She was visibly relieved. And didn't answer. The answer was unthinkable.

For weeks after, I shook with the reverberations from that afternoon in the kitchen with my mother, pained by the memory of her shocked expression and, most of all, her silence. My longing was wrong in the eyes of my mother, whose hazel eyes were the eyes of the world, and if that longing continued unchecked, the unwieldy shape of my fate would be cast, and I'd be subjected to a lifetime of scorn.

During the remainder of the semester, I became the scientist of my own desire, plotting ways to change my yearning for boys into a yearning for girls. I had enough evidence to believe that any habit, regardless of how compulsive, how deeply ingrained, could be broken once and for all: The plastic cigarette my mother purchased at the Thrifty pharmacy—one end was red to approximate an ember, the other tan like a filtered tip—was designed to wean her from the real thing. To change a behavior required self-analysis, cold resolve, and the substitution of one thing for another: plastic, say, for tobacco. Could I also find a substitute for Grady? What I needed to do, I figured, was kiss a girl and learn to like it.

This conclusion was affirmed one Sunday morning when my father, seeing me wrinkle my nose at the pink slabs of lox he layered on a bagel, tried to convince me of its salty appeal. "You should try some," he said. "You don't know what you're missing."

"It's loaded with protein," added my mother, slapping a platter of sliced onions onto the dinette table. She hovered above us, cinching her housedress, eyes wet from onion fumes, the mock cigarette dangling from her lips.

My father sat there chomping with gusto, emitting a couple of hearty grunts to dramatize his satisfaction. And still I was not convinced. After a loud and labored swallow, he told me I may not be fond of lox today, but sooner or later I'd learn to like it. One's tastes, he assured me, are destined to change.

"Live," shouted my mother over the rumble of the Mixmaster. "Expand your horizons. Try new things." And the room grew fragrant with the batter of a spice cake.

The opportunity to put their advice into practice, and try out my plan to adapt to girls, came the following week when Debbie Coburn, a member of Mr. Hubbley's algebra class, invited me to a party. She cornered me in the hall, furtive as a spy, telling me her parents would be gone for the evening and slipping into my palm a wrinkled sheet of notebook paper. On it were her address and telephone number, the lavender ink in a tidy cursive. "Wear cologne," she advised, wary eyes darting back and forth. "It's a make-out party. Anything can happen."

The Santa Ana wind blew relentlessly the night of Debbie's party, careening down the slopes of the Hollywood hills, shaking the road signs and stoplights in its path. As I walked down Beachwood Avenue, trees thrashed, surrendered their leaves, and carob pods bombarded the pavement. The sky was a deep but luminous blue, the air hot, abrasive, electric. I had to squint in order to check the number of the Coburns' apartment, a three-story building with glitter embedded in its stucco walls. Above the honeycombed balconies was a sign that read BEACHWOOD TERRACE in lavender script resembling Debbie's.

From down the hall, I could hear the plaintive strains of Little Anthony's "I Think I'm Going Out of My Head." Debbie answered the door bedecked in an Empire dress, the bodice blue and orange polka dots, the rest a sheath of black and white stripes. "Op art," proclaimed Debbie. She turned in a circle, then proudly announced that she'd rolled her hair in orange juice cans. She patted the huge unmoving curls and dragged me inside. Reflections from the swimming pool in the courtyard, its surface ruffled by wind, shuddered over the ceiling and walls. A dozen of my classmates were seated on the sofa or huddled together in corners, their whispers full of excited imminence, their bodies barely discernible in the dim light. Drapes flanking the sliding glass doors bowed out with every gust of wind, and it seemed that the room might lurch from its foundations and sail with its cargo of silhouettes into the hot October night.

Grady was the last to arrive. He tossed a six-pack of beer into Debbie's arms, barreled toward me, and slapped my back. His hair was slicked back with Vitalis, lacquered furrows left by the comb. The wind hadn't shifted a single hair. "Ya ready?" he asked, flashing the gap between his front teeth and leering into the darkened room. "You bet," I lied.

Once the beers had been passed around, Debbie provoked everyone's attention by flicking on the overhead light. "Okay," she called. "Find a partner." This was the blunt command of a hostess determined to have her guests aroused in an orderly fashion. Everyone blinked, shuffled about, and grabbed a member of the opposite sex. Sheila Garabedian landed beside me—entirely at random, though I wanted to believe she was driven by passion—her timid smile giving way to plain fear as the light went out. Nothing for a moment but the heave of the wind and the distant banter of dogs. I caught a whiff of Sheila's perfume, tangy and sweet as Hawaiian Punch. I probed her face with my own, grazing the small scallop of an ear, a velvety temple, and though Sheila's trembling made me want to stop, I persisted with my mission until I found her lips, tightly sealed as a private letter. I held my mouth over hers and gathered her shoulders closer, resigned to the possibility that, no matter how long we stood there, Sheila would be too scared to kiss me back. Still, she exhaled through her nose, and I listened to the squeak of every breath as though it were a sigh of inordinate pleasure. Diving within myself, I monitored my heartbeat and respiration, trying to will stimulation into being, and all the while an image intruded, an image of Grady erupting from our pool, rivulets of water sliding down his chest. "Change," shouted Debbie, switching on the light. Sheila thanked me, pulled away, and continued her routine of gracious terror with every boy throughout the evening. It didn't matter whom I held—Margaret Sims, Betty Vernon, Elizabeth Lee—my experiment was a failure; I continued to picture Grady's wet chest, and Debbie would bellow "change" with such fervor, it could have been my own voice, my own incessant reprimand.

Our hostess commandeered the light switch for nearly half an hour. Whenever the light came on, I watched Grady pivot his head toward the newest prospect, his eyebrows arched in expectation, his neck blooming with hickeys, his hair, at last, in disarray. All that shuffling across the carpet charged everyone's arms and lips with static, and eventually, between low moans and soft osculations,

I could hear the clack of tiny sparks and see them flare here and there in the dark like meager, short-lived stars.

I saw Theresa, sultry and aloof as ever, read three more books—*North American Reptiles, Bonjour Tristesse,* and *MGM: A Pictorial History*—before she vanished early in December. Rumors of her fate abounded. Debbie Coburn swore that Theresa had been "knocked up" by an older man, a traffic cop, she thought, or a grocer. Nearly quivering with relish, Debbie told me and Grady about the home for unwed mothers in the San Fernando Valley, a compound teeming with pregnant girls who had nothing to do but touch their stomachs and contemplate their mistake. Even Bobby Keagan, who took Theresa's place behind me in algebra, had a theory regarding her disappearance colored by his own wish for escape; he imagined that Theresa, disillusioned with society, booked passage to a tropical island, there to live out the rest of her days without restrictions or ridicule. "No wonder she flunked out of school," I overheard Mr. Hubbley tell a fellow teacher one afternoon. "Her head was always in a book."

Along with Theresa went my secret, or at least the dread that she might divulge it, and I felt, for a while, exempt from suspicion. I was, however, to run across Theresa one last time. It happened during a period of torrential rain that, according to reports on the six o'clock news, washed houses from the hillsides and flooded the downtown streets. The halls of Joseph Le Conte Junior High were festooned with Christmas decorations: crepe-paper garlands, wreaths studded with plastic berries, and one requisite Star of David twirling above the attendance desk. In Arts and Crafts, our teacher, Gerald (he was the only teacher who allowed us—*required* us—to call him by his first name), handed out blocks of balsa wood and instructed us to carve them into bugs. We would paint eyes and antennae with tempera and hang them on a Christmas tree he'd made the previous night. "Voilà," he crooned, unveiling his creation from a burlap sack. Before us sat a tortured scrub, a wardrobe-worth of wire hangers that were bent like branches and soldered together. Gerald credited his inspiration to a Charles Addams cartoon he'd seen in which Morticia, grimly preparing for the holidays, hangs vampire bats on a withered pine. "All that red and green," said Gerald. "So predictable. So *boring*."

As I chiseled a beetle and listened to rain pummel the earth, Gerald handed me an envelope and asked me to take it to Mr. Kendrick, the drama teacher. I would have thought nothing of his request if I hadn't seen Theresa on my way down the hall. She was cleaning out her locker, blithely dropping the sum of its contents—pens and textbooks and mimeographs—into a trash can. "Have a nice life," she sang as I passed. I mustered the courage to ask her what had happened. We stood alone in the silent hall, the reflections of wreaths and garlands submerged in brown linoleum.

"I transferred to another school. They don't have grades or bells, and you get to study whatever you want." Theresa was quick to sense my incredulity.

"Honest," she said. "The school is progressive." She gazed into a glass cabinet that held the trophies of track meets and intramural spelling bees. "God," she sighed, "this place is so . . . barbaric." I was still trying to decide whether or not to believe her story when she asked me where I was headed. "Dear," she said, her exclamation pooling in the silence, "that's no ordinary note, if you catch my drift." The envelope was blank and white; I looked up at Theresa, baffled. "Don't be so naive," she muttered, tossing an empty bottle of nail polish into the trash can. It struck bottom with a resolute thud. "Well," she said, closing her locker and breathing deeply, "bon voyage." Theresa swept through the double doors and in seconds her figure was obscured by rain.

As I walked toward Mr. Kendrick's room, I could feel Theresa's insinuation burrow in. I stood for a moment and watched Mr. Kendrick through the pane in the door. He paced intently in front of the class, handsome in his shirt and tie, reading from a thick book. Chalked on the blackboard behind him was THE ODYSSEY BY HOMER. I have no recollection of how Mr. Kendrick reacted to the note, whether he accepted it with pleasure or embarrassment, slipped it into his desk drawer or the pocket of his shirt. I have scavenged that day in retrospect, trying to see Mr. Kendrick's expression, wondering if he acknowledged me in any way as his liaison. All I recall is the sight of his mime through a pane of glass, a lone man mouthing an epic, his gestures ardent in empty air.

Had I delivered a declaration of love? I was haunted by the need to know. In fantasy, a kettle shot steam, the glue released its grip, and I read the letter with impunity. But how would such a letter begin? Did the common endearments apply? This was a message between two men, a message for which I had no precedent, and when I tried to envision the contents, apart from a hasty, impassioned scrawl, my imagination faltered.

Once or twice I witnessed Gerald and Mr. Kendrick walk together into the faculty lounge or say hello at the water fountain, but there was nothing especially clandestine or flirtatious in their manner. Besides, no matter how acute my scrutiny, I wasn't sure, short of a kiss, exactly what to look for—what semaphore of gesture, what encoded word. I suspected there were signs, covert signs that would give them away, just as I'd unwittingly given myself away to Theresa.

In the school library, a *Webster's* unabridged dictionary lay on a wooden podium, and I padded toward it with apprehension; along with clues to the bond between my teachers, I risked discovering information that might incriminate me as well. I had decided to consult the dictionary during lunch period, when most of the students would be on the playground. I clutched my notebook, moving in such a way as to appear both studious and nonchalant, actually believing that, unless I took precautions, someone would see me and guess what I was up to. The closer I came to the podium, the more obvious, I thought, was my endeavor; I felt like the model of The Visible Man in our science class, my heart's undulations, my overwrought nerves legible through transparent skin. A couple of kids riffled through the card catalogue. The librarian, a skinny woman whose perpetual whisper and rubber-soled shoes caused her to drift through the room like a phantom, didn't seem to register my presence. Though I'd looked up dozens of words before, the pages felt strange beneath my fingers. *Homer* was the first word I saw. *Hominid. Homogenize.* I feigned interest and skirted other words before I found the word I was after. Under the heading HO • MO • SEX • U • AL was the terse definition: *adj. Pertaining to, characteristic of, or exhibiting homosexuality.*—n. *A homosexual person.* I read the definition again and again, hoping the words would yield more than they could. I shut the dictionary, swallowed hard, and, none the wiser, hurried away.

As for Gerald and Mr. Kendrick, I never discovered evidence to prove or dispute Theresa's claim. By the following summer, however, I had overheard from my peers a confounding amount about homosexuals: They wore green on Thursday, couldn't whistle, hypnotized boys with a piercing glance. To this lore, Grady added a surefire test to ferret them out.

"A test?" I said.

"You ask a guy to look at his fingernails, and if he looks at them like this"—Grady closed his fingers into a fist and examined his nails with manly detachment—"then he's okay. But if he does this"—he held out his hands at arm's length, splayed his fingers, and coyly cocked his head—"you'd better watch out." Once he'd completed his demonstration, Grady peeled off his shirt and plunged into our pool. I dove in after. It was early June, the sky immense, glassy, placid. My father was cooking spareribs on the barbecue, an artist with a basting brush. His apron bore the caricature of a frazzled French chef. Mother curled on a chaise longue, plumes of smoke wafting from her nostrils. In a stupor of contentment she took another drag, closed her eyes, and arched her face toward the sun.

Grady dog-paddled through the deep end, spouting a fountain of chlorinated water. Despite shame and confusion, my longing for him hadn't diminished; it continued to thrive without air and light, like a luminous fish in the dregs of the sea. In the name of play, I swam up behind him, encircled his shoulders, astonished by his taut flesh. The two of us flailed, pretended to drown. Beneath the heavy press of water, Grady's orange hair wavered, a flame that couldn't be doused.

I've lived with a man for seven years. Some nights, when I'm half-asleep and the room is suffused with blue light, I reach out to touch the expanse of his back, and it seems as if my fingers sink into his skin, and I feel the pleasure a diver feels the instant he enters a body of water.

I have few regrets. But one is that I hadn't said to Theresa, "Of course I'm a fag." Maybe I'd have met her friends. Or become friends with her. Imagine the meals we might have concocted: hamburger Stroganoff, Swedish meatballs in a sweet translucent sauce, steaming slabs of Salisbury steak.

FOR JOURNALING AND DISCUSSION

1. Cooper begins his narrative with Theresa Sanchez, a classmate whose dress, reading interests, and "knowing" smile make her seem older than her peers. When Theresa leaves the school, it is rumored that she was "knocked up" by an older man and that she "flunked out" because "her head was always in a book." Why are sexuality and self-chosen books so feared in high school students? What did Theresa represent?

2. Cooper describes his friendship and crush on Grady, calling his friend's life "a testament to normalcy." Write in your journal about your own memories of myths or rituals of normalcy. Grady explains how "normal" boys look at their own nails; what tests of normalcy can you remember? Why is normalcy so important during adolescence?

3. When the teenage Cooper delivers a message from one of his male teachers to another, the "knowing" Theresa implies they are gay, and Cooper reflects, "This was a message between two men, a message for which I had no precedent. . . ." Why is the lack of a precedent or model so significant?

4. Cooper describes the adolescent awkwardness of his growing body: "my arms and legs would sometimes act of their own accord, knocking over a glass at dinner or flinching at an oncoming pitch." Do you have early memories of your body becoming unruly and unmanageable? Describe these memories, and then analyze why adolescence is such a hard time for bodies.

5. By the end of the essay, Cooper wishes he had opened up to Theresa about his sexuality, but the description of his family and school more than explains why he remained closeted. Why is difference, especially sexual difference, feared in high school? Draw from your own experience of struggling with individuality and conformity as a teen to support your argument.

FOR RESEARCH AND EXPLORATION

1. When Theresa first asks the teenage Cooper if he is a "fag," he says no and then asks his mother what the word means, assuring her that not he but Bobby Keagan was the recipient of the question. The naive Cooper knows little about homosexuality, but is clearly aware of the danger surrounding it and therefore disassociates himself from the situation. Research teen suicide and depression, and report on the incidence of these problems among homosexual teens.

2. Cooper connects the "normalcy" of Grady Rogers with his heterosexuality and his family background. Why were the Rogers more "normal" in suburban Hollywood than Cooper's "clan of Eastern European Jews, a dark and vociferous people who ate with abandon. . ."? Research anti-Semitism in the United States, especially in California, during the 1950s.

3. Cooper describes some class distinctions along with sexuality and ethnicity differences in his piece. Look at Katherine Newman's "Illegitimate Elites and the Parasitic Underclass" in Chapter 3, and, drawing evidence from both texts, explain how income and sexuality affect the "American Dream."

A Normal Lesbian

Norah Vincent

Vincent is a contributor to The New Republic *and an assistant editor for* The Free Press.

"Crate and Barrel," I said. "That sounds like a lesbian store, doesn't it?" "Sounds like what a lesbian would wear," said Susan. Susan and I are best friends, and both lesbians. We joke this way often. We are incessant watchers, curious about other lesbians and whether we can literally tease them out of the crowd. There are always crude symbols to go by, of course: rainbow flags, pink triangles, pink ribbons. And, naturally, the rote slogans of a cause—"THE LESBIAN AVENGERS. WE RECRUIT." Hence the jokes, a kind of bitter relief from orthodoxy.

But, for me, there is an urgent question under the jokes, a question the so-called "lesbian community" does not ask: Who am I?

If the straight world (and sometimes the gay male world) has defined lesbians falsely, even maliciously, then lesbians have, to some degree, acquiesced, by forgetting the I and playing into stereotypes. Lesbians have labels for everyone, it seems: "bull dyke," "granola dyke," "baby dyke," "power dyke," "butch," "soft butch," "femme," "lipstick lesbian." It goes on and on, and these are the same labels that make it easy for straight people, and gay men, to misrepresent lesbians. If we want the truth about lesbians, labels will not lead us to it, or at least not to an answer that will make any human difference.

If the question is—What does it mean to be a lesbian?—then the answer is semantic, and the same for everyone: a primary, sexual and emotional attraction to women. Reductive as it sounds, this is the only answer that will give lesbians the equality they demand. Only the simplicity of what the word "lesbian" means can make being a lesbian a neutral fact of life to which all other traits, lifestyles, professions, proclivities are incidental and beside the point. Only this literal definition will make the word "lesbian" a nonissue in public life because it threads lesbianism so completely through the fabric of "the norm" that it cannot be separated from it.

The straight world has taken lesbians, a numeric minority, and made them, by false argument, a moral, social and political minority; and in retreating to the entrenched haven of groupthink, the "lesbian community" has colluded in this sophistry. But, if I am an individual, if "lesbian" is reduced to one among many words that describe me, it ceases to so effectively define and marginalize me.

No doubt, some lesbians will label this a "back to the closet argument," i.e., if you want straight rights, then act straight. But heterocloning is not my answer to the problems lesbians face: individualism is. To straights, lesbianism may never be as innocuous as left-handedness, but ghettoization merely aggravates prejudice.

Defining oneself beyond lesbianism, however, is anathema to the group. Behaviors not sanctioned by lesbian codes of conduct are suspect in the "lesbian community," because they smack of conformity to straight life and so-called "patriarchal" notions of womanhood. Lesbianism, for many, has become an isolationist lifestyle, complete with its own vocabulary, food, clothing, politics, medicine and psychology. Dissent is no laughing matter.

About a year ago, a woman bought me a beer in a lesbian bar and taught me quickly this cool lesson of conformity. After setting the beer in front of me, she seemed suddenly distraught. She asked me if my jacket was made of leather. I said it wasn't. She then looked down at my shoes and my belt and asked if *they* were made of leather. I admitted they were, which prompted her to take back my beer: she couldn't buy a drink for anybody wearing animal hide, she explained, and pinned to my shirt a button bearing a save the animals slogan. Then she turned and offered the beer to the woman next to me. (The satisfying coda to the story is that *this* woman returned the beer, saying that she couldn't accept it in good conscience, since her parents were furriers.)

I had failed the lesbian test because in the "lesbian community" political loyalty to a particular set of causes is a prerequisite for inclusion. The veterans of everything from butch/femme in the 1950s to radical feminism in the 1970s are its esteemed matriarchs—older, seasoned women, disrespectful of the young and uninitiated. While in the gay male culture youth and beauty are absurdly apotheosized, in the "lesbian community" they are often resented and denigrated. How many times have these older women said to me: "Yeah, well God knows where you were in the '70s," or casually dropped a degrading reference to youth and its assumed concomitants, social and political ignorance?

Recently, I attended a fund-raising event for a lesbian foundation, featuring a staged reading of a new lesbian screenplay. The story, touted as a lesbian *Big Chill*, took place at a house in the Berkshires where a group of old friends gathered to celebrate one couple's new baby. The script was filled with lesbian clichés. Half the women had been paired off as lovers at one time or another and were still working through old resentments. Most were political refugees of the 1970s. Several were either alcoholics or proselytizing twelve-steppers. In one scene they sat around the porch with a guitar, warbling Holly Near tunes and recounting their coming-out stories.

The comic centerpiece was a 23-year-old corporate-bimbo type with a glen plaid suit, high heels and a pageboy haircut. The much younger lover of one of the old friends, she was many other things she wasn't supposed to be: well-groomed, attractive and straight-looking. She was also many of the things the writer believed must naturally follow from these qualities: vapid, spoiled, uninformed and complacent.

Many a poorly made lesbian film has embarrassed me of late, but this script was conspicuous because it embodied so much of the "lesbian community's" worst conformism. The writer's message was clear: don't be young, don't accept beauty, don't trespass, don't be yourself: instead, be disgruntled and carping, self-deprecating in your dress and demeanor, avoid anything that passes for accomplishment or assimilation in the mainstream, be a real lesbian and sing along.

As a young lesbian, my answer is this: be original, and write something that is a profound, intelligent depiction of the human spirit in a lesbian milieu, or if you prefer comedy, at least produce something that is clever enough not to become a parody of itself. If lesbians truly want equal rights and equal treatment, they should step into the real world, make a case for their humanity first and even learn to take a joke.

FOR JOURNALING AND DISCUSSION

1. From the outset of this piece Vincent raises questions about the "rote slogans" and "orthodoxy" of lesbian communities. Write about your own experience with slogans and orthodoxy to explain the problems with fixed definitions of a community.
2. Exploring the stereotyping of lesbians, Vincent writes, "Lesbians have, to some degree, acquiesced, by forgetting the I and playing into stereotypes." Have you ever "played into stereotypes" about your own gender/race/region or other central feature of your identity? Why or why not?
3. Only by threading lesbianism "so completely through the fabric of 'the norm,' " Vincent argues, will the stereotyping of lesbians end. What are some of the potential problems with this attempt at mainstreaming lesbianism?

FOR RESEARCH AND EXPLORATION

1. Vincent's argument is based on the goal of making lesbianism "a neutral fact of life," yet same-sex marriage is the subject of controversy in local district courts, state legislatures, the U.S. Congress, and the White House. Research recent court decisions and legislation on this issue, focusing specifically on your state's position.
2. Many of the social movements of the 1960s and 1970s are now fractured by generational, race, and class differences. Research lesbianism of the 1960s and 1970s, and offer an explanation of what Vincent claims is the "esteemed matriarchs'" assertion of a fixed orthodoxy and loyalty to a "particular set of causes."
3. If people of color and women have been fighting for rights and recognition since the 1960s and 1970s, the "Queer Rights" movement has been more prevalent in the 1980s and 1990s. Both the Stonewall riot and the murder of Harvey Milk were central to this growing prominence, and both centered largely on gay male oppression. Research equally significant moments in lesbian activism.

Asian Women in Film: No Joy, No Luck

Jessica Hagedorn

Hagedorn's first novel, Dogeaters, *was nominated for a National Book Award in 1990 and was voted the best book of the year by the Before Columbus Foundation. A well-known performance artist, poet, and playwright, and formerly a commentator on "Crossroads," a syndicated weekly magazine on National Public Radio, she is also the author of* Danger and Beauty: Poetry and Prose *and* The Gangster of Love, *as well as the editor of* Charlie Chan Is Dead: An Anthology of Contemporary Asian American Fiction. *Hagedorn lives in New York City.*

Pearl of the Orient. Whore. Geisha. Concubine. Whore. Hostess. Bar Girl. Mama-san. Whore. China Doll. Tokyo Rose. Whore. Butterfly. Whore. Miss Saigon. Whore. Dragon Lady. Lotus Blossom. Gook. Whore. Yellow Peril. Whore. Bangkok Bombshell. Whore. Hospitality Girl. Whore. Comfort Woman. Whore. Savage. Whore. Sultry. Whore. Faceless. Whore. Porcelain. Whore. Demure. Whore. Virgin. Whore. Mute. Whore. Model Minority. Whore. Victim. Whore. Woman Warrior. Whore. Mail-Order Bride. Whore. Mother. Wife. Lover. Daughter. Sister.

As I was growing up in the Philippines in the 1950s, my fertile imagination was colonized by thoroughly American fantasies. Yellowface variations on the exotic erotic loomed larger than life on the silver screen. I was mystified and enthralled by Hollywood's skewed representations of Asian women: sleek, evil goddesses with slanted eyes and cunning ways, or smiling, sarong-clad South Seas "maidens" with undulating hips, kinky black hair, and white skin darkened by makeup. Hardly any of the "Asian" characters were played by Asians. White actors like Sidney Toler and Warner Oland played "inscrutable Oriental detective" Charlie Chan with taped eyelids and a singsong, chop suey accent. Jennifer Jones was a Eurasian doctor swept up in a doomed "interracial romance" in *Love Is a Many Splendored Thing.* In my mother's youth, white actor Luise Rainer played the central role of the Patient Chinese Wife in the 1937 film adaptation of Pearl Buck's novel *The Good Earth.* Back then, not many thought to ask why; they were all too busy being grateful to see anyone in the movies remotely like themselves.

Cut to 1960: *The World of Suzie Wong,* another tragic East/West affair. I am now old enough to be impressed. Sexy, sassy Suzie (played by Nancy Kwan) works out of a bar patronized by white sailors, but doesn't seem bothered by any of it. For a hardworking girl turning nightly tricks to support her baby, she manages to parade an astonishing wardrobe in damn near every scene, down to matching handbags and shoes. The sailors are also strictly Hollywood, sanitized and not too menacing. Suzie and all the other prostitutes in this movie are cute, giggling, dancing sex machines with hearts of gold. William Holden plays an earnest, rather prim, Nice Guy painter seeking inspiration in The Other. Of course, Suzie falls madly in love with him. Typically, she tells him, "I not important," and "I'll be with you until you say—Suzie, go away." She also thinks being beaten by a man is a sign of true passion, and is terribly disappointed when Mr. Nice Guy refuses to show his true feelings.

Next in Kwan's short-lived but memorable career was the kitschy 1961 musical *Flower Drum Song*, which, like *Suzie Wong*, is a thoroughly American commercial product. The female roles are typical of Hollywood musicals of the times: women are basically airheads, subservient to men. Kwan's counterpart is the Good Chinese Girl, played by Miyoshi Umeki, who was better playing the Loyal Japanese Girl in that other classic Hollywood tale of forbidden love, *Sayonara*. Remember? Umeki was so loyal, she committed double suicide with actor Red Buttons. I instinctively hated *Sayonara* when I first saw it as a child; now I understand why. Contrived tragic resolutions were the only way Hollywood got past the censors in those days. With one or two exceptions, somebody in these movies always had to die to pay for breaking racial and sexual taboos.

Until the recent onslaught of films by both Asian and Asian American filmmakers, Asian Pacific women have generally been perceived by Hollywood with a mixture of fascination, fear, and contempt. Most Hollywood movies either trivialize or exoticize us as people of color and as women. Our intelligence is underestimated, our humanity overlooked, and our diverse cultures treated as interchangeable. If we are "good," we are childlike, submissive, silent, and eager for sex (see France Nuyen's glowing performance as Liat in the film version of *South Pacific*) or else we are tragic victim types (see *Casualties of War,* Brian De Palma's graphic 1989 drama set in Vietnam). And if we are not silent, suffering doormats, we are demonized dragon ladies—cunning, deceitful, sexual provocateurs. Give me the demonic any day—Anna May Wong as a villain slithering around in a slinky gown is at least gratifying to watch, neither servile nor passive. And she steals the show from Marlene Dietrich in Josef von Sternberg's *Shanghai Express*. From the 1920s through the '30s, Wong was our only female "star." But even she was trapped in limited roles, in what filmmaker Renee Tajima has called the dragon lady/lotus blossom dichotomy.

Cut to 1985: There is a scene toward the end of the terribly dishonest but weirdly compelling Michael Cimino movie *Year of the Dragon* (cowritten by Oliver Stone) that is one of my favorite twisted movie moments of all time. If you ask a lot of my friends who've seen that movie (especially if they're Asian), it's one of their favorites too. The setting is a crowded Chinatown nightclub. There are two very young and very tough Jade Cobra gang girls in a shoot-out with Mickey Rourke, in the role of a demented Polish American cop who, in spite of being Mr. Ugly in the flesh—an arrogant, misogynistic bully devoid of any charm—wins the "good" Asian American anchorwoman in the film's absurd and implausible ending. This is a movie with an actual disclaimer as its lead-in, covering its ass in advance in response to anticipated complaints about "stereotypes."

My pleasure in the hard-edged power of the Chinatown gang girls in *Year of the Dragon* is my small revenge, the answer to all those Suzie Wong "I want to be your slave" female characters. The Jade Cobra girls are mere background to the white male foreground/focus of Cimino's movie. But long after the movie has faded into video-rental heaven, the Jade Cobra girls remain defiant, fabulous images in my memory, flaunting tight metallic dresses and spiky cock's-comb hairdos streaked electric red and blue.

> *Mickey Rourke looks down with world-weary pity at the unnamed Jade Cobra girl (Doreen Chan) he's just shot who lies sprawled and bleeding on the street: "You look like you're gonna die, beautiful."*
>
> *Jade Cobra girl: "Oh yeah? [blood gushing from her mouth] I'm proud of it."*
>
> *Rourke: "You are? You got anything you wanna tell me before you go, sweetheart?"*
>
> *Jade Cobra girl: "Yeah. [pause] Fuck you."*

Cut to 1993: I've been told that like many New Yorkers, I watch movies with the right side of my brain on perpetual overdrive. I admit to being grouchy and overcritical, suspicious of sentiment, and cynical. When a critic like Richard Corliss of *Time* magazine gushes about *The Joy Luck Club* being "a fourfold *Terms of Endearment,*" my gut instinct is to run the other way. I resent being told how to feel. I went to see the 1993 eight-handkerchief movie version of Amy Tan's best-seller with a group that included my ten-year-old daughter. I was caught between the sincere desire to be swept up by the turbulent mother-daughter sagas and my own stubborn resistance to being so obviously manipulated by the filmmakers. With every flashback came tragedy. The music soared; the voice-overs were solemn or wistful; tears, tears, and more tears flowed on-screen. Daughters were reverent; mothers carried dark secrets.

I was elated by the grandness and strength of the four mothers and the luminous actors who portrayed them, but I was uneasy with the passivity of the Asian American daughters. They seemed to exist solely as receptors for their mothers' amazing life stories. It's almost as if by assimilating so easily into American society, they had lost all sense of self.

In spite of my resistance, my eyes watered as the desperate mother played by Kieu Chinh was forced to abandon her twin baby girls on a country road in war-torn China. (Kieu Chinh resembles my own mother and her twin sister, who suffered through the brutal Japanese occupation of the Philippines.) So far in this movie, an infant son had been deliberately drowned, a mother played by the gravely beautiful France Nuyen had gone catatonic with grief, a concubine had cut her flesh open to save her dying mother, an insecure daughter had been oppressed by her boorish Asian American husband, another insecure daughter had been left by her white husband, and so on. . . . The overall effect was numbing as far as I'm concerned, but a man sitting two rows in front of us broke down sobbing. A Chinese Pilipino writer even more grouchy than me later complained, "Must ethnicity only be equated with suffering?"

Because change has been slow, *The Joy Luck Club* carries a lot of cultural baggage. It is a big-budget story about Chinese American women, directed by a Chinese American man, cowritten and coproduced by Chinese American women. That's a lot to be thankful for. And its box office success proves that an immigrant narrative told from female perspectives can have mass appeal. But my cynical side tells me that its success might mean only one thing in Hollywood: more weepy epics about Asian American mother-daughter relationships will be planned.

That the film finally got made was significant. By Hollywood standards (think white male; think money, money, money), a movie about Asian Americans even when adapted from a best-seller was a risky proposition. When I asked a producer I know about the film's rumored delays, he simply said, "It's still an *Asian* movie," surprised I had even asked. Equally interesting was director Wayne Wang's initial reluctance to be involved in the project; he told the New York *Times*, "I didn't want to do another Chinese movie."

Maybe he shouldn't have worried so much. After all, according to the media, the nineties are the decade of "Pacific Overtures" and East Asian chic. Madonna, the pop queen of shameless appropriation, cultivated Japanese high-tech style with her music video "Rain," while Janet Jackson faked kitschy orientalia in hers, titled "If." Critical attention was paid to movies from China, Japan, and Vietnam. But that didn't mean an honest appraisal of women's lives. Even on the art house circuit, filmmakers who should know better took the easy way out. Takehiro Nakajima's 1992 film *Okoge* presents one of the more original film roles for women in recent years. In Japanese, "okoge" means the crust of rice that sticks to the bottom of the rice pot; in pejorative slang, it means fag hag. The way "okoge" is used in the film seems a reappropriation of the term: the portrait Nakajima creates of Sayoko, the so-called fag hag, is clearly an affectionate one. Sayoko is a quirky, self-assured woman in contemporary Tokyo who does voice-overs for cartoons, has a thing for Frida Kahlo paintings, and is drawn to a gentle young gay man named Goh. But the other women's roles are disappointing, stereotypical "hysterical females" and the movie itself turns conventional halfway through. Sayoko sacrifices herself to a macho brute Goh desires, who rapes her as images of Frida Kahlo paintings and her beloved Goh rising from the ocean flash before her. She gives birth to a baby boy and endures a terrible life of poverty with the abusive rapist. This sudden change from spunky survivor to helpless, victimized woman is baffling. Whatever happened to her job? Or that arty little apartment of hers? Didn't her Frida Kahlo obsession teach her anything?

Then there was Tiana Thi Thanh Nga's *From Hollywood to Hanoi,* a self-serving but fascinating documentary. Born in Vietnam to a privileged family that included an uncle who was defense minister in the Thieu government and an idolized father who served as press minister, Nga (a.k.a. Tiana) spent her adolescence in California. A former actor in martial arts movies and fitness teacher ("Karaticize with Tiana"), the vivacious Tiana decided to make a record of her journey back to Vietnam.

From Hollywood to Hanoi is at times unintentionally very funny. Tiana includes a quick scene of herself dancing with a white man at the Metropole hotel in Hanoi, and breathlessly announces: "That's me doing the tango with Oliver Stone!" Then she listens sympathetically to a horrifying account of the My Lai massacre by one of its few female survivors. In another scene, Tiana cheerfully addresses a food vendor on the streets of Hanoi: "Your hairdo is so pretty." The unimpressed, poker-faced woman gives a brusque, deadpan reply: "You want to eat, or what?" Sometimes it is hard to tell the difference between Tiana Thi Thanh Nga and her Hollywood persona: the real Tiana still seems to be playing one of her B-movie roles, which are mainly fun because they're fantasy. The time was certainly right to explore postwar Vietnam from a Vietnamese woman's perspective; it's too bad this film was done by a Valley Girl.

1993 also brought Tran Anh Hung's *The Scent of Green Papaya,* a different kind of Vietnamese memento—this is a look back at the peaceful, lush country of the director's childhood memories. The film opens in Saigon, in 1951. A willowy ten-year-old girl named Mui comes to work for a troubled family headed by a melancholy musician and his kind, stoic wife. The men of this bourgeois household are idle, pampered types who take naps while the women do all the work. Mui is a male fantasy: she is a devoted servant, enduring acts of cruel mischief with patience and dignity; as an adult, she barely speaks. She scrubs floors, shines shoes, and cooks with loving care and never a complaint. When she is sent off to work for another wealthy musician, she ends up being impregnated by him. The movie ends as the camera closes in on Mui's contented face. Languid and precious, *The Scent of Green Papaya* is visually haunting, but it suffers from the director's colonial fantasy of women as docile, domestic creatures. Steeped in highbrow nostalgia, it's the arty Vietnamese version of *My Fair Lady* with the wealthy musician as Professor Higgins, teaching Mui to read and write.

And then there is Ang Lee's tepid 1993 hit, *The Wedding Banquet*—a clever culture-clash farce in which traditional Chinese values collide with contemporary American sexual mores. The somewhat formulaic plot goes like this: Wai-Tung, a yuppie landlord, lives with his white lover, Simon, in a chic Manhattan brownstone. Wai-Tung is an only child and his aging parents in Taiwan long for a grandchild to continue the family legacy. Enter Wei-Wei, an artist who lives in a grungy loft owned by Wai-Tung. She slugs tequila straight from the bottle as she paints and flirts boldly with her young, uptight landlord, who brushes her off. "It's my fate. I am always attracted to handsome gay men," she mutters.

After this setup, the movie goes downhill, all edges blurred in a cozy nest of happy endings. In a refrain of Sayoko's plight in *Okoge,* a pregnant, suddenly complacent Wei-Wei gives in to family pressures—and never gets her life back.

> "It takes a man to know what it is to be a real woman."
> —Song Liling in *M. Butterfly*

Ironically, two gender-bending films in which men play men playing women reveal more about the mythology of the prized Asian woman and the superficial trappings of gender than most movies that star real women. The slow-moving *M. Butterfly* presents the ultimate object of Western male desire as the spy/opera diva Song Liling, a Suzie Wong/Lotus Blossom played by actor John Lone with a five o'clock shadow and bobbing Adam's apple. The best and most profound of these forays into cross-dressing is the spectacular melodrama *Farewell My Concubine,* directed by Chen Kaige. Banned in China, *Farewell My Concubine* shared the prize for Best Film at the 1993 Cannes Film Festival with Jane Campion's *The Piano.* Sweeping through 50 years of tumultuous history in China, the story revolves around the lives of two male Beijing Opera stars and the woman who marries one of them. The three characters make an unforgettable triangle, struggling over love, art, friendship, and politics against the bloody backdrop of cultural upheaval. They are as capable of casually betraying each other as they are of selfless, heroic acts. The androgynous Dieyi, doomed to play the same female role of concubine over and over again, is portrayed with great vulnerability, wit, and grace by male Hong Kong pop star Leslie Cheung. Dieyi competes with the prostitute Juxian (Gong Li) for the love of his childhood protector and fellow opera star, Duan Xiaolou (Zhang Fengyi).

Cheung's highly stylized performance as the classic concubine-ready-to-die-for-love in the opera within the movie is all about female artifice. His sidelong glances, restrained passion, languid stance, small steps, and delicate, refined gestures say everything about what is considered desirable in Asian women—and are the antithesis of the feisty, outspoken woman played by Gong Li. The characters of Dieyi and Juxian both see suffering as part and parcel of love and life. Juxian matter-of-factly says to Duan Xiaolou before he agrees to marry her: "I'm used to hardship. If you take me in, I'll wait on you hand and foot. If you tire of me, I'll . . . kill myself. No big deal." It's an echo of Suzie Wong's servility, but the context is new. Even with her back to the wall, Juxian is not helpless or whiny. She attempts to manipulate a man while admitting to the harsh reality that is her life.

Dieyi and Juxian are the two sides of the truth of women's lives in most Asian countries. Juxian in particular—wife and ex-prostitute—could be seen as a thankless and stereotypical role. But like the characters Gong Li has played in Chinese director Zhang Yimou's films, *Red Sorghum, Raise the Red Lantern,* and especially *The Story of Qiu Ju,* Juxian is tough, obstinate, sensual, clever, oafish, beautiful, infuriating, cowardly, heroic, and banal. Above all, she is resilient. Gong Li is one of the few Asian Pacific actors whose roles have been drawn with intelligence, honesty, and depth. Nevertheless, the characters she plays are limited by the possibilities that exist for real women in China.

"Let's face it. Women still don't mean shit in China," my friend Meeling reminds me. What she says so bluntly about her culture rings painfully true, but in less obvious fashion for me. In the Philippines, infant girls aren't drowned, nor were their feet bound to make them more desirable. But sons were and are cherished. To this day, men of the bourgeois class are coddled and prized, much like the spoiled men of the elite household in *The Scent of Green Papaya*. We do not have a geisha tradition like Japan, but physical beauty is overtreasured. Our daughters are protected virgins or primed as potential beauty queens. And many of us have bought into the image of the white man as our handsome savior: G.I. Joe.

BUZZ magazine recently featured an article entitled "Asian Women/L.A. Men," a report on a popular hangout that caters to white men's fantasies of nubile Thai women. The lines between movies and real life are blurred. Male screenwriters and cinematographers flock to this bar-restaurant, where the waitresses are eager to "audition" for roles. Many of these men have been to Bangkok while working on film crews for Vietnam War movies. They've come back to L.A., but for them, the movie never ends. In this particular fantasy the boys play G.I. Joe on a rescue mission in the urban jungle, saving the whore from herself. "A scene has developed here, a kind of R-rated *Cheers*," author Alan Rifkin writes. "The waitresses audition for sitcoms. The customers date the waitresses or just keep score."

Colonization of the imagination is a two-way street. And being enshrined on a pedestal as someone's Pearl of the Orient fantasy doesn't seem so demeaning, at first; who wouldn't want to be worshiped? Perhaps that's why Asian women are the ultimate wet dream in most Hollywood movies; it's no secret how well we've been taught to play the role, to take care of our men. In Hollywood vehicles, we are objects of desire or derision; we exist to provide sex, color, and texture in what is essentially a white man's world. It is akin to what Toni Morrison calls "the Africanist presence" in literature. She writes: "Just as entertainers, through or by association with blackface, could render permissible topics that otherwise would have been taboo, so American writers were able to employ an imagined Africanist persona to articulate and imaginatively act out the forbidden in American culture." The same analogy could be made for the often titillating presence of Asian women in movies made by white men.

Movies are still the most seductive and powerful of artistic mediums, manipulating us with ease by a powerful combination of sound and image. In many ways, as females and Asians, as audiences or performers, we have learned to settle for less—to accept the fact that we are either decorative, invisible, or one-dimensional. When there are characters who look like us represented in a movie, we have also learned to view between the lines, or to add what is missing. For many of us, this way of watching has always been a necessity. We fill in the gaps. If a female character is presented as a mute, willowy beauty, we convince ourselves she is an ancestral ghost—so smart she doesn't have to speak at all. If she is a whore with a heart of gold, we claim her as a tough feminist icon. If she is a sexless, sanitized, boring nerd, we embrace her as a role model for our daughters, rather than the tragic whore. And if she is presented as an utterly devoted saint suffering nobly in silence, we lie and say she is just like our mothers. Larger than life. Magical and insidious. A movie is never just a movie, after all.

FOR JOURNALING AND DISCUSSION

1. This piece covers over forty years of film-making, jumping across decades with the phrases "Cut to 1960," "Cut to 1985," "Cut to 1993." Explain how this style both fits the subject of Hagedorn's essay and furthers her thesis.
2. Write in your journal about your earliest memory of an Asian woman in a film. Which film was it? What do you remember about how the character was portrayed? Can you see some of what Hagedorn argues is the one-dimensionality of these characters?
3. Hagedorn notes that early films had white actors "with taped eyelids and a singsong, chop suey accent" playing Asian characters. This is also true of many films depicting Native American characters. What are some of the effects this has had on the stories told on the screen, on the communities being represented, and on audiences in general?

FOR RESEARCH AND EXPLORATION

1. Watch videos of at least two of the films mentioned in this essay. Record specific characteristics and bits of dialogue that you think illustrate the stereotyping of the Asian women whom Hagedorn explores.
2. Research the contemporary U.S. military presence in Asia and the Pacific Islands, specifically examining the profitable sex industry in these regions to discover the breadth of the problems Hagedorn cites.
3. Read Caffilene Allen's "First They Changed My Name" in Chapter 8, and relate it to Hagedorn's claim that "colonization of the imagination is a two-way street." Discuss how region or place and sexuality intersect when one dominant culture defines others as "decorative, invisible, or one-dimensional."

CHAPTER 5

Religion and Spirituality

Religion is deeply woven into American identity. In the Pledge of Allegiance, which all schoolchildren once recited on a daily basis, and on our money, we announce that we are "one nation under God." The Constitution of the United States was partially patterned after the system of governance in the *Book of Order* of the Church of Scotland (the Presbyterian Church). Less well known is its similarity to the constitution of the Iroquois Nation. During the nineteenth century, religious arguments were the basis for the abolitionist movement. Many feminist suffragists argued that since the scriptures defined women as humans, too, they were therefore equal to men and entitled to vote. Religious arguments were also one justification for nearly annihilating Native American culture and substituting Christianity for its spiritual traditions. In this century, Madeline Murray O'Hare was denounced as "the devil incarnate" from many pulpits and described as a "pariah" in the press because she advocated equal rights for atheists. When John F. Kennedy ran for president, one of his major campaign concerns was whether a Catholic could be elected in a historically Protestant country. Jimmy Carter was the subject of ridicule after his interview in *Playboy* in which he revealed his Southern Baptist belief that he had "sinned" by lusting in his heart after a woman. The most divisive question in the United ———a woman's right to choose to have an abortion—is largely argued ————ous definitions of human life, as is the status of gays, lesbians, bi-gender people.

No American president has thus far aligned with a religion other than Christianity, but it is not inconceivable to imagine one doing so in the future. Considering how many Jewish Americans have served in state and federal legislatures, we can imagine that a Jewish president is a likely possibility. And given the increasing numbers of Muslims, Buddhists, and Hindus in the country, we could see a president who comes out of a tradition other than the Judeo-Christian heritage. Shortly after the turn of the millennium, for example, Muslims will outnumber Presbyterians in the United States. As "mainline" churches shrink in membership, new "megachurches" with no apparent connection to a particular denomination are springing up across the country. And "hybrids" such as the Kwanza movement and African American and Native American churches mix a variety of traditions that are a part of American experience.

Clearly, Americans' views toward the connection between church and state have changed in over two hundred years. In a more pluralistic society, we now have to ask, "Which God"? And even, "Any God?" Public schools have already acknowledged these changes by banning public school prayer and forbidding the celebration of exclusively Christian holidays such as Christmas and Easter. At most educational institutions, including our own, students have the right to be excused for any religious holiday, no matter what the religion. Even though these changes have been made in the name of equity and religious freedom, principles upon which our nation was founded, they are not without their critics. For example, members of the "Christian Right" describe the move away from a Judeo-Christian heritage as a sign that the foundations of the nation are crumbling. As we look at our own nation's history and at the history of other nations, no single factor, other than perhaps language, seems to be more linked with national identity than religion.

Religion and/or spirituality are also a major part of one's personal or cultural identity. Even when people denounce a personal connection to organized religion, they are surrounded by the trappings and influences of others' beliefs. Because many choose not to be identified with organized religion, we have also used the term "spirituality" in this chapter to embrace a more personal connection to mystical traditions and other forms of suprarational consciousness. The rise of spirituality in the last few years is evident in feminist groups who are celebrating goddess traditions and newly recovered works by religious women such as Julian of Norwich and Hildegard of Bingen.

We also distinguish between those who say they are "culturally" part of a historical religious tradition (e.g., Judaism or Catholicism), but don't acknowledge or practice it as a religious or spiritual part of their lives. As you reflect on the readings in this chapter, consider whether the authors are discussing formal religious traditions, their own spirituality, and/or thei own culture.

SUMMARIES OF SELECTIONS ON RELIGION
AND SPIRITUALITY

In "Unveiling Islam," **Zainab Ali** describes the basic beliefs of Muslims for a non-Muslim audience. Her goal is to dispel many of the myths about Muslims. Interestingly, however, she does not take up many of the questions about gender roles in Muslim societies.

Judith Plaskow, in "Im and B'li," uses these terms, which refer to services "with girls" and "without girls," respectively, as she describes the status of women in the changing traditions of Conservative Judaism. The decision in 1983 to ordain women as rabbis was a momentous occasion, but, as we might expect, the realities have been somewhat less than what Jewish feminists had hoped.

James McBride's mother was a Polish Jewish immigrant. His father was African American, and in "The Color of Water: A Black Man's Tribute to His White Mother," he acknowledges that there were times when he was younger that he wished he had not come from two worlds, but that, as a grown man, he finally feels privileged that he has.

In "My Jesus Was Jim Crowed," **Nicholas Cooper-Lewter** shows us how a person named Renée has applied Jim and Jane Crow laws to come up with a Black Jesus who fits into her African American experience of Christianity. This "Jim Crowing of Jesus made her just like him, that is, black and breaking the white rules."

In contrast, **Usry Alleyne**'s Jesus, as he describes in "Atheism and Me," never made the color transformation: "God was white. In all of the pictures of Jesus, he had white skin, blue eyes, and long, stringy hair." As an African child in Guyana, he was forced to attend sunday school, but as an adult he has rejected Christianity for himself. As you read this piece along with Cooper-Lewter's, consider whether any of the differences in their positions stem from an African versus as African American heritage.

Tisha, in **Arthenia Bates**'s story "A Ceremony of Innocence," also rejects Christianity, but finds another religion in Islam. Her faith is contrasted to "Mother" Georgia's African American Baptist Christianity. Tisha leaves, after a visit to her dying cousin, confident that she has made the right choice.

Adrian Louis's account of his Native American spirituality is in sharp contrast to the acceptance of or resistance to organized Judeo-Christian traditions. His "Earth Bone Connected to the Spirit Bone" is a meditation on his personal, contemporary experience of spirituality.

Diane Glancy presents a combination of traditional religion and spirituality in "The Bible and Black Elk." She draws an analogy between Black Elk's words, as written down by a Christian translator, and the Christian New Testament's Book of Revelation. Even though many Native Americans reject the translation because it says more about what the translator thought than it does about what Black Elk spoke, his words have meaning for Glancy. Her faith is an unusual hybrid that reflects her own hybrid heritage.

Finally, in "Should Physicians Prescribe Prayer for Health?" **Charles Marwick** reports in the *Journal of the American Medical Association* that prayer, regardless of the kind, has a positive effect on health and recovery. He wonders how these benefits can be obtained in the secular world of medicine.

RHETORICAL QUESTIONS

In this chapter, we recommend that you focus on the *audiences* for these essays. In nearly all of them, the writers are trying to inform an audience that they assume knows little about the authors' religious or spiritual heritage. How much background do they supply? Are the writers aware of multiple audiences? For example, Glancy acknowledges alternative Native American views on *Black Elk Speaks*. How much does she accommodate the other stances? What is her position as a speaker who comes from two worlds? What about the other writers who come from multiple worlds? Are they addressing the communities from which they come as often as they are addressing outsiders? If you write about your own religious or spiritual beliefs, or lack thereof, who would be your audience?

Secondarily, you might want to look at the *methods* the writers use to construct their positions. How do they use personal experience? How does Cooper-Lewter use Renée's voice in making his points? How do the fictional essays compare to the nonfiction on similar themes? What special accommodations does Marwick use when he writes to a scientific audience about prayer?

Unveiling Islam: What Muslims Believe

Zainab Ali

Ali is a graduate of the University of Minnesota, where as a student she worked on the staff of the Minnesota Daily. *She is a freelance writer today.*

As-Shahadan la ilaha ill al-lah. Wa Mohammedan rasul al-lah. This phrase is called the Shahadah. When *iman* (faith) and *ihsan* (right-doing) culminate, the two become manifest in *ibadat,* worship. Faith and right-doing are articulated in the phrase, *As-Shahadan la ilaha ill al-lah. Wa Mohammedan rasul al-lah.*

Zainab Ali, "Unveiling Islam: What Muslims Believe" from *Colors* (May-June 1994). Reprinted with the permission of the author.

These are the first words spoken in the ears of a newborn baby and the last from the lips of the dying. The sentence is also said by those converting to Islam. "There is no god but Allah, and Mohammed is his Prophet." The phrase is simple, Arabic or English, but its implications are far-reaching. Professing the first part makes one a muslim—one who submits to God; saying the second makes one a Muslim, one who adheres to the religion of Islam.

In other words, according to Islam, anyone who believes in God and submits to his will is a muslim, whether you call yourself Christian or Jewish. Yet beyond that, believing in Prophet Mohammed as God's messenger, makes one a Muslim: obligated to acknowledge and apply the two basic fundamentals of belief and action.

In today's world the headlines in Western papers are occupied with the Middle East—the Gulf War, oil, peace talks—and with Muslims—the bombing of New York's World Trade Center, the film *Malcolm X*, and even Louis Farrakhan. As a result of the media coverage, a region and religion that have thus far been misunderstood and invisible to Western eyes have suddenly become laden with stereotypes—and remain misunderstood. This shortcoming of public perception is unfortunate. Islam is the fastest growing religion in the United States, and Muslims are predicted to become the second-largest religious group in the nation, outnumbering Jews, second only to Christians. Even in Minnesota, the Muslim community is two-thirds as large as the Jewish community. Interestingly, although others misunderstand Islam, the Quran is very close to the Bible in content. Indeed, Muslims believe in most of the Biblical stories and prophets, while expanding on both of them. Thus Islam is directly related to Christianity and Judaism. In fact, while Judaism does not believe in Jesus, Muslims do believe he is a very important prophet who brought Christianity to the world.

Fear, however, seems to be the undercurrent of today's misunderstanding. Many people believe Muslims are terrorists, anti-Semites, and fanatics. CNN television news and most newspapers support and perpetuate this stereotype. But relating Islam to terrorism is unfair: Islam teaches peace and tolerance. When a Muslim violates this teaching, that *person* should be accused, not an entire religious group. Blaming Islam for anti-Semitism and terrorist misdeeds is like blaming Christianity for the Waco catastrophe and David Koresh. Pointing fingers at Islam for terrorist acts is like fearing all black people because inner-city violence is portrayed in the media as a black problem. Indeed, when a group is systematically stereotyped in the media, people should question the media, not default to prejudice.

The Quran states that the people of the book are Muslims, Christians, and the Jews. Not only does this speak for tolerance, but it delineates Islam's embrace of two other monotheistic religions. If Louis Farrakhan preaches anti-Semitism, it's because he misunderstands Islam or has chosen to exploit it. In this country Black Muslims and Jews have clashed repeatedly. Yet the black nationalism supported by Farrakhan's Nation of Islam stops short of being Islamic and instead is self-indulgent and exploitative.

In the past decade Islam has come to be seen as the religion of the black man. But a close understanding of the Nation of Islam sees it as a social and political movement exploiting Islam to advance its cause. Since the inception of the Nation of Islam, disputes have occurred between it and orthodox Muslims. Muslims accuse the Nation of being unorthodox, of following a religion that it little understands, and of using Islam as a means of attaining black supremacy.

As Malcolm X realized when he traveled to Mecca, Islam is color-blind. Islam is no more the religion of the black man than it is a religion for the white man, the brown man, or the yellow man. Islam encourages unity within races, and does not privilege one color above another. This unity is best illustrated in Hajj, the holy pilgrimage to Mecca, where people of all colors stand side-by-side, dressed in simple white sheets that express equality.

As with Hajj, Islam encourages communal bonding in daily life. A Muslim community is called an *umma*. The *umma* is a requirement for all Muslims, because it stimulates an individual's sense of belonging, while strengthening Muslims' awareness of Islam. The *umma* puts unity and community among Muslims of all races above individualism. As part of an *umma*, Muslims must follow the Islamic Law, the Shari'ah. The Shari'ah is Islam's constitution, providing legislation for a Muslim's spiritual and secular life.

However, meeting the devotional requirements of the faith is the basic prerequisite of being a Muslim: There are five pillars of Islam.

First, the Shahadah, the testimony to the unity of God. "There is no god but Allah, and Mohammed is his prophet." Islam's God is the same God as the God of Christianity and Judaism. Allah is the Arabic word for God. Although Allah's attributes are many, the simple concept of God is this:

Allah is kind, omnipresent, one; he has no partners, no son, no daughter, no parents; he existed before he created time and space, and he is now as he always has been; his glorious attributes are free from all imperfections; he is free from all human attributes, without form or face; he is everlasting.

Muslims must worship God and follow Islamic doctrines, while also believing in God's angels, scriptures, and the day of judgment—when Prophet Mohammed will return with Jesus and Moses, each leading his people separately to God. More than 90 percent of Muslim theology speaks of Allah as the real God who is indivisible in nature.

The second pillar of Islam is Salah, or daily prayers. Muslims must pray five times a day; a Muslim who does not is no longer a practicing Muslim. Prayer is said at prescribed times of the day: dawn, midday, mid-afternoon, sunset, and nightfall. A Muslim who misses a prayer can make it up later in the day. Prayer consists of short verses and the confession of the Shahadah. Each movement is regulated with a rendering of a specific Quranic verse. For example, at the point of bowing and kneeling before God each Muslim recites in Arabic that he or she will not kneel or bow before anything or anyone other than Allah. At the end of each prayer a Muslim may make a *du'a,* a personal invocation to God.

The Azan, the call to prayer, that is called over a loudspeaker from a minaret consists of the following words: "God is great (four times). I bear witness that there is no god but Allah (twice). I bear witness that Mohammed is his prophet (twice). Come to prayer (twice). Come to contentment (twice)." Muslims may perform prayer anywhere; the only time a Muslim is required to pray with others is at the noon service on Friday.

Zakat is the third pillar of Islam. Zakat refers to "poor-due," almsgiving. Zakat means that a Muslim must pay back to Allah—by giving money to the poor and needy—a portion of God's bounty, thereby purifying the almsgiver's material possessions. Although the exact amount of Zakat is not explicit in the Quran, Muslims follow the example of Prophet Mohammed and give at least 2.5 percent of their annual income.

Fasting, or sawm, is the fourth pillar. Ramadan is the month of fasting, and Muslims fast from sunrise to sunset. No food, drink, sexual relations, smoking, or other physical indulgence can take place between these hours. Because Muslims follow the lunar calendar, Ramadan may fall during short days of winter or the long days of summer—causing summer fasters severe mental and physical strain. (Pregnant women, those traveling, the ill, and the very young are all exempt from fasting.)

However, denying oneself these comforts is a means of attaining self-purification and of learning sympathy with people who hunger. This year Ramadan fell from mid-February to mid-March. From personal experience I can say that fasting does increase sensitivity to poverty issues. For example, when I was at work and saw everyone around me eating lunch or drinking, I wanted also to drink and eat. But I couldn't. Each time I said no, I felt sympathy for the person who could not afford food or simply could not get it. And each time I felt lucky because I would soon break fast and eat, while those in hunger could not. It made me realize how these people need the help of those more fortunate.

The final pillar of Islam is Hajj, the sacred pilgrimage to Mecca. About two months after Ramadan, Hajj takes place on a specific day of a specific month. Every able-bodied Muslim must perform this duty once in a lifetime. A central ritual of the pilgrimage is to circle the Kabah (literally the cube), an ancient structure enclosed in a wall at the middle of a square. The Hajj requires many complicated ritual acts. Nevertheless, when pilgrims don the two seamless white cloths that Muslims must wear to perform Hajj, Islam's proclamation of communal unity for all races is realized.

The Hajj is to commemorate Abraham, not Prophet Mohammed. Abraham, considered the first Muslim, was willing to sacrifice his son for God's will. Remembering him, Muslims sacrifice lambs as part of Hajj and distribute meat to the poor and to orphans.

Each Muslim must practice the five pillars to become a true Muslim, a true submitter. We are Muslims, followers of Islam, the surrender to Allah. To call Muslims Mohammedans is incorrect. The mistake comes from a false analogy with Christians as the worshippers of Christ. But Muslims do not worship Mohammed. They worship Allah only.

Following the five pillars creates God-conscious people, possessed of piety and discipline. Islam imbues Muslims with feelings of community, equality, and moral responsibility. Unfortunately, some exploit Islam—Saddam Hussein, Louis Farrakhan—preaching division or violence in its name. But what Muslims have in common is tolerance for difference, acceptance of other races and religions, and an understanding that Islam is not simply a religion, but a way of life not to be compromised.

FOR JOURNALING AND DISCUSSION

1. Why is Ali writing this essay? What does she want non-Muslims to think about Islam? How do you know this? What rhetorical strategies does she use to explain her faith?
2. Have real and alleged acts of terrorism by Arab Muslims influenced your perceptions of Islam? Have real and alleged acts of terrorism by Irish Catholics influenced your perceptions of Christianity? Discuss your answers.
3. Charity toward the poor plays an important, if not required, role in both Islam and Christianity. Given the number of practicing Christians and Muslims in the United States, why does poverty still exist? How would these religions have to change if poverty were eradicated?

FOR RESEARCH AND EXPLORATION

1. Who is Louis Farrakhan? What is the Nation of Islam? Research the history of this leader and this group. Write an essay explaining why Farrakhan and the Nation of Islam both worry and offend many Christians, Jews, and Muslims, like Ali, who chose to distance themselves from him.
2. Because of the United States's commitment to diversity, we try to be inclusive of the holidays and holy days of other religions. Read about Ramadan. Does your school or place of employment include Ramadan on its calendar?
3. Do Muslims consider themselves members of a spiritual nation that transcends national boundaries in the same way that many Native Americans do?

Im and *B'li:* Women in the Conservative Movement

Judith Plaskow

A professor of religious studies at Manhattan College in Brooklyn, Plaskow is a longtime Jewish feminist-activist. She has written many books and articles about feminism and theology in general and about Jewish feminism in particular.

At a Solomon Schechter school on Long Island, the new principal of Jewish studies, a rabbi, was hired with the board's proviso that she not *daven* [pray] in the morning *minyan* [group of ten people, usually men, necessary for the service] wearing *tallit* (prayer shawl) and *tefillin* (phylacteries). The issue was not that girls are forbidden to wear these at the school, but that the board wanted them to come to any decision on their own, free from the influence of a female role model.

This convoluted logic is emblematic of the deep and continuing ambivalence of the Conservative movement toward women's full participation in Jewish religious life. Eleven years after the Jewish Theological Seminary's decision to admit women to the rabbinical school, there are many signals that the movement's institutions remain undecided about what they want and expect from and for their girls and women.

- Item: The spring 1994 issue of *Ramah: The Magazine* featured profiles of women rabbis and cantors who were graduates of Ramah summer camps. Ramah Canada refused to distribute the issue because it feared the article would be "bad publicity" for the camp. The Ramah commission did not intervene.
- Item: At a Yom-Hashoah concert co-sponsored by two Conservative synagogues, the cantor of the visiting synagogue was not permitted to sit on the *bimah* [the pulpit or stage] because the host cantor refused to recognize her as clergy.
- Item: Camp Ramah in the Berkshires has two *minyanim* [the body of people who participate in services], an *im minyan,* in which girls can lead

services and read from the Torah if they have taken on themselves the obligation to pray three times daily, and a *b'li minyan,* in which boys who may or may not have any sense of obligation can lead or read as they are able. Although *im* and *b'li* are meant to signify *with aliyot* [the right to go up to participate in the service] for girls and *without aliyot* for girls, in fact, the terms convey the message: with and without girls themselves.

- Item: For the last few years, women graduates of the Jewish Theological Seminary's rabbinical school have been the last students placed. Senior rabbis often function as "gatekeepers" in the placement process, choosing not to interview women candidates because their congregations are "not ready." Rather than seeing the decision to ordain women as an implied contract requiring ongoing preparation and education of congregations, the movement (including both the seminary and United Synagogue) has left ordained women to make their own way.

- Item: Following discussion with movement leaders at the 1994 Rabbinical Assembly, a group of women rabbis sent a letter to the Leadership Council of the Conservative Movement asking them to set up a commission to evaluate and address the status of women. Ismar Schorsch, chancellor of the seminary, replied that the council is not interested in a movement-wide approach at this time. He asserted that individual problems should instead be dealt with as they arise through the relevant arm of the movement. Thus, inequities at Ramah would be dealt with by the Ramah Commission, problems in hiring of rabbis by the Rabbinical Assembly, and so on.

This unwillingness to think through the role of women in Conservative Judaism in a systematic way was already evident in the original decision to ordain in 1983. That step was not premised on a commitment to religious equality, but on the narrower argument that women who accept all *mitzvot* (commandments) as obligatory should be counted in a *minyan* and allowed to exercise religious leadership on the same basis as men. The effect of the decision was to create two distinct categories of women—those who would choose to become like men and those who would choose to remain Other. In acting on this basis, the seminary both foreclosed the possibility that women might explore and exercise their obligations in new and distinctive ways and set up two problematic options that could only reinforce its own ambivalence.

What was lacking in both the decision to ordain women and its implementation was that vision or sense of educational mission that one expects to find in religious and educational institutions. On the one hand, the ordination decision was the culmination of a process of increasing women's education and participation that had been going on since the founding of the movement. On the other hand, and more profoundly, it also should have marked the beginning of a deliberate program of preparing both women and men to enter into new roles and new forms of communal relationship.

   In the absence of commitment to such a process, the movement defends its ambivalence on specific issues of women's participation on the grounds of making room for "pluralism." But it is one thing to continue to accept non-egalitarian congregations from the Conservative Movement and another to neglect the creation of an educational program that would allow individuals and communities to work through the emotional, ethical, and halakhic issues connected with major change. It is one thing to make room for opponents of the ordination of women and another not to support or stand with pride behind women the seminary has ordained. It is one thing to allow girls to make their own decisions concerning religious practice and another not to articulate the movement's goals for women's religious practice.

   There is a Catch-22 at work here. As former Ramah director Debby Hirshman points out, the Conservative Movement needs to take a systematic and sustained approach to implementing women's full participation. It needs to examine each institution within it, to evaluate existing policies and practices, and to ask where intervention is possible. It cannot formulate consistent policy or bring about substantive change without working systematically over time. But, of course, it cannot implement such an approach without some animating commitment and vision.

   In the absence of such commitment at the center—and, indeed, even were it there—there is still ample opportunity to apply both pressure and creativity at a grass-roots level. Parents at local Solomon Schecter schools can work to ensure that gender issues are part of staff training and are integrated into the curriculum. Schools might also sponsor meetings to discuss girls' expectations. Should they wear *kippot* [skull caps], or should they not? What sense of themselves is conveyed by the indifference or conflicting messages communicated by individual schools and the movement as a whole? Ramah camps could be structured to provide girls with the skills and encouragement they need to take on religious leadership and could also be addressing gender issues. Businesses, non-profit organizations, and educational institutions across the country have been hiring facilitators to help them deal with the challenges of an increasingly diverse and multicultural work force. The Conservative Movement should send its own facilitators into synagogues, camps, and schools to help work through the issues and conflicts that arise out of the new roles for women. Lectureships and scholar-in-residence programs could also address these questions.

   There are also important opportunities for change at the Conservative Movement's institutions of higher learning that should not be overlooked. The seminary recently received a $15-million grant for graduate studies in Jewish education. As Rabbi Lori Forman points out, this represents a chance for the seminary to think through the place of gender issues in the Jewish education of the future. How will the school of education integrate the new research on Jewish women's history into its own teaching? Will it encourage and participate in the preparation of new materials for every educational level? Will it train teachers in gender sensitivity and encourage them to think through their hopes and expectations of girls?

Moreover, this past fall, at the Rabbinical and Cantorial Schools' retreat, Chancellor Schorsch announced two decisions that potentially have far-reaching implications for the role of women in the movement. He decided that prayer leaders in the Seminary *minyan* can, at their discretion, include the *imahot* (matriarchs) in the davening. And—based on an article by Judith Hauptmann in the winter 1993 issue of *Judaism*—Schorsch announced that women no longer formally have to take on the obligation to pray daily but are seen by the tradition as obligated. Since, as Rabbi Nina Beth Cardin points out, this second decision alters the basis on which women are admitted to the seminary, it opens the possibility—hinted at in the first decision—that women's covenant may be developed and lived out in other ways than simply taking on formerly male roles.

Once again, then, as was the case eleven years ago, the Conservative Movement stands at a crossroads. The increasingly visible gap between the promise of equality and the willingness to implement it in a consistent and thorough way makes clear the need for renewed action. Whether this was intended or not, the decision to ordain was received by the movement's women as a statement of commitment to their full religious participation. The struggle continues to clarify and strengthen that pledge, however ambivalently made, and to turn it into a reality.

FOR JOURNALING AND DISCUSSION

1. Do you believe individual congregations have the right to reject particular ordained clergy?
2. In the next selection in this chapter, "The Color of Water," James McBride writes about his Jewish-born mother and her feelings about her first faith. What were Plaskow's attitudes about her Jewish identity?
3. Plaskow states, "The effect of the decision was to create two distinct categories of women—those who would choose to become like men and those who would choose to remain Other." How is Plaskow using the word "Other"? What special meaning does it carry in feminist theory and literature?
4. Write about a same-sex role model who has made a difference in your life. In what ways did that person expand your possibilities as a man or a woman?
5. In what ways does Andrew Kimbrell, in his article "A Time for Men to Pull Together: A Manifesto for the New Politics of Masculinity" in Chapter 4, support Plaskow's position?

FOR RESEARCH AND EXPLORATION

1. Is religion the only area where a decision for equality has been difficult to implement? Research another area of your life that has been touched by this problem, and write about how it has affected you.

2. Like the ordination of women, the ordination of gays and lesbians has divided congregations. Find two articles, one for and the other against the ordination of sexual minorities, and compare and contrast the authors' arguments with those of Plaskow.
3. View the movie *Yentl*, directed by and starring Barbra Streisand. In what time period is this story set? What motivated this character to do what she did? What happened at the end of the movie?

The Color of Water: A Black Man's Tribute to His White Mother

James McBride

James McBride grew up as one of twelve children in the all-black housing projects of Red Hook in Brooklyn. An award-winning professional saxophonist and former staff writer for the Boston Globe, *McBride is the son of a black minister and a woman who would not admit she was white. His mother, Rachel Shilsky McBride, the daughter of a failed Orthodox rabbi in rural Virginia, ran away to Harlem and, with his father, founded an all-black Baptist church in their living room.*

In Suffolk, they had a white folks' school and a black folks' school and a Jewish school. You called the Jewish school "shul" in Yiddish. It wasn't really a school. It was just the synagogue where Tateh taught Hebrew lessons and gave Bible study to children and taught cantoring to boys and that sort of thing. He'd practice his singing around the house sometimes, singing "do re mi fa sol," and all that. You know, they'd let him circumcise children too. That was part of his job as a rabbi, to go to people's houses and circumcise their kids. He had special knives for it. He'd also kill cows in the kosher faith for the Jews in town to eat, and we often kept a cow in the yard behind the store. We'd lead the cow to the Jaffe slaughterhouse down the road and the butchers would tie it from the ceiling by its hind legs. Tateh would open his knife case—he had a special velvet case with knives just for this purpose—and carefully select one of those big, shiny knives. Then he'd utter a quick prayer and plunge the knife blade into the cow's neck. The cow would shudder violently and blood would spurt down his [*sic*] neck and through his nose into a drain in the cement floor and he'd die. The butchers would then set upon him and slit his stomach and yank out his intestines, heart, liver, and innards.

I was almost grown before I could eat meat. The sight of my father plunging his knife into that cow was enough to make me avoid it for years. I was terrified of my father. He put the fear of God in me.

The Jewish school didn't really count with the white folks, so I went to the white school, Thomas Jefferson Elementary. If it was up to Tateh he would have kept me out of school altogether. "That gentile school won't teach you anything you can use," he scoffed. He paid for us to take private lessons in sewing and knitting and record keeping from other people. He was tight with his money, but when it came to that kind of thing, he wasn't cheap, I'll say that for him. He would rather pay for us to study privately than to go to school with gentiles, but the law was the law, so I had to go to school with the white folks. It was a problem from the moment I started, because the white kids hated Jews in my school. "Hey, Ruth, when did you start being a dirty Jew?" they'd ask. I couldn't stand being ridiculed. I even changed my name to try to fit in more. My real name was Rachel, which in Yiddish is Ruckla, which is what my parents called me—but I used the name Ruth around white folk, because it didn't sound so Jewish, though it never stopped the other kids from teasing me.

Nobody liked me. That's how I felt as a child. I know what it feels like when people laugh at you walking down the street, or snicker when they hear you speaking Yiddish, or just look at you with hate in their eyes. You know a Jew living in Suffolk when I was coming up could be lonely even if there were fifteen of them standing in the room, I don't know why; it's that feeling that nobody likes you; that's how I felt, living in the South. You were different from everyone and liked by very few. There were white sections of Suffolk, like the Riverview section, where Jews weren't allowed to own property. It said that on the deeds and you can look them up. They'd say "for White Anglo-Saxon Protestants only." That was the law there and they meant it. The Jews in Suffolk did stick together, but even among Jews my family was low because we dealt with *shvartses* [Yiddish for black people]. So I didn't have a lot of Jewish friends either.

When I was in the fourth grade, a girl came up to me in the schoolyard during recess and said, "You have the prettiest hair. Let's be friends." I said, "Okay." Heck, I was glad someone wanted to be my friend. Her name was Frances. I'll never forget Frances for as long as I live. She was thin, with light brown hair and blue eyes. She was a quiet gentle person. I was actually forbidden to play with her because she was a gentile, but I'd sneak over to her house anyway and sneak her over to mine. Actually I didn't have to sneak into Frances's house because I was always welcome there. She lived past the cemetery on the other side of town in a frame house that we entered from the back door. It seemed that dinner was always being served at Frances's house. Her mother would serve it on plates she took out of a wooden china closet: ham, chicken, potatoes, corn, string beans, sliced tomatoes, lima beans, white bread, and hot biscuits with lots of butter—and I couldn't eat any of it. It was *treyf*, not kosher for a Jew to eat. The first time her mother served me dinner I said, "I can't eat this," and I was embarrassed until Frances piped out, "I don't like this food either. My favorite food is mayonnaise on white bread." That's how she was. She'd do little things to let you know she was on your side. It didn't bother her one bit that I was Jewish, and if she was around, no one in school would tease me.

I would take pennies from the store cash register so Frances and I could go to the Chadwick Movie Theater—it cost only ten cents. Or we would cut through the town cemetery on the way home from school so Tateh wouldn't see us; we'd spend a lot of afternoons sitting on the headstones talking. You know I'm spooked around dead folks. To this day you can't get me near a graveyard. But when I was with Frances, it didn't bother me a bit. It seemed like the easiest, most natural thing in the world, to sit on somebody's headstone under the cool shade of a tree and chat. We always lingered till the last minute and when it was time to go, we'd have to run in separate directions to get home, so I'd watch her go first to make sure no ghosts were trying to catch her. She'd back away, facing me, asking, "Any ghosts behind me, Ruth? Is it clear?" I'd say, "Yeah. It's clear."

Then she'd turn around and scamper off, dodging the headstones and yelling over her shoulder, "You still watching, Ruth? Watch out for me!"

"I'm watching! No ghosts!" I'd shout. Then after a few seconds I'd yell, "I'm counting now!" I'd count to ten like this: "One two three four five . . . ten!"—and fly home! Fly through that cemetery!

Frances's family wasn't rich. They were like a lot of white folks back then. Farming-type folks, poor. Not poor like you see today. Back then it was a different kind of poor. A better kind of poor, but poor just the same. What I mean by that is you didn't need money as much, but you didn't have any neither. Just about everyone I knew was poor. A lot of our customers were so poor it wasn't funny. Black and white were poor. They got their food from the Nansemond River down the hill from our store. The men would go fishing and crabbing at the wharf and catch huge turtles and take them home and make soup and stew out of them. There was a man who all he did was haul in turtles. He'd walk home carrying a huge turtle under his arm the way you carry a schoolbook, and me and Dee-Dee would gawk. Sometimes he'd stop at the store and buy various ingredients for his turtle soup, various spices and garnishes. That turtle would still be alive, kicking and trying to get away while the man was standing in the store, poring over the vegetables, buying garlics and peppers to cook it up with. I used to feel sorry for the turtles. I wanted him to throw them back in the water, but I wouldn't say that. You crazy? Shoot! He wouldn't throw them back in the water for nobody. They were his dinner.

Folks were poor, and starving. And I have to admit I never starved like a lot of people did. I never had to eat turtles and crabs out of the wharf like a lot of folks did. I never starved for food till I got married. But I was starving in another way. I was starving for love and affection. I didn't get none of that.

Back in the 1960s, when she had money, which was hardly ever, Mommy would take us down to Delancey Street on Manhattan's Lower East Side to shop for school clothes. "You have to go where the deals are," she said. "They won't come to you."

"Where are the deals?" we asked.

"The Jews have the deals."

I thought Jews were something that was in the Bible. I'd heard about them in Sunday school, through Jesus and such. I told Ma I didn't know they were still around.

"Oh, they're around," she said. She had a funny look on her face.

The Hasidic Jewish merchants in their black yarmulkes would stare in shock as Mommy walked in, trailed by five or six of us. When they recovered enough to make money, she would drive them to the wall, haggling them to death, lapsing into Yiddish when the going got tough. "I know what's happening here! I know what's happening!" she snapped when the merchants lapsed into Yiddish amongst themselves during negotiations over a pair of shoes. She angrily whipped off some gibberish and the merchants gawked even more. We were awed.

The first time it happened, we asked, "Ma, how'd you learn to talk like that?"

"Mind your own business," she said. "Never ask questions or your mind will end up like a rock. Some of these Jews can't stand you."

Looking back, I realize that I never felt any kinetic relationship to Jews. We were insulated from their world and any other world but our own. Yet there was a part of me that recognized Jews as slightly different from other white folks, partly through information gleaned from Mommy, who consciously and unconsciously sought many things Jewish, and partly through my elder siblings. My sister Rosetta's college education at the all-black Howard University was completely paid for—tuition, books, even school clothes—by the Joseph L. Fisher Foundation, which was run out of the Stephen Wise Free Synagogue of Manhattan. In addition, my oldest brother, Dennis, guru of wisdom and source of much of our worldly news in the 1960s, came home from college with respect for Jewish friends he'd met. "They support the civil rights movement," he reported. Mommy was for anything involving the improvement of our education and condition, and while she would be quick to point out that "some Jews can't stand you," she also, in her crazy contradictory way, communicated the sense to us that if we were lucky enough to come across the right Jew in our travels—a teacher, a cop, a merchant—he would be kinder than other white folks. She never spoke about Jewish people as white. She spoke about them as Jews, which made them somehow different. It was a feeling every single one of us took into adulthood, that Jews were different from white people somehow. Later as an adult when I heard folks talk of the love/hate relationship between blacks and Jews I understood it to the bone not because of any outside sociological study, but because of my own experience with Jewish teachers and classmates—some who were truly kind, genuine, and sensitive, others who could not hide their distaste for my black face—people I'd met during my own contacts with the Jewish world, which Mommy tacitly arranged by forcing every one of us to go to predominantly Jewish public schools.

It was in her sense of education, more than any other, that Mommy conveyed her Jewishness to us. She admired the way Jewish parents raised their children to be scholastic standouts, insulating them from a potentially harmful and dangerous public school system by clustering together within certain communities, to attend certain schools, to be taught by certain teachers who enforced discipline and encouraged learning, and she followed their lead. During the school year she gave us careful instructions to bring home every single paper that the teachers handed out at school, especially in January, and failure to follow these instructions resulted in severe beatings. When we dutifully arrived with the papers, she would pore over them carefully, searching—"Okay . . . okay . . . here it is!"—grabbing the little form and filling it out. Every year the mighty bureaucratic dinosaur known as the New York City Public School System would belch forth a tiny diamond: they slipped a little notice to parents giving them the opportunity to have their kids bused to different school districts if they wanted; but there was a limited time to enroll, a short window of opportunity that lasted only a few days. Mommy stood poised over that option like a hawk. She invariably chose predominantly Jewish public schools: P.S. 138 in Rosedale, J.H.S. 231 in Springfield Gardens, Benjamin Cardozo, Francis Lewis, Forest Hills, Music and Art. Every morning we hit the door at six-thirty, fanning out across the city like soldiers, armed with books, T squares, musical instruments, an "S" bus pass that allowed you to ride the bus and subway for a nickel, and a free-school-lunch coupon in our pocket. Even the tiniest of us knew the subway and local city bus schedules and routes by heart. *The number 3 bus lets you off at the corner, but the 3A turns, so you have to get off* . . . . By age twelve, I was traveling an hour and a half one way to junior high school by myself, taking two buses each direction every day. My homeroom teacher, Miss Allison, a young white woman with glasses who generally ignored me, would shrug as I walked in ten minutes late, apologizing about a delayed bus. The white kids stared at me in the cafeteria as I gobbled down the horrible school lunch. Who cared. It was all I had to eat.

In this pre-busing era, my siblings and I were unlike most other kids in our neighborhood, traveling miles and miles to largely white, Jewish communities to attend school while our friends walked to the neighborhood school. We grew accustomed to being the only black, or "Negro," in school and were standout students, neat and well-mannered, despite the racist attitudes of many of our teachers, who were happy to knock our 95 test scores down to 85's and 80's over the most trivial mistakes. Being the token Negro was something I was never entirely comfortable with. I was the only black kid in my fifth-grade class at P.S. 138 in the then all-white enclave of Rosedale, Queens, and one afternoon as the teacher dutifully read aloud from our history book's one page on "Negro history," someone in the back of the class whispered, "James is a nigger!" followed by a ripple of tittering and giggling across the room. The teacher shushed him and glared, but the damage had been done. I felt the blood rush to my face and sank low in my chair, seething inside, yet I did nothing. I imagined what my siblings would have done. They would have gone wild. They would have found that punk and bum-rushed him. They never would've allowed anyone to call them a nigger. But I was not them. I was shy and passive and quiet, and only later did the anger come bursting out of me, roaring out of me with such blast-furnace force that I would wonder who that person was and where it all came from.

Music arrived in my life around that time, and books. I would disappear inside whole worlds comprised of *Gulliver's Travels*, *Shane*, and books by Beverly Cleary. I took piano and clarinet lessons in school, often squirreling myself away in some corner with my clarinet to practice, wandering away in Tchaikovsky or John Philip Sousa, trying to improvise like jazz saxophonist James Moody, only to blink back to reality an hour or two later. To further escape from painful reality, I created an imaginary world for myself. I believed my true self was a boy who lived in the mirror. I'd lock myself in the bathroom and spend long hours playing with him. He looked just like me. I'd stare at him. Kiss him. Make faces at him and order him around. Unlike my siblings, he had no opinions. He would listen to me. "If I'm here and you're me, how can *you* be there at the same time?" I'd ask. He'd shrug and smile. I'd shout at him, abuse him verbally. "Give me an answer!" I'd snarl. I would turn to leave, but when I wheeled around he was always there, waiting for me. I had an ache inside, a longing, but I didn't know where it came from or why I had it. The boy in the mirror, he didn't seem to have an ache. He was free. He was never hungry, he had his own bed probably, and his mother wasn't white. I hated him. "Go away!" I'd shout. "Hurry up! Get on out!" but he'd never leave. My siblings would hold their ears to the bathroom door and laugh as I talked to myself. "What a doofus you are," my brother Richie snickered.

Even though my siblings called me "Big Head" because I had a big head and a skinny body, to the outer world I was probably on the "most likely to succeed" list. I was a smart kid. I read a lot. I played music well. I went to church. I had what black folks called "good" hair, because it was curly as opposed to nappy. I was light-skinned or brown-skinned, and girls thought I was cute despite my shyness. Yet I myself had no idea who I was. I loved my mother yet looked nothing like her. Neither did I look like the role models in my life—my stepfather, my godparents, other relatives—all of whom were black. And *they* looked nothing like the other heroes I saw, the guys in the movies, white men like Steve McQueen and Paul Newman who beat the bad guys and in the end got the pretty girl—who, incidentally, was always white.

One afternoon I came home from school and cornered Mommy while she was cooking dinner. "Ma, what's a tragic mulatto?" I asked.

Anger flashed across her face like lightning and her nose, which tends to redden and swell in anger, blew up like a balloon. "Where'd you hear that?" she asked.

"I read it in a book."

"For God's sake, you're no tragic mul—What book is this?"

"Just a book I read."

"Don't read that book anymore." She sucked her teeth. "Tragic mulatto. What a stupid thing to call somebody! Somebody called you that?"

"No."

"Don't ever ever use that term."

"Am I black or white?"

"You're a human being," she snapped. "Educate yourself or you'll be a nobody!"

"Will I be a black nobody or just a nobody?"

"If you're a nobody," she said dryly, "it doesn't matter what color you are."

"That doesn't make sense," I said.

She sighed and sat down. "I bet you never heard the joke about the teacher and the beans," she said. I shook my head. "The teacher says to the class, 'Tell us about different kinds of beans.'

"The first little boy says, 'There's pinto beans.'

" 'Correct,' says the teacher.

"Another boy raises his hand. 'There's lima beans.'

" 'Very good,' says the teacher.

"Then a little girl in the back raises her hand and says, 'We're all *human* beans!' "

She laughed. "That's what you are, a *human* bean! And a *fartbuster* to boot!" She got up and went back to cooking, while I wandered away, bewildered.

Perplexed to the point of bursting, I took the question to my elder siblings. Although each had drawn from the same bowl of crazy logic Mommy served up, none seemed to share my own confusion. "Are we black or white?" I asked my brother David one day.

"*I'm* black," said David, sporting his freshly grown Afro the size of Milwaukee. "But *you* may be a Negro. You better check with Billy upstairs."

I approached Billy, but before I could open my mouth, he asked, "Want to see something?"

"Sure," I said.

He led me through our house, past Mommy, who was absorbed in changing diapers, past a pile of upended chairs, books, music stands, and musical instruments that constituted the living room, up the stairs into the boys' bedroom, and over to a closet which was filled, literally, from floor to ceiling, with junk. He stuck his head inside, pointed to the back, and said, "Look at this." When I stuck my head in, he shoved me in from behind and slammed the door, holding it shut. "Hey, man! It's dark in here!" I shouted, banging at the door and trying to keep the fear out of my voice. Suddenly, in the darkness, I felt hands grabbing me and heard a monster roar. My panic zoomed into high-level terror and I frantically pounded on the door with all my might, screaming in a high-pitched, fervent squawk, "BILLLLLYYYYYYYY!" He released the door and I tore out of the closet, my brother David tumbling out behind me. My two brothers fell to the floor laughing, while I ran around the house crying for Ma, zooming from room to room, my circuits blown.

The question of race was like the power of the moon in my house. It's what made the river flow, the ocean swell, and the tide rise, but it was a silent power, intractable, indomitable, indisputable, and thus completely ignorable. Mommy kept us at a frantic living pace that left no time for the problem. We thrived on thought, books, music, and art, which she fed to us instead of food. At every opportunity she loaded five or six of us onto the subway, paying one fare and pushing the rest of us through the turnstiles while the token-booth clerks frowned and subway riders stared, parading us to every free event New York City offered: festivals, zoos, parades, block parties, libraries, concerts. We walked for hours through the city, long meandering walks that took in whole neighborhoods which we would pass through without buying a thing or speaking to anyone. Twice a year she marched us to the Guggenheim dental clinic in Manhattan for free care, where foreign dental students wearing tunics and armed with drills, picks, and no novocaine, manned a row of dental chairs and reduced each of us to a screaming mass of tears while the others waited in line, watching, horrified.

They pulled teeth like maniacs, barking at us in whatever their native tongues were while they yanked our heads back and forth like rag dolls'. They once pulled my brother Billy's tooth and then sent him out to Ma in the waiting room, whereupon she looked into the mouth full of gauze and blood and discovered they had yanked the wrong tooth. She marched back in and went wild. In summer she was the Pied Piper, leading the whole pack of us to public swimming pools, stripping down to her one-piece bathing suit and plunging into the water like a walrus, the rest of us following her like seals, splashing and gurgling in terror behind her as Mommy flailed along, seemingly barely able to swim herself until one of us coughed and sputtered, at which time she whipped through the water and grabbed the offending child, pulling him out and slapping him on the back, laughing. We did not consider ourselves poor or deprived, or depressed, for the rules of the outside world seemed meaningless to us as children. But as we grew up and fanned out into the world as teenagers and college students, we brought the outside world home with us, and the world that Mommy had so painstakingly created began to fall apart.

The sixties roared through my house like a tidal wave. My sister Helen's decision to drop out of school and run off at age fifteen, though she returned home five years later with a nursing degree and a baby girl, was the first sign of impending doom. Now the others began to act out, and the sense of justice and desire for equal rights that Mommy and my father had imparted to us began to backfire. Kind, gentle, Sunday school children who had been taught to say proudly, "I am a Negro," and recite the deeds of Jackie Robinson and Paul Robeson now turned to Malcolm X and H. Rap Brown and Martin Luther King for inspiration. Mommy was the wrong color for black pride and black power, which nearly rent my house in two.

One by one, my elder siblings broke with her rules, coming home bearing fruits of their own confusion, which we jokingly called their "revolution." An elder brother disappeared to Europe. Another sister had an affair at college and came home with a love child, fairly big news in 1967. My brother Richie got married at eighteen over Mommy's objections, divorced, then entered college, and was home on summer break when he got stopped by two cops while walking down the street with a friend. A group of boys who were walking about ten yards in front of Richie and his friend had ditched what appeared to be a bag of heroin as the cop car approached. The cops grouped the boys together, lined them up against a fence, and demanded to know which of them had jettisoned the bag, which later turned out to be filled with quinine, not heroin. All denied it, so the cops searched them all and found ninety dollars of Richie's college-bank-loan money in his pocket. When the policeman asked him where he got the money from, Richie told him it was his college money and he'd forgotten he'd had it. If you knew Richie, you'd nod and say, "Uh-huh," because it was perfectly in character for him to forget he was carrying around ninety precious dollars, which was a huge sum in those days. We used to call him "the Mad Scientist" when he was little. His science experiments would nearly blow up the house because whatever he created, he'd leave it bubbling and boiling while he went to search for food, forgetting it completely. He could remember the toughest calculus formulas and had nearly perfect pitch as a musician, but he literally could not remember to put his pants on. He would play John Coltrane–type solos on his sax for hours and be dressed in a winter jacket and gym shorts the whole time. He was that kind of kid, absentminded, and very smart, and later in life he became a chemist. But to the cops, he was just another black perpetrator with a story, and he was arrested and jailed.

Mommy paced the house all night when she got the news. She showed up early at Richie's arraignment the next day and took a seat right behind the defense table. When they brought him out in handcuffs and she saw him cuffed and dirty after being in the holding pen all night, she could not contain her grief and began muttering like a crazy woman, wringing her hands. Through her reverie of mumbo jumbo she heard the court-appointed lawyer lean over to Richie and offer two words of legal advice: "Plead guilty." She jumped up and screamed, "Wait!" She charged past the court officers, shouting to the judge that it was a mistake, that none of her kids had ever been in trouble with the law before, that her son was a college student, and so forth. The white judge, who had noticed Mommy sitting in the largely black courtroom, released Richie to her custody and the charges were later dropped.

But that experience made Mommy bear down on the younger ones like me even more. She was, in retrospect, quite brilliant when it came to manipulating us. She depended heavily on the "king/queen system" which she established in our house long before I was born: the eldest sibling was the king or queen and you could not defy him or her, because you were a slave. When the eldest left for college, the next ascended to the throne. The king/queen system gave us a sense of order, rank, and self. It gave the older ones the sense that they were in charge, when in actuality it was Mommy who ruled the world. It also harked back to her own traditional Orthodox upbringing where the home was run by one dominating figure with strict rules and regulations. Despite the orchestrated chaos of our home, we always ate meals at a certain time, always did homework at a certain time, and always went to bed at a certain time. Mommy also aligned herself with any relative or friend who had any interest in any of her children and would send us off to stay with whatever relative promised to straighten us out, and many did. The extended black family was Mommy's hole card, and she played it as often as the times demanded because her family was not available to her. As I grew older, it occurred to me at some point that we had some relatives we had never seen. "How come we don't have any aunts and uncles on your side?" I asked her one day.

"I had a brother who died and my sister . . . I don't know where she is," she said.

"Why not?"

"We got separated."

"How's that?"

"I'm removed from my family."

"Removed?"

"Removed. Dead."

"Who's dead?'

"I'm dead. They're dead too by now probably. What's the difference? They didn't want me to marry on the black side."

"But if you're black already, how can they be mad at you?"

Boom. I had her. But she ignored it. "Don't ask me any more questions."

My stepfather, a potential source of information about her background, was not helpful. "Oh, your mama, you mind her," he grunted when I asked him. He loved her. He seemed to have no problem with her being white, which I found odd, since she was clearly so different from him. Whereas he was largely easygoing and open-minded about most worldly matters, she was suspicious, strict, and inaccessible. Whenever she stepped out of the house with us, she went into a sort of mental zone where her attention span went no farther than the five kids trailing her and the tightly balled fist in which she held her small bit of money, which she always counted to the last penny. She had absolutely no interest in a world that seemed incredibly agitated by our presence. The stares and remarks, the glances and cackles that we heard as we walked about the world went right over her head, but not over mine. By age ten, I was coming into my own feelings about myself and my own impending manhood, and going out with Mommy, which had been a privilege and an honor at age five, had become a dreaded event. I had reached a point where I was ashamed of her and didn't want the world to see my white mother. When I went out with my friends, I'd avoid telling her where we were playing because I didn't want her coming to the park to fetch me. I grew secretive, cautious, passive, angry, and fearful, always afraid that the baddest cat on the block would call her a "honky," in which case I'd have to respond and get my ass kicked. "Come and let's walk to the store," she said one afternoon.

"I can go by myself," I said. The intent was to hide my white mom and go it alone.

"Okay," she said. She didn't seem bothered by my newfound independence. Relieved, I set off to a neighborhood grocery store. The store owner was a gruff white man who, like many of the whites in St. Albans, was on his way out as we blacks began to move in. He did not seem to like black children and he certainly took no particular liking to or interest in me. When I got home, Mommy placed the quart of milk he sold me on the table, opened it up, and the smell of sour milk filled the room. She closed the carton and handed it to me. "Take it back and get my money back."

"Do I have to?"

"Take it back." It was an order. I was a Little Kid in my house, not a Big Kid who could voice opinions and sway the master. I had to take orders.

I dragged myself back to the store, dreading the showdown I knew was coming. The owner glared at me when I walked in. "I have to return this," I said.

"Not here," he said. "The milk is opened. I'm not taking it back."

I returned home. Ten minutes later Mommy marched into the store, doing her "madwalk," the bowlegged strut that meant thunder and lightning was coming—body pitched forward, jaw jutted out, hands balled into tight fists, nose red, stomping like Cab Calloway with the Billy Eckstein band blowing full blast behind him. I followed her sheepishly, my plan to go it alone and hide my white mother now completely awash, backfired in the worst way.

She angrily placed the milk on the counter. The merchant looked at her, then at me. Then back at her. Then at me again. The surprise written on his face changed to anger and disgust, and it took me completely by surprise. I thought the man would see Ma, think they had something in common, then give her the dough and we'd be off. "That milk is sold," he said.

"Smell it," Ma said. "It's spoiled."

"I don't smell milk. I sell milk."

Right away they were at each other, I mean really going at it. A crowd of black kids gathered, watching my white mother arguing with this white man. I wanted to sink into the floor and disappear. "It's okay, Ma . . ." I said. She ignored me. In matters of money, of which she had so little, I knew it was useless. She was going full blast—". . . fool . . . think you are . . . idiot!"—her words flying together like gibberish, while the neighborhood kids howled, woofing like dogs and enjoying the show.

After a while it was clear the man was not going to return her money, so she grabbed my hand and was heading toward the door, when he made another remark, something that I missed, something he murmured beneath his breath so softly that I couldn't hear, but it made the crowd murmur "Ooohhhh." Ma stiffened. Still holding the milk in her right hand, she turned around and flung it at him like a football. He ducked and the milk missed him, smashing into the cigarette cabinet behind him and sending milk and cigarettes splattering everywhere.

I could not understand such anger. I could not understand why she didn't just give up the milk. Why cause a fuss? I thought. My own embarrassment overrode all other feelings. As I walked home, holding Mommy's hand while she fumed, I thought it would be easier if we were just one color, black or white. I didn't want to be white. My siblings had already instilled the notion of black pride in me. I would have preferred that Mommy were black. Now, as a grown man, I feel privileged to have come from two worlds. My view of the world is not merely that of a black man but that of a black man with something of a Jewish soul. I don't consider myself Jewish, but when I look at Holocaust photographs of Jewish women whose children have been wrenched from them by Nazi soldiers, the women look like my own mother and I think to myself, *There but for the grace of God goes my own mother—and by extension, myself.* When I see two little Jewish old ladies giggling over coffee at a Manhattan diner, it makes me smile, because I hear my own mother's laughter beneath theirs. Conversely, when I hear black "leaders" talking about "Jewish slave owners" I feel angry and disgusted, knowing that they're inflaming people with lies and twisted history, as if all seven of the Jewish slave owners in the antebellum South, or however few there were, are responsible for the problems of African-Americans now. Those leaders are no better than their Jewish counterparts who spin statistics in marvelous ways to make African-Americans look like savages, criminals, drags on society, and "animals" (a word quite popular when used to describe blacks these days). I don't belong to any of those groups. I belong to the world of one God, one people. But as a kid, I preferred the black side, and often wished that Mommy had sent me to black schools like my friends. Instead I was stuck at that white school, P.S. 138, with white classmates who were convinced I could dance like James Brown. They constantly badgered me to do the "James Brown" for them, a squiggling of the feet made famous by the "Godfather of Soul" himself, who back in the sixties was bigger than life. I tried to explain to them that I couldn't dance. I have always been one of the worst dancers that God has ever put upon this earth. My sisters would spend hours at home trying out new dances to Archie Bell and the Drells, Martha Reeves, King Curtis, Curtis Mayfield, Aretha Franklin, and the Spinners. "Come on and dance!" they'd shout, boogying across the room. Even Ma would join in, sashaying across the floor, but when I joined in I looked so odd and stupid they fell to the floor laughing. "Give it up," they said. "You can't dance."

The white kids in school did not believe me, and after weeks of encouragement I found myself standing in front of the classroom on talent day, wearing my brother's good shoes and hitching up my pants, soul singer–style like one of the Temptations, as someone dropped the needle on a James Brown record. I slid around the way I'd seen him do, shouting "Owww—shabba-na!" They were delighted. Even the teacher was amused. They really believed I could dance! I had them fooled. They screamed for more and I obliged, squiggling my feet and slip-sliding across the wooden floor, jumping into the air and landing in a near split by the blackboard, shouting "Eeeee-yowwww!" They went wild, but even as I sat down with their applause ringing in my ears, with laughter on my face, happy to feel accepted, to be part of them, knowing I had pleased them, I saw the derision on their faces, the clever smiles, laughing at the oddity of it, and I felt the same ache I felt when I gazed at the boy in the mirror. I remembered him, and how free he was, and I hated him even more.

FOR JOURNALING AND DISCUSSION

1. McBride asks his mother, "Ma, what's a tragic mulatto?" Compare McBride's identity politics with those of Reginald McKnight in his essay "Confessions of a Wannabe Negro" in Chapter 2.
2. McBride and his mother paint a very different picture of poverty than does Dorothy Allison in her essay "River of Names" in Chapter 3. Discuss the similarities and differences. Is poverty only about a lack of money?

3. Analyze the two voices in the book, McBride's and his mother's. How are they different? Are these gendered and/or raced voices?
4. Ruth McBride Jordan was born Rachel Deborah Shilsky (Ruchel Dwajra Zylska) in Poland. She moved to the United States when she was two and married Andrew McBride, an African American, after high school. After McBride's death she married again and took the name Jordan. As a Jew married to an African American and the mother of mixed-race children, her racial identity is complicated. Compare and contrast her racial identity to those of people interviewed by Lise Funderburg in her profiles of mixed-race people in "Parents and Family" in Chapter 2.
5. Do you come from a mixed-race, mixed–socioeconomic class, or mixed-faith family? If so, how has your hybridity affected who you are in relationship to others and how you express your spirituality?

FOR RESEARCH AND EXPLORATION

1. McBride talks about his mother being "removed" from her family or being "dead" to them. What do those terms imply in Jewish culture? Why was she dead to them?
2. Research the Holocaust. Which groups of people besides Jews were targeted for extermination?
3. McBride discusses how the Black Pride and civil rights movements influenced him and his brothers and sisters while they were growing up. Research how these movements viewed African Americans' relationships to Christianity.

My Jesus Was Jim Crowed!

Nicholas Cooper-Lewter

An African American Ph.D., the author of this selection is president of Cooper-Lewter Rites of Passage, Inc., a nonprofit organization founded to help youth move from childhood into a responsible adulthood in which they in turn give back to the community. Trained in psychology, social work, and theology, he is a nationally recognized educator, psychotherapist in private practice, ordained clergyman, and writer. Cooper-Lewter's interest in human potential led him to develop "soul therapy"—an African American approach to freeing people from master/slave cultural residues and core beliefs.

> If you're black, get back!
> If you're brown, stick around!
> If you're yellow, you're mellow!
> If you're white, you're all right!

Nicholas Cooper-Lewter, "My Jesus Was Jim Crowed!" from *Colors* (May-June 1994). Reprinted with the permission of the author.

Renée startled the pastor with her interpretation. "When did Jewish, Semitic, and Middle Eastern rule out being African? And just what was an African American supposed to look like?" How about the flight into Egypt to escape persecution? Matthew contains the Old Testament passage of Hosea 11:1— Out of Egypt I called my son. One could say, "Out of Africa I called my son."

The pastor was most comfortable with the hegemony that created a Middle East, a non-black Egypt, and even a non-black Ethiopia. In any case, Renée believed that in antiquity, more than today, Egypt was culturally, linguistically, and racially a part of Africa.

The pastor's position illustrated how much Jim and Jane Crow were in Renée's church. The Crows symbolized why early African Americans stopped trying to worship with European Americans and black religion's feud with institutionalized victimization. Renée knew Jim and Jane Crow rules. She saw how religion and American culture encouraged a need for blacks to construct and struggle with their own church identities. Renée did not believe it took a rocket scientist to know that any form of Christianity that endorsed or permitted racism was simply a cultural phenomenon and not very Christian at all.

She thought that a culture's religion was a group of people's entire way of doing things, including feelings and beliefs that influence their definition of reality. When people in a Judeo-Christian nation had to be made to abolish chattel slavery, and made to stop supporting Jim Crow laws, and made to support civil rights legislation, and made to understand why there was a need for a National Association for the Advancement of Colored People, or an Urban League, or Marcus Garvey's United Negro Improvement Association, or a Malcolm X, or a Martin Luther King, Jr., it called into question a religion's respect for God's ability, or desire, to judge injustice.

What can a slave who converts to Christianity do? Patiently endure bondage until God sets her free? Or resist the evil and escape? Africans were forced to shape African American religious responses as a challenge to white Christianity. By commission or omission the white faith required a change of heart, a conversion, but not an active refusal to support the evil of privilege dependent on codependent cousins—racism and sexism.

In the Americas, their own religion was a consistent friend to people of African ancestry traumatized by capture and enslavement. Black religion in the beginning of the African American experience assumed that God meant to counteract the terror of chattel slavery.

> [African Americans] share the reality of a common historical taproot, which extends deep into the nurturing center of the African soil. The community of faith can attest to the strength and sturdiness of this root by the nurturing it continues to provide Africans in diaspora. Although languages, religions, customs, and institutions were diverse, many African societies shared certain virtues, ideals, cultural expressions, and outlooks on the past, present, and future which provided spiritual armor capable of surviving the impact of slavery.[1]

Theology and slavery were merged to confuse the new Americans. A white God and a white savior had given black people a white master to look out for them in all matters of existence. The effect was tragic for master and slave. Slaveholders came to think of themselves as omniscient and omnipotent, like gods who ruled over slaves the way God ruled over humankind. They were gods, and their wives, ways, and region were therefore the best possible. Slaves and land were the measures of a white man in the South, and his paternalistic society was inevitable.

A white God, a white savior, and a white master functioned as one. The white trinity was the property of the white culture. Out of this context, black religion united core beliefs that made hope and eternal realities possible while facing daily impossibilities. Prophetic liberators like Moses represented the hope of most black religious responses.

Those most successful with white people felt safe enough to throw away the African idea of the collective "I" in favor of the individual "I." "I got mine; too bad you didn't get yours!" Their acceptance of the basic rules of culturally correct etiquette between white and black benefited them, and they were proud.

The slaves and their descendants who remained sensitive to the presence and effects of chattelization never took for granted that they would be trusted or could trust others. The need to trust for psychological health—called faith and hope in theology—created dialectical tensions for soul theologians. These gatekeepers of soul routinely held polar opposites in tension, constantly shifting as necessary. Black people could not trust white people, black people who wanted to be white, or black people who acted white. Yet soul therapy was based on fully trusting the Almighty. The Bible insisted that ". . . faith is the assurance of things hoped for, the conviction of things not seen." (Hebrews 11:1)

According to James H. Cone, this was "precisely the quality of childlike trust that Jesus declared to be a precondition for entering the Kingdom of God. From this perspective there is nothing immature or demeaning about black folks having the humility and faith of children when they approach the throne of the Almighty."[2]

Renée believed that people who fully trusted God did not need the assurance of racism or sexism to succeed. Under the pressure of a master/slave paradigm, regular core-belief refills were necessary to prepare for and process the daily psycho-spiritual insults to her self-image.

Masochistically, Renée found humor in the importance of one drop of African blood in the United States. Defined according to the one-drop rule, black people were a socially constructed category in which there was wide variation in racial traits, and therefore were not strictly a race. An African American could look like a person of any so-called race. Renée's courses on internalized victimization led her to appreciate the vitality of law transformed into cultural mandates. The permutations around color reminded her of stories she had heard as a child about struggles between the almost-white, high yellow, brown, and black people. The Jesus they worshipped offered a Sunday morning release from woe. But the shouting never provided a lasting resolution of their internalized color prejudices.

Renée applied the one-drop rule and Jim Crow standards to Jesus of Nazareth: Jesus did not have the right attitude and therefore could not be excused if he made a mistake as to form. He was not a "good" Negro, one who knew his place and stayed in it. He did not agree to treat every white person as his superior. He did not accept the idea that love should never be expected to be the love of equals for each other where white people and people of color were concerned. He did not accept the idea that he could never assert or intimate that a white person might be lying. He did not accept the idea that he could never impute dishonorable intentions to a white person. He did accept the idea that he could never lay claim to, or overtly demonstrate, superior knowledge or intelligence. And he did not give up his ministry because the penalties for not following proper etiquette were severe, often death.

Renée rejoiced that the Jim Crowing of Jesus made her just like him, that is, black and breaking the white rules. Providentially, the Jim-Crowed Jesus was the Almighty's answer to the perverted use of scripture. Africans were trained, taught, and terrorized to function as ugly ducklings with the help of the Bible. Renée's joy was in the tradition of adaptive, counter-aggressive, interrelated, highly therapeutic, psychologically significant religious responses to the African American experience.

One traditional response was "theomusicotherapy," a modern form of the ancient "soul therapy." Theomusicotherapy was the reconnecting celebration that used altered states of consciousness. Rhythm, tone, voice, silence, and movement were used to invite the state of mind that promoted healing and harmony.[3] Theologically informed music made use of internal and external expression to fortify, communicate, celebrate, protect, heal, and engender the holistic aims of a providential God's gift of soul therapy.

Soul therapy counteracted the effects of apartheid and menticide and had to do with an attitude about harmonious partnerships with the Creator and creation and how information should be organized for health, wholeness, and ways to prevent, counteract, cope, and overcome insults to people's identity, the nature of interpersonal relationships, and any God-given potential. In that tradition, African American soul therapy involved finding ways to neutralize and remove dissonance promoted by the interplay of mind, body, spirit, and environment. Soul therapy was brought into the United States in the hearts of black African slaves. Soul therapy was dynamic and holistic and had as one of its objects the development of a set of intuitively affirmed ways to prevent psycho-spiritual pathology. Soul therapy concerned itself with healing. The resulting core belief was the basis of having "soul." Soul therapy made sure that the necessary resources were available for personal and familial biological, psychological, sociological, and spiritual health.

Renée rejoiced that healthy black religion—soul therapy—represented the capacity of African Americans to balance, be healthy, and prosper while their hearts and minds were under attack. Deceit and self-deception relentlessly worked to plant the intergenerational trauma of American slavery in the psyches of black people. But a healthy black religion knew this sin and fought against it with passionate precision.

Thank you, Jesus, for the African American church! A Jim-Crowed Jesus counter-commands culture. If you are black, brown, yellow, red, or white, you are all right!

NOTES

1. Costen, Melva Wilson. African American Christian Worship. Nashville: Abington Press, 1993.
2. Cone, James H. The Spirituals and the Blues. Maryknoll: Orbis Books, 1991.
3. Chernoff, John Miller. African Rhythm and African Sensibility. Chicago: University of Chicago Press, 1979.

FOR JOURNALING AND DISCUSSION

1. Analyze the author's relationship to his character Renée. When is Renée talking to us? When is Cooper-Lewter? When do you think Cooper-Lewter agrees with Renée? disagrees? What elements of his writing style lead you to these conclusions?
2. Write a dialogue between Usry Alleyne, whose essay "Atheism and Me" appears next in this chapter, and Renée, in which they discuss the color of God and Christianity. Take a side in this argument, and write a defense of your position.
3. Can African Americans and Euro-Americans successfully worship side-by-side in the same church?
4. Who are Jim and Jane Crow? In what ways does Eddy L. Harris discuss Jim Crow laws in his essay "South of Haunted Dreams" in Chapter 8?
5. Renée discusses white Christianity's role in oppressing black slaves. What would she have to say to "Mother" Georgia, who appears in Arthenia Bates's essay "A Ceremony of Innocence" later in this chapter? Would her message be different from that of Tisha, another character in Bates's story? If so, in what ways?

FOR RESEARCH AND EXPLORATION

1. Work in a group and research which religions and spiritual beliefs enslaved Africans brought to the Americas. Have any remained in either pure or hybrid forms?
2. Have you ever attended a religious service or spiritual gathering where you felt you were—or where you were viewed as—a member of a minority group? Write about this experience, or ask friends or relatives if you can accompany them to their place of worship. What was done, or could have been done, to alleviate your feelings of being a spiritual outsider?
3. Hate crimes, such as the burning of black churches or the defacing of synagogues, are still occurring in the United States, despite our Constitution's guarantee of religious freedom. Research cases where the perpetrators were apprehended and prosecuted. What justifications did they give for their actions?

Atheism and Me: Why I Don't Believe in God

Usry Alleyne

Born in Guyana, South America, Alleyne moved to the United States to study engineering, but soon decided to pursue a degree in fine arts. Presently, he is an artist-in-residence at the Pillsbury House Service Center in Minneapolis, working with people of color and the economically disenfranchised. He feels his work, which is primarily as a videographer and composer, is a way to give something back to the community now that he is a privileged, educated man of color who has reached the age of thirty. Most of Alleyne's writing is personal and not intended for publication.

"Jesus loves me, this I know, because the Bible tells me so."

I don't know if Jesus loves me and I don't really care. My concerns in life are very earth-bound. What happens when I'm alive is of the most importance. Jesus died almost 2,000 years ago. Why are Christians around the world obsessed with his life? Why do so many people believe that he had an omnipotent father who made us all in his image? Why should I believe this nonsense? Why do so many black people believe in the Father, Son, and Holy Ghost? Should I be concerned that I don't believe?

As a child I was made to attend Sunday school and, later, church. I hated it. All the fuss that was made before I had to go: being dressed in my Sunday best, getting coconut oil rubbed on my legs, having the comb dragged through my hair, all so that I could sit in a big building and listen to tales about stuff that happened 2,000 years ago.

Churches seemed so big when I was a child. They were dark, and the preachers were so far away and high up that I hardly ever saw any of them. In the Anglican church in England the preacher was on a high, ornately carved pulpit. When I finally ended up in a pew from which I could see the preacher, I spent most of my time staring at the mural on the wall behind him, which made me nervous. The mural was of two big white hands holding an open Bible. I was told that no one had ever seen God, but still there were those white man's hands holding a book.

God was white. In all of the pictures of Jesus, he had white skin, blue eyes, and long, stringy hair. Why should his father look any different? When my

Usry Alleyne, "Atheism and Me: Why I Don't Believe in God" from *Colors* (May-June 1994). Reprinted with the permission of the author.

great-aunt brought copies of *Watchtower* to our house, there were pictures in them of white people praying or looking repentant or standing on the edge of a cliff basking in brilliant light, happy and content. The little figures that they pasted on the felt boards during Sunday school were white people dressed like Arabs. Most of the preachers I came across were white. All of the high church officials or the priests of the Catholic churches—the most prestigious churches in Guyana—were white. The pope was white.

My scoutmaster was a white Catholic priest, whom we were to call "Father." That I wasn't about to do. Everything I learned as a child that was important to the Christian religion had something to do with white folks.

As a child sitting in these churches and listening, I got a lot of confusing messages. I was told that God was everywhere and that he knew everything, but I knew that nobody could be everywhere. I was told that God was in me, but I had a hard time believing it. I never heard any voices in my head other than my own or my mother's telling me what not to do. I spent a lot of time looking up at the sky, because I thought God was up there. But I also knew that people had landed on the moon and that the sky was not solid. "God is a spirit. You can't see him," they said. But my mother, grandfather, and other relatives claimed that *they* could see spirits. I was told that God was all powerful and could do anything, but when I made even the simplest of requests I never got any answers. I was told that God works in strange ways and that I just didn't believe hard enough.

They were right, I didn't believe hard enough. I had no reason to believe that what I was told about God was true. Some of the adults I knew lied a great deal. Most of them broke all the rules that they tried to make me learn. One family member lied, stole, and committed adultery, all while attending church every Sunday. Which part of this adult fiction should I believe?

Adults controlled my world. There were punishments for non-compliance and rewards for subservience. I took things apart, especially toys, to find out how they worked, and was punished for my curiosity, for being "destructive." To question what was said to me about God was sinful. Yet every new tale I was told about the acts of God led to more questions. Walking on water I believed. I tried it and failed. Parting an ocean with a few words I didn't even bother trying. As for healing the sick, my mother always put some salt or mercurochrome on the cut and sent me back out to play. In the Bible, snakes became sticks and fish multiplied without having sex, and so did a woman. Why should I believe any of this? All of it contradicted what I saw and experienced. I should learn to accept what was said to me without question, and for a short period during my late teens I complied.

But at the same time I was afraid to speak up, to investigate, even to question. It started when I went to services where everyone was babbling and fainting and catching the spirit. My cousin said they were speaking in tongues. I was impressed and confused, but it somehow strengthened my faith. I was also very vulnerable to suggestion and looking for love. I was malnourished. I weighed less than 100 pounds and remember feeling hungry for weeks at a time. My mother had moved to the United States—I hadn't seen her in a year—and was working to get visas for my sister and me. I was ready for God.

One Sunday in church, I began to feel very happy. I thought it had something to do with finding God, but I had also found a girlfriend. It could have been hormones or Jesus, but I felt happy anyway, and I attributed it to God because I was told that when I found God and his love I would be happy. I wasn't told that having female companionship could have the same effect.

Shortly after my discovery of God my parents arranged for my sister and me to be reunited with the rest of the family.

The eight of us ended up in my aunt's one-bedroom apartment. My uncle lived upstairs. His wife was a black woman from the south who always had something to say about Jesus. Her zeal was remarkable. Her conviction made me nervous. How could someone, particularly a black woman, be that committed to this Christian religion? Especially in a country where white folks weren't just the people in *Watchtower*—they were real. She had pictures in her house of white Jesuses, but by the way she spoke you would think that he was black.

The aunt whom I lived with downstairs always had her radio tuned to a twenty-four hour inspirational station. Every Sunday for the six months that we lived there everyone went to church on Sunday, everyone except me. I liked peace and quiet. I watched Reverend Fred Price on tv, but I refused to go to church, to the dismay of my father and my aunts. I was afraid of all that zeal. I'd had enough from the Baptist church in Guyana. Besides, now I had bread, hot dogs, corned beef, candy bars, and so many girls all around—all colors, sizes, and shapes. Living in Brooklyn was the beginning of my shift away from the mythology of the Christian religion.

This might seem strange especially since everyone around me went to church. There were also churches on every other corner. At school, people shot each other. Outside the school, almost every afternoon there were a half dozen, mostly white, police officers outside the school yard. Many of my teachers were Jewish. Most were white. Nobody talked about religion, which I found out later was the law. I started reading a great deal in that school and found out about the mythologies of other religions. My curiosity increased and so did my awareness about the animosity between groups of people with different metaphysical belief systems. I still continued to believe in God, mostly because of the common-sense style of the few tv preachers whom I watched. Even though most of these preachers said the same thing, their denominations looked very different. The black Baptist church seemed to full of working-class black folks. The black middle class preferred less showmanship during the delivery of the message. The white middle class preferred white-haired, sedate, kindly, smiling, old, white ministers like Rev. Schuler. I stuck with Rev. Price's good common sense, at least that [was] what I thought until I turned eighteen.

One of my classes in college was taught by a nice middle-aged white man. At least that's what I thought when I first entered his philosophy class. He turned out to be everyone's nightmare, at least everyone whose belief system was based on faith. From day one this man was trouble, asking a ton of questions. We spent very little time studying philosophy, or so I thought. He made several students angry when he asked them their reasons for going to church. Most couldn't answer. They just did it because they had always done it. He had been trained in religious studies and in philosophy, and knew more about Christianity than most fanatics that I've come across to this day. He also had a passion for life. He said he did, and he lived by his word. He seem content and very happy, and when I found out that he had metaphysical convictions my brain went wild. Within the first few weeks of his class I started to question every belief that I had about my faith in God.

I had gone to church because I was told that it was the right thing to do. I had complied with everyone else's wishes purely as a way to avoid punishment. I had grown sick and tired of hearing that the wages of sin are death. White folks in this country and all over the world had done an awful lot of sinning. But they were still in charge of everything. They were outside of my schools as cops, and they had killed black kids in Brooklyn with impunity. Isn't there a commandment that says that we shouldn't kill? The cops were the law, the Ten Commandments were law, what's wrong here? They were supposed to protect me, but I felt threatened instead. Theirs were the hands holding the Bible in that big Sunday-school painting. They had written the damned thing and they were the ones telling everybody that it was the word of God. Why should I believe them?

One of the most annoying directives of the Bible is that we should be happy and content with what we have, that it's all for a good reason. I could no longer accept that. Everything that was wrong around me had root causes that were obvious once I began looking for them. What happened didn't happen because of fate or divine discretion. Things happened because people worked for them to be that way. I didn't pass tests because I prayed; I passed because I studied. I wasn't punished so severely as a child because it was the right thing to do; I was punished because I had broken rules that I had no part in making and that were designed primarily for the peace of mind of those who created them.

This is how I began to see the Bible and those who placed it before me as the answer to all questions. On a global scale, it was a book of rules designed to secure the comfort of white people. On a personal scale it was designed for believers to accept the notion of unquestioning compliance to authority, particularly male authority. Mary didn't have a choice about having a baby. It was placed there without her active participation. Jesus didn't die for his father because he wanted to or he would not have asked while on the cross why he had been forsaken.

The more I looked at the Bible the more I saw compliance with a singular authority as its major push. Abraham nearly murdered his son because he heard a voice in his head. When Moses went up on the mountain people started to do their own thing. And Moses broke the first copy of the Ten Commandments in anger when he saw that democracy was taking root among his people. When Jesuit priests went into the Brazilian rain forests or Minnesota missionaries go to visit primitive people somewhere off in the Third World they're always armed with their Bibles. Suppose missionaries left their metaphysics at home. What if they went to learn, instead of to impose their order? And what if this had happened four, five, or six centuries ago, what would the world be like today?

I always felt very stupid when I was praying, and I never found out what prayer is for. It wasn't like asking my mother for something, because she gave distinct answers—yes, no, or maybe later. I could also influence her choices by my behavior. I could also receive cues from her to help me properly pose my question. Every child learns to do this. With God there was no telling what would happen when he was asked a question. And I found myself praying for things that I had no influence over. I was throwing wishes in the air. Instead of going out with my hands and head and trying to figure out a solution to a problem, I would sit quietly, close my eyes, and talk to myself. How idiotic! Instead of trying to find a way to empower myself, I prayed for others to have less power. Instead of studying, I was praying for the test to be easy. Ridiculous!

I stopped praying, and began to see that a structure that demanded compliance was not one that I wished to be part of. Males wanted compliance from females. My male friends thought women were inferior. My white friends thought black people were close to apes. My Christian friends didn't want to rock the boat for fear they might do something to hurt their chances of getting to heaven. My Christian friends are always saying prayers for me, as is my mother, who is now more fervent than ever. Ironically, she is the one who always insisted that if I fail I should try again and again, a concept that is probably most responsible for my belief in human effort rather than divine intervention.

I'm not going to rise above anyone or anything by adopting a mythology. I'm not going to perpetuate the concept of life's mystery by stifling my curiosity. The more one knows, even about one's metaphysical convictions, the better. Divinity was dear to me because I was ignorant about my dependence upon other human beings. I was told that I could succeed by myself, especially if I had omniscient authority—God—by my side. I wasn't told that people working together could do just about anything.

The day I decided I was atheist was a good day. I woke up, got dressed, and went to class. I was sitting there daydreaming when something clicked.

Religion was excuses—for not working hard enough; for not being my brother's keeper; and under the guise of keeping the faith and being true to only one god, for not learning what others had to offer, for bad habits, carelessness, ignorance, greed, selfishness, intolerance, bigotry, and all kinds of other correctable human tendencies. It called these tendencies "sin" and said that God would forgive us for them.

I'm not one to forgive, but I will accept an apology or just put you out of my mind. Forgiveness is stupid. We all make mistakes, but forgiveness just leads to silencing the issue. If you are a Christian woman, should you forgive your husband for his adultery or use of pornography, or should you demand a written apology and an agreement that he works to correct his ways? If you are black, should you forgive white folk for their bigotry or demand that they become educated about the issue?

Throwing wishes in the air has no effect upon human problems that demand hard work by everyone. One day I believed in God, the next day the concept of transcendence and divinity seemed like utter garbage. I have no clue about an afterlife, and I don't really care. What matters most is what I do today. We can't look at the Bible as a catalog of solutions to life's problems. Sears got rid of their catalog, and so should we.

FOR JOURNALING AND DISCUSSION

1. Alleyne, who is from Guyana, relates typical conversations he had with his family over Christianity that failed to alleviate his doubt. " 'God is a spirit. You can't see him,' they said. But my mother, grandfather, and other relatives claimed that *they* could see spirits." Discuss whether this passage might point to an attempted and perhaps imperfect synthesis of religious cultures under colonialism that added to Alleyne's loss of faith.
2. Alleyne charges that the Christian Bible is a set of rules that benefits only white people and teaches compliance to male authority. Do you agree or disagree with his position?
3. "Mythology" is a term Alleyne applies to Christianity. What is the difference between mythology and religion? Do Christians typically refer to their faith as mythology?
4. Alleyne notes that the various denominations within Christianity seem to be segregated according to stereotypical class tastes and preferences. In the essay "First They Changed My Name" in Chapter 8, Caffilene Allen describes her mother in terms of her fundamentalist Baptist faith. Does Allen support Alleyne's position?
5. In the next essay in this chapter, Arthenia Bates's "A Ceremony of Innocence," "Mother" Georgia tells Tisha, "You were raised to know that no colored folks can't rule the world by theirself. My folks told me white folks is a mess, but a nigger ain't nothing." How do her words support Alleyne's critique of Christianity?

FOR RESEARCH AND EXPLORATION

1. Alleyne complains that Jesus and God are always pictured as blue-eyed white people. Research art history books, local stores that sell popular religious art, and black, Native American, and Asian Christian churches. Do you find any variety in the face of the Christian God?
2. Research the history of Guyana before it became British Guiana. Write about the indigenous forms of faith before the island was taken over by the English.
3. What is an atheist? Research famous Americans who became atheists. Despite the fact that this country was partially founded by those fleeing religious persecution, have American atheists been persecuted for their denial of faith?

A Ceremony of Innocence

Arthenia J. Bates

Born in South Carolina, Bates is the author of The Deity Nodded, Seeds Beneath the Snow, *and* Such Things from the Valley. *She taught high school from 1942 to 1946 and taught college English and writing from 1947 to 1980. Among her achievements are the 1981 Award and Presidential Citation from the National Association for Equal Opportunities in Higher Education.*

The thick evergreens screened Georgia Ann McCullum's front porch so well that Tisha did not see her sitting in the porch swing until she reached the top step—the eighth, because she had once measured her age by these steps. She had practiced the salutation "Mother" Georgia to pay honor to this distant cousin who had reached the highest point of distinction for a woman in Chute Bay. She had been made the "mother" of Chute Bay Memorial Baptist Church, which had been built by the people in the Bay on a pay-as-you-go basis during the Depression years.

Tisha stood quietly hugging herself in a full-length Natural Emba Autumn Haze mink coat as she waited for the old woman to recognize her. Even though it was a bright day, the temperature held at 23 degrees above zero and a stiff breeze blew in from the north.

The noise of a truck coming down Bay Road jostled the swinger from an apparent reverie. She slipped from the swing and started forward, then recognized Tisha. Their eyes met and held long enough for the old woman to make a good guess. She fumbled in her mind and grunted, then, caught by pain, she backed back to the swing to steady herself. The swing moved backward, almost causing her to miss her seat.

Tisha rushed to clasp her in a bear hug.

"Don't fall, Mother Georgia—please don't fall," she pleaded.

"Don't tell me," Mother Georgia said, "you Flora Dee's baby. Ain't you now?"

"Yes, Mother Georgia," she answered, and relaxed her grip, helping the old woman to set herself in the swing.

"This here Tisha. Sweet little Tisha. Just as pretty, too. You look good enough to eat. Your grandpa still call you his 'little spicy gal'?"

"Grandpa hasn't come close to me since I've been home, Mother Georgia."

"That's your own doings. But thang God. Thang God. Thang God. I talk to Him the other night 'bout you, and here He done sent you already. I ain't scared of you just 'cause you gone astray." She cradled Tisha in her arms and nuzzled her thin cheeks with a bottom lip packed hard with Railroad Mill snuff. Coins hit the porch and began to roll as they reeled in this odd pantomime of genuine affection. She finally held Tisha away at arm's length and gloating over her, told of the wonders that had come with the title "Mother" Georgia.

Old white men whose shirts she had ironed until arthritis twisted both of her wrists—who had brought shirts to her even though a one-day service laundry had opened in Crystal Hill—who brought handouts to supplement the $54.00 a month from the "government"—even they used the title of honor "Mother" Georgia, when they had for decades called her "Aunty."

After this rehearsal, Tisha began to pick up the coins from the floor. She found several nickels and a dime, but Mother Georgia said that that was not all.

"Don't bother yourself," she told Tisha, "go on in and make yourself at home. You needn't act like company, when this your second home. I'm slow but I'm coming."

Tisha walked into the front room, a room she knew by heart before she left Chute Bay. She glanced about, noticing that it was the same. She waited a minute for Mother Georgia, then brushed the bottom of a chair with her fingers to test it for dust. Her fingertips were black with coal dust. She walked to the door to check on the old woman's delay. She did not want to be caught cleaning the chair. She walked to the door and looked out in time to see Mother Georgia crawling about slowly on her knees and fumbling up and down the porch planks with her drawn hands.

"Mother Georgia, can I help—?"

"No, Sugar, I got all but two pennies. Hope the Lord them two didn't roll off the porch. If it was Mr. Pogue' truck, I'd get my coal if I was a few cents short. But this truck want every cent. I don't know who it b'long to."

"Come on in, Mother Georgia," Tisha said. "I'll give you what you need for the coal man." She then went out and helped her up from the floor.

"Sugar, they got them ole engines what pull theirself. If they was still using coal like they used to, I'd be out there up and down them tracks with my bucket, picking me up all the coal I want."

"Yes ma'm," Tisha replied. "Now tell me now much the coal cost, and I'll sit out there and wait for the truck."

"No, Sugar. You so dressed up, he might not stop if he don't see me. You just sit tight, and soons he come I'm going to make up a great big fire in the heater. It ain't cold, is it? I got on plenty clothes, and you got on that big fine coat. Don't get hetted up 'cause I got to ask you for myself 'bout that Allie what Flora worried to death 'bout. She worried plumb stiff 'bout that God've yours, just like she can't put you back in your place. Humph. I said send her to me when she come home. I'll get her straight before she go back out yonder."

Tisha pat her feet as Mother Georgia talked, because her toes were getting stiff from cold. A minute later a truck pulled up, and she let Tisha give the driver $1.25 for a crocker sack of coal and a bunch of lightwood splinters. She built a fire in the heater with two splinters and a few lumps of coal. She washed her hands in a basin on the washstand, then sat down to watch Tisha.

"Lord, Sugar, you look good enough to bite on the jaw. The only thing got me bothered is what your ma told me 'bout that Allie. You know you got her nearly distracted? What's that, anyhow, child—talking 'bout goin'ta serve Allie? That ain't no God. You know Mother Georgia ain't goin'ta tell you nothing wrong 'long's I had my hand on the gospel plough. That was 'fore they spanked your ma, so you know I'm a soldier. You got no business turning your back on God."

"Allah, Mother Georgia, is the true God. You see, I know He's the right God because of what He's done for me. Okay?" Tisha started to stand, but the old woman waved her back to her chair. "He helps us to have heaven right here on earth, and that's what I want because I can enjoy life everyday of my life."

"What I'm telling you—that is, what Mother Georgia, ambassador to Christ, is telling you, is that ain't no God you found up the road. Your ma learned you 'bout the right God from your cradle, and it ought to be good enough to take you to your grave. You see what He's done for me, don't you, child? That Allie you heard tell of way out yonder is just a make-shift God the crowd hark'ning after. And I'm trying to tell you better 'cause, you, Flora and every child she got rest close to my heart. We kin as cousins, but I been a mother to her and to y'all before I come a mother to the church. You better turn to the true and living God 'fore it's a day and hour and eternity too late."

Tisha started to let the argument rest, but she felt that she would be a shameful volunteer for Allah if she let this occasion pass without sharing her idea of his worth.

"I'm serving Allah," she persisted, "and I hope to serve Him better. I'm twenty-two now, and I hope to be that many times stronger in His grace before I'm twice that old."

"I'm going on these here knees, little Miss, to the Master I know who'll open your eyes. Look at me." Mother Georgia hoisted her huge frame from the rocker and fastened her sharp bird eyes on Tisha. "I'm seventy-six-odd years old. How you reckon I make it without the Lord? You see that sack of coal? The Lord sent it here. Let me tell you, the Pastor—I reckon you don't know Reverend Sarks—anyway, he come here faithful as the days is long and brings me ration just like he take it home. And Mr. Dwyer—I guess you forgot him— he sends me all the bones from his store to feed these six dogs I got on the yard for company. Some of them oxtails 'n stuff the dogs don't see 'cause I make me a pot've soup."

"Well, let's not get excited," Tisha said. "I brought a present for you. Let's look after that." Tisha handed her a small Christmas-wrapped package which the old woman shook.

"What these? Drawers?" she asked.

Tisha shook her head. "You see," she told Mother Georgia, "we don't have Christmas, but you do."

"You mean Allie don't let y'all have no Christmas? How do you do when you don't ever have no Christmas? How can you live with no Christmas?"

"Everyday ought to be important in this life." Tisha had lost her ardor.

"Oh, these them pretty head rags? Well, I'm going to wear this cotton one to Prayer Meeting and the silk one on Communion Sunday." She rewrapped the gift in the same paper.

"That will be nice." Tisha was pleased with her happiness over the small gift. It was one of the things she always cherished about Mother Georgia.

It was warm enough now for Tisha to remove her coat. The old woman got up to leave for the kitchen, but Tisha tried to persuade her to relax or, if she insisted on making coffee, to make it on the heater, but she would not listen.

"You're company now," she maintained, "and a fine lady at that, so I'll treat you like one, no matter if you did used to help me out. You make yourself at home now while I get straight in the kitchen. And you get up and turn that coat insadouter so's no smoke'll hit it."

"Yes ma'm," she answered.

Tisha sat there remembering the room as she had known it years before. This room was full of furniture. There was an upright grand piano, a three-piece bedroom suite, a washstand, two rocking chairs, and a davenport with sugar-starched crocheted pieces on the arm rests. The center table held a large metal oil lamp on the top and a big family Bible on the bottom tier. The old green wool rug was practically eaten away from the floor, and the wallpaper of unidentified color was smoky and filled with rainwater circles.

There was an array of several pretty vases on the mantlepiece, of odd shapes and sizes, and pictures hung indiscriminately wherever a nail could be placed to hold them. High above the mantle was a picture of Cupid asleep, with the bow and arrow besides him. Glancing around the wall, she found the pictures of undertakers, ministers, church groups, family members, movie stars and flowers. There was a lone insurance policy hanging above the doorsill going to the middle room. She tried to evaluate the holdings of this room in terms of financial worth—the most valuable possessions in the house secured from a lifetime of satisfactory labor. They hardly added up to dollars and cents.

After a while Mother Georgia came in with a cup of coffee and a plate of cake on a tray.

"I made your coffee on the hot plate. I got 'lectric, you know," and she pointed to the bulb hanging on a suspended wire in the center of the room. "I have my lamp lighted half the time before I remember I can pull that little chain to get some light." She watched Tisha a minute, then encouraged her to eat the five slices of cake because she had baked the cakes herself. They were her specials: raisin, chocolate, pineapple, coconut and strawberry jelly.

"Mother Georgia," she said, "you remember the time I ate a whole plateful of cake when I was a child? Well, it was the best cake I'd ever had in my life at that time. And since then I've found out how to enjoy life the way I enjoyed that first plate of cake you gave me. As long as you enjoy this life, there's nothing to worry about."

"I don't want to spoil your appetite, but you're gone from your raising. You're caught in the web of sin. And you know what that mean. You sitting there all pretty, but you dying, Sugar." The old woman shook her head.

Dying! Tisha turned and looked at Georgia Ann McCullum. *She* was dying. The old woman was dying—dying as she had done every day of her life, though she was too good a minstrel man to know it. Her ugly life was death. She no doubt would have a beautiful funeral according to their pattern, with a nice long obituary, good remarks from the deacons, a wailing eulogy from the preacher and honest tears from unknown visitors at the grave; but her life was, and always had been, an ugly death.

"Thang God you come through, Sugar. Look—put your cake you left in a bag and take it home with you. And when you go back up the road, you'll remember what God has done for me and you'll forget about that Allie and the Mooselims. They'll run the world off the map if you not careful. You were raised to know that no colored folks can't rule the world by theirself. My folks told me white folks is a mess, but a nigger ain't nothing."

"Yes ma'm," Tisha said as she put on her coat to leave. She was not going to argue with the old lady because, more than anyone else, Mother Georgia had given her the final proof that she had chosen the right path—the path away from the religion of the Cross. God, the God of Mother Georgia, the God of her parents, the God who had let His only Son be crucified by wicked men, was uncaring. Then, as now, she told herself, if He was up there, He was oblivious of all the Georgia Ann McCullums in the universe.

She pulled the mink closer to her ears as she faced the cold, crisp air on the walk to her parents' home down Bay Road, happy in the thought that she had learned to praise Allah, who cared for His black children enough to help them find heaven on earth.

FOR JOURNALING AND DISCUSSION

1. As Tisha and "Mother" Georgia visit over coffee and cake, they argue over Tisha's abandonment of Christianity and her embrace of Islam. Like many conversations, theirs operates on two levels; what is the other, deeper conversation between these two women?

2. What is the significance of Tisha's "full-length Natural Emba Autumn Haze mink coat"? Why is it mentioned at the beginning of the story? Was owning such a coat typical for a black woman in Chute Bay at the time? What is the relationship of the coat to the women's discussion of religion?

3. Tisha seems to enjoy material comfort. If money is not a problem for her, why did she select the gift she did for "Mother" Georgia?
4. In "Unveiling Islam" earlier in this chapter, Zainab Ali paints a very different picture of Islam than do "Mother" Georgia and Tisha. Compare and contrast these perceptions.
5. Both Tisha and Eddy L. Harris, in "South of Haunted Dreams" in Chapter 8, travel home to the south to confront their pasts. How do their pasts differ? How are they the same?

FOR RESEARCH AND EXPLORATION

1. Research the role of black women within the African American Baptist faith. Are their positions within their congregations powerful ones?
2. Why does Islam appeal to many African Americans? Research the historical and current relationship between Islam and African Americans. If you are an African American Muslim, research when and why your family embraced this faith.
3. Research the role of women within Islam. Does Tisha dress and act in accordance with Islamic custom? In "Unveiling Islam," Ali emphasizes that a Muslim is one who submits, not necessarily one who enjoys; why might Tisha stress the importance of Muslims finding "heaven right here on earth"?

Earth Bone Connected to the Spirit Bone

Adrian C. Louis

Louis is a mixed-blood Indian, an enrolled member of the Lovelock Paiute Indian Tribe. He earned an M.A. in creative writing at Brown University and has published eight books of poetry and two novels. Among Louis's awards is a Pushcart Prize and fellowships from the South Dakota and Nebraska Arts Councils, the Bush Foundation, the National Endowment for the Arts, and the Lila Wallace–Reader's Digest Foundation. He is a teacher at Ogala Lakota College on the Pine Ridge Reservation in South Dakota.

When America died, I was passed out and I never noticed. Was it a meteor or an invisible wand that waved past our eyes and blinded everyone? I awoke one morning and electrical maggots were spurting from the mind-control machine in our disheveled living room. We are off the Rez in Rushville,

Adrian C. Louis, "Earth Bone Connected to the Spirit Bone" from *Ploughshares* 22, no. 1 (Spring 1996). Copyright © 1996 by Adrian Louis. Reprinted with the permission of the author.

Nebraska, eighteen miles from Pine Ridge. Under the carcinogenic mist of the cropdusters, this lame-brained bordertown staggers and smiles. There is only one restaurant—at the bowling alley—and it has shanky, subhuman food. The high school team is nicknamed "The Longhorns." The steaks and hamburger in the largest grocery store in town are Third World. This is the heart of cattle country. A ripened, diseased American heart.

From eighteen miles south, I watch the Rez gangbangers come to town— pallid, goofy reflections of the gang scum they've seen on TV. Sedated by sweating daylight, they rise to moonlight's murderous soul. Broken, the sacred circle is. Broken, the sacred circle is light years from mending. We all play Indian roulette. Red fluid of life. Black fluid of death. My wheel spins into middle-aged sameness. Still, there is something I want to say about love. It is the cruelest drug and I have used and abused it. And now I am spinning, afraid to die alone or together. And we are all the same, even our leaders, the tribal politicians. Our chiefs are big, brown ants in panties. Flint-skinned mutants of the sacred song. Insects. Hear me. Where is my HUD house? Where are our warriors? Where are the ancestor spirits who should be guiding us? Where is the love?

O Reservation. Home, home, hell. Eighteen miles north resides our howl and hovel where everything changes except the rusty bars across the moon. Listen, listen to the rabid coyote in the frozen Badlands. It is singing a love song to us. A wild-ass cowboy and Indian tune. We can still hear it at this Nebraska Street Dance. Yeeeeeee-hawwwww! Cowpokes all over the butt-fucking place. Huge, hairy galoots, veritable Blutos under straw Stetsons. On horses by day, on heifers tonight.

And glimmering in the eastern mist is Oz—no, I mean Lincoln, Nebraska. Beyond green cornfields that white city gleams. Midwestern Cambridge. Home of *Cliffs Notes*. City of lame, homespun poets and other plains jokers. The catapult where state income taxes launch Huskers to Orange Bowls. Great American city with a parched cornfield soul: O rasping, generic America. Home of the hospital we visit and leave with pills to flower false hope.

You are upstairs on your Prozac and Haldol. I'm forty-eight years old and groggy from napping after self-flagellation. The two Bible thumpers at the front door graze on my nakedness. God help me if you can, I mumble at them. I am scaling the black glass canyons of hell and doing tolerably well, almost enjoying myself as they titter and quickly turn whiter than white.

God bless our Indian democracy. The red sun rises. Since the diagnosis, neither of us work. The bathtub is yellow. The bills are white. They mount and mount as do my collection of books. Writers I don't know send me their books from every corner of this mad nation. I am too busy caring for you to read. Our fieldstone basement is crumbling under the weight of their books. I wish they would send money, not books.

*   *   *

You have taken to wandering. Vanished for the third time this month. You are out there someplace shimmering in your own haze of dead memory. It does no good to call the cops. I've learned my lesson. Twice they've brought you back from the video store. I sit and wait for your return, trying the mindless anesthetic of MTV. I watch the music in black and white. In Seattle, young grunge nihilists are experiencing impotence before their time. In L.A., young black rappers sing grunts of the vengeful cock—a self-demonizing sort of urban Mandingo lingo that reservation kids are now mouthing, too. Rap scares me. How is it possible to age with grace? Where is the desperado I was? Where are you now, my love? And how is it still possible for me to hate? Worn by the daily agitation of your slow-motion, terminal disease, I retain my anger. I turn off the tube and I think of one enemy in particular. The bastard is thirteen years older than me and I will not be speaking ill of the dead when I piss on his grave. I will be merely dousing the white devils which possessed him. Their names were greed, success, material goods, and Jesus H. Christ.

Still waiting, I call my friend Simon to see if he's seen her. He asks to borrow money. He needs medicine to get well, but no, no money, Cousin. You already owe me. No, I ain't giving you no twelve-step quick-step. Only the bottom, hard, harsh, and swift. Then you get up or don't, either one better than now. Oh, how you love living death. Oh, how you live loving death. Simon said he fell down and broke his crown and awoke at the VA hospital in a room filled with decrepit old men in wheelchairs. "I was one of them," he said and chuckled.

So I then said to Simon: "The information superhighway leads to consciousness overflowing the toilet *or* true denial. The murderous nature of man craves Nature's death. I know where you're coming from. Every day I also fight the urge to drink. Every minute of every day. Sometimes I think: What if I got cancer? If I did, the first one to know would be a bartender. I'd be just like you." And after an insufferable silence, Simon said at least he wasn't coughing up blood, but he did go into seizures: "The earth was dying—and its children, too. The earth was dying—and its children, too."

I'm sweating bullets at the Social Security office in the nearest large city. This homely white woman's got me bent over her desk and is banging me good. No, we're not legally married, I tell her. No, I'm not her legal guardian. Just approve the damn papers, please. Christ!—I just wish someone would have asked this bureaucrat to her high school prom. These gray-faced government mutants are all the slime-fucking-same. Hey, their souls are powdered milk and we are the water they crave. In this hallucination of midlife, I whitewash all fatalistic interrogatives. There is no primeval carnage of carcasses in caves. The black crust entombing blood lies upon a sesame seed bun. I am plastic America. I am the holy man among the hollow men who worship at the altar of greed. For many years I possessed the true Holy Grail and drank beer from it. Now I am the toad Prince. Kiss me and fuck me till I'm raw, darling dearest fed employee, but God please approve the paperwork.

I come and go like the pavement in winter. No longer greaseblack at the intersection of blood leaves and salt-peppered snow, I sometimes dye my sideburns, my soul. Smirking ancestors appear and disappear. My dogs are turning gray and swimming slowly throughout the house. There were many women I loved, but I think they all had the same name. I love you. I love you. They were all you and now you are slowly vanishing. Vanishing.

From a bleached fence post aimed at the gunpowder sky, an eagle explodes upward. Our car is speeding down the ice road when we see a small plume dancing earthward. Your circle is almost full. That is the message of the feather, yet I continue to pretend that I don't understand it. This dreadful curse of middle age is no joking matter. I'm no longer young and my mind can't grasp that fact. There is not one truth, but many truths. There are no lies—just fearful shadings of the truth. I learned all my banks. I learned all the English I needed in eight ball and snooker.

This, thus, is what I learned. You are dying and you are not dying. I wish I could have you do the rest. This is your poem. Here are the words, this is the vision. Hey, this *is* the poem. Ride it if you can. All your worlds are vanishing. I am not sad, but it is getting hard to love you. Do you understand? Do you? I remember your father said, "Long as I can remember, us Indians leased our land to the white man." He said, "The *wasicu* grows hay and gets rich." He used to run circles around these round bales when he was a kid getting in shape for high school basketball—the famed 1936 State Champs. He said, "Sometimes, just at dusk, these bales look like ghosts of the buffalos or . . . something, you know?" Now he is dead.

Darling, it seems my only reason for living is to help you remember. Do you recall that white man who said how come at every powwow you honor the American flag? This has always been a puzzle to me, he said. You are the people who fell through the crack in the Liberty Bell. You are always the first to invoke the Washita River or Bosque Redondo or Wounded Knee when you perceive injustice against your people. God, despite the centuries of atrocities this country committed against you Indian people, you still love to honor that flag. I just don't get it, the white man said to us.

There was no way to answer him. What could we say? Someone said Sitting Bull said:

> If the Great Spirit had desired me to be a white man, he would have made me so in the first place.
>
> It is not necessary for eagles to be crows.

Most of us know Sitting Bull wasn't bullshitting, but we still don't know which way to go. We are torn between two different worlds and between the past and the future. At least that's what we tell ourselves when we fail. We never mention the fact that it was Indians who killed Mr. Bull.

On Sundays the caterwauling from this bordertown church down the street is fearless, fearful, fearsome. In that eternal fear they call Christian love, they yodel to forget who they are and screech the wondrous lie that all of us are their God's children. If their God is real, why doesn't he help us? We are paying taxes here, too. It is all a bland joke. I have heard these same poor whites say Skins don't want to work and curse us, sputtering that if it weren't for the government handouts, we'd starve to death. And on Friday nights I've seen flocks of these same angel-addled sodbusters drunk and desperate for Indian pussy and worse. Last winter a mid-February thaw startled cows into dropping early calves onto the muddy plains. Even trees were tricked into budding. That week a cop in Gordon, Nebraska, murdered an Indian guy. Shot him square in the back and got away with it.

When I was young I could always tell who the real cowboys were. They always smelled like cowshit. These days they wear nylon panties under their jeans and draw their guns as if their redneck lives had meaning. Damn this chapped-ass cowboy hell. Damn this cowturd state of mind, this verbal puke, this pain.

Once the Rez sun rose bloated and angered. Like a neglected child, it pouted over the purple hills surrounding Pine Ridge Village. Dogs ran looking for cars to crush them. Soon it would be too hot to do anything but find shade and suffer, yet Adrian would survive. He had enough beer stocked up to get drunk and sleep through the heat of the day and get drunk again at night. Adrian was one smart Indian alkie. A flesh and blood oxymoron. O sweetheart, remember?

Note to a young Rez writer:
        Hey, Cuz, I thought they were eagles circling above, a sign of good luck for Skins, but closer inspection revealed them to be the turkey vultures of broken English. Hey, Cuz, I remember once you sent me a hand-scrawled note saying you were out of typewriter ribbons and I sent you off fifty bucks that same day and you wrote back saying you got the ribbons and some Big Macs to boot. Young brother, now I am saddened down to the core of my sour-wine soul. Young brother. Young brother. You've become famous before your time.

My ancient mower refuses to eat any more lawn. It belches and farts and quits. The rusty steel teeth have had their fill. Sweating dusk sedates me so I nap on the couch and wake to the pine-goosed moon. With aching old muscles and a young heart slightly crazed by my own funk and thirst, I head out for the Stockman's Saloon in Rushville, Nebraska. It is quiet there when I walk in and order a nonalcohol beer and an *Omaha World-Herald*. In this newspaper made from blood of trees, I read about Johnnie Cochran and Marcia Clark in Los

Angeles. I have lived in that mutant world of concrete canyons. The bartender says L.A. deserves a thermonuclear enema. He is white and has green teeth. Me, I'd vote for Las Vegas or Nazi Serbia.

The pale professor who claimed to be Cherokee was spelunking in baleen. When she decried the whiteness of the whale and scrimshawed the blackboard, my sad soul tittered at her blubber butt jiggling. The poor woman would never see that Melville's big fish was an Indian whale. I should've let her taste the ripe redness of my hapless harpoon. Yippie-ki-yi-yo. I should've bowed, kissed her hand, and whispered that before he shipped out with Ahab, Queequeg had his lonely sperm frozen. And that I am one of his clones. Screw it all. I have written this several times before, but again I say that downtown, inside the Rez post office, a poster displays new stamps: romantic Indian war bonnets in hues never seen by our ancestors. Outside, bruised and bumbling winos trod by with Hefty bags full of flattened cans. Again I say that when Crazy Horse was murdered at Fort Robinson, the last living free Indian died. Except for me, darling. Except for me, sweetheart. All my life I have been young and this year I no longer am. The summer is putrid and I'm toying with six years of good behavior. Sweating and drinking near beer, I'm in the oven of a bordertown bar and I don't know why I crawled in. Maybe it has something to do with courage but the air is harsh and purple. I'm wedged in a narrow passage and it's purple-black and scurrying sounds are dancing in the darkness. I know Jehovah is dead so I'm praying to the television, yes, goddamn it, I'm praying to Phil Donahue that I won't start drinking:

> Help me, Phil. Let me free to be me! I'm an Indian morsel trapped in the guts of a cannibal called America who, for rabid religious reasons and a touch of trickledown economics, has shoved a pickle past its tight sphincters. I don't want to drink. No I don't, so help me, Phil. Clinch your lust-mongering, liberal fangs upon that dill, Phil, and yank the mother out.

Earth bone connected to the spirit bone. That's what I say in the chest-pain night. Heart bone connected to the ghost bone! And I pray that I could take all the imposed infirmities of flesh, all the little cancers, the tooth cavities, the blackheads, the failing kidneys, the wrinkling skin, the allergies, the aphasia, take all those bad things from one's body, suck them out by cosmic means, compress all those negatives into a compact ball of black star mass and hurl it into the sun. Then they would all pay . . . I mean pray. And the molten-golden dew of love would cover this land. But life is not so TV-easy. We cannot remove decay. Still, it is the wish of newness we desire. Like, if everything in our worn house could automatically become new: the sunken couch arises, the flickering TV becomes clear, the dog-stained rug becomes immaculate, and the walls are freshly painted . . . but life is not so TV-easy. And no. No molten-golden dew of love will ever cover this land.

Ponce de Leon was not searching for gold when he came trudging up the Everglades humming papal torture songs. We know that he was searching for the "fountain of youth." And so what (in my hours of darkness, when the computer of memory scrolls your ancient flashbacks) do I focus on, wish a return to? A moment of stolen sex, or an accidental hand-touching, or a wistful glance of some unrequited love? Maybe a touchdown pass in a high school football game? No! For the most part, I seem to want to return to pained points of failure. Earth bone connected to the spirit bone, indeed . . . and often the doors of memory are of no consequence.

I, Adrian, live in the land of the common doorbell. Every time the doorbell rings on a TV commercial, my dogs go wild and I jump up off the couch looking for a place to hide. Me, a middle-aged man acting like it's 1962: I'm a sophomore in high school, it's Saturday, and I'm in my cubbyhole of a room off the enclosed porch of the old railroad shack whacking off and the dogs start barking and I see a pickup churning up our dirt road. I am in my sanctuary, connecting my groin bone to the heaven bone. I do not worry until there is a pounding on the small pine door to my room. My Nutty-Putty heart ricochets around my half-breed rib cage. I pull up my pegged Levi's and peek out the door. There is Chris Brandon, fellow soph but a white boy, dressed in his usual, starched, button-down clothes. I smell the Vitalis on his flat-top with wings. He is no friend, only someone I pass in the halls, but what the hell is he doing here? On the porch outside my room is a bucket of soiled diapers from one of my little sisters. The entire corridor is swamped with shit-smell. The whole house is in dirty disarray. Burning shame makes my eyeballs flutter. In the living room I can see my illiterate, drunken white stepfather making small talk with Brandon's father. My brown mother is scurrying after the smaller kids and she's wearing a tattered gingham dress. Her black hair is electric and she's pregnant although the baby she's holding is less than a year old and the flypaper above my head is so covered with flies that it couldn't hold another, and worst of all, I've still got a boner, and Brandon looks down and spots it. At that instant I pray for nuclear attack. A complete devastation of mankind, of Adrian, of Brandon, of my entire known world existing in the midst of that Nevada Indian poverty thirty-three years ago. So, now I live in the land of the common doorbell. I live in the land of the common death. This is still Indian country and it is to the Indian spirits that I must pray. I must fill our home with prayer. Death and madness are hovering above our house. And I have the need of prayer. Earth bone connected to the spirit bone. I must pray for the woman I love. Her very mind is vanishing. I must burn sweet grass, sage, and pray with the pipe. And so I pray:

GRANDFATHER OF THE WEST—

In the setting sun of my birth, in the red blood air of my birth, I am praying to you. Pity me. Help me, please. Help me to help another whose mind is evaporating like rain on these July plains. Help me to help another who truly needs my help. With this first clump of tobacco into the pipe I pray for her.

GRANDFATHER OF THE NORTH—

Grandfather of this land of the pines and cold winds. Take pity on me. I do not pray for myself. I am praying for wholeness for all of us thus fractured. We are many, Grandfather. We are ghost warriors in the setting sun, an endless army of broken Skins. This second clump of tobacco goes in the pipe.

GRANDFATHER OF THE EAST—

Who lives where the sun rises and darkness is eased. This third clump is for you. Again, I pray for wholeness and for sanity. I pray for another who needs your help. I pray for a woman who needs your healing. She is a good woman, your Indian daughter. She has made her mistakes, but her heart is good. Upon all that is holy, I say she is kind. Upon all that is holy, she deserves to be whole.

GRANDFATHER OF THE SOUTH—

One toward whom we all face. I pray for wholeness and good health for someone I love dearly. This is not a prayer for myself. Please listen, Grandfather. This fourth clump of tobacco for you. Help her, please.

GRANDFATHER, WHO IS THE GREAT SPIRIT—

One who I call *Numanah,* and my woman calls *Tunkasila,* I pray to you. You are the Creator, you are the Great Spirit. You are our God. Pity me. Help me. Help me to be a good, strong man to an ailing woman. This fifth clump is to open your ears.

GRANDMOTHER EARTH—

Mother of us all. I pray to you, I pray for your feminine assistance. Pity me. Help me. Help me to help one of your daughter-sisters. And now the pipe is loaded. Now it is ready to be smoked. And now a second round of prayers. It is needed. Dear spirits, it is needed.

O SPIRITS OF THE WEST WIND—

Receive this pipe and have pity on your people. From you comes the Thunderbird who purifies the *inipi* and the earth. You correct our mistakes. We are frail and weak humans and we sometimes do not do things right. You keep us from doing wrong. You are the giver of rain and the beginning of life. The thunder of your Horse People from the Black Mountains fills us with awe. You are mighty. Send the Black Eagle to help us. We await your arrival.

SPIRITS OF THE NORTH—

You live in the sacred Red Mountains. From you comes the good, red road—the holy road of our people. It is with you the Sacred Buffalo Calf Woman stands. It is you who lead the Buffalo People out of lost darkness. Help me be strong and steady under this adversity. Enable me to walk the good, red road with a straight face. Let me not talk out of both sides of my mouth. Let me truly be humble and honest. Show me the starlight path that leads to the good land. Send your messenger, the Golden Eagle, to guide us. Help me as I pray to you with your sacred pipe. I am praying for one I love who, in her frailty, needs my love and strength.

SPIRITS OF THE EAST—

From you comes the Morning Star which radiates wisdom. From you comes the sun filling our dark world with light. From you comes the moon that gives us help and protection at night. In your Yellow Mountains the powerful Elk People shake their great horns. Send the Bald Eagle and help me gain wisdom that I may find the things to do and say to help the one I love. This is my need. This is what I pray for.

SPIRITS OF THE SOUTH—

Land where all living things face, where all the animal spirits live, have pity on me, and turn your face toward me. Send your messenger, the White Crane. Help me, in my need, help me to help the one I love. Help me to be strong for her and not against her. Let not my fear turn into anger. Let my love fly into her heart. Hear me, O Spirits of the South.

GRANDFATHER, GREAT SPIRIT—

Have pity on the lowly piece of crap that I am. Accept this humility as my true state and not some conjured prayer stick. You are powerful and above all things. All things come from you. You are the most holy. You are the most holy. Let your Spotted Eagle look down upon me and hear my prayer. You can do all things. Help me in my need to help the one I love.

GRANDMOTHER EARTH—

It is from you that we come, and it is to your arms that one day we shall return. From you comes all our food and all that grows. From you comes the medicine plants, the winged creatures, the four-legged, the things that swim and crawl. Grandmother, help me for I am pitiful. It is to your arms that one day we shall return, Grandmother, but for the one I love this is not the time. Spirits, I smoke this pipe and pray to you. My earth bone is connected to your spirit bone. *Mitakuye oyas'in.* For all my relations, but for one in particular.

And so it begins or ends . . . If I am not prayer, at least the prayer has been launched. Earth bone connected to the spirit bone. The rest is up to the spirits. I listen to the ghost talk of tumbleweeds, nightcrawling, rasping across the dry desert heart of my distant homelands. I listen and listen, but there is no real amen. A word comes, an English word with harsh Germanic overtones. A solitary word comes and erases the connection between earth bone and spirit bone. That word is Teutonic and Nazi-sounding. That word is Alzheimer's.

And now, fuck all the words I've ever uttered, it becomes the only word in our world.

FOR JOURNALING AND DISCUSSION

1. To whom does Louis pray? Compare the tone of his language when he is addressing either the "you" in his essay or us, his readers, to the tone of his prayers. How does his tone change?

2. As Louis's monologue unfolds, we learn that his mate suffers from a memory-robbing disease such as Alzheimer's. It is possible to interpret the "you" in this story as the woman he loves. Who or what else might he be addressing?
3. Louis offers us a different vision of Native American faith in relationship to mainstream American culture than does Diane Glancy, whose essay "The Bible and Black Elk" appears next in this chapter. How are their visions different? Why might they be different?
4. Is Louis angry? at what? at whom? Compare his anger to the emerging anger of the young man named John in Sherman Alexie's story "Integration" in Chapter 2.

FOR RESEARCH AND EXPLORATION

1. Research Chief Sitting Bull. What were his politics toward Euro-Americans? Why was he killed? Why is he important to Louis's story?
2. Louis defines himself as a middle-aged man trying to understand a reality of "many truths." Read a book about Native American spirituality written by a Native American; does Louis's Native American faith offer him different role model(s) than Christianity, Judaism, or Islam offer their followers? If you are Native American, discuss Louis's essay in terms of your family's and/or your own faith.
3. What is the meaning of Louis's title, "Earth Bone Connected to the Spirit Bone"? Find the lyrics to the old popular song "Dry Bones." How might this song be a clue to the meaning of his title?

The Bible and Black Elk

Diane Glancy

Diane Glancy is part-Cherokee, part-German, and part-English, and teaches at Macalester College in St. Paul, Minnesota. She is the author of two novels, three books of short stories, two collections of essays, and six books of poetry. She has won the Capricorn Prize for poetry and was the first recipient of the North American Indian Prose Award.

I think *Black Elk Speaks* is the Native American version of the Bible, especially the Book of Revelation. In fact, I think it is America's version of Revelation. Black Elk belongs to our continent. He was born in 1863. His vision dates from just over 100 years ago. John Neihardt's transcription of Black Elk's words was published in Nebraska in 1932. Black Elk is recent history.

Diane Glancy, "The Bible and Black Elk" from *Colors* (May-June 1994). Reprinted with the permission of the author.

It happened during climactic, tragic years of Plains Indian history. It happened in the years that led to the Battle of Wounded Knee, 1890, in South Dakota, when the U.S. cavalry opened fire on Dakota ghost dancers, who were trying to make their world come back.

Among Native people in those years there had been visions of the spirit world and prophecies of a coming doom. One of the seers was Black Elk. Like the Book of Revelation's John on Patmos, Black Elk left the earth in a vision. He says, "While I was there, I saw more than I can tell, and I understood more than I saw; for I was seeing in a sacred manner the shapes of all things in the spirit."

Black Elk's life, as well as his vision, centered around the change in the way of life that was coming for the Indian. Cataclysmic events. During the massacre at Wounded Knee, an Indian people and their lifestyle passed into the other world. Yes, the Indian people also survived, and their culture is still vital. But they suffered an apocalypse. Much of what they had known was over.

In Black Elk's vision the spirit world was revealing the end of one focus, and was the beginning of another. Describing one part of his vision, Black Elk said:

> I saw . . . a sacred man who was painted red all over his body, and he held a spear as he walked into the center of the people, and there he lay down and rolled. And when he got up, it was a fat bison standing there, and where the bison stood a sacred herb sprang up right where the tree had been in the center of the nation's hoop.
>
> I know now what this meant, that the bison were the gift of a good spirit and were our strength, but we should lose them, and from the same good spirit we must find another strength. (*Black Elk Speaks*, 1961 edition, pages 38–39)

Which gets to my point:

I cannot read *Black Elk Speaks* without thinking about the Bible, especially Revelation.

This is John on the isle of Patmos:

> After this I looked and, behold, a door was opened in heaven; and the first voice that I heard was, as it were, of a trumpet talking with me; which said, "Come up here, and I will show thee things which must be hereafter." And immediately I was in the Spirit, and behold, a throne was set in heaven, and one sat on the throne. (Rev. 4:1–2)

As a Christian, I visualize this man painted red and think of John's vision of Christ in Revelation: "And he was clothed with a vesture dipped in blood: and his name is called the Word of God." (Rev. 19:13)

Black Elk was a holy man of the Oglala Sioux. Dakota, they're called now. No, Lakota. He lived between the towns of Manderson and Pine Ridge, where John Neihardt, a white historian, went in 1930 to hear him. I know some Native Americans say that in changing Black Elk's words from oral to written form, the white man Neihardt didn't get it right. In fact, when Black Elk told his story, it was interpreted for Neihardt through Black Elk's son Ben, sometimes supplemented by other Black Elk friends, and transcribed by Enid, Neihardt's daughter. Then Neihardt retold it in his own words, and maybe the text shifted somewhat, and maybe Black Elk didn't mean what *Black Elk Speaks* says. But that isn't known for sure.

To complicate matters further, I'm interpreting the book from my own heritage—part Christian and white, part Cherokee, not Lakota. But that's what story is. You speak your voice in the midst of others, and some of your voice comes off. That's the way the Bible, the holy book of the white man (or some of the white men), is written. The four gospels tell the story of Jesus, each in its own voice, the way the creation story is told and retold, or added to, in Genesis. It's the accumulation style.

And this is Black Elk in his chapter, "The Great Vision":

> There were two men coming from the clouds, head-first like arrows slanting down, and I knew they were the same that I had seen before. . . . They came clear down to the ground this time and stood a little way off and looked at me and said: "Hurry! Come! Your Grandfathers are calling you!"
> Then there was nothing but air and the swiftness of the little cloud that bore me . . . where white clouds were piled like mountains . . . and the thunder beings lived and leaped and flashed. (page 22)

The two men in Black Elk's vision are alone with Black Elk in the middle of a great plain with snowy hills. Black Elk sees a horse, and then twelve horses in each of the four directions, some wearing elkteeth necklaces, some with manes that live and grow like trees and grasses. And then there are dancing horses without number. They change into animals and birds. Then the clouds around Black Elk change into a teepee, and a rainbow is the open door of it; and through the door are six old men, which are the powers of the world. One of the Grandfathers speaks and tells Black Elk he will be a healer of his people. Then the elder says:

> "Behold the earth!" So I looked down and saw it lying yonder like a hoop of peoples, and in the center bloomed the holy stick that was a tree. (page 29)

Compare that image with Revelation's:

> And he showed me a pure river of water of life, clear as crystal, proceeding out of the throne of God and of the Lamb. In the midst of the street of it, and on either side of the river, was there the tree of life, which bore twelve kinds of fruits, and yielded her fruit every month: and the leaves of the tree were for the healing of nations. (Rev. 22:1–12)

I define Christianity as salvation through faith in the blood of Christ—recognition that Christ's death on the cross is the basis for God's acceptance of me. "Jesus said, 'I am the way, the truth and the life: no man cometh unto the Father, but by me.' " (John 14:6). In other words, the Great Spirit has a world I'm invited to—but I cannot enter except on his terms.

I sometimes think of Indian tradition as the Old Testament, so to speak. Yes, the bison is the ark of the covenant for the Indian. And some Indians have rejected Black Elk's sacred red man, just as many Jews rejected Christ. I think John of Patmos and Black Elk each saw Christ in his own way.

Listen to this:

> In the Sierras before you come to the big water, there was a sacred man among the Paiutes who had talked to the Great Spirit in a vision, and the Great Spirit had told him how to make the wasichus [white man] disappear and bring back the bison and the people who were dead and how there would be a new earth. . . . The people sent three men, Good Thunder, Brave Bear and Yellow Breast to see this sacred man. . . .
>
> They said they traveled until they came to a great flat valley, and there they saw the Wanekia, who was the son the Great Spirit and they talked to him. Wasichus called him Jack Wilson, but his name was Wovoka. He told them that there was another world coming, just like a cloud. It would come in a whirlwind out of the west and would crush out everything on this world, which was old and dying. . . .
>
> This sacred man gave some sacred red paint and two eagle feathers to Good Thunder. The people must put this on their faces and they must dance a ghost dance that the sacred man taught to Good Thunder, Yellow Breast, and Brave Bear. If they danced, they could get on this other world when it came, and the wasichus would not be able to get on, and would disappear. . . .
>
> I heard the gossip that was everywhere now, and people said it was really the son of the Great Spirit who was out there; that when he came to the wasichus a long time ago, they had killed him; but he was coming to the Indians this time and there would not be any wasichus in the new world that would come like a cloud in a whirlwind and crush out the old earth that was dying. (pages 236–239)

Indians who ghost-danced were killed in cold blood at Wounded Knee. But if you look at it through apocalyptic Christian eyes, maybe the bison and ancestors were there to meet them at the door of death under the South Dakota sky. Who knows?

. . . I always thought there was something going on behind what I could see. I always needed to think so anyway. I got it from the Bible and from books like *Black Elk Speaks*. From instinct. From a feeling of incompleteness without it. From a hollowness in my own heart. From trips to my father's Cherokee people, hated by my white mother because of their superstition.

"Superstition" seems to me now the hard fact that other things happen. We have connections to earth and sky and ancestors. My father's people were Christian, not Traditional. But there were connectives between both heritages of my family, between Sunday School and Native story, between the creation explanations, Genesis and Cherokee:

> Let the waters under the heaven be gathered together into one place, and let the dry land appear. (Genesis 1:9)

> A piece of mud was placed on the water which grew into land. (Cherokee myth)

In other words, there was nothing, and then there was something.

There also are passages similar to each other about the sky in the midst of water:

> Let there be a firmament in the midst of the waters, and let it divide the waters from the waters. (Genesis 1:6)

> Now there was a wooden cup in his hand and it was full of water and in the water was the sky. (page 26)

I have always wondered how it was possible to combine both religions: The down-home Bible-belt Christianity; The Indian no-boundaried magical. But I had to do it. To make a dry ground in the midst of the uncertainty of my own life, and my belief system or spirituality.

It still isn't easy. Part of the liturgy at Mazakute Church, where I attend—a Native Christian congregation in St. Paul, served by [a] Native Episcopal priest—says: "We pray that all members of creation will be respected as relatives to all-that-is." So how does the Christian who has Native blood hear the Christian apostle Paul? According to him, in his Letter to the Romans, to honor animals may mean to worship the creation more than the Creator. How can such opposite thoughts be reconciled?

But much that Black Elk says sounds like the Bible.

He speaks of his people finding safety and peace "as little chickens under the mother sheo's [prairie hen's] wing" (page 34). In the Old Testament the Psalmist seeks refuge "in the shadow of thy wings" (Psalm 57:1). In the New, Jesus asks, "How often I have gathered my children together, even as a hen gathereth her chickens under her wings?" (Matthew 23:37)

Black Elk and the Bible both warn against the danger of following purely personal visions. Black Elk: ". . . each one seemed to have his own little vision that he followed and his own rules; and all over the universe I could hear the winds at war like wild beasts fighting" (page 37). The book of Judges laments a time when "there was no king in Israel, but every man did that which was right in his own eyes" (Judges 17:6).

Both the Bible and Black Elk use the image of grass for the transience of the body. "It does not matter where his body lies," says Black Elk of Crazy Horse, "for it is grass. But where his spirit is, it will be good to be" (page 149). "As for a man," says Psalm 103, "his days are like the grass."

Black Elk and Paul share a sense of receiving great power from the Spirit. Paul's boasts that "I can do all things through Christ who strengtheneth me" (Philippians 4:13). Black Elk recounts that in the midst of battle, coming to the aid of a fellow fighter under fire, "Just then, for a little while, I was a wanekia [life-giver, savior]" (page 275).

And in both the holy men there's humility as well. "I got off my horse," Black Elk says, "and rubbed earth on myself, to show the powers that I was nothing without their help" (page 271). Paul writes to his congregation, "I was with you in weakness, and in fear, and in much trembling. And my speech and my preaching were not with enticing words of man's wisdom, but in demonstration of the Spirit and of power" (I Corinthians 2:3–4).

When I read in Black Elk (page 41) that "his voice was not loud, but it went all over the universe and filled it," I think of Elijah hearing God's "still small voice" (I Kings 19:12) and of the voice in Revelation that had "the sound of many waters" (Rev. 1:15).

I also think of the similarity between Black Elk's and the Bible's concept of faith and works. According to Black Elk, "A man who has a vision is not able to use the power of it until after he has performed the vision on earth for the people to see" (page 208). According to Jesus, "Not every one that saith unto me, Lord, Lord, shall enter into the kingdom of heaven, but he that doeth the will of my Father, who is in heaven" (Matthew 7:21).

Now this emphasis on good works is in the same Bible that says, "By grace are ye saved through faith; and that not of yourselves . . . not of works, lest any man should boast" (Ephesians 2:8).

I like the contradictions in the Bible, the many voices telling, the unsureness as to actuality, the relative, the changing, turned-back-upon itself. That's what storytelling is.

I also like the personal uncertainty. I feel in Black Elk. The humanity. Black Elk agrees with the apostle Paul in this sense of "wretched man that I am" (Romans 7:24):

> But now that I can see it all as from a lonely hilltop, I know it was the story of a mighty vision given to a man too weak to use it; of a holy tree that should have flourished in a people's heart with flowers and singing birds, and now is withered; and of a people's dream that died in bloody snow. (page 2)

Black Elk had a vision given to a man who didn't understand. He regretted that he saw more than he could comprehend. But that's vision—to see somewhere out of this world. Part of it moving. A changing pattern that leaves us with the feeling of defeat and inadequacy, because we just can't pick up and go with it, or when we speak we're dumbfounded with all the incongruent things going on. And who would believe?

I believe Jesus loved Black Elk's people so much that he came to them before their apocalypse. I think he's done the same for me because I also need that same assurance. Something from part of my heritage was lost. There are many voices around me. Many things pulling at my life. I'm often uncertain. I feel the changing shapes. The brokenness.

> And I saw that the sacred hoop of my people was one of many hoops that made one circle, wide as daylight and as starlight, and in the center grew one mighty flowering tree to shelter all the children of one mother and one father. And I saw that it was holy. (page 43)

> In my father's house are many mansions. (John 14:2)

It's disarming and decentering to know that our way is only one of many. But that's what we need to see to be opened from the confinement of our hoop. It's what I think of when I see the bread broken during communion. It was Christ himself who was first broken.

It's not denomination or group that finally matters, but Christ as spirit, as story, as the living being of the word. Sometimes, blasted by the prayer and heat in the sweat-lodge ceremony, I feel the weighty, humbling matters that we face as we live.

> Two men were coming from the east, head-first like arrows flying and between them rose the daybreak star. They came and gave a herb to me and said: "With this on earth you shall undertake anything and do it." It was the daybreak-star herb, the herb of understanding, and they told me to drop it on earth. I saw it falling far, and when it struck the earth it rooted and grew and flowered, four blossoms on one stem, a blue, a white, a scarlet, and a yellow; and the ray from these streamed upward to the heavens so that all creatures saw it and in no place was there darkness. (page 43)

> Then the daybreak star was rising, and a Voice said: "It shall be a relative to them; and who shall see it, shall see much more, for thence comes wisdom; and those who do not see it shall be dark." (page 35)

I think Christ is that daybreak star. I think, "It is he who sitteth upon the circle of the earth" (Isaiah 40:22). I hear him proclaim, "I am the bright and morning star." (Rev. 22:16)

I treasure the multiplicity I find in meaning in Black Elk and in the Bible: the truths within Truth that I can live by. Whether from a personal apocalypse, or as one of the Native nation, I seek an escape, a lifting from this earth. Instead of a teepee with a rainbow door, I see a city (Rev. 21:22–23) of which God and the Lamb are the temple and the light. But the teepee and the city are the same.

I want that hope, anyway.

FOR JOURNALING AND DISCUSSION

1. Glancy is responding to a text that is based on Black Elk's words, interpreted by his son and written down by a white Christian man. What are some of the problems that you face as you try to understand what Black Elk might have really said? How is this like other kinds of historical work?
2. How much of what you read here is Glancy's projection of the Bible onto Black Elk's words? How many of the comparisons are convincing to you?
3. Can you reconcile Glancy's "inclusive" approach with some Christian doctrines that are "exclusive"? Consider for example, this translation of Christ's words: "I am the way, the truth and the life: no man cometh unto the Father, but by me" (John 14:6).

FOR RESEARCH AND EXPLORATION

1. Get a copy of *Black Elk Speaks* and a copy of the Christian *New Testament,* and read the passages that Glancy refers to in context. How does having the larger context confirm or reject her reading from your perspective? Write a paper in which you accept or reject her reading.

2. Do some further research on the process that was used to get the text of *Black Elk Speaks*. Write a paper about this, including some background from disciplines such as ethnography that deal with many of the issues that arise in this case, including authenticity, intention, and the interviewer's biases.
3. Investigate the beliefs of some Native American churches. What are some of the variations in addition to the one Glancy attends, which is led by a Native American Episcopalian priest? What is the connection between early Christian missionaries and some Native American churches?

Should Physicians Prescribe Prayer for Health? Spiritual Aspects of Well-Being Considered

Charles Marwick

A graduate of the University of Edinburgh and the Journalism School at Columbia University, Marwick has specialized in science writing for thirty years. He is a member of the National Association of Science Writers and since 1983 has been a biomedical science correspondent for the Journal of the American Medical Association *in Washington, D.C.*

Should physicians write "prayer" or "more frequent participation in religious observances" when prescribing for their patients? Some physicians, chaplains, pastoral workers, and sociologists would answer affirmatively.

"There is at work an integration of medicine with religion, of spirituality with medical practice, the twin guardians of healing through the ages," said Dale Matthews, MD, associate professor of medicine, Georgetown University School of Medicine, Washington, DC, at a meeting presented as "the first conference on Spiritual Dimensions in Clinical Research."

The meeting, meant to "explore the current body of knowledge and emerging trends in the area of spirituality and health," was held in Leesburg, Va, by the National Institute for Healthcare Research, a private organization devoted to examining the role of religious commitment in improving patient care and well-being. The agenda concentrated on three general areas: alcohol and other drug abuse, mental health, and physical health. Conferees reviewed the current status of the role of prayer and religious observance in maintaining health and outlined future research needs.

That there is considerable interest in this topic is illustrated by the fact that, apart from the Leesburg meeting, there have been three recent national conferences on the spiritual aspects of health. One was called Methodological Approaches to the Study of Aging, Health, and Religion and held by the National Institute on Aging (part of the National Institutes of Health, Bethesda, Md); another, held by hospital chaplains, was entitled Spiritual Assessments in Health Care Settings; the third meeting, The Roles of Religiosity and Spirituality in Medical Rehabilitation and the Lives of Persons With Disabilities, was held early this month by the National Center for Medical Rehabilitation Research.

RESPECT THE RELIGIOUS

"There is a need for primary care physicians to consider and respect the religious and spiritual beliefs of patients. To do otherwise might be considered unethical or even negligent," said speaker Stephen Post, PhD, associate professor, Center for Biomedical Ethics, Case Western Reserve University School of Medicine, Cleveland, Ohio. The evidence suggests that spirituality is an important medical tool that should be considered when developing a therapeutic regimen for the patient, he said.

Authoritative surveys have confirmed that Americans are highly religious. Gallup polls conducted in 1944 and again in 1981 showed consistently that around 95% believe in God, and 42% attend worship services weekly.

George Gallup, Jr, who also spoke at the meeting, reviewed a number of the surveys his organization has done since the 1930s that have sought to measure the religious beliefs of people in the United States. During a 35-year period, the Gallup Poll has surveyed Americans 12 times about their belief in God.

"We find that large majorities of Americans say that prayer is an important part of their lives, that they believe that miracles are performed by the power of God, and that they are sometimes conscious of the presence of God," Gallup said. Most of those surveyed named religious practices such as prayer, meditation, and reading the Bible as their way to deal with depression, said Gallup.

"Psychiatrists no longer dismiss out of hand the importance of religious faith in recovery from emotional illness and the healing power of forgiveness; there is a recognition of the connection between prayer and healing. A strong faith can have a profound effect on our lifestyles and outlook in terms of health," he added.

However, these earlier surveys did not probe deeply, Gallup said. "Many studies that link religious practices to health do not go far enough. We have been negligent about exploring this spiritual area of life. But this is changing rapidly. The public is being increasingly drawn to the nonmaterial aspects of existence."

Some psychiatrists may indeed no longer dismiss the importance of religion, as Gallup maintains, but by and large the profession remains skeptical. A survey by the American Psychiatric Association showed that only 43% of respondents said they believed in God—half that of the general population—and in a review of the published studies in four major psychiatric journals, only between 2.5% and 1.5% included a religious commitment variable, said David B. Larson, MD, president of the National Institute for Healthcare Research. In the primary care and family practice literature, the figure was even less—1%.

RELIGION AS A VARIABLE

In a review of 115 articles that included religion as a variable, 37 showed a positive effect on health, 47 showed a negative effect, and 31 had no positive relationship. However, Georgetown's Matthews pointed out that the measures of religiousness used in these studies were limited to noting such factors as attendance at worship. "Such single-item religiosity measures are not very effective; religious factors are multidimensional," he said.

If religion is not important to physicians, it is probably not a particularly influential factor in the health and well-being of others, said another speaker at the meeting, Jeffrey S. Levin, PhD, associate professor of family and community medicine, Eastern Virginia Medical School, Norfolk. Even if physicians acknowledge the importance of religion to patients, they may not regard it as a phenomenon that could promote healing and health, he said.

But for the most part, the speakers were positive regarding the influence of religion on health. Levin has made a study of the epidemiology of religion and health. He reviewed data on the effects of religion on outcomes in a number of conditions, including heart disease, cancer, tuberculosis, and suicide.

"Out of 27 studies that included a religious variable, such as church affiliation or regular religious involvement, 22 reported a significant, positive effect, and four had a positive effect, although the studies were not large enough to be statistically significant. This suggests, although it doesn't prove, that lack of religious involvement seems to be a risk factor [for poorer health]," he said.

Another example of the beneficial effect of religious commitment came from studies among the elderly reported by Harold G. Koenig, MD, assistant professor of psychiatry and internal medicine, Duke University Medical Center, Durham, NC. Many surveys have shown, Koenig said, that older people are by and large more religious than younger persons. "Belief in God increases as people get older. Bible reading and worship attendance increases with age," he said.

He pointed out that 50% of older adults attend church at least weekly. "That's an astounding figure," he said. "It means that every Sunday half the population of the entire United States over 65 is in church. One investigator figured out that the number of people attending church on one Sunday was equal to the number attending sports events during the entire year in the United States."

At the same time, Koenig noted that it is not clear whether this is because people do in fact become more religious as they get older, or simply that the studies are identifying an older cohort that is more religious.

Koenig has done a study of these older people that suggests that despite the presence of chronic disabling disorders, such as heart disease and diabetes, they are less likely to become depressed if they score high in religious coping. He defined "coping" as the use of religion to adapt to stress, such as prayer, faith in God, and Bible reading—"typical types of Judeo-Christian behavior," he said.

"One of the strongest predictors of depression is disability. In our study, we showed that those with the most severe disabilities, such as heart disease or diabetes, and who scored high in religious coping, were less likely to become depressed compared with those who scored low in religious coping," Koenig said.

"There is an inverse relationship between religious coping and depression that was strongest among the most disabled persons. It did not necessarily prevent the disability, but it did prevent or reduce the depression that accompanies disability," he said.

There also seems to be a dynamic effect. In a 6-month follow-up study of 200 people, those who scored high in religious coping suffered less depression. "This finding is probably more important than the cross-sectional finding," Koenig said. "Over time, those who were good religious copers became less depressed."

There have been similar studies elsewhere. "This is not an isolated phenomenon," he said. "It has been demonstrated by at least 50 different studies in many parts of the United States."

CALL FOR COLLABORATION

Koenig called for steps to educate health care providers concerning the effects of religion and for a collaboration between religious institutions and social service agencies to screen for health problems and to demonstrate that governmental agencies and religious bodies can work together.

"Spirituality and religion have important health benefits and more detailed studies using more accurate measures of this are warranted," said Larson. "The question today is not whether there are health benefits, it is how these benefits can be obtained. We can no longer afford to neglect this important clinical variable."

FOR JOURNALING AND DISCUSSION

1. How does Joseph P. Whelen's account of his and his sister's battles with cancer and the disease's effect on their spiritual life ("How I Pray Now," Chapter 7) support Marwick's conclusions?
2. Many faiths sponsor "prayer chains," or groups of people who come together specifically to pray for the recovery of an individual faced with a medical crisis.

Do individuals who are the focus of such prayer groups do better medically than individuals who face a crisis alone?

3. If you pray, keep a journal of your prayers. Are your communal prayers different from your private prayers? Are your prayers ever expressed metaphorically through other artistic mediums or always through the medium of words?

4. Revisit Adrian C. Louis's essay "Earth Bone Connected to the Spirit Bone," which appeared earlier in this chapter. In what ways do you think his prayers helped him cope with his distress?

5. Discuss how a patient might ask medical caregivers to include prayer in his or her treatment plan. Do you think having prayer officially recognized as part of a treatment plan by medical personnel can be of further benefit to the patient? What problems or complications might occur?

FOR RESEARCH AND EXPLORATION

1. Marwick quotes a doctor who refers to medicine and spirituality as "the twin guardians of healing through the ages." Research the historical relationship between medical science and religion. Did they have a compatible or competitive relationship? Write about your findings.

2. What happens physically and emotionally when a person enters into a state of prayer or spiritual meditation? Explore the physiological research that has been done, and write a paper about your findings.

3. Marwick analyzes why religion appears to be not very important to physicians, and he suggests that the surveys used to determine a doctor's relationship to religion are inadequate. Research the use of surveys as a measurement tool. What are some of the strengths and weaknesses of survey use in research?

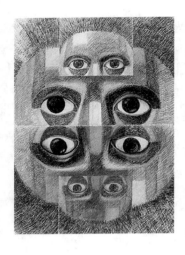

CHAPTER 6

Age

While some of the other factors that determine identity are indeed subject to change, age is, of course, *defined* as change over time. A person can have a certain outlook as a youth and then change it with age. Life experiences, education, tragedies, triumphs, and random accidents can alter a life's course. In this chapter we look at some of the changes that people have undergone as they age, as well as certain stereotypes of both young people and the elderly.

The United States is, according to many experts, obsessed with youth. Even though aging "babyboomers" outnumber young people in this country, advertisers cater to a youthful image and the boomers strive to keep up, joining health clubs and gobbling vitamins in record numbers. "Generation X-ers" struggle to define themselves in contrast to their parents and to shed dated images. Stereotypes of youth (wild, out of control) and age (decrepit, slow) can be found throughout history, but the particulars of these stereotypes vary from one generation to another.

In the introduction to this book, we stressed that all of the identity factors interact with each other. Gender, for example, is one of the defining factors in age stereotypes. Feminists in the women's movement have attempted to disrupt some of the stereotypes about aging women, reclaiming words such as "crone" and "hag" and using them as positive descriptors. A plethora of new books describe the postmenopausal woman as entering into a period of wisdom and freedom unavailable to younger women. While men have more often been venerated for the wisdom that comes with age, in the latter half of the twentieth century, being an "old boy" has not been a good thing.

Attitudes about age also vary with social class. In the community described in Tina Rosenberg's essay "On the Row," for example, a twenty-year-old is an adult, ready to marry, to drink, to bear arms and children—and to receive the death penalty for a crime committed as a juvenile. In middle- and upper-middle-class communities, however, many twenty-year-olds are still students supported by their parents, a few years away from "full" adult status.

In some regional and ethnic communities, elders are treated with more respect than they are in the general population, and children are taught to carry on this tradition. As you read these essays, consider how age, gender, race, class, religious or spiritual beliefs, region, and nationality influence your view of aging.

SUMMARIES OF SELECTIONS ON AGE

In "The Changing Seasons of Liberal Learning," **David D. Cooper** describes the generational "changing of the guard" within the academy. His description of a university "Shantytown," erected to heighten "awareness of various social issues after a long winter of Big-Ten basketball and political hibernation," reveals the conflicts that arise from differences in perspective, public policy, and conceptions of human morality. He contrasts today's students, and their variety of attitudes, with the "baby boomer" generation of professors who are now running the nation's colleges and universities, and bemoans the current fate of the liberal arts.

Terry McMillan's first-person story is told in the voice of a "wise crone" who describes the economic reality of many seniors. The title character of "Ma' Dear" is an African American woman who takes in boarders to supplement her income. Although she's a bit lonely, remembers her youth and beauty nostalgically, and is somewhat critical of today's generation, she's comfortable with who she is now and takes good care of herself.

In her autobiographical, first-person essay "Beauty: When the Other Dancer Is the Self," **Alice Walker** describes how her identity and her relationship to beauty have changed over time. As a child, she tells her father, "Take me, Daddy, . . . I'm the prettiest!" But then, everything changes one day when her brother shoots her in the eye with a BB gun. Her story reveals how as an adult she makes peace with this childhood trauma.

Bailey White's memoir about summers in her childhood, "An Old Lepidopterist," describes the respectful relationship she had with an aging man, who catalogued butterflies in Georgia, and his wife, who taught Bailey and her cousins needle crafts. During those enchanted days, Mr. Harris tells great stories about his youthful experiences as a lepidopterist and takes Bailey away from needles in search of butterflies. By the end of his life, he has forgotten everything he ever knew about butterflies, but his legacy lives on with White and with monarch butterflies in coastal Georgia.

Dan Fost's "Farewell to the Lodge" shows the impact of shifting economic and demographic conditions, as well as changing gender roles, on all-male lodges. He cites evidence that attitudes toward civic and social responsibility have changed in the generations after World War II. Subsequent generations of American men are not attracted to all-male, "old boy" clubs and to conformity. And yet substitutes such as the "virtual community" on the Internet are not satisfactory replacements.

Tina Rosenberg uses Joseph Hudgins's story to illustrate life "On the Row" for young murderers, some of whom were legally children when they committed their crimes. She writes that people today consider young people dangerous: "crazier, with more bravado and less conscience." She describes the "collective history" of many juvenile offenders as being "littered with abusive parents, uninterested doctors, and neglectful or bungling bureaucrats," none of whom "has ever been indicted as an accessory to murder."

RHETORICAL QUESTIONS

As you analyze the essays in this chapter, consider the *stance* of each writer. What are their attitudes and beliefs about aging? about other factors? From what vantage point do they write? If they are writing from the perspective of the aged person, for example, as do McMillan and Walker, what details do they provide from an insider's perspective? In McMillan's case, the character is fictitious; in Walker's, she herself is the focus. How do these two ways of presenting a point of view differ?

White writes about two older people from the vantage point of an adult remembering them from her childhood. How does memory affect her presentation of these characters? How does her recollection compare to Walker's memories of her childhood?

Fost, Cooper, and Rosenberg are reporting for magazines, but their stances are very different. Cooper and Rosenberg are present in the communities they describe, but Cooper is an insider and Rosenberg is an outsider. Fost is a relatively detached reporter, and we cannot be sure whether he has ever attended a lodge meeting. Consider how their stances determine the kinds of details they include and the tone they use with their subjects.

If you write about personal experiences, you will need to determine whether you will write in the present tense, as though you are a participant and events are happening around you, or in the past tense, as though they are history. If you report others' experiences and data, you will have to determine what your relationship is to the material. Are you an insider or an outsider? What are your attitudes and beliefs about the subject? How will you reveal these to your reader? Or will you?

The Changing Seasons of Liberal Learning

David D. Cooper

Cooper, a native of Phoenix, received his Ph.D. from Brown University in 1977. He is the author of Thomas Merton's Art of Denial: The Evolution of a Radical Humanist, *and the editor of* James Laughlin and Thomas Merton: Selected Letters. *In 1991, Cooper was the Eli Lilly Distinguished Visitor of Religion and American Culture at Berea College. He was also a Woodrow Wilson Fellow, and includes among his awards and honors grants from the National Endowment for the Humanities.*

In the spring of 1990, several student groups at my campus erected shanties on a newly reclaimed "People's Park." Growing out of a protest symbolism spurred by the anti-apartheid and endowment divestiture movements that briefly flourished on college campuses nationwide during the mid-1980s, the People's Park shanties were aimed initially at heightening awareness of various social issues after a long winter of Big-Ten basketball and political hibernation.

The first five shanties were united into a community "Shantytown" by a common protest discourse and shared political alignments. The groups included H.U.R.T. (Helping to Understand Racism Today). The Democratic Socialists of America set up a shanty protesting homelessness in America and promoting an alternative social vision of what its members felt was fairer economic justice. Another shanty, organized by the student Committee for Education on Latin America (C.E.L.A.), stood as a memorial to the late Salvadorian archbishop and martyred social democrat Oscar Romero. Sponsored by the local chapter of Take Back the Night and a proactive environmental group, the remaining two shanties advanced this theme of political dissent and consciousness-raising linked to underclass empowerment.

The first counter-protest shanty appeared barely two weeks after People's Park was reclaimed as the protest turf of liberal student organizations. Built by C.A.S.H. (Conservative Anti-Shanty Haters), the anti-shanty shanty differed as much in visual appearance as in political alignment from those erected earlier. Instead of a jury-rigged A-frame, C.A.S.H.'s shanty was scaled along lines of a conventional suburban ranch, looking like something out of a Bob Vila cassette. It was painted white. The window frames and fascia were neatly trimmed in the school colors, Spartan Green. Plastic geraniums sprouted from window flower boxes flanking the front door. A white picket fence ran the perimeter of the shanty's mock front yard. Tidy stepping stones led from the gate to a front door welcome mat. *The Wall Street Journal* was cradled in a mailbox which bore a street number—1899—and a nicely painted "fleur-de-lis." On the roof, the initials "C.A.S.H." and "P.O.L.O." were nicely lettered in the block-style of the famous Spartan "S." (The latter acronym, like a gap-toothed word puzzle on the popular TV quiz show "Wheel of Fortune," was the subject of much speculation in the student newspaper.) Two chaise lounges graced the front yard, one garnished tastefully by another edition of *The Wall Street Journal* opened to the stock tables. The C.A.S.H. architects placed a placard on the front lawn that carried the anti-shanty shanty's visual imagery into verbal territory. Pro-corporate, anti-rain forest, pro-deforestation slogans were bolstered by anti-liberal sentiment clothed in the popular cant of ardent nationalism, including "Cry Me a River: The American Way of Life is the Only Way" and "Support Your Constitution and Your Flag." More bellicose were reminders of C.A.S.H.'s social agenda: "Scum: Go Back to Where You Belong" (an apparent allusion to C.E.L.A.'s memorial to Oscar Romero) and a swipe at the feminist orientation of Take Back the Nighters, "Put the 'e' back in Womyn." An anti-affirmative action slogan directed against H.U.R.T. elicited a comment spraypainted on the sidewalk in front of C.A.S.H.'s gate: "Fear of a Black Planet!" That graffiti, in turn, drew an irate response in a letter to the student newspaper from a "sophomore computer science major" who complained about vandalism to the university's sidewalks. "People's Park is ugly enough," he protested. "Must we make the ugliness permanent?"

Other anti-shanty shanties quickly proliferated. The organizer of S.A.L.T. (Students Against Liberal Trash) was quoted in the campus newspaper as saying, "I am willing to be publicly viewed as an idiot just to get people thinking and also to heighten their awareness about issues." His martyrdom, his efforts at consciousness raising, and his calculation of personal IQ inspired the following hieroglyphics inscribed on S.A.L.T.'s own anti-shanty shanty: "Affirmative Action Sucks," "Get Help Gays," and "Minority in a Minute" with an arrow pointing to a bucket of black paint.

The counter-current of conservative student animus stirred by C.A.S.H. and S.A.L.T. soon unleashed a nastier undercurrent of intolerance from anonymous quarters of the student body. A final anti-shanty shanty was surreptitiously constructed one night, and the next morning People's Park was greeted by the following comments:

> "White Niggers Go Too!"
> "Fuck Affirmative Action. Let Them Work Like We Do"
> "5,000,000, Wasn't Enough"

(That latter statistic was apparently an anti-Semitic allusion to the six million Jews who perished in the Holocaust. But who's keeping count? Hard-working students don't have time to track down *every* statistic.)

"We Can't Have Queers Protecting Our Country or Flag"
"I'm Not Racist. But I Keep My Genes Clean"
"If You Are Looking for Problems in America, Check the Jew and Nigger Community"

The campus administration, citing anti-obscenity regulations, moved quickly (and properly) to dismantle the last shanty erected before the entire issue of the People's Park revival languished into summer vacation, and then completely disappeared.

Today's neoconservative, indeed reactionary campus outfits like C.A.S.H. and S.A.L.T. reveal the stark changes that have swept over college campuses, like a great social tsunami, in the past twenty years or so. For those undergraduates of my generation who rode out the campus storms of the late sixties and early seventies, who entered academic life in a flush of intellectual vitality leavened by social idealism, who hunkered down and (barely) survived the prolonged (and continuing) famine of the academic job market that began in the mid-seventies, who managed somehow to stay awake (and employed, even if marginally) during the eighties when the intellectual climate in Arts and Humanities was dominated by ponderous, narcoleptic theoretical abstractions, and who now find themselves—politically ambivalent, ideologically winded, intellectually adrift, publicly excoriated—on the doormat of what promises to be a new era of fiscal retrenchment and metaphysical revolution, the past couple of decades seem like nothing less than a complete flip-flop in the moral tonality—the "feel"—that defines the life of institutions of higher education. The political cartoonist Gary Trudeau captured something of that kaleidoscopic shift in consciousness and mood when, in one of his last panels before taking an extended vacation from the Op-Ed pages, he had Mike Doonesbury, a consummate Babyboomer, grasp his head—partly in confusion, partly in recognition, partly in desperation—and declare, "I have become my parents!" For those 1970s Ph.D.s whom *The Chronicle of Higher Education* not long ago labeled collectively as "the lost generation," I wonder: have students become our parents too?

Linear metaphors that measure progress, growth, transformation, and synthesis are inadequate to describe the changes that are the ballast to Doonesbury's epiphany. Metaphors of transmutation or antithesis—like the Uroboros, the symbol of a snake swallowing its tail, or, more simply, of a sock being turned inside out—seem more appropriate and accurate. One wonders if the vapid material determinism, the ethical relativism, and the moral self-enclosure of today's college students are *transmutations* of the iconoclastic mysticism that animated—powerfully, if only briefly—my generation and scribed its ideological trajectory: the return of the hipster in a three-piece suit. Can we reach back into the sixties and grasp tightly to idealism and communitarianism—"Ask not what your country can do for you but what *you* can do for your country"—and pull forward through two decades to find them transmuted into an antithetical fatalism, acquisitive individualism, uncritical conformism? "Ask not what you can do for your country, but what's in it for me." Has Allen Ginsberg become Madonna?

Such transmutations look entirely different, however, from the vantage point of a present generation struggling to emerge into self-definition from the ominous shadow cast by a previous generation whose rebelliousness must feel almost like a moral obligation to today's students. Imagine what a legacy of social activism feels like to today's understandably cynical undergraduates who have learned a sour lesson about the possibilities for social change from their own generation's defining historical moments, from gas lines, Watergate, and a Hostage Crisis to Iran-Contra, the S & L fiasco, and Rubbergate. Sometimes it seems as if the only viable alternative for them is self-enclosure, withdrawal from the social arena altogether, or a retreat into privacy, nihilism, or the tenuous rewards of careerism.

Raised on TV culture where reality comes at them through the webless seam of television news, today's students are drawn into, according to Neil Postman, "an epistemology based on the assumption that all reports of cruelty and death are [transient and] greatly exaggerated and, in any case, not to be taken seriously or responded to sanely." Pessimism about the future is reinforced by a pervasive historical pessimism among many adults to whom the past looks no better than the future. Historical pessimism is especially heightened—indeed *warranted*—as the current generation views the past from the vantage point of a present where debate rages over the deterioration of values, the loss of ethical standards in business, and the general decline of civility in America suggested by the popular slogans of a president imagining a kinder, gentler nation during a decade of governmental gridlock, record-breaking murder and suicide rates, and bracket creep among statistics that track violent crime. Not to mention the terribly confusing signals sent by an advertising industry intent on linking the empowerment of women and minorities to consumerism and the cult of celebrity, and the equally confusing signals sent by pundits like Rush Limbaugh and Maxine Waters who argue over differences between riots and insurrections while America's inner cities seethe with resentment and despair. Consider too the unprecedented hammering of Generation X starting with *Nation at Risk,* continuing unabated throughout the 80s, buttressed by a high-brow pummelling handed out by Allan Bloom in his best seller *The Closing of the American Mind,* and tracked with great precision by Alexander Austin and the Higher Education Research Institute at UCLA, whose annual logarithms suggest that each year's high school graduation class appears generally stupider and more socially disengaged than the previous year's. Is it any wonder Leon Botstein reluctantly concludes that "a sense of decline, deterioration, and futility hangs over the American classroom"?

Few young persons have managed as clean a breakthrough as twenty-something writer Arion Berger, who has come to feel "less need to borrow identities" from the omnipresent earth-rattling Sixties culture, "less fear that I'll wake up and be someone I did not create and cannot change. I've learned that underneath the fakery I've rented there's something that's mine alone. . . ." For most people Ms. Berger's age, however, there are other lessons to be learned from the cultural fault lines that separate college students today from the Babyboomer professoriate just now rising to demographic—and political—prominence on campus. Perhaps more to the point is the confused animosity felt by a senior at Cornell University sparked by forty-three-year-old Jim Klein's film "Letter to the Next Generation." The student fired off a letter of his own to Klein (and *his* generation) immediately after the film first aired on public television in July, 1990. While in many ways moved by the film's challenges to his generation, the student's letter eventually turns to the intergenerational anxieties of influence that are too often unacknowledged irritants in faculty/student relations today. "I do hate to say it," the senior letter-writer admits, but "many in my generation resent the generation before—the Baby Boomers."

> Many young people [today] see the Boomers as a generation that grew up in the Levittowns with no cares, went to college as a matter of course and denounced the wealth they always knew their families could give them in a bind, played activist for a while and became investment bankers when they got tired of it, while continually stopping on the way to dump tons of garbage on Woodstock, develop a sexist-as-hell hippie culture, and generally chew up the world and spit it out as they saw fit. Baby Boomers still have news reports about them, have a special edition of Trivial Pursuit just for them, have a Top 40 pop song (Billy Joel's "We Didn't Start the Fire") about the span of their lives and how they really are absolved of all responsibility for all that's happened, etc., etc., etc., etc. Who in our ignored generation *wouldn't* feel irritated, angered, and insecure enough to just want to buy all the dinosaurs out and shut them up once and for all? Or so goes the diatribe of many of my contemporaries, and yes, I sympathize, and even share some of the sentiments. . . . It's what happens when you are part of a generation without a name, overshadowed by another generation that refuses to fade away.

There is plenty in the film that justifies, although may not completely warrant, the letter-writer's own diatribe, for in fairness to Klein his film—which chronicles a return to Kent State University twenty years after the infamous May 4th killings of four students by National Guardsmen during an antiwar rally—is as introspectively questioning of his own generation as it is bluntly critical of contemporary Kent State students with their ball caps on backwards, singing "The Brady Bunch," theme song for Generation X. Part of the film's strength is its parallel avenues of insight into both a past generation's difficulty in letting go of its post-adolescent iconoclasm and its indefatigable mystique of nonconformity, and a present generation's cynical detachment from social concerns and its desperate search for ways to fit in—insights at loggerheads in the film until mediated by a charge to the "Next Generation" to step meaningfully into the breach.

But the film is mostly about intergenerational antagonism, about two generations uneasily eyeing each other from across a values divide that seems, at times, unbridgeable, without a common language or a binding history, without a shared moral discourse that might otherwise fill the awkward moments when fortysomething faculty (and filmmakers) and students stare blankly, even smugly, at each other, the dialogue silenced by faculty disillusionment on one side and student skepticism on the other.

The film is loaded with imagery that, frankly, indulges the stock values stereotypes often exploited by mass media (e.g., *Time* magazine's 16 July 1990 cover story on twentysomething angst) to market the Thirteenth Generation's crisis of disbelief. Those stereotypes include the ubiquitous (and ironic) dualism that pits what one student calls "the regular world" against the fast-food corporate wonderland of campus life; the self-enclosure, vanity, apathy, and cynicism routinely ascribed to today's college students, along with their disconnection from history, their obsessive career orientation and penchant for résumé-building; the prevalence of the corporate paradigm at Kent State with its ethic of efficiency, cost-effectiveness, style-brand recognition, team work, professionalism, productivity, regulated consumption, and its clearly demarcated lines of decision-making, authority, reward; and, not the least, the majority of Kent students' insensitivity to and general unconcern for issues of race/class/gender pressed unrelentingly by the campus left. As on most campuses, that latter trend is countervailed at Kent State by a small minority of students whose commitments to wider social concerns put to rout the charge of pervasive self-interest and political disengagement too often leveled at college students today by disaffected Babyboomers. It was this juxtaposition of conflicting commitments that prompted another college senior to write Klein barely two hours after the film aired. "Your mixture of the negatives and positives that exist in the reality of our generation," she said, "touched hard. The way you looked at the events that shaped (and are still shaping) our generation into a primarily capitalistic and financial-success oriented society were so understandable. . . . Your film is an inspiration to those of us who *see*," she concluded, "as well as those who have yet to."

"Letter to the Next Generation" is full of more treatments of intergenerational friction than are possible to explore in much detail here. But there are three episodes which might serve as a vivid backdrop to the discussion that follows, maybe part of the sociomoral scenery that Gary Trudeau had in mind when he staged Mike Doonesbury's initiation into nineties adulthood and his sudden realization of what it's really like growing up absurd.

In the first scene, Klein takes his camera into "Kent's Electric Beach," a tanning salon on the campus perimeters where, we are told, about a hundred students a day work on their tans. A student lies on a tanning bed that looks like a cross between a neon clam shell and an iron lung. She is wearing a bikini and eye-cups.

FEMALE ON TANNING BED: I just really enjoy the tan and I enjoy having color in my skin. It makes me feel a lot better about myself and it's also a lot healthier looking. . . .

FILMMAKER TO TANNING GUYS: What types of women do you like?

TANNING GUYS: Tan. Definitely tan. . . .

I could pass a tan for other things.

If she doesn't have a tan . . . we'll get her a tan.

That's a big question. What do we like them for? I mean, like them to keep. Two or three years from now I'll be looking for a wife, look for a nice little homebody to settle down with but right now it's hot . . . definitely hot. . . .

FEMALE ON TANNING BED: Well, I like to keep myself in shape and I like to look great and I like to exercise.

Later, Klein visits a class session for a sociology course on Utopian Societies. The professor first came to Kent State in 1967. While teaching sociology, he also took part in early demonstrations against the Vietnam war and was indicted for incitement to riot after the May 4th shootings.

PROFESSOR AT THE BLACKBOARD: The idea is to reward everyone at least similarly. . . . Regardless of ability. Don't reward ability.

STUDENT: If you don't reward ability you won't have any incentive . . . why would a doctor want to be a doctor? or a lawyer be a lawyer when we're all going to get the same amount of money?

STUDENT: Chances are a lot of people who would be doctors and be good doctors won't become doctors.

PROFESSOR IN FRONT OF CLASS: . . . if you're doing something that is rather interesting and being a medical doctor is probably pretty interesting—I know being a Ph.D. is interesting. Then that's kind of its own reward. If you think of yourself as having to measure up to standards, you're playing their game by their rules, you have to take the system as given and you never will try to change it. You'll just try to make yourself comfortable within it. This is what the professional does. This is what I do. I make myself comfortable within a rotten system and I get off the hook by telling others that we should all ban together and change this as best we can.
(Students take notes.)

After class, Klein asks the Sociology Professor what kinds of questions his students ask. "Not many," he replies.

   Near the end of the film, Klein interviews a student in his dorm room. He comments on a poster taped to the wall, a sumptuous photograph of two sports cars flanked by a phrase printed elegantly along the top.

STUDENT: I thought it was kind of unique, you know. That little saying up top, you know, "The Rewards of a Higher Education" . . . you make it through this is what you're going to get, you know. . . . My mama bought that for me for a Christmas gift. . . .

FILMMAKER: What do you see your goal coming out of college to be?

STUDENT: Wow, like goals is like materials or like within me?

FILMMAKER: Whatever. . . .

STUDENT: Getting a good job. . . . Feel like I had done something, you know, for the corporation.

FILMMAKER: You know what I see missing? The thing I'm really interested that you don't say is that . . . what would make you feel a success . . . if you had really helped change somebody's life . . . or made a difference say in the society or like that . . . do you ever think about that?

STUDENT: Like helping someone out . . . like philantropic {*sic*} like that way, you know? . . . No, I've never really thought about helping my fellow man if that's what you're bringing up, which is I can see what you're getting at. . . . That is missing I think definitely from the college student of the 80s.

During the Free Speech and Anti-War Movements of the Sixties, some faculty members, like Richard Sewall, a professor of literature at Yale, misread the dramatic upheavals on college campuses as a new millennialism, "a coming of age," he put it then, "on the part of students, a putting away of the trivia inherited from the past [and] a real desire to enter into and share the true spirit of the University community." Peter Clecak, a historian at the University of California, Irvine (which, during the mid-sixties, not incidentally, was gearing up a building program to fulfill Clark Kerr's vision of the "true spirit" of the new American "multiversity"), correctly assessed the connection between student unrest over the Viet Nam War and the numbing bureaucratization of academic life. Clecak wrote sympathetically of students who complained vociferously about "a lack of 'identity' and an absence of 'community' " on college campuses. Student agitation, he figured, derived from an encounter with "the institution of the 'system' [as] confusing, impersonal, and depersonalizing." Students resent, he noted, "those of us [on the faculty] who fail to develop—or even to seek—a style adequate to what we profess and adequate to the students' need for admirable and imitable adults. In short, they find the faculty morally corrupt, emotionally stunted and intellectually sterile—irrelevant . . . to their lives."

The same charges stick today. Except, like role models and generational heroes—Clecak's "imitable adults"—the charges have to be turned inside out. Paraphrasing Sewell, faculty today are likely to view *students* as thriving on conventions and trivia inherited from the past and possessing, at best, a reluctance, at worst, a repugnance to enter into and share in the "true spirit" of a university community. Faculty today are more inclined to deride *students* for what students twenty years ago derided *faculty* for: namely, as having no desire to seek or develop what faculty profess as adequate, admirable, and "imitable" young persons! Most astonishingly, students today still find faculty, for the most part, emotionally inept, intellectually sterile, and especially irrelevant to their lives. But in the topsy-turvy world of the academic establishment and the poster industry over the last two decades, it is an irrelevancy turned completely inside out. Clecak sensed an irrelevancy of "being" in the student critiques of faculty during the heady days of campus unrest and political agitation. Students today, pounding the career fast-track, are much more likely to dismiss faculty, instead, with an irrelevancy of "doing," a perception that professors, in the humanities and social sciences in particular, are cut off from "the regular world," alien to the status quo, too politically and ideologically supercharged, incomprehensibly theoretical, out of the real action and, hence, totally irrelevant as "imitable adults." That conflict of relevancies is painfully present in the Kent State sociology class on Utopian Societies when students argue in favor of the incentives and rewards accruing to a professional class of doctors and lawyers, while the professor struggles awkwardly to explain the intrinsic satisfactions of doctoring and "being a Ph.D." before degenerating into confused, cynical self-contradiction.

The glacial changes in the tenor of academic life that my generation has both witnessed and inspired can be seen most vividly, as a friend suggests, by contrasting the parasitic institutions that have always clustered around campus fringes like commercial barnacles. Twenty years ago campus environs were encrusted with falafel stands, co-ops, book stores, coffee houses, and head shops. Today: Taco Bells, tee-shirt emporiums, copy house franchises, chicken joints, and the ubiquitous tanning salon. Such trivialities underscore larger and more meaningful changes in institutional life that reflect cultural shifts away from a communal orientation to a new corporate establishment. Even in its own small way, the evolution from falafel stands to tan-in-the-cans illustrates a paradigmatic shift that Jurgen Habermas tracks away from crumbling "Lifeworld" structures (family, parish, synagogue, civic associations) to ascendent "Systemworld" bureaucracies, vehicles to status, wealth, professional expertise, and career mobility that reward today's professors as much as they inspire today's students in their fast-track baccalaureate worlds of food systems delivery and turf grass management.

In 1964, Mario Savio, the leader of the Free Speech Movement at the University of California, Berkeley, waxed incessantly about a "community of love" engendered among students tired of the alienation between faculty and the student body brought on by a post-Sputnik retooling of higher education into the new superefficient megaversity—sprawling, specialized, microengineered, depersonalized—that I entered in Fall, 1966, an integer in a vast sea of other Freshman units. Fast-forward to 1991 and the zebra-coded corporate model that now dominates campus life, a model in which very few students are in the least troubled [by], much less question, the student/faculty separation that prevails everywhere on campuses fractured and shrink-wrapped into what Stephen Toulmin calls "specialized modes of abstraction": divisions, units, programs, taskforces, departments, and committees where "broad and general questions about . . . 'interrelatedness' . . . have been superseded by other, more specialized, disciplinary questions."

That evolution from community to corporation, from interrelatedness and generalization to subspecialization and efficiency, can also be seen in prevailing styles of scholarship, especially in the humanities, and the connection—or, as the case may be now, the radical *disconnection*—between what faculty authors write and what students read. During the falafel era, a high water table of scholarship, much of it produced by certified academics, fed the springs of undergraduate bookshelves. Upon reflection, the bibliography looks remarkably eclectic, if not terribly resilient, and includes familiar names like McLuhan, Chomsky, Marcuse, Roszak, Sontag, Toffler, and Carson, along with less well known authors like George Leonard and William Irvin Thompson and even some transgenerational intellectuals like C. Wright Mills, Dwight MacDonald, Louis Mumford, Michael Harrington, and Jane Jacobs, many of whom were decidedly anti-academic-establishment but whose work could hardly be considered non-scholarly or intellectually dumbed down. Consider, for example Norman O. Brown's *Love's Body*. Unsurpassed in erudition, Brown's book made a tremendous impact on college campuses when first published in 1966. It was read and discussed widely by faculty *and* undergraduates. Brown's integration of philosophical discourse, literary analysis, and psychoanalytic investigation, played out against the backdrop of intellectual history and cultural politics, established a model of interdisciplinary scholarship that would fall out of fashion in the late seventies when "interdisciplinary" suddenly became synonymous with "undisciplined" or "unspecialized." Today it is virtually impossible to identify a work of contemporary academic scholarship that is known, much less read, by even a narrow swath of undergraduates. (Allan Bloom's *The Closing of the American Mind* naturally comes to mind, although I have yet to meet an undergraduate who's read it, much less quarrels with its conclusions. While not strictly interdisciplinary, recent books by Deborah Tannen and Stephen Hawking are rare exceptions which prove the rule.) Interdisciplinary scholarship on the order of *Love's Body* has given way to a species of metacritical discourse practiced by a fairly tight circle of theoretically-inclined, annoyingly self-referential, and unwriterly academic superstars whose work remains cloistered in the netherworld of advanced graduate theory seminars convened at advanced humanities institutes, marooned on lists of Works Cited or in the reduced fonts where academic immortality resides, cryogenically suspended in databases. In lieu of *Of Grammatology*, today's undergraduates opt for clarity in their reading, like Matt Groenig's phenomenally successful cartoon collections—*School Is Hell*, for example—depicting school life as a values wasteland and adulthood generally as a grinding, laughable bore. Or nicely packaged business primers that fuse entrepreneurial savvy and the cult of personality into potent best sellers, like Thomas Peters and Robert Waterman, Jr.'s *In Search of Excellence*, or *The Seven Habits of Highly Effective People* by Steven Covey. Meanwhile, pitched battles flare up around campus over such things as canon revision, curriculum reform, phallocratic culture, logocentric signifiers, and the social construction of human consciousness.

Whether post-Sputnik Babyboomers took the push for "relevancy" in education seriously or not, at least they listened intently to radical critiques of their schooling during a decade when discussions about educational reform were acrimonious, heated, usually prickly, sometimes otiose, but they never seemed to run cold. Radical reformers like Paul Goodman (*Compulsory Mis-Education*), Charles Silberman (*Crisis in the Classroom*), and Paulo Freire (*Pedagogy of the Oppressed*) fanned the reform discourse so effectively because they treated the school environment not, like today, as a boot camp for American corporations, but as a place where the demands of the society met the needs of individuals in a creative and critical tension. To Goodman and the others, school needed to become an ontological moratorium for young persons when identity and duty—the *termini ad quem* of moral and social life— could be hammered out through a humane conflict between students and the environing polity. "The current movements of rebellion, especially those of youth," Freire wrote, "manifest in their essence [a] preoccupation with men as beings in the world and with the world—a preoccupation with *what* and *how* they are 'being.' " Paul Goodman blasted the educational establishment because the bureaucratic machinery of the modern school had come to resemble less a moral encounter between student and status quo and more an administration of the status quo itself, like a department store where students were customers, the curriculum was the merchandise, and the teachers comprised the sales force. Charles Silberman best summed up the agitation for school reform as a *humanizing* of education when he wrote, "education should prepare people not just to earn a living but to live a life—a creative, humane, and sensitive life." It hardly seems fair or even useful to contrast Goodman, Silberman, and Freire's critiques of schooling with Matt Groenig's and his pointy-headed cartoon clones who thumb their noses at substitute teachers and celebrate themselves as underachievers.

In the nineties, the ethic that powers the *raison d'être* of schooling in our society has been, once again, completely inverted from Silberman's humanizing model and its understanding of school as a place to *individuate* into an apprentice model and its treatment of schooling more as a *process* of matriculating into a career. Paul Goodman's polis has been elbowed out by The Donald's office penthouse as the symbolic venue for the examined life. Once conceived of as an institution that "leads out," school has increasingly become a place that "leads to." It is this transmutation of driving spirit from "being" to "doing" that is partly responsible, I believe, for the current discontinuity of generational commitments and the gradual desensitizing of moral discourse I find among my own students. The values mismatch in the undergraduate classroom is accompanied by a new fascination with applied management theories and techniques among administrators struggling to redefine the academic mission in an era of shrinking resources, a time of capital campaigns, retooling, downsizing, and total quality management. Meanwhile, the distinction between academic and vocational education begins to blur as professional educationists cozy up to industry captains. University business parks are as commonplace as the revolving door between the university presidency and the corporate board room. Academic superstars are traded like NBA players. The much-rued extinction of the "public intellectual" in America has given way to a dubious new class of academic celebrities like Stanley Fish and Camille Paglia steered through the campus lecture circuit by publicity agents at a few grand a pop. There is no serious competition for the résumé and the memorandum as the most popular genre among undergraduates.

In short, Cardinal Newman's claim that knowledge is its own end no longer anchors the social contract of liberal learning in today's university. Instead, "applied learning" is the new idiom of educational accountability that fuses classroom and workplace into a trajectory of pedagogical competencies stressing team-work, problem solving, metacognition, time management, resource allocation, exit exams, and, generally, the ubiquitous litmus of vocational relevancy—what one observer has called "workplace correctness."

This moral turn from being to doing, or from reflection to consumption, also helps explain the lowering threshold of boredom and tolerance that students today bring to the liberal arts generally. Traditionally the animating spirit of education, the liberal arts disciplines have become instead the *animus* of undergraduate life. Students today, for the most part, revile a liberal arts curriculum. It has become a barrier to the real work of an undergraduate education: securing gainful—and one hopes meaningful—work in "the regular world." The denigration of liberal arts among today's students wouldn't be nearly so disturbing if the liberal arts consisted only of a knowledge base that spanned the humanistic disciplines, growing (admittedly) more irrelevant by the day. But a liberal arts education concerns more the *context* of a learning experience than the *content* of a curriculum, more an *epistemology*, indeed an *axiology*, than a discrete course of study either multicultural or anglocentric. A liberal education trains and shapes an individual's attitude toward learning itself. A liberal education prepares one to grapple with the crises of distraction and disinterest which become the real adversaries of adult life and citizenship in a consumer society and an information age. The liberal arts disciplines teach self-education and establish patterns of life-long learning. As such, they cultivate the capacity, desire, and drive for independent learning. A liberal education teaches us how to dig out what we need to know, and how to assess what's *worth* knowing, from the blizzard of irrelevant trivia and disinformation that constantly surrounds us. A liberal education teaches us to think for ourselves, independent of the opinions of others, yet at the same time squaring our own needs and aims in the world with the aspirations of others. "The lesson educators can teach," writes Amy Gutmann in an assessment of the liberal arts tradition and its contributions to "moral education," "is how to publicly defend one's convictions and simultaneously respect the convictions of others with whom one reasonably disagrees." Moreover, these pragmatic and moral considerations are underpinned by the ethical claim of liberalism itself. "The vision behind liberalism," Charles Frankel said on the threshold of the nuclear age, "is the vision of a world progressively redeemed by human power from its classic ailments of poverty, disease, and ignorance." As David Bromwich recently notes in a powerful meditation on learning, morality, and tradition, the solidarity of generations is also a formative virtue of a liberal education. Liberalism enfolds personal autonomy and commitment to others into a social ethic that joins, Bromwich writes, "what is good for me with what is good for others in the long run."

"Unfortunate is the youth," Jacques Maritain lamented, "who does not know the pleasure of the spirit and is not exalted in the joy of knowing and the joy of beauty, the enthusiasm for ideas, and quickening experience in the first love, delight and luxury of wisdom and poetry." The liberal arts, then, is about pleasure, exaltation, joy, enthusiasm, delight, social justice, responsibility, conviction, and commitment, along with the luxury—what St. Augustine called a "learned unhurriedness"—of knowing those things in life which are, from a strictly utilitarian standpoint, *completely useless*. And *realizing that those things are worth knowing*.

Maritain's claim for the intrinsic satisfactions of liberal learning, Frankel's liberal progressivism, and Bromwich's and Gutmann's communitarian ethic might be dismissed by most students today as either incredibly hokey or hopelessly idealistic. That deft dismissal is cued by combined forces, both within the university itself and outside in the society at-large, that have virtually transmogrified the spirit of higher education during the past twenty years and inverted the liberal ideal of the university as an institution of reflection, exploration, and observation, into the corporate view of the university as a place of action, application, praxis, profit, and personal aggrandizement. That inversion of attitude toward learning and its consequent impact on liberal education in America was vividly illustrated by a column in my own campus newspaper that, not coincidentally, appeared during the early blush of the anti-shanty movement in People's Park. Written by the paper's sports editor, the column applauded the decline of Liberal Arts disciplines. The writer vigorously defended the triumph of "the hard sciences" as "a change for the better" among undergraduates competing for "jobs, wages and luxurious lifestyles." Sports writers are known for their effective metaphors. His column is punched up with some fine metaphors, like the shiny new engineering building contrasted with the musty old basement with a crumbly ceiling where the philosophy department is housed. Such geomoral constructions reveal, to his mind, truly meaningful status valuations. "Do the rantings and ravings of a few dead poets and philosophers," he asks rhetorically, "mean anything in today's world? The 21st century is coming fast and those who are successful will be on the cutting edge. The connoisseurs of modern art don't care about discipline.

They don't learn anything. They don't teach anything. They don't *do* anything." A relentless pounding is capped off by the sports writer's *coup de grace:* arts and letters majors don't *earn* much, "unless," he rabbit-punches, "they spend more time at grad school getting a Ph.D., which," he has it on good authority and by living example, "my history professor warned me is 'the quickest and surest way to destroy your brain.' "

FOR JOURNALING AND DISCUSSION

1. Write an educational biography of you and your family. Are you a first-generation college student? If you are, write about the expectations you and your family had about college life, and compare those expectations to the realities you have encountered. If you are not a member of the first generation of your family to attend college, compare your academic goals and realities with those of your parents and grandparents. How do these realities differ? How are they the same?
2. Cooper claims, "This moral turn from being to doing, or from reflection to consumption, also helps explain the lowering threshold of boredom and tolerance that students today bring to the liberal arts generally." What do you think about the value of a liberal arts education? What is the purpose of a college education? Is it to train citizens to have careers that pay well or to become socially aware? Can it do both?
3. Who belongs to the "babyboomer" generation? Who belongs to "Generation X"? What are the stereotypes applied to each generation? Where do you fit in?
4. Cooper discusses the role of "imitable adults" in the lives of younger people. Compare and contrast Ben and Bernard Hamper's relationship in "Rivethead" in Chapter 3 to that of Caffilene and de Sara Allen in "First They Changed My Name" in Chapter 8.
5. Tim O'Brien, in his autobiographical essay "On the Rainy River" in Chapter 9, gives a human face to Cooper's "babyboomer" college student of the 1960s. Imagine the young O'Brien in People's Park; write about the shanty he would construct.

FOR RESEARCH AND EXPLORATION

1. As a class, view Jim Klein's film *Letter to the Next Generation*. Discuss what was happening within and outside of the United States during the Kent State University confrontation. What purpose does this film serve in Cooper's essay?
2. Construct a brief and informal questionnaire that asks students why they are attending college, and then ask a professor if you can ask class members to complete it during class time. What do the results say about why students want a college education?
3. Compare economic conditions today to those during the 1960s and 1970s. Consider factors such as the availability of health care, the cost of raising children, and the cost of higher learning. Write a short essay on how economic conditions might influence career choice.

Ma'Dear

Terry McMillan

The author of Mama, Disappearing Acts, *and* Waiting to Exhale, *African American writer McMillan has been a Fellow at Yaddo and MacDowell Colony. She was also the editor of* Breaking Ice: An Anthology of Contemporary African American Fiction. *McMillan has received grants from the PEN American Center, the Authors' League, the Carnegie Fund, the New York Foundation for the Arts, and the National Endowment for the Arts. She currently lives with her son, Solomon.*

Last year the cost of living crunched me and I got tired of begging from Peter to pay Paul, so I took in three roomers. Two of 'em is live-in nurses and only come around here on weekends. Even then they don't talk to me much, except when they hand me their money orders. One is from Trinidad and the other is from Jamaica. Every winter they quit their jobs, fill up two and three barrels with I don't know what, ship 'em home, and follow behind on an airplane. They come back in the spring and start all over. Then there's the little college girl, Juanita, who claims she's going for architecture. Seem like to me that was always men's work, but I don't say nothing. She grown.

I'm seventy-two. Been a widow for the past thirty-two years. Weren't like I asked for all this solitude, just that couldn't nobody else take Jessie's place is all. He knew it. And I knew it. He fell and hit his head real bad on the tracks going to fetch us some fresh picked corn and okra for me to make us some succotash, and never come to. I couldn't picture myself with no other man, even though I looked after a few years of being alone in this big old house, walking from room to room with nobody to talk to, cook or clean for, and not much company either.

I missed him for the longest time and thought I could find a man just like him, sincerely like him, but I couldn't. Went out for a spell with Esther Davis's ex-husband, Whimpy, but he was crazy. Drank too much bootleg and then started memorizing on World War I and how hard he fought and didn't get no respect and not a ounce of recognition for his heroic deeds. The only war Whimpy been in is with me for not keeping him around. He bragged something fearless about how he coulda been the heavyweight champion of the world. Didn't weigh but 160 pounds and shorter than me.

Chester Rutledge almost worked 'ceptin' he was boring, never had nothing on his mind worth talking about; claimed he didn't think about nothing besides me. Said his mind was always clear and visible. He just moved around like a zombie and worked hard at the cement foundry. Insisted on giving me his paychecks, which I kindly took for a while, but when I didn't want to be bothered no more, I stopped taking his money. He got on my nerves too bad, so I had to tell him I'd rather have a man with no money and a busy mind, least I'd know he's active somewheres. His feelings was hurt bad and he cussed me out, but we still friends to this very day. He in the home, you know, and I visits him regular. Takes him magazines and cuts out his horoscope and the comic strips from the newspaper and lets him read 'em in correct order.

Big Bill Ronsonville tried to convince me that I shoulda married him instead of Jessie, but he couldn't make me a believer of it. All he wanted to do was put his big rusty hands all on me without asking and smile at me with that big gold tooth sparkling and glittering in my face and tell me how lavish I was, lavish being a new word he just learnt. He kept wanting to take me for night rides way out in the country, out there by Smith Creek where ain't nothing but deep black ditches, giant mosquitoes, loud crickets, lightning bugs, and loose pigs, and turn off his motor. His breath stank like whiskey though he claimed and swore on the Bible he didn't drank no liquor. Aside from that his hands were way too heavy and hard, hurt me, sometimes left red marks on me like I been sucked on. I told him finally that I was too light for him, that I needed a smaller, more gentle man, and he said he knew exactly what I meant.

If you want to know the truth, after him I didn't think much about men the way I used too. Lost track of the ones who upped and died or the ones who couldn't do nothing if they was alive nohow. So, since nobody else seemed to be able to wear Jessie's shoes, I just stuck to myself all these years.

My life ain't so bad now 'cause I'm used to being alone and takes good care of myself. Occasionally I still has a good time. I goes to the park and sits for hours in good weather, watch folks move and listen in on confidential conversations. I add up numbers on license plates to keep my mind alert unless they pass too fast. This gives me a clear idea of how many folks is visiting from out of town. I can about guess the color of every state now, too. Once or twice a month I go to the matinee on Wednesdays, providing ain't no long line of senior citizens 'cause they can be so slow; miss half the picture show waiting for them to count their change and get their popcorn.

Sometimes, when I'm sitting in the park, I feed the pigeons old cornbread crumbs, and I wonders what it'll be like not looking at the snow falling from the sky, not seeing the leaves form on the trees, not hearing no car engines, no sirens, no babies crying, not brushing my hair at night, drinking my Lipton tea, and not being able to go to bed early.

But right now, to tell you the truth, it don't bother me all *that* much. What is bothering me is my case worker. She supposed to pay me a visit tomorrow because my nosy neighbor, Clarabelle, saw two big trucks outside, one come right after the other, and she wondered what I was getting so new and so big that I needed trucks. My mama used to tell me that sometimes you can't see for looking. Clarabelle's had it out to do me in ever since last spring when I had the siding put on the house. I used the last of Jessie's insurance money 'cause the roof had been leaking so bad and the wood rotted and the paint chipped so much that it looked like a wicked old witch lived here. The house looked brand-new, and she couldn't stand to see an old woman's house looking better than hers. She know I been had roomers, and now all of a sudden my case worker claim she just want to visit to see how I'm doing, when really what she want to know is what I'm up to. Clarabelle work in her office.

The truth is my boiler broke and they was here to put in a new one. We liked to froze to death in here for two days. Yeah, I had a little chump change in the bank, but when they told me it was gonna cost $2,000 to get some heat, I cried. I had $862 in the bank; $300 of it I had just spent on this couch I got on sale; it was in the other truck. After twenty years the springs finally broke, and I figured it was time to buy a new one 'cause I ain't one for living in poverty, even at my age. I figured $200 was for my church's cross-country bus trip this summer.

Jessie's sister, Willamae, took out a loan for me to get the boiler, and I don't know how long it's gonna take me to pay her back. She only charge me fifteen or twenty dollars a month, depending. I probably be dead by the time it get down to zero.

My bank wouldn't give me the loan for the boiler, but then they keep sending me letters almost every week trying to get me to refinance my house. They must think I'm senile or something. On they best stationery, they write me. They say I'm up in age and wouldn't I like to take that trip I've been putting off because of no extra money. What trip? They tell me if I refinance my house for more than what I owe, which is about $3,000, that I could have enough money left over to go anywhere. Why would I want to refinance my house at fourteen and a half percent when I'm paying four and a half now? I ain't that stupid. They say dream about clear blue water, palm trees, and orange suns. Last night I dreamt I was doing a backstroke between big blue waves and tipped my straw hat down over my forehead and fell asleep under an umbrella. They made me think about it. And they asked me what would I do if I was to die today? They're what got me to thinking about all this dying mess in the first place. It never would've layed in my mind so heavy if they hadn't kept reminding me of it. Who would pay off your house? Wouldn't I feel bad leaving this kind of a burden on my family? What family they talking about? I don't even know where my people is no more.

I ain't gonna lie. It ain't easy being old. But I ain't complaining neither, 'cause I learned how to stretch my social security check. My roomers pay the house note and I pay the taxes. Oil is sky-high. Medicaid pays my doctor bills. I got a letter what told me to apply for food stamps. That case worker come here and checked to see if I had a real kitchen. When she saw I had a stove and sink and refrigerator, she didn't like the idea that my house was almost paid for, and just knew I was lying about having roomers. "Are you certain that you reside here alone?" she asked me. "I'm certain," I said. She searched every inch of my cabinets to make sure I didn't have two of the same kinds of food, which would've been a dead giveaway. I hid it all in the basement inside the washing machine and dryer. Luckily, both of the nurses was in the islands at the time, and Juanita was visiting some boy what live in D.C.

After she come here and caused me so much eruptions, I had to make trip after trip down to that office. They had me filling out all kinds of forms and still held up my stamps. I got tired of answering the same questions over and over and finally told 'em to keep their old food stamps. I ain't got to beg nobody to eat. I know how to keep myself comfortable and clean and well fed. I manage to buy my staples and toiletries and once in a while a few extras, like potato chips, ice cream, and maybe a pork chop.

My mama taught me when I was young that, no matter how poor you are, always eat nourishing food and your body will last. Learn to conserve, she said. So I keeps all my empty margarine containers and stores white rice, peas and carrots (my favorites), or my turnips from the garden in there. I can manage a garden when my arthritis ain't acting up. And water is the key. I drinks plenty of it like the doctor told me, and I cheats, eats Oreo cookies and saltines. They fills me right up, too. And when I feels like it, rolls, homemade biscuits, eats them with Alga syrup if I can find it at the store, and that sticks with me most of the day.

Long time ago, used to be I'd worry like crazy about gaining weight and my face breaking out from too many sweets, and about cellulite forming all over my hips and thighs. Of course, I was trying to catch Jessie then, though I didn't know it at the time. I was really just being cute, flirting, trying to see if I could get attention. Just so happens I lucked up and got all of his. Caught him like he was a spider and I was the web.

Lord, I'd be trying to look all sassy and prim. Have my hair all did, it be curled tight in rows that I wouldn't comb out for hours till they cooled off after Connie Curtis did it for a dollar and a Budweiser. Would take that dollar out my special savings, which I kept hid under the record player in the front room. My hair used to be fine, too: long and thick and black, past my shoulders, and mens used to say, "Girl, you sure got a head of hair on them shoulders there, don't it make your neck sweat?" But I didn't never bother answering, just blushed and smiled and kept on walking, trying hard not to switch 'cause mama told me my behind was too big for my age and to watch out or I'd be luring grown mens toward me. Humph! I loved it, though, made me feel pretty, special, like I had attraction.

Ain't quite the same no more, though. I looks in the mirror at myself and I sees wrinkles, lots of them, and my skin look like it all be trying to run down toward my toes but then it changed its mind and just stayed there, sagging and lagging, laying limp against my thick bones. Shoot, mens used to say how sexy I was with these high cheeks, tell me I looked swollen, like I was pregnant, but it was just me, being all healthy and everything. My teeth was even bright white and straight in a row then. They ain't so bad now, 'cause ain't none of 'em mine. But I only been to the dentist twice in my whole life and that was 'cause on Easter Sunday I was in so much pain he didn't have time to take no X-ray and yanked it right out 'cause my mama told him to do anything he had to to shut me up. Second time was the last time, and that was 'cause the whole top row and the fat ones way in the back on the bottom ached me so bad the dentist yanked 'em all out so I wouldn't have to be bothered no more.

Don't get me wrong, I don't miss being young. I did everything I wanted to do and then some. I loved hard. But you take Jessie's niece, Thelma. She pitiful. Only twenty-six, don't think she made it past the tenth grade, got three children by different men, no husband and on welfare. Let her tell it, ain't nothing out here but dogs. I know some of these men out here ain't worth a pot to piss in, but all of 'em ain't dogs. There's gotta be some young Jessies floating somewhere in this world. My mama always told me you gotta have something to give if you want to get something in return. Thelma got long fingernails.

Me, myself, I didn't have no kids. Not 'cause I didn't want none or couldn't have none, just that Jessie wasn't full and couldn't give me the juices I needed to make no babies. I accepted it 'cause I really wanted him all to myself, even if he couldn't give me no new bloodlines. He was satisfying enough for me, quite satisfying if you don't mind me repeating myself.

I don't understand Thelma, like a lot of these young peoples. I be watching 'em on the streets and on TV. I be hearing things they be doing to themselves when I'm under the dryer at the beauty shop. (I go to the beauty shop once a month 'cause it make me feel like thangs ain't over yet. She give me a henna so the silver have a gold tint to it.) I can't afford it, but there ain't too many luxuries I can. I let her put makeup on me, too, if it's a Saturday and I feel like doing some window shopping. I still know how to flirt and sometimes I get stares, too. It feel good to be looked at and admired at my age. I try hard to keep myself up. Every weekday morning at five-thirty I do exercises with the TV set, when it don't hurt to stretch.

But like I was saying, Thelma and these young people don't look healthy, and they spirits is always so low. I watch 'em on the streets, on the train, when I'm going to the doctor. I looks in their eyes and they be red or brown where they supposed to be milky white and got bags deeper and heavier than mine, and I been through some thangs. I hear they be using these drugs of variety, and I can't understand why they need to use all these thangs to get from day to day. From what I do hear, it's supposed to give 'em much pleasure and make their minds disappear or make 'em not feel the thangs they supposed to be feeling anyway.

Heck, when I was young, we drank sarsaparilla and couldn't even buy no wine or any kind of liquor in no store. These youngsters ain't but eighteen and twenty and buys anything with a bite to it. I've seen 'em sit in front of the store and drank a whole bottle in one sitting. Girls, too.

We didn't have no dreams of carrying on like that, and specially on no corner. We was young ladies and young men with respect for ourselfs. And we didn't smoke none of them funny cigarettes all twisted up with no filters that smell like burning dirt. I ask myself, I say Ma'Dear, what's wrong with these kids? They can read and write and do arithmetic, finish high school, go to college and get letters behind their names, but every day I hear the neighbors complain that one of they youngsters done dropped out.

Lord, what I wouldn'ta done to finish high school and been able to write a full sentence or even went to college. I reckon I'da been a room decorator. I know they calls it be that fancy name now, interior designer, but it boil down to the same thang. I guess it's 'cause I loves so to make my surroundings pleasant, even right pretty, so I feels like a invited guest in my own house. And I always did have a flair for color. Folks used to say, "Hazel, for somebody as poor as a church mouse, you got better taste in thangs than them Rockefellers!" Used to sew up a storm, too. Covered my mama's raggedy duffold and chairs. Made her a bedspread with matching pillowcases. Didn't mix more than two different patterns either. Make you dizzy.

Wouldn't that be just fine, being an interior designer? Learning the proper names of thangs and recognizing labels in catalogs, giving peoples my business cards and wearing a two-piece with white gloves. "Yes, I decorated the Hartleys' and Cunninghams' home. It was such a pleasant experience. And they're such lovely people, simply lovely," I'da said. Coulda told those rich folks just what they needed in their bedrooms, front rooms, and specially in the kitchen. So many of 'em still don't know what to do in there.

But like I was saying before I got all off the track, some of these young people don't appreciate what they got. And they don't know thangs like we used to. We knew about eating fresh vegetables from the garden, growing and picking 'em ourselves. What going to church was, being honest and faithful. Trusting each other. Leaving our front door open. We knew what it was like to starve and get cheated yearly when our crops didn't add up the way we figured. We suffered together, not separately. These youngsters don't know about suffering for any stretch of time. I hear 'em on the train complaining 'cause they can't afford no Club Med, no new record playing albums, cowboy boots, or those Brooke Shields–Calvin Klein blue jeans I see on TV. They be complaining about nonsense. Do they ever read books since they been taught is what I want to know? Do they be learning things and trying to figure out what to do with it?

And these young girls with all this thick makeup caked on their faces, wearing these high heels they can't hardly walk in. Trying to be cute. I used to wear high heels, mind you, with silk stockings, but at least I could walk in 'em. Jessie had a car then. Would pick me up, and I'd walk real careful down the front steps like I just won the Miss America pageant, one step at a time, and slide into his shiny black Ford. All the neighbors peeked through the curtains 'cause I was sure enough riding in a real automobile with my legitimate boyfriend.

*   *   *

If Jessie was here now I'd have somebody to talk to. Somebody to touch my skin. He'd probably take his fingers and run 'em through my hair like he used to; kiss me on my nose and tickle me where it made me laugh. I just loved it when he kissed me. My mind be so light, and I felt tickled and precious. Have to sit down sometime just to get hold of myself.

If he was here, I probably woulda beat him in three games of checkers by now and he'd be trying to get even. But since today is Thursday, I'd be standing in that window over there waiting for him to get home from work, and when I got tired or the sun be in my eyes, I'd hear the taps on his wing tips coming up the front porch. Sometime, even now, I watch for him, but I know he ain't coming back. Not that he wouldn't if he could, mind you, 'cause he always told me I made him feel lightning lighting up his heart.

Don't get me wrong, I got friends, though a heap of 'em is dead or got tubes coming out of their noses or going all through their bodies every which-a-way. Some in the old folks' home. I thank the Lord I ain't stuck in one of them places. I ain't never gonna get that old. They might as well just bury me standing up if I do. I don't want to be no nuisance to nobody, and I can't stand being around a lot of sick people for too long.

I visits Gunther and Chester when I can, and Vivian who I grew up with, but no soon as I walk through them long hallways, I get depressed. They lay there all limp and helpless, staring at the ceiling like they're really looking at something, or sitting stiff in their rocking chairs, pitiful, watching TV and don't be knowing what they watching half the time. They laugh when ain't nothing funny. They wait for it to get dark so they know it's time to go to sleep. They relatives don't hardly come visit 'em, just folks like me. Whimpy don't understand a word I say, and it makes me grateful I ain't lost no more than I have.

Sometime we sits on the sun porch rocking like fools; don't say one word to each other for hours. But last time Gunther told me about his grandson what got accepted to Stanford University, and another one at a university in Michigan. I asked him where was Stanford and he said he didn't know. "What difference do it make?" he asked. "It's one of those uppity schools for rich smart white people," he said. "The important thang is that my black grandson won a scholarship there, which mean he don't have to pay a dime to go." I told him I know what a scholarship is. I ain't stupid. Gunther said he was gonna be there for at least four years or so, and by that time he would be a professional. "Professional what?" I asked. "Who cares, Ma'Dear, he gonna be a professional at whatever it is he learnt." Vivian started mumbling when she heard us talking, 'cause she still like to be the center of attention. When she was nineteen she was Miss Springfield Gardens. Now she can't stand the thought that she old and wrinkled. She started yakking about all the places she'd been to, even described the landscape like she was looking at a photograph. She ain't been but twenty-two miles north of here in her entire life, and that's right there in that home.

* * *

Like I said, and this is the last time I'm gonna mention it. I don't mind being old, it's just that sometime I don't need all this solitude. You can't do everything by yourself and expect to have as much fun if somebody was there doing it with you. That's why when I'm feeling jittery or melancholy for long stretches, I read the Bible, and it soothes me. I water my morning glories and amaryllis. I baby-sit for Thelma every now and then, 'cause she don't trust me with the kids for too long. She mainly call on holidays and my birthday. And she the only one who don't forget my birthday: August 19th. She tell me I'm a Leo, that I got fire in my blood. She may be right, 'cause once in a while I gets a churning desire to be smothered in Jessie's arms again.

Anyway, it's getting late, but I ain't tired. I feel pretty good. That old case worker think she gonna get the truth out of me. She don't scare me. It ain't none of her business that I got money coming in here besides my social security check. How they 'spect a human being to live off $369 a month in this day and age is what I wanna know. Every time I walk out my front door it cost me at least two dollars. I bet she making thousands and got credit cards galore. Probably got a summer house on the Island and goes to Florida every January. If she found out how much I was getting from my roomers, the government would make me pay back a dollar for every two I made. I best to get my tail on upstairs and clear everything off their bureaus. I can hide all the nurses's stuff in the attic; they won't be back till next month. Juanita been living out of trunks since she got here, so if the woman ask what's in 'em, I'll tell her, old sheets and pillowcases and memories.

On second thought, I think I'm gonna take me a bubble bath first, and dust my chest with talcum powder, then I'll make myself a hot cup of Lipton's and paint my fingernails clear 'cause my hands feel pretty steady. I can get up at five and do all that other mess; case worker is always late anyway. After she leave, if it ain't snowing too bad, I'll go to the museum and look at the new paintings in the left wing. By the time she get here, I'ma make out like I'm a lonely old widow stuck in a big old house just sitting here waiting to die.

FOR JOURNALING AND DISCUSSION

1. McMillan writes her story in the first person, which gives us the illusion that Hazel is addressing us directly. Through her narrative, we learn that she cheats a bit on her social security. Does McMillan's use of the first person influence our response to Hazel's behavior in ways a third-person narrative cannot?

2. Hazel seems very critical of the younger generation, especially younger women. In what ways do her criticisms seem hypocritical?

3. Does Hazel identify with other senior citizens? Compare her attitudes on aging with those of "Mother Georgia" in "A Ceremony of Innocence" in Chapter 5.

4. In what ways does Hazel, as a senior citizen, feel victimized by society in general? Compare her analysis of her victimization to Michael Lind's analysis of how the

American overclass controls the American underclass in his essay "To Have and Have Not" in Chapter 3.

5. Hazel expresses very negative feelings about old people in nursing homes. She describes their physical limitations and disabilities, but not their inner lives. How does her portrayal of the elderly support Mike Ervin's critique of "quality-of-life" assessments in his essay "Who Gets to Live? Who Will Decide?" in Chapter 7?

FOR RESEARCH AND EXPLORATION

1. Are older people in American culture respected and sought out as sources of wisdom? Interview two or more older family members or friends. How do we collectively treat our collective grandfathers and grandmothers?
2. Research the types of crime and fraud perpetrated against senior citizens, particularly those who live alone. Write about how this group of people is especially vulnerable.
3. Foreign visitors and cultural critics have observed that the United States is a youth-oriented culture preoccupied with looking, acting, and staying young. Form a small group, and collect and analyze various pop culture artifacts, such as magazine advertisements, videotapes of movies and television shows, and newspaper articles. Do you agree or disagree with this observation?

Beauty: When the Other Dancer Is the Self

Alice Walker

Born in Georgia, Walker studied for her B.A. at Spelman College and Sarah Lawrence College. She has worked for social justice as a voter registration worker in Georgia and as a Head Start worker in Mississippi. Walker was also on the staff of New York City's Welfare Department. Among her numerous awards and honors, she has received the Pulitzer Prize and the American Book Award, both in 1983, for her novel The Color Purple. *She is also co-producer of the film documentary* Warrior Marks.

It is a bright summer day in 1947. My father, a fat, funny man with beautiful eyes and a subversive wit, is trying to decide which of his eight children he will take with him to the county fair. My mother, of course, will not go. She is knocked out from getting most of us ready: I hold my neck stiff against the pressure of her knuckles as she hastily completes the braiding and then beribboning of my hair.

My father is the driver for the rich old white lady up the road. Her name is Miss Mey. She owns all the land for miles around, as well as the house in which we live. All I remember about her is that she once offered to pay my mother thirty-five cents for cleaning her house, raking up piles of her magnolia leaves, and washing her family's clothes, and that my mother—she of no money, eight children, and a chronic earache—refused it. But I do not think of this in 1947. I am two and a half years old. I want to go everywhere my daddy goes. I am excited at the prospect of riding in a car. Someone has told me fairs are fun. That there is room in the car for only three of us doesn't faze me at all. Whirling happily in my starchy frock, showing off my biscuit-polished patent-leather shoes and lavender socks, tossing my head in a way that makes my ribbons bounce, I stand, hands on hips, before my father. "Take me, Daddy," I say with assurance; "I'm the prettiest!"

Later, it does not surprise me to find myself in Miss Mey's shiny black car, sharing the back seat with the other lucky ones. Does not surprise me that I thoroughly enjoy the fair. At home that night I tell the unlucky ones all I can remember about the merry-go-round, the man who eats live chickens, and the teddy bears, until they say: that's enough, baby Alice. Shut up now, and go to sleep.

It is Easter Sunday, 1950. I am dressed in a green, flocked, scalloped-hem dress (handmade by my adoring sister, Ruth) that has its own smooth satin petticoat and tiny hot-pink roses tucked into each scallop. My shoes, new T-strap patent leather, again highly biscuit-polished. I am six years old and have learned one of the longest Easter speeches to be heard that day, totally unlike the speech I said when I was two: "Easter lilies/pure and white/blossom in/the morning light." When I rise to give my speech I do so on a great wave of love and pride and expectation. People in the church stop rustling their new crinolines. They seem to hold their breath. I can tell they admire my dress, but it is my spirit, bordering on sassiness (womanishness), they secretly applaud.

"That girl's a little *mess*," they whisper to each other, pleased.

Naturally I say my speech without stammer or pause, unlike those who stutter, stammer, or, worst of all, forget. This is before the word "beautiful" exists in people's vocabulary, but "Oh, isn't she the *cutest* thing!" frequently floats my way. "And got so much sense!" they gratefully add . . . for which thoughtful addition I thank them to this day.

It was great fun being cute. But then, one day, it ended.

I am eight years old and a tomboy. I have a cowboy hat, cowboy boots, checkered shirt and pants, all red. My playmates are my brothers, two and four years older than I. Their colors are black and green, the only difference in the way we are dressed. On Saturday nights we all go to the picture show, even my mother; Westerns are her favorite kind of movie. Back home, "on the ranch," we pretend we are Tom Mix, Hopalong Cassidy, Lash LaRue (we've even named one of our dogs Lash LaRue); we chase each other for hours rustling cattle, being outlaws, delivering damsels from distress. Then my parents decide to buy my brothers guns. These are not "real" guns. They shoot "BBs," copper pellets my brothers say will kill birds. Because I am a girl, I do not get a gun. Instantly I am relegated to the position of Indian. Now there appears a great distance between us. They shoot and shoot at everything with their new guns. I try to keep up with my bow and arrows.

One day while I am standing on top of our makeshift "garage"—pieces of tin nailed across some poles—holding my bow and arrow and looking out toward the fields, I feel an incredible blow in my right eye. I look down just in time to see my brother lower his gun.

Both brothers rush to my side. My eye stings, and I cover it with my hand. "If you tell," they say, "we will get a whipping. You don't want that to happen, do you?" I do not. "Here is a piece of wire," says the older brother, picking it up from the roof; "say you stepped on one end of it and the other flew up and hit you." The pain is beginning to start. "Yes," I say. "Yes, I will say that is what happened." If I do not say this is what happened, I know my brothers will find ways to make me wish I had. But now I will say anything that gets me to my mother.

Confronted by our parents we stick to the lie agreed upon. They place me on a bench on the porch and I close my left eye while they examine the right. There is a tree growing from underneath the porch that climbs past the railing to the roof. It is the last thing my right eye sees. I watch as its trunk, its branches, and then its leaves are blotted out by the rising blood.

I am in shock. First there is intense fever, which my father tries to break using lily leaves bound around my head. Then there are chills: my mother tries to get me to eat soup. Eventually, I do not know how, my parents learn what has happened. A week after the "accident" they take me to see a doctor. "Why did you wait so long to come?" he asks, looking into my eye and shaking his head. "Eyes are sympathetic," he says. "If one is blind, the other will likely become blind too."

This comment of the doctor's terrifies me. But it is really how I look that bothers me most. Where the BB pellet struck there is a glob of whitish scar tissue, a hideous cataract, on my eye. Now when I stare at people—a favorite pastime, up to now—they will stare back. Not at the "cute" little girl, but at her scar. For six years I do not stare at anyone, because I do not raise my head.

Years later, in the throes of a mid-life crisis, I ask my mother and sister whether I changed after the "accident." "No," they say, puzzled. "What do you mean?" *What do I mean?*

I am eight, and, for the first time, doing poorly in school, where I have been something of a whiz since I was four. We have just moved to the place where the "accident" occurred. We do not know any of the people around us because this is a different county. The only time I see the friends I knew is when we go back to our old church. The new school is the former state penitentiary. It is a large stone building, cold and drafty, crammed to overflowing with boisterous, ill-disciplined children. On the third floor there is a huge circular imprint of some partition that has been torn out.

"What used to be here?" I ask a sullen girl next to me on our way past it to lunch.

"The electric chair," says she.

At night I have nightmares about the electric chair, and about all the people reputedly "fried" in it. I am afraid of the school, where all the students seem to be budding criminals.

"What's the matter with your eye?" they ask, critically.

When I don't answer (I cannot decide whether it was an "accident" or not), they shove me, insist on a fight.

My brother, the one who created the story about the wire, comes to my rescue. But then brags so much about "protecting" me, I become sick.

After months of torture at the school, my parents decide to send me back to our old community, to my old school. I live with my grandparents and the teacher they board. But there is no room for Phoebe, my cat. By the time my grandparents decide there *is* room, and I ask for my cat, she cannot be found. Miss Yarborough, the boarding teacher, takes me under her wing, and begins to teach me to play the piano. But soon she marries an African—a "prince," she says—and is whisked away to his continent.

At my old school there is at least one teacher who loves me. She is the teacher who "knew me before I was born" and bought my first baby clothes. It is she who makes life bearable. It is her presence that finally helps me turn on the one child at the school who continually calls me "one-eyed bitch." One day I simply grab him by his coat and beat him until I am satisfied. It is my teacher who tells me my mother is ill.

My mother is lying in bed in the middle of the day, something I have never seen. She is in too much pain to speak. She has an abscess in her ear. I stand looking down on her, knowing that if she dies, I cannot live. She is being treated with warm oils and hot bricks held against her cheek. Finally a doctor comes. But I must go back to my grandparents' house. The weeks pass but I am hardly aware of it. All I know is that my mother might die, my father is not so jolly, my brothers still have their guns, and I am the one sent away from home.

"You did not change," they say.

Did I imagine the anguish of never looking up?

I am twelve. When relatives come to visit I hide in my room. My cousin Brenda, just my age, whose father works in the post office and whose mother is a nurse, comes to find me. "Hello," she says. And then she asks, looking at my recent school picture, which I did not want taken, and on which the "glob," as I think of it, is clearly visible, "You still can't see out of that eye?"

"No," I say, and flop back on the bed over my book.

That night, as I do almost every night, I abuse my eye. I rant and rave at it, in front of the mirror. I plead with it to clear up before morning. I tell it I hate and despise it. I do not pray for sight. I pray for beauty.

"You did not change," they say.

I am fourteen and baby-sitting for my brother Bill, who lives in Boston. He is my favorite brother and there is a strong bond between us. Understanding my feelings of shame and ugliness he and his wife take me to a local hospital, where the "glob" is removed by a doctor named O. Henry. There is still a small bluish crater where the scar tissue was, but the ugly white stuff is gone. Almost immediately I become a different person from the girl who does not raise her head. Or so I think. Now that I've raised my head I win the boyfriend of my dreams. Now that I've raised my head I have plenty of friends. Now that I've raised my head classwork comes from my lips as faultlessly as Easter speeches did, and I leave high school as valedictorian, most popular student, and *queen,* hardly believing my luck. Ironically, the girl who was voted most beautiful in our class (and was) was later shot twice through the chest by a male companion, using a "real" gun, while she was pregnant. But that's another story in itself. Or is it?

"You did not change," they say.

It is now thirty years since the "accident." A beautiful journalist comes to visit and to interview me. She is going to write a cover story for her magazine that focuses on my latest book. "Decide how you want to look on the cover," she says. "Glamorous, or whatever."

Never mind "glamorous," it is the "whatever" that I hear. Suddenly all I can think of is whether I will get enough sleep the night before the photography session: if I don't, my eye will be tired and wander, as blind eyes will.

At night in bed with my lover I think up reasons why I should not appear on the cover of a magazine. "My meanest critics will say I've sold out," I say. "My family will now realize I write scandalous books."

"But what's the real reason you don't want to do this?" he asks.

"Because in all probability," I say in a rush, "my eye won't be straight."

"It will be straight enough," he says. Then, "Besides, I thought you'd made your peace with that."

And I suddenly remember that I have.

I remember:

I am talking to my brother Jimmy, asking if he remembers anything unusual about the day I was shot. He does not know I consider that day the last time my father, with his sweet home remedy of cool lily leaves, chose me, and that I suffered and raged inside because of this. "Well," he says, "all I remember is standing by the side of the highway with Daddy, trying to flag down a car. A white man stopped, but when Daddy said he needed somebody to take his little girl to the doctor, he drove off."

I remember:

I am in the desert for the first time. I fall totally in love with it. I am so overwhelmed by its beauty, I confront for the first time, consciously, the meaning of the doctor's words years ago: "Eyes are sympathetic. If one is blind, the other will likely become blind too." I realize I have dashed about the world madly, looking at this, looking at that, storing up images against the fading of the light. *But I might have missed seeing the desert!* The shock of that possibility—and gratitude for over twenty-five years of sight—sends me literally to my knees. Poem after poem comes—which is perhaps how poets pray.

ON SIGHT

I am so thankful I have seen
The Desert
And the creatures in the desert
And the desert Itself.

The desert has its own moon
Which I have seen
With my own eye.
There is no flag on it.

Trees of the desert have arms
All of which are always up
That is because the moon is up
The sun is up
Also the sky
The stars
Clouds
None with flags.

If there *were* flags, I doubt
the trees would point.
Would you?

But mostly, I remember this:

I am twenty-seven, and my baby daughter is almost three. Since her birth I have worried about her discovery that her mother's eyes are different from other people's. Will she be embarrassed? I think. What will she say? Every day she watches a television program called "Big Blue Marble." It begins with a picture of the earth as it appears from the moon. It is bluish, a little battered-looking, but full of light, with whitish clouds swirling around it. Every time I see it I weep with love, as if it is a picture of Grandma's house. One day when I am putting Rebecca down for her nap, she suddenly focuses on my eye. Something inside me cringes, gets ready to try to protect myself. All children are cruel about physical differences, I know from experience, and that they don't always mean to be is another matter. I assume Rebecca will be the same.

But no-o-o-o. She studies my face intently as we stand, her inside and me outside her crib. She even holds my face maternally between her dimpled little hands. Then, looking every bit as serious and lawyerlike as her father, she says, as if it may just possibly have slipped my attention: "Mommy, there's a *world* in your eye." (As in, "Don't be alarmed, or do anything crazy.") And then, gently, but with great interest: "Mommy, where did you *get* that world in your eye?"

For the most part, the pain left then. (So what, if my brothers grew up to buy even more powerful pellet guns for their sons and to carry real guns themselves. So what, if a young "Morehouse man" once nearly fell off the steps of Trevor Arnett Library because he thought my eyes were blue.) Crying and laughing I ran to the bathroom, while Rebecca mumbled and sang herself off to sleep. Yes indeed, I realized, looking into the mirror. There *was* a world in my eye. And I saw that it was possible to love it: that in fact, for all it had taught me of shame and anger and inner vision, I *did* love it. Even to see it drifting out of orbit in boredom, or rolling up out of fatigue, not to mention floating back at attention in excitement (bearing witness, a friend has called it), deeply suitable to my personality, and even characteristic of me.

That night I dream I am dancing to Stevie Wonder's song "Always" (the name of the song is really "As," but I hear it as "Always"). As I dance, whirling and joyous, happier than I've ever been in my life, another bright-faced dancer joins me. We dance and kiss each other and hold each other through the night. The other dancer has obviously come through all right, as I have done. She is beautiful, whole and free. And she is also me.

FOR JOURNALING AND DISCUSSION

1. Walker says of her eye, "And I saw that it was possible to love it: that in fact, for all it had taught me of shame and anger and inner vision, I *did* love it." In this passage, she accepts as an adult how much she *is* her blind eye. Discuss the adult that Walker might have become had she not lost her sight in one eye.
2. Write about something negative that happened to you in childhood. Did it alter your adult personality? Do you think Walker's reaction is typical?
3. Walker states that she did not have a gun because she was a girl; therefore, she became the Indian hunted by her brothers. Do you think gender played a role in her blinding?
4. Compare Walker's mother to the mother in Lilliana Heker's "The Stolen Party" in Chapter 3. How do these mothers deal with their daughters' perceptions of reality?

5. Walker expects her daughter to be cruel. Compare Rebecca to the young John Hassler in his story "Rufus at the Door" in Chapter 7. How do you think children learn cruelty?

FOR RESEARCH AND EXPLORATION

1. Read one of Walker's novels, and compare how she uses race in that book and in this story.
2. Many psychologists believe childhood trauma results in adult dysfunction. Research a popular form of therapy, and write about the role childhood memories play in the therapeutic process.
3. As a child, Walker takes great pride in her cuteness and her clothes. Research ways our culture rewards little girls for being "pretty little women."

An Old Lepidopterist

Bailey White

In Sleeping at the Starlight Motel and Other Adventures on the Way Back Home *and* Moma Makes Up Her Mind, *White proves herself to be a gifted observer of Southern eccentricities. She has been nominated for a Southern Book Award and an ABBY Award. White teaches elementary school in Georgia and is a regular commentator on National Public Radio's "All Things Considered."*

One summer when I was a little girl, an old lepidopterist rented a cabin in the woods up the road from us. He moved down from Atlanta with his tiny, perfectly round wife, and a station wagon full of nets, spreading boards, and killing jars. He was finishing up his life's work, an exhaustive study of the butterflies of Georgia, and he was, we learned later, an eminently respected and renowned scientist in his field. But to the children in my neighborhood that summer, he was just a very kind old man with a lot of interesting stuff on his back porch, which he was happy to show off and explain to us.

His wife was a great homemaker and needleworker, and as soon as she had settled in and sent Mr. Harris off into the pine woods with his butterfly net and two pimento cheese sandwiches, she began baking exquisite little cookies and knitting little pink sweaters for me and all my cousins.

In the late afternoons of that summer, when it began to cool off, Mr. Harris would come back with his jar full of buckeyes and checkerspots and hairstreaks, and the children from up and down the road would wander onto the Harrises' porch. Mrs. Harris would serve lemonade and cookies in the shapes of flowers and butterflies of no known species. Mr. Harris would sit in his chair and arrange his day's catch, and Mrs. Harris would teach my cousins and me to do needlework. We sat for hours, scowling with concentration, cross-stitching cute little scenes and heartfelt sayings on squares of linen. Mrs. Harris's knitting needles would go *click click click*, Mr. Harris would deftly pin butterfly after butterfly into the grooves on his cork spreading boards, and the ice would melt in our thin lemonade glasses.

Mrs. Harris finished our sweaters, but it turned out she had made them all in her shape and size—short and wide. My stringy arms and knobby wrists sticking out of the dainty little pink cable-stitched sleeves had a startling effect, like one of those clever tricks of mimicry butterflies use to frighten birds.

And after many weeks my sampler was finished. Through the snagged threads and blood stains you could barely make out the words HOME SWEET HOME. Below, what was supposed to be a cute potbellied wood cookstove in a cozy country kitchen looked like a wrecked 1941 Ford in a scrap yard. My clever cousins moved on to crewel embroidery and petit point, but for my second project, Mrs. Harris tactfully started me on something called huck toweling, which turned out to be nothing but a dishrag on which I was to stitch a border of giant red X's. After many rows I got tired of red and looked with longing at the shimmering pinks and dense purples of my cousins' satin-stitched Persian flowers. But Mrs. Harris said I must set a goal for myself. When my X's reached a certain standard of consistency, then I could switch to green thread, "for a nice Christmasy effect," she said. By the time I got to green, my cousins were doing appliqué and cutwork, and something called tatting, which resulted in long bands of delicate lace.

In spite of the humiliating needlework, I kept going back again and again to the Harrises' porch that summer. I kept going back because on some afternoons Mr. Harris would tell about his adventures as a young lepidopterist. He would tell about his mentor and friend, Professor P. W. Fattig, and their entomological expeditions together. He told about the time an enormous beetle, unknown and undescribed in the scientific literature, flew by right in front of him and Professor Fattig and then disappeared in the swampy thickets.

Mr. Harris's voice fell to a husky whisper: " 'Harris,' Professor Fattig said to me, 'did you see that?' "

" 'Fattig,' I said to Professor Fattig, 'I did.' "

Mr. Harris was a wonderful storyteller, and as the afternoon wore on, my red and green X's would begin to loop and tumble over each other, until finally, when Mr. Harris got to the story of Professor Fattig and the wasp with the inch-long stinger, I wove my needle into the huck toweling, folded my hands, and just listened.

The next summer Mr. Harris rescued me from the torment of needlework by inviting me to come with him to catch butterflies. He was very particular about his recordkeeping; after every capture he noted down the time of day, location, date, and any unusual circumstances. He showed me the yucca plant, host to the *Megathymus harrisi,* a skipper butterfly that had been named for Mr. Harris after his observations of it in its pupal stage proved it to be a distinct species from the similar-appearing *Megathymus cofaqui.* In the backyard of the Harrises' little cabin we planted a butterfly garden—buddleia, pentas, and lantana for their nectar; and rabbit tobacco and passionflower, the food plants for the larvae of the gulf fritillary and painted lady. For the monarchs, Mr. Harris brought down from Atlanta a special tall-growing variety of milkweed I had never seen before.

By the end of that summer, Mr. Harris's work on the butterflies of the coastal region was complete, and the Harrises gave up their little cabin. The next year his book, *Butterflies of Georgia,* was published. Not long after that Mr. Harris's mind began to wander. He didn't know me when I went to Atlanta to see him. Then he didn't know Mrs. Harris. She got too frail to take care of him at home, and he was put in a nursing home. By the end of his life he had forgotten everything he had ever known about butterflies.

Every year when school starts in September, I teach a special science unit to my first graders called Butterflies of Georgia. I try to teach them everything I learned from Mr. Harris in those summers of listening to his stories and holding his notebook and his killing jar while he dashed through the woods making wild swats with his big net.

The little house up the road that the Harrises rented for those summers is gone now, and wisteria has taken over the yard, but those milkweed plants Mr. Harris brought down from Atlanta reseed every year, and in August and September the woods and fields around the house site are transformed into a monarch butterfly paradise. The butterflies are everywhere, floating over the red and yellow flower clusters with their characteristic leisurely glide, looping and soaring and lighting and laying eggs. The plants are covered with monarch larvae of all sizes, fatly munching out neat half-moons from the edges of the leaves. The chrysalides hang like little jewels, changing color according to the light—lime green, emerald green, aqua green—with the golden spots and perfect golden stitching around the caps glinting and flashing.

I feel a kind of reverence in late summer when I visit that abandoned butterfly garden. I feel cheered and comforted, as if, somewhere up in heaven, with his tattered nets and stretching boards, an old lepidopterist is still looking after me.

FOR JOURNALING AND DISCUSSION

1. White gives us clues about how Mrs. Harris enforced society's expectations for girls. What were they? In what ways did Mrs. Harris step outside of her prescribed gender role?

2. The young girl is infatuated with Mr. Harris's stories and passes them on to her students when she becomes a teacher. Write about a teacher whose stories inspired your interest in something. Did this teacher influence your career choices?
3. White uses the word "stitching" to describe both needlework and the markings on chrysalides. What point is she trying to make with the dual application of this word?
4. The old lepidopterist's mind began to wander toward the end of his life, and he lost his knowledge of butterflies. Compare White's use of memory loss with that of Adrian C. Louis in his essay "Earth Bone Connected to the Spirit Bone" in Chapter 5.
5. In what ways does the old lepidopterist serve as a role model for the young girl? Compare and contrast their relationship to the relationship between Caffilene Allen and her teachers in "First They Changed My Name" in Chapter 8.

FOR RESEARCH AND EXPLORATION

1. What percentage of women choose careers in science? How are today's girls encouraged to take science classes? Was this true in your high school?
2. What is a lepidopterist? What does such a career entail?
3. Research the stages of a butterfly's development. In what ways did the young Bailey White duplicate these stages in her own growing up?

Farewell to the Lodge

Dan Fost

Fost is a freelance journalist and a frequent contributor to American Demographics.

Robert Grafton's grandfather and father belonged to the Elks. When World War II ended and Grafton left the service, he joined up, too. "I got married and we had our first child. My wife stayed home, and I was able to go to meetings at night and be heavily involved with the Elks," says Grafton, 68, of Micanopy, Florida.

Times change.

Grafton's 32-year-old son also belongs to the Elks, but the younger man cannot give the lodge as much time as his father did. "When I was his age, I had already been a leader of an Elks Lodge in West Palm Beach. He has not been able to become active in assuming an office," Grafton says.

Membership in the Benevolent and Protective Order of Elks peaked 15 years ago at 1.65 million. This year [1996], membership stood at 1.3 million, a

Dan Fost, "Farewell to the Lodge" from *American Demographics* 1 (1996). Copyright © 1996. Reprinted with the permission of *American Demographics*.

21 percent decline. "It's a tough situation," says Grafton, the Elks' spokesman, "but we're not out there by ourselves."

Membership in a variety of civic and fraternal organizations is on the decline. The reasons have to do with fundamental changes in attitudes toward work, leisure, and the roles of American men.

Other groups suffering membership declines include the Lions, off 12 percent since 1983; the Shriners, off 32 percent since 1979; the Jaycees, off 44 percent since 1979; and the Masons, down 39 percent since 1959. Male Kiwanis membership has also dropped since 1970, although total membership has grown, thanks to the addition of women.

Lean times have not befallen every lodge. Membership in the Knights of Columbus has increased 20 percent since 1991, according to Christopher Kauffman, author of a history of the group. Rotary International has grown 12 percent since 1985—but only 3 percent in the past five years, and less than 1 percent in 1994.

The declining membership in men's groups and civic groups is an ominous sign, according to Robert D. Putnam, director of the Center for International Affairs at Harvard University. He describes it as a loss of "social capital" in a well-known essay entitled "Bowling Alone." The title refers to the fact that while more Americans are bowling than ever before, league bowling plummeted 40 percent between 1980 and 1993. In addition to fraternal groups, Putnam cites falling numbers of parent-teacher associations, volunteers with the Red Cross and the Boy Scouts, and labor union membership.

"There is a stark generational difference between people who grew up before 1945, who were and continue to be unusually civic, and those who grew up after that, who have always been much less civic," Putnam says. "The pre-1945 generation peaked as a fraction of the adult population in 1965 and is now rapidly passing from the scene. They leave behind the successively less civic generations raised in the 1950s, 1960s and 1970s. Thus, the trend toward disengagement is likely to continue for some years to come."

FIGHTING FOR SURVIVAL

Several forces have eroded America's "social capital," says Putnam. The movement of women into the labor force hurt groups like PTAs and the League of Women Voters most. But many leaders of fraternal groups say it also added to men's responsibilities around the house, allowing them less time for club activities.

Another possible factor is mobility, or what Putnam calls "the re-potting hypothesis." "It takes time for an uprooted individual to put down new roots," he writes. "It seems plausible that the automobile, suburbanization, and the movement to the Sunbelt have reduced the social rootedness of the average American." One problem with this theory is that residential stability and home-ownership have actually risen since the 1950s. But so have average commuting times.

Demographic shifts and economic changes also play a role. Declining marriage rates, persistently high divorce rates, and smaller families may make Americans less sociable. So might lower real wages. Putnam sees a decline in sociability when chain stores replace locally owned business institutions. But the biggest reason by far, he says, is " the technological transformation of leisure," or television.

"Television is the primary culprit for the declining social connectedness of baby boomers and Generation X," says Putnam. "It is no accident that the problem of civic disengagement is almost nonexistent among those generations raised before the advent of television. Each hour one spends in front of the tube is linked, statistically speaking, to reduced trust and social engagement. By contrast, each hour spent reading a newspaper is associated with greater trust and engagement." Putnam sums up his views on TV in a recent essay called "Tuning In, Tuning Out."

These issues are more than academic for nonprofit and membership groups. Many once-proud organizations are shrinking, a few are fighting for survival, and all are searching for ways to stem their losses.

Last year, the Shriners, headquartered in Tampa, commissioned a poll from Louis Harris and Associates to seek the cause of a drop in membership from 942,000 in 1980 to 660,000 in 1994. The results were grim. Only 6 percent of the Shrines' target market said that they would be very likely to join an organization closely matching the Shrine.

The survey interviewed 1,009 men aged 35 to 55. It did not mention the Shrine by name, so its conclusions are a warning to Elks, Eagles, Moose, and other endangered species.

More than three-fourths of the men surveyed do not belong to any civic or fraternal organization, and 57 percent are not involved in volunteer activities. Most are employed fathers or have other ongoing commitments. Their leisure is part of a hectic schedule, and they view it as a precious commodity. Yet roughly half of men aged 35 to 55 participate in sports and more than three-fourths watch television to relax. They watch an average of 2.5 hours a day.

Perhaps the most striking finding is that only 5 percent of men aged 35 to 55 regard "spending time with other men" as a very important component of leisure time. "Men do not want policies for membership that are exclusionary in any way or hint at elitism," according to the Louis Harris report. "In particular, men are not interested in belonging to organizations that accept only male members."

The distinctive features of the Shrine, such as the fez and elaborate and challenging membership requirements, are turning off baby boomers. Charitable activities such as the Shriners hospitals for children were dismissed by respondents as appealing but insufficient to join an organization. The few men who find most of the Shrine's characteristics appealing are slightly younger than average, lower income, less-educated, and more likely to belong to a minority group.

It's possible the Shriners could change in response to the survey's findings, but one thing is certain: the fez will stay. "It's a symbol of our organization," says spokesman Michael Andrews. When there's a Shriners' convention in town, "You certainly know we're there because of the unique headgear. There's no hint at this time of dropping it."

"I've talked to friends of mine in their 30s," Andrews says. "I ask them: 'If you could get into the Shrine and didn't have to wear the fez—Is that it?' That's not it at all. They don't have the time to go through all the steps of Masonry." (Applicants must become Masons before they can join.) Men of the GI generation "didn't have cable TV, didn't have health clubs, and didn't spend much time with their kids," he says. "I spend much more time with my kids than my dad spent with me."

The Shriners hope to reach young people by recruiting at college fraternities, but this effort has not yet gained momentum. And despite the survey, the Shrine has not followed other civic groups in admitting women members.

OPENING THE DOOR TO WOMEN

Women now account for the bulk of growth in some formerly all-male organizations. For the current generation, the move to co-ed membership is just common sense.

"More younger men have been dealing with women at work. They are associated with women," says Connecticut College president Claire Gaudiani. "The idea of men being together doesn't have the same play for this generation as it does for men 55 and older."

Gaudiani sees a co-ed society firmly established on campus, where men and women often play intramural sports together. "It seems to me it's a healthy thing," she says, "but it puts aside going to a men's club."

"It's not clear that going to Elks or VFW meetings once a week was transformative for people," Gaudiani says. "If the groups create communities of support and add to the quality of life in their community, their loss is a problem. The volunteer work they organize is helpful to society."

But, she says, "I'm not sure that we're going to miss Elks clubs. It may be their demise will be a tribute to profound improvements in society. Many of these clubs were racially exclusive. A lot of young people will not belong to something that omits women or men or blacks or Jews." She credits that change to growing numbers of college-educated people who are less tolerant of segregation.

The Elks voted in September to allow women to join. "I think it's the appropriate time for a change," says Robert Grafton. He says that while the vote may have the effect of increasing membership, that was not the purpose.

"You're viewed in this day and age as archaic if women aren't eligible to be part of your organization," he says. "That creates a lot of problems." Grafton is a former national leader of the Elks—in Elk parlance, as he reluctantly admits, a grand exalted ruler. "That's probably another archaic title," he says.

Another reason for decline of lodges is a new generation's dislike of conformity. "People are less willing to deal with the tight rules of the organizations, like a song and a handshake and a hat and you have to be there every Tuesday for lunch," says Gaudiani. "People need more flexibility. That's why you see these companies with 800 numbers, that are open 24 hours. It's 2 in the morning, and you call the damn number and get the shoes sent to you. People under 45 demand a lot more flexibility."

Groups like Rotary International still operate on a routine. Local clubs meet once a week, and members must attend 60 percent of the meetings. If they miss one, they can make it up in another town, and many Rotarians enjoy attending meetings in other states and countries. But the requirement is a stringent one for those whose schedules are already chaotic. And "people don't go out for hour-and-a-half or two-hour lunches any more," says Jack McAboy, past president of the Oakland, California Rotary Club.

Rotary is trying to change its demographics, McAboy says, but it's an uphill battle. "The public's view of Rotary is largely incorrect. They think that it's a white, middle-aged-to-older male-dominated luncheon club," he says. "For years, that was an accurate description." But a U.S. Supreme Court decision in 1988 allowed women to join, and they now make up 11 percent of U.S. Rotary membership. Shortly after the decision, new women members signed up 20 times faster than men. Women Rotarians increased 10 percent in the past year, according to Rotary spokesman, Martin Kantor.

Ethnic diversity is harder to come by. "If you go by our population" in Oakland, McAboy says, "our club should be 50 percent African-American, and it's probably 5 percent. We should have a very strong Asian presence, and we have 7 or 8 Asian members. It's been difficult to reach out to those communities, although we've tried."

As president, McAboy launched an initiative in Oakland's mostly minority Lowell Middle School, offering $10,000 college scholarships to any student who makes it through high school drug-free and with a good grade point average. "That's the kind of thing that will bring people in," he says.

PERSONAL BENEFITS

In a business sense, Rotary has actually become less diverse. Each club once claimed lawyers, bankers, and real estate executives—but the Oakland club is now dominated by attorneys. The Oakland club, founded in 1908, is the third-oldest in the world. It had 400 members 20 years ago. "Now we fight to stay over 300," McAboy says.

Once largely a club of business owners, Rotary has suffered as business has changed. McAboy calls the notion of Rotary as a place to conduct business a "throwback." Even so, "I won't tell you Rotarians don't do business with Rotarians. If I need a service, I will always look to a Rotarian first." New members should not expect a flood of business from Rotarians, however. They must prove themselves as volunteers before the business connection grows.

In the 1970s, McAboy says, clubs like Rotary, Kiwanis, and Lions "all had an element of prestige. You were part of the 'in' group. I think it's just the opposite today." The phrase "old boys' network" has become pejorative, and Rotary is still seen as fostering one. That image, too, has roots in the truth. "I know some people who have been in Rotary 40 or 50 years and seen all the changes, and they would just as soon go back to the way things were," McAboy says. "That's one of the obstacles."

Groups that are growing despite the anti-joiner trend offer their members significant personal benefits. The Catholic-based Knights of Columbus remain strong, in large part because of a robust insurance business that sets them apart from other groups, according to Christopher Kauffman, a professor at the Catholic University of America in Baltimore and author of *Faith and Fraternalism,* the official history of the Knights.

The Knights' life insurance program is only available to members and has about $27 billion in force, Kauffman says. "The insurance feature is one that energizes a lot of local development," he says. "Insurance agents promote new development."

Kauffman offers two other theories for the Knights' growth in the 1980s: a strong charismatic national leader, Virgil Dechant; and a value system in line with a national movement to celebrate small-town values. Even with the successful insurance business driving membership, the Knights of Columbus and other groups remain strongest outside the large metropolises.

As many groups lament their losses, they note with some poignancy the good works they do. Perhaps even more than the fez and wacky parades, the Shriners are known for their hospitals for children. Lions Clubs have the overarching goal of helping the blind and vision-impaired, while local chapters may pick their own cause. But times have changed, says Lions spokeswoman Karen Goldsmith. "People think volunteering is a great idea, but it's basically easier just to write a check."

Even groups with a reputation for partying stress their civic involvement. George Lapadula, 61, of Middletown, Connecticut, joined the Elks in 1980 because they raised a lot of money for Newington Children's Hospital, a cause he supports. Lapadula also enjoys his time with the Elks, cooking at fund-raising dinners and breakfasts. "You make a lot of new friends," he says. "It's amazing, the people you meet from all walks of life. It's like a family."

LONGING FOR CONNECTION

It may be a longing for fellow feeling that has men flocking in surprising numbers to football stadiums. They go for emotional ceremonies in which they promise to resume their traditional roles as husbands and fathers. More than 700,000 took part in Promise Keepers events in the first eight months of 1995, and organizers can't quite figure out why. "There's an element that's hard to explain," says spokesman Roger Chapman. "We just believe that God is involved in this process."

"The big events are exciting, and people make some emotional decisions," Chapman says. "The struggle point comes at home several weeks later in a crisis. We're trying to follow up with actual promise keeping. We're focusing on small local church groups."

Promise Keepers is powerful evidence that some Americans still want the feeling of community. They are seeking those connections in new ways, says writer Howard Rheingold of Mill Valley, California.

Rheingold's book, *The Virtual Community,* describes his experience as an online pioneer with the Well, an intimate and highly literate computer conferencing service. "Maybe I meet some people at PTA meetings," Rheingold says, "but not a lot, particularly not a lot of men who I have values in common with. A lot of people, including men I hang out with in real life, are people I met through the Well."

"The need for connectedness is definitely part of why online services are growing so quickly," Rheingold says. "It's a cafeteria-style connectedness. You can pick people who are baseball fans, fathers of daughters, Democrats, or Republicans."

Rheingold says that many men have replaced nightly chats at a lodge with a 21st century substitute. Men used to go out every night," he says. "Now, Dad may go into his den for 20 minutes and log on." This is all fine, Rheingold says, "as long as you don't mistake the tool for the task. Sitting in front of the screen is not a substitute for human relationships. You need to look at what you're accomplishing."

FOR JOURNALING AND DISCUSSION

1. How did traditional gender roles help to sustain civic and fraternal organizations? What impact has the transformation of gender roles had on these organizations?
2. In what ways might fraternal organizations keep whites separate from people of color? How might these organizations be reimagined to promote interracial relationships and friendships?
3. Do men and women of any age need single-sex organizations? Should everything be co-ed? Do our needs for same-sex affiliations change as we age? Why or why not?

4. Fost relates our television viewing to our declining social connectedness. Compare and contrast this view of television with the opinions of Caffilene Allen and Adrian C. Louis in their respective autobiographical essays "First They Changed My Name," in Chapter 8, and "Earth Bone Connected to the Spirit Bone," in Chapter 5.

FOR RESEARCH AND EXPLORATION

1. Interview a family member or friend about his or her affiliation with a group such as the Knights of Columbus, the Masons, or the Shriners. What future does he or she envision for the organization?
2. Working in a group, research a charitable institution such as the Shriners' Hospital for Crippled Children and interview staff members. Who is served by this group? What impact would the loss of this institution have on the community?
3. Who are the Promise Keepers? Is this an organization for younger men? older men? white men? Research women's concerns over this group's beliefs about gender roles.

On the Row

Tina Rosenberg

A freelance journalist, Rosenberg won the 1996 Pulitzer Prize for nonfiction for her book The Haunted Land: Facing Europe's Ghosts After Communism, *which also won a National Book Award. She is also the author of* Children of Cain, *a book about violence in South America. Rosenberg was the first freelance writer to receive a MacArthur "genius" Award, and she is currently a Fellow at the World Policy Institute of the New School.*

Big day on "General Hospital"—the wealthy, powerful and handsome Ned, scion of the Quartermaine family, finally took his vows in a Catholic church with Lois, the rock-band manager from Brooklyn, N.Y. Joseph Hudgins savors every minute. It's his favorite soap; he's watched it since he was little. Now it cuts the boredom of his afternoons, every day from 3 to 4 on Channel 25, WOLO, in Columbia, S.C.

Mornings are better. Breakfast comes at about 7—grits, eggs, two biscuits—pretty much the same all the time. Then Joseph can go outside. He usually plays doubles handball and talks to his friends, fellow handball players or men who read the same science-fantasy books he does. He's 3,500 pages into a series by Robert Jordan. Lunch comes at 11:30—mystery meat, boiled vegetable, white bread.

Besides watching *General Hospital,* there is little to do after lunch. Joseph can't go out, so he lies in bed and reads, listens to Garth Brooks or Little Texas tapes on the boombox his sister Renee gave him, or paints—eagles and deer—with the acrylic paints that she also sent along with a book on sketching. The hours until dinner comes at around 4:30 move slowly, especially in the humid summers, and he spends a lot of them stretched out on his bed, thinking.

Joseph has a lot to think about and, at the age of 20, both too much and too little time to do it. For the past two years, Joseph Hudgins has been on death row at the Broad River Correctional Institution for the murder of a policeman. When he was sentenced to death at the age of 17 on July 27, 1993, Joseph was the youngest resident of death row in the nation. He is still the youngest in the state. Now the electric chair awaits him 250 yards from his cell.

"Before I got there I had all these thoughts running through my head about prison," Joseph tells me during a telephone conversation. "And then the first thing they say is, 'Take your clothes off for a strip-search.' One guard told me, 'I used to work in law enforcement, and if we'd gotten hold of you, you'd never have made it here.' "

"When I first got to death row, I was scared of everything," Joseph says. "The judge had just set an execution date for a month later, and my lawyers didn't explain to me about the appeals process. I was scared of physical assault, sexual assault, being locked up the rest of my life, not being able to see my family again or even going crazy."

Joseph was put in a suicide-watch cell with lights and camera surveillance 24 hours a day. He was terrified. "The next morning the other inmates came by my cell, asking me if I needed anything, coffee or anything else," he says. "The inmates try to look out for me." Inmates, and even some guards, told him how things worked. His lawyers came and told him that he could file an appeal. He felt better. "It has not lived up to my fears," he says.

After two weeks, Joseph was put in a regular cell on the 49-man death row, which is segregated from the rest of the prison. His cell, 14 feet by 6 feet, contains a metal bed, a locker for his clothes (South Carolina is unusual in allowing inmates to wear their own clothes, though uniforms will be required by the end of the year), a metal writing table, chair, toilet, sink and TV stand. For the first time in his life, he goes to church and Bible study, every Wednesday. "I had to learn to control my temper," he says. "I used to pop off pretty much, but now if I get mad at another inmate, I stay away a few days and cool down."

On Fridays, Conny Hudgins, Joseph's father, drives two hours from the city of Anderson to the maximum-security prison, usually with Joseph's sister Cathy or sister-in-law, Susan, and their kids. The prison, part of a complex of maximum- and medium-security prisons, is bordered by two fences, with one coil of razor wire on the inner fence and four coils on the tall outer one.

Visitors must pass through a metal detector and at least 11 steel doors before reaching the visiting cell of death row.

The cell has a Polaroid camera, and Conny's stack of pictures at home shows an increasingly rotund Joseph, a chin beard covering his acne, wearing a Hard Rock Cafe shirt or a work shirt and jeans, smiling with various nephews and siblings. At Christmas the wall behind him sports paper cutouts of Santa and his reindeer. In one picture, Joseph is holding up two fingers behind Conny's head.

I never met Joseph; the Department of Corrections would not allow the press to go into the prison to see him. We communicated through letters and the collect phone calls he was permitted to make. In one call I asked him what he missed most. "Everything," he says. "Getting to be around the kids. I'd always played with them. I had them saying 'Joseph' before 'Mommy' and 'Daddy.' Christmas is bad, New Year's is bad. Thanksgiving is pretty bad."

One of Joseph's fellow inmates, Sylvester Adams, was put to death Aug. 18 by lethal injection, now an alternative to the chair, so the prospect of death is real enough. "The electric chair seems very concrete to me," Joseph writes. "I know it's there and worry about it all the time. Dad don't like me to talk about it or even think about it, but I do."

The men on death row don't talk about their crimes much, but they do talk about their punishment. "Other people come up to me and say, 'You're so young, there's so much you haven't done,' " Joseph says. "Then I start thinking about it, and when I get depressed, I get in bad shape."

Joseph Hudgins is one of 42 inmates nationwide on death row who were legally children at the time of their offenses—a number that is likely to increase dramatically in years to come. More and more states are adopting the death penalty—New York became the 38th this year—and legislatures are applying it to a broader range of crimes.

It is also being used increasingly against children. Four states permit the execution of youths who were 17 at the time of their crimes; 21 states permit it for 16 year olds. In the race for governor of Texas last year, both the then incumbent governor, Ann Richards, and George Bush Jr., who defeated her, said they'd think about using the death penalty for children as young as 14.

Until a few years ago, most people in the United States considered young people less dangerous than adults. Today that perception is reversed: Young criminals are considered crazier, with more bravado and less conscience. Although violent crime has dropped substantially nationwide, juvenile crime is rising in many places, and with it rises the national concern about juvenile killers. The justice system, once dedicated to protecting and rehabilitating young offenders, is increasingly handing children adult-size penalties.

The United States is virtually alone in the world in taking this position. In the last 15 years, only Iraq and possibly Iran have executed more minors, and only six other countries have executed even one. Some of the very qualities that make juvenile criminals most terrifying—their impulsiveness, a tendency to fall under the sway of others and a need to prove their toughness to the group—raise questions about their suitability for a punishment that the law reserves for a small group of the most morally culpable killers. Minors are thought too immature to sit on a jury, vote, buy beer or watch an X-rated movie, yet they are considered responsible enough to pay for their crimes with their lives.

The case of Joseph Hudgins illustrates all these issues. His rashness, lack of judgment and susceptibility to the domination of others might have brought him to kill 21-year-old police officer Christopher Taylor. But there is more to his story, a plot twist that raises the most basic questions about the death penalty. It is just as likely that Joseph Hudgins' youth led him not to kill but to confess to a murder he did not commit.

Anderson's main roads and its exits off the interstate look like an American Everycity: Wendy's, the Quality Inn, Wachovia Bank with drive-through and automatic tellers. The steakhouse on Sunday afternoons overflows with black families fresh from church, the little girls in white lacy dresses and pigtails. Anderson Mall is filled with teenage boys buying outfits for their girlfriends. But on the back roads there are still signs of hardscrabble Anderson, a poor and undereducated town south of the Blue Ridge Mountain foothills near the Georgia border. Off the interstate a sign announces that these two miles of highway are maintained by the Cathedral of Love. Fishermen and their families live in tents on the banks of Lake Hartwell. Here a man's prized possession is his set of carpentry tools, and his evenings and weekends are spent working on the house or car.

Anderson is not a place where folks sit around fretting about the moral dilemmas posed by the execution of a juvenile offender. A few years ago a man here thought his wife was messing around on him. He killed her, stuffed her body in the back seat of his car and drove her around town to show other residents what he had done. A boy of 17 is no kid here. Upon high school graduation the common plan is to marry, buy a trailer and park it on the property of your parents or spouse's parents, all the while saving up for a plot of land. At 17 you find the job at the textile mill or Bi-Lo supermarket which you will keep for the next 50 years.

A few hundred yards down South Carolina's Highway 24 from where police officer Taylor was shot, there is a cluster of stores selling liquor, fireworks, and guns and boat canvases, plus a video-game room and a pawnshop. At the edge of the parking lot there is a street, Pearl Harbor Way, that snakes around to the top of a hill and ends at the property of Joseph's father. Conny's scrubby six-acre spread comprises the main house, cars and trucks in various stages of repair, a few sheds, a barrack-like building that is Conny's ceramics shop, a gray trailer perched on piles of blocks with lumber stacked underneath and, across a small creek and into the family's adjoining three acres, a dilapidated A-frame house with a yard strung with wash. At the time of Joseph's arrest, his whole family lived on the property. His sister Renee and her husband, Oral Tollison—whom she married 21 years ago, at age 15—lived with their daughter in a trailer while Oral finished the house he was building with his own hands. Joseph's brother, David, and his wife, Susan, lived in another trailer with their children. His sister Cathy and her husband, Micheal Greer, lived in the A-frame with their boys. The Hudgins' compound looks like a lot of the property in Anderson—except for THE DEATH PENALTY IS DEAD WRONG bumper stickers on Conny's GMC van.

Renee's and David's families have since moved to their own houses, but Cathy and Micheal still live in the A-frame, and Conny is still in the big house. He is an engaging, likable and talkative man of 59. The house is full of his ceramics: Grandpa in overalls and a bandanna sits in a rocker; an Indian stands in the corner. Unpainted eagles and Christs on the cross cram the dining table.

Amnesty International books on the death penalty are stacked on the kitchen counter, and Conny's main room is a shrine to Joseph. The walls are dotted with some of the Polaroids from the visiting-room camera. Joseph's senior picture, taken a few months before the murder, sits on the TV. His hair is choppily cut in the short-top, long-back style favored in Anderson, and pimples dot his chin. He looks about 14.

Right before Joseph's trial, Conny quit his job working breakfast at Burger King. His health, always precarious, worsened, and his diet is none too good to begin with—I've seen him eat sandwiches of potato chips on white bread, dry. Most of all, he is nervous. He lies awake nights and, when he is not working at his new job at a Speedway truck stop, he spends his days making phone calls to help his son.

Conny is a loving father, but Joseph grew up in a weird, scary and lonely house. When he was 7 weeks old, his mother, Virginia, died of a brain tumor. Conny already suffered from what Southerners call nerves—along with emphysema, brown-lung disease and back pain. With his wife's death his depression became even more intense. From 1975, the year of Joseph's birth, to 1992, Conny's medical records include prescriptions for 22 different kinds of drugs including 11 types of mood-elevating and tranquilizing pills. As a baby, Joseph would often cry, and Conny, asleep on the couch, wouldn't wake up.

When Joseph was 4, Conny married Carolyn, a widow working at the textile mill, who moved into the house with four of her children. Conny and Carolyn divorced, got back together and then split again. As of several years ago, Carolyn was still sending Conny notes through the Burger King drive-up window.

Conny and Carolyn fought mostly about religion. Since 1962, Conny had been a follower of Brother William Marrion Branham, who preached a Holiness gospel at the Branham Tabernacle, in Jeffersonville, Ind. Many weekends, Conny would pack his family in the car and drive about 400 miles each way to Jeffersonville. (Joseph tended to fall asleep during services.) After Conny married Carolyn, they went to the Light Tabernacle, a small house with beige vinyl siding in a run-down neighborhood in Anderson. Inside it one

Sunday morning, about two dozen worshipers—all the women in long skirts with long hair and no makeup—sat in pews before a raised, carpeted altar with large pictures of equal size of Jesus, Brother Branham and Manuel Burdette, the church's preacher, now deceased. A young man with an electric guitar led a small ensemble with drums and piano in song and quoted Brother Branham's sermons. A table in the foyer held dozens of Branham's pamphlets for people to borrow. Holiness worshipers separate themselves from sin, "unlike the Baptists, who shoot pool, drink, cuss and let their women wear makeup and cut their hair," explains one Anderson follower. Conny has about 100 sermon tapes, which he constantly listened to when Joseph was growing up. When I visited Conny, he usually had one in the tape player.

Carolyn followed Brother Branham, too, but there were other voices buzzing in her head. "Religion sent her crazy," Joseph says of his stepmother. Family members say Carolyn used to walk around the house saying she was Joan of Arc and would be burned at the stake naked.

Before the age of 15, Joseph had spent only two nights away from home, but in high school he found friends outside his family. One day he was supervising a children's party at Burger King, where he worked some weekends and after school, bringing the kids cake and playing games with them. His way with the kids charmed the birthday boy's older sister, a pretty girl with long, wavy brown hair and glasses. She slipped him a napkin with her phone number. From then on, Joseph was over at Stephanie Spearman's house every day.

And then Joseph found his soul mate, Terry Cheek. Joseph had met Terry in seventh grade, but the two really became friends in eighth, when they were in the same homeroom. Skinny as a cat in a bath, Terry was nearly a year older than Joseph. He didn't talk much himself, but he made Joseph feel important. "He'd listen to what I had to say," Joseph testified at his trial. "If I wanted to talk about something, I could go to Terry. I couldn't go to any of my family, really."

In the summer between Joseph's junior and senior years, Stephanie left him for an older boy she met at the beach. Joseph got a handful of pills out of Conny's medicine chest. It was Terry, who came over with his family, who coaxed Joseph out of taking them.

School was incidental. Joseph got A's when he worked at it, but he didn't work at it much. When he went, he hung out with other people, since Terry didn't go to school very often. Even after the breakup he saw Stephanie every morning. She was in his Lunch Bunch, and he'd walk her to the parking lot, where her mother waited every afternoon. Joseph liked to fix up cars, and he wrecked a couple before losing his license for accumulating too many points, mostly for speeding. Most of his time, however, went to an activity in which he truly excelled: stealing.

Joseph began stealing pencils off desks when he was about 7. By seventh grade, Joseph, Terry and some friends were going to the Jockey Lot, Anderson's huge flea market, to see who could steal the most. By 10th grade, Joseph was meeting Terry almost every night and weekend to steal. At the trial,

Joseph admitted that he and Terry bought a pair of bolt cutters; Terry claimed they belonged to Joseph but that both used them to cut the locks on gates and the backs of trucks before helping themselves to the merchandise. Terry claimed Joseph used a ski mask for break-ins where there were surveillance cameras. According to one school friend, Joseph took advantage of his job installing car stereos to go to his clients' houses, break into their cars and steal back the stereos. He even figured out how to take $100 from the cash register at Burger King without getting caught.

"He'd come in every Monday and brag about what he'd stolen over the weekend," says one Westside High School friend. "People would come up to him: 'Can you get this piece of stereo equipment? I'll give you $75 for it.'. . . He did it more for the thrill."

"I guess I bragged about stealing in school for attention," Joseph writes to me. "I knew stealing was wrong—I was taught that all my life. I guess I justified it by only stealing from places where insurance would cover it. Well, most of the time—places like car lots and businesses."

The standard view in the Hudgins family is that this was the doing of Terry and his family. "We weren't exposed to a lot of the same things other people were," says Renee. " Joseph, being very gullible, went along for the ride." Renee's husband, Oral, says that if Terry came to his shop, he would always check to see if the tools were still there afterward. Conny believed that Joseph would have spent quiet evenings at home if it weren't for Terry. "Terry would come over at 6 and pick him up," Conny says. "I'd say, 'Now, you have school tomorrow, son,' and Joseph would say, 'I'll just be gone a few minutes.' " Conny would sit up fuming till 2 A.M., when Joseph would come back. Sometimes he wouldn't come back at all. Terry's family told me the same story with the names reversed: Terry was the quiet follower held in Joseph's sway.

But just about everyone agrees about Terry's mother, Brenda. She and Terry Sr.—by all accounts a decent, hard-working man—were one week away from legal divorce when he was found dead in his house in February 1992. The coroner's office ruled his death a suicide, but state officials are still investigating. Around the time of her husband's death, Brenda spoke to her friend Sherri Spearman, Stephanie's mother, of his $100,000 life-insurance policy. A few months after his death, Brenda found out that the policy was a myth. "She showed up at my house, devastated," Sherri says. It was one of the many stories swirling around Anderson about Brenda Cheek and her new boyfriend, Joey Fortner.

When Joseph and Terry were in 11th grade, Brenda began to live with Joey, a skinny man with slicked-back hair. Terry's friends could hang out anytime—even during the school day—to drink or have sex. According to court testimony, Joey encouraged Terry and Joseph to steal stereos and VCRs and would store the stolen goods in Brenda's rented self-storage warehouse until he could sell them. "Brenda and Joey would say, 'Get us a stereo, and we'll pay you $400 or $500,' " says Lora Shiflet, who hung out there and started dating Joseph after he and Stephanie broke up. Brenda once threw a fit because Joseph was getting more money from a burglary than she was. According to Joseph, Joey even helped the boys buy an Uzi; Terry claimed the Uzi was Joseph's. "Joey knew a guy who had one, and we had just sold a bunch of stolen stuff, so me and Terry bought it," writes Joseph. "Terry kept it either in his house or behind the seat in his truck." Joey would often tell the boys about his glorious days working in the marijuana trade.

The sense of freedom at Brenda and Joey's was heady. Joseph told me that Joey's praise wasn't all that important to him but admitted that the boys sought it. Joey was no fool. "Bet you can't break into that car," Joey would say, according to a member of Joseph's family. "Well, good for you! I didn't think you could!"

Joseph got into trouble with the law three times. In late 1991, he, Terry and two other friends were caught stealing hunters' deer stands from the back of a truck. Then Joseph was caught driving a motorcycle while his license was suspended. Both times, Conny paid fines of several hundred dollars. And several weeks before Taylor's murder, Joseph was picked up for shoplifting fishing gear at Kmart. The manager had seen two shoplifters but caught only the younger one, Joseph, who would not tell the police the name of his confederate. Joseph's brother, David, went to talk to him. "He's letting you take the fall," David argued. Joseph broke down and cried—but he didn't talk. Later his lawyers would seize on this and other examples of Joseph's code of silence in arguing that he was all too eager to take the rap for a friend.

On Sunday, Dec. 6, 1992, at around 3 A.M., Terry and Joseph stole an Orkin Exterminating truck and parked it on a back road. Toward midnight they drove out to the truck to joy ride around again. One of the two took the .25-caliber semiautomatic pistol they shared from Terry's truck. The Orkin truck's hose was dragging from the reel on the back, and Officer Chris Taylor spotted it as he was driving down Highway 24 a few miles west of Anderson. Taylor stopped them. Terry told him the truck belonged to his daddy. The three examined the truck, and, presumably because it was raining, Taylor asked them to sit down in the back of his patrol car. As they were standing by the vehicles, a passing driver saw them.

Less than five minutes later, the same driver returned. Seeing no one around, he stopped the car—nearly hitting Chris Taylor, who was lying stretched out in the middle of the road. The driver called 911 on his car phone. Taylor had been shot in the face. He was gasping for air as blood and membrane flowed from his nose and mouth. He was dead before sunrise.

Joseph and Terry ran to Joseph's house. Conny, waiting up as usual, found his son sopping wet. Once away from Conny, Joseph opened a window, and Terry climbed in. Joseph called Joey Fortner. "Get over here quick and pick up Terry," Joseph said. Terry waited in the rain at the edge of Conny's property for Joey to arrive.

One Valentine's Day, Chris Taylor took Tracy Owens, his girlfriend since he was 14, on a drive out South Carolina's Highway 187. He stopped the car at a tree with a big red bow around it. "Happy Valentine's Day," Chris said. Three and three quarters of an acre—that was her present. Chris and Tracy, a beautician, had been married a year and a week when he was killed. Tracy's doctor had told her she couldn't conceive, but a few weeks before Chris died, they learned that she was pregnant, and they were thrilled. They told his parents by bringing them a present—a bib with I LOVE GRANDPA and I LOVE GRANDMA on it. Chris and Tracy had just been approved for a loan to build their house.

Chris Taylor, 21, was a weightlifter, a stocky 5 feet 10 inches with a small mustache and a bulldog face, who loved hunting, fishing and country music. Everyone in Anderson knows his daddy, Ray, a former policeman and now a game warden, and therefore one of the county's most important men. Since he was 10, Chris Taylor had talked about joining the sheriff's department, itching to turn 21 so he could become a policeman. When he was 20 he became a dispatcher in the department radio room, and the following year he was made a deputy sheriff. He was the voice of Officer Mac, the police robot that talked to young kids in schools and churches. If his baby was a girl, he'd wanted to name her Miranda, after the legal rights police read to suspects—that's how much he'd loved being a cop. No one in Anderson could recall a death that had hit the community as hard as Chris Taylor's did. All the Anderson TV stations broadcast hours of live coverage of the manhunt—the largest in the area's history—with bloodhounds in the woods and helicopters overhead.

That Monday morning, Renee drove Joseph to school. The police stopped them at a checkpoint and waved them on. "Good thing you don't fit the description," Renee said. She lectured him about stealing and how it can lead to more serious crimes. "Here are two guys, stole a truck, got pulled over and panicked, and shot a police officer," she said.

"A thief is not a murderer," Joseph told his sister. He said it twice.

The next day, Joseph felt sick and stayed home from school. He and Conny watched Chris Taylor's funeral on TV. People packed the church and stood outside in the cold. Policemen wept openly. A policeman turned chaplain came up from Charleston, S.C., to counsel the deputies. Now, if people in Anderson saw a patrol car stopped, they pulled over to make sure the officer was all right.

On Thursday afternoon, Joseph and Terry were called out of class to the principal's office, supposedly to talk about their attendance records. Eight or 10 policemen awaited them. A few minutes later the local TV stations broke into their programming with shots of the boys being escorted from police cars into the sheriff's headquarters. Some classmates had called the Crime Stoppers hot line and told about Joseph and Terry's burglaries, and the police found a fingerprint on the Orkin truck's ignition that matched Joseph's.

The city was stunned. Joseph and Terry were typical students who went to the same school that Taylor's brother, Chad, did. Neither had any previous record of violence.

At the sheriff's headquarters, Joseph at first denied any connection to the crime. The captain interrogating Joseph told him about finding his fingerprint on the ignition of the Orkin truck. Then Joseph said he wanted to confess.

They went over the statement a few times. Another officer wrote as Joseph dictated, and Joseph signed it: "We followed him back to his car, and when he opened the back door of the car, I shot him. We then ran up the hill to the condominiums . . ." No details were asked; none seemed necessary. By the day's end the police had found a .25-caliber in the rain gutter of Hudgins' house.

Joseph called Conny later that day. "I know good and well you didn't do this," said Conny.

"Yeah, I did, Daddy. I done it," Joseph replied.

"Oh, no, Joseph," Conny said. "Ain't no way you're gonna convince me."

Joseph and Terry were put in separate jails outside Anderson County for their own protection. Conny's children gathered and sat up talking till 5 that morning and the next. Westside High offered counseling to any student who wanted it. Students walked around in a daze. How could their own classmates—not model boys, but boys—have put a gun in Chris Taylor's face and pulled the trigger?

America's first documented execution of a juvenile took place in 1642. Thomas Graunger, 16, was hanged in the Plymouth colony for having carnal knowledge of a cow and a horse. About 350 juvenile offenders have been executed since that time—three-fourths of them were minorities, almost all the victims white. At least 43 of those executed were never even convicted of murder but of rape or attempted rape. None of these were white, and all the victims but one were.

South Carolina's last execution of a juvenile offender was the 1986 electrocution of James Terry Roach, who at the time of his crime was 17, mentally retarded, suffering from a deteriorating brain disease and under the domination of an older "friend" who had injected him with PCP before the crime. The state legislature was at the time considering a bill prohibiting capital punishment for juveniles; still, Gov. Richard Riley—today, President Clinton's secretary of education—wouldn't sign a stay of execution to await the vote.

Roach's history is a common one for death row. A Human Rights Watch report describes one juvenile offender on Texas' death row—abandoned by his mother, skull fractured by a truck, a first-grade dropout, brain damaged, schizophrenic, regularly sexually assaulted by his stepfather and grandfather, regularly sniffed glue—who told a psychiatrist he could not remember anything good that ever happened to him. The collective history of most juvenile offenders on death row is filled with such tragedy. It is littered with abusive parents, uninterested doctors, and neglectful or bungling bureaucrats. None of these people has ever been indicted as accessory to murder.

The state appointed and paid two lawyers for Joseph: Robert Gamble, a profane, curmudgeonly public defender in his 50s, and Bob Lusk, a young private attorney.

Gamble and Lusk pondered how to make the best of a bad hand. Death penalty trials have two phases. If the jury finds the defendant guilty, it then sits for a second trial to determine the sentence. Gamble and Lusk's strategy was to concentrate on getting Joseph a prison term instead of the death penalty.

They planned a defense revolving around Joseph Hudgins' youth: that it was his naiveté, eagerness to please, lack of judgment and child's view of loyalty that led him to fall under the spell of Terry, Brenda and Joey. They planned to argue that a boy with no history of violence deserved to live to earn another chance.

That was the strategy, anyway, until July 1993, two days before jury selection was to begin, when Joseph's defense team met in a motel parking lot to re-create the moment of the shooting. "And then we sat down with our mouths open," says Hyatt Whetsell, an investigator working with the lawyers. "Joseph Hudgins could not have pulled that trigger."

Taylor had been shot during his attempt to open the back door of the patrol car. The defense team parked two cars and reenacted the shooting, using what they knew about the position of the body (feet near the car, stretched out at a 30-degree angle from the car), the angle of the shot (slightly upward from behind Taylor's right eye) and the placement of the spent shell (next to the rear left tire). When they were finished, they concluded there was only one possibility: The shooter had to have been standing between Taylor and the rear of the car. According to what both Joseph and Terry had said and maps both boys drew, the one standing there was the one who was about to get into the back seat, Terry Cheek.

Lusk and Whetsell drove to see Joseph in jail that night. "We got proof you didn't do it," Lusk kept repeating into Joseph's face. To their astonishment, Joseph kept insisting he was guilty—until Lusk told him about the witness list: Terry Cheek was on for the prosecution. "I felt betrayed," Joseph testified at his trial, explaining why he changed his story. "I mean, here I am taking the blame, and he's going to testify and try to send me to the electric chair." He told Lusk and Gamble that he and Terry, who was 18, had agreed later on the day of the murder that if they were arrested, Joseph would take the rap. "I've been in trouble before," Joseph says. "But I never had any problems because I'm a juvenile." Joseph wrote to me that it wasn't hard to lie to the police: "I told them exactly what they wanted to hear. . . . The only thing that was going through my head was to stick to the plan we had worked out." The tough part, he wrote, was lying to his dad: "I mean, I had lied to him before, but this was hard. The good thing is Dad never believed it."

By the time the attorneys left Joseph's cell, they had a new case.

The publicity made finding an impartial jury in Anderson County impossible. Instead of moving the trial, a jury was chosen from Lexington County—a conservative white suburb of Columbia. In its 14 previous death-penalty cases, Lexington County jurors had sent 13 men to death row.

The courtroom atmosphere left little doubt about Anderson's sentiments. Spectators wore buttons with Chris Taylor's picture. During trial breaks, people debated whether Joseph should simply be electrocuted or also tortured first. "I would go into a restaurant, and people at the next booth would be talking about killing those boys," says Charles Whiten, Terry's lawyer. "I got phone threats: 'This case won't ever make it to court.' Some people I'd wanted to testify came to my house and said they were afraid someone in the community would harm them if they showed up. . . . It went beyond the normal community anger. You ask people what should happen, people say they should be shot on the square."

Anderson's fury made Joseph's situation even more precarious. When he confessed, police investigators quite naturally stopped looking any further. Prosecutors, therefore, decided to allow Terry to plead guilty to accessory after the fact and gave him a guarantee that he could never be prosecuted for anything related to the murder. Although Joseph's lawyers asked the judge to allow the jury to be able to find that Joseph was an accessory after the fact, the judge refused. "Mr. Hudgins either committed this murder, or he didn't," the judge told Joseph's lawyers. He allowed jurors the options of convicting Joseph of murder or finding him innocent—they could not say, "We think Terry Cheek should be tried" or "We think Joseph had minor participation." So if the jurors didn't convict Joseph, they were telling Anderson that no one would pay for Chris Taylor's death.

Joseph, dressed in an uncomfortable-looking jacket and tie, his hair freshly cut, stared ahead for most of the trial. On the stand he said he confessed to save his best friend and said of Taylor, "I'd give my own life for his life to be back."

"I can't remember a lot of it—it's blacked out," Joseph tells me about the trial. "I was concentrating on the testimony. I was concentrating on keeping my emotions down. As soon as a recess came, my family would come up to me, and I'd burst out crying."

Stephanie's testimony was the hardest. "You love him?" the assistant prosecutor asked, trying to discredit her testimony. "Yes," Stephanie said. Tears welled up in Joseph's eyes. The jurors I spoke with said the most damning testimony was given by three of Joseph's Westside classmates, who all said that he told them one day in class that since policemen wore bulletproof vests, he would shoot one in the head if he got caught stealing. The best Gamble and Lusk could do in cross-examination was to get them to admit they were all friends of Chad Taylor, Chris' younger brother. I called all three. One said he didn't want to talk about it. One said he stands by his testimony. The third, reversing what he'd said on the stand, told me he'd never heard Joseph make that statement.

Jurors later told me that they had not been convinced by the physical evidence that was at the heart of the defense. Joseph's lawyers had pegged Terry as the shooter in part because a .25 ejects its shells behind and to the right—if the gun had been in Joseph's hand, the shell would have been found away from the car, not next to the rear tire. In test firings, they said, a .25 had ejected the shell 13 times in a row to the same position. But jurors did their own test. "We went into the bathroom, which had a hard floor," juror Frank Peters tells me. "We dropped the shell from the sink several times. Each time it rolled and ended up in a different place." After eight hours of deliberation, the jurors returned with their verdict. Joseph stared straight ahead as they pronounced him guilty of murder.

The drama in the second phase of the trial—for sentencing—came from the emotional testimony of Tracy and Ray Taylor and one of Chris' colleagues. If the jury had any doubts about the sentiment of Anderson, it didn't after Tracy talked about the hundreds of letters she received and the child who made her angels to hang on the wall, and after Capt. Vick Wooten talked about the size of the funeral and the psychological counseling that deputies required. The testimony was of questionable legality—to avoid putting community pressure on juries, victim-impact statements are supposed to be limited. In theory the law places an identical value on each human life; a drug dealer's life is worth the same as Mother Teresa's, and their murderers should be subject to the same punishments, even if the drug dealer did not leave behind grieving friends and families, or a community screaming for the defendant's head.

George Ducworth, the chief prosecutor, summed up. "He had four weapons that he took with him," he said of Joseph. "Those bolt cutters, this ski mask, that gun and one more that's not so readily apparent. And that is the shield of youth. Should he receive extra credit because he was able to kill somebody at a younger age than a lot of other people are when they kill somebody?" No credit, the jury said after eight more hours of deliberation. Death.

Three months later, Terry pleaded guilty to accessory after the fact, auto theft and a series of burglaries and was sentenced to 30 years. He has earned his high school equivalency degree in McCormick Correctional Institution. He is taking college courses and has joined the Jaycees. He expects to be out on work release next year and is eligible for parole in 1998.

On July 24 this year, the South Carolina Supreme Court affirmed Joseph's conviction. Because Gamble and Lusk had failed to raise objections at the trial, the Supreme Court was barred from even considering most arguments raised by Joseph's new lawyers such as the legality of the extensive statements from Taylor's family.

Brenda Cheek did not attend her son's hearing. According to Terry's grandmother, who visits him every other week, Brenda went to see Terry in prison three times in his first two years there. Although Brenda came to Joseph's trial once, and Joey attended some days—once even sitting with a sheriff's department investigator, apparently laughing and trading jokes—neither was arrested nor even called to the stand to testify. The police waited till three days after Terry's arrest to search their house. Today, Brenda and Joey have disappeared from Anderson. No one I talked to, not even Brenda's father, said they knew where she was.

Tracy Taylor still cries every time she hears Chris' name or picks up a magazine that mentions him. Her pension as a widow of a slain policeman helped her to open her own beauty shop and build the house she and Chris had been planning. On June 4, 1993, she gave birth to Christopher Taylor Jr., and they now live on the property Chris gave her that Valentine's Day.

Death row has been eventful lately. In South Carolina, as all over the country, prisoners are losing their privileges. The state brought in a new prison commissioner from Texas, whose new rules have cut back on visits, phone calls, out-of-cell time and hair length. Joseph's hair is now Marine short. In April five prisoners (none of them on death row) led a revolt against the new hair rules. "Some of the religious segregations [*sic*] were saying that it was against their religion," Joseph says. The prisoners attacked five guards with kitchen knives, baseball bats and boiling water—and held three workers hostage during the 11-hour standoff. All prisoners were locked in their cells for the next two weeks.

Joseph Hudgins is still hoping the courts will grant him a new trial and still thinks about life after the row. He writes to Lora Shiflet, the girl he dated after Stephanie, and she has visited him. "Her parents only let me call once a month, but I really look forward to it," Joseph writes. "I think about her a lot."

Stephanie switched high schools, to McDuffie, in a different part of the city, where she was voted Miss McDuffie. She had to get away from Westside, from the memories and taunts of "killer's girlfriend." "Joseph and Terry weren't there to face the other students, so they took it out on her," says Sherri, her mother. Stephanie visited Joseph a few times in the beginning but hasn't gone now in a year. Joseph had Conny buy her white and pink carnations for her high school graduation. "I think about Stephanie all the time, but I don't let it bother me that she doesn't come and see me," Joseph writes me. "I understand that she should get on with her life, and I just hope she's happy." He knows it's been hard for her. He knows kids can be so cruel.

FOR JOURNALING AND DISCUSSION

1. What is "tone"? Discuss Rosenberg's tone throughout her article, and consider whether her selection of key words and phrases (for example, "a weird, scary and lonely house") betrays a possible bias about the Hudgins case and the death penalty for juvenile offenders.
2. If Tracy Taylor (the widow of slain officer Chris Taylor) were to read Rosenberg's essay, how do you think she would respond? Write a letter from Tracy to Rosenberg.
3. Rosenberg describes Anderson as "hardscrabble," "a poor and undereducated town south of the Blue Ridge Mountain foothills near the Georgia border." Compare her construction of place with that of Polly Stewart in "Regional Consciousness as a Shaper of Local History" in Chapter 8. How are these descriptions tied to violent crime?

4. Dorothy Allison, in her essay "River of Names" in Chapter 3, describes the taken-for-granted, everyday violence that dominated her youth as a poor white person. Rosenberg also discusses Anderson's criminal activities as a possible mitigating circumstance in Joseph Hudgins's development. Write an imagined dialogue between Allison and Rosenberg about criminals, their victims, and the law.
5. Discuss the possible ways that local expectations about masculinity might have contributed to Hudgins's murder of Chris Taylor. How do you think Andrew Kimbrell, the author of "A Time for Men to Pull Together" in Chapter 4, would explain Hudgins's behavior?

FOR RESEARCH AND EXPLORATION

1. Research current statistics on juvenile crime. Do you agree or disagree with applying the death penalty to juvenile offenders? Write a position paper on this issue, and support your decision with facts gathered from your research.
2. As a class, view the films *Dead Man Walking* and *Just Cause*. Discuss how each film treats the subject of capital punishment. Discuss their social impact.
3. What role do race and class play in how the death penalty is applied to both adult and juvenile offenders in the United States? Are more adults and juveniles of color sentenced to death? more poor adults and juveniles? Do these statistics change when collected for states or regions rather than for the nation as a whole?

CHAPTER 7

Ability and Disability

Our sense of who we are is intimately bound up with our abilities and disabilities. Some abilities, such as a high IQ or artistic talent, are generally considered positive by the dominant culture, while others are considered impediments. Some people want their differences to be identified as assets, while others want them to be labeled as disabilities. How we define these conditions—as either advantages and disadvantages—is yet another result of the way meaning is socially constructed. For example, many members of the deaf community and many little people construct meanings from their own perspectives; they consider themselves "normal" and everyone else "different."

Sometimes, because they are the recipients of privileges (such as reserved parking spaces or access to restricted elevators) or financial support, people are forced to accept the label "disabled" (or the euphemism "differently abled") when they do not view themselves as disadvantaged. Still other members of a community might hope for a cure for their condition or wish they were not as they are. Clearly, in the case of a condition such as fetal alcohol syndrome (FAS), it is hard to imagine anyone who would not want to prevent it, and yet there are those who celebrate the special gifts of FAS children. The contributors to this chapter present a remarkable range of definitions for ability and disability.

SUMMARIES OF SELECTIONS ON ABILITY AND DISABILITY

In "Deafness as Culture," **Edward Dolnick** traces attitudes toward deafness ranging from Samuel Johnson's view that deafness is "one of the most desperate of human calamities" to the deaf community's celebration of the condition as a cultural identity. He analyzes the "fault lines" that run through the heterogeneous world of the deaf. Issues such as whether a person is "authentically deaf" and which language is best for deaf children illustrate the conflict between assimilation and separatism.

In the opening line of "Up with People," **David Berreby** states, "Identity politics has been good for people with disabilities." The "rhetoric of pride" makes sense to him, but, like Dolnick, he demonstrates how some identity categories are different from others. For example, even though the deaf community objects strenuously, deafness is still something people sometimes try to cure. In contrast, being female or being gay is not generally something people want to "cure," although there are exceptions. Berreby writes about the conflict between those who think of being a little person as a positive thing, a marker of identity that establishes community, and those who think of it as a condition to be cured or avoided through abortion.

Nancy Mairs writes "On Being a Cripple" in the voice of someone who has nearly made her peace with herself, even though she hates her multiple sclerosis. She chooses to call herself a "cripple" instead of any of the possible euphemisms, such as "differently abled," which she describes as "pure verbal garbage designed, by its ability to describe anyone, to describe no one." Unlike others more involved in the "disability movement," Mairs would take a cure "in a minute." She writes, "I may be a cripple, but I'm only occasionally a loony and never a saint."

Laura Hershey's essay "Choosing Disability" illustrates an important point: diversity exists within any identity "community." Hershey identifies with three groups—the disability community, the women's movement, and the prochoice movement. As a disabled person who might well have been aborted as a fetus, she challenges women to consider giving birth to a disabled child. The choice not to bear a child just because tests indicate a possible disability is offensive to her and to other disabled people, but as a feminist, she supports a woman's right to make her own reproductive choices.

In "Who Gets to Live? Who Will Decide?" **Mike Ervin** moves the debate about what constitutes a "severe" or "life-threatening" disability to the legal and legislative arenas as he describes attempts to limit health care and services in cases in which the benefits to society are not thought to be worth the costs. The money question in health care begins to resemble a war in which "people are making decisions as to who's worth saving and who's not. It's just another form of triage," according to one expert on disability issues.

In his book *Paper Trail,* from which the selections here on fetal alcohol syndrome were chosen, **Michael Dorris** connects his personal history to issues that are important to all of us. First, he writes about FAS from the perspective of a citizen demanding that the nation confront the problem. Then he describes the heartbreak he and his wife, the novelist Louise Erdrich, endured as the parents of children with FAS. Using all of his skills as a writer, Dorris presents a stunning array of evidence, from statistics to personal experience to analogies, to make his case for prevention. Someone else will have to write the rest of the story about his broken family in the aftermath of Dorris's deep depression and suicide in 1997.

Joseph P. Whelen, a well known Catholic author, describes in "How I Pray Now" another kind of disability—the inability to think or to verbalize because of the overwhelming presence of cancer and pain in his life. As he faces the end of his life, the terminally ill Whelen struggles to perform the most routine tasks and, most importantly, finds that he can no longer pray as he has prayed all his life.

In "Rufus at the Door," **John Hassler** tells the story of his high school field trips to the "insane asylum." After the first trip, Rufus, a person from his home town, is institutionalized, and on the second trip, he and Hassler make eye contact. Hassler is unable to respond to Rufus, and his denial is far too familiar to most of us. The story reveals much about the ways our society has changed with regard to "mentally challenged" people. We no longer use the terms "moron," "idiot," and "imbecile" that were common during the author's adolescence, but our reactions to someone like Rufus may be very similar to Hassler's.

RHETORICAL QUESTIONS

As you consider the *rhetoric* of these readings, you will obviously have to deal with the issue of *authority.* Who gets to speak in these essays, and what would happen if people in other positions attempted to say the same things? Is Dolnick deaf? Does it matter? And is Berreby a dwarf? What claim does Ervin have to this turf? How can journalists establish the authority to cover sensitive topics like these?

Given the relatively high incidence of FAS among Native American children, does it help that Dorris identified himself as partly Native American? How has the publicity surrounding Dorris's suicide affected his authority in his writing for children? Mairs can use the word "cripple" because she claims the word, but can an able-bodied person use it in the same way? Hershey positions herself in several camps. Does this help or hurt her authority to write about abortion? How do your answers change if you consider two kinds of readers—insiders and outsiders, people with disabilities and people without obvious ones? Hassler is the only author who writes from the position of an observer, an outsider. How does he establish his authority?

And finally, what is the purpose of each of these essays? Some have a clear call for action, and others have an implied message. Are the rhetorical appeals appropriate for the authors' purposes? What other kinds of appeals might they have used? What might Whelen have hoped to accomplish with his interview? What was Hassler's goal?

Deafness as Culture (Debate)

Edward Dolnick

Dolnick is a freelance writer and regular contributor to Slate.

In 1773, on a tour of Scotland and the Hebrides Islands, Samuel Johnson visited a school for deaf children. Impressed by the students but daunted by their predicament, he proclaimed deafness "one of the most desperate of human calamities." More than a century later Helen Keller reflected on her own life and declared that deafness was a far greater hardship than blindness. "Blindness cuts people off from things," she observed. "Deafness cuts people off from people." *Hinders social activity*

For millennia deafness was considered so catastrophic that very few ventured to ease its burdens. Isolation in a kind of permanent solitary confinement was deemed inevitable; a deaf person, even in the midst of urban hub-bub, was considered as unreachable as a fairy-tale princess locked in a tower. The first attempts to educate deaf children came only in the sixteenth century. As late as 1749 the French Academy of Sciences appointed a commission to determine whether deaf people were "capable of reasoning." Today no one would presume to ignore the deaf or exclude them from full participation in society. But acknowledging their rights is one thing, coming to grips with their plight another. Deafness is still seen as a dreadful fate.

Lately, though, the deaf community has begun to speak for itself. To the surprise and bewilderment of outsiders, its message is utterly contrary to the wisdom of centuries: Deaf people, far from groaning under a heavy yoke, are not handicapped at all. Deafness is not a disability. Instead, many deaf people now proclaim, they are a subculture like any other. They are simply a linguistic minority (speaking American Sign Language) and are no more in need of a cure for their condition than are Haitians or Hispanics.

[Handwritten in left margin: Rhetorical strategy]

That view is vehemently held. "The term 'disabled' describes those who are blind or physically handicapped," the deaf linguists Carol Padden and Tom Humphries write, "not Deaf people." (The upper-case D is significant: it serves as a succinct proclamation that the deaf share a culture rather than merely a medical condition.) So strong is the feeling of cultural solidarity that many deaf parents cheer on discovering that their baby is deaf. Pondering such a scene, a hearing person can experience a kind of vertigo. The surprise is not simply the unfamiliarity of the views; it is that, as in a surrealist painting, jarring notions are presented as if they were commonplaces.

The embrace of what looks indisputably like hardship is what, in particular, strikes the hearing world as perverse, and deaf leaders have learned to brace themselves for the inevitable question. "No!" Roslyn Rosen says, by shaking her head vehemently, she *wouldn't* prefer to be able to hear. Rosen, the president of the National Association of the Deaf, is deaf, the daughter of deaf parents, and the mother of deaf children. "I'm happy with who I am," she says through an interpreter, "and I don't want to be 'fixed.' Would an Italian-American rather be a WASP? In our society everyone agrees that whites have an easier time than blacks. But do you think a black person would undergo operations to become white?"

The view that deafness is akin to ethnicity is far from unanimously held. "The world of deafness often seems Balkanized, with a warlord ruling every mountaintop," writes Henry Kisor, the book editor for the *Chicago Sun-Times* and deaf himself. But the "deaf culture" camp—Kisor calls it the "New Orthodoxy"—is in the ascendancy, and its proponents invoke watchwords that still carry echoes of earlier civil-rights struggles. "Pride," "heritage," "identity," and similar words are thick in the air.

Rhetoric aside, however, the current controversy is disorientingly unfamiliar, because the deaf are a group unlike any ethnic minority: 90 percent of all deaf children are born to hearing parents. Many people never meet a deaf person unless one is born to them. Then parent and child belong to different cultures, as they would in an adoption across racial lines. And deaf children acquire a sense of cultural identity from their peers rather than their parents, as homosexuals do. But the crucial issue is that hearing parent and deaf child don't share a means of communication. Deaf children cannot grasp their parents' spoken language, and hearing parents are unlikely to know sign language. Communication is not a gift automatically bestowed in infancy but an acquisition gained only by laborious effort.

This gulf has many consequences. Hearing people tend to make the mistake of considering deafness to be an affliction that we are familiar with, as if being deaf were more or less like being hard of hearing. Even those of us with sharp hearing are, after all, occasionally unable to make out a mumbled remark at the dinner table, or a whispered question from a toddler, or a snatch of dialogue in a movie theater.

[handwritten marginal note: A sort of disconnect between a parent\child]

To get a hint of blindness, you can try making your way down an unfamiliar hall in the dark, late at night. But clamping on a pair of earmuffs conveys nothing essential about deafness, because the earmuffs can't block out a lifetime's experience of having heard language. That experience makes hearing people ineradicably different. Because antibiotics have tamed many of the childhood diseases that once caused permanent loss of hearing, more than 90 percent of all deaf children in the United States today were born deaf or lost their hearing before they had learned English. The challenge that faces them—recognizing that other peoples' mysterious lip movements *are* language, and then learning to speak that language—is immeasurably greater than that facing an adult who must cope with a gradual hearing loss.

Learning to speak is so hard for people deaf from infancy because they are trying, without any direct feedback, to mimic sounds they have never heard. (Children who learn to speak and then go deaf fare better, because they retain some memory of sound.) One mother of a deaf child describes the challenge as comparable to learning to speak Japanese from within a soundproof glass booth. And even if a deaf person does learn to speak, understanding someone else's speech remains maddeningly difficult. Countless words look alike on the lips, though they sound quite different. "Mama" is indistinguishable from "papa," "cat" from "hat," "no new taxes" from "go to Texas." Context and guesswork are crucial, and conversation becomes a kind of fast and ongoing crossword puzzle.

"Speechreading is EXHAUSTING. I hate having to depend on it," writes Cheryl Heppner, a deaf woman who is the executive director of the Northern Virginia Resource Center for Deaf and Hard of Hearing Persons. Despite her complaint, Heppner is a speech-reading virtuoso. She made it through public school and Pennsylvania State University without the help of interpreters, and she says she has never met a person with better speech-reading skills. But "even with peak conditions," she explains, "good lighting, high energy level, and a person who articulates well, I'm still guessing at half of what I see on the lips." When we met in her office, our conversation ground to a halt every sentence or two, as if we were travelers without a common language who had been thrown together in a train compartment. I had great difficulty making out Heppner's soft, high-pitched speech, and far more often than not my questions and comments met only with her mouthed "Sorry." In frustration we resorted to typing on her computer.

For the average deaf person, lip-reading is even less rewarding. In tests using simple sentences, deaf people recognize perhaps three or four words in every ten. Ironically, the greatest aid to lip-reading is knowing how words sound. One British study found, for example, that the average deaf person with a decade of practice was no better at lip-reading than a hearing person picked off the street.

Unsurprisingly, the deaf score poorly on tests of English skills. The average deaf sixteen-year-old reads at the level of a hearing eight-year-old. When deaf students eventually leave school, three in four are unable to read a newspaper. Only two deaf children in a hundred (compared with forty in a hundred among the general population) go on to college. Many deaf students write English as if it were a foreign language. One former professor at Gallaudet, the elite Washington, D.C., university for the deaf, sometimes shows acquaintances a letter written by a student. The quality of the writing, he says, is typical. "As soon as you had lend me $15," the letter begins, "I felt I must write you to let you know how relievable I am in your aid."

Small wonder that many of the deaf eagerly turn to American Sign Language [ASL], invariably described as "the natural language of the deaf." Deaf children of deaf parents learn ASL as easily as hearing children learn a spoken language. At the same age that hearing babies begin talking, deaf babies of parents who sign begin "babbling" nonsense signs with their fingers. Soon, and without having to be formally taught, they have command of a rich and varied language, as expressive as English but as different from it as Urdu or Hungarian.

At the heart of the idea that deafness is cultural, in fact, is the deaf community's proprietary pride in ASL. Even among the hearing the discovery of ASL's riches has sometimes had a profound impact. The most prominent ally of the deaf-culture movement, for example, is the Northeastern University linguist Harlan Lane, whose interest in the deaf came about through his study of ASL. When he first saw people signing to one another, Lane recalls, he was stunned to realize that "language could be expressed just as well by the hands and face as by the tongue and throat, even though the very definition of language we had learned as students was that it was something spoken and heard." For a linguist, Lane says, "this was astonishing, thrilling. I felt like Balboa seeing the Pacific."

Until the 1960s critics had dismissed signing as a poor substitute for language, a mere semaphoring of stripped-down messages ("I see the ball"). Then linguists demonstrated that ASL is in fact a full-fledged language, with grammar and puns and poems, and dignified it with a name. Anything that can be said can be said in ASL. In the view of the neurologist and essayist Oliver Sacks, it is "a language equally suitable for making love or speeches, for flirtation or mathematics." *more of a sub culture*

ASL is the everyday language of perhaps half a million Americans. A shared language makes for a shared identity. With the deaf as with other groups, this identity is a prickly combination of pride in one's own ways and wariness of outsiders. "If I happened to strike up a relationship with a hearing person," says MJ Bienvenu, a deaf activist speaking through an interpreter, "I'd have considerable trepidation about my [deaf] parents' reaction. They'd ask, 'What's the matter? Aren't your own people good enough for you?' and they'd warn, 'They'll take advantage of you. You don't know what they're going to do behind your back.' "

Blind men and women often marry sighted people, but 90 percent of deaf people who marry take deaf spouses. When social scientists ask people

Holds and groups them together

who are blind or in wheelchairs if they wish they could see or walk, they say yes instantly. Only the deaf answer the equivalent question no. The essence of deafness, they explain, is not the lack of hearing but the community and culture based on ASL. Deaf culture represents not a denial but an affirmation.

Spokespeople for deaf pride present their case as self-evident and commonsensical. Why should anyone expect deaf people to deny their roots when every other cultural group proudly celebrates its traditions and history? Why stigmatize the speakers of a particular language as disabled? "When Gorbachev visited the U.S., he used an interpreter to talk to the President," says Bienvenu, who is one of the directors of an organization called The Bicultural Center. "Was Gorbachev disabled?"

UNEASY ALLIES

Despite the claims made in its name, though, the idea that deafness is akin to ethnicity is hardly straightforward. On the contrary, it is an idea with profound and surprising implications, though these are rarely explored. When the deaf were in the news in 1988, for instance, protesting the choice of a hearing person as president of Gallaudet, the press assumed that the story was about disabled people asserting their rights, and treated it the same as if students at a university for the blind had demanded a blind president.

The first surprise in the cultural view of deafness is that it rejects the assumption that medical treatment means progress and is welcome. Since deafness is not a deprivation, the argument runs, talk of cures and breakthroughs and technological wizardry is both inappropriate and offensive—as if doctors and newspapers joyously announced advances in genetic engineering that might someday make it possible to turn black skin white.

Last fall, for example, *60 Minutes* produced a story on a bright, lively little girl named Caitlin Parton. "We don't remember ever meeting [anyone] who captivated us quite as much as this seven-year-old charmer," it began. Caitlin is deaf, and *60 Minutes* showed how a new device called a cochlear implant had transformed her life. Before surgeons implanted a wire in Caitlin's inner ear and a tiny receiver under her skin, she couldn't hear voices or barking dogs or honking cars. With the implant she can hear ordinary conversation, she can speak almost perfectly, and she is thriving in school. *60 Minutes* presented the story as a welcome break from its usual round of scandal and exposé. Who could resist a delightful child and a happy ending?

Activists in the deaf community were outraged. Implants, they thundered in letters to *60 Minutes,* are "child abuse" and "pathological" and "genocide." The mildest criticism was that Caitlin's success was a fluke that would tempt parents into entertaining similar but doomed hopes for their own children. "There should have been parades all across America," Caitlin's father lamented months later. "This is a miracle of biblical proportions, making the

The deaf want to remain deaf?

deaf hear. But we keep hearing what a terrible thing this is, how it's like Zyklon B,[*] how it has to be stopped."

The anger should have been easy to anticipate. The magazine *Deaf Life*, for example, runs a question-and-answer column called "For Hearing People Only." In response to a reader's question well before *60 Minutes* came along, the editors wrote, "An implant is the ultimate invasion of the ear, the ultimate denial of deafness, the ultimate refusal to let deaf children be Deaf . . . . Parents who choose to have their children implanted, are in effect saying, "I don't respect the Deaf community, and I certainly don't want my child to be part of it. I want him/her to be part of the hearing world, not the Deaf world."

The roots of such hostility run far deeper than the specific fear that cochlear implants in children are unproved and risky. More generally, the objection is that from the moment parents suspect their child is deaf, they turn for expert advice to doctors and audiologists and speech therapists rather than to the true experts, deaf people. Harlan Lane points to one survey that found that 86 percent of deaf adults said they would not want a cochlear implant even if it were free. "There are many prostheses from eyeglasses and artificial limbs to cochlear implants," Lane writes. "Can you name another that we insist on for children in flagrant disregard of the advice of adults with the same 'condition'?"

The division between the deaf community and the medical one seems to separate two natural allies. Even more surprising is a second split, between deaf people and advocates for the disabled. In this case, though, the two sides remain uneasy partners, bound as if in a bad marriage. The deaf community knows that whatever its qualms, it cannot afford to cut itself off from the larger, savvier, wealthier disability lobby. **Separation ≠ Equality**

Historically, advocates for every disabled group have directed their fiercest fire at policies that exclude their group. No matter the good intentions, no matter the logistical hurdles, they have insisted, separate is not equal. Thus buildings, buses, classes, must be accessible to all; special accommodations for the disabled are not a satisfactory substitute. All this has become part of conventional wisdom. Today, under the general heading of "mainstreaming," it is enshrined in law and unchallenged as a premise of enlightened thought.

Except among the deaf. Their objection is that even well-meaning attempts to integrate deaf people into hearing society may actually imprison them in a zone of silence. Jostled by a crowd but unable to communicate, they are effectively alone. The problem is especially acute in schools, where mainstreaming has led to the decline of residential schools for the disabled and the deaf and the integration of many such students into ordinary public schools. Since deafness is rare, affecting one child in a thousand, deaf students are thinly scattered. As a result, half of all deaf children in public school have either no deaf classmates at all or very few.

[*]Editor's Note: The Nazis used Zyklon B, a deadly insecticide, to murder Jews on a massive scale at Auschwitz during World War II.

"Mainstreaming deaf children in regular public-school programs," the prominent deaf educator Leo Jacobs writes, will produce "a new generation of educational failures" and "frustrated and unfulfilled adults." Another deaf spokesman, Mervin Garretson, is even harsher. The danger of mainstreaming, he contends, is that deaf children could be "educationally, vocationally, and emotionally mutilated."

THE CASE FOR ASL

In his brilliant and polemical book *The Mask of Benevolence,* Harlan Lane, the chief theoretician of the deaf-culture movement, makes his case seem as clear-cut as a proposition in formal logic. Deaf children are biologically equipped to do everything but hear, he argues; spoken language turns on the ability to hear; therefore spoken language is a poor choice for deaf children. For good measure, Lane throws in a corollary: Since an alternative language, ASL, is both available and easy for the deaf to learn, ASL is a better choice for a first language.

For the parents of a deaf child, though, matters are far from simple. (Lane is childless.) Parents have crucial decisions to make, and they don't have the luxury of time. Children who learn a language late are at a lifelong disadvantage. Deafness is, in one scholar's summary, "a curable, or rather a preventable, form of mental retardation."

Osmond and Deborah Crosby's daughter was born in July of 1988. "Dorothy Jane Crosby," the birth announcement began, "Stanford class of 2009, track, academic all-American, B.S. in pre-astronautics, Cum Laude, 2008 Olympics (decathlon), Miss Florida, Senate hopeful."

"You can chuckle about that announcement," Oz Crosby says now, "but we all have expectations for our kids. That card was a message from my unconscious—these are the kinds of things I'd like to see, that would make me proud, in my child. And the first thing that happened after DJ's deafness was diagnosed was that I felt that child had died. That's something you hear a lot from parents, and it's that blunt and that real."

Crosby, fifty, is tall and athletic, with blond hair and a small, neat moustache. A timber executive who now lives in the suburbs of Washington, D.C., he is a serious and intelligent man who had scarcely given deafness a thought before it invaded his household. Then he plunged into the deafness literature and began keeping a journal of his own.

He found that every path was pocked with hazards. The course that sounds simplest, keeping the child at home with her parents and teaching her English, can prove fantastically difficult. Even basic communication is a constant challenge. In a memoir called *Deaf Like Me,* a man named Thomas Spradley tells of raising a deaf daughter, Lynn. One Saturday morning , shortly after Lynn had begun school, Spradley and his wife, Louise, found her outdoors, waiting for the school bus. Lynn stood at the end of the driveway, scanning the street every few seconds. After half an hour she gave up and came indoors. For weeks Lynn repeated the same futile wait every Saturday and Sunday, until her parents finally managed to convey the concept of "weekday" and "weekend." Words like "car" and "shoes" were easy; abstractions and relationships were not. The Spradleys knew Lynn loved her grandparents, for instance, but they had no idea if she knew who those devoted elderly people were. When Lynn once had to undergo a spinal tap, her parents could not explain what the painful test was for.

As much trouble as Thomas and Louise Spradley had in talking with their daughter, she was just as frustrated in trying to communicate with them. "How do you tell Mommy that you don't like your cereal with that much milk on it?" Spradley writes. "How do you ask Daddy to swing you upside down when all he seems to understand is that you want to be held? How do you tell them that you want to go to other people's houses like [her older brother]? How do you make them understand you want the same kind of Kool-Aid that you had two weeks ago at your cousin's house and just now remembered? How do you say, 'I forgot what I wanted'?"

Making matters more frustrating still, no one seems able to tell parents how successful their child will be in speaking and understanding English. "I'd ask, 'What's the future for us?'" Crosby says, "and they'd say, 'Every deaf child is different.'" Though given to measured, even pedantic, phrasing, Crosby grows angry as he recalls the scene. "It seemed like such a cop-out. I wanted to grab them by the throat and shout, 'Here's the bloody audiogram. How's she going to talk?'" All deaf cases are different

The truth, Crosby has reluctantly come to concede, is that only a few generalizations are possible. Children who are born deaf or who lose their hearing before learning to speak have a far harder time than those deafened later. Children with a profound hearing loss have a harder time than children with a mild loss. Children who cannot detect high-pitched sounds have problems different from those of children who cannot detect low pitches. Finally, and unaccountably, some deaf children just happen to have an easier time with spoken English than others.

Hence few overall statistics are available. Those few are not encouraging. In one study, for example, teachers of the deaf, evaluating their own pupils, judged the speech of two thirds of them to be hard to understand or unintelligible. Timothy Jaech, the superintendent of the Wisconsin School for the Deaf, writes, "The vast majority of deaf children will never develop intelligible speech for the general public." Jaech, who is deaf, speaks and reads lips. "To gamble 12 to 15 years of a deaf child's life is almost immoral," he says. "[My sister] and I were among the lucky ones. What of the other 99 percent?"

Still, it is indisputable that many profoundly deaf adults participate fully and successfully in the hearing world, as lawyers and engineers and in dozens of other roles. Do these examples show what parents might expect for their own child? Or are they inspiring but irrelevant tales that have as little bearing on the typical deaf child as Michael Jordan's success has on the future of a ten-year-old dreaming of NBA glory?

The case of ASL has problems of its own. ASL is certainly easier for the deaf child to learn, but what of the rest of the family? How can parents say anything meaningful to their child in a foreign language they have only begun to study? Moreover, many hearing parents point out, even if deaf culture is rich and vital, it is indisputably not the majority culture. Since spoken language is the ticket to the larger world, isn't giving a child ASL as a first language a bit risky?

The choices are agonizing. "I understand now how people choosing a cancer therapy for their child must feel," Crosby says. "You can't afford to be wrong." To illustrate the dilemma, Crosby wrote what he calls a parable:

A fake example of the hard decisions these parents make

> Suppose that your one-year-old, who has been slow to walk, has just been diagnosed with a rare disorder of the nervous system. The prognosis is for great difficulty in muscular control of the arms and legs due to tremors and impaired nerve pathways. With the help of special braces, physical therapy, and lots of training, she will be able to walk slowly, climb stairs haltingly, and use her hands awkwardly. In general, she will be able to do most of the things other kids do, although not as easily, smoothly, or quickly. Some children respond to this therapy better than others, but all can get around on their legs after a fashion. Even though they will never run or play sports, they will have complete mobility at a deliberate, shuffling pace.
>
> There *is* an alternative, however. If her legs are amputated right away, the tremors will cease, and the remaining nerve pathways will strengthen. She will be able to use a wheelchair with ease. She can even be a wheelchair athlete, "running" marathons, playing basketball, etc., if she desires. Anywhere a wheelchair can go is readily available to her. There is easy access to a world that is geographically smaller. On the other hand, she can't climb simple stairs, hike trails slowly, or even use public transportation without special assistance.

"Now, Mr. and Mrs. Solomon," Crosby concluded, "which life do *you* choose for your child?"

CUED SPEECH

Crosby and his wife have chosen a compromise, a controversial technique called cued speech, in which spoken English is accompanied by hand signals that enable a deaf person to distinguish between words that look alike on the lips. The aim is to remove the guesswork from lip-reading by using eight hand shapes in different positions near the face to indicate that the word being spoken is, say, "bat" rather than "pan."

The technique, which is spread by a tiny but zealous group of parents with deaf children, has several advantages. It's easy to learn, for one thing, taking only twenty or so hours of study. A parent who sets out to learn American Sign Language, in contrast, must devote months or years to the project, as he would have to do in order to learn any foreign language. And since cued speech is, essentially, English, parents can bypass the stilted, often useless phrases of the beginning language student. Instead of stumbling over "*la plume de ma tante*," they can talk to their deaf child from the beginning about any subject in the world.

Moreover, because cued speech is simply English transliterated, rather than a new language, nothing has to be lost in translation. A deaf child who learns cued speech learns English, along with its slang and jargon and idioms and jokes, as his native language. "It's a way to embrace English, the language your whole country runs on, instead of trying to pretend it doesn't exist," says Judy Weiss, a woman in Washington, D.C., who has used cued speech with her son since he lost his hearing as a ten-month-old.

This method, which was invented at Gallaudet in 1965–1966, is nonetheless out of favor with the deaf community. It's seen as a slap at ASL and as just a new version of the despised "oralism," in which deaf students were forced for hour upon hour to try to pronounce English words they had never heard. But the proponents of cued speech insist that these objections are political and unfounded. They point to a handful of small studies that conclude that deaf children who learn cued speech read as well as hearing students, and they mention a small group of highly successful deaf students who rely on cuing. Perhaps the most accomplished of all is a Wellesley undergraduate named Stasie Jones. Raised in France by an American mother and a British father, she speaks French and English and is now studying Russian and Spanish.

But the system is no godsend. "The trap I see a lot of cuing families fall into," Crosby says, "is to say, 'Johnny understands everything we say, we understand everything he says, he's getting *A*s at school—what's the problem?' The problem is, Johnny can't talk to someone he meets on the street and Johnny can't order a hamburger at McDonald's."

Still a disconnection

TOTAL COMMUNICATION

Cued speech is used only in a relative handful of schools. By far the most common method of teaching the deaf today is called "total communication." The idea is that teachers use any and all means of communication with their students—speech, writing, ASL, finger-spelling. Total communication was instituted in the 1970s as a reaction to a century of oralism, in which signing was forbidden and the aim was to teach the deaf child to speak and lip-read.

Oralism still has zealous adherents, but today it is used mainly with hard-of-hearing students and only rarely with deaf ones. Its dominance began with the Congress of Milan, an international meeting of educators in 1880, which affirmed "the incontestable superiority of speech over sign" and voted to banish sign language from deaf education. The ban, notorious to this day among the deaf, was effective. In 1867 every American school for the deaf taught in ASL; by 1907 not a single one did.

When total communication came along, the two rival camps in deaf education accepted it warily. Those who favored English reasoned that at least teachers would be speaking to their students; those who preferred ASL were pleased that teachers would be signing. Today hardly anyone is pleased, and one of the few points of agreement in the present debate is that deaf education is distressingly bad. The Commission on Education of the Deaf, for example, which reported to the President and Congress in 1988, began its account, "The present status of education for persons who are deaf in the United States is unsatisfactory. Unacceptably so. This is [our] primary and inescapable conclusion." . . .

The world of the deaf is heterogeneous, and the fault lines that run through it are twisted and tricky. Now politics has worsened the strains. Frances Parsons, for example, is a much honored Gallaudet professor who, though deaf herself, has denounced "the extremists fanatically hawking ASL and Deafism." Such views have brought her hate mail and denunciatory posters and, once, a punch in the neck. Parsons sees her attackers as cultists and propagandists; they call her and her allies traitors and Uncle Toms.

Much of the dispute has to do with who is authentically deaf. Parsons is suspect because she speaks and has hearing parents. To be the deaf child of deaf parents has cachet, because this is as deaf as one can be. (The four student leaders of the 1988 Gallaudet protest were all "deaf of deaf.") To use ASL is "better" than to use a manual language that mimics English grammar and arranges ASL signs in English word order. "Those born deaf deride those who become deaf at six years or twelve years or later," the Gallaudet psychologist Larry Stewart observed last year in a bitter essay titled "Debunking the Bilingual-Bicultural Snow Job in the American Deaf Community." "ASL-users who do not use lip movements scorn those who sign with mouthed English, or, the other way around. Residential school graduates turn up their nose at mainstream graduates, or the reverse. And so it goes; a once cohesive community now splintered apart by ideology."

Still, there is some common ground and even room for optimism. Captioning on television is universally welcomed; so are TTYs, keyboard devices that allow the deaf to use the telephone, provided the person called also has a TTY. In most states phone companies provide a free "relay" service, in which an operator with a TTY serves as a link between a deaf person with a TTY and a hearing person without one.

"Things are getting better," Roslyn Rosen says. "When I check into a hotel, because of the Americans with Disabilities Act, I expect the TV in the room will have captions, there'll be a TTY, the phone and the fire alarm will have flashing lights, and all that. And soon there will be TV-phones, which will be a wonderful boon for people who use sign language."

What's the difference between these technologies, which Rosen welcomes, and such a device as the cochlear implant, which she denounces? "An implant," she says, "alters *me*. The critical point is, it changes me instead of changing the environment. Therefore the problem is seen as belonging to the deaf person, and *that's* a problem."

To an outsider, this sounds a bit forced. Do eyeglasses, say, belong to one moral category and eye surgery to another? A more useful distinction may be between approaches that allow deaf people to participate in the world and

you can succeed in your world only?

Imagery

those that leave them stranded on the sidelines. "Part of the odyssey I've made," Cheryl Heppner says, "is in realizing that deafness is a disability, but it's a disability that is unique." It is unique in that a deaf person, unaided and independent, can travel wherever he wants, whenever he wants. The question is whether he will be able to communicate with anyone when he gets there.

Deaf can still do things but their social life is disabled

FOR JOURNALING AND DISCUSSION

1. If the deaf majority do not think of deafness as a disability, what impact might this attitude have on federal and state funding for education and other programs that benefit deaf individuals?
2. Apply folklorist William Hugh Jansen's "esoteric-exoteric factor," as discussed by Polly Stewart in her essay "Regional Consciousness as a Shaper of Local History" in Chapter 8, to the deaf community's relationship with the hearing majority.
3. What accommodations has your college or university made for deaf students?
4. Discuss the tension between hearing parents' wishes for their deaf children and the parental role that deaf adults sometimes assume toward all deaf children.
5. Analyze the relationship Ben Hamper has with his family in "Rivethead" in Chapter 3. Does this family really "hear" each other? In what ways can deafness be interpreted as a psychological disability?

FOR RESEARCH AND EXPLORATION

1. Research Gallaudet University's Internet site, and write an essay comparing your school's admission standards, tuition, classes, faculty, and student body with Gallaudet's.
2. Dolnick mentions that "90 percent of deaf people who marry take deaf spouses." View the film *Children of a Lesser God*, the story of a relationship between a deaf woman and a hearing man. Write about their problems and the ways they coped and did not cope.
3. Research statistics on the adoption of deaf children. Are they adopted by deaf or hearing parents? Write about the issues surrounding these adoptions.

Up with People

David Berreby

Born in France, Berreby earned a degree in English literature from Yale University in 1981. He has worked as a reporter, editor, theater critic, and freelance journalist for newspapers and general interest publications.

Identity politics has been good for people with disabilities. For fending off prejudice, finding community and organizing politically to win things like universal wheelchair access and an accessible cash machine, the rhetoric of pride and rights makes sense. But insisting that deafness, for example, is an identity rather than a disability leads to political and cultural conflicts other communities don't face. After all, nobody tries to cure women of being female, and only a few cranks are still working on homosexuality. Genetics and medical technology are, however, gaining on disabilities. Is deafness an identity that needs protecting from doctors? Who gets to say so? To these contentious questions, another is now being added: Should dwarves be accepted or made taller? Is dwarfism a defect or a destiny?

About one birth in 10,000 in this country results in a baby with dwarfism, who will grow up with exceptionally short limbs (dwarves don't reach an adult height taller than 4′6″), though often with an average-size head and torso. A variety of medical complications can result from the condition, such as bowed legs, ear problems and spinal curvature. Most dwarves, however, are perfectly able to function normally with these conditions, and we have belatedly begun to overcome the stereotypes they once invoked. Little people, to use the correct term, were commonly shuffled off into entertainment (remember the munchkins? the endearing Australian sport of dwarf-tossing?), or relegated to a life of isolation. "Dropping out of school because they couldn't take the ridicule from the other kids, never learning to drive, living with their families and babysitting for their sister, that kind of life," says Ruth Ricker, a technical assistance specialist for the federal Department of Education's Office of Civil Rights in Boston. Though most dwarves score no differently than other people on intelligence tests, some were shunted into institutions for the retarded.

A group of people, in other words, ripe for the benefits of solidarity. A dwarfed actor named Billy Barty saw that prospect and in 1957 founded the Little People of America [LPA], which has now grown into a nationwide organization of some 5,000 families. The LPA sponsors monthly meetings of its fifty chapters and a week-long national convention, publishes a newsletter and maintains an Internet bulletin board. The group helps dwarfed couples adopt babies (some average-height couples give up dwarfed children) and provides psychological and social counseling.

But the LPA is also a political and cultural organization, the NAACP or NOW of little people. "We work to change building codes, for instance," explains Angela Muir Van Etten, a lawyer and LPA activist in Rochester, New York. "We request ATMs, pay phones, elevator buttons that can be reached by little people." The annual convention includes dances, talent shows, athletic events— the trappings not of a hospital but a community. The group's mission statement speaks of assistance and guidance for little people, but also of "peer support" and "personal example," and of networking to "enhance knowledge and support of short statured individuals."

LPA activists know the rhetoric of identity. "If there were a magic pill that would make me wake up tomorrow and be tall, I would not take it," says Robert Van Etten, an engineer who is married to Angela Muir Van Etten. "Height has made me what I am." They even have their heroes culled from history. "You know who was a dwarf, although we don't like to talk about it?" Barty told *The Los Angeles Times* in 1994. "Attila the Hun."

Some 80 percent of dwarves are born to parents who are of what the movement carefully calls "average" height. So membership in the LPA was a lifeline for many people who, like many deaf people and many gay people, were alone in their families. "I joined when I was 6. Knowing all these adults as role models my whole life certainly helped me," says Ricker, now, in her 30s, the president of the LPA.

Four decades of activism seem to have worked. "In the 1950s, most of our people were in entertainment," Ricker tells me. "A lot were not educated." Now, parents are less likely to send a dwarf child off to classes for the retarded. Dwarves are far more likely to be lawyers, engineers and other white-collar sorts. And, if mainstream America isn't yet saying "little person" the way it knows to say "African American," dwarf-friendly plots have made it into the recent film *Living in Oblivion* and onto episodes of TV shows as distinct as "Baywatch" and "Seinfeld." "There's a lot of people in LPA who don't consider short stature a disability," Ricker declares.

But, she adds, only some 10 percent of the country's little people are in the organization, and there are many who still grow up in isolation, treated like freaks or morons. The Human Growth Foundation, an organization for families with children, cites studies showing that shorter people are literally not given as much space as others: people stand closer to them than they do to taller people. A study published in the *Journal of Pediatrics* in 1990 reported that men over six-feet earn starting salaries 12 percent higher than shorter men. A study by Linda Jackson and Kelly Ervin of Michigan State found that people rate tall men more attractive, accomplished, fit and masculine than short men. They rate tall women as being higher-class and more physically attractive than short women. These prejudices against short people are redoubled in the experience of dwarves, who are even shorter and who look different. "The reason little people have so many problems is not size," says Angela Muir Van Etten. "You can deal with the physical aspects. The hardest thing is people's attitudes. You can go out and get yourself an education and prepare yourself for the job market and find people who won't hire you."

So activism has given little people the same kinds of choices faced by members of other groups—assimilation or insistence on one's difference. Do you militantly insist on difference and demand your place at the table ("we're queer, we're here, get used to it"), or do you stress the common ground ("hath not a Jew eyes? If you prick us, do we not bleed?")? But this choice—once theoretical—has suddenly become real. Advances in medical technology are giving us the option to make dwarves taller or to prevent them from being born at all.

First, in the 1980s, came a surreal-sounding surgical procedure that literally stretches dwarves' arms and legs. A surgeon cuts small incisions through skin and muscle to reach the bone, which he slices into two sections. Then he implants high-tension wires into the two sections of bone. These are connected to a "fixator": a frame, roughly resembling the Eiffel Tower, that goes around the limb like a cast. The fixator pulls the two sections of bone apart—with help from the patient, who has to turn screws on the apparatus every day to keep tugging the bone along. The body's natural healing mechanisms do the rest of the work, growing extra bone, muscle and skin as the tension continues. At the rate of about a millimeter a day, over a span of several months, the bone can be extended to as much as a foot longer than it would have been without "the human erector set," as some professional papers call it.

Developed in the 1950s and '60s by Gavril Abramovich Ilizarov, an orthopedist in the city of Kurgan, 1,000 miles east of Moscow, the technique came to Western Europe in the 1980s and was first tried in this country in 1987 by Dror Paley, now a Baltimore surgeon and an associate professor at the University of Maryland's medical school. There are a number of variations on the method, Paley says, but they all derive from Ilizarov. It has caught on fast, replacing much bloodier and less successful approaches like the Wagner Method, in which, Paley says, "you just cut through everything and crank it out at about two millimeters a day." Now, hundreds of the operations are performed every year. Paley himself—now a co-director of the Maryland Center for Limb Lengthening and Reconstruction at the Kernan Hospital in Baltimore—has performed some 1,500 since 1987.

The vast majority of the operations, though, reassemble shattered limbs or straighten bones deformed by infections, cancer surgery or birth defects. (A common use is to lengthen an injured leg so it will be as long as its counterpart.) Why, the LPA activists like to ask, should a little person put him or herself through it? After all, the Ilizarov technique is no day at the beach. The treatment takes months and is demanding in many ways, "especially," one journal abstract adds helpfully, "for the patient." Some people who've been through it say the lengthening bone merely aches; others say the pain is far worse than that. The patient can walk after a few days (the Ilizarov apparatus bounces along with each step like a trampoline), but the procedure requires physical therapy, and there can be complications, such as temporary palsies and other odd nerve behavior, infections from the wires, difficulty standing on the toes. The surgery is also expensive ($80,000 to $130,000 to lengthen a pair of legs, Paley says), though insurers often cover it. Most poignantly, as a way of making dwarves taller, it can only be performed on kids. After age 20 the bones aren't flexible enough to stand the stretching.

The LPA take on the surgery invokes the rhetoric honed in movements of the gay and the deaf: the image of a lone swan amid uncomprehending ducklings, unaware what others of his kind are about. After all, the child on whom Ilizarov surgery is to be done is likely surrounded by average-height parents, siblings and doctors. "Many of these decisions about leg lengthening are being taken by parents long before a child is of age to really know," says Angela Muir Van Etten. "We're not just talking about size, we're talking about identity. It's like saying, 'I wish I weren't born.' "

But not all LPA members want to play the identity card as thoroughly as the leadership does. They say being several inches taller makes a lot of things, from driving to reaching the second shelf to getting a job, a lot easier. And they point to signs that the surgery can help forestall some of the back problems dwarves often develop later in life.

So the LPA confines itself to pointing out the drawbacks and recommending that dwarves who want the surgery have it done in the experimental program at the University of California at Los Angeles, which is run by David Rimoin, professor of pediatrics at UCLA and a member of the LPA medical advisory board. Rimoin said he was "totally opposed" to limb-lengthening surgery until he attended a conference on achondroplasia* several years ago where he was impressed by how pleased and pain-free some European patients were. He takes only patients 12 years old or older and includes psychological counseling in his program ("a waste of time," says Paley, who stopped counseling years ago). Rimoin stresses that he considers the technique a medical experiment, whose long-term effects aren't known.

"We can't say no member of the LPA has ever had it done," Ricker concedes. "Though certainly no second-generation person has had it done." Arguments over the procedure have broken out on the group's Internet bulletin board, she says, and what she then describes is the familiar identity-politics drama of someone discovering that the sturdy scaffolding the group provides can also feel like a cage: "There was a guy on the board who had had it done, and there were people infuriated at him that he had had it done. And he got mad, too. He basically said, 'Don't psychoanalyze me when you don't even know me.' "

After leg-lengthening surgery got established in the late '80s, the '90s brought medical advances that may have an even more profound impact on dwarves: the genes that cause the condition are being identified. In the summer of 1994, for example, a team headed by John Wasmuth, a geneticist at the University of California at Irvine, found the gene that causes achondroplasia, which is responsible for more than half the incidence of dwarfed babies in the United States. Five or six other genes are responsible for another 30 percent of dwarfism, and they're eagerly being sought. Later that same year, for instance, another important dwarfism gene was found by a team from MIT and the University of Helsinki in Finland.

There was never any doubt that a fetal test for the achondroplasia gene would be developed, because a fetus conceived by two dwarf parents has a 25 percent chance of inheriting the mutated gene from both mother and father,

---

*Editor's Note: "Achondroplasia" is the term used to describe the failure of cartilage to develop, the cause of dwarfism.

which dooms the baby to an early death. (He or she has a 50 percent chance of inheriting one copy of the gene, resulting in dwarfism, and a 25 percent chance of not receiving the mutation from either parent.) But the prospect of an amniocentesis test for dwarfism raises the question: How deep do "average-height" Americans' laissez-faire attitudes about identity go?

Ricker points out that the question presents itself not as a simple yes-no switch, but as a continuum: there are some 200 genetic anomalies that can cause rarer forms of dwarfism, each with its own character. "For example, diastrophic dysplasia is another condition. This is typically more disabling orthopedically than achondroplasia. People who have it use crutches. They wear special shoes. But we don't see this as any big deal." But, as the joke goes, what mean we? An average-height doctor trying to give prospective parents an estimate of "quality of life"—the kind of cost-benefit analysis beloved of HMOs—might see it as a bigger deal. So might those parents themselves.

The prospect is considered remote by some geneticists, but it nagged at Wasmuth. In the journal *Cell*, in which he announced his team's discovery, he went out of his way to argue that only dwarf parents should be given the option of testing a fetus for the gene. Wasmuth, who died last year at 49, often spoke about the dangerous prospect of "personal selection" interfering with "natural selection," and to illustrate his point he said he knew of at least one dwarf couple who wanted amniocentesis so they could abort *unless* the fetus was dwarfed. "I don't know anybody that would do that," Ricker told me. "Or that would publicly say they would, anyway."

This little tale of role reversal, though, does underscore an irony of this identity-happy era: achondroplastic dwarves, having the same mutation, literally share a gene. In this respect, they are more genetically isolatable right now than any ethnic group or gay people. And their condition is far more amenable to surgical reversal. Once stereotyped as little more than freaks, dwarves are now on the edge of the dilemma of science and identity. How their culture finally determines the question could have ramifications far beyond their small world.

FOR JOURNALING AND DISCUSSION

1. Does Berreby ever identify himself as part of the dwarf community? Does your response to his essay change according to his possible status?
2. Does American culture place a value on being tall for both men and women? What sources can you point to that support your conclusion? Write about your height and how this one facet of your total being has helped to shape your life and expectations.
3. Look at your picture books from childhood. Do the mythical creatures called trolls resemble dwarves? Were they portrayed as being smarter than humans?
4. Berreby discusses the censorship and ostracism little people face from their peers when they decide to undergo Ilizarov surgery. Using the stories in Lise Funderburg's "Parents and Family" in Chapter 2 and James McBride's "The

Color of Water" in Chapter 5, write about what sometimes happens to individuals who choose to step outside of their group's "identity politics."

5. As a class, view the film *Ship of Fools,* based upon the novel by Katherine Anne Porter. The movie is narrated by a character who is a dwarf. Discuss why this person narrates the story.

FOR RESEARCH AND EXPLORATION

1. Research the cast that played the "Munchkins" in the film *The Wizard of Oz.* Write a paper about these actors.
2. From whom do little people buy their clothes and furnishings? Use the Internet and little people organizations to research the names of businesses and industries that cater to them. Do such special interest groups contribute to the growth of the American economy?
3. Research the physical and genetic differences between dwarves and midgets. While some may see these terms as synonyms, is this correct? Does our culture treat dwarves and midgets in the same way?

On Being a Cripple

Nancy Mairs

Mairs, who has written a poetry collection entitled In All the Rooms of the Yellow House, *earned an M.F.A. in creative writing and a Ph.D. in English literature in 1984. She has taught high school and college courses in writing and also worked as a technical writer.*

The other day I was thinking of writing an essay on being a cripple. I was thinking hard in one of the stalls of the women's room in my office building, as I was shoving my shirt into my jeans and tugging up my zipper. Preoccupied, I flushed, picked up my book bag, took my cane down from the hook, and unlatched the door. So many movements unbalanced me, and as I pulled the door open I fell over backward, landing fully clothed on the toilet seat with my legs splayed in front of me: the old beetle-on-its-back routine. Saturday afternoon, the building deserted, I was free to laugh aloud as I wriggled back to my feet, my voice bouncing off the yellowish tiles from all directions. Had anyone been there with me, I'd have been still and faint and hot with chagrin. I decided that it was high time to write the essay.

First, the matter of semantics. I am a cripple. I choose this word to name me. I choose from among several possibilities, the most common of which are "handicapped" and "disabled." I made the choice a number of years ago, without thinking, unaware of my motives for doing so. Even now, I'm not sure what those motives are, but I recognize that they are complex and not entirely flattering. People—crippled or not—wince at the word "cripple," as they do not at "handicapped" or "disabled." Perhaps I want them to wince. I want them to see me as a tough customer, one to whom the fates/gods/viruses have not been kind, but who can face the brutal truth of her existence squarely. As a cripple, I swagger.

But, to be fair to myself, a certain amount of honesty underlies my choice. "Cripple" seems to me a clean word, straightforward and precise. It has an honorable history, having made its first appearance in the Lindisfarne Gospel in the tenth century. As a lover of words, I like the accuracy with which it describes my condition: I have lost the full use of my limbs. "Disabled," by contrast, suggests any incapacity, physical or mental. And I certainly don't like "handicapped," which implies that I have deliberately been put at a disadvantage, by whom I can't imagine (my God is not a Handicapper General), in order to equalize chances in the great race of life. These words seem to me to be moving away from my condition, to be widening the gap between word and reality. Most remote is the recently coined euphemism "differently abled," which partakes of the same semantic hopefulness that transformed countries from "undeveloped" to "underdeveloped," then to "less developed," and finally to "developing" nations. People have continued to starve in those countries during the shift. Some realities do not obey the dictates of language.

Mine is one of them. Whatever you call me, I remain crippled. But I don't care what you call me, so long as it isn't "differently abled," which strikes me as pure verbal garbage designed, by its ability to describe anyone, to describe no one. I subscribe to George Orwell's thesis that "the slovenliness of our language makes it easier for us to have foolish thoughts." And I refuse to participate in the degeneration of the language to the extent that I deny that I have lost anything in the course of this calamitous disease; I refuse to pretend that the only differences between you and me are the various ordinary ones that distinguish any one person from another. But call me "disabled" or "handicapped" if you like. I have long since grown accustomed to them; and if they are vague, at least they hint at the truth. Moreover, I use them myself. Society is no readier to accept crippledness than to accept death, war, sex, sweat, or wrinkles. I would never refer to another person as a cripple. It is the word I use to name only myself.

I haven't always been crippled, a fact for which I am soundly grateful. To be whole of limb is, I know from experience, infinitely more pleasant and useful than to be crippled; and if that knowledge leaves me open to bitterness at my loss, the physical soundness I once enjoyed (though I did not enjoy it half enough) is well worth the occasional stab of regret. Though never any good at sports, I was a normally active child and young adult. I climbed trees, played hopscotch, jumped rope, skated, swam, rode my bicycle, sailed. I despised team sports, spending some of the wretchedest afternoons of my life, sweaty and humiliated, behind a field-hockey stick and under a basketball hoop. I tramped alone for miles along the bridle paths that webbed the woods behind the house I grew up in. I swayed through countless dim hours in the arms of one man or another under the scattered shot of light from mirrored balls, and gyrated through countless more as Tab Hunter and Johnny Mathis gave way to the Rolling Stones, Creedence Clearwater Revival, Cream. I walked down the aisle. I pushed baby carriages, changed tires in the rain, marched for peace.

When I was twenty-eight I started to trip and drop things. What at first seemed my natural clumsiness soon became too pronounced to shrug off. I consulted a neurologist, who told me that I had a brain tumor. A battery of tests, increasingly disagreeable, revealed no tumor. About a year and a half later I developed a blurred spot in one eye. I had, at last, the episodes "disseminated in space and time" requisite for a diagnosis: multiple sclerosis. I have never been sorry for the doctor's initial misdiagnosis, however. For almost a week, until the negative results of the tests were in, I thought that I was going to die right away. Every day for the past nearly ten years, then, has been a kind of gift. I accept all gifts.

Multiple sclerosis is a chronic degenerative disease of the central nervous system, in which the myelin that sheathes the nerves is somehow eaten away and scar tissue forms in its place, interrupting the nerves' signals. During its course, which is unpredictable and uncontrollable, one may lose vision, hearing, speech, the ability to walk, control of bladder and/or bowels, strength in any or all extremities, sensitivity to touch, vibration, and/or pain, potency, coordination of movements—the list of possibilities is lengthy and, yes, horrifying. One may also lose one's sense of humor. That's the easiest to lose and the hardest to survive without.

In the past ten years, I have sustained some of these losses. Characteristic of MS are sudden attacks, called exacerbations, followed by remissions, and these I have not had. Instead, my disease has been slowly progressive. My left leg is now so weak that I walk with the aid of a brace and a cane; and for distances I use an Amigo, a variation on the electric wheelchair that looks rather like an electrified kiddie car. I no longer have much use of my left hand. Now my right side is weakening as well. I still have the blurred spot in my right eye. Overall, though, I've been lucky so far. My world has, of necessity, been circumscribed by my losses, but the terrain left me has been ample enough for me to continue many of the activities that absorb me: writing, teaching, raising children and cats and plants and snakes, reading, speaking publicly about MS and depression, even playing bridge with people patient and honorable enough to let me scatter cards every which way without sneaking a peek.

Lest I begin to sound like Pollyanna, however, let me say that I don't like having MS. I hate it. My life holds realities—harsh ones, some of them—that no right-minded human being ought to accept without grumbling. One of them is fatigue. I know of no one with MS who does not complain of bone-weariness; in a disease that presents an astonishing variety of symptoms, fatigue seems to be a common factor. I wake up in the morning feeling the way most people do at the end of a bad day, and I take it from there. As a result, I spend a lot of time *in extremis* and, impatient with limitation, I tend to ignore my fatigue until my body breaks down in some way and forces rest. Then I miss picnics, dinner parties, poetry readings, the brief visits of old friends from out of town. The offspring of a puritanical tradition of exceptional venerability, I cannot view these lapses without shame. My life often seems a series of small failures to do as I ought.

I lead, on the whole, an ordinary life, probably rather like the one I would have led had I not had MS. I am lucky that my predilections were already solitary, sedentary, and bookish—unlike the world-famous French cellist I have read about, or the young woman I talked with one long afternoon who wanted only to be a jockey. I had just begun graduate school when I found out something was wrong with me, and I have remained, interminably, a graduate student. Perhaps I would not have if I'd thought I had the stamina to return to a full-time job as a technical editor; but I've enjoyed my studies.

In addition to studying, I teach writing courses. I also teach medical students how to give neurological examinations. I pick up freelance editing jobs here and there, I have raised a foster son and sent him into the world, where he has made me two grandbabies, and I am still escorting my daughter and son through adolescence. I go to Mass every Saturday. I am a superb, if messy, cook. I am also an enthusiastic laundress, capable of sorting a hamper full of clothes into five subtly differentiated piles, but a terrible housekeeper. I can do italic writing and, in an emergency, bathe an oil-soaked cat. I play a fiendish game of Scrabble. When I have the time and the money, I like to sit on my front steps with my husband, drinking Amaretto and smoking a cigar, as we imagine our counterparts in Leningrad and make sure that the sun gets down once more behind the sharp childish scrawl of the Tucson Mountains.

This lively plenty has its bleak complement, of course, in all the things I can no longer do. I will never run again, except in dreams, and one day I may have to write that I will never walk again. I like to go camping, but I can't follow George and the children along the trails that wander out of a campsite through the desert or into the mountains. In fact, even on the level I've learned never to check the weather or try to hold a coherent conversation: I need all my attention for my wayward feet. Of late, I have begun to catch myself wondering how people can propel themselves without canes. With only one usable hand, I have to select my clothing with care not so much for style as for ease of ingress and egress, and even so, dressing can be laborious. I can no longer do fine stitchery, pick up babies, play the piano, braid my hair. I am immobilized by acute attacks of depression, which may or may not be physiologically related to MS but are certainly its logical concomitant.

These two elements, the plenty and the privation, are never pure, nor are the delight and wretchedness that accompany them. Almost every pickle that I get into as a result of my weakness and clumsiness—and I get into plenty—is funny as well as maddening and sometimes painful. I recall one May afternoon when a friend and I were going out for a drink after finishing up at school. As we were climbing into opposite sides of my car, chatting, I tripped and fell, flat and hard, onto the asphalt parking lot, my abrupt departure interrupting him in mid-sentence. "Where'd you go?" he called as he came around the back of the car to find me hauling myself up by the door frame. "Are you all right?" Yes, I told him. I was fine, just a bit rattly, and we drove off to find a shady patio and some beer. When I got home an hour or so later, my daughter greeted me with "What have you done to yourself?" I looked down. One elbow of my white turtleneck with the green froggies, one knee of my white trousers, one white kneesock were bloodsoaked. We peeled off the clothes and inspected the damage, which was nasty enough but not alarming. That part wasn't funny: The abrasions took a long time to heal, and one got a little infected. Even so, when I think of my friend talking earnestly, suddenly, to the hot thin air while I dropped from his view as though through a trap door, I find the image as silly as something from a Marx Brothers movie.

I may find it easier than other cripples to amuse myself because I live propped by the acceptance and the assistance and, sometimes, the amusement of those around me. Grocery clerks tear my checks out of my checkbook for me, and sales clerks find chairs to put into dressing rooms when I want to try on clothes. The people I work with make sure I teach at times when I am least likely to be fatigued, in places I can get to, with the materials I need. My students, with one anonymous exception (in an end-of-the-semester evaluation), have been unperturbed by my disability. Some even like it. One was immensely cheered by the information that I paint my own fingernails; she decided, she told me, that if I could go to such trouble over fine details, she could keep on writing essays. I suppose I became some sort of bright-fingered muse. She wrote good essays, too.

The most important struts in the framework of my existence, of course, are my husband and children. Dismayingly few marriages survive the MS test, and why should they? Most twenty-two- and nineteen-year-olds, like George and me, can vow in clear conscience, after a childhood of chicken pox and summer colds, to keep one another in sickness and in health so long as they both shall live. Not many are equipped for catastrophe: the dismay, the depression, the extra work, the boredom that a degenerative disease can insinuate into a relationship. And our society, with its emphasis on fun and its association of fun with physical performance, offers little encouragement for a whole spouse to stay with a crippled partner. Children experience similar stresses when faced with a crippled parent, and they are more helpless, since parents and children can't usually get divorced. They hate, of course, to be different from their peers, and the child whose mother is tacking down the aisle of a school auditorium packed with proud parents like a Cape Cod dinghy in a stiff breeze jolly well stands out in a crowd. Deprived of legal divorce, the child can at least deny the mother's disability, even her existence, forgetting to tell her about recitals and PTA meetings, refusing to accompany her to stores or church or the movies, never inviting friends to the house. Many do.

But I've been limping along for ten years now, and so far George and the children are still at my left elbow, holding tight. Anne and Matthew vacuum floors and dust furniture and haul trash and rake up dog droppings and button my cuffs and bake lasagna and Toll House cookies with just enough grumbling so I know that they don't have brain fever. And far from hiding me, they're forever dragging me by racks of fancy clothes or through teeming school corridors, or welcoming gaggles of friends while I'm wandering through the house in Anne's filmy pink babydoll pajamas. George generally calls before he brings someone home, but he does just as many dumb thankless chores as the children. And they all yell at me, laugh at some of my jokes, write me funny letters when we're apart—in short, treat me as an ordinary human being for whom they have some use. I think they like me. Unless they're faking . . . .

Faking. There's the rub. Tugging at the fringes of my consciousness always is the terror that people are kind to me only because I'm a cripple. My mother almost shattered me once, with that instinct mothers have—blind, I think, in this case, but unerring nonetheless—for striking blows along the fault-lines of their children's hearts, by telling me, in an attack on my selfishness, "We all have to make allowances for you, of course, because of the way you are." From the distance of a couple of years, I have to admit that I haven't any idea just what she meant, and I'm not sure that she knew either. She was awfully angry. But at the time, as the words thudded home, I felt my worst fear, suddenly realized. I could bear being called selfish: I am. But I couldn't bear the corroboration that those around me were doing in fact what I'd always suspected them of doing, professing fondness while silently putting up with me because of the way I am. A cripple. I've been a little cracked ever since.

Along with this fear that people are secretly accepting shoddy goods comes a relentless pressure to please—to prove myself worth the burdens I impose, I guess, or to build a substantial account of goodwill against which I may write drafts in times of need. Part of the pressure arises from social expectations. In our society, anyone who deviates from the norm had better find some way to compensate. Like fat people, who are expected to be jolly, cripples must bear their lot meekly and cheerfully. A grumpy cripple isn't playing by the rules. And much of the pressure is self-generated. Early on I vowed that, if I had to have MS, by God I was going to do it well. This is a class act, ladies and gentlemen. No tears, no recriminations, no faint-heartedness.

One way and another, then, I wind up feeling like Tiny Tim, peering over the edge of the table at the Christmas goose, waving my crutch, piping down God's blessing on us all. Only sometimes I don't want to play Tiny Tim. I'd rather be Caliban, a most scurvy monster. Fortunately, at home no one much cares whether I'm a good cripple or a bad cripple as long as I make vichyssoise with fair regularity. One evening several years ago, Anne was reading at the dining-room table while I cooked dinner. As I opened a can of tomatoes, the can slipped in my left hand and juice spattered me and the counter with bloody spots. Fatigued and infuriated, I bellowed, "I'm so sick of being crippled!" Anne glanced at me over the top of her book. "There now," she said, "do you feel better?" "Yes," I said, "yes, I do." She went back to her reading. I felt better. That's about all the attention my scurviness ever gets.

Because I hate being crippled, I sometimes hate myself for being a cripple. Over the years I have come to expect—even accept—attacks of violent self-loathing. Luckily, in general our society no longer connects deformity and disease directly with evil (though a charismatic once told me that I have MS because a devil is in me) and so I'm allowed to move largely at will, even among small children. But I'm not sure that this revision of attitude has been particularly helpful. Physical imperfection, even freed of moral disapprobation, still defies and violates the ideal, especially for women, whose confinement in their bodies as objects of desire is far from over. Each age, of course, has its ideal, and I doubt that ours is any better or worse than any other. Today's ideal woman, who lives on the glossy pages of dozens of magazines, seems to be between the ages of eighteen and twenty-five; her hair has body, her teeth flash white, her breath smells minty, her underarms are dry; she has a career but is still a fabulous cook, especially of meals that take less than twenty minutes to prepare; she does not ordinarily appear to have a husband or children; she is trim and deeply tanned; she jogs, swims, plays tennis, rides a bicycle, sails, but does not bowl; she travels widely, even to out-of-the-way places like Finland and Samoa, always in the company of the ideal man, who possesses a nearly identical set of characteristics. There are a few exceptions. Though usually white and often blonde, she may be black, Hispanic, Asian, or Native American, so long as she is unusually sleek. She may be old, provided she is selling a laxative or is Lauren Bacall. If she is selling a detergent, she may be married and have a flock of strikingly messy children. But she is never a cripple.

Like many women I know, I have always had an uneasy relationship with my body. I was not a popular child, largely, I think now, because I was peculiar: intelligent, intense, moody, shy, given to unexpected actions and inexplicable notions and emotions. But as I entered adolescence, I believed myself unpopular because I was homely: my breasts too flat, my mouth too wide, my hips too narrow, my clothing never quite right in fit or style. I was not, in fact, particularly ugly, old photographs inform me, though I was well off the ideal; but I carried this sense of self-alienation with me into adulthood, where it regenerated in response to the depredations of MS. Even with my brace I walk with a limp so pronounced that, seeing myself on the videotape of a television program on the disabled, I couldn't believe that anything but an inch-worm could make progress humping along like that. My shoulders droop and my pelvis thrusts forward as I try to balance myself upright, throwing my frame into a bony S. As a result of contractures, one shoulder is higher than the other and I carry one arm bent in front of me, the fingers curled into a claw. My left arm and leg have wasted into pipe-stems, and I try always to keep them covered. When I think about how my body must look to others, especially to men, to whom I have been trained to display myself, I feel ludicrous, even loathsome.

At my age, however, I don't spend much time thinking about my appearance. The burning egocentricity of adolescence, which assures one that all the world is looking all the time, has passed, thank God, and I'm generally too caught up in what I'm doing to step back, as I used to, and watch myself as though upon a stage. I'm also too old to believe in the accuracy of self-image. I know that I'm not a hideous crone, that in fact, when I'm rested, well dressed, and well made up, I look fine. The self-loathing I feel is neither physically nor intellectually substantial. What I hate is not me but a disease.

I am not a disease.

And a disease is not—at least not singlehandedly—going to determine who I am, though at first it seemed to be going to. Adjusting to a chronic incurable illness, I have moved through a process similar to that outlined by Elizabeth Kübler-Ross in *On Death and Dying*. The major difference—and it is far more significant than most people recognize—is that I can't be sure of the outcome, as the terminally ill cancer patient can. Research studies indicate that, with proper medical care, I may achieve a "normal" life span. And in our society, with its vision of death as the ultimate evil, worse even than decrepitude, the response to such news is, "Oh well, at least you're not going to *die*." Are there worse things than dying? I think that there may be . . . .

The absence of a cure often makes MS patients bitter toward their doctors. Doctors are, after all, the priests of modern society, the new shamans, whose business is to heal, and many an MS patient roves from one to another, searching for the "good" doctor who will make him well. Doctors too think of themselves as healers, and for this reason many have trouble dealing with MS patients, whose disease in its intransigence defeats their aims and mocks their skills. Too few doctors, it is true, treat their patients as whole human beings, but the reverse is also true. I have always tried to be gentle with my doctors, who often have more at stake in terms of ego than I do. I may be frustrated, maddened, depressed by the incurability of my disease, but I am not diminished by it, and they are. When I push myself up from my seat in the waiting room and stumble toward them, I incarnate the limitation of their powers. The least I can do is refuse to press on their tenderest spots.

This gentleness is part of the reason that I'm not sorry to be a cripple. I didn't have it before. Perhaps I'd have developed it anyway—how could I know such a thing?—and I wish I had more of it, but I'm glad of what I have. It has opened and enriched my life enormously, this sense that my frailty and need must be mirrored in others, that in searching for and shaping a stable core in a life wrenched by change and loss, change and loss, I must recognize the same process, under individual conditions, in the lives around me. I do not deprecate such knowledge, however I've come by it.

All the same, if a cure were found, would I take it? In a minute. I may be a cripple, but I'm only occasionally a loony and never a saint. Anyway, in my brand of theology God doesn't give bonus points for a limp. I'd take a cure; I just don't need one. A friend who also has MS startled me once by asking, "Do you ever say to yourself, 'Why me, Lord?' " "No, Michael, I don't," I told him, "because whenever I try, the only response I can think of is 'Why not?' " If I could make a cosmic deal, who would I put in my place? What in my life would I give up in exchange for sound limbs and a thrilling rush of energy? No one. Nothing. I might as well do the job myself. Now that I'm getting the hang of it.

FOR JOURNALING AND DISCUSSION

1. In Chapter 6, Alice Walker writes in her essay "Beauty: When the Other Dancer Is the Self " about how her accident changed her self-image and how she interacted with the world. How is Walker's situation different from and similar to Mairs's? How have these women's children made a difference in their adjustment to their situations?

2. In this chapter, we have been introduced to people who have had to cope with being disabled from birth and to others who became disabled later in life. Divide the essays into these two categories, and compare the attitudes of each group. What insights have you reached?

3. Do you think there is a relationship between our cultural obsession with physical beauty and our wish to eradicate physical disabilities?

4. If a cure for MS were found, Mairs states she would take it "in a minute." How does her attitude differ from that of the deaf community Edward Dolnick writes about in his essay earlier in this chapter?

5. In Chapter 4, Sallie Tisdale writes about excess weight as a social disability in her essay "A Weight That Women Carry." Compare how Mairs and Tisdale feel about themselves as worthwhile people when they don't measure up to our cultural beauty standards.

FOR RESEARCH AND EXPLORATION

1. Select three or four magazines designed and written for different types of readers. Analyze the ads. Are any of the models disabled? If so, describe them. Are any of the ads directed toward the disabled community? What messages do the magazines give to readers with disabilities?

2. Mairs discusses how accommodating the physical demands of MS has changed her body: "When I think about how my body must look to others, especially to men, to whom I have been trained to display myself, I feel ludicrous, even loathsome." Research what benefits physically attractive people receive. Write a personal essay about how American standards of beauty have influenced your life.

3. What is MS? Research MS and the toll it takes on young adults and their families.

Choosing Disability

Laura Hershey

Hershey is a freelance writer, a consultant specializing in access issues for peo-
ple with disabilities, and a poet whose work can be found on the World Wide
Web site for the on-line magazine Howlings: Wild Women of the West.

In 1983, when I was in college, local antiabortion protestors commemorated
the tenth anniversary of *Roe* v. *Wade* with a rally. Our student feminist organization held a small counterdemonstration. Frantic in their zeal, anti-choice
protesters assailed us with epithets like "slut" and "bitch." But the most hostile
remark was directed at me. I was confronted by an angry nun whose "Abortion
Is Murder" sign hung tiredly at her side. She stopped in front of me and aimed
a pugnacious finger. "You see?" she announced. "God even let you be born!"

I'm not sure the sister realized that I had been part of the pro-choice
demonstration. All she saw in me was a poster child for her holy crusade. I must
have seemed to her an obvious mistake of nature: a severely disabled person,
who, through a combination of divine intervention and legal restrictions, had
been born anyway.

That was my first inkling of how attitudes about disability function in the
volatile debate over reproductive rights. I understood that the nun and her co-
crusaders were no friends of mine. To her, I was a former fetus who had escaped
the abortionists. No room in that view for my identity as an adult woman; no
room for the choices I might make. Now, more than a decade later, antiabortion
groups are courting the disability community. The approach has become less
clumsy, emphasizing respect for the lives of people with disabilities, and some activists have accepted the anti-choice message because they find it consistent with
the goals of the disability rights movement. As a feminist, however, I recoil at the
"pro-life" movement's disregard for the lives and freedom of women.

But I cannot overlook the fact that when a prenatal test reveals the possibility of a "major defect," as the medical profession puts it, the pregnancy almost always ends in "therapeutic abortion." The prospect of bearing a child
with disabilities causes such anxiety that abortion has become the accepted
outcome—even among people who oppose abortion rights in general.

Indeed, fear of disability played a key role in the legalization of abortion
in the United States in the 1960s. When thousands of pregnant women who
had taken thalidomide (a drug used in tranquilizers) or had contracted

rubella (German measles) gave birth to children with "defects," doctors called for easing abortion laws.

Today, despite three decades of activism by the disability community, and substantial disability rights legislation, avoiding disability is an important factor in the use and regulation of abortion. In a 1992 Time/CNN survey, for example, 70 percent of respondents favored abortion if a fetus was likely to be born deformed.

This is the quandary we face: the choices we all seek to defend—choices individual women make about childbirth—can conflict with efforts to promote acceptance, equality, and respect for people with disabilities. I am inseparably committed to the empowerment of both people with disabilities and women. Therefore, my pro-choice stance must lie somewhere in the common ground between feminism and disability rights. I want to analyze social and scientific trends, and to vocalize my troubled feelings about where all of this may lead. I want to defy patriarchy's attempts to control women, and also to challenge an age-old bias against people with disabilities. I want to discuss the ethics of choice—without advocating restrictions on choice. To draw a parallel, feminists have no problem attacking sex-selective abortion used to guarantee giving birth to a child of the "right" sex (most often male), but we try to educate against the practice, rather than seek legislation.

In an effort to clarify my own thinking about these complex, interlocking issues, I have been reading and listening to the words of other disabled women. Diane Coleman, a Nashville-based disability rights organizer, is deeply concerned about the number of abortions based on fetal disability. Coleman sees this as "a way that society expresses its complete rejection of people with disabilities, and the conviction that it would be better if we were dead." I find myself sharing her indignation.

Julie Reiskin, a social worker in Denver who is active in both disability rights and abortion rights, tells me, "I live with a disability, and I have a hard time saying, 'This is great.' I think that the goal should be to eliminate disabilities." It jars me to hear this, but Reiskin makes a further point that I find helpful. "Most abortions are not because there's something wrong with the fetus," she says. "Most abortions are because we don't have decent birth control." In other words, we should never have to use fetal disability as a reason to keep abortion legal: "It should be because women have the right to do what we want with our bodies, period," says Reiskin.

We are a diverse community, and it's no surprise to find divergent opinions on as difficult an issue as abortion. Our personal histories and hopes, viewed through the lens of current circumstances, shape our values and politics. Like all the women I interviewed, I must be guided by my own experiences of living with disability. At two years old, I still could not walk. Once I was diagnosed—I have a rare neuromuscular condition—doctors told my parents that I would live only another year or two. Don't bother about school, they advised; just buy her a few toys and make her comfortable until the end.

My parents ignored the doctors' advice. Instead of giving up on me, they taught me to read. They made sure I had a child-size wheelchair and a tricycle. My father built a sled for me, and when the neighborhood kids went to the park to fly downhill in fresh snow, he pulled me along. My mother performed much of my physical care, but was determined not to do all of it; college students helped out in exchange for housing. She knew that her own wholeness and my future depended on being able to utilize resources outside our home.

Now my life is my own. I have a house, a career, a partner, and a community of friends with and without disabilities. I rely on a motorized wheelchair for mobility, a voice-activated computer for my writing, and the assistance of Medicaid-funded attendants for daily needs—dressing, bathing, eating, going to the bathroom. I manage it all according to my own goals and needs.

My life contradicts society's stereotypes about how people with disabilities live. Across the country, thousands of other severely disabled people are surviving, working, loving, and agitating for change. I don't mean to paint a simplistic picture. Most of us work very hard to attain independence, against real physical and/or financial obstacles. Too many people are denied the kind of daily in-home assistance that makes my life possible. Guaranteeing such services has become a top priority for the disability rights movement.

Changes like these, amounting to a small revolution, are slow to reach the public consciousness. Science, on the other hand, puts progress into practice relatively quickly. Prenatal screening seems to give pregnant women more power—but is it actually asking women to ratify social prejudices through their reproductive "choices"? I cannot help thinking that in most cases, when a woman terminates a previously wanted pregnancy expressly to avoid giving birth to a disabled child, she is buying into obsolete assumptions about that child's future. And she is making a statement about the desirability or the relative worth of such a child. Abortion based on disability results from, and in turn strengthens, certain beliefs: children with disabilities (and by implication adults with disabilities) are a burden to family and society; life with a disability is scarcely worth living; preventing the birth is an act of kindness; women who bear disabled children have failed.

Language reinforces the negativity. Terms like "fetal deformity" and "defective fetus" are deeply stigmatizing, carrying connotations of inadequacy and shame. Many of us have been called "abnormal" by medical personnel, who view us primarily as "patients," subject to the definitions and control of the medical profession. "Medical professionals often have countless incorrect assumptions about our lives," says Diane Coleman. "Maybe they see us as failures on their part." As a result, doctors who diagnose fetuses with disabilities often recommend either abortion or institutionalization. "I really haven't heard very many say, 'It's O.K. to have a disability, your family's going to be fine,' " Coleman says.

The independent living movement, which is the disability community's civil rights movement, challenges this medical model. Instead of locating our difficulties within ourselves, we identify our oppression within a society that refuses to accommodate our disabilities. The real solution is to change society—to ensure full accessibility, equal opportunity, and a range of community support services—not to attempt to eliminate disabilities.

The idea that disability might someday be permanently eradicated—whether through prenatal screening and abortion or through medical research leading to "cures"—has strong appeal for a society wary of spending resources on human needs. Maybe there lurks, in the back of society's mind, the belief—the hope?—that one day there will be no people with disabilities. That attitude works against the goals of civil rights and independent living. We struggle for integration, access, and support services, yet our existence remains an unresolved question. Under the circumstances, we cannot expect society to guarantee and fund our full citizenship.

My life of disability has not been easy or carefree. But in measuring the quality of my life, other factors—education, friends, and meaningful work, for example—have been decisive. If I were asked for an opinion on whether to bring a child into the world, knowing she would have the same limitations and opportunities I have had, I would not hesitate to say, "Yes."

I know that many women do not have the resources my parents had. Many lack education, are poor, or are without the support of friends and family. The problems created by these circumstances are intensified with a child who is disabled. No woman should have a child she can't handle or doesn't want. Having said that, I must also say that all kinds of women raise healthy, self-respecting children with disabilities, without unduly compromising their own lives. Raising a child with disabilities is difficult, but raising any child is difficult; just as you expect any other child to enrich your life, you can expect the same from a child with disabilities. But the media often portray raising a child with disabilities as a personal martyrdom. Disabled children, disabled *people,* are viewed as misfortunes.

I believe the choice to abort a disabled fetus represents a rejection of children who have disabilities. Human beings have a deep-seated fear of confronting the physical vulnerability that is part of being human. This terror has been dubbed "disabiliphobia" by some activists. I confront disabiliphobia every day: the usher who gripes that I take up too much room in a theater lobby; the store owner who insists that a ramp is expensive and unnecessary because people in wheelchairs never come in; the talk-show host who resents the money spent to educate students with disabilities. These are the voices of an age-old belief that disability compromises our humanity and requires us to be kept apart and ignored.

Disabiliphobia affects health care reform too. In the Clinton health plan [proposed early in his first term as President] only people disabled through injury or illness—not those of us with congenital disabilities—will be covered. Is this exclusion premised on the assumption that those of us born with disabilities have lesser value and that our needs are too costly?

People with severe disabilities do sometimes require additional resources for medical and support services. But disabiliphobia runs deeper than a cost-benefit analysis. Witness the ordeal of Bree Walker, a Los Angeles newscaster with a mild physical disability affecting her hands and feet. In 1990, when Walker became pregnant with her second child, she knew the fetus might inherit her condition, as had the first. She chose to continue the pregnancy, which led talk-show hosts and listeners to feel they had the right to spend hours debating whether Walker should have the child (most said no). Walker received numerous hostile letters. The callers and letter writers seemed to be questioning her right to exist, as well as her child's.

Walker's experience also pointed out how easily disabiliphobia slips from decisions about fetuses with disabilities to decisions about people with disabilities. That's why abortion is an area where we fear that the devaluation of our lives could become enshrined in public policy. Pro-choice groups must work to ensure that they do not support legislation that sets different standards based on disability.

A case in point is Utah's restrictive 1991 antiabortion law (which has since been declared unconstitutional). The law allowed abortions only in cases of rape, incest, endangerment of the woman's life, a profound health risk to the woman—or "fetal defect." According to Susanne Millsaps, director of Utah's NARAL [National Abortion and Reproductive Rights Action League] affiliate, some disability rights activists wanted NARAL and other pro-choice groups to join in opposing the "fetal defect" exemption. The groups did not specifically take a stand on the exemption; instead they opposed the entire law. I would agree that the whole statute had to be opposed on constitutional and feminist grounds. But I would also agree that there should have been a stronger response to the fetal disability exemption.

To group "fetal defect" together with rape, incest, and life-endangering complications is to reveal deep fears about disability. As Barbara Faye Waxman, an expert on the reproductive rights of women with disabilities, says: "In this culture, disability, in and of itself, is perceived as a threat to the welfare of the mother. I find that to be troublesome and offensive."

There is more at stake here than my feelings, or anyone else's, about a woman's decision. Rapidly changing reproductive technologies, combined with socially constructed prejudices, weigh heavily on any decision affecting a fetus with possible disabilities. While some women lack basic prenatal and infant care, huge amounts of money are poured into prenatal screening and genetic research. Approximately 450 disorders can now be predicted before birth. In most cases the tests reveal only the propensity for a condition, not the condition itself. The Human Genome Project aims to complete the DNA map, and to locate hundreds more physical and developmental attributes. There is little public debate about the worth or ultimate uses of this federally funded multibillion-dollar program. But there are issues with regard to abortion that we can no longer afford to ignore:

- Does prenatal screening provide more data for women's informed choices, or does it promote the idea that no woman should risk having a disabled child?
- Who decides whether a woman should undergo prenatal screening, and what she should do with the results?
- Are expensive, government-funded genetic research projects initiated primarily for the benefit of a society unwilling to support disability-related needs?
- Is society attempting to eradicate certain disabilities? Should this ever be a goal? If so, should all women be expected to cooperate in it?

The January/February 1994 issue of *Disability Rag & Resource,* a publication of the disability rights movement, devoted several articles to genetic screening. In one, feminist lawyer Lisa Blumberg argues that women are being coerced into accepting prenatal tests, and then pressured to terminate their pregnancies when disabling conditions appear likely. "Prenatal testing has largely become the decision of the doctor," Blumberg writes, and "the social purpose of these tests is to reduce the incidence of live births of people with disabilities."

A woman faced with this choice usually feels pressure from many directions. Family, friends, doctors, and the media predict all kinds of negative results should her child be disabled. At the same time, she is unlikely to be given information about community resources; nor is she encouraged to meet individuals who have the condition her child might be born with. This lack of exposure to real-life, nonmedical facts about living with a disability should make us wonder whether women are really making "informed" choices about bearing children with disabilities.

Few outside the disability community have dealt with these issues in any depth. "We are all aware of the potential for abuses in reproductive technology and in genetic testing," says Marcy Wilder, legal director for NARAL's national office in Washington, D.C. "I don't see that there have been widespread abuses—but we're certainly concerned." That concern has not led to any coalition-building with disability rights groups, however.

Many feminist disability rights activists report chilly responses when they attempt to network with pro-choice groups. Too often, when we object to positions that implicitly doubt the humanity of children born disabled, we are accused of being anti-choice. One activist I know recently told me about her experience speaking at a meeting of a National Organization for Women chapter. She mentioned feeling discomfort about the widespread abortion of disabled fetuses—and was startled by the members' reactions. "They said, 'How could you claim to be a feminist and pro-choice and even begin to think that there should be any limitations?' I tried to tell them I don't think there should be limitations, but that our issues need to be included."

On both sides, the fears are genuine, rational, and terrifying—if not always articulated. For the pro-choice movement, the fear is that questioning the

motives and assumptions behind any reproductive decision could give ammu-
nition to antiabortionists. Defenders of disability rights fear that the widespread use of prenatal testing and abortion for the purpose of eliminating disability could inaugurate a new eugenics movement. If we cannot unite and find
ways to address issues of reproductive screening and manipulation, we all face
the prospect that what is supposed to be a private decision—the termination
of a pregnancy—might become the first step in a campaign to eliminate people with disabilities.

I am accusing the pro-choice movement not of spurring these trends, but
of failing to address them. Most pro-choice organizations do not favor the use
of abortion to eliminate disabilities, but their silence leaves a vacuum in which
fear of disability flourishes.

Disabiliphobia and the "genetics enterprise," as activist Adrienne Asch calls
it, have also had legal implications for the reproductive rights of all women. The
tendency to blame social problems such as poverty and discrimination on individuals with disabilities and their mothers has made women vulnerable to the
charge that they are undermining progress toward human "perfectibility"—
because they insist on a genuine choice. Some legal and medical experts have
developed a concept called "fetal rights," in which mothers can be held responsible for the condition of their unborn or newborn children. According to Lisa
Blumberg, "fetal rights" could more accurately be called "fetal quality control."
For women with hereditary disabilities who decide to have children this concept
is nothing new. Society and medical professionals have often tried to prevent us
from bearing and raising children. Disabled women know, as well as anyone,
what it means to be deprived of reproductive choice. More broadly, decisions involving our health care, sexuality, and parenting have been made by others
based on assumptions about our inabilities and/or our asexuality.

The right to control one's body begins with good gynecological care. Low
income, and dependence on disability "systems," restrict access to that care.
Like many women of disability, my health care choices are limited by the accessibility of medical facilities, and by providers' attitudes toward disability and
their willingness to accept the low reimbursement of Medicaid. And Medicaid
will not cover most abortions, a policy that discriminates against poor women
and many women with disabilities.

Paradoxically, policy is often undermined by practice. Although public
funding rarely pays for abortions, many women with disabilities are encouraged to have them—even when they would prefer to have a child. Doctors try
to convince us an abortion would be best for "health reasons"—in which case,
Medicaid will pay for it after all. "Abortions are easier for disabled women to
get," says Nancy Moulton, a health care advocate in Atlanta, "because the medical establishment sees us as not being fit parents." Most women grow up amid
strong if subtle pressures to become mothers. For those of us with disabilities,
there is an equal or greater pressure to forgo motherhood. This pressure has
taken the form of forced sterilization, lost custody battles, and forced abortion.

Consequently, for women with disabilities, reproductive freedom means more than being able to get an abortion. It is hard for many of us to relate to those in the reproductive rights movement whose primary concern is keeping abortions legal and available. But I believe our different perspectives on reproductive freedom are fundamentally compatible, like variations on a single theme.

Whatever the reason, feminist organizations seem inclined to overlook disability concerns. Feminist speakers might add "ableism" to their standard list of offensive "isms," but they do little to challenge it. Now more than ever, women with disabilities need the feminist movement's vigorous support. We need you to defend our rights as if they were your own—which they are. Here are a few suggestions:

- Recognize women with disabilities' equal stake in the pro-choice movement's goals. That means accepting us as women, not dismissing us as "other," or infirm, or genderless. Recognize us as a community of diverse individuals whose health needs, lifestyles, and choices vary.
- Defend all our reproductive rights: the right to appropriate education about sexuality and reproduction; to gynecological care, family planning services, and birth control; the right to be sexually active; to have children and to keep and raise those children, with assistance if necessary; and the right to abortion in accessible facilities, with practitioners who are sensitive to our needs.
- Remove the barriers that restrict the access of women with disabilities to services. Help to improve physical accessibility, arrange disability awareness training for staff and volunteers, and conduct outreach activities to reach women with disabilities.
- Continue struggling to build coalitions around reproductive rights and disability issues. There is plenty of common ground, although we may have to tiptoe through dangerous, mine-filled territory to get to it.
- Question the assumptions that seem to make bearing children with disabilities unacceptable.

Despite our rhetoric, abortion is not strictly a private decision. Individual choices are made in a context of social values; I want us to unearth, sort out, and appraise those values. I wouldn't deny any woman the right to choose abortion. But I would issue a challenge to all women making a decision whether to give birth to a child who may have disabilities.

The challenge is this: consider all relevant information, not just the medical facts. More important than a particular diagnosis are the conditions awaiting a child—community acceptance, access to buildings and transportation, civil rights protection, and opportunities for education and employment. Where these things are lacking or inadequate, consider joining the movement to change them. In many communities, adults with disabilities and parents of disabled children have developed powerful advocacy coalitions. I recognize that, having weighed all the factors, some women will decide they cannot give birth to a child with disabilities. It pains me, but I acknowledge their right and their choice.

Meanwhile, there is much work still to be done.

FOR JOURNALING AND DISCUSSION

1. Why is disability a class issue?
2. Earlier in this chapter, David Berreby, in "Up with People," discusses little people who wanted to abort a fetus that did not have the achondroplasia gene. Write a letter from Hershey to a dwarf couple faced with this decision.
3. Why is Hershey, a feminist, often at odds with pro-choice individuals and organizations?
4. Discuss the scene between Hershey and the pro-life nun in terms of Usry Alleyne's perspective on Christianity in his essay "Atheism and Me" in Chapter 5.

FOR RESEARCH AND EXPLORATION

1. Research the Human Genome Project. How might this project influence future cultural decisions about conception, health care, and programs for the disabled?
2. Interview a person who works with an organization like the Special Olympics that caters to the needs and abilities of the disabled. Why was he or she motivated to do that work, and what rewards does he or she receive?
3. In several cultures, a female fetus is considered a cultural disability, and the mother is urged to have an abortion. Research two countries where this is an accepted practice, and write a paper discussing why abortion based on gender is practiced in both societies.

Who Gets to Live? Who Will Decide?

Mike Ervin

Ervin is a freelance writer and disabilities activist in Chicago. An MS-disabled former poster child who, in retrospect, became disillusioned by the experience, Ervin helped to start Jerry's Orphans, a grassroots group formed to express opposition to the way telethons and other charity fundraisers degrade and exploit the disabled. He also helped to found ADAPT, a national group committed to taking people out of nursing homes and other institutions and placing them back into the community.

Mike Ervin, "Who Gets to Live? Who Will Decide?" from *The Progressive* 58, no. 10 (1994). Copyright © 1994. Reprinted with the permission of *The Progressive*, 409 East Main Street, Madison, WI 53703.

"People with disabilities are in a war for our lives," says Carol Gill, a clinical psychologist in Chicago who specializes in disability issues. "Like in a war, people are making decisions as to who's worth saving and who's not. It's just another form of triage."

Gill is referring to the sort of health-care "reform" passed last year by the Oregon legislature, which "rations" Medicaid benefits. As originally drafted, the Oregon plan ranked several hundred medical conditions and drew a line below which a condition would not be covered. The placement of the line was to be determined by estimates of what a year's state Medicaid budget would be.

State bureaucrats would prioritize conditions by, among other things, a telephone survey of 1,001 Oregonians who would be asked their perceptions of the quality of life of a person with those conditions. Treatment decisions would be driven not by what was medically necessary but by other people's *perceptions* of life with a chronic medical condition or a permanent disability.

The plan was criticized by former Secretary of Health and Human Services Louis Sullivan because its provisions violate the rights of people with disabilities under the Americans with Disabilities Act (ADA).

Bob Griss, an official of the Washington, D.C.–based Center on Disability and Health, agrees. "It's important that access to health care be viewed as a Federal civil-rights issue," he says. "Otherwise we're all going to be politically vulnerable."

When it comes to rationing schemes, he says, no ground should be given without a fight, because such schemes reduce the complexity of health-care delivery to a question of "Who gets thrown out of the lifeboat?" Proponents of rationing justify it as a way to face up to inevitable tough choices, when they're really just taking the easy way out.

While no one involved in the national health-care debacle seriously proposed a plan like Oregon's, both the House and Senate considered a form of fluctuating coverage that weighed the costs of treatments against their effect on the Federal deficit.

However, when the Oregon plan, in revised form thanks to lobbying by Griss and other activists, did become state law, U.S. Senator Bob Packwood said, "Sooner or later, the rest of America is going to come to what Oregon is trying."

And that's exactly what disability activists are worried about. There's ample recent precedent for them to fear the disabled will be the "dead weight" that gets tossed overboard. The more the desire for supported, dignified death à la Dr. Kevorkian is seen as the logical emotional response to the prospect of life with a disability, the more the desire for supported, dignified life will seem radical and unreasonable.

It has happened before. "Permitting the Destruction of Unworthy Life" is the title of a 1920 essay by Alfred Hoche, M.D., in which he made his case for the elimination through euthanasia of the "dead weight existences" of "incurables" in Germany.

"Our situation resembles that of participants in a difficult expedition," Hoche wrote. "The greatest possible fitness of everyone is the inescapable condition of our endeavor's success, and there is no room for half-strength, quarter-strength, or eighth-strength members . . . . Eliminating those who are completely mentally dead is no crime, no immoral act, no emotional cruelty, but is rather a permissible and useful act."

By "incurables," Hoche meant mentally retarded people or people with emotional disabilities who are "empty human shells" who "stand on an intellectual plane we first discover only far down in the animal kingdom."

Skip to 1977, to the Children's Hospital of Oklahoma, where children born with spina bifida were used in a secret "quality-of-life" experiment conducted there between 1977 and 1982. Many were left untreated until they died.

Some doctors at the hospital had invented the eugenicist's dream—a mathematical formula for determining whose life was worth living and whose wasn't. The miracle formula was: $QL = NE \times (H + S)$—that is, Quality of Life is: one's Natural Endowment, multiplied by Home contribution plus Society's contribution.

"Natural Endowment" was a euphemism for ability—or, actually, disability, so the more severe a person's potential disability, the lower his or her natural endowment. "Home" contribution basically meant the financial resources and education level of the parents—the more the better. "Society" contribution was an estimation of how much public support the child was likely to need to be able to live—the less the better.

Just last year, the U.S. Supreme Court refused to hear, and thus killed, a lawsuit filed by the parents of children the Oklahoma hospital allowed to die.

Babies born with spina bifida need immediate surgery to survive, surgery that often renders them paraplegic. So doctors, using the QL formula, gave poorer, less-educated parents, who were therefore more dependent on public resources, a more pessimistic prognosis than they gave more affluent parents of babies with the same disability.

In all, twenty-four of the twenty-five babies whose parents, on doctors' advice, elected not to have them treated died. All thirty-six of those who were fully treated in this experiment lived.

The parents who filed the lawsuit dismissed in 1993 all said they had known nothing about the formula or the experiment. But it took no muckraking or legal coercion to reveal what had happened: The doctors reported the experiment in detail—and bragged about it—in an article published in the October 1983 edition of *Pediatrics*, a prestigious medical journal.

To be blunt, that means the hospital killed two dozen children with disabilities, strutted and crowed about it, and got away with it.

And the Supreme Court's silence was eerily reminiscent of the 1927 majority opinion written by Justice Oliver Wendell Holmes upholding a Virginia law calling for mandatory sterilization of people with mental disabilities. Holmes's rationale in the test case involving Carrie Buck: "Three generations of imbeciles are enough."

So what's next? Maybe a game show, sort of a perverse *Queen for a Day* in which two people with similar medical conditions beg for treatment and an audience vote decides who gets it and who doesn't.

Why not? There already has been such a show in the Netherlands. Called *A Matter of Life and Death,* it was partly financed by the Dutch Ministry of Health. One episode featured two women with cancer stating their cases—why one should be treated before the other. Then they watched as the results of the audience vote appeared on an electronic scoreboard.

Disability activists are on red alert, but they know the bigotry that spans the century can be most dangerous when it comes in a seemingly innocuous package like the Oregon rationing plan.

When the Bush Administration rejected the original plan, its architects resubmitted it with a strange and convoluted tie-breaking system—as if deciding who gets treatment is comparable with deciding who makes the football playoffs. If money shortages dictated the need for decisions about which people with similar needs would get treatment, the tie would be broken in favor of those with the better chance of not having residual effects—which, of course, the state would have to deal with later.

Bob Griss and others argue that this still violated ADA because it devalued those with permanent disabilities. He uses the example of two people who need surgery for cancer, one requiring amputation and one not. Why should the person needing amputation be deemed less worthy of treatment when the only difference between the two after treatment is one less limb?

The Clinton Administration agreed, and nixed the second plan.

The version finally approved in March 1993, however, retains the fluctuating cut-off line. And that's one of the greatest dangers of the Oregon plan, according to Griss, because it is justified by prejudice—a prejudice that people with chronic conditions or permanent disabilities deserve fewer guarantees, that they may be deemed worthy of coverage in one year and not the next.

Griss takes some satisfaction from playing his role in lobbying for the revisions that lessened the plan's severity, but he wishes those efforts had invalidated the very idea of rationing. "If you don't recognize the true driving points of health-care costs, like administrative waste and excess profits, you're not going to solve the problem," he says.

The sort of pigeonholing sanctioned by the Oregon plan is what makes people with disabilities, who are fighting for the absolute right to medical care, feel that they cannot rely on anyone but themselves to secure that right. They've learned they can't always rely on courts and legislatures. And they've found that bureaucracies and even family members are often all-too-ready to dilute that right.

Social psychologist Elaine Makas inserted herself into the case of Corey Brown, in her hometown of Lewiston, Maine. Corey is a twelve-year-old girl disabled by cerebral palsy and scoliosis. Her doctor issued a "do-not-resuscitate" order should anything happen to Corey. Her mother agreed it was in Corey's best interest. Nowhere was it expressed what Corey thinks. Elaine Makas doubts that anyone ever asked Corey.

Late last year, the school board of Lewiston held a hearing on whether to honor the order while Corey is in school. The board eventually voted that it would, which meant that Corey was the only student in her school not entitled to lifesaving measures should she need them.

Some teachers were defiant and said they would do whatever they could to save Corey if such a situation arose. Makas filed an ADA complaint and spread the word about the case to disability activists and organizations around the country, who responded with angry letters to the school board. Some of them went to Lewiston to testify at a hearing held to reconsider the school board's decision.

The board did reverse itself to a degree, and Makas thinks the pressure of all these various factors is what led it to that decision.

"My argument has always been with the policy, not the people involved," Makas says. "Having a disability is not sufficient reason to let somebody die." Maine law allows the issuance of such "do-not-resuscitate" orders for people in a persistent vegetative state or people who are terminally ill.

Obviously, someone like Corey Brown, who attends school every day, is not in a persistent vegetative state. "But," says Makas, "people are making an equation that having a severe disability is the same as being terminally ill. There's a perception that they are better off dead."

As things are now, and depending on future developments, Corey will receive almost the same emergency treatment in school as any other student. But Makas calls it a small victory, since Corey's do-not-resuscitate order still stands in every other arena of her life. And Makas knows of at least two other Lewiston children with disabilities who live under similar orders issued by Corey's doctor.

Not even a small victory can be claimed in the case of *In re C.A.* in Illinois. C.A. is a girl who was born in October 1990, HIV-positive and addicted to cocaine. Today, according to her lawyer and guardian ad litem Thomas Holum, she needs to be fed through a tube, but other than that, she's as active as any girl her age.

Because she is a ward of the state, the Illinois Department of Children and Family Services petitioned the courts in 1991 for the right to decide whether she should be resuscitated in a medical emergency. Holum opposed the motion because, he says, "Bureaucracies shouldn't be the ones to decide. Bureaucracies aren't known for their sensitivity and compassion. They're designed to manage large numbers of people. They're interested in the bottom line." Holum fears that a bureaucracy has too much incentive to just cut loose a burdensome child like C.A. He wanted to establish the right of a child in a situation like C.A.'s to a hearing at which all sides could be heard before a judge makes a decision.

But Holum lost. Today or tomorrow, C.A. could be allowed to die without Holum being notified, without her foster parents being notified, without anyone who cherishes her being notified.

Cases like these keep the National Legal Center for the Medically Disabled and Dependent busier than ever. The Center, based in Indianapolis, specializes in cases involving the civil rights of people with disabilities—especially those who are indigent and need life-sustaining treatment.

Staff attorney John Altomare sees the slippery slope of euthanasia getting steeper and slicker. "I think there's a desire to escape the paternalism of physicians and a desire for autonomy. But I think the ethics of euthanisia are starting to catch up to it, as the discussion is becoming one of economics and control."

The cases Altomare finds most alarming are those that enter the realm of involuntary euthanasia of competent adults.

Michael Martin is a forty-two-year-old man who lives in a long-term-care facility near Grand Rapids, Michigan. He sustained a brain injury when his car was hit by a train in 1987.

He can move only his right arm and leg and uses a wheelchair for mobility. He can't speak but communicates by nodding his head or spelling on an alphabet board. John Hess, Martin's attorney in Grand Rapids, says his client enjoys watching Detroit Tigers baseball (or did until the recent strike) and plays cards; his IQ has been tested at sixty-three. Lately he has been complaining about not having enough to do.

One day, Hess says, Martin spelled out the word AFRAID on his board. He was questioned until he managed to explain that what he was afraid of was that someone would force him to die against his will.

Martin waits like a man on death row because his wife, who is his legal guardian, has petitioned Michigan courts to give her the power to end his life by disconnecting the tube through which he receives nourishment. She claims he once said, before his accident, that he would not want to live in a condition like the one he's in.

But Hess says Martin has changed his mind. He now states consistently that he wants to live. "People forget how adaptable the human spirit is," says Hess. "Michael is not in a condition people would choose. But when you're in that situation, you can see where you can have a full and rewarding life."

The latest court decision favored Martin's wife. Martin was not considered competent enough to have the right to change his mind. If his wife prevails, Hess says, "Michael could starve and dehydrate to death," whether he likes it or not.

"Where do you draw the line?" Hess asks. "If we can take Michael out at sixty-three IQ, then why not seventy-three or seventy-five or eighty or ninety?"

Access to fast and easy euthanasia is gaining esteem as an alternative to living with physical and even emotional pain. Freedom of choice, says Carol Gill, is not the issue anymore: "A lot of people with disabilities internalize the devaluation of their bodies or get burned out from the struggle and want to give up. In that case, I don't think they're in the best position to decide. So what if they're rational? It's possible to be rational and seriously depressed."

But isn't it strange, she continues, that the competence and rights of people with disabilities who want to live face increasing challenges, while those who want to die are rarely questioned?

FOR JOURNALING AND DISCUSSION

1. What might be biased or unethical about a telephone survey that asks for people's perceptions on the quality of life of others who are permanently disabled or who have a chronic medical condition?
2. The stories and perspectives of Corey Brown's mother and Michael Martin's wife are not presented by Ervin. Why might they have made the decisions they did? Do you know anyone who has been the primary caretaker of a severely disabled person? How has his or her loved one's disability affected the quality of the caretaker's life?
3. Ervin describes himself as an activist for the disabled community. Discuss the additional barriers he might face when he confronts able-bodied people in power positions.
4. Just as Ervin discusses the disabled's increasing vulnerability in the face of Medicaid cuts, David D. Cooper, in "The Changing Seasons of Liberal Learning" in Chapter 6, examines the growing fiscal and political conservatism of contemporary college students. Do Cooper's findings support Ervin's observations?

FOR RESEARCH AND EXPLORATION

1. Find the 1920 essay by Alfred Hoche, M.D., that Ervin mentions. Write a paper about the influence that Hoche's thinking had on Adolf Hitler.
2. What is a eugenicist? Research and write about eugenics as an ideology.
3. Are the disabled segregated from the able-bodied in our country? Take a survey of people in another of your classes. How many of the able-bodied students have an ongoing relationship with a disabled person other than a family member? Are disabled and able-bodied people easily accessible to one another for friendship? Why or why not?

Fetal Alcohol Syndrome: A National Perspective
Fetal Alcohol Syndrome: A Parent's Perspective

Michael Dorris

While single, anthropologist and writer Dorris adopted three Native American children; his son Abel's battle with Fetal Alcohol Syndrome is described in The Broken Cord *and a made-for-TV movie. Dorris is the author of* Paper Trail *and* A Yellow Raft in Blue Water. *After he married writer Louise Erdrich (see the essay "Big Grass" in Chapter 8), they co-authored* The Crown of Columbus *and added three additional children to their family. Erdrich also adopted Dorris' Native American children. Their son Abel was tragically struck and killed by a car in 1991. In April of 1997, on the brink of a divorce from Erdrich, Dorris took his own life. Allegations of sexual misconduct circulated after his death, but Erdrich's only public comments were: "Michael did a huge amount of good in the world. He also suffered from severe depression" (* Time, *4/28/97, p. 62).*

A NATIONAL PERSPECTIVE

At the time I adopted my oldest son, Abel, in 1971, I knew that his birth mother had been a heavy drinker, but even the medical textbooks in those days stated that exposure to alcohol could not damage a developing fetus. I knew that Abel had been born small and premature, had "failed to thrive," and was an initially slow learner, but for ten years as a single parent I convinced myself that nurture, a stimulating environment, and love could open up life to my little boy.

It wasn't true. At the University of Washington and elsewhere, biochemists and psychologists now confirm that for some women even moderate doses of prenatal exposure to alcohol can permanently stunt a human being's potential. According to the U.S. surgeon general, *no* level of ethanol is guaranteed to be "safe."

My grown son has a full range of physical disorders: seizures; curvature of the spine; poor coordination, sight, and hearing. But his most disabling legacy has to do with his impaired ability to reason. Fetal alcohol syndrome (FAS) victims are known for their poor judgment, their impulsiveness, their persistent confusions over handling money, telling time, and in distinguishing right from wrong.

Since the publication of *The Broken Cord* last August [1989], I have received an outpouring of wrenching letters from literally hundreds of readers—rural and urban, religious and agnostic, of all ethnic and economic backgrounds— who share experiences of heartache, grief, and frustration uncannily identical to my wife's and mine. Their sons, daughters, or grandchildren have been repeatedly misdiagnosed with the same amorphous labels: retarded, sociopathic, attention-deficit, unteachable troublemakers.

A majority of full-blown FAS victims are adopted or in state care, but many children who are less drastically impaired (i.e., with fetal alcohol effect [FAE]) remain with their natural parents. Depending on the term of pregnancy in which the harmful drinking occurred, these individuals may look perfectly healthy and test in the normal range for intelligence, yet by early adolescence they show unmistakable signs of comprehension problems or uncontrollable rage. It is currently estimated that in the United States some eight thousand babies are born annually with full FAS and another sixty-five thousand with a degree of FAE. Nothing will ever restore them to the people they might otherwise have been.

And it seems that's far less than the half of it. An additional three hundred thousand babies prenatally bombarded with illegal drugs will be born in this country in 1990. Recent studies indicate that crack cocaine, if smoked during pregnancy, causes learning deficits in offspring similar to those caused by alcohol. The "first generation" of children from the 1980s' crack epidemic is about to enter public school, and these children are consistently described as "remorseless," "without a conscience," and passive, apparently lacking that essential empathy, that motivation toward cooperation, upon which a peaceful and harmonious classroom—and society—so depends.

No curriculum or training program has so far proven to be completely effective for people with this totally preventable affliction, and a Los Angeles pilot education project costs taxpayers $15,000 a year per pupil. However, the price of doing nothing, of ignoring the issue, is beyond measure.

Nothing like crack—a baby shower gift of choice in certain populations because it is reputed to speed and ease labor—has occurred before. According to one survey, upwards of 11 percent of all U.S. infants in 1988 tested positive for cocaine or alcohol the first time their blood was drawn. A New York City Health Department official estimated that births to drug-abusing mothers had increased there by about 3,000 percent in the past ten years.

Why? Some explanations have to do with a paucity of available services and support. Too many fathers regard their baby's health as solely their partner's concern. Only one residential treatment program specifically for chemically dependent pregnant women exists in New York City, where the State Assembly Committee on Alcoholism and Drug Abuse estimates that "twelve thousand babies will be born addicted . . . in 1989, and the number of children in foster care has doubled in two years from twenty-seven thousand in 1987 to more than fifty thousand today, mainly because of parental drug abuse." The system has broken down. Sixteen percent of all American mothers have had insufficient prenatal medical attention—increasing to 33 percent for unmarried or teenage mothers, 30 percent for Hispanic women, and 27 percent for black women.

At last, thanks to a 1989 act of Congress, liquor bottle labels must include a warning, and signs posted in many bars proclaim the hazards of alcohol to unborn children. But what happens when public education doesn't work as a deterrent, when a pregnant woman herself is a victim of FAS or prenatal crack and therefore cannot understand the long-term disastrous consequences for the life of another resulting from what she drinks or inhales? It isn't that these women don't love the *idea* of their babies. They just can't foresee the cruel realities.

The conflict of competing rights—of protecting immediate civil liberty versus avoiding future civil strife—is incredibly complex, with no unambiguously right or easy answers, but as a nation it's unconscionable to delay the debate. If we close our eyes we condemn children not yet even conceived to existences of sorrow and deprivation governed by prison, victimization, and premature death.

My wife and I think of these tragedies as we wait for our son to have brain surgery that may reduce the intensity of his seizures, though not eliminate them. At twenty-two, despite all of our efforts and his best intentions, he remains forever unable to live independently, to manage a paycheck, or to follow the plot of a TV sitcom, and we worry about the very fabric of society when hundreds of thousands of others with problems similar to his or worse become teenagers, become adults, beyond the year 2000.

*   *   *

FETAL ALCOHOL SYNDROME: A PARENT'S PERSPECTIVE

Unlike so many good people—scientists and social workers and politicians—who have chosen out of the kindness of their hearts and the dictates of their social consciences to become knowledgeable about fetal alcohol syndrome [FAS] and fetal alcohol effect [FAE], to work with their victims, to demand prevention, I was dragged to the subject blindfolded, kicking and screaming. I'm the worst kind of expert, a grudging, reluctant witness, an embittered amateur, and, above all else: a failure. A parent.

I'm a living, breathing encyclopedia of what hasn't worked in curing or reversing the damage to one child prenatally exposed to too much alcohol. Certain drugs temporarily curbed my son's seizures and hyperactivity but almost certainly had dampening effects on his learning ability and personality development. Fifteen years of special education—isolation in a classroom, repetitive instruction, hands-on learning—maximized his potential but didn't give him a normal IQ. Psychological counseling—introspective techniques, group therapy—had no positive results, and may even have encouraged his ongoing confusion between what is real and what's imagined.

Brain surgery hasn't worked.

Anger hasn't worked.

Patience hasn't worked.

Love hasn't worked.

When you're the parent of an FAS or FAE child, your goals change with the passing years. You start with seeking solutions: ideas and regimens to penetrate the fog that blocks your son's or daughter's ability to comprehend rules, retain information, or even be curious. You firmly believe—because it has to be true—that the answers are "out there." It's just a matter of locating them. You go through teachers and their various learning theories like so many Christmas catalogues received in the mail, determined to find the perfect gift, the right combination of toughness and compassion, optimism and realism, training and intuition. Once you find a likely prospect, you badger her (in my experience, most teachers of "learning disabled" [LD] children seem to be women), demand results, attempt to coerce with praise or threat. You become first an ally, then increasingly a pain in the neck, a judgmental critic, an ever-persistent, occasionally hysterical, nuisance. When the teacher, worn out and frustrated, eventually gives up on your child, decides he's beyond her ability or resources to help, she's as glad to see *you* go as she's relieved that your son won't be back to remind her of her limitations. "With a crazy, irrational parent like that," you imagine her saying to her colleagues, "no wonder the kid has problems."

Do I sound paranoid, cynical? I wasn't always this way, but I'm the product of a combined total of fifty years of dealing with alcohol-damaged children—for not only does the son I wrote about in *The Broken Cord* suffer from fetal alcohol syndrome, but his adopted brother and sister are, to a lesser and greater extent, victims of fetal alcohol effect.

For years, my wife and I and our extended families had no choice but to become a kind of full-time social service agency specializing in referrals, the admissions policies of various expensive institutions, the penalties meted out under the juvenile justice system, the nightmares of dealing with uninformed, often smug, bureaucrats given by default responsibility for people who can't make it on their own in contemporary America. We were forced to progress from attending increasingly sour PTA meetings to learning the intricacies of intelligence testing—hoping that the score will come in below 70 and thus qualify a child for legal disability. We've had to become acquainted with the admissions policies and maximum length of stays at institutions like Covenant House, Boystown, and the Salvation Army. We've paid out well over $150,000, not counting what our insurance has covered, for our children's primary and secondary special school tuitions, counseling, doctors of every sort, experimental medical procedures, Outward Bound for Troubled Youth, and private camps for the learning disabled. We have managed to try every single avenue that's been suggested to us by well-meaning people who should know what might benefit our sons and daughter, and nothing—*nothing*—has consistently worked for more than a few months.

Our older children, now all adults or nearly so, often cannot function independently, cannot hold jobs, tell the truth, manage money, plan a future. They have all at one time or another been arrested or otherwise detained for shoplifting, inappropriate sexual conduct, and violent behavior. Despite all our efforts to protect them, they have periodically come under the influence of people who, for instance, worship Satan or take advantage of them physically, mentally, and/or financially. They maintain no enduring friendships, set for themselves no realistic goals, can call upon no bedrock inner voice to distinguish moral from amoral, safe from dangerous.

Okay: maybe it's us. Maybe we're incredibly dysfunctional parents. We've spent years feeling guilty and inadequate, holding on to the belief that if only we could become better, more resourceful, more sympathetic, more enlightened in our expectations and requirements, we could alter the bleak future that seems to lie in store or have already arrived for our adopted children. Like every self-reflective father and mother, we can recall our failures, our lapses, our losses of temper, and time after time we have added up these shortcomings to see if they balance the devastating total of our sons' and daughter's current situations. *The Broken Cord* was written, at least in part, to further this process, to assign guilt—if not wholly to us, then to somebody, something—to make not just sense of a senseless waste, but a difference. If every avenue of investigation were explored, maybe something would be discovered that could reverse the fate of not just any anonymous afflicted fetus, child, or adult, but of *our* children.

But what the book yielded was worse than the least I had expected. Not only was there no magic trick, no scientific breakthrough that could produce a "cure," but from the outpouring of letters that have come from around the country it is clear that our family's private sorrow is far from unusual. In the year and a half since *The Broken Cord* was published, we have heard from more than two thousand parents of FAS and FAE victims. All love their children, and almost none have given up hope. But none of them knows what the hell to do next.

The hardest group to answer are the parents of very young children, children who seem from the symptoms described to be clearly fetal alcohol affected. I recognize these parents: in the early stages of denial, full of the surety that answers exist. They want practical advice, experts to consult, books to read, innovative doctors to visit. They want to head off the unpleasant disappointments chronicled in my book, to save their child—and themselves—from such a miserable chain of events. If *The Broken Cord* had been written by somebody else, I would have mailed just such a letter to its author. I would have been skeptical of his pessimism, sure that I could do better, last longer, be smarter, succeed where he had failed. So when I answer the letters I receive, I root for those parents, applaud their confidence, ask them to write back and tell me when things improve. So far, there has been no good news.

Almost equally difficult to absorb is the mail I receive from parents whose FAS and FAE children are older than ours. They write with the weary echo of experience, the products of many cycles of raised expectations followed by dejection. They tell of their "fifty-two-year-old child," or their FAE adult daughter who's just given birth to her third FAS baby and is pregnant again and still drinking. They tell of children serving twenty-year prison terms or, in one case, of a "sweet" son sentenced to the death penalty for an impulsive murder for which he has never shown the slightest remorse. They tell of children raised in privilege who are now lost among the homeless on a distant city's streets, of children once so loving and gentle who have been maimed from drug use or knife fights, or, as is so often the case, who have been raped. They tell of innocents become prostitutes, of suicide attempts, and always, always, of chemical dependency. They tell of children whose whereabouts are unknown, or who are dead at twenty-five. This is not the way it was supposed to happen, these parents cry. It's not fair. It's not right.

We read these letters and wonder: is *this* in store?

I've even heard from adults diagnosed with fetal alcohol effect—one of them with a Ph.D. from Harvard and several others with master's degrees. These are highly intelligent people, the Jackie Robinsons of FAE, who have had to become specialists on themselves. Through years of observing their own trials and errors, of watching how "normal" people behave in a given context and analyzing how that contrasts with their own uncertain reactions, some of them have worked out complicated formulas to simulate a greater connection to the world than they in fact possess. One woman carries in her purse a card on which is typed a series of questions she explicitly asks herself in an attempt to gauge the consequences of her possible responses to an unprecedented situation: What would so-and-so do in this instance? What will people probably think if I do *x, y,* or *z?* She's compensating for life in a universe that's slightly, almost imperceptibly alien, and trying to speak a language whose idiom and nuance are forever just beyond her automatic reach.

The correspondence we've received from around this country, and lately from around the world, has magnified exponentially our particular family experience, but hasn't contradicted it. The letter I've waited for but which has yet to arrive is the one that begins, "I've read your book and you're dead wrong," or "My child was diagnosed as having FAS but we fixed it by doing the following things and now, five years later, he's perfectly fine."

*   *   *

To what extent does this preventable scourge affect American Indian people? The answer, like so much about FAS, is ambiguous. On the one hand, prenatal exposure to ethanol impairs a fetus in exactly the same ways whether its mother is a member of a country club in Greenwich, Connecticut, or an ADC [Aid to Dependent Children] mom on the White Earth reservation. Every human being during development is vulnerable, fragile, easy to poison; ethnicity acts as neither a shield nor a magnet. Yes, "drinking age" matters, diet counts, smoking and other drug use will exacerbate the damage done by alcohol, but all things considered, no woman is physically destined to give birth to an FAS baby.

The factors that really make a difference have to do with ephemeral things: strong family and community support for abstinence, access to good prenatal care and chemical dependency treatment, clear and widespread information on the dangers of drinking during pregnancy. And it's here that Native American women are at a severe disadvantage. Health programs on reservations have been among the first things cut when the federal budget gets tight; clinics are shut down, counselors laid off, preventive educational campaigns scrapped. Access to organizations like Planned Parenthood is, in many tribal communities, impossible. Poverty, unemployment, despair—familiar elements in the daily lives of too many Indian people—lead to alcohol and other drug abuse. The causes of the problem, and the solutions, are so much bigger and more complex than just saying no.

When you factor in to the statistics on FAS and FAE those having to do with prenatal exposure to crack cocaine—which seems to produce in children many of the same learning disabilities as too much alcohol—we are looking at hundreds of thousands of impaired babies born in this country annually. In ten years that's three million people. By the time the first generation counted is twenty years old, it's six million, and that's assuming a stable rate—not the current geometrically accelerating one. How does our society handle this onslaught, on either a local or a national level? How do we make laws that apply equally to those of us who can understand the rules and to a significant minority who, through no fault of their own, can't? How do we preserve individual liberty, free choice, safe streets, mutual trust, when some members of society have only a glancing grasp of moral responsibility? How do we cope with the growing crime rate among young people, with "wilding," with trying to teach the unteachable?

The thorny ethical issue that has troubled me most in thinking about the social impact of FAS and other such lifelong but preventable afflictions concerns responsibility. When, if ever, are we, one-on-one or collectively, obliged to intervene? It's becoming increasingly clear that FAS victims beget more FAS victims: a pregnant woman who can't calculate the long-term consequences of her decisions is a hard case for prenatal counseling. It is difficult if not impossible to convince her to defer an immediate gratification because nine months or nine years later her hypothetical child might suffer from a night of partying. That child is an abstraction, a hazy shadow at best, and the argument is a great deal less compelling than the draw of another drink or fix.

Some studies have suggested that compared with the "average" woman, female FAS and FAE victims start having children younger, continue for a longer period of years to produce them, and ultimately conceive and bring to term more offspring. They are less likely to seek prenatal care, to abstain from dangerous activities during their pregnancies, and to keep custody of their babies. Statistically a woman who's given birth to an FAS baby has almost an eight out of ten chance to do so again, if she continues drinking, and subsequent siblings are likely to be even more impaired than the first.

These often abandoned or removed children, whether adopted or institutionalized, are ultimately our culture's victims and therefore are its responsibility. How to cope? At the absolute minimum, how do we—especially in a tight economy—pay the medical bills, build the prisons, construct the homeless shelters? How do we train special education teachers to function indefinitely with no hope of success, or ordinary citizens how to forgive behaviors that are irritating at best, threatening or dangerous at worst? How do we teach compassion for a growing class of people who are likely to exhibit neither pity nor gratitude, who take everything society has to offer and have almost nothing constructive to give back? How do we maintain the universal franchise to vote, the cornerstone of our political system? How do we redefine "guilty or not guilty" to apply to heartless acts committed by people who are fundamentally incapable of comprehending the spirit of the law?

To me these questions can be understood if not answered by a simple analogy: Imagine we saw a blind woman holding a child by the hand attempt to cross a busy street. The traffic was fast, she guessed wrong, and before our eyes her child was struck by a truck and killed. A tragedy we would never forget. Then a year later we come by the same intersection again, and again there's the woman, but with a new child. The light is against her but she doesn't see and tries to cross to the other side. The child is hit, terribly injured, as we stand by helplessly and watch. The next year it happens again, and the next, and the next. How many times must it happen before we become involved? Before we take the woman's arm or hold up our hand to stop the cars or carry her child or at least tell her when the signal is green? How many children are too many? When do their rights to safe passage assert themselves? And how long before the mother herself is killed?—for remember, she's a victim and at grave risk, too. It does no good to blame her, to punish her for the result of her blindness. Once the street is crossed the child is dead. The mother needs help and we need to find a decent way to provide it. If we turn our backs, we stop being innocent bystanders and become complicit in the inevitable accident, accessories after the fact.

* * *

Despite all his recent fame since *The Broken Cord*'s publication, [my son] Abel continues to be fired from menial jobs, to lose places to live. He hasn't made a single lasting friend, hasn't received a friendly personal phone call, hasn't read a book unless you count *Garfield*. He's twenty-three and lonely, without being able to think of the name to describe that emotion or figure out and persevere in any action to alleviate it.

My wife and I had to go out of town on business last week. When we returned we called Abel's new residence and were greeted by the chilling report that he had apparently "forgotten" to eat from Thursday through Sunday and had lost a considerable amount of weight.

Abel isn't considered to be sufficiently impaired to qualify for a state-run facility for the disabled, so his only option is to board in a private home close enough to walk to the truck stop where he works part-time. As it happened, the perfectly nice husband and wife who maintain this home had a family emergency that necessitated that they be gone the same weekend that Louise and I were away. They left Abel's food, clearly marked for each day, on a special shelf in the refrigerator, but in their absence—that is, without the cue of their direct, repeated instructions at meal time—it had not occurred to our adult son that the hunger he had to have felt could be sated simply by feeding himself.

And Abel is the easy one, the most fortunate of our three adopted children, because he is at least unambiguously diagnosable. The state of New Hampshire, financially strapped as it is, has no choice but to examine him and conclude "LD." Minimal services are provided: a social worker takes him to the dentist and checks on his living situation a couple of times a month. He's finally eligible for social security and Medicaid benefits, providing he doesn't earn more than $500 a month. Strangers and friends who interact with him think, "Ah, retarded," instead of "stupid," "rude," or "dangerous." They make allowances.

Our two other older children, however, are another story. Their respective birth mothers drank in sprees while pregnant—not heavily enough to produce full FAS symptoms in their offspring, but . . . heavily enough. Almost certainly fetal alcohol affected, our son and daughter are now nineteen and almost sixteen, respectively, and they have fallen apart, right on the FAE schedule. My son has been on the street since, at seventeen, he chose to quit the last of the many special schools and treatment centers we found for him, starting at age fourteen. That final place was the only one that didn't kick *him* out. He's intellectually capable of a normal life, but he often lacks judgment, empathy, perspective, the patience to set long-term goals and then work to accomplish them.

Our daughter, at Boystown for the last two years after having been expelled from three "regular" schools for shoplifting or for failing to pass any courses since the sixth grade, has recently discovered satanism. She has carved an upside-down cross into her arm with a ballpoint pen, twice. After seeing *Dances with Wolves* she's become convinced that the reservation where she was born (and where her birth mother is currently in jail again for drunk and disorderly conduct) is like the happy community in the movie, and so has refused to cooperate with her house parents in any way because she hopes to be sent to South Dakota. Helpful people from the Omaha Indian Center, as well as Louise and I and a dozen others, have tried to explain to her the huge gap between fantasy and fact, between antiseptic fiction and the ragged poverty of Rosebud reservation, but it doesn't penetrate.

Every parent is helpless, that's a given, virtually a cliché. The children of hippies become CPAs or join the army, rural kids move to the city as soon as they can buy a ticket, passing on their way the teenage urban cowboys en route to the wide open spaces. But the utter helplessness of an FAS or FAE parent is of another magnitude. We stand by, throwing one temporary impediment after another into the path of boys and girls seemingly bent upon engineering their own destruction. Many of us hear at one time or another the standard advice of the stumped psychological counselor: let your kids sink to the bottom, then they'll start to work their way back up. Well, we come to discover that in the case of our "special" children, the bottom is very deep indeed. At each plateau, a new descent is immediately sought, and if the levels of Dante's *Inferno* spring to mind, it's not inappropriate. For an FAS or FAE child who doesn't understand rules or morality, honesty or loyalty (except as applying to the exigencies of the moment), the drop is that of an elevator once the cable has been severed.

Louise and I are not the persons to consult for a benign or inspirational message. Hope has become our enemy—a trickster who lies in wait, who reappears in dreams and then pulls the rug from under us time after time. Our afflicted children are beyond placebos, beyond the reach of platitude. Our sons and oldest daughter were brainwashed by alcohol before they were born, casualties in this battle. We have fought the aftereffects of their prenatal exposure to ethanol for twenty years—tried every tactic we could think of or that was suggested to us by specialists—and we barely made a dent in their fates.

When one son calls me from a reservation phone booth and speculates about how he might steal a car and drive to Seattle, it's not much consolation to think that the sum of all our efforts may have merely forestalled this moment in his life by a year or so. We know that buried within the brooding adult Abel resides a sweet little boy, capable of responding with affection if the right buttons are pushed—but try to convince his co-workers when he forgets to punch in on time.

Let us make no mistake about one point: we're not *facing* a crisis, we're *in* one, though official statistics can be deceiving. A couple of years ago South Dakota, a state with at that time no resident dysmorphologist (the only doctor, except for a geneticist, fully trained to diagnose FAS or FAE), reported a grand total of two FAS births—during the same period in which my friend Jeaneen Grey Eagle, director of Project Recovery in Pine Ridge, estimated that somewhere between one-third and one-half of the infants born in certain communities of her reservation were at high risk due to heavy maternal drinking. Underdiagnosis, unfortunately, does not equal small numbers.

But what can we do about it? Each person must provide his or her own answers. Some of us—the scientists—can study the biochemistry involved in fetal damage from drugs, learn to predict which women are most at risk and when, figure out how much ethanol, if any, is tolerable. Others—advocates and politicians—can address the issue of prevention: get out the word, make pests of ourselves, speak up even when it makes our friends uncomfortable, fight for the future of a child not yet even conceived. Still others—social workers, psychologists, and educators—can tackle the needs of the here and now, of the tens of thousands of FAS and FAE men, women, and children who exist on the margins of society. We can devise effective curricula, learning regimens, humane models for dependent care.

If we, today, put our minds to it, if only we did our part, we might not obliterate fetal alcohol syndrome on a global level, but, in all candor, we could save many lives, many mothers, many babies. All it takes is nine months of abstinence, a bit longer if a mother breast feeds. Three hundred thousand separate and discrete solutions, three hundred thousand miracles, and it's a clean year.

And finally some of us, the parents into whose care these children have been given, whether by birth or adoption, can try to get through another day, to survive the next unexpected catastrophe, to preserve a sense of humor. We laugh at things that really aren't funny—quite the contrary—but we laugh, without malice, for relief. When Abel went with me last fall to his annual case management meeting, he was asked to list all the accomplishments in the past twelve months about which he felt especially proud. He drew a blank.

"Then, tell us what you've been doing since we met here last year," the man directed—and Abel complied.

"Well, I went down the stairs and I opened the door," he began. "Then I got into the car and my father took me home. For supper we had . . . ." Abel tried to remember that anonymous meal he polished off some 365 days before, stalled, and looked to me for help.

"Next question," I suggested, and the social worker consulted his list.

"Tell me what things you really *don't* like to do," he invited.

Abel's eyes lit. This was an easy one. "I don't like to dig up burdocks," he stated.

I blinked in surprise. Abel hadn't dug up burdocks in three years. He was simply using a response that had worked in the past.

"Wait a minute," I said. "Abel, thousands of people all over the country have read your chapter at the end of the book about how you dug up those burdocks to help us. People liked that part so much I think that's why they gave our book that prize you have sitting on your dresser. People are very proud of you for what you did. I know it wasn't fun to dig up those plants, but you should feel good that you did it."

Abel was having an especially polite day. He smiled at me, cocked his head, and asked: "What book would that be?"

The grind doesn't get easier and it doesn't go away. FAS victims do not learn from experience, do not get well. Louise keeps a diary and a while ago she glanced back over the past four years. That can be dangerous, because there are some things you don't notice until you take the long view. It turned out that as a family we hadn't had a single period longer than three consecutive days in all that time when one of our alcohol-impaired children was not in a crisis—health, home, school—that demanded our undivided attention. It often seems to us that their problems define our existence as well as their own, and in that respect perhaps we are in a small way the forecast of things to come for this country. How many children of chemically dependent parents have perished in house fires, from malnutrition, from lack of medical care, from exposure? Are these, also, options protected under the rubric of an adult's right to choose to drink or take drugs beyond the point of responsible self-control? Who are these lost babies but the victims of "victimless" crime? Certainly if they survive, the penalties they suffer are ongoing. The prisons to which they are confined exist without the possibility of parole.

FAS is not a problem whose impact is restricted to its victims. It's not just a woman's issue, not just a man's. No one is exempted. These are everybody's children.

I am descended from the Modoc tribe on my father's side, and I can't help but think of a historic parallel to my present circumstances. In the late nineteenth century the Modocs were engaged in what history calls "the Last Indian War." It consisted of about fifty hungry men, women, and children leaving the Oregon reservation to which they had been assigned—a reservation owned and operated by their traditional enemies, the Klamath—and returning to the Northern California lands they had previously occupied. As was the custom in those days, they were pursued by the cavalry and a full military force—who had a terribly hard time locating them, since the Modocs were hiding in a moonscape of lava beds. But find them they eventually did.

A few of the captured leaders were executed without trial, but what to do with the rest? A group of about twenty adult Modocs were given a choice: either be shipped to a cholera-ridden prison camp in Indian Territory (now Oklahoma) or work the vaudeville circuit with A. B. Meacham, the former Indian agent who had been the source of many of the tribe's troubles. Meacham, you see, had a dynamite idea: America had read in newspapers about the savage Modocs, now the public must be allowed to see them in person.

For more than a year, in cities and towns throughout this country, between a troop of jugglers and a knife-throwing act, the final agonized moments of the "war" were restaged. The Modoc POWs were assigned new, more "Indian-sounding" names, costumed in the kind of fringe-and-feather outfits the audience expected Indians to wear, and commanded to re-create, twice a day, six nights a week, plus two additional matinee performances, the moment of their final defeat.

I know how they must have felt.

People have asked me whether it was "cathartic" to write *The Broken Cord* and then see it have some impact on national awareness. The answer is no. There's no catharsis when you're the parent of an FAS or FAE child or adult.

On my book tour, I one day found myself on a Seattle TV talk show. During the commercial break the hostess chided me for not revealing enough of my *feelings* about the plight of my oldest son. "You want feelings, get Barry Manilow," I told her, but it did no good. The next time I looked at the monitor, there was my face, and lest anyone miss the point, it had a caption: *Tragic Dad.*

That's hardly the identity I expected when I became a father. I speak out publicly today as a living anecdote, a walking warning label, a Chatty Cathy doll who spews forth a version of the same cautionary tale whenever the string is pulled. Our unhappy personal chronicle, the struggle of many well-intentioned and initially optimistic people to alter for the better the life of one damaged little boy, has to the great surprise of my wife and myself become a kind of flagship sound bite for prenatal sobriety, and yet mostly my role is not to warn but to mourn—and that's easier done in private. To be best known for one's saddest story is not the road to notoriety anyone would willingly choose.

FOR JOURNALING AND DISCUSSION

1. Dorris states, "The conflict of competing rights—of protecting immediate civil liberties versus avoiding future civil strife—is incredibly complex, with no unambiguously right or easy answers, but as a nation it's unconscionable to delay the debate." Whose competing rights does his essay address? Why is the issue complex?

2. Should mothers who use alcohol or drugs while pregnant and who birth damaged children be legally prosecuted? Do race, class, and gender considerations figure into your decision?

3. Research statistics on FAS/FAE in the Native American population compared to other populations. What conclusions can you draw? How might these statistics and those for "crack babies" relate to the phenomenon of internalized oppression discussed by Itabari Njeri in "Sushi and Grits" in Chapter 9?

4. Dorris mentions that access to organizations like Planned Parenthood is impossible in many Native American communities. In Thomas King's essay "Borders" in Chapter 9, his mother argues that her Blackfoot identity supersedes her forced Canadian identity. How might belonging to a nation within a nation work against FAS/FAE children and their parents?

5. In Tina Rosenberg's essay "On the Row" in Chapter 6, Joseph Hudgins is convicted of murder at the age of seventeen and sentenced to die for his crime. Compare what Rosenberg reveals about Hudgins with what Dorris tells us about his son and other FAS adolescents.

FOR RESEARCH AND EXPLORATION

1. Do companies that manufacture alcoholic beverages target certain groups for their advertising campaigns? Research how alcohol is marketed specifically to Native American or African American consumers, and how these groups are resisting such campaigns.
2. Over the years, Dorris and his wife came to understand the meaning of the African proverb, "It takes a village to raise a child." Why would Dorris believe that this disability is everyone's concern?
3. Compare FAS/FAE to disabilities like spina bifida and polio. How are they alike? How are they different? As a nation, do you think we have the ethical responsibility to care for all disabled people even if their disability could have been prevented?

How I Pray Now: A Conversation
Joseph P. Whelen, S.J.

Father Whelen, now deceased after a long struggle with lung cancer, held a doctorate in ascetical theology from the University of London, and taught and wrote extensively about prayer. He entered the Jesuit Novitiate in 1954 and was ordained to the priesthood in 1965. After serving as provincial superior of the Society of Jesus and then regional assistant for the United States to the superior general of the Society, Whelen became a fellow at the Woodstock Theological Center, Washington, D.C.

As you know, I did an earlier essay on how I pray [published under the title "Not Everyone Who Says Lord, Lord . . . " New Catholic World, 1977], and—I would say—in a highly self-conscious manner, both in thinking about my experience of prayer at that time and in putting it in literary form. There is nothing of that here.

While certain things that I will say about my prayer apply to the past 20 or 30 years, and certainly the past 2 or 3, nevertheless I am a very sick man—with cancer—and that's what is in my heart, that's what is on my mind, that's the life that I'm living. That reality will be very much at the center of what I can now say about prayer, talking as someone who very possibly isn't going to live much longer.

The distinction between prayerfulness and prayer becomes ever more useless, I find. Nothing will do except prayer. Being "prayerful" leaves me quite unsatisfied, and I want to do something about it. Prayer always falls apart as one grows a little bit. One is always trying to learn to pray—we all know that. "I don't know how to pray, Father," we'll say. One tries to be near Jesus and be taught by Him.

But with the sickness, and what happens to your mind and your memory— even if you're not medicated a lot, as I often am, and I am going to medicate myself this afternoon because the pain is getting too difficult—I've found the prayer just falls apart in a special way.

There's a new inability with sickness, an inability to think. I can't think anymore. There's an inability to remember very much. There's a greatly reduced ability to verbalize. I can sit here and grasp and grasp and grasp and then finally ask you, by circumlocutions, "What's the word I'm looking for?" and you will give it to me because I simply can't find it.

There's the inability to concentrate. When my sister was dying of cancer, I remember her telling me that, when she was in the hospital, the thing she craved more than anything else was people to help her pray. And almost no one would. Priests would come in, sisters would come in, good Catholic daily communicants would come in, and she would ask them to help her pray, and they would pat her on the head and tell her what a good person she was and go on to other things. And she said: "I cannot get through the Our Father. I cannot get through the Hail Mary. I cannot concentrate. And nobody will help." I never forgot it, and I have the same experience.

I hold the rosary in my hands a lot, and sometimes it's nothing more than that, fingering the beads, because even with the beads I can't get through the Hail Mary or the Our Father. Vocal prayer is certainly a blessing, but it's by no means a solution because I can't get through it. I'll start something like the "Memorare" 10, 15 or 20 times. It's not discouraging really, a little bit frustrating [with a small laugh]. It doesn't induce low spirits or anything like that.

I have been very much helped by something from Meister Eckhart that George Aschenbrenner [a friend, also living at Wernersville, PA] gave me. It's where Eckhart says, "Do the next thing." When you think about your life and you look at the next week coming up or at the month, you say, "I just don't see how I can get through all that." But can you do the "next thing"? If the next thing were to listen to me for 20 minutes, could you do that? Ordinarily you'd be able to say, "Yeah, I can do that." So I find that the prayer I most frequently say is: "With your help, dear Lord Jesus, I can do the next thing." Then I try to see what the next thing is, and I try to do it, because I often can just get no further than that.

For eight years now I have been looking at those two prints [hung side by side over his desk, Cimabue's Christ crucified and a detail of the same painting showing Christ's face], and they are like mantras, you know. You look at them and look at them and then you don't see them anymore, but nevertheless they gather you—in my room at Rome, and then at Woodstock and now here. They're wonderful for me. I've never found them depressing, these prints of Cimabue, not gloomy at all, since the glory is there in its fullest for me. But I've been aware in this sickness, which is so grave, that I do need to look at the Resurrection once in a while—well, a fellow I met at Woodstock who's spent eight months in Italy has found a print of Piero's "Resurrection" from San Sepolcro, and I'm going to hang it over there. I'll be able to look at both. I do need to look at the Resurrection when I get afraid.

In the sickness, fears and weaknesses loom larger. There's no doubt about that, what with the possibility of an imminent death—the doctors don't talk of my being terminal and they don't say when, but things are not going well, they are willing to tell me that—so I get afraid. But then faith comes in wonderful waves, and I am not afraid. It comes and goes.

I find that in times of intense prayer—and there aren't many of them, I'm too scattered and fragmented, but when they come—good things, bad things, ugly things (but I don't mean morally ugly because the poor are not morally ugly, at all) will hover in the prayer in a way that I've never been gifted with before. Some of the prayer with the poor comes into my heart much more than it ever has before. I've wanted that, I've asked for that. I had hoped to have a life that might have included being with them, and I never have. I never have.

You know that I wrote *Benjamin* [a series of prose poems on prayer, published in book form in 1971], and I have some pieces that could have provided an expanded second edition. Of course, inclusive language would have had to be taken care of—in 1971 there was no thought of that—but I determined very shortly after I wrote it that I would never publish again unless I not only knew much more about the poor but unless I knew the poor themselves in some way that I didn't then. But my life, taking me from Baltimore to Rome to Washington and now here to Wernersville, sick with cancer—you know, I'm not going to know the poor in the way I would have liked. I would have liked to write about prayer again, but only if the Lord had given me that ministry, and it didn't come.

At the end of that article I wrote in 1977, I mentioned that I had lost Mary for the preceding decade. You know, it was after Vatican II, and so many things in me got secularized in a bad way as many things got secularized in a good way. Mary got tossed around a good deal, mainly by neglect. But I have found in reading feminist exegesis—I've not read a lot, but I've read more than a little and I intend to read more in the life remaining to me (I have Elizabeth Johnson's *She Who Is*, and I have a wonderful book here called *The Woman's Bible Commentary*, which I am well into)—and in reading other contemporary exegesis, not just feminist, that I believe Mary is going to come off well from all that is happening. There is some bizarre stuff, and that, I think, will simply fall by the wayside. But I think not only of her ignorance of who Jesus was and what He was about, but of the terrible suffering involved and her disapproval— probably even that. I think of what she saw Him doing and her understanding of it and of how her heart and her whole being remained His. Well, I just think she's going to come off looking greater than she ever has in history, as we grow in the awareness of what was asked of her—the spiritual, mental and intellectual sufferings, and the distance and the strain and the stress between them.

So she's in my life quite a bit now, and I find that she's a good companion for turmoil, for tough stuff. A real woman, a real friend.

On a different note entirely, I do nothing an enormous amount of the time in this stage of my life as a sick man with a good deal of pain. In the hospital—I've had 14 hospitalizations since September 1992—I have not been able to turn on the television set five times. I find the noise, the images, the voices on television drain my energy and never nourish me. The one exception would be baseball. I can turn on a baseball game with great pleasure. I turn the sound down low so that I can hear it but can ignore it if I want to and just watch the wonderful images—of a game without a clock. The American game seems so un-American when you look at other things like football or even basketball. I'm only a baseball fan.

I see this Roger Angell baseball book on your desk. I didn't know that about you.

Oh, yeah, I've read about five of his, a lot of Tom Boswell. That's one of the pleasures when George [Aschenbrenner] and I go away on vacation together. We usually bring a baseball book and read it to each other, and so we have the pleasure of reading the same thing at the same time.

I don't listen to music, beautiful music. I have the same experience as with television. I can't bear it. It takes energy, it doesn't give me energy, it doesn't give me nourishment. It causes pain, it doesn't console—most of the time.

To read someone quite serious, like Elizabeth Johnson, here at home or at the hospital is usually completely out of the question now—not to mention Lonergan. Even to read novels that are well within my grasp and competence, from being a reader over many years—somebody like Edith Wharton, not nearly so difficult as Henry James—I usually find that, within a page and a half, it has exhausted me.

And so what do I do? I do nothing. I sit here, and I am not bored. When I think of doing something else, I almost always think, "Well, why don't you pray first?" And then I start praying first, and then I usually don't do anything else. And I can't pray. But I don't want to do anything else. And when I start to think of doing something else, it's usually a little distasteful to me, and then I go back to trying to pray. So between nothing and God, I don't know what the distinction is.

As I mentioned in the 1977 article, Jesus is always there. I find that between 1977 and 1993, almost 16 years, that's both more true and less true. He was never more central than He is now. I can't imagine the prayer that wouldn't seek to find Him at the center. At the same time, any discursive elements to being with Him are impossible. They just elude me. So there's a presence, but there aren't any ideas. Afterward, sometimes, but not during prayer.

During this whole experience, I have had the blessing of a lot of friends. You know, there's a sense in which you don't call your brothers in Christ "friends" because a lot of them you don't see for years and you don't spend any time with them. But they're your brothers, and they're very dear and beloved. Well, I have a number of friends like that, and they have been enormously good to me, with phone calls and letters and cards. What's been simply astounding is, over the 13 months, not only Jesuits from other parts of the country, and some from Europe, but over 200 of my own brother Jesuits from the Maryland Province have written me a letter, and maybe more than one. Dozens of them are of a beauty that's really quite unbearable. So that's intimately within the ambit of prayer. I haven't saved the letters. I can't bear to, they're so beautiful and I'm so undeserving of them. I usually read them twice, and then I throw them away because I don't know what to do with them. They engulf me like a tidal wave. I get to thank some of these people who have come by, but there are wonderful letters from people I have never seen to say "thank you." I write no letters, I write no cards. I make no phone calls.

I would not want to have a conversation like this come and go without some mention of the Eucharist. I often cannot attend Mass. When I am in the hospital, of course, there's no question of getting there, and often when I am home, I'm simply not well enough to go downstairs. But whether in the hospital or in the house, I am always given Communion by someone, and, again, I'm filled with distraction. Not humiliation. I don't find it humiliating to be so overwhelmingly a body in sickness of this kind. Your body just looms enormously as it overwhelms and silences your mind and breaks it in pieces. But I don't find it humiliating at all. It seems to me a good incarnationalism goes right along with this. I'm not interested in any resurrection that doesn't include my body, and the body of Jesus and the body of people I love.

So, usually the Eucharist is very distracted, with a lot of pain and discomfort. I can't get the right position in bed or the chair. But I get so hungry for it. And I miss it so—just the once or twice that it hasn't been there. Its unity between me and those I love, its unity between me and Jesus, and between Jesus and the Father, doesn't explain life; it's the meaning of life and, to a very great extent then, the meaning of all eternity for me.

Could you explain more of what you mean by the distinction between prayerfulness and prayer?

Well, when a man is really in love with his wife or vice versa—I'll take it the first way—there's a quality of presence to his wife, if he marries her well and marries her daily and chooses her as his best friend ceaselessly, that will simply permeate his walking down the street, his playing basketball with the guys and the very detailed concentration of his work if he's a doctor or an engineer or a trial lawyer or whatever. But all of that, it seems to me, is dependent upon something else. All of that is inadequate unless he sits down on the sofa regularly and looks her in the eye. He cannot successfully over time be doing everything for her unless he chooses time to be with her, in a face-to-face relationship. Then the shoulder-to-shoulder relationship or the relationship of nonphysical presence can flourish wonderfully—and we see that. But friends need to take time, husbands and wives need to take time, to be each other's best friend.

Well, I find more and more that to say I'm being prayerful is not the answer unless there is a lot of prayer. So I guess that's what I mean.

You said at one point that Jesus is ever more a presence for you and yet "there are no ideas." Are there any words from you to Him?

At the beginning, usually I try, but they break down either through distraction or because I can't find what I want to say. So when it goes very well, there's nothing to say, and when it doesn't go well at all, I'm too distracted [with a laugh] to know what to say. I've been praying a long time so, you know, that's no great achievement on my part. For goodness' sake, it ought to be happening by this time that when prayer goes well it would be largely of a simple and not of a discursive kind. When it doesn't go well, of course, because of weakness or selfishness—I look elsewhere or I can't collect myself or I can't feel the grace of being collected by our dear God—well, then it's hard to find words.

Joe, what do you mean when you say about good music, which I know you love, that you "can't bear it"?

In its most primitive meaning, even the most beautiful music since I've been sick comes in as sound, and I'm too sick to be able to process that sound without pain. It draws from me, it exhausts me, it hurts.

At another level the reason "I can't bear it"—like the letters from my brothers—is that there's so much there in beautiful music. It's potentially a way of life—a quite inadequate one frankly, I think. But it can make a very good run for the money as a way of life. I certainly went through that temptation when I was in my early 20's and took music very seriously and was well trained professionally as a pianist. The only way I got through it was not playing the piano for two years, and I have never played it again except to sight-read music. I have never again tried to learn anything Mozart wrote. And after I was able to go back to it, I didn't listen to Mozart for a good 10 years. Now I can listen to him, and I can thumb my nose at him and keep him at his distance. But there was a time when he would just make everything else seem pointless.

One last question, about Mary. How will she be exalted all the more out of the present turmoil? I was taken with your saying that she's a "good companion for turmoil."

It seems to me history and good scholarship are showing that she has entered and explored more and more and more dimensions of the human than we ever imagined. She did it with this clarity and innocence of heart that, it seems to me, is Catholic faith. That is where the Catholic faith about Mary is: What is her heart?

Her heart is perfectly holy by the redemptive grace of her Son. But in everything else, it seems to me, we're finding she entered into the terrible darkness and ambiguity that goes with being human, which included the relationships with her own Son.

It's as if we're discovering now not only Christology "from below" but Mariology "from below."

That's exactly right. It just seems to me she's going to become greater than ever as we see the stunning generosity of her heart before the darkness and the pain and the simple mystification that He presented her with.

FOR JOURNALING AND DISCUSSION

1. Do Whelen's feelings about prayer support the research on prayer and well-being that Charles Marwick discusses in "Should Physicians Prescribe Prayer for Health?" in Chapter 5?
2. From the scattered bits of personal information about Father Whelen in this essay, speculate about his class background. Why did he consider a ministry with the poor, which was denied him, so central to his work?
3. Father Whelen states, "I don't find it humiliating to be so overwhelmingly a body in sickness of this kind. Your body just looms enormously and silences your mind and breaks it into pieces." Compare this statement with Laura Hershey's feelings about her body in her essay "Choosing Disability" earlier in this chapter.
4. Compare Father Whelen's feelings about Mary's role in Christianity with that of Usry Alleyne in "Atheism and Me" in Chapter 5.
5. Father Whelen writes, "I don't mean morally ugly because the poor are not morally ugly, at all . . . . " Assume the persona of Dorothy Allison as she configures herself and her history in "River of Names" in Chapter 3, and write a letter to Father Whelen about this statement. Account for their differences in gender, class, and religious callings.

FOR RESEARCH AND EXPLORATION

1. Locate reproductions of Cimabue's *Christ Crucified* and Piero's *Resurrection*. Compare the two works. Why might Father Whelen want to see the Piero image at this stage of his life?
2. What is a disability? Do invisible disabilities exist? If so, what are some of these conditions? Does our culture have a more difficult time emotionally with visual signs of impairment or with the lack of visual signs?
3. Is cancer Father Whelen's prime disability? To him, what is worse than the pain and limitation of terminal cancer?

Rufus at the Door

John Hassler

Hassler is Regents' Professor of English and Writer-in-Residence at St. John's University in Collegeville, Minnesota. He was educated in Minnesota and North Dakota, and began his teaching career in 1955. The author of two books for young adults and nine novels, including The Love Hunter, Rookery Blues, North of Hope, *and* Staggerford, *Hassler lives with his wife, Gretchen.*

Each year the ninth and 11th grades of Plum High School were loaded on a bus and driven to Faribault for a tour of what was then called the insane asylum. The boys' health teacher, Mr. Lance, and the girls', Miss Sylvestri, led us single file through a series of gloomy wards and hallways where we were smiled at, scowled at, lunged at and jeered by all manner of the mentally deficient.

I recall much more about my ninth-grade trip than I do about my 11th. I recall, for example, how the faces of the retarded absorbed the elderly Mr. Lance, how he gazed at them the way we freshmen did, as though he were seeing them for the first time, and yet how he displayed none of our pity or shock or revulsion; his gaze, like a good many of those it met, was intense but neutral. I remember the middle-aged Miss Sylvestri bouncing along at the head of our column and—as though reading labels at the zoo—calling out the categories: "These are morons, class, and over there you have the imbeciles. In the next room they're all insane." I remember my relief when the tour ended, for the place had given me a severe stomach ache.

As we boarded the bus, Miss Sylvestri turned back for a last look and waved cheerily at a balloonlike face peering out the window of the broad front door and said, "That's a waterhead, class, and now we'll go downtown for lunch."

Mr. Lance drove the bus, and Miss Sylvestri stood at his shoulder and delivered an unnecessary lecture about how lucky we were to have been spared from craziness and retardation. She wore a long coat of glistening black fur, and the shape of her tall hat fit the definition, in our geometry text, of a truncated cone. She asked if any of us realized that we had a moron living in Plum.

Pearl Peterson's hand shot up. Pearl was the ninth grade's foremost sycophant. "Henry Ahman," she said. "Henry Ahman is a moron."

"No, I'm sorry, Pearl. Henry Ahman is an epileptic, there's no comparison. Come now, class, I'm asking for a moron."

I knew the right answer, but I kept my mouth shut for fear of losing face with my friends. This was the year a lot of us boys were passing through our anti-achievement phase. We had vowed never to raise our hands.

"Please, Miss Sylvestri," said Pearl, "would you tell us again what a moron is?"

Swaying with the traffic, Miss Sylvestri said that morons were a little smarter than idiots and a lot smarter then imbeciles. She said that morons could do things like run errands for their mothers while idiots and imbeciles couldn't leave the house.

The impassive Mr. Lance found his way downtown and parked in front of the Green Parrot Cafe. He looked into the mirror that showed him his whole load, even those of us way in back, and he said, "Chow time." But Miss Sylvestri begged to differ. She said nobody was having lunch until somebody came up with a moron.

My friends and I groaned anonymously.

Pearl suggested the Clifford girl.

"No, I'm sorry, the Clifford girl is an out-an-out imbecile."

Somebody else, a junior, said, "Gilly Stone."

"No, Gilly Stone's problem is polio."

Finally out of hunger—the jolting bus had settled my stomach—I shouted, "Rufus Alexander."

"That's correct—Rufus Alexander is very low on the scale but he's still higher than an idiot. He's what you call a low-grade moron."

We were permitted to eat.

At the west edge of Plum, Rufus Alexander lived with his mother in a little house near the stockyards. Rufus was about 35, and his mother was very old, yet his hair was turning gray at the same rate as hers. On Saturday afternoons they walked together to the center of the village to shop—the tall, bony-faced Mrs. Alexander striding along with her shoulders hunched and her skirts flowing around her shoetops; her tall, grinning son stepping along at her side, his back so straight that he seemed about to tip over backward.

Though he walked fast to keep pace, there was in each step he took an almost imperceptible hesitation, a tentativeness that lent a jerky aspect to his progress down the street and reminded me of old films of the Keystone Kops. Whenever he came to a stop, he always clasped his hands behind his back and stood as though at attention; from a distance, in his long gray coat and white scarf, he might have been mistaken for a diplomat or a funeral director. At home Rufus sat in a deep chair by the front window and listened all day to the radio. Passing the house on my bike, I used to see him there, looking out and grinning.

Mrs. Alexander had raised three older sons, but it was Rufus she loved best. He was hard of hearing and mute, though on rare occasions he made guttural noises, which his mother took to be words.

In order to go about her Saturday shopping unencumbered by Rufus, who couldn't turn a corner without being steered, Mrs. Alexander would deposit him either in the pool hall or in my father's grocery store. She would look in at the pool hall first, because there Rufus could sit on one of the chairs around the card table, but if she saw that her card-playing son—her eldest son, Lester—hadn't come to town, she would lead Rufus down the street to our store and place him in my father's care.

Not that he needed care. He was content to stand at the full-length window of the front door, looking out. For as long as two hours he would remain there as though enchanted, his hands clasped behind him, his eyes directed at a point slightly above the passing people, his face locked in its customary grin. When someone entered or left the store, Rufus would shuffle backward and allow himself to be pressed for a moment between the plate glass in front of him and the glassine doors of the cookie display behind him, and then as the door went shut he would shuffle forward, keeping his nose about six inches from the glass.

Although our customers were greeted week after week by this moronic face, and although he obscured the cookie display, I don't think Rufus had an adverse effect on our business. Everybody was used to him. In a village as small as Plum the ordinary population didn't outnumber the odd by enough to make the latter seem all that rare. We became, as villagers, so accustomed to each other's presence, so familiar with each other's peculiarities, that even the most eccentric among us—Henry Ahman, who often had his fits in public; the Clifford girl, who was an out-and-out imbecile—were institutions rather than curiosities. I noticed that most of our customers ignored Rufus as they came through the door, while a few, like me, gave him a fleeting smile in return for his incessant grin.

He had an odd face. His round, prominent cheekbones were rosy, healthy-looking, but his eyes were skeletal—deep-set eyes under brows like ledges, blue eyes perfectly round and (I thought) perfectly empty. I never saw him—except once—that he wasn't grinning. Though I told myself that this was an unconscious grin, that he probably grinned all night in his sleep, I couldn't help responding to it. Returning time and again to the store after carrying out the groceries, I smiled. As an exercise in will power, I would tell myself that his grin was not a sign of good will but an accident of nature, and I would attempt a neutral stare, like Mr. Lance's, but it was no use. (I could never resist smiling at clowns either, even though I knew their joy was paint.)

I asked my father one time if he thought Rufus ever had anything on his mind, if he understood what he was staring at—or staring slightly above. My father said he had wondered the same thing himself and concluded that Rufus was only two-dimensional; there was no depth to him at all. And this, for a time, I believed.

Then one Monday morning—it was around the time of my first trip to the insane asylum—word spread through town that Rufus had another dimension after all. It was said that during a Sunday picnic in Lester Alexander's farmyard, Rufus had flown into a rage. The picnic was attended by scads of Alexanders from far and near, and three or four of his little cousins began to taunt Rufus. They made up a song about his ignorance and sang it to him again and again. He rolled his great round eyes, it was said, and he made a mysterious noise like a groan or a belch (it was not reported whether he lost his grin) and he set out after his cousins, brandishing the long knife his mother had brought along for slicing open her homemade biscuits.

Hearing about it, I couldn't believe that anyone had actually been in danger. I pictured Rufus tipping backward as he ran, too slow to catch his quick little cousins; I pictured the knife—a bread-slicer, dull at the tip; I pictured the many Alexander men—strapping farmers all—who could easily have restrained him. But on the other hand, I could also imagine the alarm. I had attended a few of these farmyard picnics, invited by friends, and I imagined how it must have looked to a bystander; the afternoon hazy and hot; dozens of relatives deployed across the sloping, shady lawn; the children shirtless under their bib overalls; the women at the outdoor table, uncovering their tepid hot dishes and their runny gelatins; the men smoking under the trees; then suddenly this heightened racket among the children and everyone turning and seeing, to their terror, the youngsters scattering and shrieking (half in fright, half in glee) and Rufus hopping jerkily over the grass, the bread knife in his hand, the blade glinting in the sun as he thrust it stiffly ahead of him, stabbing the air.

As it was told the next day, Rufus' wild mood quickly passed and a half hour later he and the smaller children, full of food, lay down together for a nap in the shade. But he had given his brothers and their wives a terrible fright. Rufus would have to be put away, his brothers told their mother. He would have to be taken to the insane asylum.

Never. As long as she lived, said Mrs. Alexander, Rufus would never leave her side. Not once in his life had he disobeyed her; never had he been anything but gentle. How would any of them like it, she wanted to know, if they were teased and attacked by a bunch of impudent snips? No, if anyone was coming to take Rufus away, they were coming over her dead body.

And there the matter rested. The three sons refrained from saying what they foresaw. They foresaw the day when their mother would die, and Rufus would be whisked off to Faribault.

After the upheaval of that Sunday afternoon, Mrs. Alexander no longer left Rufus at the pool hall, for it was card-playing Lester who had been the first to speak about putting him away. In my father's keeping, then, Rufus was placed each week without fail. Now and then I would glance up from my work and see him there and wonder how it would end. Morons, according to Miss Sylvestri, sometimes died young. Maybe his mother would survive him, and wouldn't that be a blessing? His brothers' secret intention—like all secrets in Plum—had become public knowledge, and I didn't see how Rufus, after all these years of fixed habits and mother love, could adapt himself to the gruesome life of the asylum, particularly now that he had exhibited strong emotion.

Hearing of his anger at the picnic, I now suspected that Rufus was capable of perceptions and emotions beyond what my father and I (and probably most of the village) had formerly believed. Now, though his eyes were consistently shallow and his grin steady, I had a hard time thinking of him in only two dimensions. This was a man who knew things, who felt things, I told myself, and therefore if he outlived his mother he was bound to come to grief. I didn't ask my father what he thought about this. I was afraid he would agree.

In the autumn of my junior year Mrs. Alexander died. Rufus apparently didn't recognize death when he looked it in the face, for although the coroner said she had been dead since midnight it wasn't until the following noon that Rufus went next door and by his moaning and wild look alerted Mrs. Underdahl. No one could say for certain how Rufus, waiting for his mother to wake up, had spent the forenoon, but judging later by the evidence and what we knew of his habits, the village imagined this:

Rufus got out of bed on his own and went into his mother's room to see why she hadn't awakened him, why she hadn't started breakfast. The depth of her sleep puzzled him. He was capable of a number of things; he could dry dishes and dress himself, but he couldn't figure out why his mother lay so late in bed. He put on his clothes and breakfasted on biscuits and milk (or rather cream, for he opened a full bottle and swigged off the top), and he evidently passed the rest of the time listening to the radio. In my mind's eye I see him sitting in his favorite chair by the window, soothed by the voice of Arthur Godfrey. I see him grinning when the audience laughs and grinning when it doesn't.

At noon he went back into his mother's bedroom and pulled her by the arm, and when she didn't respond, he tugged harder. He pulled her out of bed and onto the floor. Then, seeing her there at his feet, twisted among the sheets, he perceived something new. A door in his dense thinking opened on an emotion he had never felt before. Not anger this time, but fear. He went straight to Mrs. Underdahl's house and called up the same belching groan he had uttered at the picnic. His great blue eyes were rolling, Mrs. Underdahl later told my father in the store, as though he sensed that this day marked the end of his childhood and now, in his late 30s, he would have to face the world alone—far off from his mother's house, which had been arranged to fit so well his simple needs, far off from his mother's love.

I was one of the altar boys at Mrs. Alexander's funeral. I looked for Rufus among the mourners, but he wasn't there. I supposed, correctly as it turned out, that he had already been taken to Faribault. At the cemetery it rained. There were dozens of Alexanders standing three-deep around the grave. The little cousins, wearing short pants and neckties, were as antic as ever. While the priest blessed the grave and read aloud the prayers of burial, the cousins shrieked and played tag among the tombstones. Impudent snips, their grandmother had called them.

Six months later my classmates and I were bused to Faribault for our second look at the unfortunates. Over the years I have tried to figure out why everyone who went through school in Plum during the Lance-Sylvestri era was twice required to pass through this gauntlet of retarded and insane humanity. Surely all of us had been sufficiently impressed the first time by the smells and vacant faces of this dismal congregation, sufficiently impressed by our own good luck at having been spared.

One thing we did learn on this second trip—and this may have been the lesson our teachers had in mind (particularly Mr. Lance, who taught it by example)—was how to look impassive in the face of chaos. I had the same pain in my stomach that I had had two years earlier, and one of the inmates leaped at me and tried to pull off my jacket, but like most of my classmates I played the stoic from the time I entered the broad front door until I departed.

I acted this way because I was 16, the age when nothing seems quite so crucial—especially if freshmen are watching you—as appearing to be above it all; nothing seems quite so clever—if joking would be out of place—as disdain. I discovered that I could be really quite good at looking neutral. The trick was simply to tell myself that none of these crouching, drooling, gawking people were experiencing the misery that visitors pitied them for. They had no knowledge—no memory—of life as it was lived among the normal—life, say, in Plum. Unaware of any better form of existence, they were content. Brainless, they possessed the peace that passes understanding.

But then I saw Rufus. We were boarding the bus when Miss Sylvestri suddenly pointed behind us at the broad front door and said, "Why, that's Rufus Alexander." I turned and saw two men on the doorstep with their backs to us. One was an orderly, the other a tall, white-haired man with a straight spine and his hands clasped behind his back. It was Rufus, all right, and I was surprised— not only because his hair had turned white, but because he had slipped my mind over the winter; I had forgotten that he lived here now. Where had he been during our tour? Outside, strolling the grounds? Or had he been present in one of the crowded wards we passed through, and had a familiar face told him that we were the Plum delegation? Had he tried to follow us out to the bus? The orderly had him tightly by the elbow and was steering him in through the door we had just come out of, but he seemed reluctant to go. Though he didn't struggle, there was a hint of unwillingness in his movements, a hesitation in his step.

This time Miss Sylvestri did not lecture us as Mr. Lance started the bus, but she sat visiting with Pearl Peterson in the front seat on the driver's side. I sat in the back, next to a window, and looked straight at Rufus. The broad front door was now locked and he was standing behind the glass. Our two windows were scarcely thirty feet apart. He didn't look as healthy as he used to. The color was gone from his face and his ledgelike brows were sharper, deeper. While the whiteness of his hair was alarming (in six months it had grown much whiter than his mother's had been), the astonishing thing was the look on his face. He wasn't grinning. His face, without the grin, was that of a much older man, the jaw hanging slack, the cheeks hollow. In his round blue eyes, without the grin, there was something obviously very deep, like yearning. Obvious to me, at least, because his eyes were aimed directly at mine—not slightly above me, the way he used to look at things—and they told me that he had indeed tried to follow us out to the bus; moreover, they told me that mine was the face that reminded him of Plum. I looked away. Mr. Lance shifted gears, and I never saw Rufus again.

FOR JOURNALING AND DISCUSSION

1. Describe your relationship with a mentally or emotionally challenged person. What was your emotional response to Hassler's depiction of Mr. Lance and Miss Sylvestri? Have people's attitudes changed since Hassler was a boy growing up in Plum?
2. In what ways did the village speculate Rufus had spent the twelve hours from his mother's death until he alerted Mrs. Underdahl? Imagine and write about a different series of events.
3. During his second visit to Faribault, Hassler says he "played the stoic." But confronted with the now alone and aging Rufus, he concludes that Rufus's eyes "told me that mine was the face that reminded him of Plum." Why did the young Hassler look away?
4. Compare Hassler's essay with Katherine Newman's "Illegitimate Elites and the Parasitic Underclass" in Chapter 3. Why is it dangerous to ever conclude, like Hassler's father did about Rufus, that someone is only two-dimensional and without depth?
5. Discuss how Rufus's siblings and their families treat him before and after their mother's death. How would Usry Alleyne, whose essay "Atheism and Me" appears in Chapter 5, interpret this treatment?

FOR RESEARCH AND EXPLORATION

1. Find a newspaper article that discusses the emotional, sexual, or physical abuse of institutionalized persons by their caregivers. Why might Rufus's mother have been so unwilling to have her son taken to Faribault?
2. Research an article or book written by or about a person with a mental disability. Are these people really oblivious to how others treat them or what others think about them?
3. Hassler notes that everyone was poor in Plum; the state hospital in Faribault was all that was available to Rufus. Research the differences in cost between private and public facilities for people deemed mentally incapable of caring for themselves.

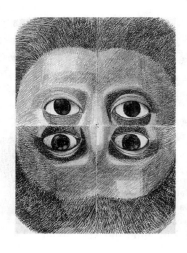

CHAPTER 8

Region

Like the other categories in this anthology, regional identity is complicated and difficult to define. It varies with race, ethnicity, class, age, and ability, as do all the other identity categories. Often it is most effectively described in terms of what it is not, or by the ways that one region's identity is different from others'. Cartographers rely on geographical and legal data to define a region, but the people who live there often think in historical, social, and cultural terms about the meaning of "place," defining themselves in opposition to or in contrast to residents of other regions. For example, some southerners maintain their regional identity more tenaciously than do people from other parts of this country. This is partly because of the heritage of slavery, the Civil War (or, as some southerners prefer, "The War Between the States"), and the conflict, sometimes perceived as ongoing, with the North.

Some white southerners see themselves as oppressed and discriminated against by northerners (or "Yankees"), outsiders who want to come in and tell them how to run their lives. Although slavery was the central issue leading to the Civil War, another significant issue in the eyes of some southern whites was the need to be able to govern themselves without interference or dictation from a central government that they felt was largely controlled by the North. Most black southerners, however, have an entirely different response to government intervention because the Civil War freed their ancestors and because federal civil rights legislation has resulted in improvements in such areas as education and housing. And yet black and white southerners share many cultural similarities, including tastes for certain food, language, hospitality toward strangers, and love of the land.

The conflict between regions and the national government is largely something that is inherent in our governmental system. In fact, the founders built it in. Many of the early struggles around the formation of this country focused on what kind of government we would have—one that invested power primarily at the state level or one that focused on the national level. Our current system was created to provide numerous checks and balances between state, regional, and federal power. We still struggle with this division of power, as seen in the debates in recent elections about returning power to the states.

Anywhere that this "us versus them" mentality takes root, a stronger sense of regionalism develops, particularly among people who see themselves as a kind of oppressed minority in relation to the nation as a whole. Westerners, for example, have recently come into increased conflict with the federal government over land use and environmental issues. The West also has a long history of media images, now turned cultural stereotypes, that portray strong, silent cowboys, tender-hearted dance hall madams, and ferocious Indians as the dominant inhabitants of the lands west of the Mississippi. Nearly every region has to deal with such stereotypical conceptions. As you plan a project for this topic, you might consider the ways films such as the following have influenced your view of regional identity: *Gone with the Wind, Mississippi Burning, Dances with Wolves, Fargo, A Walk in the Clouds, Grumpy Old Men,* and any cowboy movie from the 1950s and 1960s.

Dialect and region, although still significant issues in this country, seem to be becoming less important. The ever-present force of the national media (and even the local media to some extent), which uses a "midwestern broadcast standard" for American English, has started to erode regional dialectic differences in many parts of the country. Certain dialects have traditionally been associated with class, especially with lower socioeconomic status (Appalachian, for example), and some southerners have consciously attempted to avoid discrimination by altering their dialects to fit a media standard—or at least the southern phonological version of standard English. However, some recent research indicates that Black English Vernacular ("Ebonics"), with its roots in the South, is more resistant to change because of the intense connection between this dialect and identity.

More and more, certain regions of the country are feeling overwhelmed by outsiders moving in from other sections. These newcomers are for the most part moving out of large cities and into areas that they believe will provide them with a safer, cleaner, more traditional life style. For example, many are moving to the West and South from large cities in California and the east coast. Many of the long-term residents of these regions resent the newcomers, whom they believe are bringing big-city problems and conflicts to their peaceful hometowns. For example, wealthy Californians have flocked to Montana, Colorado, and Arizona, skyrocketing the price of real estate and often pricing local, middle-income people out of the housing market. In addition, these newcomers are demanding many of the amenities that they enjoyed in their previous homes—swimming pools, golf courses, freeways, and the like—that put a severe strain on the ecosystem in their new region. The conflict is sometimes framed as the clash of urban versus rural values. As the conveniences of the cities and suburbs are brought to the country, the country is no longer the place it once was.

This kind of internal regional conflict also occurs when large numbers of an immigrant group begin to settle in a specific area. The increasing numbers of Mexican and South American immigrants moving into California have resulted in the passing of Proposition 187, which denies government benefits such as health care and education to illegal immigrants. There is also constant conflict in southern Florida between Cuban immigrants and other ethnic groups. These tensions are further discussed in Chapter 10, which examines the connections between nation and identity.

SUMMARIES OF SELECTIONS ON REGION

Paul Gruchow shows in "Discovering One's Own Place" that too often we are raised with no real knowledge or understanding of the towns, cities, and regions in which we are raised. He claims that the Midwest is particularly guilty of undervaluing its own achievements and history, noting that while in school—from primary school through university—he was never taught the history, literature, or biology of his home state of Minnesota. For some reason we are taught to value the distant instead of the close. His essay's elegant simplicity may inspire you to try your own version of this combination of narration and description.

In "Big Grass" **Louise Erdrich** describes the prairie—the extensive grasslands that have been destroyed by farming and settlement. She contrasts this process to some of the traditions and values of Native American peoples. Her beautiful descriptions are a good starting place for your own regional writing.

Polly Stewart covers some important ideas about how regional identities are formed and maintained through a series of insider/outsider conflicts. In "Regional Consciousness as a Shaper of Local History," she uses three significant events—a mass murder and two lynchings on Maryland's Eastern Shore in the 1930s—to demonstrate these issues. Outsiders claimed that this violence was a result of the Eastern Shoremen's racism and ignorance, whereas the Eastern Shoremen believed that it was a direct response to unwanted outside interference in their internal affairs.

Jonathan Raban details how much of the West was settled. He explains in "The Unlamented West" the politics of bringing in settlers to farm nonarable land in order to build the railroads' wealth. He links these past policies, which caused great suffering and hardship among many westerners, to current antigovernment feeling in the West.

Dorothy Allison describes the views of "Yankee" tourists that she developed while working as a waitress when she was a teenager. In "I'm Working on My Charm," she links these observations to her later experiences as a college student in the North and to northerners' expectations that a certain type of southerner should be charming, genteel, and gracious. She knows, however, these are not the expectations that people have of the group named in the title of her book: *Trash*.

Another southerner, **Caffilene Allen,** examines the costs of education: changing her name, leaving her family, learning a "new" language. These changes, as she discusses in "First They Changed My Name," have, to some extent, divided her from her home and her past. Now that she is educated, for example, it is more difficult for her to talk with her mother.

"South of Haunted Dreams" is the first chapter in **Eddy L. Harris**'s novel describing his motorcycle journey through the South. In this chapter Harris, who is African American, gives an overview of the treatment of blacks in the South—some history, some personal experience. Harris embodies the mixed images that the South evokes in many blacks—of home and roots, but also of violence and racism.

In "A Place of Grace," **Jill Nelson** talks about life on Block Island, Rhode Island, away from the busy city, and the islanders' efforts to maintain its peace. Like many other inhabitants of private places, they are losing the battle to preserve its traditional way of life.

Edward Hougland deals with the archetypal place that people are abandoning in search of the countryside—New York City. New Yorkers, as he discusses in "New York Blues," are becoming more and more cut off from one another by class distinctions. Life in this big city has inured people to the terrible living conditions of the poor and the homeless. Instead of compassion, people feel disgust for the underclass. Class divisions continue to contribute to neighborhood disintegration and a lack of community within the city. Despite this, New York is still a major destination for immigrants around the world—symbolizing the American dream with all its problems and hope.

RHETORICAL QUESTIONS

Questions about *context* and *stance* are the most obvious ones to consider in this chapter. First, what is the setting for the piece of writing? Is the author an insider writing from the regional location? or an outside observer? or someone living somewhere else and remembering "home"? Is the writer kind to or critical of the people in the region—or some bittersweet combination of the two? Does the writer identify with or reject (or both) the regional identity? Does this stem from being an insider or an outsider?

Where does regional writing appear? Consider the kind of writing that you can find in local or regional magazines (e.g., *Southern Living*) or in fiction categorized as "regional" by your local bookstore. Much of this writing focuses on a sense of place and identity. What is the difference between regional writing that remains in a local market versus writing that appeals to a national audience? How can you account for the popularity of Dorothy Allison's books about "southern white trash" or Garrison Keillor's descriptions of shy Scandinavian Minnesotans in *Lake Wobegon Days?*

Who are some of the writers in your regional "home"? You may or may not consider "home" to be the place where you are now living. How does distance alter your regional identity? If you have moved frequently, what kinds of regional assumptions affect you? How do you define "home"? What kinds of memories or impressions of home are important enough to write about? Are they more about the place itself or the values and culture of the people?

Discovering One's Own Place

Paul Gruchow

Gruchow, who lives on a farm in Northfield, Minnesota, is a writer, teacher, and frequent lecturer on rural issues and literature. He has published hundreds of essays and articles as well as four books, including Journal of a Prairie Year *and* The Necessity of Empty Places.

The schools in which I was educated were by most standards first-rate. But they were, as our schools generally are, largely indifferent to the place and to the culture in which they operated.

Among my science courses I took two full years of biology, but I never learned that the beautiful meadow at the bottom of my family's pasture was remnant virgin prairie. We did not spend, so far as I can remember, a single hour on prairies—the landscape in which we were immersed—in two years of biological study.

I took history courses for years, but I never learned that one of the founders of my town and for decades its leading banker—the man who platted the town and organized its school system, its library, its parks, and its fire department—was also the author of the first comprehensive treatise on Minnesota's prairie botany. I can only imagine now what it might have meant to me—a studious boy with a love of nature—to know that a great scholar of natural history had made a full and satisfying life in my town. I did not know until long after I left the place that it afforded the possibility of an intellectual life.

I read, in the course of twelve years of English instruction, many useful and stimulating books, but I never learned that someone who had won a National Book Award for poetry—Robert Bly—was living and working on a farm only thirty miles from our house. The countryside was full of writers, I would later discover, but I did not meet anybody who had written a book until I went away to college. I had not imagined, or been encouraged to imagine, that it was possible to live in the country and to write books, too. Nor did I suspect that it was possible to write books about *our* countryside. We read Sir Walter Scott, John Steinbeck, and Robert Frost, but not O. E. Rolvaag or Black Elk, Lois Hudson or Thomas McGrath, Meridel LeSueur or Frederick Manfred. We did not read them at the University of Minnesota, either. I was left to unearth by my own devices, years later, the whole fine literature of my place.

I took a six-quarter survey of Western thought at the University of Minnesota in which the only nature that came up for consideration was human nature. When we got to the Americans, we skipped right over Whitman and Melville, Emerson and Thoreau, and got down, first thing, to T. S. Eliot and Henry James. The great writers, I learned, were not rural and were not interested in nature; in the American instance, they were even expatriate.

I studied industrial arts with a man who taught me how to make a wooden nightstand and an electric motor; I did not learn until many years later that on his own time he made wonderful lithographs and woodblock prints of the prairie landscape. I grew up believing that scenery consisted of mountains and waterfalls and deer, and that there was nothing worth seeing in our own tedious flatlands.

I studied vocational agriculture. I learned how to identify thirty common weeds and how to formulate a good pig ration, but nothing of the history of farming and nothing that might have encouraged me to think critically about how we farm. My father was an organic farmer. What I mainly learned from my vocational agriculture classes was that he was a nut.

Nothing in my education prepared me to believe, or encouraged me to expect, that there was any reason to be interested in my own place. If I hoped to amount to anything, I understood, I had better take the first road east out of town as fast as I could. And, like so many of my classmates, I did.

Here is a symptom of the thinness with which we have settled rural America: we have made communities that we have always in some sense thought of as disposable. Many of the first white towns of the Midwest were established by speculators, either railroad companies or individual opportunists; in the case of the railroads as the efficient collectors of farm commodities, in the case of individuals as short-term real estate ventures. Our towns were planned, by and large, as profit centers, not as communities. They flourished for two or three decades and, by the 1920s, when both the psychic and the economic energy of the nation had begun to flow from the countryside into the great cities, they were already starting to fail.

We said then, as we do now, that those who fought to preserve the vitality of rural towns were victims of nostalgia, unable or unwilling to keep up with the times. We still have not noticed that the phrase "bedroom community," a place merely to sleep, is an oxymoron: a community is by definition a population with a common interest distinct from that of the larger world; it is a place with more than convenience at its heart; it has some shared work to do; and it has a shared history. If one follows the word *community* to its Latin root, one finds that it literally means a group of people who have made together the rite of passage from adolescence into adulthood.

Here is another symptom: we have occupied this continent now for four centuries, but with the exception of the sunflower we have yet to make significant use of any of its thousands of native plants as a source of food. Ninety-five percent of our nutrition comes from thirty plants, all of them originating in what we call the Third World. That we have made so little use of our land's biotic wealth is a striking measure of how little we have settled into it. Ironically, even the weeds that plague our imported crops have been imported. When we came here, we packed up even our troubles and brought them along.

Here is yet another symptom: only about one-tenth of one percent of the native tallgrass prairie that covered the central United States at the time of white settlement remains. The tallgrass prairie region was once exactly comparable in size to the Amazon rain basin, now similarly threatened. Although we have squandered half the topsoil that lay beneath its virgin sod in our first century of farming, it remains the richest agricultural land on the planet. Had we had any appreciation for the place we were appropriating, had we been thinking from the beginning in terms of making real homes here, we would have felt compelled to preserve at least representative samples of the land we found for the future. We might even have imagined, as we have yet to do, that the life that was prospering here when we arrived might have had some instruction to offer us about how to succeed in this strange new world.

FOR JOURNALING AND DISCUSSION

1. Why do you think that schools tend to be so indifferent to the place and culture in which they are located?
2. Do you live in a community that fits Gruchow's definition? What do you think defines a community?
3. Using Gruchow's essay as a model, describe your own place. What have you learned about your home town or region that has surprised you?

FOR RESEARCH AND EXPLORATION

1. Find a local newspaper that has been published for at least fifty years. Read one week's worth of the issues from fifty years ago. What were the major concerns of the community then? What has changed? What has stayed the same?
2. Examine some school history and geography textbooks. How is your home place or region described? What information is included? What important things are left out? What impression do you think that outsiders will receive based on these textbooks?
3. Interview friends, grandparents, and teachers who have lived in your region for a long time. What did you discover about your community? Has this information changed your views or impressions of it?

Big Grass

Louise Erdrich

Louise Erdrich grew up in North Dakota and is of German-American and Chippewa descent. She has a master's degree in creative writing from Johns Hopkins University and has subsequently worked as a poet in the schools, giving poetry workshops to school children throughout North Dakota. She has written several novels including Love Medicine, Tracks, *and* The Beet Queen. *She was married to the author Michael Dorris, who took his own life in 1997. They had a large family and a productive career together as writers (see the comments on Dorris in Chapter 7). At the time of his death, a neighbor expressed the feelings of thousands of admirers: "We feel profoundly sad for them all" (*Time, *April 28, 1997, p. 62).*

My father loves the small and receding wild places in the agribusiness moonscape of North Dakota cropland, and so do I. Throughout my childhood, we hunted and gathered in the sloughs, the sandhills, the brushy shelterbelts and unmowed ditches, on the oxbows and along the banks of mudded rivers of the Red River valley. On the west road that now leads to the new Carmelite monastery just outside of Wahpeton, we picked prairie rosehips in fall and dried them for vitamin C–rich teas in the winter. There was always, in the margins of the cornfield just beyond our yard, in the brushy scraps of abandoned pasture, right-of-ways along the railroad tracks, along the river itself, and in the corners and unseeded lots of the town, a lowly assertion of grass.

It was big grass. Original prairie grass—bluestem and Indian grass, side oats grama. The green fringe gave me the comforting assurance that all else planted and tended and set down by humans was somehow temporary. Only grass is eternal. Grass is always waiting in the wings.

Before high-powered rifles and a general dumbing down of hunting attitudes, back when hunters were less well armed, and anxious more than anything to put meat on their tables, my father wore dull green and never blaze orange. He carried a green fiberglass bow with a waxed string, and strapped to his back a quiver of razor-tipped arrows. Predawn on a Saturday in fall he'd take a child or two into the woods near Hankinson, Stack Slough, or the cornfields and box elder and cottonwood scruff along the Wild Rice or Bois de Sioux rivers. Once, on a slim path surrounded by heavy scrub, my father and I heard a distant crack of a rifle shot and soon, crashing toward us, two does and a great gray buck floated. Their bounds carried them so swiftly that they nearly ran us over.

The deer huffed and changed direction midair. They were so close I felt the tang of their panic. My father didn't shoot—perhaps he fumbled for his bow but there wasn't time to aim—more likely, he decided not to kill an animal in front of me. Hunting was an excuse to become intimate with the woods and fields, and on that day, as on most, we came home with bags of wild plums, elmcap mushrooms, more rosehips.

Since my father began visiting the wild places in the Red River valley, he has seen many of them destroyed. Tree cover of the margins of rivers, essential to slow spring runoff and the erosion of topsoil—cut and leveled for planting. Wetlands—drained for planting. Unplowed prairie (five thousand acres in a neighboring Minnesota county)—plowed and planted. From the air, the Great Plains is now a vast earth-toned Mondrian painting, all strict right angles of fields bounded by thin and careful shelterbelts. Only tiny remnants of the tallgrass remain. These pieces in odd cuts and lengths are like the hems of long and sweeping old-fashioned skirts. Taken up, the fabric is torn away, forgotten. And yet, when you come across the original cloth of grass, it is an unfaded and startling experience. Here is a reminder that before this land was a measured product tended by Steiger tractors with air-cooled cabs and hot-red combines, before this valley was wheat and sugar-beet and sunflower country, before the drill seeders and the windbreaks, the section measures and the homesteads, this was the northern tallgrass prairie.

It was a region mysterious for its apparent simplicity.

Grass and sky were two canvases into which rich details painted and destroyed themselves with joyous intensity. As sunlight erases cloud, so fire ate grass and restored grass in a cycle of unrelenting power. A prairie burned over one year blazes out, redeemed in the absolving mist of green the next. On a warm late-winter day, snow slipping down the sides of soft prairie rises, I can feel the grass underfoot collecting its bashful energy. Big bluestem, female and green sage, snakeweed, blue grama, ground cherry, Indian grass, wild onion, purple coneflower, and purple aster all spring to life on a prairie burned the previous year.

To appreciate grass, you must lie down in grass. It's not much from a distance and it doesn't translate well into most photographs or even paint, unless you count Albrecht Dürer's *Grosses Rasenstuck*, 1503. He painted grass while lying on his stomach, with a wondering eye trained into the seed tassles. Just after the snow has melted each spring, it is good to throw oneself on grass. The stems have packed down all winter, in swirls like a sleeper's hair. The grass sighs and crackles faintly, a weighted mat, releasing fine winter dust.

It is that smell of winter dust I love best, rising from the cracked stalk. Tenacious in its cycle, stubborn in its modest refusal to die, the grass embodies the philosopher's myth of eternal return. *All flesh is grass* is not a depressing conceit to me. To see ourselves within our span as creatures capable of quiet and continual renewal gets me through those times when the writing stinks, I've lost my temper, overloaded on wine chocolates, or am simply lost to myself. Snow melts. Grass springs back. Here we are on a quiet rise, finding the first uncanny shoots of green.

My daughters' hair has a scent as undefinable as grass—made up of mood and weather, of curiosity and water. They part the stiff waves of grass, gaze into the sheltered universe. Just to be, just to exist—that is the talent of grass. Fire will pass over. The growth tips are safe underground. The bluestem's still the scorched bronze of late-summer deer pelts. Formaldehyde ants swarm from a warmed nest of black dirt. The ants seem electrified, driven, ridiculous in tiny self-importance. Watching the ants, we can delight in our lucky indolence. They'll follow one another and climb a stem of grass threaded into their nest to the end, until their weight bows it to the earth. There's a clump of crested wheatgrass, a foreigner, invading. The breast feather of a grouse. A low hunker of dried ground cherries. Sage. Still silver, its leaves specks and spindrels, sage is a generous plant, releasing its penetrating scent of freedom long after it is dried and dead. And here, the first green of the year rises in the female sage, showing at the base in the tiny budded lips.

Horned larks spring across the breeze and there, off the rent ice, the first returning flock of Canada geese search out the open water of a local power plant on the Missouri River. In order to recreate as closely as possible the mixture of forces that groomed the subtle prairie, buffalo are included, at Cross Ranch Preserve, for grazing purposes. Along with fire, buffalo were the keepers of the grass and they are coming back now, perhaps because they always made sense. They are easier to raise than cattle, they calve on their own, and find winter shelter in brush and buffalo-berry gullies.

From my own experience of buffalo—a tiny herd lives in Wahpeton and I saw them growing up and still visit them now—I know that they'll eat most anything that grows on the ground. In captivity, though, they relish the rinds of watermelon. The buffalo waited for and seemed to know my parents, who came by every few days in summer with bicycle baskets full of watermelon rinds. The tongue of a buffalo is long, gray, and muscular, a passionate scoop. While they eat watermelon, the buffalo will consent to have their great boulder foreheads scratched but will occasionally, over nothing at all, or perhaps everything, ram themselves into their wire fences. I have been on the other side of a fence charged by a buffalo and I was stunned to a sudden blank out at the violence.

One winter, in the middle of a great snow, the buffalo walked up and over their fence and wandered from their pen by the river. They took a route through the town. There were reports of people stepping from their trailers into the presence of shaggy monoliths. The buffalo walked through backyards, around garages, took the main thoroughfares at last into the swept-bare scrim of stubble in the vast fields—into their old range, after all.

Grass sings, grass whispers. Ashes to ashes, dust to grass. But real grass, not the stuff that we trim and poison to an acid green mat, not clipped grass never allowed to go to seed, not this humanly engineered lawn substance as synthetic as a carpet. Every city should have a grass park, devoted to grass, long grass, for city children haven't the sense of grass as anything but scarp on a boulevard. To come into the house with needlegrass sewing new seams in your clothes, the awns sharp and clever, is to understand botanical intelligence. Weaving through the toughest boots, through the densest coat, into skin of sheep, needlegrass will seed itself deep in the eardrums of dogs and badgers. And there are other seeds, sharp and eager, diving through my socks, shorter barbs sewn forever into the laces and tongues of my walking boots.

Grass streams out in August, full grown to a hypnotizing silk. The ground begins to run beside the road in waves of green water. A motorist, distracted, pulls over and begins to weep. Grass is emotional, its message a visual music with rills and pauses so profound it is almost dangerous to watch. Tallgrass in motion is a world of legato. Returning from a powwow my daughter and I are slowed and then stopped by the spectacle and we drive side roads, walk old pasture, until we find real grass turned back silver, moving, running before the wind. Our eyes fill with it and on a swale of grass we sink down, chewing the ends of juicy stems.

Soon, so soon.

Your arms reach, dropping across the strings of an air harp. Before long, you want your lover's body in your hands. You don't mind dying quite so much. You don't fear turning into grass. You almost believe that you could continue, from below, to express in its motion your own mesmeric yearning, and yet find cheerful comfort. For grass is a plant of homey endurance, pure fodder after all.

I would be converted to a religion of grass. *Sleep the winter away and rise headlong each spring. Sink deep roots. Conserve water. Respect and nourish your neighbors and never let trees gain the upper hand.* Such are the tenets and dogmas. As for the practice—*grow lush in order to be devoured or caressed, stiffen in sweet elegance, invent startling seeds*—those also make sense. *Bow beneath the arm of fire. Connect underground. Provide. Provide. Be lovely and do no harm.*

FOR JOURNALING AND DISCUSSION

1. Erdrich clearly feels closely connected to the land in which she grew up. Reflect on a natural place that is somehow connected to your youth. Write an essay describing its importance to you.
2. Erdrich's love of the land is also closely linked to her childhood memories of her father. Reflect on how our memories of place are connected to the personal relationships that we have formed there.
3. Vine Deloria, a Native American writer and researcher has said, "White people in this country are so alienated from their own lives and so hungry for some sort of real life that they'll grasp at any straw to save themselves. But high tech society has given them a taste for the 'quick fix.' They want their spirituality prepackaged in such a way as to provide instant insight, the more sensational and preposterous the better."* Contrast this description of one kind of spirituality with the spirituality that Erdrich describes when she talks about the grasslands of her childhood.

FOR RESEARCH AND EXPLORATION

1. Find a description of the great prairies and grasslands of the Upper Midwest written by some of the original white settlers and explorers. What was their reaction to this land? How are their responses different from Erdrich's? What do their responses suggest about the differences between their world view and Erdrich's?
2. Erdrich refers to our current obsession with "humanly engineered" grass— maintained largely by overfertilization and an excessive use of chemicals as a perversion of nature. Do some research on the effects of this chemical use on the environment. Write an essay in which you either agree with or dispute her claim.
3. Erdrich says that in her experience "hunting was an excuse to become intimate with the woods and fields . . . ." How does this contrast (if indeed it does) with the approach of most contemporary hunters? Interview some hunters about why they hunt. How do their statements mesh or conflict with Erdrich's views?

*From "Spiritual Hucksterism" by Ward Churchill, *Z Magazine,* December 1990, 94–98.

Regional Consciousness as a Shaper of Local History: Examples from the Eastern Shore

Polly Stewart

Stewart earned a Ph.D. in English from the University of Oregon and currently teaches at Salisbury State University in Maryland. She has produced folklife festivals and published articles on such subjects as the politics of folklore scholarship, Idaho family folk song traditions, and women in ballads.

The simple principle that *a region's consciousness of itself defines the region* offers a sensible and effective means for interpreting local historical events. Regional consciousness bears no necessary relation to artificial administrative lines imposed by governments; for analytical purposes it is just as isolating as occupation, ethnic heritage, age, sex, or any of the factors that come into play when cultural groups identify themselves. It crosses all ethnic, class, and economic lines, and the highly educated are just as much imbued with it as are the unlettered. Regional consciousness is less a matter of geography than it is a state of mind. It is therefore possible to speak of "folk regions" as distinct from geographic or political regions.

The lands surrounding the Chesapeake Bay provide an unusually fertile field for examination of folk regional consciousness. The land immediately west of the bay is home to the nation's capital and to a portion of the megalopolis that sprawls between Richmond and Boston—the Eastern Seaboard. The largely rural peninsula situated east of the bay comprises the entire state of Delaware, nine counties of Maryland, and two counties of Virginia, and is called, from syllables in the three states' names, "Delmarva." (Border communities, by the same principle, are given names like Mardela, Delmar, Marydel.) Residents often decry the carving up of Delmarva to meet various political demands, and for many decades there has been talk of merging the three political units into a new "State of Delmarva." But Delmarva includes an informal subregion known as the "Eastern Shore" or simply "the Shore." Its geographic boundaries are not obvious to the uninitiated, yet its cultural boundaries are deeply felt and passionately defended by its residents. An outsider who might innocently confuse the Eastern

Shore with the Eastern Seaboard will not, in the presence of an Eastern Shoreman, make the same mistake twice. Such loyalty to a folk region makes it unlikely that Eastern Shoremen would be politically any happier in a State of Delmarva than they presently are in the State of Maryland.

Everything one can observe about the Shore validates it as a folk region. To begin with, in the minds of Shoremen the Shore encompasses only eight of the nine Maryland counties on Delmarva (the northernmost county is viewed as part of the megalopolis) and excludes all but the southern edge of Delaware. The portion of Virginia that extends south to the tip of the peninsula is called the "Eastern Shore of Virginia" and is regarded, for various political and economic and cultural reasons, as a different domain. The Maryland part of Delmarva divides itself into two Shores, Upper and Lower; the latter comprises four counties, Worcester, Wicomico, Somerset, and Dorchester. The county seats of the first three—Snow Hill, Salisbury, and Princess Anne—play a large role in the present study.

Originally settled by English colonists in the 1640s, the Shore existed for over three centuries in relative geographic isolation. Until 1952, when the Bay Bridge was opened, the only routes west were by ferry across the Chesapeake or overland across the head of the bay; a bridge-tunnel leading south to Norfolk was not opened until 1965. Today, ineluctably connected to the western mainland, the Eastern Shore is as easy to reach by automobile as Lane County, Kansas. But while the Shore is no longer geographically isolated, its people remain, on the whole, culturally isolated by choice. In saying this I do not wish to suggest in any way that Shoremen are not knowledgeable about the rest of the world, but rather that, whatever their level of education, Shoremen take an unusual degree of pride in setting themselves apart from the rest of the world. Membership in the group is rigidly determined: the only way one can be a Shoreman is to have been born in the Shore. (It should be pointed out that the term is generic, as in, "She's a Shoreman, but her husband isn't.") Those who find it necessary to secure employment away from the Shore yearn to come back, and many do come back upon retirement, because of the "sand between their toes."

The attitude of Shoremen toward outsiders is pervasive and unsubtle, though not necessarily unkind. Young people who come from the megalopolis to attend college in the Eastern Shore quickly learn that they are "Western Shoremen," a term they may never before have had applied to them. Shoremen are given to expressing their feeling about outsiders in a song, sung to the tune of "The Old Gray Mare," that states, "We don't give a damn about the whole state of Maryland,/ . . . We're from the Eastern Shore." This song is performed annually at the close of the state legislative session in Annapolis by members of the Eastern Shore delegation—to the delight of the assembled throng—as a gesture of regional pride, but it can also be heard ardently sung in Eastern Shore taverns by men and women who have been discussing strategies for blowing up the Bay Bridge. Shoremen are inclined to exhibit more condescension toward Baltimoreans than to outsiders from other locales; the term "Baltimoron" is more or less good-naturedly bandied about, and one can hear many stories about "Baltimore hunters" who drive up to Shore game-checking stations with goats or cows strapped to their fenders.[1]

The principle of regional consciousness has great potential as an analytical tool. But when we add to it three others, two from the study of folklore and one from anthropology, the possibilities become especially powerful for interpreting local historical events in an unprecedented way. The first of these, invented by the late William Hugh Jansen, is known to folklorists as "the esoteric-exoteric factor"—a technical term for the "us-them" dichotomy that pervades the thinking of groups.[2] Sometimes exquisitely subtle, sometimes painfully overt, the esoteric-exoteric factor always operates as groups are perceiving themselves, perceiving other groups, and imagining how other groups perceive them. Because regional consciousness involves a sense of belonging to a place, it automatically posits an "other," a class of persons who do not belong. Jansen postulated that the more a group sees itself as beset by hostile outside forces, the stronger will be its esoteric, or in-group, identification and the stronger its need to construct defenses against those outside forces.

The second analytical tool—awareness of the importance of the number three in shaping Euro-American perception and behavior—has been examined by (among many others) folklorist Alan Dundes.[3] Citing Bronislaw Malinowski's observation that "Nothing is as difficult to see as the obvious," Dundes provides many examples of ways in which the number three pervades Western culture, even to the point of causing apparently objective students of natural and cultural phenomena to create analytical categories with three parts, whether warranted or not. (Witness the present analysis.) Everyday life is organized into patterns of threes, and people are likely to make sense of unusual or stressful events by noticing when such events occur in threes. As Dundes notes, "The child is conditioned by his folklore to expect three and his culture does not disappoint him."[4] The importance of the number three in the present study will be made plain.

The anthropologist Edward T. Hall has provided the third useful tool in interpreting regional historical events. He has argued persuasively that much of the experience of everyday life is processed so far below the level of consciousness ("out of awareness" is the term Hall uses) that many events cannot be subjected to rational analysis by even the most rational among us, that we respond instead, for good or for ill, according to deep-seated cultural predispositions that we do not recognize.[5] Such response, powerful enough in individuals, is likely to be even more powerful among groups acting under the esoteric-exoteric force mentioned above. In stressful circumstances entire populations, particularly in such strongly self-identified regions as the Shore, can be caught up in courses of thought and action that they might not otherwise follow. Regional consciousness can thus figure significantly in the playing out of historical events. More pointedly, historical events can actually be shaped by regional consciousness.

Some historical events are less pleasant to talk about than others. The three major events of the present discussion—a mass murder and two lynchings, which occurred in the Lower Shore between 1931 and 1933—are unpleasant in the extreme. My purpose in presenting them here is not merely to exhume, and certainly not to sensationalize, painful historical memories, but to illustrate the premises of regional consciousness mentioned at the opening of this essay. I offer the discussion in hopes not only of explaining these local events but also of showing that their causes differ markedly from the causes of apparently similar events that were occurring elsewhere in the United States during the same troubled period; many parts of the nation, during the late twenties and early thirties, were in the grip of lynchings and other violent outbreaks.[6]

The oral history of the Eastern Shore events is extremely guarded, though anyone from the Lower Shore is likely to know about them either through personal memory or through the oral narratives of others. I learned initially about the oral history through reading student folklore collections in the archives at Salisbury State University. I subsequently read a valuable unpublished manuscript by John R. Wennersten, a historian at the University of Maryland, Eastern Shore, in Princess Anne; in preparing his manuscript Wennersten had consulted newspaper accounts and transcripts of hearings and had also conducted oral interviews. Still later I conducted interviews of my own and studied printed accounts from the day in the three Lower Shore newspapers—the *Snow Hill Democratic Messenger,* the *Salisbury Daily Times,* and the *Princess Anne Marylander and Herald*—as well as in the *Baltimore Sun.* Because the Eastern Shore events attracted the attention of the American liberal press, I was also able to read outside observers' comments in the *Nation* and *New Republic,* which typically discussed the events in connection with others seemingly like it around the country.

As the various press accounts demonstrate, the violence in the Shore was explicitly and consistently interpreted by insiders as evidence of justified local reaction to outside interference, and by outsiders as evidence of backwardness and racism in the Shore. A clearer example of Jansen's esoteric-exoteric factor—"us against them"—could scarcely be found anywhere.

The first of the violent incidents was a multiple murder in Worcester County. On October 10, 1931, four members of a prominent and well-liked white farm family—father, mother, and two teenage daughters—were found shot in their beds. The only suspect in the crime was an employee of the family, an itinerant black laborer who had lived in the area for several weeks, named Euel (or Yuel) Lee. Items of clothing and jewelry identified as the property of murdered family members were found in the boardinghouse where Lee was staying. After several hours of questioning by local law-enforcement officers, Lee signed a confession and was jailed. There he was interviewed by

Bernard Ades, a lawyer from the International Labor Defense League (ILD), a communist organization that was waging an extensive labor, civil-rights, and antilynching campaign in the South at that time. Local sentiment against Lee was exceptionally high because of the popularity of the murdered family and, I believe, because of Lee's apparently unremorseful presentation of self; he was described in the *Salisbury Times* as a "cool, self-possessed man" who showed "little, if any, signs of emotion" (October 16, 1931). Perhaps for these reasons the court-appointed local defense lawyer had demonstrated little interest in preparing a case on Lee's behalf, and Ades was soon granted authority to take on the case. Lee subsequently changed his plea to not guilty. Ades contended that a fair trial would be impossible for Lee in the Eastern Shore and further charged that Lee was being used as "an example to keep negroes in Eastern Shore counties in their places." The ILD engineered Lee's extradition out of Worcester County to Baltimore, and over the next two years, by the use of various technicalities, it succeeded in keeping the Lee case in litigation (and Lee away from the gallows; there is little to suggest he was not guilty of the murders).[7] Lee was eventually executed in Baltimore—exactly two years and two weeks after the murders—but people throughout the Eastern Shore were outraged that the case had been taken away from them by outsiders.

In the meantime, two months after the slayings in Worcester County, when it had become apparent that the accused Lee was not going to be brought swiftly to justice in the Shore, a second violent incident occurred, this time in Salisbury. Daniel J. Elliott, a prominent and well-respected white lumber dealer, was shot and killed, allegedly by a black employee named Matthew Williams. There were no witnesses to the murder, but Williams himself somehow sustained a gunshot wound and was taken to the local hospital. The local papers later offered speculation that Williams had accidentally or intentionally shot himself after shooting Elliott, but in the folk memory the culprit in both shootings was Elliott's own son. The following account from the Salisbury State University archives, collected in 1973 from a sixty-two-year-old white woman, is typical of about half of the several dozen narratives of the incident (in the other half, Williams shoots Elliott):

> Everybody claimed the colored man had killed Dan Elliott at the lumber mill on Lake Street and had robbed him. But it ain't so because an old colored lady we had known for years told us what happened. She said that the colored man had saved money from working at the mill and had asked Dan Elliott to keep it for him. So on that day the colored man went to get his money, but it was gone. It seems that Dan Elliott's son had stolen the money and when he was confronted by his father, he shot the father and then shot the colored man.[8]

Whether or not Williams actually had committed the murder will never be known, for within hours after Williams was hospitalized, a mob of about three hundred gathered at the hospital, got Williams out, dragged him several blocks to the county courthouse, hanged him from a tree on the courthouse lawn, and burned his body.

Local newspaper reports and editorials of the time indicate strongly a belief that this lynching would not have happened were it not for the pending Lee case. An editorial from the *Chestertown Enterprise,* reprinted in the *Salisbury Times* on December 11, 1931, typifies this position: "The Eastern Shore wants nothing more at this time than to be left alone in the settling of its problems. Outside interference which caused the delay in the case of the Worcester murderer of four was directly responsible for the deplorable lynching in Salisbury." In the oral record the message was blunter still: according to one account, collected in the early 1970s, "Well, you see, there was this other family that was murdered over [in Worcester County] and a black man had been accused of killing them but he got off. And so they decided, some people around town, that this man wasn't gonna get off."

Local news reports on the lynching suggest that outsiders were "responsible" in yet another way: it became known that the night before the Elliott shooting a meeting was held in Salisbury attended only by local blacks, during which outsiders identified as communists told the blacks they were being economically exploited by their white employers and exhorted them to take steps to end their oppression. Matthew Williams was reported to have been there, though no connection between the meeting and the shooting could be established once Williams was dead.

One day after the lynching, on December 5, 1931, the *Baltimore Sun* published an editorial, "Disgrace," which said, in part, "The lowest and least civilized elements [took] command; and that remains true whether or not men of position participated in the Salisbury lynching or tacitly approved it." Several letters to the editor followed, one of which, signed "A Reader," was captioned, "Very, Very Bold, But Not Enough So to Use His Name to This Letter"—an indication of the *Sun's* negative attitude toward the writer (December 7, 1931). Though the letter was datelined Baltimore, it apparently was written by a Shoreman and I believe it represents the feelings of many Shoremen:

> It seems to me that you have taken only one side of the question, and also you condemn the whole Eastern Shore for this particular case . . . . The case of Yuel Lee hacking to death a complete white family was but a stimulus to the mob . . . . If this Negro had been promptly tried and hanged, there would not have been a lynching yesterday . . . . Negroes on the Eastern Shore are well-behaved. Where I come from the Negro steps aside and raises his hat . . . . I predict that there won't be any more white people shot down by Negroes for some time, for they know what is their due if they should.

Four days after the lynching a vitriolic new editorial, "The Eastern Shore Kultur," signed by H. L. Mencken, appeared in the *Baltimore Sun.* (It was reprinted in full on the front page of the *Salisbury Times* on the following day, December 8, 1931.) Well-known for his free use of immoderate language, Mencken here let out all the stops, attacking the Shore as a place "wherein there are no competent police, little save a simian self-seeking in public office, no apparent intelligence on the bench, and no courage and decency in the local press." He alleged that the lynching occurred in a milieu of social degeneration that had permitted "ninth-rate men" to come to power. And he argued for a concerted effort "to educate" the Eastern Shore: "The majority of people, even in Wicomico, are probably teachable." In his attack, Mencken did what many other outside observers did in writing about the lynching—he condemned the entire population for it, including those in high positions, not merely those who had actually participated in it. From the local perspective, outsiders were blaming the Shore for something that had been caused by outsiders.

The Wicomico County state's attorney conducted a grand-jury investigation to determine who had been responsible for the lynching, but witness after witness failed to identify any participant, saying the lynchers' faces were unfamiliar. It was reported in the local press that eyewitnesses thought the perpetrators had come from out of town, possibly from the Eastern Shore of Virginia. Fifty years later the state's attorney's son told me the same thing, stressing that people honestly did not know who the lynchers were. Oral accounts in the Salisbury State University folklore archives sustain this view as well; for example, a man who was in his teens when the lynching occurred said in 1972, "I right now could not tell you a single person I saw . . . . Amazing thing about a crowd—you don't see individuals, you just see a crowd."

No indictments were found in the grand-jury investigation, and in late January 1932 the Salisbury lynching case was closed. Outsiders were furious. Broadus Mitchell, a liberal professor of political science at Johns Hopkins University, conducted a brief survey of Salisbury for the Federal Council of the Churches of Christ in America and published a report critical of the town (and, by implication, the region). The *Salisbury Times* responded with a front-page editorial, "In Rebuttal to Prof. Broadus Mitchell," on January 30, 1932, which said, in part, "It is extremely difficult for any blue-blooded American to sit idly by and witness the spectacle of a wholesale indictment of the ideals and the institutions established by his progenitors . . . . The professor . . . concludes after interviewing a dozen persons during a three day visit here, that Salisbury is lacking in 'civic morality,' its residents are mentally deficient and they fail to 'apply religion to life,' and he tries to find an explanation for this in what he terms our 'isolation.' " The editorial then devotes considerable space to discrediting Mitchell as a commentator, citing his membership in the American Civil Liberties Union (a "communist organization") and connecting the ACLU with "the International Labor Defense, another known communist organization." But the real sentiment of the editorial is felt in the following: "The report may be worthy of a citation for the distinguished service its author has rendered to the cause of the Soviet government, but what about the humiliation it has brought a Christian, English speaking people here in Salisbury . . . . [W]e do not relish the injury Prof. Mitchell has inflicted upon us."

To recapitulate: the Salisbury lynching was not resolved to the satisfaction of outsiders and as events proceeded the collective feelings of the Eastern Shore had been battered; the Lee murder case had been usurped by outsiders and was to drag on in Baltimore for nearly two more years. Euel Lee eventually was found guilty of murder, but even after his conviction the lawyers from ILD kept staying his execution through a series of appeals to various state and federal courts. For two years, Eastern Shoremen had been reading of these trials and appeals, and it does not seem likely that the length of time it was taking to bring Lee to justice was doing anything to abate their resentment about the conduct of the case. After several last-ditch appeals, reported agonizingly in the daily papers, Lee was at last hanged in Baltimore on October 27, 1933.

The execution of Euel Lee, which presumably would have eased the anger and resentment of people in the Shore, came too late for George Armwood, a black man who died at the hands of a lynch mob in Princess Anne on October 18.

The events immediately prior to this second lynching are reported differently by blacks and whites. Were it not for the research efforts of John R. Wennersten, who conducted "ten confidential interviews of blacks resident at Princess Anne at the time of the lynching," we might never have a record of the black version.[9] According to this version, a white farmer in Somerset County, John Richardson, persuaded George Armwood, a farm worker, to help him rob an elderly white woman. The woman, who owned rental properties, was known to carry cash as she walked from property to property collecting rents. Richardson's plan for robbing her was preposterous, and Armwood, who was described by Wennersten's black informants as "slow-witted," would doubtless never have agreed to participate in it had he had all his faculties. The plan was this: Armwood would lurk in the forest waiting for the woman, Mrs. Denston, to come by. Disguised by a wool cap pulled down over his face, he would grab her money, take the money to Richardson, and split the proceeds with him. In the enactment of the crime, however, things did not work out as planned. Mrs. Denston struggled and Armwood succeeded only in disrobing her and having his pitiful disguise pulled off his face.

In the version published in newspapers (October 17–20, 1933), which we may take to be the white version, no mention was made of the Richardson-Armwood conspiracy; only the black man's attack on the elderly white woman was reported. Richardson's only reported role in the story was as an accessory after the fact, for Armwood had gone to him and asked for help in escaping, and Richardson had transported him several miles south to the farm of his brother, James Richardson, near the Maryland-Virginia border. It took only a few hours for the police to find and arrest Armwood, but in the meantime a rumor had gone abroad that Armwood had raped Mrs. Denston, who was variously reported as being seventy-two, eighty-two, and ninety-two years old.

Emotions in Princess Anne were therefore high, but they rose even higher when an officer of the State Police, fearing for Armwood's safety because of the Euel Lee case and the Salisbury lynching, telephoned the governor of Maryland and secured his permission (though the governor had no authority to grant it) to take Armwood to Baltimore under cover of night, which was done. The next day the Somerset County sheriff traveled to Baltimore with a writ of habeas corpus, properly issued by the Somerset County state's attorney, and brought Armwood back to Princess Anne. That night a mob of about two thousand people stormed the county jail, brought Armwood out, hanged him, and burned his body.

As a human being, I cannot help finding these facts appalling. As a folklorist I cannot help noticing that the Armwood lynching was the third in a series of nationally reported events, each contributing to the rage of Eastern Shoremen who, whatever their social standing or occupation, found themselves the object of ridicule and attack by outsiders. It seems that the power of the number to shape perception, the esoteric-exoteric factor that can foster "us against them" thinking, and the irrational way people can act upon cultural impulses below the level of consciousness all combined in the Armwood case. It is little wonder that Shore citizens, in editorials and letters to the editor over the 1931–33 period, claimed repeatedly that outside interference in the Lee case had been the root cause of the violence that followed. Matthew Williams and George Armwood were implicated in crimes at the wrong moment in history. Both became victims to misdirected anger against outsiders—a circumstance that, I believe, sets these two lynchings apart from others that happened elsewhere in the country during the same period.

The aftermath of the Princess Anne lynching constituted an exercise in ironic futility. As with the Salisbury lynching, a locally conducted grand-jury investigation found no indictments. This time, however, officials at the state level were determined to prosecute, and after a series of machinations that might be the stuff of comic opera were they not so grim, several Somerset County men were implicated in the lynching. At issue was whether the state or the county had authority to prosecute. Local feeling against the state's action was so great that the governor sent a detachment of three hundred National Guardsmen to the Shore in an effort to keep the peace as the men were being transported to Baltimore. Violence erupted at the Salisbury National Guard Armory, however; a crowd of two thousand was tear-gassed and shots were fired. The attorney general of Maryland, who was present at the incident, escaped with his life. (He later dropped his campaign to prosecute lynchers, and the Princess Anne case was closed early in 1934.) The anger generated in the Shore was so great that it contributed to the governor's losing his 1934 bid for reelection.

The anger of Shoremen was not directed solely at the governor, however; the *Baltimore Sun* was blamed locally for inflammatory reporting and for being prejudiced against the Shore. As one oral informant, a young woman at the time of the incident, said in 1971, "I still won't buy a *Baltimore Sun*. They were terrible about it—they called us everything in the book, said we were beating everyone with hoses, rakes, shovels—and if they hadn't exaggerated everything that happened it would have died down a lot quicker. The Baltimore papers sent reporters, and the militia was sent in to quiet us down. But the Eastern

Shore people would have none of other people telling them what they should and should not do."

Even if the facts of the Eastern Shore events could be fully established and agreed upon (an unlikely eventuality, since the folk memory differs from the printed record and the black memory differs from the white), the interpretation of the facts would remain problematical. During the 1930s the Eastern Shore was racially segregated, but even the most thoughtful white Eastern Shoremen honestly did not see segregation as a valid issue and they earnestly and consistently denied that racism had anything to do with the violence reported in the news. Their position was, and continues to be, that the issue should be discussed in terms of local and county authority as opposed to the authority of the state (or, more broadly, to the putative authority of the Western Shore). Outsiders, by contrast, persisted in seeing the events in racial and cultural terms, and this profound difference in approach to interpretation of facts contributed heavily to the Shore's resentments.

That seems to be the real issue—resistance to and resentment of being meddled with by outsiders. I learned this myself several years ago, the hard way. The setting was the annual meeting of one of the Lower Shore county historical societies, a respected group of local white residents, many of whom hold high positions in the community. I was there because I had been invited to deliver the major address. I had been a Lower Shore resident for ten years at that time. Many members of the society were known to me through community service and through social contact, so I felt at ease with them both as individuals and as a group. I was excited by my topic, for I had been studying the Princess Anne lynching and was just starting to apply the theory of regional consciousness to it (I had not at that point connected it with the other two events). Knowing that everyone present would be familiar with the Princess Anne incident, I thought the annual meeting would be a perfect place to discuss the regional theory. Following my incisive and enlightening presentation, my well-educated and reasonable audience would see the historical event with new eyes and would come away with a new respect for themselves as tradition bearers.

That was my plan. What actually happened was that everybody in the audience stopped listening as soon as I said "Princess Anne lynching"—about halfway through the talk—and spent the rest of the time getting ready for assault. Years afterward it is still hard to write about this. I was hurt and mystified at the vehemence of their reaction, horrified at the irrationality of their anger. These people were my friends, and they were turning on me. Some responded with more anger than others, but it was clear that everyone there was really upset with me. Some of them still are.

Had I not ignored two key points in the theory of regional consciousness— that it applies universally in a region by crossing all class and educational lines, and that it operates without reference to reason—I could have avoided so egregious a blunder. But I misjudged my audience and became, in their eyes, yet another outsider telling local people what was what.

NOTES

1. Stories of the out-of region hunter can be found in a variety of regional settings, where they serve to mark identity boundaries between insiders and outsiders. See Jan Howard Brunvand, *Curses! Broiled Again! The Hottest Urban Legends Going* (New York: Norton, 1989), 138–141.

2. William Hugh Jansen, "The Esoteric-Exoteric Factor in Folklore," *Fabula: Journal of Folktale Studies* 2 (1959), 205–211; reprinted in *The Study of Folklore*, ed. Alan Dundes (Englewood Cliffs, NJ: Prentice-Hall, 1965), 43–51.

3. Alan Dundes, "The Number Three in American Culture," in *Every Man His Way: Readings in Cultural Anthropology*, ed. Alan Dundes (Englewood Cliffs, NJ: Prentice-Hall, 1968), 401–424.

4. Ibid., 159.

5. Edward Hall, *The Silent Language* (Garden City, NY: Doubleday, 1959).

6. See also Trudier Harris's fine *Exorcising Blackness: Historical and Literary Lynching and Burning Rituals* (Bloomington: Indiana Univ. Press, 1984). Arthur F. Raper, *The Tragedy of Lynching* (1933; repr., New York: Arno, 1969).

7. Quotation from the *Salisbury Times*, Oct. 20, 1931. It seems clear that the International Labor Defense League used the Lee case to bring to national attention the need to end Jim Crowism. Because of developments in the Lee case, the ILD helped establish legal precedents for black civil rights in Maryland and elsewhere thirty years before these became customary. For example, it got the Lee case transferred out of the Shore on the argument that no black could receive a fair trial there; it invalidated Lee's first trial on the argument that blacks had been excluded from the jury pool; and it challenged his second trial on the argument that blacks, while included in the pool, had not been selected to serve on the jury.

8. This and all subsequent quotations are from the confidential files of the Folklore Archives at Salisbury State University. The interviews were conducted with the understanding that narrators' anonymity would be protected.

9. John R. Wennersten, "Tidewater Somerset: A County History, 1850–1976" (manuscript), 392.

FOR JOURNALING AND DISCUSSION

1. Stewart claims that regional consciousness "crosses all ethnic, class, and economic lines, and the highly educated are just as much imbued with it as are the unlettered. Regional consciousness is less a matter of geography than it is a state of mind." How has your regional consciousness helped to shape your identity? Is regional identity as important as race, class, gender, age, nation, religion, and ability in determining people's sense of themselves?

2. In what ways is the region in which you live set off from the rest of the country? How much of its individuality is a result of geography?

3. Do you think that some parts of the country have a stronger sense of region—a clearer regional identity—than others? Which ones? What creates a stronger regional sense?

4. What effect does a region's racial make-up have on its identity? Do different races perceive the same region differently?

FOR RESEARCH AND EXPLORATION

1. Find someone on your campus who comes from a different part of the country than you do. Interview this person about his or her perceptions of *your* home region. How do his or her perceptions differ from yours? How did your interviewee get these views?
2. In an essay, apply Stewart's views on regional consciousness and insider/outsider conflict to the situation Katherine Newman describes in "Illegitimate Elites and the Parasitic Underclass" in Chapter 3. Why are the people of Pleasanton so threatened by the outsiders' arrival? What role does race play in compounding an already tense situation?
3. Research a historical event in your region that would probably be viewed differently by outsiders than by those who live there. Find examples of both national and local reports and editorials about this event. How was this event portrayed differently by the various groups? Explain why you think those different perceptions exist.

The Unlamented West
Jonathan Raban

Raban is a British writer and academic who has dealt with such topics as literary criticism, history, social commentary, travel, and exploration. His publications include Arabia: A Journey Through the Labyrinth; God, Man, and Mrs. Thatcher; *and* Hunting Mr. Heartbreak.

Most mornings at this time of year, I gut the skinny national edition of the New York *Times* on my third-floor deck—looking east, over the green Seattle suburbs, to the spindrift snowcaps of the Cascade Range. Past the Cascades, sagebrush takes hold, in the dry coulees and lumpy prairie country of eastern Washington. The land turns green again in Idaho, in the fir-clad foothills of the Rocky Mountains. And after the Rockies, it's back to dust and sagebrush on the arid plains of eastern Montana and the Dakotas. I've driven that route so often that the intervening mountains offer no serious impediment to the thousand-mile view from the deck: on a good day, I can see clear to the North Dakota badlands—to Dickinson, Minot, Bismarck, and the coffee-colored gleam of the Missouri River, where the Midwest begins.

For people on this fertile coast, most of "The West" is, as people like to say, Back East. It belongs to the past. It is where parents and grandparents lived and—mostly—failed, leaving a forlorn trail of abandoned homesteads, bankrupt businesses, exhausted mines, and empty logging camps behind them. Serial failure is the driving theme in the family narratives of a great many of my immediate neighbors: high hopes dashed, rekindled, dashed again, as families crawled westward, in meagre increments of a hundred miles or so, until at last they found a modestly secure anchorage somewhere between the Cascades and the Pacific.

It is an unquiet past. The news from the Back-East West that finds its way into the *Times* reads like a string of bubbles of bad gas, rising from the depths of the grandfather era and bursting noxiously into the present. Angry disputes over land use, grazing rights, logging, mineral royalties . . . . The strangely antique figures of James (Bo) Gritz, Randall Weaver, the Freemen of Justus Township, the Trochmann brothers and their homemade army, Ted Kaczynski reading Thackeray and the Bible in his red plywood cabin. Photographs of these characters should be printed in sepia. They belong to that sad and unlamented West where bitterness and fury were the natural offspring of impossibly great expectations.

I

From the spring of 1907 through the fall of 1908, the Chicago, Milwaukee & St. Paul railroad lumbered through the Dakotas and into Montana. From the top of any butte, one could have seen its course through the badlands: the lines of horse-drawn wagons, the heaps of broken rock for the roadbed, the gangs of laborers, engineers, surveyors. From a distance, the construction of the new line looked like a disaster of war.

As the Milwaukee Road advanced, it flung infant cities into being at intervals of a dozen miles or so. Trains needed to be loaded with freight and passengers, and it was the essential business of the railroad company to create instant communities of people whose lives would be dependent on the umbilical of the line. So the company built skeletal market centers on company-owned land. Its creations were as arbitrary as those described in Genesis. The company said, "Let there be a city": and there was a city.

Each was a duplicate of the last. Main Street was a line of boxes, wood and brick, laid out on the prairie, transverse to the railroad line. The boxes housed a post office, a hotel, a saloon, a general store, a saddlery, a barbershop, a church, a bank, a schoolhouse, and a jail. Beside the line, sites were earmarked for the grain elevator and the stockyard. A few shacks, and the city was done. Photographed from the proper angle, with railroad workers for citizens, it could be promoted as the coming place in the New West.

The railroad moved into Montana like Caesar marching through Gaul, freely inventing the land it occupied as it went along. Like Gaul, this part of Montana had been named long ago—by the Indians, by the United States Army, and by ranchers, who had raised cattle, sheep, and horses there for the last forty years. But the railroad ignored the existing names, preferring to adorn the landscape with bright new coinages of its own. It canvassed directors and senior managers for the names they had given their daughters. The president of the railroad, Albert J. Earling, had two daughters, Isabel and May. The girls' names were fused to produce Ismay, which sounded modern and tripping on the tongue, although someone might have warned the company that it could, sometime in the far future, be vulnerable to the addition of a spray-painted initial "D." The recent offspring of other Milwaukee Road officials seem to have included a Lorraine, an Edina, and a Mildred . . . .

Nearly a century after they were born, these towns are still haunted by the accidental nature of their conception. Their brickwork has grown old, the advertisements painted on the sides of their buildings have faded pleasantly into antiques, yet the towns seem insufficiently attached to the earth. Such lightness is unsettling. It makes one feel too keenly one's own contingency in the order of things.

As the railroads pushed farther west, into open rangeland that grew steadily drier and steadily emptier, the rival companies clubbed together to sponsor an extraordinary body of popular literature. In school atlases just a few years earlier, the area had been called the Great American Desert—an imaginative vacancy, without any flora or fauna. Railroad writers and illustrators were assigned to come up with a new picture of free, rich farmland—a picture so attractive that readers would commit their families and their life savings to it, sight unseen.

The pamphlets were distributed by railroad agents all over the United States and Europe. They were translated into German, Swedish, Norwegian, Danish, Russian, Italian. They turned up in bars and barbershops, in doctors' waiting rooms, in the carriages of the London tube and the New York subway. Newspapers carried advertisements for them: by filling in and returning a coupon, you could receive a free copy by post.

When a pamphlet arrived, it was bigger than one had expected. What slid from the manila envelope had the glamorous, bang-up-to-date look of a bestseller. Its cover was dominated by a warm golden yellow—the color of sunshine, ripe wheat, money. The land from the Dakotas to the Pacific was drawn as a single, enormous field, and across it ran the straight line of the Milwaukee Road. The main body of the picture showed a fresh-faced young man steering a plow drawn by two horses. As the virgin earth peeled away from the blade of the plow, it turned into a breaking wave of gold coins.

One would have to be a fool to take the cover seriously. Yet, the more you looked at the text inside, the less fantastic the claim made by the cover came to seem. It was in black-and-white—facts and figures, and testimonies of experts and of new settlers already coining money from their homesteads. At the Great New York Land Show, held in Madison Square Garden, Montana had carried off the prizes for the best wheat, best oats, best barley, and best alfalfa in the United States. In print, these crops took on a solid, succulent weight. "Oats grow to perfection. There is something about the climate that favors them and produces a bright, plump, heavy berry that averages forty pounds to the bushel." As for alfalfa, the "noted alfalfa grower" I. D. O'Donnell turned in a lyrical prose poem:

> Alfalfa is the best mortgage lifter ever known. It is better than a bank account, for it never fails or goes into the hands of a receiver. It is weather proof, for cold does not injure it and heat makes it grow all the better. A winter flood does not drown it and a fire does not kill it . . . . Cattle love it, hogs fatten upon it, and a hungry horse wants nothing else.

Some pamphlets were aimed at readers with firsthand experience of farming: Southern sharecroppers; tenants and paid hands in rural Iowa and Minnesota; Scandinavian wheat farmers bankrupted by the devastating success of the American grain belt. But many were addressed to the wider audience of urban daydreamers—people who, cut off from nature, yearned for a draught of country air and the daily intimacies of village life. The pamphlets sought out the haggard schoolteacher, the bored machinist, the clerk, the telegrapher, the short-order cook, and the printer, and promised to turn each of them into the prosperous squire of his or her own rolling acres.

"Uncle Sam gives you a cordial invitation . . . ." The terms of the Enlarged Homestead Act, passed by Congress in 1909, after a great deal of lobbying by the railroad companies, were generous. The size of a government homestead on "semi-arid land" was doubled, from a quarter section to a half section; from a hundred and sixty acres to three hundred and twenty. One did not have to be an American citizen to stake a claim—though it was necessary to become one within five years, when the homestead was "proved up." The proving-up was a formality that entailed the payment of a small fee and an inspection of the property to verify that it had been kept under cultivation. That done, the full title to the land was granted to the homesteader.

Three hundred and twenty acres. In such a space one could imagine a dozen big fields, filled with rippling crops of wheat, oats, alfalfa, barley; ample pastureland for sheep and cattle to wander over; a tree-shaded house, a red barn, a walled kitchen garden for vegetables. There would be poultry scratching in the yard, beehives in the clover, a winding gravel drive . . . . It wouldn't be a farm, it would be an estate. It was an astounding free offer by any reckoning . . . .

II

Mike Wollaston and I have been wrangling all morning. Mike is the grandson of a homesteader, and we've just spent an hour in the wrong township. We are now, we think, in the right one: Township 9, north of Range 53 East, southern half of Section 2, eleven miles northwest of Ismay. The land was proved up by Mike's grandfather, Ned Wollaston, on April 27, 1917, and granted to him, and to his heirs and assigns forever, under the Presidential seal of Woodrow Wilson. We are definitely on the Wollaston place, but the homestead has gone missing.

A photograph was taken by Mike's father, Percy Wollaston, in the late nineteen-thirties. In the chemical gloaming of underexposure stands a trim two-story farmhouse with barns and outbuildings.

We expected to find the place in ruins, but there isn't so much as the ruin of a ruin in sight. The open range, green now, in May, and splashed with yellow and purple wildflowers, is empty except for a herd of cattle two or three miles off. As we try to match the topography to the photograph, bump for bump, the missing homestead slides about over the prairie like an egg on hot oil. Maybe the swale has changed its course. Maybe grass has grown over the exposed rock of the ridge. Mike and I, both fifty-something, shiver at the discovery that a mere half century is sufficient to consign his grandfather's farm to the realm of archeology. . . .

When he was a small child, shortly after Pearl Harbor, Mike was evacuated from Great Falls to Ismay, along with his elder brother and two sisters, and they all lived there with their maternal grandmother for the duration of the war. Though the homestead was only a short ride away, they were never taken to see it, nor was it spoken of.

"Look." Mike has found a small rusted metal frame on which a single plank dangles loosely from a bolt. "My father's sled."

"Rosebud," I say, and wish I hadn't.

For a full minute, he stands silent, cradling his father's sled. Then he lays it back in the grass as carefully as one might lay down a sleeping child. "It's better where it is." He affects a hardboiled grin. "My father only talked once about the homestead. We were sitting up late over a glass of whiskey. There was a silence. Then he said he hoped he'd never again have to see anything like his mother down on her knees day after day praying for rain. That was it." . . .

III

Mike and I tack east, then south, then east again as the road makes ninety-degree turns along the section lines. One can no longer get really lost on the prairie: these roads, with their slavish devotion to the cardinal points of the compass, have converted the land into a full-scale map of itself.

Our course converges with a drab-green rift of cottonwoods along O'Fallon Creek. We cross a bridge—the creek is now a river, swollen and turbid from recent rains—then jolt over the one-track line of the old Milwaukee Road, and we are in Ismay, or what was Ismay but is Ismay no longer. The name on the sign has been painted out and replaced with "Joe. Population 28."

Easy come, easy go. When it first came into the world, Ismay was idly, capriciously named, as if it were a goldfish or a hamster. It nearly jettisoned its name in 1912, when the Titanic went down and Bruce Ismay, the chairman of the shipping line, allegedly elbowed his way ahead of women and children in the race for the lifeboats. Then the town voted to remain Ismay and tough out the jokes at its name's expense. Ismay even made it into the gazetteer of the

"Times Atlas of the World," sandwiched between Ismaning, Germany, and Ismetpaşa, Turkey. But the glue on the name lost its sticking power, and Ismay is now Joe.

In 1993, when the Kansas City Chiefs acquired the quarterback Joe Montana from the San Francisco 49ers, three Kansas City disk jockeys came up with the idea of turning Joe Montana—or, rather, a Joe, Montana—into a place on the map. What was needed was an ailing townlet, just big enough to have a United States post office, for souvenir-mail frankings. It could become the object of tourist pilgrimages. It could build a museum of Joe Montana memorabilia. It could make a killing with Joe, Montana, T-shirts. This was an offer that no ailing townlet could afford to turn down. The station called one-stoplight towns and then no-stoplight towns, and met with gruff refusals. People are attached to the names that had served their parents and grandparents, even when the names are of the kind that you might think anyone would have been glad to be rid of: Molt, Iron, Straw, Yaak, Stumptown, Twodot, Agency, Crackerville. Zero, Montana, might have been a likely taker, but it had lost its post office in 1957. Finally, they got through to Ismay, the smallest incorporated city in the state, six miles from the nearest blacktop road, and largely in ruins. Ismay bought the pitch and in July, 1993, changed its name . . . .

The town now has an agent—a man in Billings. Not since 1910 has Ismay been the focus of such publicity.

The whole town was flown to Kansas City, where it watched the Chiefs play, had an audience with Joe Montana, and returned home with a clutch of autographed footballs . . . .

This year's Joe Montana Day is July 3rd. The first Joe Montana Day, held in 1993, drew some two thousand visitors; even though it was advertised only locally, the town sold boxes and boxes of T-shirts, sweatshirts, bumper stickers, baseball caps, and souvenir mugs. The town did a fine trade in commemorative cards and letters franked "Joe, Montana". . . .

When Mike's grandfather, Ned Wollaston, arrived here with his family, in September, 1910, he had more reason than most of his neighbors to be thinking big.

Ned was born in England, the thirteenth child of a Liverpool shipping agent and son of the cloth. Ned was aged four in 1876, when his father, aged fifty-one, brought his family to the United States. Hawk-nosed, tombstone-bearded, and with plenty of capital, Ned's father arrived in the brand-new town of Fairmont, Minnesota, and took the place by storm.

He began by building a house the size of a palace, with sixteen rooms and a wraparound porch supported by elaborately ornamented timber columns. He then started a bank, founded the Episcopal church of St. Martin's, opened a general store, and farmed four hundred and sixty acres of wheat and barley. But what people would remember best was his windmill—a Norfolk-style saltshaker with thirty-foot sails. The tireless Englishman, a whirligig of businesses and projects, was a Minnesota landmark.

To be a child of such a father must have been a tough assignment. None of the sons bore much resemblance to a windmill. One became a grocer, one a surveyor, one a Colorado miner. And so it went. When Ned was sixteen, he enlisted in the Minnesota National Guard, and in five years he climbed to the rank of sergeant. After his discharge, in 1893, he knocked about the Dakotas working as a cook, a carpenter, and a cowhand on ranches there. And then, in 1900, responsibility settled on Ned all of a sudden, when, at twenty-eight, he married a Fairmont widow, Mrs. Dora Marietta, and found himself the stepfather of her three children. Dora was keen to have more. For a year, the Wollastons ran a store in Madison, South Dakota, and then they rented a small mixed farm a couple of miles south of the town. Percy, Mike's father, was born in that farmhouse, in September, 1904.

Ned must have felt that he was still living in the shadow of his father. His land was not his, and it was a handkerchief-size scrap compared with the Wollaston holdings in Minnesota. By 1908, he would have been following the newspaper reports on the proposed Enlarged Homestead Act. The bill endured a rough passage through Congress, with the big ranchers and their Washington lobbyists opposing it at every stage. The railroad interests needed the bill, and feared bankruptcy if it failed to pass; the ranching interests saw in it the ruination of the West.

When Theodore Roosevelt, himself a onetime Dakota Territory rancher, finally signed the bill into law, on February 19, 1909, Ned Wollaston was euphoric to get the news—but it was shortly followed by his father's death. Ned had always seen himself showing his father around his own acres.

Mike's father tells of hearing Ned and Dora talk in the evenings at the time of the Homestead Act:

> I remember my parents discussing something about "taking up a claim." The imagination and curiosity of a four- or five-year-old boy began to conjure up pictures of some vague object being taken up bodily . . . . On another evening Mother said, "Percy and I could hold down the claim if you had to go somewhere to find work," and I envisioned Mother and myself trying to hold down a huge tarp or canvas in a terrific wind.

Unlike the schoolteachers and clerks, barbers and bottle washers who were jumping aboard the emigrant trains, Ned was an experienced farmer, and he could see the difficulties ahead. Although eastern Montana was only four hundred miles northwest of Madison, its climate was a lot drier, and he would have to make do with, on average, five or six inches less rainfall a year. With twenty inches or more, you'd be in clover. With fifteen or less, you could be in trouble. The latest rainfall figures for Miles City, Montana, were: 1907, 14.75 inches; 1908, 19.08 inches; 1909, 13.31 inches. Right on the margin. But nearly all this rain had fallen in the growing season—and Mildred and Ismay generally did better, by as much as an inch, than Miles City. There should be enough. Just.

In the spring of 1910 Ned rode the train alone to Mildred, where he scouted out the land, now crowding with homeseekers. The lobby of the Mildred hotel was a polyglot din of Russian, Swedish, German, Irish, English, Greek, and American voices. Ned found a glorious site for a farm, ten miles out of town. Old buffalo trails and newer cattle tracks converged on a spring that was shaded by a gnarly cottonwood tree. A coulee bisected the half section, making a green valley where the cornflowers were in bloom. He hired a loca- tor to check the property, filed his claim at the Miles City Land Office, and rode back in an exultant mood to Madison, and saw his crops through to har- vest. When the harvest was done, Ned and Dora put most of their goods and livestock up for auction, keeping only the animals, tools, and furniture that would fit into a single emigrant car.

Building his own house on his own land that fall, Ned thought often of his father. Among the first crops raised in the virgin soil of the homestead were some freakishly big turnips. One weighed twenty-one pounds. In 1912, Ned took the train back to Minnesota, to buy more cattle at the South St. Paul stockyards. He made a detour to Fairmont, to present one of these amazing vegetables, scrubbed clean and sliced in half to prove its integrity, to the new president of the bank founded by his father. For several weeks, the turnip stood on exhibition in the window of his father's old place of business, an em- blem of the bounty of the Western plains. You could raise a four-figure loan on the surety of such a turnip.

The yards of the hardware stores in Ismay and Mildred were packed with bales of fencing wire. Freight cars laden with wire stood in the railroad sidings. The wire, double-stranded, with barbs twisted on one strand, was shipped from the Glidden factory, in Illinois. Its trade name was The Winner.

Each homestead needed between five and seven miles of fences. For every mile of fence, one needed to cut and haul some eleven hundred posts— in a country where timber grew in isolated pockets, often many miles from any homestead. The new arrivals lived and breathed fencing. It was hard, cold, te- dious labor—a much bigger job than the building of a house and barns. But in the course of it this ill-assorted bunch of dazed railroad passengers was slowly transformed into a coherent society.

The fences are still a wonder. You can sight along a surviving line of posts, and not a single one is out of true, though the ground on which they're set dips, rolls, and breaks, and the unwavering vertical of the fence keeps on be- ing lost to sight, then pops up again, exactly—but *exactly*—on its marks. People were proud of their fences. The fences were not merely functional. They were a statement of the belief that this unruly land could be subdued and civilized.

The ranchers watched with affected disdain as the newcomers stole the range from under their noses. They'd lost the political battle against the Enlarged Homestead Act. They were outnumbered by the homesteaders. In the eighteen-eighties, "fence wars" in Texas and elsewhere had only rallied public opinion to the homesteaders' side. The ranchers were cast as villains long before they reached for their wirecutters. So in 1910 the Montana ranchers' best hope was that the homesteaders would quickly fail, pack their bags, and take the damnable train back to wherever it was they had come from. The ranchers fought mostly on the morale front, losing no opportunity to broadcast the view that the prairie soil was far too dry to farm, that even a small herd of cows would starve on a miserable half section of land, and that the homesteaders were poor fools—unwitting dupes of a bunch of conniving politicians and railroad barons—whose only hope was to get out as fast as possible, before they were overtaken by inevitable ruin . . . .

IV

The first week of June, 1995, brings perfect spring weather to the prairie. The weather is a stroke of luck for me, for I'm seeing the prairie as the homesteaders saw it during their first Montana spring. They arrived in a run of moist years—1910, 1911, 1912—and the land was living up to its descriptions. The old hands—the ranchers and the early, quarter-section honyockers*—couldn't remember a time when it had been so wet and green, and the newly arrived settlers were able to look at the brimming creeks and fenced squares of tender wheat, and see them as a prophecy come to pass. It was *as it was written*—a conclusive rebuttal of all those jaundiced critics who had argued, in Congress and elsewhere, that this country was unsuitable for the small farmer.

In this age of belief in the efficacy of Science and the march of Progress, the homesteaders' bible was an eccentric, self-published little book entitled "Campbell's 1907 Soil Culture Manual," by Hardy Webster Campbell. The "Campbell Method" of dry-farming urged on its adherents a mystical faith in the power of capillary attraction and an abhorrence of the devilish works of evaporation.

Immediately following a shower of rain, you were to harness your horses to a disk harrow and pulverize and loosen the surface of the soil. This was to prevent the loss of precious moisture, to open the soil to the nitrogen in the air, and to prepare the ground for the next shower. Rain falling on loosened earth would percolate faster into the subsoil, where it would top up the building "reservoir" of stored water. Give in to evaporation, and you are on the road to ruin . . . .

That initial, exceptional spell of fair weather came close to living up to its glowing description by the Milwaukee Road's in-house pamphleteer ("The clear, dry air is extremely invigorating and, combined with the large percentage of bright days, makes the climate one of the most healthful and pleasant in the world"), and people built their houses for Montana's "pleasant" climate. From 1910 to 1915, they spread themselves over the land, started their repayments, and

---

*Editors' Note: "Honyockers" was a term used by ranchers in the West to ridicule homesteaders. Probably a blend of "hunk" (for Hungarian people) and "Pollack" (for Polish people), it was meant to characterize newcomers as "ridiculous oafs, saps, and dimwits" according to the author in the complete version of this long essay.

generally felt their adventure to be turning into a success. It was the winter of 1916 that gave the settlers their first taste of the pitiless, extreme character of the Montana climate. When stable, high-pressure Arctic air settled in over the prairie, it brought blue-sky days without a cloud to insulate the earth at night. There was almost no precipitation. And the north wind, with no shelter belts of trees to divert it, raked the homesteads, keening and whistling through every crack in their amateur carpentry, prying off their tarpaper siding. The temperature dropped, and went on dropping: past zero, into the tens, twenties, thirties, forties.

The Wollastons, bred to the big-minus-number winters of the northwestern interior, took the bitter weather in their stride. Their neighbors from the eastern states and from Britain, southern Sweden and Norway, and Germany had never known that cold could be so cold. They had expected snow, ice, the pitcher frozen in the morning, earth standing as hard as iron, water like a stone. But the cold of Montana, when it finally came, was an insult and a shock.

Lynn Householder, whose Log Cabin Ranch had begun as a half section, homesteaded by his father in 1911, told me how people used to keep going. "The wind blew for three days. Thirty below, and night and day it never changed. They had newspapers and cardboard glued up on the inside walls of the houses, but that cold keeps coming through. In those winter blizzards, you feel very much alone. You listen to the walls move—and that's in a modern house. The potbellied stoves would run out of fuel, and people would have to tear down the fences that they'd put up in the summer."

But the cold was the least destructive element in Montana's repertoire of violent weather. Lightning-strikes set the prairie ablaze, cyclones whirled away farm buildings, and hailstorms, coming out of nowhere in the sweetest, moistest summers, took just a few minutes to put an end to a family's dreams . . . .

Wind, fire, lightning, ice . . . . At first, Montana's fierce and capricious climate was seen to come with the territory. People battened down for these assaults, and came to accept them as part of the annealing process. Urban types took pride in coming through each new calamity. They were learning to be farmers. It was exhilarating just to find that one could cope. Facing up to the wrecked wheat field after a hailstorm, burning the fence to keep warm in winter, digging a fire trench to keep off the flames in summer were emblems of the homesteaders' growing know-how.

Until 1917. That year, barely five inches of rain fell between May and August, and the harvest was disappointingly thin. The arid summer was then followed by another winter of shocking cold . . . .

But some viewed the weather in a more constructive light.

Wynona Breen's father, Henry Zehm, along with her uncles and grandparents, had filed on claims near the Wollaston place. Like the Wollastons, the Zehms had come to Montana from Fairmont, Minnesota. The Zehms, devout Seventh-Day Adventists, were, at least by the Episcopalian Wollastons' standards, religious cranks. Back East, in Fairmont, the Zehms might have been considered funny peculiar. When the rain stopped and the grasshoppers descended on the earth, Wynona Breen's grandfather quietly rejoiced. A plague of locusts ate the miserable remains of the spring wheat. Lightning bolts set fire to the dry buffalo grass. Hailstones pounded the buildings. The papers carried reports of the carnage of the First World War. Everything was set fair for the sounding of the last trump, the rending of the sky, the great shout of the descending Lord, come to whisk the righteous off to their eternal home. The Second Coming was at hand.

"The righteous will rise up and live for a thousand years—I never knew exactly where, but not on this earth—and the earth will be cleansed by fire and made new," Wynona Breen said. "It's all in the Bible."

We were talking in the bare but cozy living room of the original house on the Zehm homestead—old stove, old rocker, old table, old prints on the walls. Only a pile of rental videos, ready for return to the store in Terry, gave away the fact that we were in 1995. Mrs. Breen herself, nut brown, with big, capable hands, had put a distance between herself and her Adventist upbringing; she, alone among her siblings, had drifted from the Church. Her independence of mind and her humor showed in her broad face, which was weathered in the style of the local landscape, fissured with gullies and dry coulees. With her round glasses and curly gray hair, she was still the even-toned schoolmistress, weighing each sentence carefully as she spoke it.

"So the worse the weather got, the happier it made your parents?" I said.

"Well, there was certainly a good deal of satisfaction at things like the grasshoppers. My folks never hesitated to mention those things, and quote the texts."

"But the Zehms would be saved on Judgment Day?"

"Oh, yes. We were the saved, among the righteous."

In 1993, during "the Waco deal," Wynona felt a spasm of sympathy for David Koresh and his flock.

"My husband, Charlie, and I were in Dallas at the time, staying with our daughter, who is a lawyer there. And she, of course, would have gone out with her little gun and shot Koresh herself. But Charlie and I couldn't help telling her, 'Now, that man has the right to live there any way he pleases. He built that place, and paid for it.' So far as we know, he wasn't doing anything terrible. He was on his own property, and was trying to keep anybody else from coming on, even if the people trying to come on it were officials."

I realized that I had missed something very obvious in the furor over the Waco siege. The Branch Davidian "compound" was in essence a homestead. "It was built and paid for": the labor that Koresh's followers had put into its construction entitled them to enjoy freedom on their own land; and, like so many homesteads—like the house in which Wynona and I were sitting—it was a sanctuary for unconventional religious beliefs and social attitudes. People like the Zehms chose to come to the West at least partly because they felt themselves to be outsiders back East, and the isolated homestead set them free from the conformist values of the small town. When Westerners watched the confrontation near Waco on CNN, they could see their own family histories reflected in the Koresh place in the Texas prairie, and when the Bureau of Alcohol, Tobacco, and Firearms and the FBI moved in it was as if the family homestead were being violated. People felt tenderness for the Branch Davidians—not merely out of some Neanderthal dogma about property rights but because their sense of themselves as Westerners was under siege.

That Koresh had chosen to await Armageddon in what looked like a badly constructed motel in the wilderness was for most non-Westerners an alienating image: it was a feature of the Branch Davidians' general dangerous craziness. But it wouldn't look like that to a Westerner with a homestead on the Plains in his or her family background: it would look like Grandpa's farm—where, perhaps, Armageddon had been as eagerly awaited as it was in Waco.

Percy Wollaston had confided to his son, close to midnight and over whiskey, that his memory was haunted by the sight of his mother, on her knees every day praying for rain. Writing his memoir for the grandchildren, he didn't disclose that scene. He wanted his readers to enjoy the homestead as an adventure, and in his writing the faces of Ned and Dora are sometimes colored by anxiety and disappointment but never by despair. Perhaps he needed to rescue from his boyhood something wholesome and of heritable value precisely because his keenest memories of homestead life were too bleak to bear . . . .

In 1917, less than twelve inches of rain fell. Though the numbers fluctuate slightly, each subsequent year (1918, 1919, 1920) was worse than the last one, with too little rain falling on ground already parched beyond hope. Fifteen inches of rainfall was the make-or-break rule of thumb. Much less than that, and the topsoil turned to dust. . . .

Rain suddenly chose to come back to the prairie in 1927. The Wollastons were tired. Ned was fifty-four, Dora sixty-two. They were grizzled, lonely, and undeceived by this show of kindly weather. With the copious spring rains, eastern Montana was again promoted as the new Eden, and it was painful to watch new people move in, as guileless as the homesteaders of 1910. Although Ned's attachment to his land was as strong as ever, he could not subject Dora to another evil winter, and he hardly had the stomach for it himself. But he could not sell. When he talked of moving, strangers called at the house and made offers, which rankled in his soul. Eight thousand dollars for his valley, his home, his fields, his hives on the hill, for the best years of his and Dora's life? From the moment he set foot on the claim, Ned had seen the homestead as the estate that he would pass on to his son.

He agreed to rent the farm on a year-by-year basis to a young couple named Shumaker. He sold them his stock, horses, and implements. He would keep the bees. Three wagonloads of books and furniture went to Mildred, to be loaded on a boxcar. Then Ned packed the Ford until it resembled a top-pling haystack of assorted household goods, and in March, 1927, he and Dora drove sadly west.

Those homesteaders who clung on were faced with a hard reckoning. In every sense of the phrase, the railroads had taken them for a ride. They remembered the misleading pictures in the brochures. Vanity had led them to read too much into the glossy descriptions. Humbled now, and wiser, they reproached themselves more than they did the railroads or the federal government. The homesteaders now saw themselves as contrite realists. They understood, at last, how dry the land really was, and how it needed to be gentled back to health. They resolved to save for the bad years, not splurge in the good ones. From now on, they would use the plow lightly, let the soil lie fallow, and feed it with nutrients. This land might not be much, but it was theirs. They had abused it. Now they would atone for that abuse. The homesteaders who survived into the nineteen-twenties found that their attachment to the land had grown beyond reason, as love does . . . .

VI

Following the route taken by Ned and Dora Wollaston as they drove west in their Model T in 1927, I sped through the hardtack landscape of failure and abandonment—the wrecked houses, boarded-up schools, junked farm machinery—that marks the line of the Milwaukee Road on its ill-fated passage through eastern Montana. More than four hundred miles west of Ismay by road, the Continental Divide is crossed at Rogers Pass on Highway 200, and for the Wollastons, as for me, the Divide was the boundary between two worlds: the dry and the wet, the poor and the rich . . . .

I drove on west, with water, lots of it now, always at my elbow. I followed the Blackfoot to its confluence with the Clark Fork, switched to the Jocko, ran down to the Flathead, and caught up again with the Clark Fork at Paradise.

A light rain was falling. There were weeping-willow trees in people's yards, and brown bulrushes in the ditches at the roadside. The Clark Fork was full of cigar-shaped wooded islands. As the rain cleared and sunlight caught the edges of the clouds, the water turned soapstone green—reflecting the conifers on the high slopes above. Small farms were crowded into the narrow space of the valley floor. A few acres could support a family here: a dozen dairy cattle, an orchard, a plowed field sown with winter wheat, two ponies on a wood-fenced pasture—all this within the compass of a handkerchief, by prairie standards. To Ned it must have looked as green as his idea of England. Anything would grow here, if you could find a patch of soil to call your own.

At Thompson Falls, Ned and Dora took a room in the Black Bear Hotel, on Main. Land-hungry, Ned scouted around town for an affordable chunk of the place. On the twenty-fifth of April, 1927, he paid Orrie K. Goodwin a total of five hundred and fifty dollars for eight lots on the block bounded by Clay and Church Streets and by Third and Fourth Avenues. They amounted to a little less than two-thirds of an acre.

Ned's small new world was on a wooded slope with a clear view over the town and the river. The house he built is still there, snugged in among add-ons by later owners, and I saw immediately the plan that he had in mind. The front of the house looks south, as the homestead had looked south over the swale. At the back, as at Ismay, a stone path leads north from the kitchen to the henhouse. The new house was the old house, transplanted to a Rocky Mountain Eden.

Most of the homesteaders went on farther west, and I didn't want to lose sight of their continuing trail.

Nearly forty miles on from Thompson Falls, there was a sign for a town named Noxon, on the far bank of the river, and I crossed a bridge over the Clark Fork in search of a late lunch. In closeup, Noxon was less attractive than it should have been—a rambling string of bungalows and trailers, with a general store, a gunshop, and the Landmark Café.

I opened the café door on an amiable buzz of talk between the owner and three men seated around a table. The talk stopped dead. I hoisted myself onto a stool at the bar and asked for coffee and a hamburger. The owner took my order but didn't make eye contact.

The four men of Noxon closely resembled each other. All had black spade beards. All were around forty. The three at the table were dressed in camouflage caps, plaid flannel shirts, suspenders, work pants, and big black lace-up boots. I made an inventory of my own clothes: an olive-green shirt, a gray herringbone-tweed jacket from Brooks Brothers, corduroy slacks from Eddie Bauer, and a pair of blue leather deck shoes. In the Landmark Café, Noxon, I might as well have been wearing a ball gown, high heels, and a wig.

The silence behind me became an inaudible muttering, as conversation resumed in strict sotto voce. My food came. It was good, and I said so, but still the owner wouldn't catch my eye. I then remembered where I had seen the name Noxon: in the New York *Times* a few months before. Noxon was the headquarters of the Militia of Montana, which had come to sudden public attention in the aftermath of the Oklahoma City bombing. The Landmark Café was evidently the regimental mess.

When I thanked the owner for a fine lunch, he turned his back on me and busied himself with the coffee machine. To give him and his café their full due, the place was more grimly unwelcoming than any other restaurant I have eaten in in my life, but the hamburger—and the coffee, too—were beyond reproach.

I spent a short while prowling along a mountain road behind the town. At regular intervals, there were mailboxes by muddy tracks leading deep into the trees. It was prime survivalist real estate. As the homesteaders had been drawn to this valley for its easy pickings, so a later generation of surly romantics found in it the perfect site for a life in the woods. With a hunting rifle and a pair of dogs, you could sally forth from your cabin like Natty Bumppo, snacking on huckleberries. When the dogs growled in the dark, you'd go out to the stockade with night-vision binoculars, searching the forest shadows for lurking federal agents.

That version of the West, half Boy Scout playacting, half paranoia, with some queer Bible-reading thrown into the mixture, seemed to bear directly on my own theme. Its leading figures were like bad-blood descendants of the homesteaders. In their resentment of government, their notion of property rights, their harping on self-sufficiency and self-defense, as in their sense of enraged Scriptural entitlement, one could see the perverse legacy of the homesteading experience and its failure on the Plains.

When, earlier in the year, a bomb destroyed the Alfred P. Murrah Federal Building in Oklahoma City, killing a hundred and sixty-eight people, the gist of every editorial I saw was "Terror in the Heartland: How Could It Happen Here?"

In private, and closer to the so-called heartland, I heard a quite different response: "Any farm kid could have done it. You'd think it would happen more often than it does." Farmers in the West regularly make bombs. They use them to blast stumps, blow up walls of rock, and make quick work of ditchdigging. The sound of distant explosions is an everyday part of country life. "If I were to start on it now, this morning, I could have it ready to blow up a federal building by two o'clock this afternoon. So could you." Fertilizer saturated with diesel fuel and packed into a confined space (like that of a rental van) is more stable and more economical than dynamite, and needs only a detonator to set it off.

My informant fished a suitable detonator out of a drawer. "Like this." An Atlas blasting cap, the size of a refill cartridge for a fountain pen. Blasting caps could be got—against a purchaser's signature—from a rural hardware store. You push the blasting cap into the explosive mixture and complete the circuit with a battery and a doctored clock.

In fact, the heartland folk were not only already heavily armed but had virtually unlimited access to deadly explosive matériel. Given the political tensions between the country and the city, especially in the West, it seemed likely that there would be another farm-bomb horror. If it ever came to war, the country was in a position to blow the city clean out of the ground. . . .

VIII

The story of the homesteaders and their flight from the land is so American that some Americans will hardly see it as a story. These people came over, went broke, quit their homes, and moved elsewhere. So? In this country, everybody has the right to fail—it's in the Constitution.

The homesteading experience was more than that: it scorched people too deeply to be forgotten in a mere generation. It still rankles. The abandoned homesteads of eastern Montana and the Dakotas stand as a warning to the credulous. Here, on these three-hundred-and-twenty-acre plots of dust, the Western forefathers were suckered.

In 1994, on the twenty-fifth anniversary of the Apollo moon landing, the *Washington Post* concluded from the results of a poll it had recently conducted that twenty million Americans give credence to the idea that the moon walk was a hoax, perpetrated in the Arizona desert by the federal government, for the financial benefit of the powerful corporations who were the NASA contractors. In my experience, almost every bar in the West has its resident skeptic, who will expound this theory at tediously detailed length.

After all, in 1909 the government really did drop people onto an expanse of land that closely resembles the dusty surface of the moon. The homestead scheme was, indeed, pushed through Congress largely for the benefit of the great railroad companies. The corporation bosses, like Albert Earling and James J. Hill, ran their lines to the coast at—as it turned out—the expense of hundreds of thousands of innocent would-be farmers, who bought the government pitch and saw their families "starve out" on their claims.

Around the time of the first catastrophic drought, in the late teens of the century, Montana children were taught to vilify James J. Hill in the schoolyards, where they chanted:

> Twixt Hill and Hell, there's just one letter;
> Were Hill in Hell, we'd feel much better.

Those children, educated into cynicism, have not been slow in passing on their knowledge to their children and their children's children. No matter what the federal government did to make amends to the homesteaders (and the New Deal Administration, through Rexford Tugwell's resettlement program, did much), the federal government would be remembered by many in the West as a trickster, never to be trusted again. The fresh-faced young farmer plowing gold coins out of the prairie, near Ismay, would be remembered, too, as an exemplar of the enormous, treacherous power of the advertising industry.

In places like Justus Township, where people are inclined to believe in black helicopters, and in unholy conspiracies among government, big business, and the media, the bleak and haunted landscape offers its own nourishment to the paranoid political imagination. With its broken fences and splayed houses (many still furnished, with rotting clothes in the closet, and dirty dishes in the sink), it looks like a landscape in an allegory—the site of Everyman's betrayal by the giants Government and Industry, which is where, or so they say, the decline of the West began.

FOR JOURNALING AND DISCUSSION

1. Raban claims that the West's focus on religious freedom and its history of providing homes for zealots caused many in the region to sympathize with David Koresh's group rather than with the FBI. Do you agree with Raban's view that there is little sympathy in the West for the federal government?
2. Raban suggests that the survivalist movement—whose main adherents live in the West—is a direct descendant of homesteader mentality. How are these two groups related? What similarities does Raban claim they share? Do you agree?
3. Raban notes that "no matter what the federal government did to make amends to the homesteaders . . . the federal government would be remembered by many in the West as a trickster, never to be trusted again." How do we see this lack of trust in the government playing itself out in the West today?
4. How do our myths and legends about the "Wild West" still affect our perception of that region?
5. Compare Polly Stewart's description of Eastern Shoremen's response to outsider interference in "Regional Consciousness as a Shaper of Local History: Examples from the Eastern Shore" earlier in this chapter with Raban's description of a similar conflict in the West. How does the fact that both writers are essentially outsiders color the way they describe these regions?

FOR RESEARCH AND EXPLORATION

1. Find and read some of the original newspaper articles written to entice people to move to Montana. Describe the rhetoric and persuasive techniques used. Offer some theories about why people were so willing to be persuaded by the railroads to leave everything behind and move west.
2. Research the conflict that revolved around the 1909 Enlarged Homestead Act. What was the controversy? What were the significant issues? Why did the ranchers so vehemently oppose the bill? Why did Roosevelt sign it? What effects from this legislation do we still see?
3. Recently there has been a great deal of controversy between westerners and environmentalists. Many in the West feel that the federal government and environmentalists (outsiders) are coming into their states and imposing solutions on situations they do not understand. Research one of these issues, such as the reintroduction of wolves into Yellowstone National Park, the location of a national nuclear waste dump, the creation of a massive national monument in Utah, and the preservation of the spotted owl in the Northwest. Find copies of editorials in regional and national newspapers. Explain each side's contrasting views. Use the analyses by Raban and Polly Stewart (in "Regional Consciousness as a Shaper of Local History" in this chapter) to explain why the West is so sensitive about the issue.

I'm Working on My Charm

Dorothy Allison

Allison has called herself a "cross-eyed, working-class lesbian, addicted to vi-olence, language, and hope." She grew up in South Carolina and has worked as a writer, editor, and activist. Her books include Trash, Skin, *and* Bastard Out of Carolina, *which was nominated for the 1992 National Book Award, and* Two or Three Things I Know for Sure. *See Chapter 3 for another of Allison's essays; her work illustrates the interactions among race, class, region, and sexuality.*

I'm working on my charm.

It was one of those parties where everyone pretends to know everyone else. My borrowed silk blouse kept pulling out of my skirt, so I tried to stay with my back to the buffet and ignore the bartender who had a clear view of my problem. The woman who brushed my arm was a friend of the director of the organization where I worked, a woman who was known for her wardrobe and sudden acts of well-publicized generosity. She tossed her hair back when she saw me and laughed like an old familiar friend. "Southerners are so charming, I always say, giving their children such clever names."

She had a wine glass in one hand and a cherry tomato in the other, and she gestured with that tomato—a wide, witty, "charmed" gesture I do not re-member ever seeing in the South. "I just love yours. There was a girl at school had a name like yours, two names said as one actually. Barbara-Jean, I think, or Ruth-Anne. I can't remember anymore, but she was the sweetest, most soft-spoken girl. I just loved her."

She smiled again, her eyes looking over my head at someone else. She leaned in close to me, "It's so wonderful that you can be with us, you know. Some of the people who have worked here, well . . . you know, well, we have so much to learn from you—gentility, you know, courtesy, manners, charm, all of that."

For a moment I was dizzy, overcome with the curious sensation of float-ing out of the top of my head. It was as if I looked down on all the other peo-ple in that crowded room, all of them sipping their wine and half of them eat-ing cherry tomatoes. I watched the woman beside me click her teeth against the beveled edge of her wine glass and heard the sound of my mother's voice hissing in my left ear, *Yankeeeeeees!* It was all I could do not to nod.

When I was sixteen I worked counter with my mama back of a Moses Drugstore planted in the middle of a Highway 50 shopping mall. I was trying to save money to go to college, and ritually, every night, I'd pour my tips into a can on the back of my dresser. Sometimes my mama'd throw in a share of hers to encourage me, but mostly hers was spent even before we got home—at the Winn Dixie at the far end of the mall or the Maryland Fried Chicken right next to it.

Mama taught me the real skills of being a waitress—how to get an order right, get the drinks there first and the food as fast as possible so it would still be hot, and to do it all with an expression of relaxed good humor. "You don't have to smile," she explained, "but it does help." "Of course," she had to add, "don't go 'round like a grinning fool. Just smile like you know what you're doing, and never *look* like you're in a hurry." I found it difficult to keep from looking like I was in a hurry, especially when I got out of breath running from steam table to counter. Worse, moving at the speed I did, I tended to sway a little and occasionally lost control of a plate.

"Never," my mama told me, "serve food someone has seen fall to the floor. It's not only bad manners, it'll get us all in trouble. Take it in the back, clean it off, and return it to the steam table." After awhile I decided I could just run to the back, count to ten, and take it back out to the customer with an apology. Since I usually just dropped biscuits, cornbread, and baked potatoes—the kind of stuff that would roll on a plate—I figured brushing it off was sufficient. But once, in a real rush to an impatient customer, I watched a ten-ounce T-bone slip right off the plate, flip in the air, and smack the rubber floor mat. The customer's mouth flew open, and I saw my mama's eyes shoot fire. Hurriedly I picked it up by the bone and ran to the back with it. I was running water on it when Mama came in the back room.

"All right," she snapped, "you are not to run, you are not even to walk fast. And," she added, taking the meat out of my fingers and dropping it into the open waste can, "you are not, not ever to drop anything as expensive as that again." I watched smoky frost from the leaky cooler float up toward her blonde curls, and I promised her tearfully that I wouldn't.

The greater skills Mama taught me were less tangible than rules about speed and smiling. What I needed most from her had a lot to do with being as young as I was, as naive, and quick to believe the stories put across the counter by all those travelers heading North. Mama always said I was the smartest of her daughters and the most foolish. I believed everything I read in books, and most of the stuff I heard on the TV, and all of Mama's carefully framed warnings never seemed to quite slow down my capacity to take people as who they wanted me to think they were. I tried hard to be like my mama but, as she kept complaining, I was just too quick to trust—badly in need of a little practical experience.

My practical education began the day I started work. The first comment by the manager was cryptic but to the point. "Well, sixteen." Harriet smiled, looking me up and down, "At least you'll up the ante." Mama's friend, Mabel, came over and squeezed my arm. "Don't get nervous, young one. We'll keep moving you around. You'll never be left alone."

Mabel's voice was reassuring even if her words weren't, and I worked her station first. A family of four children, parents, and a grandmother took her biggest table. She took their order with a wide smile, but as she passed me going down to the ice drawer, her teeth were point on point. "Fifty cents," she snapped, and went on. Helping her clean the table thirty-five minutes later I watched her pick up two lone quarters and repeat "fifty cents," this time in a mournfully conclusive tone.

It was a game all the waitresses played. There was a butter bowl on the back counter where the difference was kept, the difference between what you guessed and what you got. No one had to play, but most of the women did. The rules were simple. You had to make your guess at the tip *before* the order was taken. Some of the women would cheat a little, bringing the menus with the water glasses and saying, "I want ya'll to just look this over carefully. We're serving one fine lunch today." Two lines of conversation and most of them could walk away with a guess within five cents.

However much the guess was off went into the bowl. If you said fifty cents and got seventy-five cents, then twenty-five cents went to the bowl. Even if you said seventy-five cents and got fifty cents instead, you had to throw in that quarter—guessing high was as bad as guessing short. "We used to just count the short guesses," Mabel explained, "but this makes it more interesting."

Once Mabel was sure she'd get a dollar and got stiffed instead. She was so mad she counted out that dollar in nickels and pennies, and poured it into the bowl from a foot in the air. It made a very satisfying angry noise, and when those people came back a few weeks later no one wanted to serve them. Mama stood back by the pharmacy sign smoking her Pall Mall cigarette and whispered in my direction, "Yankees." I was sure I knew just what she meant.

At the end of each week, the women playing split the butter bowl evenly.

Mama said I wasn't that good a waitress, but I made up for it in eagerness. Mabel said I made up for it in "tail." "Those salesmen sure do like how you run back to that steam table," she said with a laugh, but she didn't say it where Mama could hear. Mama said it was how I smiled.

"You got a heartbreaker's smile," she told me. "You make them think of when they were young." Behind her back, Mabel gave me her own smile, and a long slow shake of her head.

Whatever it was, by the end of the first week I'd earned four dollars more in tips than my mama. It was almost embarrassing. But then they turned over the butter bowl and divided it evenly between everyone but me. I stared and Mama explained. "Another week and you can start adding to the pot. Then you'll get a share. For now just write down two dollars on Mr. Aubrey's form."

"But I made a lot more than that," I told her.

"Honey, the tax people don't need to know that." Her voice was patient. "Then when you're in the pot, just report your share. That way we all report the same amount. They expect that."

"Yeah, they don't know nothing about initiative," Mabel added, rolling her hips in illustration of her point. It made her heavy bosom move dramatically, and I remembered times I'd seen her do that at the counter. It made me feel even more embarrassed and angry.

When we were alone I asked Mama if she didn't think Mr. Aubrey knew that everyone's reports on their tips were faked.

"He doesn't say what he knows," she replied, "and I don't imagine he's got a reason to care."

I dropped the subject and started the next week guessing on my tips.

Salesmen and truckers were always a high guess. Women who came with a group were low, while women alone were usually a fair twenty-five cents on a light lunch—if you were polite and brought them their coffee first. It was 1966, after all, and a hamburger cost sixty-five cents. Tourists were more difficult. I learned that noisy kids meant a small tip, which seemed the highest injustice. Maybe it was a kind of defensive arrogance that made the parents of those kids leave so little, as if they were saying, "Just because little Kevin gave you a headache and poured ketchup on the floor doesn't mean I owe you anything."

Early morning tourists who asked first for tomato juice, lemon, and coffee were a bonus. They were almost surely leaving the Jamaica Inn just up the road, which had a terrible restaurant but served the strongest drinks in the county. If you talked softly you never got less than a dollar, and sometimes for nothing more than juice, coffee, and aspirin.

I picked it up. In three weeks I started to really catch on and started making sucker bets like the old man who ordered egg salad. Before I even carried the water glass over, I snapped out my counter rag, turned all the way around, and said, "five." Then as I turned to the stove and the rack of menus, I mouthed, "dollars."

Mama frowned while Mabel rolled her shoulders and said, "An't we growing up fast!"

I just smiled my heartbreaker's smile and got the man his sandwich. When he left I snapped that five dollar bill loudly five times before I put it in my apron pocket. "My mama didn't raise no fool," I told the other women, who laughed and slapped my behind like they were glad to see me cutting up.

But Mama took me with her on her break. We walked up toward the Winn Dixie where she could get her cigarettes cheaper than in the drugstore.

"How'd you know?" she asked.

"'Cause that's what he always leaves," I told her.

"What do you mean *always?*"

"Every Thursday evening when I close up." I said it knowing she was going to be angry.

"He leaves you a five dollar bill every Thursday night!" Her voice sounded strange, not angry exactly but not at all pleased either.

"Always," I said, and I added, "and he pretty much always has egg salad."

Mama stopped to light her last cigarette. Then she just stood there for a moment, breathing deeply around the Pall Mall and watching me while my face got redder and redder.

"You think you can get along without it?" she asked finally.

"Why?" I asked her. "I don't think he's going to stop."

"Because," she said, dropping the cigarette and walking on, "you're not working any more Thursday nights."

On Sundays the counter didn't open until after church at one o'clock. But at one sharp, we started serving those big gravy lunches and went right on till four. People would come in prepared to sit and eat big—coffee, salad, country fried steak with potatoes and gravy, or ham with red-eye gravy and carrots and peas. You'd also get a side of hog's head biscuits and a choice of three pies for dessert.

Tips were as choice as the pies, but Sunday had its trials. Too often, some tight-browed couple would come in at two o'clock and order breakfast—fried eggs and hash browns. When you told them we didn't serve breakfast on Sundays, they'd get angry.

"Look girl," they might say, "just bring me some of that ham you're serving those people, only bring me eggs with it. You can do that," and the contempt in their voices clearly added, "even you."

It would make me mad as sin. "Sir, we don't cook on the grill on Sundays. We only have what's on the Sunday menu. When you make up your mind, let me know."

"Tourists," I'd mutter to Mama.

"No, *Yankees,*" she'd say, and Mabel would nod.

Then she might go over with an offer of boiled eggs, that ham, and a biscuit. She'd talk nice, drawling like she never did with me or friends, while she moved slower than you'd think a wide-awake person could. "Uh huh," she'd say, and "shore-nuf," and offer them honey for their biscuits or tell them how red-eye gravy is made, or talk about how sorry it is that we don't serve grits on Sunday. That couple would grin wide and start slowing their words down, while the regulars would choke on their coffee. Mama never bet on the tip, just put it all into the pot, and it was usually enough to provoke a round of applause after the couple was safely out the door.

Mama said nothing about it except the first time when she told me, "Yankees eat boiled eggs for breakfast," which may not sound like much, but had the force of a powerful insult. It was a fact that the only people we knew who ate boiled eggs in the morning were those stray tourists and people on the TV set who we therefore assumed had to be Yankees.

Yankees ate boiled eggs, laughed at grits but ate them in big helpings, and had plenty of money to leave outrageous tips but might leave nothing for no reason that I could figure out. It wasn't the accent that marked Yankees. They talked different, but all kinds of different. There seemed to be a great many varieties of them, not just Northerners, but Westerners, Canadians, Black people who talked oddly enough to show they were foreign, and occasionally strangers who didn't even speak English. Some were friendly, some deliberately nasty. All of them were Yankees, strangers, unpredictable people with an enraging attitude of superiority who would say the rudest things as if they didn't know what an insult was.

"They're the ones the world was made for," Harriet told me late one night. "You and me, your mama, all of us, we just hold a place in the landscape for them. Far as they're concerned, once we're out of sight we just disappear."

Mabel plain hated them. Yankees didn't even look when she rolled her soft wide hips. "Son of a bitch," she'd say when some fish-eyed, clipped-tongue stranger would look right through her and leave her less than fifteen cents. "He must think we get fat on the honey of his smile." Which was even funnier when you'd seen that the man hadn't smiled at all.

"But give me an inch of edge and I can handle them," she'd tell me. "Sweets, you just stretch that drawl. Talk like you're from Mississippi, and they'll eat it up. For some reason, Yankees got strange sentimental notions about Mississippi."

"They're strange about other things too," Mama would throw in. "They think they can ask you personal questions just 'cause you served them a cup of coffee." Some salesman once asked her where she got her hose with the black thread sewed up the back and Mama hadn't forgiven him yet.

But the thing everyone told me and told me again was that you just couldn't trust yourself with them. Nobody bet on Yankee tips, they might leave anything. Once someone even left a New York City subway token. Mama thought it a curiosity but not the equivalent of real money. Another one ordered one cup of coffee to go and twenty packs of sugar.

"They made 'road-liquor' out of it," Mabel said. "Just add an ounce of vodka and set it down by the engine exhaust for a month or so. It'll cook up into a bitter poison that'll knock you cross-eyed."

It sounded dangerous to me, but Mabel didn't think so. "Not that I would drink it," she'd say, "but I wouldn't fault a man who did."

They stole napkins, not one or two but a boxful at a time. Before we switched to sugar packets, they'd come in, unfold two or three napkins, open them like diapers, and fill them up with sugar before they left. Then they might take the knife and spoon to go with it. Once I watched a man take out a stack of napkins I was sure he was going to walk off with. But instead he sat there for thirty minutes making notes on them, then balled them all up and threw them away when he left.

My mama was scandalized by that. "And right over there on the shelf is a notebook selling for ten cents. What's wrong with these people?"

"They're living in the movies," Mabel whispered, looking back toward the counter.

"Yeah, Bette Davis movies," I added.

"I don't know about the movies." Harriet put her hand on Mama's shoulder. "But they don't live in the real world with the rest of us."

"No," Mama said, "they don't."

I take a bite of cherry tomato and hear Mama's voice again. *No,* she says.

"No," I say. I tuck my blouse into my skirt and shift in my shoes. If I close my eyes, I can see Mabel's brightly rouged cheekbones, Harriet's pitted skin, and my mama's shadowed brown eyes. When I go home tonight I'll write her about this party and imagine how she'll laugh about it all. The woman who was talking to me has gone off across the room to the other bar. People are giving up nibbling and going on to more serious eating. One of the men I work with every day comes over with a full plate and a wide grin.

"Boy," he drawls around a bite of the cornbread I contributed to the buffet, "I bet you sure can cook."

"Bet on it," I say, with my Mississippi accent. I swallow the rest of a cherry tomato and give him my heartbreaker's smile.

FOR JOURNALING AND DISCUSSION

1. Over one hundred years after the Civil War, relations between the North and South are still somewhat strained. What are the stereotypes that each group holds about the other? How are these stereotypes maintained and reinforced?
2. How does class affect our sense of region? How does class shape our regional stereotypes?
3. Harriet, one of the waitresses in this story, describes the Yankees that come through the diner by saying, "You and me, your mama, all of us, we just hold a place in the landscape for them. Far as they're concerned, once we're out of sight we just disappear." Do you think this attitude is created by regional differences, class conflicts, or both? How does Harriet's view about these wealthy Yankees fit with Robert D. Kaplan's description of the First World elites traveling in their air-conditioned limousines through Third World ghettos in "The Coming Anarchy" in Chapter 9?
4. Reginald McKnight, in "Confessions of a Wannabe Negro" in Chapter 2, describes having to deal with stereotypes about how he should behave, talk, act, and look from both blacks and whites. Allison similarly encounters stereotypes about how a southerner should act and talk. How do others' expectations and stereotypes affect both writers' behavior?
5. Polly Stewart, in "Regional Consciousness as a Shaper of Local History: Examples from the Eastern Shore" in this chapter, claims that one thing that creates a strong regional consciousness is the presence of a strong "us versus them" mentality. Considering the history of this country, how do we see the effect of this phenomenon on the South's regional identity? How is it present in Allison's story?

FOR RESEARCH AND EXPLORATION

1. Find a TV program with southern characters. How are they portrayed? Does their portrayal reinforce stereotypes about the South? How frequently do you

see southern lawyers, doctors, and other professionals in the media? What is the effect of this?

2. Research the post–Civil War period in the South. How did the northern carpet-baggers treat their southern "hosts"? Do we see any lingering effects of the abuse that the South suffered after the war in modern regional relations?

3. Interview three or four people who do not come from or live in the South. Ask them to share with you their impressions, views, and stereotypes about the South. What are the common answers? Now interview several southerners. What do they think of the outsiders' impressions? Why do they think that others hold these views?

First They Changed My Name
Caffilene Allen

Allen, who was born in McCaysville, Georgia, and grew up in Tennessee, has a bachelor's degree in journalism and a master's degree in counseling. She has worked as a journalist, editor, technical writer, career counselor, and public administrator.

Although I was born in 1951, I grew up speaking the English of an earlier century—a fact I was reminded of one Sunday afternoon at my mother's rest home. A nurse drew me aside and, blushing a little, said uncertainly, "Your mother says Esther has been 'progging' again."

Quickly, I put her mind at ease. How well I knew what progging meant. It had been the cause of all my spankings as a young child. Progging was the act of going through belongings that were not yours, digging into clothes drawers, purses, anything that contained intriguing items in its mysterious depths.

Though words like "progging" seemed strange to the nurse, the rest home was not more than 12 miles from Tumbling Creek, Tennessee, the town where I grew up. What we called "old" English was the only language that I knew until I was six years old, when I was dragged, wailing and sobbing, onto the school bus. In school, I soon discovered that the lack of communication links from Tumbling Creek to the outside world, as well as the clannish nature of the people who lived there, had allowed two separate cultures, divided by centuries, to exist within miles of each other. At the school, I heard such unfamiliar words as "church," "couch," "living room," "Christ," and "isn't." At home, we used "meetinghouse," "divanette," "front room," "the Good Man," and "ain't." I had vague memories of some of those strange words being spoken occasionally, but whoever had used them had been immediately accused of trying to be like the "town-doogers" (town dwellers). That these were the terms my teachers wanted me to use was incomprehensible.

Perhaps my confusion helps to explain why I was surprisingly meek when my teachers took it upon themselves to change my name, thinking that I had misspelled it. They were probably not too far from the truth. Coming from English, Scottish, Irish, and German stock that never left the Tennessee hill area, I inherited a linguistic pattern that was mostly oral and did not include the "th" sound. My mother was most likely trying to give me the good Irish name of Kathleen, but pronounced the "th" with an "f" sound and then spelled it phonetically for the nurse. All went well until I got to the first grade, where my teacher first decided that my name must be Caffie Lene but then settled on Kathleen. She told me I had to start writing it that way. My mother had no objection: whatever the God-Teacher said must be done—even if it meant changing my name.

In the second grade, my teacher told me that it was a law that everyone had to have a middle name, and that I should choose one for myself, so she could put it on my permanent record. I was delighted. Here was my chance to be Barbara Allen, the focus of an English ballad in which the heroine rejects "sweet William," supposedly causing his death. When they both eventually die of broken hearts, a rose grows from William's grave and a briar from Barbara Allen's. Why I wished to become the namesake of such a person is something that I have never wanted to examine too closely, but I was absolutely thrilled when my teacher wrote Kathleen Barbara Allen on my permanent record.

If I had known how much frustration would result from these changes, I would have been less thrilled. I soon discovered that Kathleen was one of the most common names in school, and that I was doomed to almost always have a number added after my name to distinguish me from the others with the same name. By the sixth grade I had developed a somewhat oversensitive approach to life, and began to notice that I was never Kathy #1 but always Kathy #2 or #3. I still had enough of my mother's awe for teachers that I was never able to express my displeasure to them.

I was given the chance to reclaim my name when, as a senior in high school, I was required to produce a birth certificate in order to graduate. By that time, I had almost forgotten about Caffilene, so I was very surprised to see the name on my birth certificate. My teachers were even more surprised, since the ones who had changed my name were long gone. A new problem loomed: I was one name on the school records and another on my birth certificate—therefore, I couldn't graduate. It took several teachers and a great deal of trouble to convince the bureaucracy I should be allowed to graduate.

Changing my name had a profound effect on my sense of identity, but my teachers had an equally long-lasting impact on my relationship with my mother, who believed that if the teacher said it was right, it was so. Having only a third-grade education obtained in a one-room country schoolhouse, she had the same reverence for schoolteachers as she had for the mysterious government, which kept her and her five children alive by sending a monthly Social Security check after my father was killed in the copper mines when I was 16 months old. To her, the government and the teachers were the keepers of some noble and powerful system upon which our survival and well-being depended, and we would be nothing less than ungrateful fools if we questioned their sterling wisdom. My four older brothers and sisters seemed to catch on sooner than I did: if my mother ever found out that the teachers she revered had a low opinion of her way of speech and life, she would be deeply hurt. For her peace of mind, my siblings learned to behave and speak one way at school and another way at home, whereas I would bound home, armed with linguistic rules that created a lifelong conflict between my mother and me. My first demand was that she allow me to call her Mommy rather than Miney (actually, her name was de Sara de Mina de Magdalene Pless Allen, but we couldn't get all of that out).

"What for?" was her reply. None of her ancestors had ever done such a thing.

"Because the teacher said I wasn't showing proper respect."

She became even more puzzled. "What does that mean?"

I had to admit that I didn't know. "But she said I was supposed to call you Mommy, and so I'm going to."

Well, the God-Teacher had said it, so it had to be.

She had an easier time with my second question. After I learned to read about Dick and Jane, I soon realized that everyone—even Jane—was sometimes referred to as "he." Having a strictly literal approach to life, I couldn't understand. When I asked my teachers why only the male pronoun was used, they laughed at me, so I took my question home to my mother. Readily, she replied with the only answer that a good Baptist could give, and one which she sincerely believed: "Because men are better than women." I soon learned to stop asking my mother questions.

By the fourth grade I had become increasingly ashamed of my mother and almost came to despise her for her manner and speech. One evening at the supper table when she was speaking improper English, chewing with her mouth open, and propping her elbows on the table, I found myself staring in open disgust. Suddenly, she stopped speaking in mid-sentence and glared at me, her face turning purple. By now, I was familiar enough with this scene to know what was going to happen next. Sure enough, I escaped from my seat just in time to miss being hit by the fork that she threw at my eyes. "Stop looking at me like I was a freak!" she screamed. Later, after the dishes were washed and put away, I went into the kitchen to get a glass of water. Through the screen door, I saw my mother sitting on the back steps, watching the sun go down behind the Blue Ridge Mountains. Her shoulders were shaking with silent sobs. For the first time, I sensed the depth of her isolation and despair; I also got my first inkling that she was not the one who was in the wrong. An intelligent, beautiful woman raised in a fundamentalist culture that assured her that she was nothing simply because she was a woman, she now was confronted with the scorn, brought

home to her by her daughter, of those whom she had once revered as her benevolent protectors. Now she was sure that she was truly worthless.

Even though that moment gave me some understanding of my mother,
it did not give me enough to change my ways totally. I continued to try to convince her that she needed to speak and act more like the people in town. I
didn't have much success by myself, but I eventually got help from a rather
surprising source. My mother had adamantly refused to get a telephone or a
car, which were becoming more and more common in Tumbling Creek by
the mid-1960s, so it was an incredible surprise to me when, one day when I
was in the seventh grade, she brought home a television. Never in my life, not
before or since, have I felt such a sense of wonder as when the television was
first turned on in our house and people showed up on the screen in my living room who were fun to watch and listen to. Suddenly, the mountains
seemed a little less lonely and my mother a little less mean.

By this time, I was pretty much considered an oddity by everyone who knew
me. Since I always ate first, with the men rather than with the women, who had to
wait until the men were finished before they could even sit down at the table, I
became a third sex; people would say, "the men, the women, and Kathy." My love
for books and writing seemed especially odd and somewhat slothlike to those
working in the fields and the house morning, noon, and night in order to survive
(which seemed to include everyone except me). And more than once, students
in my class had been sent to the principal's office for calling me a nigger-lover.
(No one in Tumbling Creek or Copperhill had ever met a person of color, but
racism existed there, and my support of the civil rights movement increased my
isolation.) But there, on the television, were people who gave me some inkling of
another world out there where I might find others with ideas like mine. Peter,
Paul, and Mary showed up singing "Blowing in the Wind" at a civil rights march.
One afternoon, while my mother and I were watching *Who Do You Trust?*, newscasters interrupted to report a confrontation between Governor George Wallace
and a black student trying to enter the University of Alabama. My spirits rose.
Although at first they all seemed to be losing, at least there were people out there
fighting for the same things that I thought were right.

I picked up "correct" pronunciation and grammar from TV, as well as an
accent that gradually replaced my east Tennessee twang. My mother, on the
other hand, changed the words to suit her own style of speech. Once, she told
me that her favorite TV show was "Feenanzie." When I told her there was no
such show, she retorted that there certainly was: "It's the one that has Hoss
Cartwright and Little Joe and advertises Chevrolets."

Nevertheless, my mother did let television temper her cultural approach
to life. She stopped trying to compliment my friends by telling them they were
"just as fat as a little pig." She learned to stop asking the kids I brought home
if they wanted a "dope," which meant a soft drink in Tumbling Creek. Most important, through TV, she learned to understand me and the ways that I had already adopted, and so television made life a little easier for both of us.

Many years have gone by. I grew up and left Tumbling Creek, as my teachers and my mother always knew I would. But even now, thinking back on those times and conflicts, I find my emotions toward my mother and my teachers still bound up in the same love-hate web most of us reserve for our families only. In a way, my teachers were my family. They were the first to encourage my love for learning, to find scholarships for me, to bring me books to read during the long, lonely summer months, to encourage my writing, to express their belief that I could even make a living as a writer. But at the same time, they taught me to hate my culture, to despise people who had a different linguistic approach to life, even if one of those people was my mother. After many long years, I have managed finally to reconcile to some extent my world with my mother's. Regaining a sense of pride in my Appalachian heritage and an appreciation for who my mother was as a person was one of the hardest and most valuable tasks of my adult life.

FOR JOURNALING AND DISCUSSION

1. As a child, Allen struggled with both loving and being embarrassed by her mother. Write an essay in which you reflect on your own similar conflicts with your family.
2. How is Allen's regional identity compounded by her social class?
3. Allen tells us that television was her window to the outside world, and that it taught her how to talk and act outside of her region. Do you think television unites this country? Do you think television has negative effects on regionalism?
4. In "Speak, That I May See Thee" in Chapter 3, Paul Fussell describes some of the links between language and class. In this essay, Allen adds the factor of region to this mix as well. Write an essay in which you apply Fussell's analysis of language and class to Allen's experiences growing up in Appalachia.

FOR RESEARCH AND EXPLORATION

1. Traditionally the American education system has been seen as the great melting pot—melting down regional, ethnic, religious, and racial differences to create one homogenized American student. Interview an elementary school teacher in your region. Ask him or her if this philosophy still prevails. What kinds of things does he or she do in the classroom to help students understand their regional identity? Does anything undermine his or her efforts to create a stronger sense of regionalism in the students?
2. Outsiders frequently believe that Appalachia is filled with uneducated, poverty-stricken hicks. Do some research into Appalachia's past and present. Why does the region have these stereotypes? To what extent are they deserved or undeserved?
3. Several years ago Brooks Eliot Wigginton, a schoolteacher in Appalachia, together with his students, began publishing the *Foxfire* books detailing the culture, crafts, and stories of the region. Do some research into this project. What were its effects on the young participants? on the region as a whole? Did these books help to alter or to reinforce our national stereotypes about Appalachia?

South of Haunted Dreams: A Ride Through Slavery's Old Back Yard

Eddy L. Harris

Harris graduated from Stanford University in 1977 and went on to study and write in London and Paris. In addition to South of Haunted Dreams, *he has written two other critically acclaimed travel books—* Mississippi Solo *and* Native Stranger. *Harris now lives in St. Louis.*

South of Owensboro, Kentucky, a wooden sign hangs from a rusted post. DAVIESS COUNTY COON HUNTERS' CLUB, the sign says, and as I ride past, a cold hand touches the small of my back. A shiver runs up my spine. The road I am on, Highway 231, goes over the Ohio River at Owensboro. I have crossed into the South.

Instinctively my hand locks tighter around the grip of my motorcycle and twists open the throttle. The engine roars. The bike—a blue BMW—quickens. I hold on tight. I crouch forward on the bike and hurry past the sign, hurry past the evil spirits that hold the thing upright and steady. These many years later, the South still owns my nightmares and haunts my memory. Like links in the heavy chains dragged by ghosts, the images form one by one and rattle round me, weighing me down, terrifying me.

Coon, Ape, Pickaninny, Darkie, Nigra, Nigger, Boy: these are a few of the names blacks were once and not so long ago called in the Deep South, and when a white man said, "We're going coon huntin' tonight, boy," a colored man in those days never knew quite how to take it. I imagine the white man's voice menacing, perhaps teasing a little, or even sporting and jocular. The knife edge of terror would slice into the backbone of even the bravest black man, as indeed now it slices into mine.

Those were the nightmare days of our history, a time not long enough ago when killing a nigger in the South was no more an offense than jaywalking. That era has passed us now, times do change (I hope), but the memory of those days has not died.

Incredibly those old times are remembered now as gentler than today, somehow looked upon fondly by many southern whites longing for the glory that has been lost and the simplicity that went with it, the chivalry, the courtesy, the gallantry, and of course the southern hospitality.

"The South shall rise again," they say, hoping once more, I suppose, for a time when white supremacy was the rule, a time when life seemed simple and easy. The lines were clearly drawn, the boundaries set: blacks and whites, Indians, Asians, Hispanics, and Jews all knew their places in society, where they could and could not go, what they could and could not do, who they could and could not be. It was a white man's country, all right, a white man's world, and if you were lucky enough to have been born white, all was right with the world. The land was prosperous and generous, peaceful for all, the bounty trickling down supposedly from rich to poor, from white to black. As long as no one upset the delicate balance, the world seemed to spin in a greased groove.

But behind the storefront of gentility hid, and perhaps still hides, an edifice of white supremacy and segregation so rigid and so codified that in 1949 the racist society of South Africa could have turned to the American South to learn the system of apartheid. Beneath the myth of chivalry and gallantry lay a reality of paternalism and repression that lent shame to the miracle of human justice and equality upon which this country was founded. Beneath the veneer of largess lurked a poverty that would rival the worst conditions of the poorest Third World nations. And beneath it all lay a core of hatred and commingled violence, and the politics of injustice.

Perhaps in a way, then, the kindly old South is responsible for the violent present we have inherited. Since the founding of the republic the South has dictated and defined us. Perhaps the South, more even than the wild wild West, more in fact than any other region, is responsible for who we are as a people and as a nation. Since the very beginning the South has compromised us.

This is the South into which I had crossed, the South of mythic reality:

In 1945, on his way home after serving his country during the Second World War, a black veteran named Isaac Woodward was attacked by a gang of angry whites at a bus station. He had used the wrong men's room. There was no men's room for coloreds and the one he had used was reserved for whites only. The white mob gouged out his eyes. He was still in uniform.

In 1955, a black male named Emmett Till went from Chicago to Money, Mississippi, to visit relatives in the South. He didn't know any better, whistled at a white woman, and that night two men dragged him from his bed and beat him savagely. They shot him, then pitched his body into the Tallahatchie River. An all-white jury found the two men innocent of murder. Emmett Till was fourteen years old.

In 1958, Jimmy Wilson was tried in an Alabama court and convicted of stealing $1.95 from Estelle Barker, a white woman. Wilson was black. He was sentenced to die. The Alabama Supreme Court upheld the conviction.

In 1955, while trying to organize blacks to vote in an upcoming election, Lamar Smith was shot dead in front of the courthouse—in broad daylight, by a white man. His assassin was never indicted. No one would admit to seeing a white man kill a black man.

There's more. There's Medgar Evers. There's Virgil Lamar Ware. There's Herbert Lee and Louis Allen.

And these are only the most notable ones.

There's the Groveland Four, the four black men in Groveland, Florida, accused of raping a white woman. They were beaten and tortured by the police until finally they confessed. And then they were sentenced to die.

There's Addie Mae Collins, Denise McNair, Carole Robertson, and Cynthia Wesley—four young children blown up when their Birmingham, Alabama, church was bombed one Sunday morning in September 1963.

The list goes on and on. And on.

Their crimes, the real crimes of all these men, women, and little children? That they were born black, already damned by the color of their skin, born nonwhite in a white man's world, a country where being black has always been the greatest curse, has always been the greatest crime, such an offense, in fact, such a heinous and damaging insult that in 1957 the South Carolina Supreme Court ruled that it was indeed a grave error to confuse a white person with a black one, and a libelous act to call the white person a Negro by mistake. Even without proof of actual harm, the injured white party could sue for damages—and win.

Being black was considered such a crime that white persons keeping company with blacks were as guilty as spies caught consorting with the enemy. In 1958 an ordinance was passed in Montgomery, Alabama, forbidding even the friendly association of blacks and whites. "It shall be unlawful," the statute read, "for white and colored persons to play together . . . in any game of cards, dice, dominoes, checkers, pool, billiards, softball, basketball, football, golf, track, and at swimming pools or in any athletic contest."

Being black determined where you could live, where your kids went to school, who you could sit next to on a bus, whom you could love and marry. It was against the law in twenty-nine states (not just in the South) for whites and blacks to marry. The law in Alabama: *"The legislature shall never pass any law to legalize marriage between any white person and a negro, or a descendant of a negro."*

White women making love with blacks in Florida, $1,000 fine. (No penalty for white men with black women.)

Ministers performing marriage ceremonies between blacks and whites in South Carolina—$500 fine, twelve months in jail.

Texas: *"If any white person and negro shall knowingly intermarry with each other in this state, or having so intermarried in or out of the state shall continue to live together as man and wife within this state, they shall be confined in the penitentiary not less than two nor more than five years."*

Georgia: *"It shall be unlawful for a white person to marry anyone except a white person."*

Being black was limitation, and one drop of black blood was enough; one African ancestor three, four, five generations ago, and you were legally shit.

Alabama: *"The term 'negro' includes mulatto . . . a person of mixed blood, descended on the part of the father or mother from negro ancestors, without reference to or limit of time or number of generations."*

Arkansas: *"The words 'person of negro race' shall be held to apply to and include any person who has in his or her veins any negro blood whatever."*

Louisiana classified blacks more carefully. Negroes, 3/4 or more Negro blood; Griffe, 1/2 Negro, 1/2 mulatto; Mulatto, 1/2 Negro, 1/2 white; Quadroon, 1/4 Negro, 3/4 white; Octoroon, 1/8 Negro, 7/8 white.

This is the South I had entered and had chosen to motorcycle across, where Governor George Wallace of Alabama had the battle flag of the old Confederacy raised as a symbol of hate, a symbol of segregation and white supremacy to fly above the dome of the capitol.

"Segregation now, segregation forever," he declared during his inauguration address. Later, for all the world to see and hear, he stood in the doorway of the University of Alabama and announced that he would defy even the authority of the U.S. Supreme Court. He would not allow the public schools in Alabama to be integrated.

In Oxford, Mississippi, riots broke out when James Meredith went to register for classes at the university there. The police refused to protect him from the armed and angry crowds shouting invectives, hurling insults and stones, threatening his life. Federal marshals had to escort him. The National Guard had to be summoned. Just so a lone black man could go to college. And not a single white voice to offer him support nor lend him courage. It was 1962. I was six years old.

I cannot remember the details of my birthday party that same year, but I have heard the stories of those angry days too many times, have seen the images often enough that I cannot forget them. I remember as if I had been there. I remember as if it had happened to me.

I remember the signs—WE CATER TO WHITE ONLY. NIGGERS MEXICANS PUERTO RICANS NOT ALLOWED—and I know the shame and the fear. I burn with the same rage, feel the degradation that generations of black men have had to endure, men like my father, a strong and arrogant man who is a hero to me and yet who had to walk lightly in the shadow of white men, sleeping in his car at the side of the road because unless he was lucky enough to find a colored hotel when he traveled, he would not have been given a room for the night, nor allowed to eat when hungry, drink when thirsty, or ever enter by the front door. He would have had to call the lowest white man "sir," would have had to remove his hat and bow his head whenever a white woman passed. Afraid of a lynching, fearing for his life, he would never have sassed back, would never have hit back, would have put up with every indignity. He knew the boundaries, as all black men did. He would not have crossed over.

As a young man during the Great Depression he hoboed around the country, as many did—no matter the color of skin. He hitchhiked. He hopped freight trains. He slept out in the rain. He tried to find a little work wherever he could, following the promise, even the rumor of a job. Eventually he found himself in the South.

"It wasn't too good for black folks up north," he used to say. "But down south! Hell, no northern black man ever wanted to spend too much time in the South."

But he went there anyway, tempting fate, testing his limits.

"It would have been about 1934 or '35," he said, repeating a story he had told many times. He would take a deep breath each time and pucker his lips to help him remember. And each time he would wince. From somewhere within a tangle of wistful melancholy, pain and shame, the memory would awaken.

"I was just a boy," he said. "Barely twenty years old. Brother . . . " (He often calls me brother.) "Brother, it's so long ago I can't even remember the name of that little town. But it was somewhere on the Ohio River, not too far from Louisville, Kentucky. And what I was doing there, I'm only guessing. Passing through, mostly."

Passing through until he met a young woman who was lovely to look at, he said, and very nice to talk to. He decided to hang around awhile.

"Yeah, she was pretty," he said. "She was very pretty."

He might not remember the name of the town, might not really want to, but this woman he will never forget.

"Her hair was shiny black, soft and wavy," he said. "Her skin was smooth and tight. She was black, but her complexion was light enough that she could have passed for white. They called them high yellow in those days. I don't know what they call them now."

My father, very light-skinned himself, and this pretty young woman started keeping company. He said they made a handsome couple.

But then one day an old black man with a limp came to warn my father to stay away from her. The old man raised the stick he used for a cane and shook it, but he never said why, and my father just ignored him.

"I must have thought he was jealous or something," said my father. "But man! That wasn't it at all."

One night as my father was walking alone down a dark road near the river, a car pulled up. Four angry white men dressed in sheets jumped out, surrounded my father, trapped him. There was nowhere to run, no way to attempt to get away without giving them an excuse to shoot. Two of the men pulled out shotguns. One man had a pistol, another carried a big stick. All they needed was half an excuse.

"Boy, didn't you get word to stop fooling around up there on that hill?"

That's what they said to him. Then they grabbed him and started shoving him back and forth.

"Ain't you just been told to stop hanging around that girl Sally Ann?"

"But, mister, that girl's colored," my father said.

"That don't mean she spends her time with nigger men. Don't you know whose colored girl that is? Don't you know who she belongs to?"

"No, sir, I sure don't."

"Then, boy, you need to find out. And you're going to find out tonight."

"Nigger, you think you could drink all the water in this here Ohio River? We're going to throw your coon ass off this damned bridge and find out."

"Naw, let's don't kill him tonight. Let's have a little sport. Let's see how fast he can skedaddle."

"Let's light a fire under his black ass and watch him squirm."

"Okay, nigger, did you hear that? We ain't going to kill you tonight. We're going give you until noontime tomorrow to get the hell out of town. If we see you around here after that, we're going to hunt you down like a dog and then we're going to drown your black ass. You got that?"

"Yes, sir," my father said. He must have said "yes, sir" ten hundred times that night.

"We're going to bind your ass with barbed wire and tie you to something that ain't going to float. Then we're going to dump you in the river. You understand?"

"Yes, sir."

"Tomorrow noon. Now you be gone."

"Mister," my father said, cowering. "Mister, I don't need that much time."

The way he said it, imitating himself so many years after, was hilarious. His eyes crinkled with shameless fear, his bowed head cocked to one side, his voice humble, trembling.

He went to the station that very night and that arrogant young man, my father, suddenly a coward, was on the next bus to anywhere.

It used to be a story we laughed about. It isn't so funny anymore.

The Black Codes of the old South defined how blacks were to act. These guidelines of etiquette between the races were established during slavery days, but they were still the order of the day a hundred years after. Louisiana's: *"Free persons of color ought never to insult or strike white people, nor pressure to conceive themselves equal to the white; but on the contrary they ought to yield to them in every occasion, and never speak or answer to them but with respect, under penalty of imprisonment according to the nature of the offense."* To act otherwise was to risk a lynching, have your home burned, your family driven out into the street. And no one, black or white, would lift a finger to help.

Jesse Brooks was raised in the South, in Eads, Tennessee. He should have known better. But he had relatives in St. Louis, not quite the North and not quite the South either, and poor Jesse spent too much time there one summer. He learned from his young cousins that it was all right to fight the white boys from the next neighborhood over.

On the corner of Ashland and Lambden was a vacant lot where the boys, black and white, played ball. When the games were over, the boys would fight— simple as that—and then go home. It was, in a way, friendly fighting, the kind of crazy thing young boys do, playing one minute, fighting the next, with some semblance of fairness, equality even. Poor Jesse. He went back to Eads,

Tennessee, and thought he could expect blacks and whites to get along the way they did in St. Louis. He got too arrogant. He fought with the white boys in Tennessee, and they didn't like it. He went too far when, like the other boys, he tried to buy candy on credit at the local grocer's.

"What makes you think you can buy candy on credit, boy? You sure you got your daddy's permission?"

"Of course I do," he said. "He's my daddy, ain't he? I can buy what I want. Just like the other boys."

They didn't like his attitude.

"You ain't like the other boys," he was told. They said he was a sassy little nigger and they chased him that day through the town.

The black folks in Eads were afraid to help him. Every door he passed was suddenly shut to him. The black folks said, "God help you, son, but please don't stop here." They were that afraid.

When the white folks caught up with Jesse they threw one end of a rope over the limb of an apple tree, the other end they tied around his neck. Maybe they just wanted to scare him. Maybe they wanted to warn him what happens to smart niggers. Maybe they hadn't intended to and went a bit too far, but they lynched him just the same and left him hanging there. He was sixteen years old. He was my father's cousin. And this was another story, not so funny, my father used to tell.

No wonder my father drinks as much whiskey as he does.

No wonder black men fear the South.

I too am afraid, for I too carry the curse of dark skin, but my fear is different.

Can you imagine how it is to waken every morning and know your father and relatives had to act the coward, had to act the "good Negro" instead of the "bad nigger," had to adopt attitudes of subservience? When Blackamericans look at themselves and at their history, this in part is what we see: this violence, these constant reminders of being unwanted and unloved, of being treated as if we were less than human, these shadows of indignation, indignity and shame. Black men and women have had to bear them like crosses and there have been too few Simons (from Cyrene) to help with the load.

Forgive me if I rant, but you cannot know how I have cried and despaired and nearly given myself over to the dark gods of bitterness and frustration. You cannot know, unless I now tell you, how the anger often wells up in me lately and I am driven to the edges of violence and hate and I want insanely to fight men bigger than myself and burn buildings down, set fire to their homes, their happiness, their way of life. They and I alike pretend not to know whence comes this anger, for it seems in my case to be especially unfounded, to make little sense. I was not born into slavery or into abject circumstance. Luckily, for me and for those around me, the gods in whose laps we sit saw fit that I should not be so cursed, for then surely I would have been a murderer, indeed a butcher.

Instead, I travel to the South to confront the source of my anger. I am half hoping to hurt someone. At the same time I am longing to find a new South, a new America, hoping with heart and soul that all is not hopelessness and despair. For if nothing has changed in these thirty years, then we as a people are living a great lie and are no different from other nations that now are crumbling in the crucible of disunity and ethnic discord. Then we are not a nation wholly joined by a common culture, but instead are separated by color and class and religion and judged by them and by them alone. How easy then it will be to surrender to the viler angels of my nature. How easy it will be to break the arm of anyone calling me "boy," or the neck of someone who calls me "nigger."

Afraid? Yes. And my fear is indeed different from my father's fear, different perhaps from the fears of other black men too, for I am afraid not only for the things that might happen to me as I wander south. I fear as well for the things I might do.

I am not my father, not of my father's generation. I was not tempered in the kiln of Jim Crow. I was instead forged in a new furnace, hammered out of a new tradition—wholly connected to the old, as all tradition must be, but so utterly different. I do not come to the South with hat in hand, head bowed, timid and humble. I stand tall and firmly planted. I am not small. I take up plenty of space. I am proud of who and what I am, as arrogant as my father ever was. And I burn with an anger that is rightfully his, but that is anger nonetheless. And I am afraid, am almost certain in fact, that before this trip ends someone will have died.

Slowly I come to realize that I am not the man I once was, not the man who once believed he was who he was from the inside out, that the blackness of my skin is merely a physical attribute like being bearded or being tall.

No. I am different now. I have awakened from my slumber.

DAVIESS COUNTY COON HUNTERS' CLUB. The sign helps to awaken me. The sign helps me remember. I am black, and being black matters.

I turn the bike around and go back—slowly this time—back to the sign and to the arrow pointing down a narrow lane that disappears around a sharp bend.

The sign is wooden, its painted letters fading in the hot sun, its post rusting. The arrow painted on it shows the way, and down this road I ride.

The countryside smells faintly of tobacco, the scent borne on a gentle wind that riffles over the fields. Kentucky is tobacco country, just about the northernmost edge, but corn country too, and the fields are green with tall stalks. The corn tops are ripening. Their tassels once flowing gold have dried and turned to brown, dangling now, swaying in the delicate breeze that blows a hush across the valley and leads the eye from wave to wave of stalks bending. Deep into the distance the eye floats over an endless sea of meadows in bloom and corn fields that change color beneath sun and cloud-shadow from gold and green to amber and orange.

The road winds through these fields on one side; trees, shrubs, and vines on the other. Beyond the trees a creek courses in the valley below. A dilapidated footbridge tries to cross the creek but has rotted with age and is ready to collapse halfway across. On the near edge of these trees there is a small white frame house for sale. Nearby, a shed with a corrugated metal roof waits to fall over. Next to the shed a small greenhouse decays. The roof has caved in, the windows are broken out, not yet boarded up. The house, now a shack, is overgrown with weeds and consumed by the undergrowth. Saplings and vines creep through the walls and climb through the gaps in the roof. Nature has staked its claim on all that once seemed it would last forever. But nothing is permanent. All eventually passes away.

When the road bends, the trees end. Cultivation runs on from there, the fields owning lines of sight from here to the horizon.

There ought to be a huge plantation house up on the hill, these fields of corn should be fields of cotton perhaps; old Negro laborers stooped over their hoes and baking in the hot sun should be happily singing their woes in these fields, for this is the South and that is the image, and down this road is the Coon Hunters' Club.

I expect that when I arrive there I will find a bunch of big-bellied rednecks sitting around an old wood-burning stove. They will be chewing tobacco and wearing caps advertising seed corn, tractors, and transmission companies. And they will be drinking beer, of course, telling stories and dreaming about the good old days, dreaming about lynching niggers.

Up on a hill a farmhouse does rise, but a modern one. Big metal silos glimmer in the sunlight. At the foot of the hill there is a sign for a school bus stop.

A car approaches and passes. The driver throws up a wave, does not stop, but goes on. From the yard surrounding a house on another hill, a child, awed, I suppose, by this big blue bike I ride, waves and runs down to the edge of the street. And I, not knowing how to take this waving, these friendly gestures, toss up my hand and continue on.

A couple of miles farther on, there is a right turn. One sign on the corner says GOD IS THE ANSWER, another sign promises GOD ANSWERS PRAYER. Just beyond the signs, the Coon Hunters' Club. Not much of a clubhouse, just a concrete box made of cinder blocks, a squat building only one story tall, four small windows on the front. But there is indeed a wood-burning stove inside, revealed by an exhaust pipe coming through a hole in the wall. An air-conditioner unit sticks out of the opposite wall and promises relief from the intense autumn heat. And perhaps there is beer inside to help with the same relief, but at this I can only guess, for the place is deserted. No one answers my knocking at the door. I will not this day get to see the inside of the Coon Hunters' Club, nor talk to any of the coon hunters. I will have to wait until some other time to be glared at, threatened, turned away, called names, and made afraid.

Some other time, of course, will be soon enough.

The motorcycle revs to its highest-pitched whine and continues on, following the road over these rolling hills and around every bend, leading me on. I have no idea where the road will go.

FOR JOURNALING AND DISCUSSION

1. What is the effect of the italicized legal excerpts that run throughout this writing? How do they complement the story Harris tells?
2. Why do you think Harris is making this journey?
3. Why is anger such a defining emotion for Harris? Why is he—even though he did not personally suffer under the Jim Crow laws—so much angrier than his father, who did?
4. Harris says, "Since the founding of the republic the South has dictated and defined us. Perhaps the South, more even than the wild wild West, more in fact than any other region, is responsible for who we are as a people and as a nation." Do you agree with this? Why or why not?
5. In "India" in Chapter 2, Richard Rodriguez, like Harris, describes being pulled back to the homeland of his parents in order to learn more about himself and his ethnicity. Harris's love/hate relationship with the South, like Rodriguez's with Mexico, is shaped by history, race, and family. Write an essay explaining how each of these writers uses place as a metaphor for his own conflicts over race and history. Where do they diverge?

FOR RESEARCH AND EXPLORATION

1. Research the history of the word "coon." Why is the "Coon Hunters' Club" sign so terrifying for Harris?
2. Interview several people about their recollections of and involvement with the civil rights movement in the 1960s. Do their perceptions change any depending on the region that they lived in at the time?
3. Harris alludes to several historical figures who were linked to the civil rights movement, including Jimmy Wilson, Lamar Smith, Medgar Evers, and the Groveland Four. Pick one and research the person. Explain why that individual was so significant to the struggle for civil rights. Why does Harris refer to him or her here?

A Place of Grace

Jill Nelson

Nelson is a freelance journalist, contributing to periodicals such as Ms., Village Voice, *and* Essence. *For over four years she worked as a staff writer for the* Washington Post. *Her memoir* Volunteer Slavery: My Authentic Negro Experience *is based on her experiences as a black woman at this nearly all-white, all-male corporation.*

Here, honking is not the horns of cars beneath the hands of impatient mo-
torists, but a goose in a garden on Grace's Point, strategically placed and guard-
ing its turf from hungry deer.

Likewise, the ever-present roar is that of wave against rock and sand as
the Atlantic Ocean pummels the circumference of this tiny island, not of too
many voices in too small a space raised in complaint or anger.

The soft, constant whispering is not of people asking, imploring, suggesting, but of the wind off the ocean as it whips across this island of few trees,
rustling the gold-red leaves of shadbush, the gray bayberry, jingling the bright
red berries that adorn the shiny-leafed black alder as Indian summer melts into
fall. The wind provides a cushion of air for the northern harriers, peregrines,
monarch butterflies, gulls—island residents—and dozens of other birds who
stop off on the long migration south.

For a city woman, this is a place first of absence. Of people, of the familiar noises and odors of the town or metropolis, of all the things there are to do
demanding to be done. It is, at first, disconcerting, this natural silence that
seems somehow unnatural. But not for long. In no time at all I am amazed,
awed, and seduced. Without distractions, I fall into the rhythm of the island,
the water, the land, the animals: being an animal too, it is not very long before
my human rhythms fall into step with those that preceded me.

Perhaps it is as it should be that for the insects, birds, and plants that
thrive here, some of them endangered species, Block Island is a place not of
absence, but of presence. A place where nature and human nature conspire to
make survival possible.

Surely the trip to Block Island, twelve miles off the coast of Rhode Island,
should have forewarned me. The trip, a bit over an hour, is about separation,
isolation, distance. There is something about islands, about being on a piece
of land in the middle of water, that simplifies everything: desires, yearnings,
thoughts. Once arrived over a roiling sea, the bow of the boat drenched with
spray, my stomach slipping slightly, ears cold and face red from the chill wind
of late October, there is a sense of finality, commitment, surety. Islands do not
suffer well the antsy or indecisive, means of escape being few and far between.
Better to submit to the will of the island, relax, and enjoy it.

Everywhere, there is the feeling of absence. It is late fall and the summer
people, fifteen thousand strong, are mostly gone, returning the island to its winter population of eight hundred. The bars, restaurants, and dockside souvenir
shops are shuttered for the winter. Nearly everyone goes to the same restaurant
for lunch because it's the only one open. Still, it is not simply the absence of
summer and people, but of structures. In a nation where it often seems a dominant credo might be summed up, "If it's beautiful, we will build," on Block
Island beauty still outweighs buildings. This is, as you might figure, by design.

There are about 1,200 houses on Block Island, double the number there
were twenty years ago, but not nearly as many as they legally could be—
2,400—or would be if development were allowed to go unchecked. Those who

grew up here, the old-timers, asked to point out buildings that weren't on the island twenty years ago, insist it's easier to point out the few that were. Guided by their mind's eye it is possible to see the island as it was: sparsely populated, the rolling, treeless hills dissected by stone fences, farmland looking like the English countryside on an island in New England, sweeping vistas of grassland, fences, cliffs, straight across to the sea.

Even so, in the here and now, many of the vistas remain. Walk up a rise on the 274-acre Lewis-Dickens Farm and you look dead across farmland to the ocean sparkling in the distance, the view unbroken, by choice and sacrifice.

Or stand at the overlook and gaze down into Rodman's Hollow, its carpet of burnt orange, red, green, an occasional yellow as fall orchestrates its colorful symphony, unbroken by condos, quaint summer cottages, Dairy Queens, or fast-food joints. It was here, in the early 1970s, that the conservation of Block Island began, hastened by the arrival of developers and spearheaded by the commitment of local working people.

The spirit began much earlier, spearheaded by Elizabeth Dickens, island resident and lover, who from 1909 until her death in 1963 kept daily records of bird sightings, who for decades taught schoolchildren what she knew about birds, nature, respect for the island. Absent for twenty years, her legacy remains present.

It seems that around every bend in the road there's a pond, "kettle holes," as they're rightly called, formed by the movement of glaciers. People here like to say there are 365, one for every day of the year; others, splitting hairs and dismissing the poetic hyperbole, say 360 is a more accurate number. The largest is Great Salt Pond, but there is Fresh Pond; Deep Pond; Sachem, Harbor, and Middle ponds; ponds everywhere. Good fresh and saltwater fishing too, clams, lobsters, an abundance of seafood almost begging to be eaten.

In the morning I drive past Seal Cove, where northern seals spend the winter, on my way to Mohegan Bluff. Illuminated in the glare of the car's lights are clumps of seaside golden rod, swamp rose, high-tide bush with its fluffy, tiny, white blossoms, salt-marsh hay. Rounding a bend, two deer stroll slowly, gracefully into the undergrowth, unconcerned. Nor am I startled, so fully has the natural beauty of this place, the juxtaposition of absence and presence, overtaken me.

Mohegan Bluff is where the original inhabitants of Block Island, the Manisse, fought off a party of fifty Mohegans in 1590. Little good it did them when the Europeans arrived. Like the Mohegans, the Manisse are long gone. But though absent, their spirit pervades in respect for the land, nature, a sense of balance.

It is cold up here on the bluff, the sky blue-black, the wind whipping off the ocean. Slowly, the sky moves from darkest to less so, peeling back layered shades of blue to reveal yellow, orange, purple, red. A single star stands sentry against the night.

The sun is a long time coming. Gulls swoop low against the ocean, settle confidently on water textured by the wind, their shrill shrieks breaking the silence as they swoop up and away.

Once the sun comes it is immediate: pale blue, yellow, purple, red, orange—*voilà!* It is risen. It moves fast, a red-orange ball on a pedestal. Ascending, it turns pale, illuminating grasslands, dunes, rocks far below on the beach drenched by sea spray, houses in the distance, showing something where, under cover of darkness, there appeared to be nothing. This is the delicate balance of absence and presence, of the important seen and equally crucial unseen, of peaceful coexistence between nature and people that Block Island struggles to achieve.

A city woman, warming up, can dig it.

FOR JOURNALING AND DISCUSSION

1. Nelson explains that her view of this island is influenced by the fact that she is a city dweller. How has her life in the city affected her perceptions? What does she notice that most islanders might miss? What things does she probably miss that they would see?
2. Nelson ends this piece by saying, "This is the delicate balance of absence and presence, of the important seen and equally crucial unseen, of peaceful coexistence between nature and people that Block Island struggles to achieve." What does she mean by this balance between absence and presence?
3. Nelson, as an outsider, sees only the beauty and isolation of Block Island. Now rewrite her essay from the point of view of an imaginary islander. Describe your home, your feelings about the island, and your reaction to the outsiders and tourists like Nelson.
4. Do you think Nelson would be able to live on this island year round? Why or why not? Would you be able to?
5. Compare Nelson's description of the attempts to keep Block Island underdeveloped with Robert D. Kaplan's description of overdevelopment and its frightening consequences in "The Coming Anarchy" in Chapter 9. In the future that Kaplan describes, will there be room for underdeveloped places like Block Island? Will they be available only to the very rich?

FOR RESEARCH AND EXPLORATION

1. Nelson describes a conflict on the island between developers and those who wish to maintain the island's natural state. This is occurring with greater and greater frequency worldwide. Research the effects—both positive and negative—that increased development has had on areas like Block Island; the Florida Keys, the Virgin Islands, and the rain forests of Africa and South America are a few examples. What happens to the local people and culture? What are the benefits? What are the costs? Should the federal government be doing more to control development in our remaining "natural" places, or should these decisions be left to the local people?
2. Nelson, like Louise Erdrich in her essay "Big Grass" and Ned Wollaston in Jonathan Raban's essay "The Unlamented West" earlier in this chapter, seems to feel almost spiritually attached to this island and its beauty. Place seems to affect

these three individuals in a similar way. Research the ways that other groups and peoples throughout history have linked spirituality and geography. Offer some suggestions as to why you think this happens.
3. This essay was originally published by an environmental group called the Nature Conservancy, which takes a unique approach to preserving our environment. Research its policies and approaches. How successful have they been? Can this approach make any real difference in preventing the kind of worldwide environmental degradation described by Kaplan in "The Coming Anarchy"?

New York Blues
Edward Hougland

Hougland, a writer and teacher, was born in New York City. His novels include Cat Man *and* Seven Rivers West, *and he has written over one hundred essays and articles as well. Hougland, who has taught at numerous colleges and universities including Columbia, Rutgers, and the universities of Iowa and California, now lives in Manhattan.*

Most of us realized early on that we are not our "brother's keeper." Yet perhaps we also came to recognize that "there but for the grace of God go I." If the jitters we experience on a particularly awful afternoon were extended and became prolonged until we couldn't shake them off, after a few drastic months we might end up sleeping on the sidewalk too. Character is fate, we like to say: hard work and fidelity (or call it regularity) will carry the day. And this is just true enough to believe. But chemistry is also fate: the chemistry of our tissues and the chemistry of our brains. We know that just as some people among us get cancer at a pitiably young age, others go haywire through no fault of their ethics, pluck, or upbringing.

Still, what do most of us do when we notice a hungry, disoriented person slumped on the street in obvious despair? Why, we pass quickly by, averting our eyes toward an advertisement, the stream of taxis, a shop's window dressing. Part of the excitement of a great metropolis is how it juxtaposes starvelings blowing on their fingers in front of Bergdorf Goodman, Saks, and Lord & Taylor; urchins shilling for a three-card monte pitchman alongside a string of smoked-glass limousines; old people coughing, freezing, next to a restaurant where young professionals are licking sherbet from their spoons to

clear their palates after enjoying the entree. Already in the eighteenth century Tom Paine wrote that in New York City "the contrast of affluence and
wretchedness is like dead and living bodies chained together." Or as is said
nowadays: Takes all kinds.

Those hungry people apparently didn't start a Keogh plan or get themselves enrolled in some corporation's pension program thirty years ago and
stick to the job. They didn't "get a degree" when they were young; they were
uncertain in direction, indecisive about money; they plotted their course badly
or slipped out of gear somewhere along the line. Or they may merely be "defective," in Hitler's sense of the term—a bit retarded, a trifle nuts. So they are
not being maintained at the requisite room temperature that society provides
for the rest of us year round. They are standing in the cold wind, hat in hand,
as the saying goes, or lined up docilely, forlornly, in front of a convent for a
baloney sandwich at 11:00 A.M.

It's not as if we had the leisure or quietude to worry overmuch about the
souls whom we are well acquainted with who, in reasonably comfortable, well-
stocked apartments, may nonetheless be drinking themselves to death. And
what could we *do* about those on the street? Empty our wallets and rush to a
money machine for more cash to give out? Run for public office on a philanthropic platform? Become social workers? Set an example in the manner of
Mahatma Gandhi? Move to the country and forget it all? I'm of a generation
of Americans that tended to ignore the magnetic model of Gandhi in favor of
his beguiling contemporary Freud, who explained or micromanaged individual psyches in a subtly satisfying, amusing way. Our living writers of choice were
the genius nay-sayers, starting with T. S. Eliot and Jean-Paul Sartre, through
Samuel Beckett, who befitted the nuclear age and gave no more guidance than
Freud for remedying a social collapse. Social collapse, or Kafkaesque mirror
tricks in the name of totalitarianism, were to be presumed. We knew that
Gandhi would not have fared well against Hitler or Stalin, and so he was considered irrelevant. Though not foreseeing the appearance of an American
Gandhi, Martin Luther King, in the 1960s, we would have thought his assassi-
nation, like Gandhi's, no surprise. (Besides, for activism, our intellectuals were
enamored of Karl Marx, even as a god that failed.)

I went against the grain of much of this. Nature redeems mankind in
many writers who mattered to me, and nature had no place among these postwar intellectuals. April was "the cruellest month," not a genuine rebirth. Life
seemed richer, too, to me with an admixture of social ideals, but Surrealism,
Black Humor, the Theater of the Absurd, Existentialism, and lately Minimalism
have all assumed the impossibility of holding viable ideals. Our mass escape
from both a nuclear holocaust and *1984* were not in their cards. Nor did the
cadre of French authors reigning in the 1950s, and Kafka, Eliot, and Beckett,
picture life in any light that has squared with my experience of school (rebel
though I was), and of the army, the open road, marriage and divorce, career
success and catastrophe, fatherhood, love affairs, suicidal spells, political un-

popularity, blindness in the form of cataracts, and religious revelation in the years since, or the elementary buoyancy with which I wake up every morning. They were waiting for Godot, and, impatient with realism, they may have missed reality, which was more complicated than their perspective allowed.

On the other hand, they were writing from a background of war, whereas we're afraid that we are witnessing a more peaceable delirium of social collapse. Nature, the redeemer, has not survived; and families, finance, and traditional faith are not doing a lot better at the moment. "New York is getting unlivable," people say. Among the privileged, an adage is that "you can't live on less than $150,000" (a year). But if this isn't swinishness talking, what is really meant is that it costs that much *not* to be in the city—to be elevated above the fracases, dolor, and grief of the streets, with sufficient "doorman" protection to shield you from the dangers, to exclude anyone with a lesser income, and to conceal from you the fact that cities *are* their streets. A city is its museums too, but in New York, Goya is in the streets.

Our ancestral wish as predators is that somebody be worse off than we are—that we see subordinates or surplus prey or rivals hungering, to assure us we're prospering. Rather in the same way that we dash sauces on our meat (Worcestershire, horseradish, A.1., or bearnaise) to restore a tartness approximating the taint of spoilage that wild meat attains, we want a city with a certain soupcon of visible misfortune, with people garishly on the skids, scouting in the gutter for a butt and needing to be "moved on" (the policeman's billy club banging on their shoes if they fall asleep on a bench). In a metropolis, in other words, there should be store detectives, collaring shoplifters while we finger our credit cards, white-haired men being bullied by midlevel executives younger than them or forced to hustle around the subway system as messengers, occasional young women selling themselves, and suffering exhibitionists publicly going mad. That quick-footed, old-eyed gentleman with the wife in a lynx coat, grabbing a cab on Sixth Avenue to go uptown after a gala evening, leaves behind a Purple Heart soldier with his broken leg in a cast, scrambling for a tip, who, at sixty, may sleep on a grating tonight in the icy cold. *You're sick? You have no co-op to go to? No T-bills, mutual funds? Where've you been?*

A city is supposed to be a little bit cruel. What's the point of "making it" at all if the servants in hotels and restaurants aren't required to behave like automatons and if plenty of people at your own place of business don't have to bootlick and brownnose? A city with its honking traffic jams, stifling air, and brutal cliffs of glass and stone is supposed to watch you enigmatically, whether you are living on veal *médaillons* and poached salmon or begged coins and hot dogs. But stumble badly, and it will masticate you. Sing a song and exhibit your sores on the subway, and it will nickel-and-dime you as you gradually starve.

All this Dickensian tough stuff, however, has often verged on the playful in American myth, because in the past it has been tied in with rags-to-riches stories. The ragamuffin enshrouded in burlap, sleeping underneath a bush at the edge of the park, might be a new immigrant who in another seven years would grab his first million in the garment trade. He had links to the Statue of Liberty, to put it bluntly, so don't be a glib fool and dismiss him. Ben Franklin entered Philadelphia that first time to make his name with one "Dutch dollar" to live on.

Or he might be a hobo, riding the rods for freedom and fun, a hero of folk songs and such, whose worst sin was stealing Mom's apple pie as it cooled on the kitchen porch and a chicken from the dooryard for his "jungle" stew. He might be a labor organizer traveling on the qt. Or if the figure asleep in the park was female, she might be Little Orphan Annie, soon to charm Daddy Warbucks and be spruced up by him. Fallen women (versus ladies in distress) did exist, but not bag ladies and mad people wandering loose in superabundance. And in hard, bad times like the Depression, the Arkie and Okie families hitting the open road for a chance at a better life—one of the most hallowed American rites—were white. For many urbanites, what makes the heart pound at being surrounded by street people is that a preponderance of them are black, and sometimes very black, by no coincidence, because their color has been a disadvantage to them from the word go. Also, when those disheartened farmers from the dust bowl indulged in what is lately called "substance abuse," hey, they were just winos, drunks. We all knew what getting three sheets to the wind, and the hangover, was like. There was nothing arcanely, explosively mind-blitzing about liquor, even during prohibition. Hillbillies (or "Legs" Diamond) smuggled it into town, not "Colombian drug lords." Besides, during the Great Depression as many as a fourth of U.S. workers were unemployed; we were all in a mess together.

Then we pulled together to fight World War II. And the veterans came back, as from previous wars, and had to start over. Even ten years after 1945 it remained easy for a white man to hitchhike anywhere—just stick out your thumb. People kept a rabbit's foot in their pocket for good luck. The random nature of death, like the Depression, had reminded everybody that success is partly a matter of luck, and may be a question of cowardice. Just as cowards come back from wartime alive, so they may get rich and sleek and influential. Yet you'll remember the happy slogan "The best things in life are free." This might be said tongue in cheek, but seldom cynically. Religious belief, for example, was surely free; so were sunshine and open spaces (though people might leave them to come to the city). Children were free, falling in love was the next thing to free, and friendship was not necessarily "networking." Movie idols played happy-go-lucky roles, with the good guys often the poor guys. Every middle-class person in the city wasn't stitched into the disciplines of a telephone-answering machine, an exercise club, and psychotherapy. People let the phone ring, let a call slip by once in a while, and walked between business appointments when they could. They weren't keyed nearly to computer tempo, fax speed.

What has also happened in New York is that we no longer assume we like most people—assume that strangers are not a cause for alarm and may be worth a second glance or tarrying over. In the old neighborhoods of mixed incomes, one's tribal affiliation was not just mercenary. All kinds of factors operated in layers to populate the place—religious, ethnic, style, and taste—and the residents didn't invariably appear as if they could raise (or not raise) a loan of a certain sum. The stores too, when rents weren't sky-high, could be handed down from father to son, acquiring a mystery or no-cash-flow look. The almighty dollar, where spoken of irreverently, was not.

But now when we take note of people on the sidewalk, we flee on past them, dodging by as if the human shape had become adversarial. And along with the dusty shops and greasy spoons and rent-stabilized buildings with a quirky variety of tenants in them has gone the idea that the smattering of bums one used to see were familiar characters, a part of the regular world. There on the corner by the subway steps stood "Buffalo Bill" or "Grover Cleveland," "Golda Meir" or "V. I. Lenin" or "Yogi Berra" to contribute to—not an encampment of war-zone refugees fighting for space on a steam vent, under a scrap of carpeting, or in a sofa carton. Statistically, New York was less violent when it was more crowded. People merely had homes.

The discovery that you could build dwellings taller and taller or sell air rights above a building was like when the Indians discovered that they could sell land: and then it was gone. Sunlight, like falling in love and raising children conscientiously, has become expensive, and with the money pressure unrelenting even in flush periods ("We have no *downtime*," as a friend who is doing O.K. expresses it), the flippant malevolence of racism increases, as well as a general sense of malaise and deterioration or imminent menace. A man with his head bandaged says at a party: "I was on my way to work, and half the world seemed to be standing around on the platform, including a Guardian Angel, while those creeps were beating me, but for a minute I had this ludicrous feeling that I was about to die."

Some days the ills of the city seem miasmally mental, a bedlam of drugs and dysfunctions, a souring in the gut like dysentery. The creeds or the oratory that ought to invigorate us seem exhausted, whether derived from Marx, Freud, or capitalism (newly perverse). Nationalism as idealism reached its nadir with the Axis powers and has not carried our own country far since Korea. Judaism has bent itself awry in the conflicted Middle East; Christianity hasn't been tried in years. "Tell it to the marines!" one of the elder statesmen of finance or marketing striding to lunch might want to tell the sad-sack young blacks wanting a coin on Fifty-first Street, but they may have already *been* in the marines. The fact that the city's former economic base of muscular industries like transport and manufacturing has been supplanted by an employment pattern of money-processing and "information" jobs—electronic paper-pushing—has made it a city of myriad keypunchers, legal assistants, commercial pulse takers: the suddenly rich, the high-skimming strivers who live by their wits, and their countless clerks, and a piggishness to suit. The leavening of physical work that was present before brought more good humor, loosened the effect of so many people whose bread and butter is their nerves.

I remember trolley cars, and business deals clinched with a handshake. New Yorkers who knew the night sky's constellations, and how easy it was to raise a thumb, catch a ride, and reach Arizona on ten bucks. I can't claim this made it a golden age or even that the city's faces were much happier then. Needless to say, I see lovers now, and business people alive to their work, and immigrants thick in speech but alight with hopes. High is handsome, and fast is fun, not just brutal. No other world city has had quite such a bounce; has been dreamed about from so very far off. A "mecca," "on the edge," and still a fine hotbed in which to be young. And that it has curdled doesn't mean it hasn't remained so rich that you could choke.

"But they're so ruthless," several of my middle-aged friends suggest, speaking of the new professionals sprinting as they start. I don't know. Planes are more ruthless than cars, but more gleeful as well, as long as they don't burn up travel itself. I love planes, arriving out of the heavens at strange locations and picking up instant friendships, easy come, easy go. Or call them battlefield alliances, if you prefer. Anyway, that's the style of the day. Look at your watch, pat your passport, and expand upon conversations you had last evening in a different country, a different climate, a different time zone, with somebody these people won't ever know.

We New Yorkers, rushing to keep up with our calendars yet pausing to open a fast-food package, and finding the plastic wrapper resists our fingers, immediately, unthinkingly, move it to our teeth. Wild we still are, but possessed by velocities too quick to stay abreast of ourselves, and strewing empathy and social responsibility behind us as we go. In losing contact with what used to be whole rafts of blood relatives and the complex, affectionate sense of diverse "walks of life" that families had—a barber uncle, an actress aunt, pig farmers, anesthesiologists, linoleum salesmen, typesetters, shoemakers—we have fractured into interest groups. Our variety is our national strength and should help to sustain the web of democracy, but without the tolerance that downhome, firsthand familiarity (even if left behind in a hometown) brings, professional insularity is added to racial prejudice as a national handicap. And airplanes and computers don't cure that.

The American dream wasn't only money. "There but for the grace of God go I" was a metaphor to mitigate the clashing claims of equality and meritocracy. It was different from the European concept of noblesse oblige, but, like the Statue of Liberty, to be useful it didn't need to be literally believed. Dog-eat-dog laissez-faire, or cradle-to-grave security—which version was our democracy meant to be? A good many of the stockbrokers and financial lawyers who commuted daily with my father on the subway from Grand Central Terminal to Wall Street during the 1950s saw their children grow up to be hippie carpenters and plumbers a decade later, just as some of the electricians and carpenters who sat across from them on that subway ride watched *their* kids become lawyers and brokers. That's been the genius of New York and America: the two-way street.

Whether as kith and kin, or else in church, or on the subway, people have somehow got to sit together for democracy to work. And now, when guns have legs on them and wander everywhere, when poverty is more anonymous than perhaps ever before and homelessness amounts to a continental phenomenon, when cousinhood and neighborhoods are disappearing, common sense has little play, and the most fundamental decencies must be enforced by litigation or legislation, it seems. There hadn't been endemic starvation in America since before Franklin D. Roosevelt's New Deal set into place an elementary safety net of programs such as Social Security in the 1930s. But now it's likely that, without them, there would be. People "on the wrong side of the tracks," as poverty used to be, were close enough to become known quite personally, not ghettoized thirty miles from a plush suburb, where it can be said, as during the 1980s by federal officials, that ketchup in a school lunch program "is a vegetable."

Money has engendered mean spirits since seashells were currency, and time has not reduced our tribalism. But we are sinking underneath the impersonality of disasters flashed in by satellite from Yugoslavia, Cambodia, Nicaragua, or wherever (Timor, Liberia, Somalia . . . Kurds, Afghans, Eritreans, Tutsis), which overflood the homegrown, street-corner miseries that we can witness in person, and blur them. Catastrophes worldwide are recapitulated. The city, any city, meanwhile surrenders its gloss, as, in a casual hour, we can visit Sydney, Hong Kong, Amsterdam, Miami, just by being couch potatoes. Bangkok, Geneva, Cape Town, Edinburgh, Kuala Lumpur: just watching the commercials. Florence, St. Petersburg, Rio . . . without truly seeing them.

FOR JOURNALING AND DISCUSSION

1. Like Robert D. Kaplan in "The Coming Anarchy" in Chapter 9, Hougland describes a radical division between the rich and the poor in the city. Are these divisions more evident in cities than in rural places?

2. Do you agree with Hougland's statement, "A city is supposed to be a little bit cruel"? What allows this cruelty to grow and fester in large cities?

3. Contrast this essay to Louise Erdrich's "Big Grass" and Paul Gruchow's "Discovering One's Own Place," in this chapter, in which they speak about the importance of land and community in a rural environment. What are the values of the city?

4. How has the media blunted our responses to poverty, misery, and disaster? Do you think, as Hougland suggests, that we feel as distant from the tragedies that happen across town as we do from those that happen on the other side of the world?

FOR RESEARCH AND EXPLORATION

1. Interview someone from a big city and someone from a small town about their sense of connectedness to the place they were raised. Did they feel as if they were part of a community? How strongly do they feel connected to their place of origin?

Do you think that life in a big city automatically leads to a sense of isolation, or is this just a myth?

2. Hougland says, "A city is its museums too, but in New York, Goya is in the streets." Goya was a famous Spanish artist who was born in 1746. After looking at some examples of Goya's paintings, write an essay explaining why you think Hougland uses this artist to describe New York. How appropriate is the comparison?

3. Do you think that racial tensions are exacerbated or lessened in cities? Are racial conflicts just as prevalent in rural areas? Find some statistics to support your position, and explain why you have taken this stand.

CHAPTER 9

Nation

From the perspective of human history, nations are a fairly recent worldwide development. Across much of the world, tribes, communities, and cities may have banded together in the past, but with the exception of colonial powers, nations did not emerge on a global basis until the twentieth century. Colonial powers imposed often artificial boundaries and nation status on the lands under their domination. Consequently, in the postcolonial era many of these nations are still struggling with artificial national constructions created by the colonizers. We need only to look at the frequent blood baths in many parts of Africa and Eastern Europe to see the results of nations created by the union of historically unfriendly peoples.

National borders become an interesting issue when applied to peoples who have never acknowledged the artificial borders imposed upon them by outside forces. For example, for centuries Blackfoot Indians freely crossed back and forth between what is now Canada and the United States; the Pueblo and other tribes moved unrestricted between Mexico and Texas. Now border patrols and passport checks limit this freedom of movement. To a large extent our increasing obsession with immigration is infringing on our valued civil rights. Do illegal aliens have rights in this country? Are we willing to sacrifice some of our own conveniences, such as unimpeded travel, to keep them out?

In an interesting twist, it seems that just as many developing countries are just beginning to establish themselves as nations, many of the developed ones are beginning to move beyond nationhood. In other words, as global corporations, markets, and policies become more and more important, the significance of nation recedes. If labor laws, environmental policies, or wages are unfavorable at home, many companies have few qualms about moving overseas (or across the border) to conduct their business. Those who engage in international business are wealthy enough to move about in a global community, which brings up an important intersection with class; as national boundaries blur, class distinctions harden. It is becoming easier to cross national borders than to cross class boundaries.

Linked to this move to globalization is a frightening move toward the destruction of the global environment. Local, regional, and national resources, along with the values and will to protect them, are often abandoned by those in power in favor of economic development. Poorer nations are willing to take the waste of richer ones. Global corporations move to countries that will allow them to pollute. Products deemed too dangerous here are freely marketed in other parts of the world. Nuclear disasters, ozone depletion, and radiation leaks acknowledge no boundaries. Neighboring nations squabble over fishing rights in polluted, overfished waters. Air pollution from major northern cities in the United States comes down as acid rain in Canada—destroying their forests and lakes. The result affects everyone worldwide. Environmental laws need to be international for real change to be accomplished. However, tougher environmental laws frequently come up against economic gains, and in country after country the marketplace wins.

Immigration is another important issue in the formation of a national identity, both in terms of the individual and in terms of the nation. When people immigrate they take on an interesting hybrid status. They have left behind the old country and embraced the new; they are now neither completely one or the other, but a combination of both. To what extent should they assimilate? To what extent should they preserve their traditional culture, language, and past? The majority culture often is threatened or economically affected by immigrant groups that do not assimilate quickly or completely enough. Attempts to regulate assimilation such as the English-only movement, California's Proposition 187, and other anti-immigration policies are an increasingly frequent response.

Patriotism is an important element in national identity. The willingness to fight for one's country or to support the troops becomes more and more entrenched when a country feels threatened from either within or without. The rhetoric used to describe the Gulf War and the aftermath of the Oklahoma City bombing are both examples of this. Our continuing obsession with passing a constitutional amendment to protect the flag also demonstrates this point. We seem to be grasping at symbolic straws in an attempt to preserve and strengthen what some see as a nation in decline.

Race and ethnicity further complicate the many issues important to national identity. For example, many Native Americans, Japanese Americans, Mexican Americans, and African Americans (to name just a few) have struggled greatly with the issue of their own national identity. How do they claim to be a part of a nation that has hurt and oppressed them? How can they go to war and fight for a country that will not give them even basic human rights in return? How can Native Americans be loyal to a government that stripped them of their land, their culture, and their way of life, inflicting genocide on their people? How can African Americans be supportive of a nation that was founded largely due to the benefits resulting from their forced slave labor?

SUMMARIES OF SELECTIONS ON NATION

In "The Coming Anarchy," **Robert D. Kaplan** predicts a future in which nations disintegrate because of environmental destruction, poverty, urbanization, crime, and ultimately anarchy. He also comments on the artificiality of maps and national borders, suggesting that ultimately national boundaries will become unimportant as environmental destruction emerges as a rampant international problem. Kaplan adds that class distinctions will become more divisive than national divisions.

Itabari Njeri moves the focus to a newly multicultural United States, raising many questions about national identity in her essay "Sushi and Grits." She discusses colorism in black communities and multiethnic people, cross-racial oppression, and Korean/black racism, and offers counseling as a partial solution. Old models of nationalism, national identity, and patriotism, Njeri argues, will no longer apply in the new millennium.

Preserving English as a national language is an issue deeply bound up with identity. With "Mute in an English-Only World," **Chang-rae Lee** responds to white Americans' anger about Korean signs in shop windows with a story about his mother's difficulties with English when she first arrived here.

As a young man, **Tim O'Brien** must choose whether to go to fight in Vietnam or to flee to Canada. He spends several days on the border between the two countries deciding, as he describes in "On the Rainy River." In the end he goes to war because he does not have the courage to flee his country, disappoint his family, and tarnish himself in the eyes of his community. However, O'Brien sees his loyalty to his nation as a fault.

Thomas King's short story, "Borders," also takes place on the border between Canada and the United States, as a Blackfoot woman and her son attempt to cross into the United States to visit her daughter in Las Vegas. At the border the guards require that she identify her nationality, and she tells them that she is Blackfoot. That answer, however, is not an option. She and her son remain caught between two borders for several days while the authorities try to figure out what to do with them.

In "The Border Patrol State," **Leslie Marmon Silko** describes many personal experiences with the abuse of power by immigration officials and border police. Pointing out that this violence on the part of the American government is taking away the freedoms of many American citizens as well, she illustrates the tension between preserving both national boundaries and individual freedom.

RHETORICAL QUESTIONS

Context again is an important consideration in the discussion of national identity. If Kaplan is right in "The Coming Anarchy," global definitions of nation will change radically in the next century. How will these changes affect the United States? How will they affect our national identity? What are some of the terms and metaphors that help us think about our future: a multicultural society? a pluralistic society? a melting pot? a salad bowl? a buffet? an armed camp? What are some of the beliefs that you have about the national identity?

Defining national identity depends to a great extent on whether you are a newcomer or an old-timer in the society, or in other words, on your *stance* in relation to the *context*. Louise Erdrich, for example, writes in "Big Grass" in Chapter 8 from the perspective of Native peoples whose history is much older than much of the rhetoric about American nationalism. The incident in King's "Borders" highlights the fact that lines on a map do not mean much to a person who defines herself as a member of a Native nation. Newcomers often clash with the Euro-American traditions and values of speaking English and practicing Christianity. And finally, O'Brien's story shows that even those who identify with the dominant images of the United States as a nation have conflicts about loyalty.

As you consider national identity, also analyze the *forms* that language might take to influence an audience. Some writers blend more than one language into their texts (see, for example, Gloria Anzaldua's book *Borderlands*) to reflect the multicultural character of areas on the borders with other nations. Others choose fiction over nonfiction to create a more powerful response on the part of the reader. Still others adopt a jarring tone as they address an allegedly complacent audience. Is "objectivity" possible when writing about national identity? If so, from whose perspective is it objective? If it is not possible, how will you deal with this problem?

The Coming Anarchy
Robert D. Kaplan

Kaplan is a freelance writer who has published books on Africa, the Middle East, and Eastern Europe, including Surrender or Starve: The Wars Behind the Famine, Soldiers of God: With the Mujahidin in Afghanistan, *and* Balkan Ghosts. *He also contributes to such national magazines as* Atlantic Monthly, New Republic, *and* Reader's Digest.

The Minister's eyes were like egg yolks, an aftereffect of some of the many illnesses, malaria especially, endemic in his country. There was also an irrefutable sadness in his eyes. He spoke in a slow and creaking voice, the voice of hope about to expire. Flame trees, coconut palms, and a ballpoint-blue Atlantic composed the background. None of it seemed beautiful, though. "In forty-five years I have never seen things so bad. We did not manage ourselves well after the British departed. But what we have now is something worse—the revenge of the poor, of the social failures, of the people least able to bring up children in a modern society." Then he referred to the recent coup in the West African country Sierra Leone. "The boys who took power in Sierra Leone come from houses like this." The Minister jabbed his finger at a corrugated metal shack teeming with children. "In three months these boys confiscated all the official Mercedes, Volvos, and BMWs and willfully wrecked them on the road." The Minister mentioned one of the coup's leaders, Solomon Anthony Joseph Musa, who shot the people who had paid for his schooling, "in order to erase the humiliation and mitigate the power his middle-class sponsors held over him."

Tyranny is nothing new in Sierra Leone or in the rest of West Africa. But it is now part and parcel of an increasing lawlessness that is far more significant than any coup, rebel incursion, or episodic experiment in democracy. Crime was what my friend—a top-ranking African official whose life would be threatened were I to identify him more precisely—really wanted to talk about. Crime is what makes West Africa a natural point of departure for my report on what the political character of our planet is likely to be in the twenty-first century.

The cities of West Africa at night are some of the unsafest places in the world. Streets are unlit; the police often lack gasoline for their vehicles; armed burglars, carjackers, and muggers proliferate. "The government in Sierra Leone has no writ after dark," says a foreign resident, shrugging. When I was in the capital, Freetown, last September, eight men armed with AK-47s broke into the house of an American man. They tied him up and stole everything of value. Forget Miami: direct flights between the United States and the Murtala Muhammed Airport, in neighboring Nigeria's largest city, Lagos, have been suspended by order of the U.S. Secretary of Transportation because of ineffective security at the terminal and its environs. A State Department report cited the airport for "extortion by law-enforcement and immigration officials." This is one of the few times that the U.S. government has embargoed a foreign airport for reasons that are linked purely to crime. In Abidjan, effectively the capital of the Côte d'Ivoire, or Ivory Coast, restaurants have stick- and gun-wielding guards who walk you the fifteen feet or so between your car and the entrance, giving you an eerie taste of what American cities might be like in the future. An Italian ambassador was killed by gunfire when robbers invaded an Abidjan restaurant. The family of the Nigerian ambassador was tied up and robbed at gunpoint in the ambassador's residence. After university students in the Ivory Coast caught bandits who had been plaguing their dorms, they executed them by hanging tires around their necks and setting the tires on fire.

In one instance Ivorian policemen stood by and watched the "necklacings," afraid to intervene. Each time I went to the Abidjan bus terminal, groups of young men with restless, scanning eyes surrounded my taxi, putting their hands all over the windows, demanding "tips" for carrying my luggage even though I had only a rucksack. In cities in six West African countries I saw similar young men everywhere—hordes of them. They were like loose molecules in a very unstable social fluid, a fluid that was clearly on the verge of igniting.

"You see," my friend the Minister told me, "in the villages of Africa it is perfectly natural to feed at any table and lodge in any hut. But in the cities this communal existence no longer holds. You must pay for lodging and be invited for food. When young men find out that their relations cannot put them up, they become lost. They join other migrants and slip gradually into the criminal process."

"In the poor quarters of Arab North Africa," he continued, "there is much less crime, because Islam provides a social anchor: of education and indoctrination. Here in West Africa we have a lot of superficial Islam and superficial Christianity. Western religion is undermined by animist beliefs not suitable to a moral society, because they are based on irrational spirit power. Here spirits are used to wreak vengeance by one person against another, or one group against another." Many of the atrocities in the Liberian civil war have been tied to belief in *juju* spirits, and the BBC has reported, in its magazine *Focus on Africa,* that in the civil fighting in adjacent Sierra Leone, rebels were said to have "a young woman with them who would go to the front naked, always walking backwards and looking in a mirror to see where she was going. This made her invisible, so that she could cross to the army's positions and there bury charms . . . to improve the rebels' chances of success."

Finally my friend the Minister mentioned polygamy. Designed for a pastoral way of life, polygamy continues to thrive in sub-Saharan Africa even though it is increasingly uncommon in Arab North Africa. Most youths I met on the road in West Africa told me that they were from "extended" families, with a mother in one place and a father in another. Translated to an urban environment, loose family structures are largely responsible for the world's highest birth rates and the explosion of the HIV virus on the continent. Like the communalism and animism, they provide a weak shield against the corrosive social effects of life in cities. In those cities African culture is being redefined while desertification and deforestation—also tied to overpopulation—drive more and more African peasants out of the countryside.

A PREMONITION OF THE FUTURE

West Africa is becoming *the* symbol of worldwide demographic, environmental, and societal stress, in which criminal anarchy emerges as the real "strategic" danger. Disease, overpopulation, unprovoked crime, scarcity of resources, refugee migrations, the increasing erosion of nation-states and international borders, and the empowerment of private armies, security firms, and international drug cartels are now most tellingly demonstrated through a West African prism. West Africa provides an appropriate introduction to the issues, often extremely unpleasant to discuss, that will soon confront our civilization. To remap the political earth the way it will be a few decades hence—as I intend to do in this article—I find I must begin with West Africa.

There is no other place on the planet where political maps are so deceptive—where, in fact, they tell such lies—as in West Africa. Start with Sierra Leone. According to the map, it is a nation-state of defined borders, with a government in control of its territory. In truth the Sierra Leonian government, run by a twenty-seven-year-old army captain, Valentine Strasser, controls Freetown by day and by day also controls part of the rural interior. In the government's territory the national army is an unruly rabble threatening drivers and passengers at most checkpoints. In the other part of the country units of two separate armies from the war in Liberia have taken up residence, as has an army of Sierra Leonian rebels. The government force fighting the rebels is full of renegade commanders who have aligned themselves with disaffected village chiefs. A premodern formlessness governs the battlefield, evoking the wars in medieval Europe prior to the 1648 Peace of Westphalia, which ushered in the era of organized nation-states.

As a consequence, roughly 400,000 Sierra Leonians are internally displaced, 280,000 more have fled to neighboring Guinea, and another 100,000 have fled to Liberia, even as 400,000 Liberians have fled to Sierra Leone. The third largest city in Sierra Leone, Gondama, is a displaced-persons camp. With an additional 600,000 Liberians in Guinea and 250,000 in the Ivory Coast, the borders dividing these four countries have become largely meaningless. Even in quiet zones none of the governments except the Ivory Coast's maintains the schools, bridges, roads, and police forces in a manner necessary for functional sovereignty. The Koranko ethnic group in northeastern Sierra Leone does all its trading in Guinea. Sierra Leonian diamonds are more likely to be sold in Liberia than in Freetown. In the eastern provinces of Sierra Leone you can buy Liberian beer but not the local brand.

In Sierra Leone, as in Guinea, as in the Ivory Coast, as in Ghana, most of the primary rain forest and the secondary bush is being destroyed at an alarming rate. I saw convoys of trucks bearing majestic hardwood trunks to coastal ports. When Sierra Leone achieved its independence, in 1961, as much as 60 percent of the country was primary rain forest. Now six percent is. In the Ivory Coast the proportion has fallen from 38 percent to eight percent. The deforestation has led to soil erosion, which has led to more flooding and more mosquitoes. Virtually everyone in the West African interior has some form of malaria.

Sierra Leone is a microcosm of what is occurring, albeit in a more tempered and gradual manner, throughout West Africa and much of the underdeveloped world: the withering away of central governments, the rise of tribal and regional domains, the unchecked spread of disease, and the growing pervasiveness of war.

West Africa is reverting to the Africa of the Victorian atlas. It consists now of a series of coastal trading posts, such as Freetown and Conakry, and an interior that, owing to violence, volatility, and disease, is again becoming, as Graham Greene once observed, "blank" and "unexplored." However, whereas Greene's vision implies a certain romance, as in the somnolent and charmingly seedy Freetown of his celebrated novel *The Heart of the Matter,* it is Thomas Malthus, the philosopher of demographic doomsday, who is now the prophet of West Africa's future. And West Africa's future, eventually, will also be that of most of the rest of the world.

Consider "Chicago." I refer not to Chicago, Illinois, but to a slum district of Abidjan, which the young toughs in the area have named after the American city. ("Washington" is another poor section of Abidjan.) Although Sierra Leone is widely regarded as beyond salvage, the Ivory Coast has been considered an African success story, and Abidjan has been called "the Paris of West Africa." Success,however, was built on two artificial factors: the high price of cocoa, of which the Ivory Coast is the world's leading producer, and the talents of a French expatriate community, whose members have helped run the government and the private sector. The expanding cocoa economy made the Ivory Coast a magnet for migrant workers from all over West Africa: between a third and a half of the country's population is now non-Ivorian, and the figure could be as high as 75 percent in Abidjan. During the 1980s cocoa prices fell and the French began to leave. The skyscrapers of the Paris of West Africa are a façade. Perhaps 15 percent of Abidjan's population of three million people live in shantytowns like Chicago and Washington, and the vast majority live in places that are not much better. Not all of these places appear on any of the readily available maps. This is another indication of how political maps are the products of tired conventional wisdom and, in the Ivory Coast's case, of an elite that will ultimately be forced to relinquish power.

Chicago, like more and more of Abidjan, is a slum in the bush: a checkerwork of corrugated zinc roofs and walls made of cardboard and black plastic wrap. It is located in a gully teeming with coconut palms and oil palms, and is ravaged by flooding. Few residents have easy access to electricity, a sewage system, or a clean water supply. The crumbly red laterite earth crawls with footlong lizards both inside and outside the shacks. Children defecate in a stream filled with garbage and pigs, droning with malarial mosquitoes. In this stream women do the washing. Young unemployed men spend their time drinking beer, palm wine, and gin while gambling on pinball games constructed out of rotting wood and rusty nails. These are the same youths who rob houses in more prosperous Ivorian neighborhoods at night. One man I met, Damba Tesele, came to Chicago from Burkina Faso in 1963. A cook by profession, he has four wives and thirty-two children, not one of whom has made it to high school. He has seen his shanty community destroyed by municipal authorities seven times since coming to the area. Each time he and his neighbors rebuild. Chicago is the latest incarnation.

Fifty-five percent of the Ivory Coast's population is urban, and the proportion is expected to reach 62 percent by 2000. The yearly net population growth is 3.6 percent. This means that the Ivory Coast's 13.5 million people will become 39 million by 2025, when much of the population will consist of urbanized peasants like those of Chicago. But don't count on the Ivory Coast's still existing then. Chicago, which is more indicative of Africa's and the Third World's demographic present—and even more of the future—than any idyllic junglescape of women balancing earthen jugs on their heads, illustrates why the Ivory Coast, once a model of Third World success, is becoming a case study in Third World catastrophe.

President Félix Houphouët-Boigny, who died last December at the age of about ninety, left behind a weak cluster of political parties and a leaden bureaucracy that discourages foreign investment. Because the military is small and the non-Ivorian population large, there is neither an obvious force to maintain order nor a sense of nationhood that would lessen the need for such enforcement. The economy has been shrinking since the mid-1980s. Though the French are working assiduously to preserve stability, the Ivory Coast faces a possibility worse than a coup: an anarchic implosion of criminal violence—an urbanized version of what has already happened in Somalia. Or it may become an African Yugoslavia, but one without mini-states to replace the whole. . . .

Ali A. Mazrui, the director of the Institute of Global Cultural Studies at the State University of New York at Binghamton, predicts that West Africa—indeed, the whole continent—is on the verge of large-scale border upheaval. Mazrui writes,

> In the 21st century France will be withdrawing from West Africa as she gets increasingly involved in the affairs [of Europe]. France's West African sphere of influence will be filled by Nigeria—a more natural hegemonic power. . . . It will be under those circumstances that Nigeria's own boundaries are likely to expand to incorporate the Republic of Niger (the Hausa link), the Republic of Benin (the Yoruba link) and conceivably Cameroon.

The future could be more tumultuous, and bloodier, than Mazrui dares to say. France *will* withdraw from former colonies like Benin, Togo, Niger, and the Ivory Coast, where it has been propping up local currencies. It will do so not only because its attention will be diverted to new challenges in Europe and Russia but also because younger French officials lack the older generation's emotional ties to the ex-colonies. However, even as Nigeria attempts to expand, it, too, is likely to split into several pieces. . . .

Part of West Africa's quandary is that although its population belts are horizontal, with habitation densities increasing as one travels south away from the Sahara and toward the tropical abundance of the Atlantic littoral, the borders erected by European colonialists are vertical, and therefore at cross-purposes with demography and topography. Satellite photos depict the same reality I experienced in the bush taxi: the Lomé-Abidjan coastal corridor—indeed, the entire stretch of coast from Abidjan eastward to Lagos—is one burgeoning megalopolis that by any rational economic and geographical standard should constitute a single sovereignty, rather than the five (the Ivory Coast, Ghana, Togo, Benin, and Nigeria) into which it is currently divided.

As many internal African borders begin to crumble, a more impenetrable boundary is being erected that threatens to isolate the continent as a whole: the wall of disease. Merely to visit West Africa in some degree of safety, I spent about $500 for a hepatitis B vaccination series and other disease prophylaxis. Africa may today be more dangerous in this regard than it was in 1862, before antibiotics, when the explorer Sir Richard Francis Burton described the health situation on the continent as "deadly, a Golgotha, a Jehannum." Of the approximately 12 million people worldwide whose blood is HIV-positive, 8 million are in Africa. In the capital of the Ivory Coast, whose modern road system only helps to spread the disease, 10 percent of the population is HIV-positive. And war and refugee movements help the virus break through to more remote areas of Africa. Alan Greenberg, M.D., a representative of the Centers for Disease Control in Abidjan, explains that in Africa the HIV virus and tuberculosis are now "fast-forwarding each other." Of the approximately 4,000 newly diagnosed tuberculosis patients in Abidjan, 45 percent were also found to be HIV-positive. As African birth rates soar and slums proliferate, some experts worry that viral mutations and hybridizations might, just conceivably, result in a form of the AIDS virus that is easier to catch than the present strain.

It is malaria that is most responsible for the disease wall that threatens to separate Africa and other parts of the Third World from more-developed regions of the planet in the twenty-first century. Carried by mosquitoes, malaria, unlike AIDS, is easy to catch. Most people in sub-Saharan Africa have recurring bouts of the disease throughout their entire lives, and it is mutating into increasingly deadly forms . . . .

Africa may be as relevant to the future character of world politics as the Balkans were a hundred years ago, prior to the two Balkan wars and the First World War. Then the threat was the collapse of empires and the birth of nations based solely on tribe. Now the threat is more elemental: *nature unchecked.* Africa's immediate future could be very bad. The coming upheaval, in which foreign embassies are shut down, states collapse, and contact with the outside world takes place through dangerous, disease-ridden coastal trading posts, will loom large in the century we are entering. (Nine of twenty-one U.S. foreign-aid missions to be closed over the next three years are in Africa—a prologue to a consolidation of U.S. embassies themselves.) Precisely because much of Africa is set to go over the edge at a time when the Cold War has ended, when environmental and demographic stress in other parts of the globe is becoming critical, and when the post–First World War system of nation-states—not just in the Balkans but perhaps also in the Middle East—is about to be toppled, Africa suggests what war, borders, and ethnic politics will be like a few decades hence.

To understand the events of the next fifty years, then, one must understand environmental scarcity, cultural and racial clash, geographic destiny, and the transformation of war. The order in which I have named these is not accidental. Each concept except the first relies partly on the one or ones before it, meaning that the last two—new approaches to mapmaking and to warfare—are the most important. They are also the least understood. I will now look at each idea, drawing upon the work of specialists and also my own travel experiences in various parts of the globe besides Africa, in order to fill in the blanks of a new political atlas.

THE ENVIRONMENT AS A HOSTILE POWER

For a while the media will continue to ascribe riots and other violent upheavals abroad mainly to ethnic and religious conflict. But as these conflicts multiply, it will become apparent that something else is afoot, making more and more places like Nigeria, India, and Brazil ungovernable.

Mention "the environment" or "diminishing natural resources" in foreign-policy circles and you meet a brick wall of skepticism or boredom. To conservatives especially, the very terms seem flaky. Public-policy foundations have contributed to the lack of interest, by funding narrowly focused environmental studies replete with technical jargon which foreign-affairs experts just let pile up on their desks.

It is time to understand "the environment" for what it is: *the* national-security issue of the early twenty-first century. The political and strategic impact of surging populations, spreading disease, deforestation and soil erosion, water depletion, air pollution, and, possibly, rising sea levels in critical, overcrowded regions like the Nile Delta and Bangladesh—developments that will prompt mass migrations and, in turn, incite group conflicts—will be the core foreign-policy challenge from which most others will ultimately emanate, arousing the public and uniting assorted interests left over from the Cold War. In the twenty-first century water will be in dangerously short supply in such diverse locales as Saudi Arabia, Central Asia, and the southwestern United States. A war could erupt between Egypt and Ethiopia over Nile River water. Even in Europe tensions have arisen between Hungary and Slovakia over the damming of the Danube, a classic case of how environmental disputes fuse with ethnic and historical ones. The political scientist and erstwhile Clinton adviser Michael Mandelbaum has said, "We have a foreign policy today in the shape of a doughnut—lots of peripheral interests but nothing at the center." The environment, I will argue, is part of a terrifying array of problems that will define a new threat to our security, filling the hole in Mandelbaum's doughnut and allowing a post–Cold War foreign policy to emerge inexorably by need rather than by design.

Our Cold War foreign policy truly began with George F. Kennan's famous article, signed "X," published in *Foreign Affairs* in July of 1947, in which Kennan

argued for a "firm and vigilant containment" of a Soviet Union that was impe-
rially, rather than ideologically, motivated. It may be that our post–Cold War
foreign policy will one day be seen to have had its beginnings in an even bolder
and more detailed piece of written analysis: one that appeared in the journal
International Security. The article, published in the fall of 1991 by Thomas
Fraser Homer-Dixon, who is the head of the Peace and Conflict Studies
Program at the University of Toronto, was titled "On the Threshold:
Environmental Changes as Causes of Acute Conflict." Homer-Dixon has, more
successfully than other analysts, integrated two hitherto separate fields—mili-
tary-conflict studies and the study of the physical environment.

In Homer-Dixon's view, future wars and civil violence will often arise
from scarcities of resources such as water, cropland, forests, and fish . . . .

While a minority of the human population will be, as Francis Fukuyama
would put it, sufficiently sheltered so as to enter a "post-historical" realm, living in cities and suburbs in which the environment has been mastered and ethnic animosities have been quelled by bourgeois prosperity, an increasingly
large number of people will be stuck in history, living in shantytowns where attempts to rise above poverty, cultural dysfunction, and ethnic strife will be
doomed by a lack of water to drink, soil to till, and space to survive in. In the
developing world environmental stress will present people with a choice that
is increasingly among totalitarianism (as in Iraq), fascist-tending mini-states (as
in Serb-held Bosnia), and road-warrior cultures (as in Somalia). Homer-Dixon
concludes that "as environmental degradation proceeds, the size of the potential social disruption will increase". . . .

. . . Quoting Daniel Deudney, another pioneering expert on the security
aspects of the environment, Homer-Dixon says that "for too long we've been
prisoners of 'social-social' theory, which assumes there are only social causes
for social and political changes, rather than natural causes, too. This social-
social mentality emerged with the Industrial Revolution, which separated us
from nature. But nature is coming back with a vengeance, tied to population
growth. It will have incredible security implications.

"Think of a stretch limo in the potholed streets of New York City, where
homeless beggars live. Inside the limo are the air-conditioned post-industrial regions of North America, Europe, the emerging Pacific Rim, and a few other isolated places, with their trade summitry and computer-information highways.
Outside is the rest of mankind, going in a completely different direction". . . .

SKINHEAD COSSACKS, JUJU WARRIORS

In the summer, 1993, issue of *Foreign Affairs,* Samuel P. Huntington, of
Harvard's Olin Institute for Strategic Studies, published a thought-provoking
article called "The Clash of Civilizations?" The world, he argues, has been moving during the course of this century from nation-state conflict to ideological
conflict to, finally, cultural conflict. I would add that as refugee flows increase

and as peasants continue migrating to cities around the world—turning them into sprawling villages—national borders will mean less, even as more power will fall into the hands of less educated, less sophisticated groups. In the eyes of these uneducated but newly empowered millions, the real borders are the most tangible and intractable ones: those of culture and tribe. Huntington writes, "First, differences among civilizations are not only real; they are basic," involving, among other things, history, language, and religion. "Second . . . interactions between peoples of different civilizations are increasing; these increasing interactions intensify civilization consciousness." Economic modernization is not necessarily a panacea, since it fuels individual and group ambitions while weakening traditional loyalties to the state. . . .

Huntington points to interlocking conflicts among Hindu, Muslim, Slavic Orthodox, Western, Japanese, Confucian, Latin American, and possibly African civilizations: for instance, Hindus clashing with Muslims in India, Turkic Muslims clashing with Slavic Orthodox Russians in Central Asian cities, the West clashing with Asia. (Even in the United States, African-Americans find themselves besieged by an influx of competing Latinos.) Whatever the laws, refugees find a way to crash official borders, bringing their passions with them, meaning that Europe and the United States will be weakened by cultural disputes. . . .

Most people believe that the political earth since 1989 has undergone immense change. But it is minor compared with what is yet to come. The breaking apart and remaking of the atlas is only now beginning. The crack-up of the Soviet empire and the coming end of Arab-Israeli military confrontation are merely prologues to the really big changes that lie ahead. Michael Vlahos, a long-range thinker for the U.S. Navy, warns, "We are not in charge of the environment and the world is not following us. It is going in many directions. Do not assume that democratic capitalism is the last word in human social evolution."

Before addressing the questions of maps and of warfare, I want to take a closer look at the interaction of religion, culture, demographic shifts, and the distribution of natural resources in a specific area of the world: the Middle East.

THE PAST IS DEAD

Built on steep, muddy hills, the shantytowns of Ankara, the Turkish capital, exude visual drama. Altindag, or "Golden Mountain," is a pyramid of dreams, fashioned from cinder blocks and corrugated iron, rising as though each shack were built on top of another, all reaching awkwardly and painfully toward heaven—the heaven of wealthier Turks who live elsewhere in the city. Nowhere else on the planet have I found such a poignant architectural symbol of man's striving, with gaps in house walls plugged with rusted cans, and leeks and onions growing on verandas assembled from planks of rotting wood. For reasons that I will explain, the Turkish shacktown is a psychological universe away from the African one.

To see the twenty-first century truly, one's eyes must learn a different set of aesthetics. One must reject the overly stylized images of travel magazines, with their inviting photographs of exotic villages and glamorous downtowns. There are far too many millions whose dreams are more vulgar, more real—whose raw energies and desires will overwhelm the visions of the elites, remaking the future into something frighteningly new. But in Turkey I learned that shantytowns are not all bad.

Slum quarters in Abidjan terrify and repel the outsider. In Turkey it is the opposite. The closer I got to Golden Mountain the better it looked, and the safer I felt. I had $1,500 worth of Turkish lira in one pocket and $1,000 in traveler's checks in the other, yet I felt no fear. Golden Mountain was a real neighborhood. The inside of one house told the story: The architectural bedlam of cinder block and sheet metal and cardboard walls was deceiving. Inside was a *home*—order, that is, bespeaking dignity. I saw a working refrigerator, a television, a wall cabinet with a few books and lots of family pictures, a few plants by a window, and a stove. Though the streets become rivers of mud when it rains, the floors inside this house were spotless.

Other houses were like this too. Schoolchildren ran along with briefcases strapped to their backs, trucks delivered cooking gas, a few men sat inside a café sipping tea. One man sipped beer. Alcohol is easy to obtain in Turkey, a secular state where 99 percent of the population is Muslim. Yet there is little problem of alcoholism. Crime against persons is infinitesimal. Poverty and illiteracy are watered-down versions of what obtains in Algeria and Egypt (to say nothing of West Africa), making it that much harder for religious extremists to gain a foothold.

My point in bringing up a rather wholesome, crime-free slum is this: its existence demonstrates how formidable is the fabric of which Turkish Muslim culture is made. A culture this strong has the potential to dominate the Middle East once again. Slums are litmus tests for innate cultural strengths and weaknesses. Those peoples whose cultures can harbor extensive slum life without decomposing will be, relatively speaking, the future's winners. Those whose cultures cannot will be the future's victims. Slums—in the sociological sense—do not exist in Turkish cities. The mortar between people and family groups is stronger here than in Africa. Resurgent Islam and Turkic cultural identity have produced a civilization with natural muscle tone. Turks, history's perennial nomads, take disruption in stride. . . .

In Turkey several things are happening at once. In 1980, 44 percent of Turks lived in cities; in 1990 it was 61 percent. By the year 2000 the figure is expected to be 67 percent. . . . This is the real political and demographic revolution in Turkey and elsewhere, and foreign correspondents usually don't write about it.

Whereas rural poverty is age-old and almost a "normal" part of the social fabric, urban poverty is socially destabilizing. As Iran has shown, Islamic extremism is the psychological defense mechanism of many urbanized peasants threatened with the loss of traditions in pseudo-modern cities where their values are under attack, where basic services like water and electricity are unavailable, and where they are assaulted by a physically unhealthy environment. . . . Beyond its stark, clearly articulated message, Islam's very militancy makes it attractive to the downtrodden. It is the one religion that is prepared to *fight.* A political era driven by environmental stress, increased cultural sensitivity, unregulated urbanization, and refugee migrations is an era divinely created for the spread and intensification of Islam, already the world's fastest-growing religion. (Though Islam is spreading in West Africa, it is being hobbled by syncretization with animism: this makes new converts less apt to become anti-Western extremists, but it also makes for a weakened version of the faith, which is less effective as an antidote to crime.). . .

THE LIES OF MAPMAKERS

Whereas West Africa represents the least stable part of political reality outside Homer-Dixon's stretch limo, Turkey, an organic outgrowth of two Turkish empires that ruled Anatolia for 850 years, has been among the most stable. Turkey's borders were established not by colonial powers but in a war of independence, in the early 1920s. Kemal Atatürk provided Turkey with a secular nation-building myth that most Arab and African states, burdened by artificially drawn borders, lack. That lack will leave many Arab states defenseless against a wave of Islam that will eat away at their legitimacy and frontiers in coming years. Yet even as regards Turkey, maps deceive.

It is not only African shantytowns that don't appear on urban maps. Many shantytowns in Turkey and elsewhere are also missing—as are the considerable territories controlled by guerrilla armies and urban mafias. Traveling with Eritrean guerrillas in what, according to the map, was northern Ethiopia, traveling in "northern Iraq" with Kurdish guerrillas, and staying in a hotel in the Caucasus controlled by a local mafia—to say nothing of my experiences in West Africa—led me to develop a healthy skepticism toward maps, which, I began to realize, create a conceptual barrier that prevents us from comprehending the political crack-up just beginning to occur worldwide.

Consider the map of the world, with its 190 or so countries, each signified by a bold and uniform color: this map, with which all of us have grown up, is generally an invention of modernism, specifically of European colonialism. . . .

. . . To the colonialist, country maps were the equivalent of an accountant's ledger books. Maps, Anderson explains, "shaped the grammar" that would make possible such questionable concepts as Iraq, Indonesia, Sierra Leone, and Nigeria. The state, recall, is a purely Western notion, one that until the twentieth century applied to countries covering only three percent of the earth's land area. Nor is the evidence compelling that the state, as a governing ideal, can be successfully transported to areas outside the industrialized world. Even the United States of America, in the words of one of our best living poets, Gary Snyder, consists of "arbitrary and inaccurate impositions on what is really here". . . .

On a recent visit to the Turkish-Iranian border, it occurred to me what a risky idea the nation-state is. Here I was on the legal fault line between two clashing civilizations, Turkic and Iranian. Yet the reality was more subtle: as in West Africa, the border was porous and smuggling abounded, but here the people doing the smuggling, on both sides of the border, were Kurds. In such a moonscape, over which peoples have migrated and settled in patterns that obliterate borders, the end of the Cold War will bring on a cruel process of natural selection among existing states. No longer will these states be so firmly propped up by the West or the Soviet Union. Because the Kurds overlap with nearly everybody in the Middle East, on account of their being cheated out of a state in the post–First World War peace treaties, they are emerging, in effect, as *the* natural selector—the ultimate reality check. They have destabilized Iraq and may continue to disrupt states that do not offer them adequate breathing space, while strengthening states that do.

Because the Turks, owing to their water resources, their growing economy, and the social cohesion evinced by the most crime-free slums I have encountered, are on the verge of big-power status, and because the 10 million Kurds within Turkey threaten that status, the outcome of the Turkish-Kurdish dispute will be more critical to the future of the Middle East than the eventual outcome of the recent Israeli-Palestinian agreement.

America's fascination with the Israeli-Palestinian issue, coupled with its lack of interest in the Turkish-Kurdish one, is a function of its own domestic and ethnic obsessions, not of the cartographic reality that is about to transform the Middle East. The diplomatic process involving Israelis and Palestinians will, I believe, have little effect on the early- and mid-twenty-first-century map of the region. Israel, with a 6.6 percent economic growth rate based increasingly on high-tech exports, is about to enter Homer-Dixon's stretch limo, fortified by a well-defined political community that is an organic outgrowth of history and ethnicity. Like prosperous and peaceful Japan on the one hand, and war-torn and poverty-wracked Armenia on the other, Israel is a classic national-ethnic organism. Much of the Arab world, however, will undergo alteration, as Islam spreads across artificial frontiers, fueled by mass migrations into the cities and a soaring birth rate of more than 3.2 percent. Seventy percent of the Arab population has been born since 1970—youths with little historical memory of anticolonial independence struggles, postcolonial attempts at nation-building, or any of the Arab-Israeli wars. . . .

. . . Whatever the outcome of the peace process, Israel is destined to be a Jewish ethnic fortress amid a vast and volatile realm of Islam. In that realm, the violent youth culture of the Gaza shantytowns may be indicative of the coming era.

The destiny of Turks and Kurds is far less certain, but far more relevant to the kind of map that will explain our future world. The Kurds suggest a geographic reality that cannot be shown in two-dimensional space. The issue in Turkey is not simply a matter of giving autonomy or even independence to Kurds in the southeast. This isn't the Balkans or the Caucasus, where regions are merely subdividing into smaller units, Abkhazia breaking off from Georgia, and so on. Federalism is not the answer. Kurds are found everywhere in Turkey, including the shanty districts of Istanbul and Ankara. Turkey's problem is that its Anatolian land mass is the home of two cultures and languages, Turkish and Kurdish. Identity in Turkey, as in India, Africa, and elsewhere, is more complex and subtle than conventional cartography can display.

A NEW KIND OF WAR

To appreciate fully the political and cartographic implications of post-modernism—an epoch of themeless juxtapositions, in which the classificatory grid of nation-states is going to be replaced by a jagged-glass pattern of city-states, shanty-states, nebulous and anarchic regionalisms—it is necessary to consider, finally, the whole question of war.

. . . The intense savagery of the fighting in such diverse cultural settings as Liberia, Bosnia, the Caucasus, and Sri Lanka—to say nothing of what obtains in American inner cities—indicates something very troubling that those of us inside the stretch limo, concerned with issues like middle-class entitlements and the future of interactive cable television, lack the stomach to contemplate. It is this: a large number of people on this planet, to whom the comfort and stability of a middle-class life is utterly unknown, find war and a barracks existence a step up rather than a step down.

. . . When I asked Pentagon officials about the nature of war in the twenty-first century, the answer I frequently got was "Read [Martin] Van Creveld." The top brass are enamored of this historian not because his writings justify their existence but, rather, the opposite: Van Creveld warns them that huge state military machines like the Pentagon's are dinosaurs about to go extinct, and that something far more terrible awaits us.

The degree to which Van Creveld's *Transformation of War* complements Homer-Dixon's work on the environment, Huntington's thoughts on cultural clash, my own realizations in traveling by foot, bus, and bush taxi in more than sixty countries, and America's sobering comeuppances in intractable-culture zones like Haiti and Somalia is startling. The book begins by demolishing the notion that men don't like to fight. "By compelling the senses to focus themselves on the here and now," Van Creveld writes, war "can cause a man to take his leave of them." As anybody who has had experience with Chetniks in Serbia, "technicals" in Somalia, Tontons Macoutes in Haiti, or soldiers in Sierra Leone can tell you, in places where the Western Enlightenment has not penetrated and where there has always been mass poverty, people find liberation in violence. In Afghanistan and elsewhere, I vicariously experienced this phenomenon: worrying about mines and ambushes frees you from worrying about mundane details of daily existence. If my own experience is too subjective, there is a wealth of data showing the sheer frequency of war, especially in the developing world since the Second World War. Physical aggression is a part of being human. Only when people attain a certain economic, educational, and cultural standard is this trait tranquilized. In light of the fact that 95 percent of the earth's population growth will be in the poorest areas of the globe, the question is not whether there will be war (there will be a lot of it) but what kind of war. And who will fight whom? . . .

Also, war-making entities will no longer be restricted to a specific territory. Loose and shadowy organisms such as Islamic terrorist organizations suggest why borders will mean increasingly little and sedimentary layers of tribalistic identity and control will mean more. "From the vantage point of the present, there appears every prospect that religious . . . fanaticisms will play a larger role in the motivation of armed conflict" in the West than at any time "for the last 300 years," Van Creveld writes. This is why analysts like Michael Vlahos are closely monitoring religious cults. Vlahos says, "An ideology that challenges us may not take familiar form, like the old Nazis or Commies. It may not even engage us initially in ways that fit old threat markings." Van Creveld concludes, "Armed conflict will be waged by men on earth, not robots in space. It will have more in common with the struggles of primitive tribes than with large-scale conventional war." While another military historian, John Keegan, in his new book *A History of Warfare,* draws a more benign portrait of primitive man, it is important to point out that what Van Creveld really means is *re-primitivized* man: warrior societies operating at a time of unprecedented resource scarcity and planetary overcrowding. . . .

Future wars will be those of communal survival, aggravated or, in many cases, caused by environmental scarcity. These wars will be subnational, meaning that it will be hard for states and local governments to protect their own citizens physically. This is how many states will ultimately die. As state power fades—and with it the state's ability to help weaker groups within society, not to mention other states—peoples and cultures around the world will be thrown back upon their own strengths and weaknesses, with fewer equalizing mechanisms to protect them. Whereas the distant future will probably see the emergence of a racially hybrid, globalized man, the coming decades will see us more aware of our differences than of our similarities. To the average person, political values will mean less, personal security more. . . .

THE LAST MAP

In *Geography and the Human Spirit,* Anne Buttimer, a professor at University College, Dublin, recalls the work of an early-nineteenth-century

German geographer, Carl Ritter, whose work implied "a divine plan for humanity" based on regionalism and a constant, living flow of forms. The map of the future, to the extent that a map is even possible, will represent a perverse twisting of Ritter's vision. Imagine cartography in three dimensions, as if in a hologram. In this hologram would be the overlapping sediments of group and other identities atop the merely two-dimensional color markings of city-states and the remaining nations, themselves confused in places by shadowy tentacles, hovering overhead, indicating the power of drug cartels, mafias, and private security agencies. Instead of borders, there would be moving "centers" of power, as in the Middle Ages. Many of these layers would be in motion. Replacing fixed and abrupt lines on a flat space would be a shifting pattern of buffer entities, like the Kurdish and Azeri buffer entities between Turkey and Iran, the Turkic Uighur buffer entity between Central Asia and Inner China (itself distinct from coastal China), and the Latino buffer entity replacing a precise U.S.-Mexican border. To this protean cartographic hologram one must add other factors, such as migrations of populations, explosions of birth rates, vectors of disease. Henceforward the map of the world will never be static. This future map—in a sense, the "Last Map"—will be an ever-mutating representation of chaos. . . .

None of this even takes into account climatic change, which, if it occurs in the next century, will further erode the capacity of existing states to cope. India, for instance, receives 70 percent of its precipitation from the monsoon cycle, which planetary warming could disrupt.

Not only will the three-dimensional aspects of the Last Map be in constant motion, but its two-dimensional base may change too. The National Academy of Sciences reports that

> as many as one billion people, or 20 per cent of the world's population, live on lands likely to be inundated or dramatically changed by rising waters. . . . Low-lying countries in the developing world such as Egypt and Bangladesh, where rivers are large and the deltas extensive and densely populated, will be hardest hit . . . . Where the rivers are dammed, as in the case of the Nile, the effects . . . will be especially severe.

Egypt could be where climatic upheaval—to say nothing of the more immediate threat of increasing population—will incite religious upheaval in truly biblical fashion. Natural catastrophes, such as the October, 1992, Cairo earthquake, in which the government failed to deliver relief aid and slum residents were in many instances helped by their local mosques, can only strengthen the position of Islamic factions. In a statement about greenhouse warming which could refer to any of a variety of natural catastrophes, the environmental expert Jessica Tuchman Matthews warns that many of us underestimate the extent to which political systems, in affluent societies as well as in places like Egypt, "depend on the underpinning of natural systems." She adds, "The fact that one can move with ease from Vermont to Miami has nothing to say about the consequences of Vermont acquiring Miami's climate."

Indeed, it is not clear that the United States will survive the next century in exactly its present form. Because America is a multi-ethnic society, the nation-state has always been more fragile here than it is in more homogeneous societies like Germany and Japan. James Kurth, in an article published in *The National Interest* in 1992, explains that whereas nation-state societies tend to be built around a mass-conscription army and a standardized public school system, "multicultural regimes" feature a high-tech, all-volunteer army (and, I would add, private schools that teach competing values), operating in a culture in which the international media and entertainment industry has more influence than the "national political class." In other words, a nation-state is a place where everyone has been educated along similar lines, where people take their cue from national leaders, and where everyone (every male, at least) has gone through the crucible of military service, making patriotism a simpler issue. Writing about his immigrant family in turn-of-the-century Chicago, Saul Bellow states, "The country took us over. It *was* a country then, not a collection of 'cultures.' "

During the Second World War and the decade following it, the United States reached its apogee as a classic nation-state. During the 1960s, as is now clear, America began a slow but unmistakable process of transformation. The signs hardly need belaboring: racial polarity, educational dysfunction, social fragmentation of many and various kinds. William Irwin Thompson, in *Passages About Earth: An Exploration of the New Planetary Culture,* writes, "The educational system that had worked on the Jews or the Irish could no longer work on the blacks; and when Jewish teachers in New York tried to take black children away from their parents exactly in the way they had been taken from theirs, they were shocked to encounter a violent affirmation of negritude."

Issues like West Africa could yet emerge as a new kind of foreign-policy issue, further eroding America's domestic peace. The spectacle of several West African nations collapsing at once could reinforce the worst racial stereotypes here at home. That is another reason why Africa matters. We must not kid ourselves: the sensitivity factor is higher than ever. The Washington, D.C., public school system is already experimenting with an Afrocentric curriculum. Summits between African leaders and prominent African-Americans are becoming frequent, as are Pollyanna-ish prognostications about multiparty elections in Africa that do not factor in crime, surging birth rates, and resource depletion. The Congressional Black Caucus was among those urging U.S. involvement in Somalia and in Haiti. At the *Los Angeles Times* minority staffers have protested against, among other things, what they allege to be the racist tone of the newspaper's Africa coverage, allegations that the editor of the "World Report" section, Dan Fisher, denies, saying essentially that Africa should be viewed through the same rigorous analytical lens as other parts of the world.

Africa may be marginal in terms of conventional late-twentieth-century conceptions of strategy, but in an age of cultural and racial clash, when national defense is increasingly local, Africa's distress will exert a destabilizing influence on the United States.

This and many other factors will make the United States less of a nation than it is today, even as it gains territory following the peaceful dissolution of Canada. Quebec, based on the bedrock of Roman Catholicism and Francophone ethnicity, could yet turn out to be North America's most cohesive and crime-free nation-state. (It may be a smaller Quebec, though, since aboriginal peoples may lop off northern parts of the province.) "Patriotism" will become increasingly regional as people in Alberta and Montana discover that they have far more in common with each other than they do with Ottawa or Washington, and Spanish-speakers in the Southwest discover a greater commonality with Mexico City. (*The Nine Nations of North America*, by Joel Garreau, a book about the continent's regionalization, is more relevant now than when it was published, in 1981.) As Washington's influence wanes, and with it the traditional symbols of American patriotism, North Americans will take psychological refuge in their insulated communities and cultures.

Returning from West Africa last fall was an illuminating ordeal. After leaving Abidjan, my Air Afrique flight landed in Dakar, Senegal, where all passengers had to disembark in order to go through another security check, this one demanded by U.S. authorities before they would permit the flight to set out for New York. Once we were in New York, despite the midnight hour, immigration officials at Kennedy Airport held up disembarkation by conducting quick interrogations of the aircraft's passengers—this was in addition to all the normal immigration and customs procedures. It was apparent that drug smuggling, disease, and other factors had contributed to the toughest security procedures I have ever encountered when returning from overseas.

Then, for the first time in over a month, I spotted businesspeople with attaché cases and laptop computers. When I had left New York for Abidjan, all the businesspeople were boarding planes for Seoul and Tokyo, which departed from gates near Air Afrique's. The only non-Africans off to West Africa had been relief workers in T-shirts and khakis. Although the borders within West Africa are increasingly unreal, those separating West Africa from the outside world are in various ways becoming more impenetrable.

But Afrocentrists are right in one respect: we ignore this dying region at our own risk. When the Berlin Wall was falling, in November of 1989, I happened to be in Kosovo, covering a riot between Serbs and Albanians. The future was in Kosovo, I told myself that night, not in Berlin. The same day that Yitzhak Rabin and Yasser Arafat clasped hands on the White House lawn, my Air Afrique plane was approaching Bamako, Mali, revealing corrugated-zinc shacks at the edge of an expanding desert. The real news wasn't at the White House, I realized. It was right below.

FOR JOURNALING AND DISCUSSION

1. Kaplan describes many forces, such as religious conflict, ethnic strife, and environmental degradation, that are working to destroy our concepts of nation and borders. What forces that he ignores are working to *stabilize* nations throughout the world?
2. How does Kaplan relate interethnic conflicts to environmental destruction?
3. There is a good deal of subtle and not-so-subtle Western ethnocentrism running through this article. While Kaplan vividly paints a picture of the horrors and disintegration of many Third World countries, he fails to mention that these conditions were to a large extent caused by Western colonialism and imperialism. Compare Kaplan's descriptions of the Western countries—France, Britain, and the United States—and the developing countries. What do you find?
4. If the United States were to dissolve as a nation, what configurations of smaller nations do you think would result? How successful do you think they would be? Would they be in conflict with each other?

FOR RESEARCH AND EXPLORATION

1. Do some research on Africa's colonial history and on how the borders of most African nations were created. Based on your discoveries, choose one of the current conflicts facing African nations and predict an outcome.
2. In "To Have and Have Not: Notes on the Progress of the American Class War" in Chapter 3, Michael Lind also predicts that borders between nations will become less and less important in the twenty-first century. His reasons are linked largely to class issues. How are Kaplan's and Lind's views about nations and what maintains them similar? Where do they diverge? Who are the people in the luxury limousine that Kaplan describes? How do they fit into Lind's views about the invisible upper classes?
3. Find an article that describes life in an American ghetto. Compare the description you find with Kaplan's details of life in African and Turkish ghettos. Are the major inner-city areas of the United States destined to experience the devastation of the African cities? Do we have any of Turkey's stabilizing factors?

Sushi and Grits: Ethnic Identity and Conflict in a Newly Multicultural America

Itabari Njeri

Njeri is a journalist and editor who describes herself as a typical descendant of the African diaspora—a person of African, East Indian, English, and

Itabari Njeri, "Sushi and Grits: Ethnic Identity and Conflict in a Newly Multicultural America" from Gerald Early, ed., *Lure and Loathing: Essays on Race, Identity, and the Ambivalence of Assimilation* (New York: Penguin Books, 1993). Copyright © 1993 by Itabari Njeri. Reprinted with the permission of the Miriam Altshuler Literary Agency on behalf of the author.

French descent. She has won numerous awards, including an Associated Press Award for feature writing, the National Association of Black Journalists Award for feature writing, and a National Endowment for the Humanities Fellowship. Her memoir, Every Good-Bye Ain't Gone, *won the 1990 American Book Award.*

At a camp in the woods of eastern Massachusetts, a woman stepped to the front of a room bathed in harsh fluorescent light and took the hand of Barbara Love. "So, tell us who you are," said Love. The woman shifted from side to side. She flashed a nervous smile. Knowing she was here to heal, knowing it was a setting of anonymity, knowing she had the complete, respectful attention of a community of people who—no matter their disparate origins—had lived some piece of her psychic terror, she spoke her name.

"Gloria.[1] I am of Creole ancestry, born in Louisiana." She was about forty-five, a handsome, statuesque woman with a hint of gold in a complexion that was brown like the crown of a well-baked biscuit. A college dean, she told the group she often mediates disputes involving issues of "race"[2] and ethnicity on campus. "I," she said, "was the darkest one in my family. All my life I heard my grandparents, my cousins, my—everyone—whispering 'nigger-nigger-nigger-nigger. . . .' " The more she said it, the more it became an aspirate hiss—" 'ni-hhger-nihhger-nihhger . . . NIHHGGER!!' " She laughed. "*Errrgggggg.*" It was the sound of someone gargling with gravel. She shivered.

"When I had my first child, it was a beautiful mahogany-colored boy. He was so beautiful. *Errrgggggg.*" She shook again. "Then I had my daughter." The woman moaned . . . .

She squealed, "Blue eyeeees. My daughter, she was vanilla-colored, like ice-cream, with red hair and blue . . . eyes." She pulled her shoulders to her ears. "And I freaked out."

"Why?"

"Why? Why?" Her voice was singsong. "Because . . ." Then, from some boxed-up corner of her soul, she let loose a scream so primal it seemed to reach back thirty thousand years . . . pierced the room's thin, dry wall . . . echoed through the woods . . . shook the leaves and scarred the trees. "Because . . ."

And then this biscuit-brown woman revealed that she'd spent the past twenty-five years of her life in mortal fear that her vanilla-ice-cream-colored child would hate her, reject her because . . .

"I'm a nigger. Oh, God, because I'm Black, because I'm so Black. . . ." And then she screamed that ancient scream again and fell into moaning for what seemed an eternity by the unyielding knot in my gut. I heaved and thought of Jeffrey, my cousin. He looked like Ricky Nelson and always wanted to be the baddest nigger on the block.

Like me, he was African American and Caribbean American or, to break it down, African, French, English, Arawak, East Indian, and probably more—a typical New World Black. When he was being sent to prison, the judge, examining his record, called him a White man. My cousin protested and pointed to our brown-skin grandmother in the courtroom. "If she's Black, I'm Black, too." Then he demanded he be treated just like any other "Negro." The judged obliged, adding a year to his sentence.

Trying to prove how bad he was in the eyes of other Black men, my cousin bought into the street life, absorbing, as they had, an oppressor's definition of a Black male: a hustler—confusing patterns of survival for culture. And since Jeffrey was a Black man growing up in Harlem during the late fifties, he saw few options but the street life. But his looks made the price of admission exceedingly high.

When they found his body on a Harlem rooftop, bloated, bullet-pierced, it was because he'd spent his too-short life trying to prove how *bad* he was. . . .

What writer Alice Walker defined as *colorism*, the preferential or prejudicial treatment of same-*race* people based on skin color, continues to this day. And as she once wrote, unless we exorcise it "we cannot as a people progress. For colorism, like colonialism, sexism and racism, impedes us."

Just four years ago, two Euro-American social scientists documented that the social and economic gap between light- and dark-skinned African Americans is as significant as "one of the greatest socioeconomic cleavages in America," the chasm between the income and status of all Blacks and Whites. A dark-skinned Black earns seventy cents for every dollar a light-complexioned African American makes, according to the 1988 study conducted by Michael Hughes and Bradley R. Hertel, professors at Virginia Polytechnic Institute and State University in Virginia. Most telling, said the two social psychologists, are the percentages for Blacks and Whites that show who is employed in professional and managerial occupations—high-status jobs.

Almost 29 percent of all Whites hold such jobs, the study found, while Blacks hold only about 15 percent. That is nearly a two-to-one ratio. Ironically, the same ratio holds true for light-skinned Blacks—27 percent of whom hold such jobs—compared with 15 percent of dark-skinned Blacks who were employed in these positions.

Significantly, when Hughes and Hertel compared their findings to studies done between 1950 and 1980 on the relationship between skin color and socioeconomic status, they concluded that nothing had "changed appreciably." The effect of "skin color on life chances of Black Americans was not eliminated by the Civil Rights and Black pride movements."

Understandably, African Americans are loath to acknowledge such disparities, even though we aren't to blame for them. It undermines the image of ethnic solidarity.

"It's absurd for any Black person to be talking about [color distinctions among African Americans] without talking about White supremacy," says Washington, D.C., psychiatrist Frances Cress Welsing, the controversial author of "The Cress Theory of Color Confrontation and Racism (White Supremacy)," which traces the roots of White racism to a fear of genetic annihilation of the planet's White minority.

"It is White people that keep saying and imposing that if you look like an African you should be at the bottom of the choice spectrum."

That is what Hughes and Hertel concluded from their study, too.

They found that skin color, like gender, acts as a "diffuse status characteristic." For example, a man is believed more competent to pilot a plane than a woman "when in fact there is no evidence that gender has anything to do with ability," Hughes said.

Skin color works this way too, and that's how Whites respond to it. "We focused on Whites because White people are the ones who are generally responsible for making upper-level management and personnel decisions. They are more likely to decide whether people get through educational institutions." In short, they are the ones in power. And when they look at a darker-complexioned Black person, Hughes and Hertel believe, they think they are seeing someone "less competent"—someone less like them than a fairer-complexioned person. . . .

When I raise the painful issue of colorism, African Americans write angry letters, call in to radio shows or attack me in person, asserting I exaggerate the problem, the problem doesn't exist, or, conversely, accuse me of airing the "race's" dirty laundry. . . .

While taking questions from listeners during one radio show, I was told, "You just raise this colorism stuff 'cause you're light with green eyes and wanna be White."

"Where did you get that impression?" I asked.

"I've seen you," the caller insisted, "on TV, in magazines."

"I'm looking at the sister," said the radio show's host, "and she looks like nothing you've described."

"I can tell from the passion in your voice that you've suffered a lot because of looking White," another caller told me. "But forgive, it'll be all right."

I have been called redbone a few times in my life. And once, from a distance, late at night, a Haitian cab driver said he almost mistook me for a White woman. (A bartender in a Tanzanian hotel actually believed I was White because I was so much lighter than he.) Those exceptions aside, no one in America has ever mistaken sapodilla-brown me (that's the color my Guyanese relatives call me) for anything but a New World Black.

I know the exact moment I was compelled to investigate the extent and impact of colorism among our people. It was 1976. I was not long out of college, living in Brooklyn, recovering from my travels as a backup singer with Major Harris of "Love Won't Let Me Wait" fame and reading Alice Walker's essay "If the Present Looks Like the Past, What Does the Future Look Like?" in *In Search of Our Mothers' Gardens.*

I wanted to know who these light-skinned Black women were that Walker wrote were insensitive to the pain of their darker-skinned sisters. As with many light-complexioned Blacks, the people in my family who looked closest to being White compensated by being aggressively Black.

But Walker wrote: "I think there is probably as much difference between the life of a black black woman and a 'high yellow' black woman as between a 'high yellow' woman and a white woman."

I put down the book and called the woman who had been my best friend since college, Celia. She was short, beautiful, charismatic, and a black-black Black woman. She was more than a dear friend. I called her Sister C.

When we hung up, I was numb. And for many days after, I would suddenly weep when alone, replaying her voice in my head. How could we have been so close and I not know how much she'd been hurt by people contemptuous of her for her color, her belligerently close-cropped hair, and the defiantly neon-bright colors she wore? And she was particularly bitter about her relatives, half of whom looked White, some of whom passed for White, and had practically disowned Celia and the other dark, poorer members of her family. Over the next decade I would watch Celia, with the help of friends but virtually none of her more affluent, fair-complexioned relatives, take care of two parents stricken with Alzheimer's and no money, nurse the children of several brothers who had been lost to the streets, put one parent in the grave, leave another in a nursing home, and finally die herself of cancer at the age of thirty-eight.

In 1988, two years before Celia's death, I remember telling a very dark-complexioned acquaintance—a fellow female journalist—how appalled I was at the pervasiveness of a problem I, too, had thought buried. She looked me up and down with silent contempt, examining pore by pore my face—a fraction past yellow, barely brown—and shot a blast of air through her nose that was a half a chuckle, half a snort. "You just finding all this out?"

While all Blacks suffer discrimination in America, the darker one's skin the more one's humanity is ignored. "You know the Links," said E. B. Attah, a Nigerian-born sociologist who has taught at Atlanta University, referring to the elite Black social-service organization. "Well, I had a member of the Links showing me pictures of different chapters. When she encountered a dark-skinned woman in a picture she'd say: 'How did *she* get in there?'

"I'm very dark-skinned and anybody in this country who is dark-skinned can tell you about encountering situations of lighter-skinned people devaluing you as a human being because of your darkness."

About a year ago, I sat in an African American braiding parlor in Los Angeles having my hair done. Two men walked in and waited for a friend. "Did you see the guy Pam brought to the party last night?" one asked.

"I was too busy jammin'. What did he look like?"

The other man chuckled. "If you'd seen him, you'd remember. The nigger looked like eleven fifty-nine."

My mouth dropped and I lifted my bent head. "You mean a shade shya midnight?"

The guy laughed. "You got it, sister."

Said one twenty-three-year-old man I interviewed, after hearing him on a radio show: "I did say I want a fair-complected Black woman." Brown-skinned, which is what he described himself as being, "is all right." He just didn't want a woman who's too dark. And his parents didn't want him dating one either.

The one time he did bring home a dark-skinned girl, his mother took him aside and said: "Don't let it go too far. We don't want any dark people in our family." Both his parents are light brown, the man said.

"My sister has two beautiful light-skinned children," and that's what he wants too. "I don't want to marry a woman who's African dark, even if she's really nice. Uh uh. Nope. I'm going to be truthful. I don't want to walk into the room at night and be scared by just the whites of her eyes."

. . . nihhgger-nihhgger-nihhgger . . . and I freaked out . . . she screamed . . . primal . . . thirty-thousand years . . . scarring the trees . . . My name is Gloria. . . .

Against this historical landscape of psychological anguish, fortified daily by continued socioeconomic discrimination based on color and "race," comes a new generation of so-called multiracial Americans demanding that they be acknowledged as a distinct "racial" group. The concerns they raise are not new within communities of color. However, that their concerns are becoming part of a national debate relates to massive population shifts that may lead to a new majority in twenty-first century America: people of color. Many demographers predict that Whites (I don't consider most Latinos White, given their largely mixed Indian, African, and European ancestry) may be a minority toward the end of the next century. Latino and Asian immigration, the higher birthrate among Latinos and Blacks and intermarriage among all groups are key factors in the rise of the multiethnic population.

Tagged an "emerging" population by social scientists, multiethnic Americans may be the most significant group to spring from a newly pluralistic America. Their demand for recognition is stimulating what I think will be a decades-long debate—one that may force all Americans to confront the myths that surround "race" and ethnicity in the United States.

High on the political agenda of many now-vocal multiethnic Americans is the demand for a new "multiracial" census category that specifically identifies ethnically and "racially" mixed citizens. The size of the "multiracial" population may be about five million—probably more than twice that number, say multiethnic activists. But the exact figures are unknown because the census requires people to either identify with one "race" or ethnic group or to check "other" when filling out data for the Census Bureau.

The ranks of multiethnic activists are being bolstered by their monoethnic kin—parents, grandparents, and spouses—who have helped form support groups in, among other places, Atlanta, Buffalo, Chicago, Houston, Los Angeles, Omaha, San Diego, Seattle, San Francisco, Pittsburgh, and Washington, D.C. Similar support groups are popping up on college campuses, particularly in California, a center of multicultural activism. While these activists failed to get a new multiethnic designation on the 1990 census, they are pushing to see one established for the year 2000.

In general, supporters of the category want recognition and political representation for people of mixed heritage. Opponents say minority groups would shrink if such a designation is allowed, leading to a loss of political representation and congressionally appropriated funds, based on the census count, used to remedy the effects of past and continuing discrimination.

These multiethnic Americans may be Mexican American and Italian American; Japanese American and Cherokee; Korean American, Armenian American, and Chinese. But the most problematic amalgams are those that include the genes of America's most stigmatized group: Negroes, Blacks, Afro-Americans, African Americans, African heritage people—a "spade" by any other name in the consciousness of still too many White Americans. The issue of a special census designation, and social recognition, is especially important to this group because of the way in which "race" has been traditionally defined in America for people of African descent: socially, any known or perceived African ancestry makes one Black—the one-drop-in-the-bucket theory of descent.

"If you consider yourself Black for political reasons, raise your hand," Charles Stewart said to a predominantly African American audience at a symposium I organized for the National Association of Black Journalists in 1990. "The overwhelming majority raised their hands," said Stewart, a Democratic Party activist in Los Angeles. "When I asked how many people here believe that they are of pure African descent, without any mixture, nobody raised their hands." The point, said Stewart, is this: "If you advocate a category that includes people who are *multiracial* to the detriment of their Black identification, you will replicate what you saw—an empty room. We cannot afford to have an empty room. We cannot afford to have a race empty of Black people—not so long as we are struggling against discrimination based on our identification as Black people."

But a woman I will call Anna Vale eschews the little-dab'll-do-you school of genetics. She is a Californian of Japanese, African American, and Native American descent. A voice from the sushi-and-grits generation, she represents the new kind of diversity challenging old "racial" conceptions. Her eyes scan me skeptically. She does not trust me. Though I have written often and sympathetically about the issues so-called "multiracial" Americans face and the problem of colorism, she fears that I, too, will "rape" her. That's what Black people have been doing to her all her life, she claims, committing political and psychological rape on her person. And I'll do it, too, she insists, by writing a piece that distorts the reality of Americans like her who assert their "biological truth" and seek an identity separate from Blacks.

"What I don't appreciate about the African American community," she tells me, "is this mentality of annexing anyone with one drop of African blood. . . . I don't know why African American people seem so obsessed with annexing other people." Yet, says Anna, when "multiracial" people want to voice their unique concerns—political support for Amer-Asian refugees, many of whom have African American fathers, funding for works of art that present the complex cultural views of, for instance, a Black-Korean American—they are told to "be quiet," and "just carry out the political and cultural agenda of African Americans."

As she sits in a Santa Monica café, Vale's delicate body belies the dragon within. "African Americans want us to be their political slaves," she says with the intensity of water at a low boil. "They are saying, 'Come join us.' But it's not because of some great brother or sister love—it's political. If their numbers decrease, their chance of getting public funds decrease—as well as political representation. To me, that's a totally unethical way of saying that you want people to be a member of your community. As far as I am concerned all slavery is over—whether it's physical slavery on the plantation or political slavery that gives one group, like African Americans, the audacity to say that they own people because they have one drop of African blood."

Of course, it was White slave owners in the antebellum South who perpetuated the little-dab'll-do-you rule. They wanted to make sure that Blacks of mixed heritage—usually the products of White masters' raping of enslaved Black women—had no special claim to freedom because their fathers were free. They inherited the status of their slave mothers and were categorized with "pure" Blacks to assure the perpetuation of the slave population. In the post-slave era, the alleged inferiority of African blood—no matter how little of it one possessed—was used to rationalize the continued social and political subordination of Blacks. Wisely, Blacks made a political virtue out of a necessity, asserting that we would not allow our heterogeneous ancestry to divide and render us politically dysfunctional—as many argue has been the case with Brazil's "Black" population.

I looked at Anna and listened to her ahistorical and apolitical diatribe. Her comments were a more extreme form of the kind of Black bashing I've often heard from multiethnics of African descent—usually ones who have had little contact with, or understanding of, the Black side of their heritage. I fear that the increasingly acrimonious nature of the debate among multiethnic Americans and African Americans is turning into a dialogue of the deaf. Pain and rage are the barriers. And though Anna often sees me as the enemy, I have always viewed her as a wounded sister. I understand the source of her rage.

Born in Japan and brought to the U.S. while in grade school, she knew little about her father's African American and Native American family. He died when she was young. Her mother, a Japanese war bride, raised Anna as only she could: to be a good Japanese daughter.

On the days Anna brought sushi to lunch, African American children teased her. But their mild teasing escalated to schoolyard terrorism: a group of Black girls pushing her down . . . cutting off her long, dark hair 'cause she swung it like a White girl. . . .

. . . a Black cop in L.A. ignoring her pleas for help after a fender bender injured her light-skinned son, then calling her a "half-breed bitch." . . .

From her perspective, the dark-brown, long-haired Polynesian-looking and Japanese-speaking woman has had the foot of an African American on her neck all her life.

"Communities of color are the most severe in doling out this kind of oppression," she says grimly. "The oppressed seem to oppress more."

In 1903, when Du Bois wrote that the "problem of the twentieth century is the problem of the color-line—the relation of the darker to the lighter races of men in Asia and Africa, in America and the islands of the sea," he referred to the domination of Whites over darker peoples. This remains true. But that domination has bred an insidious offspring: internalized oppression, that is, the installing of the oppressor's values within the psyche of oppressed people, so that—in a system of structured inequality such as ours—the psychological dynamics that help to keep the system in place function on automatic pilot. In effect, the mind becomes the last plantation. . . .

Among the consequences of internalized oppression are "the ways in which we put each other down. The ways in which we play out the dehumanization that got inflicted on *us*, at *each other*," Love continues. It's the flip side of the oppression itself.

Tall, possessing skin with the soft patina of polished mahogany and disposed to wearing flowing African gowns, Love relates that her own sister had long hair and light skin. "If she tossed her hair in a certain way, she"—like Anna—"was accused of trying to act like a White girl. And the other kids jumped her." Why? "Because we have internalized this set of notions about what it means to be beautiful," says Love. "And what it means to be beautiful in this society is to be like Whites.

"The oppression says that by definition Black people cannot be beautiful. But if someone—because of our genetically mixed heritage—comes along looking like the dominant group, we say, 'If you're Black you are not beautiful—that is, you can't have long hair and here you've got long hair. It's wrong. We'll fix it. We'll cut it off and we'll put you back in your place. Because your place is to be like us: nobody.' "

Looking to the broader community of color, what happens when two historically subjugated people, culturally dissimilar, collide? In one notorious case, a Black teenage girl in Los Angeles was killed by a Korean American merchant after a dispute over a $1.79 bottle of orange juice.

The merchant, a then fifty-year-old woman named Soon Ja Du, was the daughter of a doctor and a literature major in college before she came to the United States with her husband and three children. She never adjusted to her loss of status as an immigrant who, because of language barriers, was compelled to work in a knitting factory for many years before her family saved enough to buy two combination liquor-and-food markets.

A devout Christian, Du reportedly never felt comfortable selling liquor or having to keep a gun in the stores, one of which was in the midst of gang-plagued South-Central Los Angeles—the Empire Market and Liquor Store.

And she later told a probation officer she was afraid of, and didn't understand, the poor Blacks who frequented her store. "They look healthy, young," she said through an interpreter. "Big question why they don't work. Didn't understand why got welfare money and buying alcoholic beverages and consume them . . . instead of feeding children. . . . Didn't understand at first," she said. Eventually, she explained, "paid less attention," and decided that it was "their way of living."

Days after Black gang members had terrorized her adult son, Du saw fifteen-year-old Latasha Harlins walk into the Empire Market, take a container of orange juice from a refrigerated case, and place it in her open backpack. With the juice visible, the girl walked to the counter with two dollars in her hand. Du accused her of stealing the juice. Harlins turned halfway to show her the exposed juice container and said she was paying for it. Du did not believe her, yanked Harlins toward her, pulling the arm of the girl's sweater.

What happened then?

Years before and months after the incident, commentators insist on calling the tensions between Blacks and Koreans an essentially cultural conflict.

At root, I think the conflict stems from economic and political inequality *exacerbated* by cultural differences. And the nation's White elite are not just *tsk-tsk-tsking* spectators. It has much to do with the way capitalism works. As Edna Bonacich, professor at the University of California in Irvine and an expert on the role of middleman minorities around the world, points out, "Korean Americans, to a certain extent, are fronting for the larger White power structure. They are both beneficiaries of the arrangement and the victims of it." The sale of liquor in the Black community is but one example of how Korean immigrant merchants, like Jews before them and Arab immigrants in other parts of the country, fulfill their middleman role.

Corporate-owned liquor companies sell their products through Korean-owned liquor stores in the Black community, Bonacich says. Koreans, who then distribute liquor in a community plagued by substance abuse, "bear the brunt of the anger the African-American community rightfully has against the larger system of oppression. Koreans become sort of foot soldiers of internal colonialism," asserts Bonacich.

Cultural and ethnic difference "are no doubt a small factor in these types of conflict," Bonacich contends, "but unless you deal with the structural problems, you do not solve the conflict."

But I would argue that we have to move on all these fronts—cultural (which includes psychological issues) and structural—simultaneously. Actions rooted in bigotry usually turn these simmering hostilities into social conflagrations. Even when people of apparent goodwill try to cooperate, an aide to Los Angeles Mayor Tom Bradley admitted, there is this "impenetrable veil" of hostility, based on ethnic stereotyping, that undermines joint economic and cultural ventures.

Traditional mediation and bridge-building efforts are too superficial to penetrate that veil. They don't get at the psychological terror, fed by bigotry, that lead the Soon Ja Dus of the world to shoot the Latasha Harlinses who inhabit the planet's inner cities.

A significant part of the problem lies in a failure to address the exaggerated psychological dimensions of intraminority group tensions. Most interethnic conflicts have a psychological aspect—rigidity of thinking, low self-esteem, compensatory behavior. But I think these are especially significant in disputes between historically subordinate groups.

In the case of Korean immigrants, they carry not only the historical memory of subjugation under the Japanese but the day-to-day reality of anti-Asian prejudice in the United States and the isolation caused by language and cultural differences. African Americans carry not only the historical memory of slavery but their status as American's most stigmatized minority.

In many respects, I believe Korean Americans and African Americans to be very similar. Accustomed to being targets of abuse, members of both groups are quick to defend themselves if anyone seems ready to violate their humanity. I see it especially in the often swaggering, chip-on-the-shoulder posture of African American and Korean immigrant men. I saw it in the quick defense of Latasha Harlins when she slugged Soon Ja Du three times in the face after Du grabbed her. I saw it when the battered Du threw a stool at Harlins . . . then took a gun . . . braced herself on the counter, and as Harlins turned to leave . . . shot the girl in the back of the head. Over and over, I watched the now infamous videotape of the incident in Du's store and saw the consequences of "internalized oppression."

In other words, when a battered wife stabs her husband in the chest after he's complained that the eggs are overdone again, it's a safe bet that the murder was over more than breakfast.

There are few safe places where oppressed groups can express their distress. The nation's power elite are not going to let poor people of any color riot on Rodeo Drive. Instead, much of that rage is turned inward—alcoholism, drug abuse, suicide—or directed toward those equally or more marginalized—Black-on-Black crime, child abuse, spouse abuse, violence against Korean merchants, ethnic-bashing between Blacks and Latinos. . . .

These tensions have no easy remedies. But we have to work toward an atmosphere of cooperation rather than antagonism. If we don't, the bottom line for African Americans is this: our numbers are shrinking relative to the growth of other minorities. Like the poor, troublesome Black people are always with us, lament many Whites. But as one elderly Black xenophobe acknowledged, White people have some "new niggers" now ("I'm just a high-tech coolie," said one politically conscious Chinese American engineer)—ones that look more like them, act more like them, and don't haunt their days and nights with cries of "No justice, no peace." Know something else, in some parts of the country they vote more like conservative Whites. And when they marry into White families, some grandpas and grandmas (happy that at least their new child-in-law is not Black) are more than willing to lobby for a new mixed-race census category that might take some of the taint off their grandchild's color and may, eventually, make them honorary White people. (That's already the case with large numbers of Latinos, East Indians, and Arabs.)

Not long ago, I heard about a bumper sticker spotted on a car cruising down a Los Angeles freeway: *If I had known then what I know now, I would have picked my own cotton.*

Tired of reaping what they've sown, many White Americans will happily embrace the proliferating Asian American and Latino population in an effort to exploit intraminority conflicts and permanently marginalize Blacks, if we can't reach honorable political, social, and cultural compromises with other groups, particularly people of color.

As we approach this mine-laden social-psychological terrain, among the questions we should be asking is, What does it mean to be an African American at the end of the twentieth century? In the same breath we should ask, What does it mean to be an American? These questions are at the heart of the un-resolved tension in discussions about cultural pluralism: balancing what is perceived to be universal with ethnic particularism. . . .

Finally, the exorcising of the psychological consequences of oppression that divide communities of color is a painful matter that many of us would rather deny or argue should be done out of sight and earshot of the enemy. But Black folks are among the most studied people on the planet. Who *doesn't* know our business?

As long as colorism and conflicts with other minority groups distract us from the larger issues of social and economic justice, the nation's system of structured inequality prevails. Which is why so many among the country's White power elite smile indulgently at the notion of a "browner," "newly mul-ticultural" America. They know what the last plantation is, too.

NOTES

1. Some names and details have been changed to protect the anonymity of sources.

2. Except in direct quotations, I will place the word "race" in quotes or italics to sig-nal how problematic the use of this term is. As many social scientists have acknowledged for years, "race" is a pseudo-scientific category that has been used to justify the political subordination of non-White peoples based on superficial physical differences. "Race," of course, is a social construct of enormous political significance. But there is one race, *Homo sapiens,* and the physical variations that characterize the species do not amount to fundamental, qualitative differences, as the popular use of the term suggests.

The cultural and physical variations among humans are best contained within the concept of ethnicity, a term that can encompass shared genetic traits, culture, and his-tory—real or perceived.

Further, no one's skin color, obviously, is literally black or white. Phenotype is not a definitive indicator of one's genetic background. Recognizing, however, that social identity in the United States is based primarily on this color divide, I acknowledge it, but treat *Black* and *White* as proper nouns. Throughout this essay I use *Black* to refer to so-called *Negroid* peoples in Africa or of African descent, treating it as a generic ethnic reference to people lumped together for political reasons though, indeed, linked by history, blood, and culture—no matter how distant or diluted. Similarly, I treat *White* as a proper noun, a generic ethnic reference to so-called *Caucasoid* peoples, especially Europeans, Euro-Americans, and others claiming pure European ancestry.

Both the accepted meanings attached to "race" and ethnicity in our current social lexicon and my challenges to them are imperfect descriptors. My hope is that, by challenging our *a priori* acceptance of "race," and the social classifications that result, I will prompt discussions of "race" as a concept, "racism" as an ideology, and the false reality they create in our daily lives.

FOR JOURNALING AND DISCUSSION

1. Njeri notes that "when a battered wife stabs her husband in the chest after he's complained that the eggs are overdone again, it's a safe bet that the murder was over more than breakfast." How does this serve as an analogy for the Los Angeles riots that erupted after the Rodney King verdict?
2. Njeri claims that the melting pot no longer can work as an effective metaphor for describing American society. Create your own new metaphor to describe the ways that Americans are negotiating, assimilating, and shaping their lives together.
3. According to Njeri, many blacks do not want to acknowledge that colorism exists among them because it "undermines the image of ethnic solidarity." However, this hidden status just serves to reinforce it. How is this similar to the idea that our refusal to acknowledge that strong class differences exist in our society also just reinforces those divisions?

FOR RESEARCH AND EXPLORATION

1. Njeri quotes Barbara Love's claim that "what it means to be beautiful in this society is to be like Whites." Look through several women's magazines and cut out the pictures of black female models. Make a collage of these photographs. Attach an essay in which you use these models to demonstrate the American ideal of black female beauty.
2. Njeri claims that "the nation's power elite are not going to let poor people of any color riot on Rodeo Drive. Instead, much of that rage is directed inward—alcoholism, drug abuse, suicide—or directed toward those equally or more marginalized—Black-on-Black crime, child abuse, spouse abuse." Find the actual statistics for some of the effects of rage directed inward—alcoholism among poor blacks, for example. How do these statistics support both Njeri's views and Michael Lind's claims in "To Have and Have Not: Notes on the Progress of the American Class War" in Chapter 3 that one method of maintaining the social class structure is to turn the poor against themselves?
3. Research the ways that Latasha Harlins's killing was covered in the popular media, the black media, and the Asian media. How clear are their inherent biases? What points did each choose not to cover? How fairly did they present the perspectives of the other side?

Mute in an English-Only World

Chang-rae Lee

Lee was born in Seoul, South Korea, to a family that immigrated to the United States when he was young. He received a bachelor's degree from Yale and a master's degree from the University of Oregon. He has written two novels, Native Speaker *and* Comfort Woman.

When I read of the troubles in Palisades Park, N.J., over the proliferation of Korean-language signs along its main commercial strip, I unexpectedly sympathized with the frustrations, resentments and fears of the longtime residents. They clearly felt alienated and even unwelcome in a vital part of their community. The town, like seven others in New Jersey, has passed laws requiring that half of any commercial sign in a foreign language be in English.

Now I certainly would never tolerate any exclusionary ideas about who could rightfully settle and belong in the town. But having been raised in a Korean immigrant family, I saw every day the exacting price and power of language, especially with my mother, who was an outsider in an English-only world.

In the first years we lived in America, my mother could speak only the most basic English, and she often encountered great difficulty whenever she went out.

We lived in New Rochelle, N.Y., in the early 70's, and most of the local businesses were run by the descendants of immigrants who, generations ago, had come to the suburbs from New York City. Proudly dotting Main Street and North Avenue were Italian pastry and cheese shops, Jewish tailors and cleaners and Polish and German butchers and bakers. If my mother's marketing couldn't wait until the weekend, when my father had free time, she would often hold off until I came home from school to buy the groceries.

Though I was only 6 or 7 years old, she insisted that I go out shopping with her and my younger sister. I mostly loathed the task, partly because it meant I couldn't spend the afternoon playing catch with my friends but also because I knew our errands would inevitably lead to an awkward scene, and that I would have to speak up to help my mother.

I was just learning the language myself, but I was a quick study, as children are with new tongues. I had spent kindergarten in almost complete silence, hearing only the high nasality of my teacher and comprehending little but the cranky wails and cries of my classmates. But soon, seemingly mere months later, I had already become a terrible ham and mimic, and I would crack up my father with impressions of teachers, his friends and even himself. My mother scolded me for aping his speech, and the one time I attempted to make light of hers I rated a roundhouse smack on my bottom.

For her, the English language was not very funny. It usually meant trouble and a good dose of shame, and sometimes real hurt. Although she had a good reading knowledge of the language from university classes in South Korea, she had never practiced actual conversation. So in America, she used English flashcards and phrase books and watched television with us kids. And she faithfully carried a pocket workbook illustrated with stick-figure people and compound sentences to be filled in.

But none of it seemed to do her much good. Staying mostly at home to care for us, she didn't have many chances to try out sundry words and phrases. When she did, say, at the window of the post office, her readied speech would stall, freeze, sometimes altogether collapse.

One day was unusually harrowing. We ventured downtown in the new Ford Country Squire my father had bought her, an enormous station wagon that seemed as long—and deft—as an ocean liner. We were shopping for a special meal for guests visiting that weekend, and my mother had heard that a particular butcher carried fresh oxtails, which she needed for a traditional soup.

We'd never been inside the shop, but my mother would pause before its window, which was always lined with whole hams, crown roasts and ropes of plump handmade sausages. She greatly esteemed the bounty with her eyes, and my sister and I did also, but despite our desirous cries she'd turn us away and instead buy the packaged links at the Finast supermarket, where she felt comfortable looking them over and could easily spot the price. And, of course, not have to talk.

But that day she was resolved. The butcher store was crowded, and as we stepped inside the door jingled a welcome. No one seemed to notice. We waited for some time, and people who entered after us were now being served. Finally, an old woman nudged my mother and waved a little ticket, which we hadn't taken. We patiently waited again, until one of the beefy men behind the glass display hollered our number.

My mother pulled us forward and began searching the cases, but the oxtails were nowhere to be found. The man, his big arms crossed, sharply said, "Come on, lady, whaddya want?" This unnerved her, and she somehow blurted the Korean word for oxtail, soggori.

The butcher looked as if my mother had put something sour in his mouth, and he glanced back at the lighted board and called the next number.

Before I knew it, she had rushed us outside and back in the wagon, which she had double-parked because of the crowd. She was furious, almost vibrating with fear and grief, and I could see she was about to cry.

She wanted to go back inside, but now the driver of the car we were blocking wanted to pull out. She was shooing us away. My mother, who had just earned her driver's license, started furiously working the pedals. But in her haste she must have flooded the engine, for it wouldn't turn over. The driver started honking and then another car began honking as well, and soon it seemed the entire street was shrieking at us.

In the following years, my mother grew steadily more comfortable with English. In Korean, she could be fiery, stern, deeply funny and ironic; in English, just slightly less so. If she was never quite fluent, she gained enough confidence to make herself clearly known to anyone, and particularly to me.

Five years ago, she died of cancer, and some months after we buried her I found myself in the driveway of my father's house, washing her sedan. I liked taking care of her things; it made me feel close to her. While I was cleaning out the glove compartment, I found her pocket English workbook, the one with the silly illustrations. I hadn't seen it in nearly 20 years. The yellowed pages were brittle and dog-eared. She had fashioned a plain-paper wrapping for it, and I wondered whether she meant to protect the book or hide it.

I don't doubt that she would have appreciated doing the family shopping on the new Broad Avenue of Palisades Park. But I like to think, too, that she would have understood those who now complain about the Korean-only signs.

I wonder what these same people would have done if they had seen my mother studying her English workbook—or lost in a store. Would they have nodded gently at her? Would they have lent a kind word?

FOR JOURNALING AND DISCUSSION

1. Should the United States pass a law making English the "official" language of this nation? What would the benefits of this law be? the disadvantages?
2. In "Illegitimate Elites and the Parasitic Underclass" in Chapter 3, Katherine Newman says many of the long-term residents of Pleasanton resent that the new immigrants use their native languages. They believe newcomers should instead learn and use English. Write an editorial from the perspective of one of these people responding to Lee's article.
3. Lee notes that many of the businesses in his childhood neighborhood were run by the descendants of immigrants, many of whom had parents and grandparents who had struggled with English. Why are these people so impatient with his mother's difficulties with the language?
4. To what extent is a national identity determined by a national language?

FOR RESEARCH AND EXPLORATION

1. Several countries have two or more national languages, including Canada, Switzerland, Belgium, Ghana, and India. Research one of these countries. How

do they handle their multiple languages? What are the difficulties and benefits that result from multilingualism?

2. Bilingual education is a highly controversial issue in the United States. Do some research and write an essay explaining the main points in favor and the main points against such a program.

3. In some ways the difficulties that immigrant adults experience learning a new language creates a kind of role reversal in their families, as the children who have quickly learned English often end up translating for and taking care of their elders. This can create strained familial relations as everyone struggles with new, unfamiliar roles as well as a new culture and language. Interview a recent immigrant, and ask about the ways language affects his or her roles in both family and culture.

[handwritten: Separation between countries]

On the Rainy River: The Things They Carried *[handwritten: Title? what did they carry?]*

Tim O'Brien *[handwritten: Short story (F)]*

O'Brien grew up in Minnesota. After college he was drafted into the army and served in Vietnam. While there he rose to the rank of sergeant and was awarded a Purple Heart after receiving a shrapnel wound near My Lai. Upon returning from Vietnam, O'Brien briefly attended graduate school at Harvard, but dropped out in order to become a full-time writer. His books include If I Die in a Combat Zone, The Things They Carried, In the Lake of the Woods, *and* Going After Cacciato, *which won the National Book Award.*

[handwritten: a secret (only he knows)]

This is one story I've never told before. Not to anyone. Not to my parents, not to my brother or sister, not even to my wife. To go into it, I've always thought, would only cause embarrassment for all of us, a sudden need to be elsewhere, which is the natural response to a confession. Even now, I'll admit, the story makes me squirm. For more than twenty years I've had to live with it, feeling the shame, trying to push it away, and so by this act of remembrance, by putting the facts down on paper, I'm hoping to relieve at least some of the pressure on my dreams. Still, it's a hard story to tell. All of us, I suppose, like to believe that in a moral emergency we will behave like the heroes of our youth, bravely and forthrightly, without thought of personal loss or discredit. Certainly that was my conviction back in the summer of 1968. Tim O'Brien: a secret hero. The Lone Ranger. If the stakes ever became high enough—if the evil were evil

[handwritten: Physical and emotional weight carried]

enough, if the good were good enough—I would simply tap a secret reservoir of courage that had been accumulating inside me over the years. Courage, I seemed to think, comes to us in finite quantities, like an inheritance, and by being frugal and stashing it away and letting it earn interest, we steadily increase our moral capital in preparation for that day when the account must be drawn down. It was a comforting theory. It dispensed with all those bothersome little acts of daily courage; it offered hope and grace to the repetitive coward; it justified the past while amortizing the future.

In June of 1968, a month after graduating from Macalester College, I was drafted to fight a war I hated. I was twenty-one years old. Young, yes, and politically naive, but even so the American war in Vietnam seemed to me wrong. Certain blood was being shed for uncertain reasons. I saw no unity of purpose, no consensus on matters of philosophy or history or law. The very facts were shrouded in uncertainty: Was it a civil war? A war of national liberation or simple aggression? Who started it, and when, and why? What really happened to the USS *Maddox* on that dark night in the Gulf of Tonkin? Was Ho Chi Minh a Communist stooge, or a nationalist savior, or both, or neither? What about the Geneva Accords? What about SEATO and the Cold War? What about dominoes? America was divided on these and a thousand other issues, and the debate had spilled out across the floor of the United States Senate and into the streets, and smart men in pinstripes could not agree on even the most fundamental matters of public policy. The only certainty that summer was moral confusion. It was my view then, and still is, that you don't make war without knowing why. Knowledge, of course, is always imperfect, but it seemed to me that when a nation goes to war it must have reasonable confidence in the justice and imperative of its cause. You can't fix your mistakes. Once people are dead, you can't make them undead.

In any case those were my convictions, and back in college I had taken a modest stand against the war. Nothing radical, no hothead stuff, just ringing a few doorbells for Gene McCarthy, composing a few tedious, uninspired editorials for the campus newspaper. Oddly, though, it was almost entirely an intellectual activity. I brought some energy to it, of course, but it was the energy that accompanies almost any abstract endeavor; I felt no personal danger; I felt no sense of an impending crisis in my life. Stupidly, with a kind of smug removal that I can't begin to fathom, I assumed that the problems of killing and dying did not fall within my special province.

The draft notice arrived on June 17, 1968. It was a humid afternoon, I remember, cloudy and very quiet, and I'd just come in from a round of golf. My mother and father were having lunch out in the kitchen. I remember opening up the letter, scanning the first few lines, feeling the blood go thick behind my eyes. I remember a sound in my head. It wasn't thinking, just a silent howl. A million things all at once—I was too *good* for this war. Too smart, too compassionate, too everything. It couldn't happen. I was above it. I had the world dicked—Phi Beta Kappa and summa cum laude and president of the student

Did not believe in war, certainly wanted no part in it

body and a full-ride scholarship for grad studies at Harvard. A mistake, maybe—a foul-up in the paperwork. I was no soldier. I hated Boy Scouts. I hated camping out. I hated dirt and tents and mosquitoes. The sight of blood made me queasy, and I couldn't tolerate authority, and I didn't know a rifle from a slingshot. I was a *liberal,* for Christ sake: If they needed fresh bodies, why not draft some back-to-the-stone-age hawk? Or some dumb jingo in his hard hat and Bomb Hanoi button, or one of LBJ's pretty daughters, or Westmoreland's whole handsome family—nephews and nieces and baby grandson. There should be a law, I thought. If you support a war, if you think it's worth the price, that's fine, but you have to put your own precious fluids on the line. You have to head for the front and hook up with an infantry unit and help spill the blood. And you have to bring along your wife, or your kids, or your lover. A *law,* I thought.

I remember the rage in my stomach. Later it burned down to a smoldering self-pity, then to numbness. At dinner that night my father asked what my plans were.

"Nothing," I said. "Wait."

I spent the summer of 1968 working in an Armour meat-packing plant in my hometown of Worthington, Minnesota. The plant specialized in pork products, and for eight hours a day I stood on a quarter-mile assembly line—more properly, a disassembly line—removing blood clots from the necks of dead pigs. My job title, I believe, was Declotter. After slaughter, the hogs were decapitated, split down the length of the belly, pried open, eviscerated, and strung up by the hind hocks on a high conveyer belt. Then gravity took over. By the time a carcass reached my spot on the line, the fluids had mostly drained out, everything except for thick clots of blood in the neck and upper chest cavity. To remove the stuff, I used a kind of water gun. The machine was heavy, maybe eighty pounds, and was suspended from the ceiling by a heavy rubber cord. There was some bounce to it, an elastic up-and-down give, and the trick was to maneuver the gun with your whole body, not lifting with the arms, just letting the rubber cord do the work for you. At one end was a trigger; at the muzzle end was a small nozzle and a steel roller brush. As a carcass passed by, you'd lean forward and swing the gun up against the clots and squeeze the trigger, all in one motion, and the brush would whirl and water would come shooting out and you'd hear a quick splattering sound as the clots dissolved into a fine red mist. It was not pleasant work. Goggles were a necessity, and a rubber apron, but even so it was like standing for eight hours a day under a lukewarm blood-shower. At night I'd go home smelling of pig. It wouldn't go away. Even after a hot bath, scrubbing hard, the stink was always there—like old bacon, or sausage, a dense greasy pig-stink that soaked deep into my skin and hair. Among other things, I remember, it was tough getting dates that summer. I felt isolated; I spent a lot of time alone. And there was also that draft notice tucked away in my wallet.

You cant pick your war
However, he would go if it was Reasonable

In the evenings I'd sometimes borrow my father's car and drive aimlessly around town, feeling sorry for myself, thinking about the war and the pig factory and how my life seemed to be collapsing toward slaughter. I felt paralyzed. All around me the options seemed to be narrowing, as if I were hurtling down a huge black funnel, the whole world squeezing in tight. There was no happy way out. The government had ended most graduate school deferments; the waiting lists for the National Guard and Reserves were impossibly long; my health was solid; I didn't qualify for CO status—no religious grounds, no history as a pacifist. Moreover, I could not claim to be opposed to war as a matter of general principle. There were occasions, I believed, when a nation was justified in using military force to achieve its ends, to stop a Hitler or some comparable evil, and I told myself that in such circumstances I would've willingly marched off to the battle. The problem, though, was that a draft board did not let you choose your war.

Beyond all this, or at the very center, was the raw fact of terror. I did not want to die. Not ever. But certainly not then, not there, not in a wrong war. Driving up Main Street, past the courthouse and the Ben Franklin store, I sometimes felt the fear spreading inside me like weeds. I imagined myself dead. I imagined myself doing things I could not do—charging an enemy position, taking aim at another human being.

At some point in mid-July I began thinking seriously about Canada. The border lay a few hundred miles north, an eight-hour drive. Both my conscience and my instincts were telling me to make a break for it, just take off and run like hell and never stop. In the beginning the idea seemed purely abstract, the word Canada printing itself out in my head; but after a time I could see particular shapes and images, the sorry details of my own future—a hotel room in Winnipeg, a battered old suitcase, my father's eyes as I tried to explain myself over the telephone. I could almost hear his voice, and my mother's. Run, I'd think. Then I'd think, Impossible. Then a second later I'd think, *Run.*

It was a kind of schizophrenia. A moral split. I couldn't make up my mind. I feared the war, yes, but I also feared exile. I was afraid of walking away from my own life, my friends and my family, my whole history, everything that mattered to me. I feared losing the respect of my parents. I feared the law. I feared ridicule and censure. My hometown was a conservative little spot on the prairie, a place where tradition counted, and it was easy to imagine people sitting around a table down at the old Gobbler Café on Main Street, coffee cups poised, the conversation slowly zeroing in on the young O'Brien kid, how the damned sissy had taken off for Canada. At night, when I couldn't sleep, I'd sometimes carry on fierce arguments with those people. I'd be screaming at them, telling them how much I detested their blind, thoughtless, automatic acquiescence to it all, their simpleminded patriotism, their prideful ignorance, their love-it-or-leave-it platitudes, how they were sending me off to fight a war they didn't understand and didn't want to understand. I held them responsible. By God, yes, I *did.* All of them—I held them personally and individually responsible—the polyestered Kiwanis

did not understand the war,
unsure what to do

boys, the merchants and farmers, the pious churchgoers, the chatty housewives, the PTA and the Lions club and the Veterans of Foreign Wars and the fine up-standing gentry out at the country club. They didn't know Bao Dai from the man in the moon. They didn't know history. They didn't know the first thing about Diem's tyranny, or the nature of Vietnamese nationalism, or the long colonial-ism of the French—this was all too damned complicated, it required some read-ing—but no matter, it was a war to stop the Communists, plain and simple, which was how they liked things, and you were a treasonous pussy if you had second thoughts about killing or dying for plain and simple reasons.

Mixed Emotions   I was bitter, sure. But it was so much more than that. The emotions went from outrage to terror to bewilderment to guilt to sorrow and then back again to outrage. I felt a sickness inside me. Real disease.

Most of this I've told before, or at least hinted at, but what I have never told is the full truth. How I cracked. How at work one morning, standing on the pig line, I felt something break open in my chest. I don't know what it was. I'll never know. But it was real, I know that much, it was a physical rupture—a cracking-leaking-popping feeling. I remember dropping my water gun. Quickly, almost without thought, I took off my apron and walked out of the plant and drove home. It was midmorning, I remember, and the house was empty. Down in my chest there was still that leaking sensation, something very warm and precious spilling out, and I was covered with blood and hog-stink, and for a long while I just concentrated on holding myself together. I remem-ber taking a hot shower. I remember packing a suitcase and carrying it out to the kitchen, standing very still for a few minutes, looking carefully at the fa-miliar objects all around me. The old chrome toaster, the telephone, the pink and white Formica on the kitchen counters. The room was full of bright sun-shine. Everything sparkled. My house, I thought. My life. I'm not sure how long I stood there, but later I scribbled out a short note to my parents.

What it said, exactly, I don't recall now. Something vague. Taking off, will call, love Tim. *up and left it all*

I drove north.

It's a blur now, as it was then, and all I remember is a sense of high ve-locity and the feel of the steering wheel in my hands. I was riding on adrena-line. A giddy feeling, in a way, except there was the dreamy edge of impossi-bility to it—like running a dead-end maze—no way out—it couldn't come to a happy conclusion and yet I was doing it anyway because it was all I could think of to do. It was pure flight, fast and mindless. I had no plan. Just hit the border at high speed and crash through and keep on running. Near dusk I passed through Bemidji, then turned northeast toward International Falls. I spent the night in the car behind a closed-down gas station a half mile from the border. In the morning, after gassing up, I headed straight west along the Rainy River, which separates Minnesota from Canada, and which for me separated one life from another. The land was mostly wilderness. Here and there I passed a motel or bait shop, but otherwise the country unfolded in great sweeps of pine and birch and sumac. Though it was still August, the air already had the smell of October, football season, piles of yellow-red leaves, everything crisp and clean. I remember a huge blue sky. Off to my right was the Rainy River, wide as a lake in places, and beyond the Rainy River was Canada.

For a while I just drove, not aiming at anything, then in the late morning I began looking for a place to lie low for a day or two. I was exhausted, and scared sick, and around noon I pulled into an old fishing resort called the Tip Top Lodge. Actually it was not a lodge at all, just eight or nine tiny yellow cabins clustered on a peninsula that jutted northward into the Rainy River. The place was in sorry shape. There was a dangerous wooden dock, an old minnow tank, a flimsy tar paper boathouse along the shore. The main building, which stood in a cluster of pines on high ground, seemed to lean heavily to one side, like a cripple, the roof sagging toward Canada. Briefly, I thought about turning around, just giving up, but then I got out of the car and walked up to the front porch.

The man who opened the door that day is the hero of my life. How do I say this without sounding sappy? Blurt it out—the man saved me. He offered exactly what I needed, without questions, without any words at all. He took me in. He was there at the critical time—a silent, watchful presence. Six days later, when it ended, I was unable to find a proper way to thank him, and I never have, and so, if nothing else, this story represents a small gesture of gratitude twenty years overdue.

Even after two decades I can close my eyes and return to that porch at the Tip Top Lodge. I can see the old guy staring at me. Elroy Berdahl: eighty-one years old, skinny and shrunken and mostly bald. He wore a flannel shirt and brown work pants. In one hand, I remember, he carried a green apple, a small paring knife in the other. His eyes had the bluish gray color of a razor blade, the same polished shine, and as he peered up at me I felt a strange sharpness, almost painful, a cutting sensation, as if his gaze were somehow slicing me open. In part, no doubt, it was my own sense of guilt, but even so I'm absolutely certain that the old man took one look and went right to the heart of things— a kid in trouble. When I asked for a room, Elroy made a little clicking sound with his tongue. He nodded, led me out to one of the cabins, and dropped a key in my hand. I remember smiling at him. I also remember wishing I hadn't. The old man shook his head as if to tell me it wasn't worth the bother.

"Dinner at five-thirty," he said. "You eat fish?"

"Anything," I said.

Elroy grunted and said, "I'll bet."

We spent six days together at the Tip Top Lodge. Just the two of us. Tourist season was over, and there were no boats on the river, and the wilderness seemed to withdraw into a great permanent stillness. Over those six days Elroy Berdahl and I took most of our meals together. In the mornings we sometimes went out on long hikes into the woods, and at night we played Scrabble or listened to records or sat reading in front of his big stone fireplace. At times I felt the awkwardness of an intruder, but Elroy accepted me into his quiet routine without fuss or ceremony. He took my presence for granted, the same way he might've sheltered a stray cat—no wasted sighs or pity—and there was never any talk about it. Just the opposite. What I remember more than anything is the man's willful, almost ferocious silence. In all that time together, all those hours, he never asked the obvious questions: Why was I there? Why alone? Why so preoccupied? If Elroy was curious about any of this, he was careful never to put it into words.

My hunch, though, is that he already knew. At least the basics. After all, it was 1968, and guys were burning draft cards, and Canada was just a boat ride away. Elroy Berdahl was no hick. His bedroom, I remember, was cluttered with books and newspapers. He killed me at the Scrabble board, barely concentrating, and on those occasions when speech was necessary he had a way of compressing large thoughts into small, cryptic packets of language. One evening, just at sunset, he pointed up at an owl circling over the violet-lighted forest to the west.

"Hey, O'Brien," he said. "There's Jesus."

The man was sharp—he didn't miss much. Those razor eyes. Now and then he'd catch me staring out at the river, at the far shore, and I could almost hear the tumblers clicking in his head. Maybe I'm wrong, but I doubt it.

One thing for certain, he knew I was in desperate trouble. And he knew I couldn't talk about it. The wrong word—or even the right word—and I would've disappeared. I was wired and jittery. My skin felt too tight. After supper one evening I vomited and went back to my cabin and lay down for a few moments and then vomited again; another time, in the middle of the afternoon, I began sweating and couldn't shut it off. I went through whole days feeling dizzy with sorrow. I couldn't sleep; I couldn't lie still. At night I'd toss around in bed, half awake, half dreaming, imagining how I'd sneak down to the beach and quietly push one of the old man's boats out into the river and start paddling my way toward Canada. There were times when I thought I'd gone off the psychic edge. I couldn't tell up from down, I was just falling, and late in the night I'd lie there watching weird pictures spin through my head. Getting chased by the Border Patrol—helicopters and searchlights and barking dogs—I'd be crashing through the woods, I'd be down on my hands and knees—people shouting out my name—the law closing in on all sides—my hometown draft board and the FBI and the Royal Canadian Mounted Police. It all seemed crazy and impossible. Twenty-one years old, an ordinary kid with all the ordinary dreams and ambitions, and all I wanted was to live the life I was born to—a mainstream life—I loved baseball and hamburgers and cherry Cokes—and now I was off on the margins of exile, leaving my country forever, and it seemed so impossible and terrible and sad.

I'm not sure how I made it through those six days. Most of it I can't remember. On two or three afternoons, to pass some time, I helped Elroy get the place ready for winter, sweeping down the cabins and hauling in the boats, little chores that kept my body moving. The days were cool and bright. The nights were very dark. One morning the old man showed me how to split and stack firewood, and for several hours we just worked in silence out behind his house. At one point, I remember, Elroy put down his maul and looked at me for a long time, his lips drawn as if framing a difficult question, but then he shook his head and went back to work. The man's self-control was amazing. He never pried. He never put me in a position that required lies or denials. To an extent, I suppose, his reticence was typical of that part of Minnesota, where privacy still held value, and even if I'd been walking around with some horrible deformity—four arms and three heads—I'm sure the old man would've talked about everything except those extra arms and heads. Simple politeness was part of it. But even more than that, I think, the man understood that words were insufficient. The problem had gone beyond discussion. During that long summer I'd been over and over the various arguments, all the pros and cons, and it was no longer a question that could be decided by an act of pure reason. Intellect had come up against emotion. My conscience told me to run, but some irrational and powerful force was resisting, like a weight pushing me toward the war. What it came down to, stupidly, was a sense of shame. Hot, stupid shame. I did not want people to think badly of me. Not my parents, not my brother and sister, not even the folks down at the Gobbler Café. I was ashamed to be there at the Tip Top Lodge. I was ashamed of my conscience, ashamed to be doing the right thing.

Some of this Elroy must've understood. Not the details, of course, but the plain fact of crisis.

Although the old man never confronted me about it, there was one occasion when he came close to forcing the whole thing out into the open. It was early evening, and we'd just finished supper, and over coffee and dessert I asked him about my bill, how much I owed so far. For a long while the old man squinted down at the tablecloth.

"Well, the basic rate," he said, "is fifty bucks a night. Not counting meals. This makes four nights, right?"

I nodded. I had three hundred and twelve dollars in my wallet.

Elroy kept his eyes on the tablecloth. "Now that's an on-season price. To be fair, I suppose we should knock it down a peg or two." He leaned back in his chair. "What's a reasonable number, you figure?"

"I don't know," I said. "Forty?"

"Forty's good. Forty a night. Then we tack on food—say another hundred? Two hundred sixty total?"

"I guess."

He raised his eyebrows. "Too much?"

"No, that's fair. It's fine. Tomorrow, though . . . I think I'd better take off tomorrow."

Elroy shrugged and began clearing the table. For a time he fussed with the dishes, whistling to himself as if the subject had been settled. After a second he slapped his hands together.

"You know what we forgot?" he said. "We forgot wages. Those odd jobs you done. What we have to do, we have to figure out what your time's worth. Your last job—how much did you pull in an hour?"

"Not enough," I said.

"A bad one?"

"Yes. Pretty bad."

Slowly then, without intending any long sermon, I told him about my days at the pig plant. It began as a straight recitation of the facts, but before I could stop myself I was talking about the blood clots and the water gun and how the smell had soaked into my skin and how I couldn't wash it away. I went on for a long time. I told him about wild hogs squealing in my dreams, the sounds of butchery, slaughter house sounds, and how I'd sometimes wake up with that greasy pig-stink in my throat.

When I was finished, Elroy nodded at me.

"Well, to be honest," he said, "when you first showed up here, I wondered about all that. The aroma, I mean. Smelled like you was awful damned fond of pork chops." The old man almost smiled. He made a snuffling sound, then sat down with a pencil and a piece of paper. "So what'd this crud job pay? Ten bucks an hour? Fifteen?"

"Less."

Elroy shook his head. "Let's make it fifteen. You put in twenty-five hours here, easy. That's three hundred seventy-five bucks total wages. We subtract the two hundred sixty for food and lodging, I still owe you a hundred and fifteen."

He took four fifties out of his shirt pocket and laid them on the table.

"Call it even," he said.

"No."

"Pick it up. Get yourself a haircut."

The money lay on the table for the rest of the evening. It was still there when I went back to my cabin. In the morning, though, I found an envelope tacked to my door. Inside were the four fifties and a two-word note that said EMERGENCY FUND.

The man knew. *He never told him anything*

Looking back after twenty years, I sometimes wonder if the events of that summer didn't happen in some other dimension, a place where your life exists before you've lived it, and where it goes afterward. None of it ever seemed real. During my time at the Tip Top Lodge I had the feeling that I'd slipped out of my own skin, hovering a few feet away while some poor yo-yo with my name and face tried to make his way toward a future he didn't understand and didn't want. Even now I can see myself as I was then. It's like watching an old home movie: I'm young and tan and fit. I've got hair—lots of it. I don't smoke or drink. I'm wearing faded blue jeans and a white polo shirt. I can see myself sitting on Elroy Berdahl's dock near dusk one evening, the sky a bright shimmering pink, and I'm finishing up a letter to my parents that tells what I'm about to do and why I'm doing it and how sorry I am that I'd never found the courage to talk to them about it. I ask them not to be angry. I try to explain some of my feelings, but there aren't enough words, and so I just say that it's a thing that has to be done. At the end of the letter I talk about the vacations we used to take up in this north country, at a place called Whitefish Lake, and how the scenery here reminds me of those good times. I tell them I'm fine. I tell them I'll write again from Winnipeg or Montreal or wherever I end up.

On my last full day, the sixth day, the old man took me out fishing on the Rainy River. The afternoon was sunny and cold. A stiff breeze came in from the north, and I remember how the little fourteen-foot boat made sharp rocking motions as we pushed off from the dock. The current was fast. All around us, I remember, there was a vastness to the world, an unpeopled rawness, just the trees and the sky and the water reaching out toward nowhere. The air had the brittle scent of October.

For ten or fifteen minutes Elroy held a course upstream, the river choppy and silver-gray, then he turned straight north and put the engine on full throttle. I felt the bow lift beneath me. I remember the wind in my ears, the sound of the old outboard Evinrude. For a time I didn't pay attention to anything, just feeling the cold spray against my face, but then it occurred to me that at some point we must've passed into Canadian waters, across that <u>dotted line between</u> <u>two different worlds,</u> and I remember a sudden tightness in my chest as I looked up and watched the far shore come at me. This wasn't a daydream. It was tangible and real. As we came in toward land, Elroy cut the engine, letting the boat fishtail lightly about twenty yards off shore. The old man didn't look at me or speak. Bending down, he opened up his tackle box and busied himself with a bobber and a piece of wire leader, humming to himself, his eyes down.

It struck me then that he must've planned it. I'll never be certain, of course, but I think he meant to bring me up against the realities, to guide me across the river and to take me to the edge and to stand a kind of vigil as I chose a life for myself.

I remember staring at the old man, then at my hands, then at Canada. The shoreline was dense with brush and timber. I could see tiny red berries on the bushes. I could see a squirrel up in one of the birch trees, a big crow looking at me from a boulder along the river. That close—twenty yards—and I could see the delicate latticework of the leaves, the texture of the soil, the browned needles beneath the pines, <u>the configurations of geology and human</u> <u>history.</u> Twenty yards. I could've done it. I could've jumped and started swimming for my life. Inside me, in my chest, I felt a terrible squeezing pressure. Even now, as I write this, I can still feel that tightness. And I want you to feel it—the wind coming off the river, the waves, the silence, the wooded frontier. You're at the bow of a boat on the Rainy River. You're twenty-one years old, you're scared, and there's a hard squeezing pressure in your chest.

What would you do?

All that is considered when crossing

> Would you jump? Would you feel pity for yourself? Would you think about your family and your childhood and your dreams and all you're leaving behind? Would it hurt? Would it feel like dying? Would you cry, as I did?

I tried to swallow it back. I tried to smile, except I was crying.

Now, perhaps, you can understand why I've never told this story before. It's not just the embarrassment of tears. That's part of it, no doubt, but what embarrasses me much more, and always will, is the paralysis that took my heart. A moral freeze: I couldn't decide, I couldn't act, I couldn't comport myself with even a pretense of modest human dignity.

All I could do was cry. Quietly, not bawling, just the chest-chokes.

At the rear of the boat Elroy Berdahl pretended not to notice. He held a fishing rod in his hands, his head bowed to hide his eyes. He kept humming a soft, monotonous little tune. Everywhere, it seemed, in the trees and water and sky, a great worldwide sadness came pressing down on me, a crushing sorrow, sorrow like I had never known it before. And what was so sad, I realized, was that Canada had become a pitiful fantasy. Silly and hopeless. It was no longer a possibility. Right then, with the shore so close, I understood that I would not do what I should do. I would not swim away from my hometown and my country and my life. I would not be brave. That old image of myself as a hero, as a man of conscience and courage, all that was just a threadbare pipe dream. Bobbing there on the Rainy River, looking back at the Minnesota shore, I felt a sudden swell of helplessness come over me, a drowning sensation, as if I had toppled overboard and was being swept away by the silver waves. Chunks of my own history flashed by. I saw a seven-year-old boy in a white cowboy hat and a Lone Ranger mask and a pair of holstered six-shooters; I saw a twelve-year-old Little League shortstop pivoting to turn a double play; I saw a sixteen-year-old kid decked out for his first prom, looking spiffy in a white tux and a black bow tie, his hair cut short and flat, his shoes freshly polished. My whole life seemed to spill out into the river, swirling away from me, everything I had ever been or ever wanted to be. I couldn't get my breath; I couldn't stay afloat; I couldn't tell which way to swim. A hallucination, I suppose, but it was as real as anything I would ever feel. I saw my parents calling to me from the far shoreline. I saw my brother and sister, all the townsfolk, the mayor and the entire Chamber of Commerce and all my old teachers and girlfriends and high school buddies. Like some weird sporting event: everybody screaming from the sidelines, rooting me on—a loud stadium roar. Hotdogs and popcorn—stadium smells, stadium heat. A squad of cheerleaders did cartwheels along the banks of the Rainy River; they had megaphones and pompoms and smooth brown thighs. The crowd swayed left and right. A marching band played fight songs. All my aunts and uncles were there, and Abraham Lincoln, and Saint George, and a nine-year-old girl named Linda who had died of a brain tumor back in fifth grade, and several members of the United States Senate, and a blind poet scribbling notes, and LBJ, and Huck Finn, and Abbie Hoffman, and all the dead soldiers back from the grave, and the many thousands who were later to die—villagers with terrible burns, little kids without arms or legs—yes, and the Joint Chiefs of Staff were there, and a couple of popes, and a first lieutenant named Jimmy Cross, and the last surviving veteran of the American Civil War, and Jane Fonda dressed up as Barbarella, and an old man sprawled beside a pigpen, and my grandfather, and Gary Cooper, and a kind-faced woman carrying an umbrella and a copy of Plato's *Republic,* and a million ferocious citizens waving flags of all shapes and colors—people in hard hats, people in headbands—they were all whooping and chanting and urging me toward one shore or the other. I saw faces from my distant past and distant future. My wife was there. My unborn daughter waved at me, and my two sons hopped up and down, and a drill sergeant named Blyton sneered and shot up a finger and shook his head. There was a choir in bright purple robes. There was a cabbie from the Bronx. There was a slim young man I would one day kill with a hand grenade along a red clay trail outside the village of My Khe.

The little aluminum boat rocked softly beneath me. There was the wind and the sky.

I tried to will myself overboard.

I gripped the edge of the boat and leaned forward and thought, *Now.*

I did try. It just wasn't possible.

All those eyes on me—the town, the whole universe—and I couldn't risk the embarrassment. It was as if there were an audience to my life, that swirl of faces along the river, and in my head I could hear people screaming at me. Traitor! they yelled. Turncoat! Pussy! I felt myself blush. I couldn't tolerate it. I couldn't endure the mockery, or the disgrace, or the patriotic ridicule. Even in my imagination, the shore just twenty yards away, I couldn't make myself be brave. It had nothing to do with morality. Embarrassment, that's all it was.

And right then I submitted.

I would go to the war—I would kill and maybe die—because I was embarrassed not to.

That was the sad thing. And so I sat in the bow of the boat and cried.

It was loud now. Loud, hard crying.

Elroy Berdahl remained quiet. He kept fishing. He worked his line with the tips of his fingers, patiently, squinting out at his red and white bobber on the Rainy River. His eyes were flat and impassive. He didn't speak. He was simply there, like the river and the late-summer sun. And yet by his presence, his mute watchfulness, he made it real. He was the true audience. He was a witness, like God, or like the gods, who look on in absolute silence as we live our lives, as we make our choices or fail to make them.

"Ain't biting," he said.

Then after a time the old man pulled in his line and turned the boat back toward Minnesota.

I don't remember saying goodbye. That last night we had dinner together, and I went to bed early, and in the morning Elroy fixed breakfast for me. When I

where did the old man go?

told him I'd be leaving, the old man nodded as if he already knew. He looked down at the table and smiled.

At some point later in the morning it's possible that we shook hands—I just don't remember—but I do know that by the time I'd finished packing the old man had disappeared. Around noon, when I took my suitcase out to the car, I noticed that his old black pickup truck was no longer parked in front of the house. I went inside and waited for a while, but I felt a bone certainty that he wouldn't be back. In a way, I thought, it was appropriate. I washed up the breakfast dishes, left his two hundred dollars on the kitchen counter, got into the car, and drove south toward home.

The day was cloudy. I passed through towns with familiar names, through the pine forests and down to the prairie, and then to Vietnam, where I was a soldier, and then home again. I survived, but it's not a happy ending. I was a coward. I went to the war.

FOR JOURNALING AND DISCUSSION

1. O'Brien carefully crafts the symbolism of his job at the meat-packing factory. Reread these passages, and explain how this symbolism fits into the overt and underlying meanings of the story.
2. What does it mean to be patriotic? Can one refuse to fight for one's country and still be a patriot?
3. O'Brien believes that fundamentally he was a coward for going to war—a reversal of our usual linking of bravery with fighting. Do you agree or disagree with O'Brien's definition of bravery?
4. O'Brien says that the main reason he went to Vietnam was because he was afraid of what people would think of him if he did not go—that he was a sissy, a coward, less than a man. Why does our definition of masculinity seem so closely tied to fighting? What would Andrew Kimbrell, the author of "A Time for Men to Pull Together" in Chapter 4, have to say about Tim's dilemma?

FOR RESEARCH AND EXPLORATION

1. O'Brien makes references to terms and events that were significant to the Vietnam War—the Gulf of Tonkin, SEATO, and Ho Chi Minh, among others. Make a list of these terms and research their importance to the war.
2. Interview some people who were eighteen–twenty years old at the time of the Vietnam War. Ask them to describe the times. What options did they have? Did they know anyone who went to Canada? What was the general response to those who did flee the country? Why did they or didn't they fight in the war? Write the responses in interview format.
3. When he was president, Jimmy Carter pardoned those who had fled the draft and gone to Canada. Research the newspaper coverage at the time. How were these men portrayed—draft dodgers? cowards? moralists? pacifists? Why did Carter finally pardon them? Should he have done so?

Borders (OF COUNTRIES)

Thomas King

*King, of Cherokee, Greek, and German descent, grew up in Canada and has been a professor of American Indian Studies. His short stories have been published in both the United States and Canada, and he has written two novels—*Medicine River *and* Green Grass, Running Water. Medicine River *was made into a television movie.*

When I was twelve, maybe thirteen, my mother announced that we were going to go to Salt Lake City to visit my sister who had left the reserve, moved across the line, and found a job. Laetitia had not left home with my mother's blessing, but over time, my mother had come to be proud of the fact that Laetitia had done all of this on her own. *Up and left her home*

"She did real good," my mother would say.

Then there were the fine points to Laetitia's going. She had not, as my mother liked to tell Mrs. Manyfingers, gone floating after some man like a balloon on a string. She hadn't snuck out of the house, either, and gone to Vancouver or Edmonton or Toronto to chase rainbows down alleys. And she hadn't been pregnant.

"She did real good."

I was seven or eight when Laetitia left home. She was seventeen. Our father was from Rocky Boy on the American side.

"Dad's American," Laetitia told my mother, "so I can go and come as I please."

"Send us a postcard."

Laetitia packed her things, and we headed for the border. Just outside of Milk River, Laetitia told us to watch for the water tower.

"Over the next rise. It's the first thing you see."

"We got a water tower on the reserve," my mother said. "There's a big one in Lethbridge, too."

"You'll be able to see the tops of the flag poles, too. That's where the border is."

When we got to Coutts, my mother stopped at the convenience store and bought her and Laetitia a cup of coffee. I got an Orange Crush.

"This is real lousy coffee."

Mom thinks she is rejecting them

"You're just angry because I want to see the world."

"It's the water. From here on down, they got lousy water."

"I can catch the bus from Sweetgrass. You don't have to lift a finger."

"You're going to have to buy your water in bottles if you want good coffee."

There was an old, wooden building about a block away, with a tall sign in the yard that said "museum." Most of the roof had been blown away. Mom told me to go and see when the place was open. There were boards over the windows and doors. You could tell that the place was closed, and I told Mom so, but she said to go and check anyway. Mom and Laetitia stayed by the car. Neither one of them moved. I sat down on the steps of the museum and watched them, and I don't know that they ever said anything to each other. Finally, Laetitia got her bag out of the trunk and gave Mom a hug.

I wandered back to the car. The wind had come up, and it blew Laetitia's hair across her face. Mom reached out and pulled the strands out of Laetitia's eyes, and Laetitia let her.

["You can still see the mountain from here," my mother told Laetitia in Blackfoot. Tension with language]

"Lots of mountains in Salt Lake," Laetitia told her in English.

"The place is closed," I said. "Just like I told you."

Laetitia tucked her hair into her jacket and dragged her bag down the road to the brick building with the American flag flapping on a pole. When she got to where the guards were waiting, she turned, put the bag down, and waved to us. We waved back. Then my mother turned the car around, and we came home.

We got postcards from Laetitia regular, and, if she wasn't spreading jelly on the truth, she was happy. She found a good job and rented an apartment with a pool.

"And she can't even swim," my mother told Mrs. Manyfingers.

Most of the postcards said we should come down and see the city, but whenever I mentioned this, my mother would stiffen up.

So I was surprised when she bought two new tires for the car and put on her blue dress with the green and yellow flowers. I had to dress up, too, for my mother did not want us crossing the border looking like Americans. We made sandwiches and put them in a big box with pop and potato chips and some apples and bananas and a big jar of water.

"But we can stop at one of those restaurants, too, right?"

"We maybe should take some blankets in case you get sleepy."

"But we can stop at one of those restaurants, too, right?"

The border was actually two towns, though neither one was big enough to amount to anything. Coutts was on the Canadian side and consisted of a convenience store and gas station, a museum that was closed and boarded up, and a motel. Sweetgrass was on the American side, but all you could see was an overpass that arched across the highway and disappeared into the prairies. Just hearing the names of these towns, you would expect that Sweetgrass, which is a nice name and sounds like it is related to other places such as Medicine Hat and Moose Jaw and Kicking Horse Pass, would be on the Canadian side, and that Coutts, which sounds abrupt and rude, would be on the American side. But this was not the case.

Between the two borders was a duty-free shop where you could buy cigarettes and liquor and flags. Stuff like that.

We left the reserve in the morning and drove until we got to Coutts.

"Last time we stopped here," my mother said, "you had an Orange Crush. You remember that?"

"Sure," I said. "That was when Laetitia took off."

"You want another Orange Crush?"

"That means we're not going to stop at a restaurant, right?"

My mother got a coffee at the convenience store, and we stood around and watched the prairies move in the sunlight. Then we climbed back in the car. My mother straightened the dress across her thighs, leaned against the wheel, and drove all the way to the border in first gear, slowly, as if she were trying to see through a bad storm or riding high on black ice.

The border guard was an old guy. As he walked to the car, he swayed from side to side, his feet set wide apart, the holster on his hip pitching up and down. He leaned into the window, looked into the back seat, and looked at my mother and me.

"Morning, ma'am."

"Good morning."

"Where you heading?"

"Salt Lake City."

"Purpose of your visit."

"Visit my daughter."

"Citizenship?"

"Blackfoot," my mother told him.

"Ma'am?"

"Blackfoot," my mother repeated.

"Canadian?"

"Blackfoot."

It would have been easier if my mother had just said "Canadian" and been done with it, but I could see she wasn't going to do that. The guard wasn't angry or anything. He smiled and looked towards the building. Then he turned back and nodded.

"Morning, ma'am."

"Good morning."

"Any firearms or tobacco?"

"No."

"Citizenship?"

"Blackfoot."

He told us to sit in the car and wait, and we did. In about five minutes, another guard came out with the first man. They were talking as they came, both men swaying back and forth like two cowboys headed for a bar or a gunfight.

"Morning, ma'am."

"That's right."

"Now, I know that we got Blackfeet on the American side and the Canadians got Blackfeet on their side. Just so we can keep our records straight, what side do you come from?"

I knew exactly what my mother was going to say, and I could have told them if they had asked me.

"Canadian side or American side?" asked the guard.

"Blackfoot side," she said.

It didn't take them long to lose their sense of humor, I can tell you that. The one guard stopped smiling altogether and told us to park our car at the side of the building and come in.

We sat on a wood bench for about an hour before anyone came over to talk to us. This time it was a woman. She had a gun, too.

"Hi," she said. "I'm Inspector Pratt. I understand there is a little misunderstanding."

"I'm going to visit my daughter in Salt Lake City," my mother told her. "We don't have any guns or beer."

"It's a legal technicality, that's all."

"My daughter's Blackfoot, too."

The woman opened a briefcase and took out a couple of forms and began to write on one of them. "Everyone who crosses our border has to declare their citizenship. Even Americans. It helps us keep track of the visitors we get from the various countries."

She went on like that for maybe fifteen minutes, and a lot of the stuff she told us was interesting.

"I can understand how you feel about having to tell us your citizenship, and here's what I'll do. You tell me, and I won't put it down on the form. No one will know but you and me."

The gun was silver. There were several chips in the wood handle and the name "Stella" was scratched into the metal butt.

We were in the border office for about four hours, and we talked to almost everyone there. One of the men bought me a Coke. My mother brought a couple of sandwiches in from the car. I offered part of mine to Stella, but she said she wasn't hungry.

I told Stella that we were Blackfoot and Canadian, but she said that that didn't count because I was a minor. In the end, she told us that if my mother didn't declare her citizenship, we would have to go back from where we came. My mother stood up and thanked Stella for her time. Then we got back in the car and drove to the Canadian border, which was only about a hundred yards away.

I was disappointed. I hadn't seen Laetitia for a long time, and I had never been to Salt Lake City. When she was at home, Laetitia would go on and on about Salt Lake City. She had never been there, but her boyfriend Lester Tallbull had spent a year in Salt Lake at a technical school.

"It's a great place," Lester would say. "Nothing but blondes in the whole state."

Whenever he said that, Laetitia would slug him on his shoulder hard enough to make him flinch. He had some brochures on Salt Lake and some maps, and every so often the two of them would spread them out on the table.

"That's the temple. It's right downtown. You got to have a pass to get in."

"Charlotte says anyone can go in and look around."

"When was Charlotte in Salt Lake? Just when the hell was Charlotte in Salt Lake?"

"Last year."

"This is Liberty Park. It's got a zoo. There's good skiing in the mountains."

"Got all the skiing we can use," my mother would say. "People come from all over the world to ski at Banff. Cardston's got a temple, if you like those kinds of things."

"Oh, this one is real big," Lester would say. "They got armed guards and everything."

"Not what Charlotte says."

"What does she know."

Lester and Laetitia broke up, but I guess the idea of Salt Lake stuck in her mind.

The Canadian border guard was a young woman, and she seemed happy to see us. "Hi," she said. "You folks sure have a great day for a trip. Where are you coming from?"

"Standoff."

"Is that in Montana?"

"No."

"Where are you going?"

"Standoff."

The woman's name was Carol and I don't guess she was any older than Laetitia. "Wow, you both Canadians?"

"Blackfoot."

"Really? I have a friend I went to school with who is Blackfoot. Do you know Mike Harley?"

"No."

"He went to school in Lethbridge, but he's really from Browning."

It was a nice conversation and there were no cars behind us, so there was no rush.

"You're not bringing any liquor back, are you?"

"No."

"Any cigarettes or plants or stuff like that?"

"No."

"Citizenship?"

"Blackfoot."

"I know," said the woman, "and I'd be proud of being Blackfoot if I were a Blackfoot. But you have to be American or Canadian."

When Laetitia and Lester broke up, Lester took his brochures and maps with him, so Laetitia wrote to someone in Salt Lake City, and, about a month later, she got a big envelope of stuff. We sat at the table and opened up all the brochures, and Laetitia read each one out loud.

"Salt Lake City is the gateway to some of the world's most magnificent skiing."

"Salt Lake City is the home of one of the newest professional basketball franchises, the Utah Jazz."

"The Great Salt Lake is one of the natural wonders of the world."

It was kind of exciting seeing all those color brochures on the table and listening to Laetitia read all about how Salt Lake City was one of the best places in the entire world.

"That Salt Lake City place sounds too good to be true," my mother told her.

"It has everything."

"We got everything right here."

"It's boring here."

"People in Salt Lake City are probably sending away for brochures of Calgary and Lethbridge and Pincher Creek right now."

In the end, my mother would say that maybe Laetitia should go to Salt Lake City, and Laetitia would say that maybe she would.

We parked the car to the side of the building and Carol led us into a small room on the second floor. I found a comfortable spot on the couch and flipped through some back issues of *Saturday Night* and *Alberta Report.*

When I woke up, my mother was just coming out of another office. She didn't say a word to me. I followed her down the stairs and out to the car. I thought we were going home, but she turned the car around and drove back towards the American border, which made me think we were going to visit Laetitia in Salt Lake City after all. Instead she pulled into the parking lot of the duty-free store and stopped.

"We going to see Laetitia?"

"No."

"We going home?"

Pride is a good thing to have, you know. Laetitia had a lot of pride, and so did my mother. I figured that someday, I'd have it, too.

"So where are we going?"

Most of that day, we wandered around the duty-free store, which wasn't very large. The manager had a name tag with a tiny American flag on one side and a tiny Canadian flag on the other. His name was Mel. Towards evening, he began suggesting that we should be on our way. I told him we had nowhere to go, that neither the Americans nor the Canadians would let us in. He laughed at that and told us we should buy something or leave.

The car was not very comfortable, but we did have all that food and it was April, so even if it did snow as it sometimes does on the prairies, we wouldn't freeze. The next morning my mother drove to the American border.

It was a different guard this time, but the questions were the same. We didn't spend as much time in the office as we had the day before. By noon, we were back at the Canadian border. By two we were back in the duty-free shop parking lot.

The second night in the car was not as much fun as the first, but my mother seemed in good spirits, and, all in all, it was as much an adventure as an inconvenience. There wasn't much food left and that was a problem, but we had lots of water as there was a faucet at the side of the duty-free shop.

One Sunday, Laetitia and I were watching television. Mom was over at Mrs. Manyfingers. Right in the middle of the program, Laetitia turned off the set and said she was going to Salt Lake City, that life around here was too boring. I had wanted to see the rest of the program and really didn't care if Laetitia went to Salt Lake City or not. When Mom got home, I told her what Laetitia had said.

What surprised me was how angry Laetitia got when she found out that I had told Mom.

"You got a big mouth."

"That's what you said."

"What I said is none of your business."

"I didn't say anything."

"Well, I'm going for sure, now."

That weekend, Laetitia packed her bags, and we drove her to the border.

Mel turned out to be friendly. When he closed up for the night and found us still parked in the lot, he came over and asked us if our car was broken down or something. My mother thanked him for his concern and told him that we were fine, that things would get straightened out in the morning.

"You're kidding," said Mel. "You'd think they could handle the simple things."

"We got some apples and a banana," I said, "but we're all out of ham sandwiches."

"You know, you read about these things, but you just don't believe it. You just don't believe it."

"Hamburgers would be even better because they got more stuff for energy."

My mother slept in the back seat. I slept in the front because I was smaller and could lie under the steering wheel. Late that night, I heard my mother open the car door. I found her sitting on her blanket leaning against the bumper of the car.

"You see all those stars," she said. "When I was a little girl, my grandmother used to take me and my sisters out on the prairies and tell us stories about all the stars."

"Do you think Mel is going to bring us any hamburgers?"

"Every one of those stars has a story. You see that bunch of stars over there that look like a fish?"   *daughter on own*

"He didn't say no."   *son still here*

"Coyote went fishing, one day. That's how it all started."

We sat out under the stars that night, and my mother told me all sorts of stories. She was serious about it, too. She'd tell them slow, repeating parts as she went, as if she expected me to remember each one.

Early the next morning, the television vans began to arrive, and guys in suits and women in dresses came trotting over to us, dragging microphones and cameras and lights behind them. One of the vans had a table set up with orange juice and sandwiches and fruit. It was for the crew, but when I told them we hadn't eaten for a while, a really skinny blonde woman told us we could eat as much as we wanted.

They mostly talked to my mother. Every so often one of the reporters would come over and ask me questions about how it felt to be an Indian without a country. I told them we had a nice house on the reserve and that my cousins had a couple of horses we rode when we went fishing. Some of the television people went over to the American border, and then they went to the Canadian border.

Around noon, a good-looking guy in a dark blue suit and an orange tie with little ducks on it drove up in a fancy car. He talked to my mother for a while, and, after they were done talking, my mother called me over, and we got into our car. Just as my mother started the engine, Mel came over and gave us a bag of peanut brittle and told us that justice was a damn hard thing to get, but that we shouldn't give up.

I would have preferred lemon drops, but it was nice of Mel anyway.

"Where are we going, now?"

"Going to visit Laetitia."

The guard who came out to our car was all smiles. The television lights were so bright they hurt my eyes, and, if you tried to look through the windshield in certain directions, you couldn't see a thing.

"Morning, ma'am."

"Good morning."

"Where are you heading?"

"Salt Lake City."

"Purpose of your visit?"

Borders create blood to be shed

"Visit my daughter."

"Any tobacco, liquor, or firearms?"

"Don't smoke."

"Any plants or fruit?"

"Not any more."

"Citizenship?"

"Blackfoot."

Humans created the borders

The guard rocked back on his heels and jammed his thumbs into his gun belt. "Thank you," he said, his fingers patting the butt of the revolver. "Have a pleasant trip."

My mother rolled the car forward, and the television people had to scramble out of the way. They ran alongside the car as we pulled away from the border, and, when they couldn't run any farther, they stood in the middle of the highway and waved and waved and waved.

We got to Salt Lake City the next day. Laetitia was happy to see us, and, that first night, she took us out to a restaurant that made really good soups. The list of pies took up a whole page. I had cherry. Mom had chocolate. Laetitia said that she saw us on television the night before, and, during the meal, she had us tell her the story over and over again.

Laetitia took us everywhere. We went to a fancy ski resort. We went to the temple. We got to go shopping in a couple of large malls, but they weren't as large as the one in Edmonton, and Mom said so.

After a week or so, I got bored and wasn't at all sad when my mother said we should be heading back home. Laetitia wanted us to stay longer, but Mom said, no, that she had things to do back home and that, next time, Laetitia should come up and visit. Laetitia said she was thinking about moving back, and Mom told her to do as she pleased, and Laetitia said that she would.

On the way home, we stopped at the duty-free shop, and my mother gave Mel a green hat that said "Salt Lake" across the front. Mel was a funny guy. He took the hat and blew his nose and told my mother that she was an inspiration to us all. He gave us some more peanut brittle and came out into the parking lot and waved at us all the way to the Canadian border.

It was almost evening when we left Coutts. I watched the border through the rear window until all you could see were the tops of the flag poles and the blue water tower, and then they rolled over a hill and disappeared.

FOR JOURNALING AND DISCUSSION

1. National borders are lines drawn on a piece of paper, and, depending upon political events, they can change. In other words, national identity is somewhat arbitrary. What does this have to do with the mother's response to being asked whether she's American or Canadian?

2. Why do you think that the media became so interested in a mother and her son trying to cross the border?

3. Why do these characters have such a different experience crossing the border from the one described by Leslie Marmon Silko in "The Border Patrol State," the next essay in this chapter? Why do the young boy and his mother encounter polite guards, nice clerks, friendly reporters, and the like?
4. What is the significance of the scene in which the narrator's mother tells him the stories of the stars? How does this relate to borders?

FOR RESEARCH AND EXPLORATION

1. Research the border treaties made with the Blackfoot Indians in Canada and the United States. Why don't many Blackfoot Indians acknowledge the current border? Write an essay explaining the current state of the border treaties.
2. King is making a point about the difference between self-assigned versus arbitrarily assigned identity. Similarly, Julie Charlip in "A Real Class Act" in Chapter 3 describes her difficulty crossing the invisible border between social classes. Does Charlip manage to make this crossing with her values and sense of self intact, as King's characters do, or does crossing the border between social classes exact a different kind of price?
3. Because of the narrator's youth, his view of these events is somewhat skewed; those around him and the reader understand much more that he does about his mother's actions. Retell the story from his mother's perspective. Include her views of the treaties governing the border.

The Border Patrol State

Leslie Marmon Silko

Silko, of mixed Laguna, Mexican, and white ancestry, was born in New Mexico, and grew up on the Laguna Pueblo reservation. She received a bachelor's degree in English from the University of New Mexico, and has taught at Navajo Community College, the University of Arizona, and the University of New Mexico. Silko has published two novels, Ceremony *and* The Almanac of the Dead.

She loved to travel

I used to travel the highways of New Mexico and Arizona with a wonderful sensation of absolute freedom as I cruised down the open road and across the vast desert plateaus. On the Laguna Pueblo reservation, where I was raised, the people were patriotic despite the way the U.S. government had treated Native

Being able to travel is a Right

Americans. As proud citizens, we grew up believing the freedom to travel was our inalienable right, a right that some Native Americans had been denied in the early twentieth century. Our cousin, old Bill Pratt, used to ride his horse 300 miles overland from Laguna, New Mexico, to Prescott, Arizona, every summer to work as a fire lookout.

In school in the 1950s, we were taught that our right to travel from state to state without special papers or threat of detainment was a right that citizens under communist and totalitarian governments did not possess. That wide open highway told us we were U.S. citizens; we were free . . . .

Not so long ago, my companion Gus and I were driving south from Albuquerque, returning to Tucson after a book promotion for the paperback edition of my novel *Almanac of the Dead*. I had settled back and gone to sleep while Gus drove, but I was awakened when I felt the car slowing to a stop. It was nearly midnight on New Mexico State Road 26, a dark, lonely stretch of two-lane highway between Hatch and Deming. When I sat up, I saw the headlights and emergency flashers of six vehicles—Border Patrol cars and a van were blocking both lanes of the highway. Gus stopped the car and rolled down the window to ask what was wrong. But the closest Border Patrolman and his companion did not reply; instead, the first agent ordered us to "step out of the car." Gus asked why, but his question seemed to set them off. Two more Border Patrol agents immediately approached our car, and one of them snapped, "Are you looking for trouble?" as if he would relish it. *Why so Rude?*

I will never forget that night beside the highway. There was an awful feeling of menace and violence straining to break loose. It was clear that the uniformed men would be only too happy to drag us out of the car if we did not speedily comply with their request (asking a question is tantamount to resistance, it seems). So we stepped out of the car and they motioned for us to stand on the shoulder of the road. The night was very dark, and no other traffic had come down the road since we had been stopped. All I could think about was a book I had read—*Nunca Más*—the official report of a human rights commission that investigated and certified more than 12,000 "disappearances" during Argentina's "dirty war" in the late 1970s.

The weird anger of these Border Patrolmen made me think about descriptions in the report of Argentine police and military officers who became addicted to interrogation, torture and the murder that followed. When the military and police ran out of political suspects to torture and kill, they resorted to the random abduction of citizens off the streets. I thought how easy it would be for the Border Patrol to shoot us and leave our bodies and car beside the highway, like so many bodies found in these parts and ascribed to "drug runners."

Two other Border Patrolmen stood by the white van. The one who had asked if we were looking for trouble ordered his partner to "get the dog," and from the back of the van another patrolman brought a small female German shepherd on a leash. The dog apparently did not heel well enough to suit him,

Communism vs. free
"Boogie man" | nation

The patrol wanted to find something

and the handler jerked the leash. They opened the doors of our car and pulled the dog's head into it, but I saw immediately from the expression in her eyes that the dog hated them, and that she would not serve them. When she showed no interest in the inside of our car, they brought her around back to the trunk, near where we were standing. They half-dragged her up into the trunk, but still she did not indicate any stowed-away human beings or illegal drugs.

Connection between the dog & the main characters

Their mood got uglier; the officers seemed outraged that the dog could not find any contraband, and they dragged her over to us and commanded her to sniff our legs and feet. To my relief, the strange violence the Border Patrol agents had focused on us now seemed shifted to the dog. I no longer felt so strongly that we would be murdered. We exchanged looks—the dog and I. She was afraid of what they might do, just as I was. The dog's handler jerked the leash sharply as she sniffed us, as if to make her perform better, but the dog refused to accuse us: She had an innate dignity that did not permit her to serve the murderous impulses of those men. I can't forget the expression in the dog's eyes; it was as if she were embarrassed to be associated with them. I had a small amount of medicinal marijuana in my purse that night, but she refused to expose me. I am not partial to dogs, but I will always remember the small German shepherd that night. *The dog is a tool*

Unfortunately, what happened to me is an everyday occurrence here now. Since the 1980s, on top of greatly expanding border checkpoints, the Immigration and Naturalization Service and the Border Patrol have implemented policies that interfere with the rights of U.S. citizens to travel freely within our borders. I.N.S. agents now patrol all interstate highways and roads that lead to or from the U.S.-Mexico border in Texas, New Mexico, Arizona and California. Now, when you drive east from Tucson on Interstate 10 toward El Paso, you encounter an I.N.S. check station outside Las Cruces, New Mexico. When you drive north from Las Cruces up Interstate 25, two miles north of the town of Truth or Consequences, the highway is blocked with orange emergency barriers, and all traffic is diverted into a two-lane Border Patrol checkpoint—ninety-five miles north of the U.S.-Mexico border.

I was detained once at Truth or Consequences, despite my and my companion's Arizona driver's licenses. Two men, both Chicanos, were detained at the same time, despite the fact that they too presented ID and spoke English without the thick Texas accents of the Border Patrol agents. While we were stopped, we watched as other vehicles—whose occupants were white—were waved through the checkpoint. White people traveling with brown people, however, can expect to be stopped on suspicion they work with the sanctuary movement, which shelters refugees. White people who appear to be clergy, those who wear ethnic clothing or jewelry and women with very long hair or very short hair (they could be nuns) are also frequently detained; white men with beards or men with long hair are likely to be detained, too, because **Border Patrol agents have "profiles" of "those sorts" of white people who may help political refugees.** (Most of the political refugees from Guatemala and El

they used outward appearance to decide who could go through

the law of patrol is ignored (No boundaries)

Salvador are Native American or mestizo because the indigenous people of the Americas have continued to resist efforts by invaders to displace them from their ancestral lands.) Alleged increases in illegal immigration by people of Asian ancestry means that the Border Patrol now routinely detains anyone who appears to be Asian or part Asian, as well.

Once your car is diverted from the Interstate Highway into the checkpoint area, you are under the control of the Border Patrol, which in practical terms exercises a power that no highway patrol or city patrolman possesses: They are willing to detain anyone, for no apparent reason. Other law-enforcement officers need a shred of probable cause in order to detain someone. On the books, so does the Border Patrol; but on the road, it's another matter. They'll order you to stop your car and step out; then they'll ask you to open the trunk. If you ask why or request a search warrant, you'll be told that they'll have to have a dog sniff the car before they can request a search warrant, and the dog might not get there for two or three hours. The search warrant might require an hour or two past that. They make it clear that if you force them to obtain a search warrant for the car, they will make you submit to a strip search as well.

Traveling in the open, though, the sense of violation can be even worse. Never mind high-profile cases like that of former Border Patrol agent Michael Elmer, acquitted of murder by claiming self-defense, despite admitting that as an officer he shot an "illegal" immigrant in the back and then hid the body, which remained undiscovered until another Border Patrolman reported the event. (Last month, Elmer was convicted of reckless endangerment in a separate incident, for shooting at least ten rounds from his M-16 too close to a group of immigrants as they were crossing illegally into Nogales in March 1992.) Or that in El Paso, a high school football coach driving a vanload of his players in full uniform was pulled over on the freeway and a Border Patrol agent put a cocked revolver to his head. (The football coach was Mexican-American, as were most of the players in his van; the incident eventually caused a federal judge to issue a restraining order against the Border Patrol.) We've a mountain of personal experiences like that which never make the newspapers. A history professor at U.C.L.A. told me she had been traveling by train from Los Angeles to Albuquerque twice a month doing research. On each of her trips, she had noticed that the Border Patrol agents were at the station in Albuquerque scrutinizing the passengers. Since she is six feet tall and of Irish and German ancestry, she was not particularly concerned. Then one day when she stepped off the train in Albuquerque, two Border Patrolmen accosted her, wanting to know what she was doing, and why she was traveling between Los Angeles and Albuquerque twice a month. She presented identification and an explanation deemed "suitable" by the agents, and was allowed to go about her business.

Just the other day, I mentioned to a friend that I was writing this article and he told me about his 73-year-old father, who is half Chinese and had set out alone by car from Tucson to Albuquerque the week before. His father had become confused by road construction and missed a turnoff from Interstate 10 to

Untold Stories of colored struggles

Attention drawn to color

Interstate 25; when he turned around and circled back, he missed the turnoff a second time. But when he looped back for yet another try, Border Patrol agents stopped him and forced him to open his trunk. After they satisfied themselves that he was not smuggling Chinese immigrants, they sent him on his way. He was so rattled by the event that he had to be driven home by his daughter. This is the police state that has developed in the southwestern United States since the 1980s. No person, no citizen, is free to travel without the scrutiny of the Border Patrol. In the city of South Tucson, where 80 percent of the respondents were Chicano or Mexicano, a joint research project by the University of Wisconsin and the University of Arizona recently concluded that one out of every five people there had been detained, mistreated verbally or nonverbally, or questioned by I.N.S. agents in the past two years.

An absolute

Slang and phrases used to degrade immigrants

Manifest Destiny may lack its old grandeur of theft and blood—"lock the door" is what it means now, with racism a trump card to be played again and again, shamelessly, by both major political parties. "Immigration," like "street crime" and "welfare fraud," is a political euphemism that refers to people of color. Politicians and media people talk about "illegal aliens" to dehumanize and demonize undocumented immigrants, who are for the most part people of color. Even in the days of Spanish and Mexican rule, no attempts were made to interfere with the flow of people and goods from south to north and north to south. It is the U.S. government that has continually attempted to sever contact between the tribal people north of the border and those to the south.[1]

Neg Ref.

today = true

Now that the "Iron Curtain" is gone, it is ironic that the U.S. government and its Border Patrol are constructing a steel wall ten feet high to span sections of the border with Mexico. While politicians and multinational corporations extol the virtues of NAFTA and "free trade" (in goods, not flesh), the ominous curtain is already up in a six-mile section at the border crossing at Mexicali; two miles are being erected but are not yet finished at Naco; and at Nogales, sixty miles south of Tucson, the steel wall has been all rubber-stamped and awaits construction likely to begin in March [of 1994]. Like the pathetic multimillion-dollar "antidrug" border surveillance balloons that were continually deflated by high winds and made only a couple of meager interceptions before they blew away, the fence along the border is a theatrical prop, a bit of pork for contractors. Border entrepreneurs have already used blow-torches to cut passageways through the fence to collect "tolls," and are doing a brisk business. Back in Washington, the I.N.S. announces a $300 million computer contract to modernize its record-keeping and Congress passes a crime bill that shunts $255 million to the I.N.S. for 1995, $181 million earmarked for border control, which is to include 700 new partners for the men who stopped Gus and me in our travels, and the history professor, and my friend's father, and as many as they could from South Tucson.

It is no use; borders haven't worked, and they won't work, not now, as the indigenous people of the Americas reassert their kinship and solidarity with

No need for borders

Many reasons as to why people want to come to America

The Border Patrol State 571

one another. A mass migration is already under way; its roots are not simply economic. The Uto-Aztecan languages are spoken as far north as Taos Pueblo near the Colorado border, all the way south to Mexico City. Before the arrival of the Europeans, the indigenous communities throughout this region not only conducted commerce, the people shared cosmologies, and oral narratives about the Maize Mother, the Twin Brothers and their Grandmother, Spider Woman, as well as Quetzalcoatl the benevolent snake. The great human migration within the Americas cannot be stopped; human beings are natural forces of the Earth, just as rivers and winds are natural forces. *People should be able to move free as nature*

Deep down the issue is simple: The so-called "Indian Wars" from the days of Sitting Bull and Red Cloud have never really ended in the Americas. The Indian people of southern Mexico, of Guatemala and those left in El Salvador, too, are still fighting for their lives and for their land against the "calvary" patrols sent out by the governments of those lands. The Americas are Indian country, and the "Indian problem" is not about to go away.

One evening at sundown, we were stopped in traffic at a railroad crossing in downtown Tucson while a freight train passed us, slowly gaining speed as it headed north to Phoenix. In the twilight I saw the most amazing sight: Dozens of human beings, mostly young men, were riding the train; everywhere, on flat cars, inside open boxcars, perched on top of boxcars, hanging off ladders on tank cars and between boxcars. I couldn't count fast enough, but I saw fifty or sixty people headed north. They were dark young men, Indian and mestizo; they were smiling and a few of them waved at us in our cars. I was reminded of the ancient story of Aztlán, told by the Aztecs but known in other Uto-Aztecan communities as well. Aztlán is the beautiful land to the north, the origin place of the Aztec people. I don't remember how or why the people left Aztlán to journey farther south, but the old story says that one day, they will return.

NOTE *Limiting Rights as Americans*

1. The treaty of Guadalupe Hidalgo, signed in 1848, recognizes the right of the Tohano O'odm (Papago) people to move freely across the United States–Mexico border without documents. A treaty with Canada guarantees similar rights to those of the Iroquois nation in traversing the border between the United States and Canada.

FOR JOURNALING AND DISCUSSION

1. Why are the instances of border patrol abuse and violence rarely covered by the media?
2. What purpose do the police profiles used by border patrols serve? Whom do they affect? Why are they used when they are so easy to subvert by any determined criminal?
3. Is it possible to achieve a balance between protecting and enforcing our borders while not abusing and harassing our own people?

4. Write an essay in which you use Silko's article to demonstrate the claims that Robert D. Kaplan makes about disintegrating borders and societal conflict in "The Coming Anarchy" earlier in this chapter.

FOR RESEARCH AND EXPLORATION

1. Supporters of the North American Free Trade Act (NAFTA) claim that it will help to decrease the numbers of illegal aliens entering the United States. Do some research on this issue. What real effect has NAFTA had on our borders?
2. Find four or five newspaper accounts of illegal aliens. Write an essay analyzing how they are portrayed by the media. What rhetoric is used to describe them? What purpose does this image serve? What stereotypes are perpetuated by this kind of coverage?
3. Find the actual statistics estimating the numbers of illegal immigrants that come from Mexico, Canada, Europe, Russia, and Asia. Write an essay explaining why so much effort is spent to keep out illegal Mexicans and so little to keep out the others.

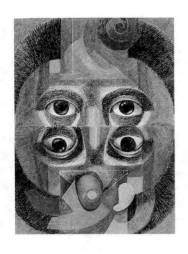

CHAPTER 10

Writing Well
in a Variety of
Academic Forms

Some people question whether there is more than one way to write well. Within the academy, there are those who believe that good writing is simply a matter of good thinking. We agree, but we also believe that there are conventions and expectations that vary from one kind of writing to another and from one kind of audience or purpose to another. We also know that genres, patterns of organization, methods, and conventions for "standard written English" evolve over time—some conventions have lasted 2,500 years; others are being invented or radically altered as we write. Beyond the academy, the forms and expectations for good writing vary considerably from those that are effective with the professoriate. Good writers know these things intuitively, but students who are learning to produce college-level writing may benefit from having some of them laid out explicitly.

The idea that there are different styles, modes, and forms for writing is as least as old as Aristotle, who first described the differences among forensic (legal, judicial), epideictic (praising, blaming, eulogistic), and deliberative (political) speeches. He had much to say about just these three in Greek public life over 2,300 years ago, and he was not dealing with the tremendous variety of written and oral communication we have today. Before him, the Sophists were famous (or infamous, depending upon their ethics) for their ability to manipulate audiences using verbal tricks designed specifically to appeal to their audiences. But Aristotle was the first to gather the received wisdom, and we have his students' notes as a record. Aristotle classified types of evidence as well as styles that were appropriate in various circumstances. He told his followers that every kind of style had to fit the audience, that every kind of style could be used "in season or out of season." The Roman rhetorician Cicero maintained that "the orator must be accomplished in every kind of discourse and every kind of culture."

A contemporary rhetorician, George A. Kennedy (1980), divides discourse into philosophical rhetoric, technical rhetoric, and letteraturizzazione, which he defines as "the tendency of rhetoric to shift its focus from persuasion to narration, from civic to personal contexts, and from discourse to literature, including poetry" (p. 5). Patricia Bizzell and Bruce Herzberg, in their book *The Rhetorical Tradition* (1990), include challenges to classical rhetoric from French feminists, deconstructionists, and African American rhetorical and linguistic traditions. If you add modern theories of epistemology and cultural difference to this mix, it hardly seems possible that there could be just one right or good type of thinking or writing. "Good writing" may boil down to effectiveness with the conventions and expectations for writing in various discourse communities.

ACADEMIC CONVENTIONS

Within the academy, there are certain conventions that most professors expect. Given their level of education and the premium they place on public communication and formal publication, it should come as no surprise that the following are nearly universal expectations:

- New information, insights, or points of view (unless the writing is for reference only)
- Sufficient information to establish what is shared by the writer and the reader or to establish the writer's credibility and authority—and no more
- Appropriate details, examples, illustrations, or evidence
- Clear patterns of organization
- Clarity in sentence structure
- Credit for other people's ideas or material
- A consistent form for references
- Standard written English grammar (unless otherwise specified)
- Careful copyediting, including punctuation and spelling

If you take a controversial position, as you no doubt will as you use this book, you are also expected to acknowledge your stance. If you are reporting factual or technical information, you are expected to convey it as accurately and objectively as possible. If you do not believe that objectivity is possible, you should make your biases clear.

From a broad perspective, it is possible to question the very existence of "objectivity." For example, when reporters from *Time* magazine cover a topic such as the O. J. Simpson trials, they select information designed to appeal to a wide readership, whereas, a writer describing the events in a magazine such as *Gentlemen's Quarterly,* aimed at an African American male audience, might use a different selection principle. The *Time* essay might present all perspectives, whereas the *GQ* article might focus on flawed investigation procedures, given the interest in the possibility of a frame-up in certain African American communities. In both cases, the evidence could be factual and still lead to different conclusions. As Aristotle knew in ancient Greece, many decisions are based on the probable rather than the provable, and one's perspective definitely influences the type of evidence one will find compelling as well as the selection principle used. A safe way to deal with this is to state your positions, your biases, your methods, and your selection principles for evidence as clearly as possible.

In this chapter, we describe some conditions for learning to write well and give you suggestions for steps in a writing process, including finding information, brief descriptions of particular types of writing, ways to get good feedback, and tips for preparing a final draft.

✸ CONDITIONS FOR LEARNING TO WRITE WELL

There are four conditions for good writing:

- Critical thinking
- Critical reading
- Critical practice
- Critical feedback

The *critical thinking* aspect is fundamental, for it is a necessary ingredient in the other three. In Chapter 1 and throughout this book, we have offered advice on *critical reading* to help you interrogate the readings, your own responses, and the possible reactions of others to your ideas. As you read critically, your thinking will be informed by others' vast knowledge and experience. Reading good prose also helps you to develop an "ear" for good style. Lots of *critical practice* will help you develop fluency, an important asset, but if you do not do more than let your ideas flow freely, you may not produce much that others would care to read, or you may not know how to improve your output. You need *critical feedback* about your writing—ideally from the intended readers, but also from peers who can simulate your readers, from the instructor who will comment on the quality of your writing, and from anyone else whose opinion you value. The more readers, the better. By giving and receiving feedback, you can learn to be a better critic of your own writing, but even the most experienced writers are grateful for the feedback they get from good editors.

CRITICAL PRACTICE

In addition to the suggestions for critical reading in Chapter 1, we recommend that as you read the essays in this book, you keep informal writing and notes in a *critical reading log* in which you do the following:

- Summarize the overall content of the essay (see our summaries in the introductions to each chapter).
- Make lists of key points.
- Record your disagreements with the writer(s).
- Note the types of evidence used.
- Write more detailed answers to the questions in Chapter 1.
- Ask, "What if . . . ?" What if the readers were different? What if the writer were someone else? What if the essay were written in a different form?
- Jot down possible ideas for formal writing projects.

Throughout the chapters, the questions "For Journaling and Discussion" should suggest many more topics that will lead you to write informally in your log. This is the place for you to record what is notable in the essay and what you have to say about it. You should spend some time thinking about what kind of format will be easiest for you to use. Some people find a three-ring notebook handy so that they can rearrange notes easily. Others like a system of cards that they can rearrange as they use them. Office supply stores and mail order houses for writers' supplies have many interesting systems that allow you to organize cards in a notebook. Some people keep their notes on laptop computers and print them only when they share them. Data bases for note-taking and informal writing are also useful to some writers. Be sure you know whether your instructor will be reading these logs so that you can be prepared to share them. Always keep a backup of computer files and any materials you turn in for evaluation.

CRITICAL WRITING

You will write critically for yourself in your reading log, but you will also want to share your positions publicly in formal papers. The questions listed as "For Research and Exploration" should suggest topics for more formal, public writing. Sometimes your instructor will design a specific assignment based on the readings. If this is the case, it is important for you to analyze key instructions in the oral or written directions for the assignment. For example, does the instructor specify that you "analyze," "compare/contrast," or "summarize"? Words like these have very specific implications for the forms that you will need to use.

In addition, your instructor may specify a purpose and an audience for your paper. If these are not clear, you should create a context for your writing and check with your instructor to be sure that you are on the right track.

If you have the freedom to design your own assignment, we recommend that you write a *proposal* for your paper and have it approved before you proceed. You can also solicit feedback about the feasibility and scope of the project. Others may also have helpful advice about the rhetorical questions you are considering and additional readings you might want to consult. A proposal might have the following parts:

- A general statement of your interest in the topic
- Your purpose in writing the essay
- Your intended audiences
- A possible thesis (If you can state one; sometimes a thesis has to evolve, and sometimes there isn't a single thesis; if your work is merely descriptive or if it's fiction, you can probably just expand the purpose statement.)
- An outline of the work that you plan to do to gather materials or evidence
- A rough idea of the form the paper might take
- A list of key books and articles that you have *already* consulted, as well as sources you hope to find. This will prompt others to give you more suggestions. Sometimes you will use these readings as sources in your text; other times they might be used as models or inspirations.

INVENTION: WAYS TO GET MATERIAL

Prewriting Activities, or Priming the Pump Any Time

There are any number of ways to begin writing (and lots of ways to avoid beginning). Some people are planners; they like to come up with a good thesis and then find the material they need to support it. Others just have a general topic, and have to read and write a great deal before a structure and a thesis finally evolve. In P. E. Vernon's *Creativity: Selected Readings,* the poet Stephen Spender observed these two ways of working in two kinds of artists that he labeled "Mozartians" and "Beethovians." Mozart conceived his symphonies during a long incubation period, during which the music remained largely in his head, so that when he actually put quill to paper, he hardly revised anything. Some writers report that they work this way; these are the folks for whom a beginning outline works very well. Once they have their concept, they can outline the parts and simply carry out the plan as they write. Beethoven's manuscripts, on the other hand, are filled with false starts, editing, and massive revisions. It is as though he had to compose through trial and error. Many writers report that they have to write to figure out what they have to say. They create all kinds of outlines that are constantly revised before they finally find a structure that works. You may be one or the other or somewhere in between, depending upon the kind of writing you are doing.

In your writing class, you may also experiment with a number of techniques for "priming the pump": free writing (writing as fast as you can for a few minutes on a topic to see what you can learn); focused free writing (asking yourself a specific question about the topic and free writing until you find answers); and the use of structural drawings to represent the relationships among your ideas (this may be called "treeing," "clustering," or "looping," depending upon the visual techniques you use).

At home, or wherever you write, you may find that some sections of the paper are easier to figure out than others. Start with them and reward yourself for making progress. Perfectionists often develop writer's block. If you keep writing, eventually you will have good material to work with.

Gathering Outside Material

The references in Chapter 1 and those cited by the authors in the selections will give you a head start on good sources. One of the secrets to finding the most important sources is to check several introductions to the subject and see which sources are cited most often. These are the ones you need to find. Comparing bibliographies will also teach you a lot about the ways experts have posed questions about the topic. The titles may also give you some indication of the scope of a typical essay. One of the main problems beginning writers have is trying to cover too much ground. Think small; think particular.

Most libraries now have on-line catalogues, so the first step in finding materials is to brainstorm some good key words for searches, whether you are looking for books in the electronic catalogue, articles in on-line periodical data bases, or helpful sites on the Internet. Each search procedure may have its own little idiosyncrasies, so a little time spent reading the directions can help you a great deal. For example, some search engines allow you to put a phrase in quotations marks (e.g., "identity politics" or "cultural pluralism") so that you will come up with sources that are really on the mark.

If you do not know how to use these electronic resources, you should enroll in a short course offered by your library, work with a reference librarian, get a friend to help you get started, or learn by doing. Often the hardest part is just making the initial connection; go to a place where someone can help you do this. You cannot be part of the information age if you are not using these tools. At the end of Chapter 1, we offer a few suggestions for searching cyberspace.

DRAFTING: PRODUCING MATERIAL AND CRAFTING A FORM

Whether you are a Beethovian or a Mozartian, you can often benefit from studying different forms for essays. Understanding the component parts helps some people develop a plan of action as they begin drafting. There are no formulas for good patterns of organization, however. The form for each paper must grow organically out of its own materials and purpose. There are some familiar patterns that we often see in prose, but the problem is that you hardly ever find them in pure form. A narrative may contain many descriptions. An analysis may contain a comparison/contrast section. An argument may call for an extended definition. Below we have listed the rhetorical forms of the essays in this collection. The number in parentheses indicates the chapter in which the author's essay appears. After this list, we describe some familiar patterns, often represented in these essays, followed by some "experimental" forms that might be fun to try.

Rhetorical Forms

Commentary: Klor De Alva, Shorris, and West (2); Kimbrell (4)
Magazine feature story: Ali (5), Fost (6), Rosenberg (6), Dolnick (7), Berreby (7), Ervin (7), Lind (3)
Academic essay journal article: D. Cooper (4)
Social, cross-cultural, or historical criticism: Newman (3), Tisdale (4), Freedman (4), Pollitt (4), Rosenberg (6), Dolnick (7), Berreby (7), Hershey (7), Ervin (7), Raban (8), Hougland (8), Kaplan (9), Njeri (9), Funderburg (2), Ali (5), Fussell (3)
Ethnography/oral history: Funderberg (2), Stewart (8)
Media criticism: Hagedorn (4)
Fiction: Allen (4), McMillan (6), King (9), O'Brien (9), Heker (3), Allison (3,8)
Memoir/autobiography/personal essay: Lee (9), Silko (9), Alexie (2), Rodriguez (2), McKnight (2), Indiana (2), Williams (2), Charlip (3), Hamper (3), Meyer (3), B. Cooper (4), Vincent (4), Walker (6), White (6), Mairs (7), Hershey (7), Whelen (7), Hassler (7), Gruchow (8), Erdrich (8), C. Allen (8), P. Allen (4), Harris (8), Nelson (8)

Frequently Used Patterns in Formal Papers

Narrative. In a narrative, time is the organizing principle. Histories, stories, and personal experiences can be put in chronological order. Sometimes, depending upon the purpose of the narrative, the time order may be rearranged, for example, by using flashbacks, or by starting with the final events for dramatic effect and then going back to tell how it all happened—or how *some* things happened. Selecting the appropriate amount of detail and the number of events to include is one of the most important tasks in writing a good narrative. Narratives also often include other types of writing, too, such as commentaries on the events, analyses, and rich descriptions of scenes. This reader is filled with narratives, but not one of them presents just the facts of something that happened. Once you have a clear purpose for telling the story and some sense of what your readers need to know, or what you want them to know, you will have ways of deciding what goes in and what stays out. Look at Tim O'Brien's essay "On the Rainy River" in Chapter 9 from this perspective.

Definition. In every chapter in this book, definition is a crucial issue. How is race defined? How is ability defined? You can write essays in which your whole subject is the way such terms are defined, and how definitions have changed historically or how they vary depending upon the person doing the defining. Once again, there must be a reason why it is important to understand the definitions you are analyzing, and you will include this in your thesis. There are many ways a term can be defined, and you will have to consider how many of these to take up and how to organize the material: what the elements of the term are; how the term functions; how it changes over time; the categories to which the term belongs; the terms that are a part of it; how its synonyms are similar although slightly different; how its opposites reveal something about the term; and so on.

Analysis. To "analyze" means, simply, to take something apart and see how it works. If you write an analytical essay about a selection in the book, for example, you could examine the accuracy of its content, the logic of its argument, the type of evidence used, the assumptions behind its premises, its objectivity, and any claims made. The rhetorical questions presented in Chapter 1 are a handy way of setting up a rhetorical analysis of a piece of writing. But, as always, your purpose dictates whether these questions are important or which deserve more attention than others.

Argument. Sometimes your point of view on a controversy is so clear that you want to write a traditional argumentative essay. The goal of such an essay is to change the reader's mind, or at least to win an argument. The mechanics of an argument are simple—lay out your case and provide better evidence than the opponent. The psychology, however, is something else. Before you choose a traditional argumentative form, consider whether there is really any chance that you can change the reader's mind. With the question of abortion, for example, it is not likely that two people will ever agree if their religious beliefs are such that they define human life differently. When there is the possibility of accepting each other's premises, a traditional argument is a good approach.

The traditional argumentative essay. An argument opens with a general introduction and presents a *thesis* that you defend. A thesis is a simple statement of your position ("Workfare is less successful than welfare because it is more likely to neglect children's needs"; "Class is a more important predictor of career choice than race or ethnicity"). Next, the nature of the problem or controversy is explicated in a few paragraphs. The main body of the argument consists of the reasons or evidence that supports the thesis. Here you can use data such as statistics, quotes from authorities, examples, and illustrations. The better your sources, the better your credibility as a person who has read enough to understand the problem. After the case is made, you should anticipate the counterarguments. If there is a controversy, there must be reasons why people do not accede to your point of view. In the penultimate sections of an argument, you should attempt to show why your position is superior to others. Finally, in the conclusion, you can summarize the outlines of your case, call for action, point out the consequences or implications of your position or the opponent's position, or end with a dramatic illustration of the need for action. Try to leave the reader with something more memorable than a simple restatement of the thesis.

Rogerian argument. Other forms of argument are more appropriate when it is not likely that you can change the reader's mind. In a *Rogerian argument,* named after the psychologist Carl Rogers, the goal is not to convert an opponent or change the reader's mind, but to establish common ground. Most academic arguments state the thesis immediately, but in a Rogerian argument, it might come later, once the common ground has been established. After the writer attempts to convince the reader that they share certain opinions or perspectives, the writer might move on to suggest alternative points of view or ways to reconcile differences. The conclusion might call for more dialogue between the parties or at least consideration for different points of view. Given the controversial nature of many of the topics in this book, and given the multiple points of view on many of them, the Rogerian argument might be a good choice for a formal paper. There are several examples of it in the selections (see Laura Hershey's essay "Choosing Disability" in Chapter 7, for example).

However you structure an argument, you should avoid easy pitfalls in logic. In her textbook *Rhetoric in the Classical Tradition* (1988), Winifred Bryan Horner describes in some detail three types of faulty arguments: material fallacies, in which the basic premises of the argument are unfounded; logical fallacies, which have defects in their chains of reasoning; and psychological fallacies, which inappropriately exploit emotions. Standard fallacies include hidden generalizations; insufficient sampling; unrepresentative sampling; forced "either/or" choices; and appeals to force, ignorance, stereotypes, authority, and emotions that mask the real issues.

Critique or review. Sometimes you will want to evaluate an issue. You can consider a critique an argumentative form (it will have some of the same parts), but it will also have an additional section in which you establish the criteria by which you are evaluating the topic. Why are these valid criteria? and to whom? Have any other criteria been applied? Why are you applying the ones you have chosen? Once you make your case for your evaluative tools, then you provide the evidence you need to evaluate the topic. Depending upon your purpose and the effect you want to have on your readers, you will have to decide whether to apply each of the criteria equally, to use only the most compelling ones, to put smaller points first, or to start with your most important material. Be sure to give your reader a road map for your essay, probably in the first paragraph. Based on the effect you hope to achieve, you will have to decide whether you want to reveal your judgment early on or at the end.

Position paper. In a position paper you take a stand or call for action. Because it is also a variation on an argumentative essay, you will want to consider what kind of argument you are making: win/lose; persuade/compromise; or agree to disagree/open dialogue. Typically, you will state a thesis early and provide your evidence in a straightforward manner. A position paper is often a fairly short document, frequently produced so that a group of people can have a conversation about whether they agree or disagree with the writer. This might be a good place to take some risks—a place where your readers know that you are floating a "trial balloon." A *problem-solution paper* is another kind of position paper. In this case, you may be opening up the discussion of proposed solutions or arguing for one over others.

Comparison/Contrast. This is a handy pattern if you want to analyze the similarities and differences of two or more things. Your thesis will most likely signal your pattern of organization to the reader right away. It will also say *why* you are comparing and contrasting. You will also need to analyze your purpose to decide exactly how to structure your materials. For example, if you are comparing the job opportunities for African Americans to those of Asian Americans, you could take several careers (e.g., teaching, health support services, and management) and describe how opportunities compare and contrast for both groups. Or you could describe opportunities for each set of careers fully for Asian Americans and then shift to African Americans.

Description. Your purpose in writing about a person, place, or emotion may simply be to record enough detail so that your reader will be able to see, feel, smell, hear, or taste the thing you are describing. You should ask yourself why you want to share this experience and select the details that enhance a few aspects, rather than everything, about your topic. As you write, consider your position in relation to your reader's. What is your stance? Patricia Williams combines description and narration in "My Best White Friend" in Chapter 2. Consider how she selected the details she included in this essay.

Experimental Forms

Sometimes your writing goals will be more "creative," or riskier. Sometimes you are ready to go public with an idea, but you are not ready to frame it in clear, argumentative terms. Or sometimes the variety of possibilities is so dizzying that you want to illustrate them in a visually interesting textual space. And finally, you may want to say something you can express only in fiction. Even though there are conventions for fiction and poetry, just as there are for academic writing, we have not designed this book for creative writing classes. You have probably enrolled to learn more about expository writing, but we include fiction in this text, and you might want to consider a creative experiment in fiction or poetry.

In addition to learning to produce familiar forms, we encourage you to create some new genres for yourself, just as some of our students have done. Here are some possibilities:

A Paper of Questions. If you do not know much about a topic, you can speculate about what you would like to know. One student of ours found himself the lone male in a class on feminist theory. Deciding to tread lightly because he was new to the material and new to the way of thinking, he wrote an entire essay in which each sentence was a question, one leading to another. Other students have written papers about their possible questions on an issue and then speculated about how they would find answers, what kind of evidence would be persuasive, and so on.

A Paper of Quotes and Commentaries. Sometimes when you are reading widely in a new field, encountering lots of new theorists or researchers, you just want to preserve these thoughts and reflect on them, without making up your mind. Particularly when classes are on the quarter system (under which we teach), we find that our students are often pressed to come up with a premature thesis and that they would be better off just deliberating over possibilities. To do this, you might gather a set of the most provocative excerpts from your reading about a topic, organize them in one column on the left (this is a word processor project), and write your own commentaries in a second column. This is a lot like the double-entry journals that scientists keep in their labs, with one column for findings, another for interpretations. One student of ours gathered all the definitions she could find of the term "rhetoric" and commented on each one in a separate column. She did not feel compelled to come up with a single, reductionist definition, but rather let the variety of ways of defining the term make the point that the word has a complex history.

Readers' Theater. Another student of ours wrote a script for a readers' theater in which Plato, Aristotle, Quintilian, and Cicero all appeared. She used direct quotes from each of them to reveal their personalities and differences, and linked them all through the adventures of "Alice in Rhetorica-Land." Occasionally, she had Jacques Derrida or Helene Cixous, contemporary theorists known for their complex and sometimes confusing ideas, drop in to confuse everything.

Parodies. Another student wrote the parody "An English Department Summa Thesis," in which she had all of the authorities on Virginia Woolf line up on opposite sides of a basketball court to hold a pep rally for opposing teams interpreting Woolf's works. This was her way of refusing to reduce her ideas to a single thesis. She did not want to bend the variety of critical readings she had found to fit a narrow thesis.

We want to stress that experiments like these are not always common outside creative writing classes. If you want to write in an experimental form—and we hope you will try it—you should prepare a proposal for your instructor and get approval for the experiment. If you can find an example of an experimental form similar to the one you want to try, append it to your proposal. We also want to stress that experiments are vital to the intellectual energy we get from academic writing. For example, there is a place for personal experience and narrative in nearly every academic field we have investigated, even though older textbooks might lead you to believe that all academic writing is expository, third person, and objective.

USING OUTSIDE SOURCES

When you use others' ideas, data, or exact wording, you must give them credit for their intellectual property. When you read something that someone else has written that any number of sources contain, you do not have to cite the reference, unless you use the same language as the source. If you borrow someone else's exact language, you must give credit. Common knowledge does not belong to anyone in particular, and you do not have to give credit for it. Determining the dividing line between an author's intellectual property and information in the public domain is often a tricky process. When in doubt, err on the side of caution and cite references. If you are overdoing it, you can raise questions about particular examples and get a better sense of the difference.

There are basically four ways to use an outside source:

- Just for *background reading,* in which case you do not even have to list it in the reference list
- As the source for a *direct quotation,* which calls for a reference
- As the basis for a *summary* of some information, which calls for a reference
- As the basis for a *paraphrase* of a key idea, which also calls for a reference.

You should consult a style manual on documentation form (see below) for specifics on the type of documentation you need.

When your paper calls for a review of the literature on your topic and you are using multiple sources to provide background, you will be borrowing lots of ideas and materials, and including many quotations. One trick that we have used is to make a list of words and phrases that can be used to introduce a quotation, rather than always relying on such phrases as "she reports" or "he argues." Study a well-written essay and develop a repertoire of techniques for weaving outside material into your own organizational structure. Remember that you must organize the material into your own text's structure. Do not just link paragraph-long quotes like beads on a string. Write your own framework, and use long quotes sparingly.

CRITICAL FEEDBACK

There are several ways you can get feedback on your writing. First, you can ask friends who are good writers to read your drafts. Sometimes it is easier to share your early efforts with someone who will be gentle. But when it is time for critical feedback, consider peer tutors, writing center tutors, and your instructors as the best sources. They will have a better sense of the rhetorical situation for your writing and can compare it to the prevailing standards.

If your instructor allows time for peer writing groups to meet, you will probably receive some specific instructions on what to do as you provide criticism. If you set up a peer group yourself, here are some things to consider:

- Put specific questions for your readers on your draft.
- Circulate copies of the papers in advance so that readers can read and comment on them in advance.
- Appoint a timekeeper who will be sure each person gets a fair share of the time.
- Have one person (not the writer) facilitate the discussion of a paper, paragraph by paragraph, or question by question if the writer has asked for specifics.
- Include two kinds of feedback: (1) *reader-based,* which is how the paper affects the reader, usually from the standpoint of content ("I didn't get what you were saying here," "I want to know more about this section," "Here, I expected something else"); and (2) *text-based,* which is commentary on the language, organization, or mechanics of the text itself. If the draft is a really early version, you need more reader-based feedback and less text-based feedback because much will change.
- At the end of discussion for each writer, have someone in the group or the writer summarize the key suggestions for revision so that the writer knows what to do next.

REVISING

Once you have had a good reading of your writing, you will want to revise your draft. Sometimes the organization works pretty well, and all you have to do is develop points, polish, and edit. Other times, your readers will tell you that they just don't get it—that they don't understand your thesis or your purpose, or that they don't think you have proved your point. When the feedback is negative, you need to go back to the drawing board—perhaps do more reading, brainstorm on the rhetorical questions in Chapter 1 (is one of them giving you problems?), or spend some time writing statements of purpose ("What I really want to say is . . . "). Often you will have lots of material you can use but just have not yet figured out what you are trying to do with it all. Or you may have the opposite problem—a good concept, but not enough material. Even if the feedback is good, our view is that we have never seen a paper, ours or a student's, that could not be improved. So leave some quality time for revision in your schedule. Do not just tinker with words and type sizes. Really look at the structure of your paper and the ways you could sharpen your focus on something important.

At the very last stages of revision, you will probably want to pay special attention to the introduction and the conclusion. As you develop the body of your paper, the thesis may need to be refined or modified. You may find exactly the right quote to work into the conclusion. You may really discover the consequences of your position. This is also the time to be sure that your transitions between paragraphs are smooth, especially if you have moved some sections around.

POLISHING AND EDITING

Polishing and editing are the final stages of writing. You may want to work through your paper several times with the following goals:

- Ferret out excess wordiness.
- Craft better sentence structure.
- Check your grammar and usage.
- Generate a title.
- Check spelling.
- Proofread for little things, like commas in the right places and typos that a spelling checker will not detect (problems with homonyms, the use of "the" for " they, " etc.).
- Generate a reference list and footnotes if you are using outside sources.

Of course, you need a good dictionary on your desk. We recommend some other tools, too:

A Grammar Handbook

Do you always remember the difference between "lie" and "lay"? "that" and "which"? "less" and "fewer"? All of us are dogged by a few little points of standard written English that we cannot seem to store in our memory banks. A good usage book will answer these questions right away. It will also help you decode editorial and proofreading marks made by your readers. There are many of these handbooks on the market. The best way to select one is to look at the indexes of several. If you can find answers to your questions efficiently, it should be a good one.

A Style Book

Sometimes handbooks contain helpful sections on sentence style, and this may be enough to help you for now. However, there are several classics in this department that are also worthwhile: Strunk and White's *Elements of Style* and Williams's *Style: Toward Clarity and Grace* are worth the money.

A Documentation Manual

These books will give you detailed examples of all the ways you might need to document the sources you use. As the media for information (books, newspapers, journals, Internet sites, Listserve messages, CD-ROMs, on-line databases) become more diverse, we find that we need to consult a style manual frequently. The following widely used sources are frequently revised and published in new editions and are available at most bookstores:

- General: *The Chicago Manual of Style*
- Humanities: *MLA Handbook for Writers of Research Papers,*
- Sciences: *Scientific Style and Format: The Council of Biology Editors Manual for Authors, Editors, and Publishers,*
- Social sciences: *The Publication Manual of the American Psychological Association*

The best way to determine which citation style you should use is to examine publications in your field. For example, every field has major journals where scholars publish their work. The specifications for submissions to these journals are usually included on the inside cover, in the editor's opening materials, or at the end. You can also ask instructors and professors in your field which styles they prefer. Sometimes they will leave the choice up to you, but if they do, that does not mean that you should use your creativity here.

We hope you will communicate with us if you find readings and sources that inspire you. Please contact us through e-mail (see our web site on page 588 for information about our cyberlives). We wish you well as you interrogate identities, write for yourself, and write for others.

REFERENCES

Bizzell, Patricia, and Bruce Herzberg, eds. *The Rhetorical Tradition: Readings from Classical Times to the Present.* Boston: Bedford Books of St. Martin's Press, 1990.

Horner, Winifred Bryan. *Rhetoric in the Classical Tradition.* New York: St. Martin's Press, 1988.

Kennedy, George A. *Classical Rhetoric and Its Christian and Secular Tradition from Ancient to Modern Times.* Chapel Hill: The University of North Carolina Press, 1980.

Vernon, P. E., ed. *Creativity: Selected Readings.* Hammondsworth, Middlesex, England: Penguin Books, Inc., 1970.

For on-line help on the Internet, go to our home page at the Center for Interdisciplinary Studies of Writing: http://CISW.cla.umn.edu. At our site you can find links to hundreds of other resources, including on-line writing centers where you can get direct help with your writing, examples of papers and documentation styles, and lots of other inspiration.

Index